SIMON&SCHUSTER
HANDBOOK
FOR WRITERS

SIMON&SCHUSTER
HANDBOOK
FOR WRITERS

LYNN QUITMAN TROYKA

PRENTICE-HALL, INC., ENGLEWOOD CLIFFS, NEW JERSEY 07632

Library of Congress Cataloging-in-Publication

Troyka, Lynn Quitman (date)
    Simon & Schuster handbook for writers.

    Includes index.
    1. English language—Rhetoric—Handbooks,
manuals, etc. 2. English language—Grammar—
1950-   —Handbooks, manuals, etc. I. Title.
II. Title: Simon and Schuster handbook for writers.
PE1408.T696 1987   808'.042   86-25589
ISBN 0-13-810409-3

Development Editor: *JOYCE F. PERKINS*
Production Editor: *HILDA TAUBER*
Interior and cover design: *LORRAINE MULLANEY*
Manufacturing Buyer: *RAY KEATING*
Associate Art Director: *FLORENCE D. SILVERMAN*
Art production assistance: *KAREN SALZBACH*

Printed in the United States of America
10 9 8 7 6 5 4 3 2

ISBN 0-13-810409-3   01

Prentice-Hall International (UK) Limited, *London*
Prentice-Hall of Australia Pty. Limited, *Sydney*
Prentice Hall Canada Inc., *Toronto*
Prentice Hall Hispanoamericana, S.A., *Mexico*
Prentice-Hall of India Private Limited, *New Delhi*
Prentice-Hall of Japan, Inc., *Tokyo*
Prentice Hall of Southeast Asia Pte. Ltd., *Singapore*
Editora Prentice-Hall do Brasil, Ltda., *Rio de Janeiro*

for David,
who makes it all possible

CREDITS

CONTENTS

III
WRITING CORRECT SENTENCES   259

■ ‖ IV
WRITING EFFECTIVE SENTENCES   301

16   CONCISENESS   302

17   COORDINATION AND SUBORDINATION   316

Coordination   317

Subordination   322

18   PARALLELISM   330

◼|| VI
PUNCTUATION AND MECHANICS 409

▄▌|| VII
WRITING SPECIAL ASSIGNMENTS   509

PREFACE

▮‖ TO THE INSTRUCTOR

Scholarship and practice in the teaching of writing have become quite sophisticated today, especially compared to forty-five years ago when handbooks for writers began to be widely used. This *Simon & Schuster Handbook for Writers* weds the best of traditional and contemporary theory to lively, accessible practice. It is a comprehensive handbook that includes all topics usually in handbooks and adds much new material.

- It starts with five chapters about the whole essay, thereby giving students a context for studying writing.
- It sets the scene by devoting a chapter to the concepts of purposes and audiences for writers, thereby explaining the *why* of writing before turning to writing as a process and to written products.
- It explains the writing process, emphasizing that the steps of composing are rarely linear and that the process varies with the writer and the writing situation.

- It offers two student papers to illustrate variations of the writing process. One paper, shown in three drafts, was written with an informative purpose; the other was written with a persuasive purpose.

- It devotes a long chapter to critical thinking, a topic of major importance today. The chapter includes a detailed discussion of critical reading skills for college work and of reasoning and logic.

- It pays extended attention to the problem of plagiarism—with a separate chapter on how to avoid plagiarism and how to paraphrase, summarize, and use quotations correctly.

- It treats the research paper from two perspectives: the research process *and* the writing process, with an illustrative student paper.

- It features the MLA parenthetical system of documentation ("new MLA"), with briefer presentations of the MLA note system ("old MLA"), the APA system, and one system for the sciences.

- It includes a long chapter for "writing across the curriculum," focusing on the similarities *and* differences in assumptions and underlying thought processes that inform the humanities, the social sciences, and the natural and technological sciences; six student samples serve as models.

Rather than preparing a grab bag of isolated components, I have sought to unify this handbook with many elements. Most of all, theory informs practice. For example, I attended to the function of context in writing situations. Therefore, 95 percent of the exercises contain connected discourse rather than random sentences. When students work the exercises, they will experience what writers face when they revise and edit. I chose the content of the exercises for its intrinsic interest, drawn from subjects "across the curriculum." I hope that while students practice skills, they will simultaneously enjoy learning about a variety of subjects. Context was also on my mind when I composed the clusters of examples written especially for this book. Most clusters have related content. This use of context means that students can focus on the instruction instead of being distracted by a new topic with each new example. As with the exercises, I have drawn the content from "across the curriculum"—and all examples are expository to the extent practical.

To reflect my conviction that learning takes place most successfully when students can make connections between disparate elements, I devised a unique dual system of presenting information about selected matters of punctuation. In addition to full chapters on each mark of punctuation, the book uses short "punctutation alerts" to help students make connections between, for example, an aspect of sentence style and the role of a comma. These alerts, and similar ones related to usage, are signaled throughout the text by the same symbol—printed in color.

I am equally convinced that students today are strongly oriented toward the visual. To accommodate this reality, I use two innovations in the *Simon & Schuster Handbook for Writers*. First, I have created over 115 tinted charts and other visual displays. These materials include guidelines, checklists, sentence patterns, summaries, flow charts, illustrations, and more. Each item is designed to help students both learn new material and refresh their memories afterwards when they want to look up information. Second, I use the visual cue of a degree mark (°) with major terms to tell students that a definition of the term appears in the "Glossary of Grammatical and Selected Composition Terms."

A more subtle but no less important concern has been my desire to make the *Simon & Schuster Handbook for Writers* inclusive of all people rather than exclusive. The explanations, the examples I wrote as illustrations, and the examples I chose by professional writers are nonsexist: *man* is not used to stand for the whole human race, and role stereotyping is avoided. Also, an approximately equal number of male and female writers are represented in the professional examples. Student writing is represented by samples of eight student papers, an unprecedented number in a handbook, and by numerous paragraphs by students.

An unusually complete collection of supplementary materials is available with the *Simon & Schuster Handbook for Writers*. The package includes a highly innovative *Annotated Instructor's Edition* which offers a rich array of resources for instructors; the *Simon & Schuster Workbook for Writers,* which is closely coordinated with this handbook; answer keys for both the *Handbook* and *Workbook;* the *Study Guide to Accompany the Simon & Schuster Handbook for Writers;* a collection of diagnostic and competency tests, four reproducible and two on software compatible with IBM and Apple microcomputers; a booklet of 100 transparency masters of important charts and other displays from the text; *Blue Pencil,* interactive editing exercises for IBM and Apple microcomputers; and much more. For information, write College English Editor, Prentice-Hall, Inc., Englewood Cliffs, NJ 07632.

When I was a college student, I never knew that handbooks for writers existed. They were not mentioned by my instructors, nor were they stocked by the campus bookstore. Not until I got to graduate school did I learn how to look up information about written conventions and about how writers make choices; only then did I get the chance to talk through concepts in class and become an independent learner. I have written the *Simon & Schuster Handbook for Writers* for this more enlightened new time, when students are encouraged early to know how to use a handbook, in class and out; when instructors teach not only what writers know but also how writers behave; and when theory can meet practice gracefully in the classroom and on a reference shelf.

Acknowledgments

The writing of this book and its related materials was the most challenging composition assignment I ever undertook. Being able to turn for advice and reactions to a community of colleagues, friends, and family sustained me, affirming once again my conviction that writing is a social act for both writer and reader. Though responsibility for any flaws rests with me, I wish to thank many people for their help.

Emily R. Gordon, Hofstra University and Queensborough Community College of The City University of New York (CUNY), co-author of the *Workbook* and author of the testing package that accompanies this *Handbook,* became a special friend as well as an astute consultant. Judith Stanford, Merrimack College, was my highly valued advisor and friend. Linda Julian, Furman University, made many excellent suggestions in the final stages of the project. The following colleagues generously offered their ideas about teaching writing: Alan Adelson, City College, CUNY; Anne Agee, Anne Arundel Community College; Duncan Carter, Boston University; Karen Anderson, Midway College; Kathleen Shine Cain, Merrimack College; Mary Kay Mahoney, University of Massachusetts at Boston; and Laura Zaidman, University of South Carolina at Sumter. Michael Goodman, Fairleigh Dickinson University, gave me skilled guidance as I prepared the chapter on business writing, a subject I have rarely taught.

For their participation in this book's pivotal "Student Writing Project," whose purpose was to gather a national sample of student writing from which to select the student work in this book, I thank Vivian Brown, Laredo Community College; Jean M. English, Tallahassee Community College; Rodney F. Farnsworth, Indiana University-Purdue University; Christine Hult, Utah State University (formerly at Texas Tech University); Joan Karbach, Indiana University-Purdue University; James E. Porter, Indiana University-Purdue University; John Reedy, State University of New York College at Buffalo; Elizabeth Wahlquist, Brigham Young University;

Carolyn West, Daytona Beach Community College; and the entire English Department at Dean Junior College. Bonnie Sunstein, Rivier College, also contributed student writing to the pool.

For their attending a Reviewer Conference at Prentice-Hall and making invaluable comments on my evolving text, I owe a special debt to Kenneth Davis, University of Kentucky; Louis Emond, Dean Junior College; Jean M. English, Tallahassee Community College; Elizabeth Penfield, University of New Orleans; and Josephine Koster Tarvers, Rutgers University at New Brunswick. Also, at various stages of the evolution of my manuscript, I had the benefit of excellent suggestions from Gary Acton, Eastern Montana College; Bruce C. Appleby, Southern Illinois University; Dorothy Bankston, Louisiana State University; Vivian Brown, Laredo Junior College; Lennet Daigle, Georgia Southwestern College; Sally Geil, Brevard Community College; G. Dale Gleason, Hutchinson Community College; Mary Ellen Grasso, Broward Community College; Dorothy M. Guinn, Florida Atlantic University; Virginia C. Hinton, Kennesaw College; Albert M. Katz, University of Wisconsin; George E. Kennedy, Washington State University; Mark L. Knapp, University of Texas at Austin; Rosemary Lanshe, Broward Community College; Joyce M. Pair, DeKalb Community College; Edgar V. Roberts, Lehman College, CUNY; Barbara Saigo, University of Northern Iowa; Roy Saigo, University of Northern Iowa; Louise Z. Smith, University of Massachusetts at Boston; Barbara R. Stout, Montgomery College; Carolyn West, Daytona Beach Community College; Stephen Worchel, Texas A&M University.

At Prentice-Hall I have had the privilege of working with a stellar team. Joyce F. Perkins has been the ultimate development editor, nurturing my vision of the book while serving as my invaluable sounding board, shoulder, and—most of all—muse. Phil Miller, Executive Editor for Humanities and English Editor, has woven his way into my creative life with his keen mind, unfailing energy, and gentle optimism. Hilda Tauber, Production Editor, has enhanced the project by giving tirelessly of her vast experience, uncommon skill, and impressive eye for detail. Others at Prentice-Hall who mattered much were Ed Stanford, President of College Book Division, who inspired me to accept the invitation to write this book; Bud Therien, former Executive Editor for the Humanities, who helped me begin; Carol Carter, Marketing Manager for Humanities, who invigorated me with her resourcefulness and enthusiasm; and Jane Baumann, Assistant to Phil Miller, who has magical powers over red tape and knotty problems.

Closer to home, I drew much strength from my colleagues at the *Journal of Basic Writing,* especially Ruth Davis and Marilyn Maiz. Randy and Phil Klein of WORDSERV guided me expertly through the word processing maze of this 150-disk project. Among the many friends who have surrounded me with the special moral support and patience that help a writer thrive were Irving Bieber, Michael and Jayne Brookes, Rita and Hy Cohen, Elliott Goldhush, Myra Kogen, Jo Ann Lavery, Claire Perlmutter, Betty Renshaw, Shirley and Don Stearns, Marilyn Sternglass, Muriel Wolfe, and Gideon Zwas. My parents, Belle and Sidney Quitman, and my sister, Edith Klausner, gave fully of their love and enthusiasm. Above all, I am grateful to my husband, David Troyka, for his discerning reader's eye and the joy of each new day with him.

▉‖ TO THE STUDENT

My purpose in writing this handbook was to give you clear, thorough, up-to-date information about how to write effectively. I discuss the *conventions* of writing—the rules and standard practices concerning grammar, punctuation, spelling, and mechanics. I also discuss *choices* that writers confront—options writers have for shaping their essays and paragraphs, crafting their sentences, and selecting words. To complete the picture of what writing entails, I also discuss how the process of writing works, how writing relates to critical thinking, and what characterizes writing in subjects other than composition.

As with all other tools, the *Simon & Schuster Handbook for Writers* works best when its systems are familiar to the user. Try to take some time right away to get to know the book's format. As you browse through the pages, notice particularly how information is presented in the book's thirty-five chapters. Within each chapter, section headings announce key information. These headings are numbered with a code that includes the chapter number and a letter (*a, b, c,* and so on). The tab at the top of each page carries the code of the nearest section head on the page, so that you can thumb through the book and easily find the section you are searching for.

How do you look up the information you want in this book? You have three ways. On the inside front covers you can see all the main parts of the book at a glance. In the Table of Contents all sections of the book are listed in greater detail, with page numbers. The Index provides an alphabetical listing of all information, referenced both to section numbers and page numbers.

On the inside back covers you will see many of the correction symbols used by instructors, with explanations of the symbols and cross-references to the related sections in this handbook. You will also find a selected list of the key guidelines, checklists, summaries, and sentence patterns which appear in shaded panels in the text.

English, like many fields, uses terms not always widely known. The first time I use such a term in this handbook, I define it. Often, however, when I reuse the term later, I do not always have space to redefine it. When you are unsure of the meaning of a term I do not define, you can look it up in the Glossary of Grammatical and Selected Composition Terms. **After a term is introduced and defined, it is marked with a degree symbol (°) to signal that you can find its definition in the Glossary of Grammatical and Selected Composition Terms.** Thus, you can move through material in this book with the confidence that you have easy access to the meaning of unfamiliar terms.

While you are gaining experience as a student writer, you are often likely to want to ask new questions. Sometimes an instructor will be available to answer them, but often the questions will occur to you when you are writing with no one around. I have, therefore, designed this handbook so that you can learn from it with your class as well as on your own. Throughout your college career and beyond, keep this handbook close by so that you can always look up what you need to know. It belongs in your permanent library, alongside your dictionary and other reference books.

If you are like I was in college, you want direct and full answers to your questions. You also want a chance to think about some useful questions that you might have overlooked. I wrote this handbook with you in mind. I hope you will find it a helpful, stimulating, and pleasurable resource now and for many years to come.

LYNN QUITMAN TROYKA
Beechhurst, New York

I ‖ Writing an Essay

1
THINKING ABOUT PURPOSES AND AUDIENCES

Why write? In this age of telephones and tape recorders, television and film, computers and communications satellites, why should you bother with writing? The answer has overlapping parts, starting with the inner life of a writer and moving outward.

Writing is a way of thinking and learning. Writing gives you unique opportunities to explore ideas and acquire information. By writing, you come to know subjects well and make them your own. Even thirty years later, many people can recall details about the topics and content of essays they wrote in college, but far fewer people can recall specifics of a classroom lecture or a textbook chapter. Thus, writing helps you learn and gain authority over knowledge. As you communicate your learning, you are also teaching. When you write for a reader, you play the role of a teacher, someone who knows the material sufficiently well to organize and present it clearly. Little is as hospitable to learning as the act of teaching.

Writing is a way of discovering. The act of writing allows you to make unexpected connections among ideas and language. As you write, thoughts emerge and interconnect in ways unavailable until the physical act of writing began. An authority on writing, James Britton, describes discovery in writing as "shaping at the point of utterance." Similarly, well-known writer E. M. Forster talked about discovery during writing by asking, "How can I know what I mean until I've seen what I said?" You can expect, therefore, many surprises of insight that come only when you write and re-write, each time trying to get closer to what you want to say.

Writing creates reading. Writing creates a permanent, visible record of your ideas for others to read and ponder. Writing is a powerful means of communication, for reading informs and shapes human thought. In an open society, everyone is free to write and thereby to create reading for other people. For that freedom to be exercised, however, the ability to write cannot be concentrated in a few people. All of us need access to the power of the written word.

Writing ability is needed by educated people. Your skill with writing is often considered to reflect your level of education. College work demands that you write many different types of assignments. Most jobs in today's technological society require writing skill for preparing documents ranging from letters and memos to formal reports. Indeed, throughout your life, your writing will reveal your ability to think clearly and use language to express ideas.

■‖ 1a
Understand the elements of writing.

What does writing do? Writing is often explained by its elements: *Writing is a way of communicating a message to a reader for a purpose.* Each word in this definition carries important meaning that can help you understand what writing is.

Communicating means sending, so a message must have a destination. The well-known writer and historian Barbara Tuchman says that it takes two to complete the function of the written word.

The **message** of writing is its content. Whether the subject you write about is your choice or is assigned, you must transform it into a message worthy of communication. You need a thesis, a central idea that serves an a unifying focus for your content. You also need sufficient content to support and elaborate that thesis. You can present your message in a variety of ways. Traditionally, forms for writing are divided into *narration, description, exposition,* and *argumentation.* Narration and description are two among many strategies for developing ideas, all of which are presented in Chapter 4. Exposition and argumentation are **purposes** for writing (see 1b). Finally, the **reader** of your writing is your audience (see 1c).

■‖ 1b

Understand purposes for writing.

Writing is often defined by its **purpose.** Writing purposes have to do with goals, often referred to as *aims of writing* or *writing intentions.* Thinking about purposes for writing means thinking about the motivating forces that move people to write. Students often think their purpose for writing is to fulfill a class assignment. But the concept of purpose means more: It refers to what the writing seeks to achieve. Purposes for writing, though varied, can be categorized into four major groups.*

- to express yourself
- to provide information for your reader
- to persuade your reader
- to create a literary work

The purposes of writing *to express yourself* and *to create a literary work* contribute importantly to human thought and culture. This handbook, however, concentrates on the two purposes most prominent and practical in your academic life: *to inform your reader* and *to persuade your reader.*

‖ 1

Recognize informative writing.

Informative writing seeks to give information and, when necessary, to explain it. This writing is known also as **expository** because it expounds on, or sets forth, ideas and facts. *Informative writing focuses on the subject being discussed.* (In contrast, persuasive writing focuses on the reader, whom the writer wants to influence; see 1b–2.) Informative writing includes reports of observations, ideas, scientific data, facts, statistics. It can be found in textbooks, encyclopedias, technical and business reports, books of nonfiction, newspapers, and magazines.

When you write exposition, you present information. You are expected to offer that information with a minimum of bias, for you are aiming to educate, not persuade. Like all effective teachers, you need to present the information completely and clearly. The material has to be accurate and verifiable by additional reading, talking with others, or personal experience. For example, consider this passage of informative writing.

*Adapted from the ideas of James L. Kinneavy, a modern rhetorician, discussed in *A Theory of Discourse.* 1971; New York: Norton, 1980.

In 1914 in what is now Addo Park in South Africa, a hunter by the name of Pretorius was asked to exterminate a herd of 140 elephants. He killed all but 20, and those survivors became so cunning at evading him that he was forced to abandon the hunt. The area became a preserve in 1930, and the elephants have been protected ever since. Nevertheless, elephants now four generations removed from those Pretorius hunted remain shy and strangely nocturnal. Young elephants evidently learn from the adults' trumpeting alarm calls to avoid humans.

—CAROL GRANT GOULD, "Out of the Mouths of Beasts"

This passage is successful because it *communicates* (sends) a *message* (about young elephants learning to avoid humans) to a *reader* (the general reading public who might be interested in the subject) for a *purpose* (to inform). In this passage, the writer's last sentence states the main idea. Each sentence before the last offers information that builds support for the main idea.

CHECKLIST FOR INFORMATIVE WRITING

1. Is its major focus the subject being discussed?
2. Is its primary purpose to inform rather than persuade?
3. Is its information complete and accurate?
4. Is its information verifiable?
5. Is its information arranged for clarity?
6. Is it interesting to read?

2
Recognize persuasive writing.

Persuasive writing seeks to convince the reader about a matter of opinion. This writing is sometimes called **argumentative** because it argues a position.

As a writer of persuasion, you deal with the debatable, that which has other sides to it. *Persuasive writing focuses on the reader, whom the writer wants to influence.* (In contrast, informative writing focuses on the subject being discussed; see 1b-1.) Persuasive writing seeks to change the reader's mind, to bring the reader's point of view closer to the writer's. Examples of persuasive writing include editorials, letters to the editor, reviews, sermons, business or research proposals, opinion essays in magazines, and books that argue a point of view.

To be persuasive, you cannot merely state an opinion. You must offer convincing support for your point of view. To argue well, your reasoning must be logical and sensible (see Chapter 5) and clearly arranged. For example, consider this passage of persuasive writing.

> Scientifically, levels of sound are measured by decibels. Starting with zero, decibels reach a very loud 150 for a jet takeoff. The degree and constancy of exposure to high decibels of noise can be the difference between good and poor health. Repeated exposure to sound levels of 85 or more decibels can cause permanent hearing loss. In the case of our young people who frequent discotheques where the decibels level usually exceeds 115, and who at home have stereo units that play to a damaging 90 decibels, the warning is out. Leading otologists throughout the country have predicted that today's teenagers and those in their early twenties face a grim future with impaired hearing—the price they will pay for their rash disregard of medically proven evidence that music that blares hath no charm whatsoever.
>
> —SYLVIA RESNICK, "Noise: It Can Kill You"

This passage is successful because it sends a *message* (about damaging sound levels) to a *reader* (especially anyone who listens, or knows people who listen, to loud music) for a *purpose* (to persuade readers that loud music can damage hearing). The writer's last sentence summarizes her opinion. Each sentence before the last offers evidence so that the reader can understand, and perhaps be persuaded to agree with, the author's conclusion. Not all people will heed the warning, but the writer has given sufficient information to sound the alert.

CHECKLIST FOR PERSUASIVE WRITING

1. Is its major focus the reader?
2. Is its primary purpose to convince rather than inform?
3. Does it offer information or reasons to support its point of view?
4. Is its point of view based on sound reasoning and logic?
5. Are the points of its argument arranged for clarity?
6. Does it motivate the reader to action or otherwise evoke the intended response?

EXERCISE 1

For each paragraph: (1) Decide if the dominant purpose is *informative* or *persuasive*. (2) Refer back to whichever of the two checklists above corresponds to the purpose you have identified. (3) Answer the questions on the checklist in relation to the paragraph, and explain each of your answers.

A. When most people think of a black hole, the Hollywood image of a spiraling tunnel into alternate dimensions comes to their minds. But we have only theory and speculation as to what a black hole really is. When a star begins to die, the matter that holds it together is burned up. The star looses its bonds and slowly expands from its constant rotation. Eventually, however, it begins to close in on itself until the process is irreversible. The size that the star expanded to before it began to contract is a black circle referred to as an "event horizon." This is what is normally seen in photographs, a black circular void that a beam of light cannot penetrate.

                                        —DAVID PHILLIPS, student

B. For the past few years, our city has been in a downward slump, especially in terms of its recreational facilities and economy. Our parks and buildings have been the target of considerable vandalism. The lake, which has been sorrowfully neglected, could be improved with more trees, better roads, and additional security. Our unemployment is the highest in the state and our economy the worst. Both situations could be improved by attracting new industries to our city. Reclaiming our land by planting orange trees, onions, and melons would help the farm economy. Our city could be one of the best places to live if it would employ its available manpower to effect these kinds of improvements.

                                        —GERARDO ANTONIO GARZA, student

C. Twenty-two million American children ride school buses every day, but fewer than 200,000—living in 24 school districts throughout the country—are required to wear seat belts. Figures for the 1982–83 academic year (the latest figures available) reveal that 13 students were killed and approximately 1,500 were injured in school bus accidents. These figures may not be staggering, but they are almost wholly preventable. Seat belts on school buses are a must.

                                        —THOMAS GOLDWASSER, "Letter to the Editor," *Washington Post*

EXERCISE 2

A. In a single issue of a newspaper, find one informative article and one persuasive article. Explain why you identify them as you do. Next, for each article, go back to the checklist above that corresponds to the purpose you have identified, and answer the questions on the checklist. Explain each answer.

B. Repeat this process with a magazine.

EXERCISE 3

Assume that you have to write on each of these topics twice, once to inform your reader and once to persuade your reader. Be prepared to discuss how your two treatments of each topic would differ.

1. fast-food restaurants
2. studying
3. space exploration
4. cancer signals
5. good manners
6. William Shakespeare
7. pollution
8. endangered species
9. automobile safety
10. Mexico

 1c

Understand audiences for writing

Good writing is often judged by its ability to reach its intended **audience.** To be effective, informative and persuasive writing (1b) need to be geared to the fact that someone is "out there" to receive the communication. If you write without considering your audience, you risk communicating only with yourself.

Experienced writers think about the background of their audience as they write. For example, a sales report filled with technical language assumes that its readers know the specialized vocabulary. The general reading public would, of course, have trouble understanding such a report. But if it were rewritten without technical terms, general readers could understand it.

As a writer for an audience, you need to be sensitive to your readers' beliefs and concerns. For example, in writing meant to persuade people to vote for a particular candidate, if you imply disrespect for people who stay home and raise children, you risk losing votes of many homemakers and their spouses. Or, if you want to persuade lawmakers that homemakers should be allowed to draw from the Social Security system, you would need to address some of the lawmakers' practical concerns, such as the impact of your proposal on the federal budget.

The more explicit information you have about your audience, the better you can think about how to reach it. Often, of course, you can only guess at the details. If you know or can take a good guess about even a few characteristics, your chances of reaching your audience improve. Here is a checklist to get your thinking started.

CHECKLIST OF AUDIENCE CHARACTERISTICS

WHO ARE THEY?

age/sex/education?
ethnic background/political philosophy/religious beliefs?
role(s): student/veteran/parent/wage earner/voter/etc.?
employment/economic status?
interests/hobbies?

WHAT INFORMATION DO THEY HAVE?

level of education?
experience with reading academic or business writing?
amount of general knowledge about the subject?
amount of specialized knowledge about the subject?
what preconceptions do they bring to the material?

1
Understand the general reading public.

The **general reading public** is educated, sometimes less and sometimes more than you. Its members are experienced readers, people who frequently read newspapers, magazines, and books. They often have some general information about the subject you are dealing with, but they enjoy a chance to learn something new or see something from a different perspective.

The general reading public expects you to know how to reach them. For example, the general reader expects material to be clear and to be free of advanced technical information. Equally important, the general reading public expects to be treated respectfully. As experienced readers, they are sensitive to your **tone**—the way what you say reflects your attitude toward the subject and the audience. If the tone implies you feel superior to your audience, your tone will be condescending and distasteful. Similarly, if your tone hints that you are uninformed or unsure, readers will lose confidence in your material. Tone is created largely by word choice (see Chapter 21). Although the general reading public enjoys lively language, it is jarred by an overly informal tone in the middle of a serious presentation of informative or persuasive writing. For example, in a newspaper report about the results of an election, you should not refer to the loser or winner as *guy* or *gal,* no matter how relaxed the candidate's demeanor. Likewise, in the middle of a serious critique, using *pretty* as a synonym for *very* or *fairly* would be out of place (as in "The weak script was helped by some pretty good acting"). An artificial tone is also a mistake (see 21d). Do not, for example, use pretentious phrases such as "the aforementioned occurrence that transpired" when you mean "the event." Also, if your language is biased or slanted (see 21a), your tone will seem underhanded, and your readers will distrust what you say. For more about the writer's role and tone, see 2e-3.

2
Understand your instructor as a reader.

When you write for a class assignment, your audience will almost certainly be your **instructor.** Sometimes, especially when you are planning or revising your work, your instructor might want other students in your class to collaborate as an audience, but your final audience usually remains your instructor.

Your instructor is a member of the general reading public and also someone who recognizes that you are an apprentice. Your instructor knows that few students are experienced writers or complete experts on their subjects. Still, your instructor always expects your writing to reflect that you took time to write well and learn the material thoroughly. In part, therefore, an instructor is a *judge,* someone to whom you must demonstrate that you are doing your best. Instructors are very experienced readers who can quickly recognize minimal efforts or a negative attitude (as when a paper carries a tone that suggests "Tell me what you want and I'll give it to you").

Inexperienced writers wrongly assume sometimes that instructors will fill in mentally what is missing on the page. Instructors expect what they read to include everything that the writer wants to say or imply, so you cannot leave out material. Even if you write immediately after your instructor has heard you give an oral report on the same subject, write as if no one is aware of what you know.

Your instructor is also an *academic,* a member of a group whose professional lives center on intellectual endeavors. You must, therefore, write within the constraints of academic writing. For example, if you are told to write on a topic of your choice, you definitely do not have total freedom to choose. Your topic must have some intrinsic intellectual interest. For example, an essay should not merely give directions on how to cut a wedding cake or use an eraser.

‖ 3
‖ Understand specialists as readers.

Specialists are members of the general reading public who have expert knowledge on specific subjects. In writing for specialists, you are expected both to know the specialty and to realize that your readers have advanced expertise.

Specialized readers often share not only knowledge but also assumptions, interests, and beliefs. For example, they may be members of a club that concentrates on a hobby, such as amateur astronomy or orchid raising. They may have similar backgrounds, such as having immigrated from another country or having fought in a particular war. They may have similar views on matters related to religion and politics. You have, therefore, to balance the necessity to be thorough with the demand that you not recapitulate matters such as technical terms and special references.

EXERCISE 4

Each of these passages was written for an instructor, and therefore, for a general reading audience. Read each paragraph and decide (a) if it has the right tone for academic writing and (b) if it assumes knowledge that only a specialist would have.

1. When contrasting Jimmy Connors' style of play to John McEnroe's style, people should remember that Jimmy Connors is a baseline player and John McEnroe is a serve and volley player. Jimmy Connors' game plan is to hit baseline shots until the chance to come to the net is achieved. He also will try to wear down the player by hitting baseline shots until he can hit a winner. In contrast, John McEnroe will serve and come to the net immediately. John comes to the net with the hope that the service return will be poor so that he can hit a winner.

—DAN DORAN, student

2. If two hockey greats were to be compared, then the unique choice would be to compare Wayne Gretzky and Gordie Howe. Both will be remembered for their hockey prowess. Gordie Howe is now retired, and Wayne Gretzky is probably just entering his prime with the Edmonton Oilers, accumulating records that will probably never be broken again.

—JOE BROOKS, student

2

PLANNING AND SHAPING

Many people assume that a real writer can pick up a pen (or sit at a typewriter or word processor) and magically write a finished product, word by perfect word. Experienced writers know better. They know that **writing is a process,** a series of activities that start the moment they begin thinking about a subject and end when they complete a final draft. Experienced writers know, also, that good writing is rewriting. Their drafts are filled with additions, deletions, rearrangements, and rewordings.

For example, on the next page you can see how the paragraph you just read was reworked into final form. Notice that two sentences were dropped, two sentences were combined, one sentence was added, and various words were dropped, changed, or added. Such activities are typical of writing.

◼‖ 2a
Understand the writing process.

Writing is an ongoing process of considering alternatives and making choices. The better you understand the writing process, the better you will write and the more you can enjoy writing. For the

~~Chapter One discusses what writing is.¶ This chapter~~

~~explains how writing happens.¶~~ Many people assume that a real

pick up a pen

writer can ~~put pen to paper~~ (or sit at ~~the keyboard of~~ a

magically—a

typewriter or word processor) and write finished product, *word*

by perfect word.

Experienced writers ~~all~~ know better. They know that writing

is a process, ~~Writing is~~ a series of activities that start

they begin

the moment thinking about a subject ~~begins~~ and end when they

complete ~~the~~ a

final draft. ~~is complete.¶~~ Experienced writers know, also,

that good writing is rewriting. *Their drafts are filled with additions, deletions, rearrangements, and rewordings.*

---

sake of explanation, the parts of the writing process are discussed separately in this chapter. In real life, you will find that the steps overlap, looping back and forth as each piece of writing evolves.

AN OVERVIEW OF THE WRITING PROCESS

Planning calls for you to gather ideas and think about a focus.

Shaping calls for you to consider ways to organize your material.

Drafting calls for you to write your ideas in sentences and paragraphs.

Revising calls for you to evaluate your draft and, based on your decisions, rewrite it by adding, cutting, replacing, moving—and often totally recasting material.

Editing calls for you to check the technical correctness of your grammar, spelling, punctuation, and mechanics.

Proofreading calls for you to read your final copy for typing errors or handwriting legibility.

Understanding writing as a multistage process allows you to work efficiently, concentrating on one activity at a time rather than trying to juggle all of the facets of a writing project simultaneously.

As you work with the writing process, rest assured that there is no *one* way to write. When you start, allow yourself to move through each stage of the writing process and see what is involved. Then as you gain experience, begin to observe what works best for you. After you master the differences that separate planning from shaping, drafting from revising, and editing from proofreading, you might want to experiment a little. For example, some people write a "discovery" draft to see what emerges before they begin shaping. Some writers outline immediately and use planning techniques to flesh out points on the outline. Many writers find during revising that they need more ideas, so they use planning techniques once again. Still other writers edit during revision because a grammar or spelling error keeps getting in the way.

Most writers struggle some of the time with ideas that are difficult to express, sentences that will not take shape, and words that are not precise. Do not be impatient with yourself and do not get discouraged. Writing takes time. The more you write, the easier it will be, but remember that experienced writers know that writing never happens magically.

An aside about the words used to discuss writing: Instructors refer to written products in different ways. Often the words are used interchangeably, but sometimes they have specific meanings for specific instructors. Listen closely and ask if you are unsure of what you hear. For example, the words *essay, theme,* and *composition* usually—but not always—refer to writing that runs from about 500 to 1,000 words. This book uses *essay.* The words *report* and *project* usually mean writing that draws on outside sources. The word *paper* can mean anything from a few paragraphs to a long and detailed report of a complex research project. This book uses *paper* to refer to research writing.

■‖ 2b
Think about writing.

Writing begins with thinking. When you are given a writing assignment, you are immediately cast into a **writing situation.** The decisions you make as you write an essay depend on the particulars of each writing situation: topic, purpose, audience, and special requirements.

Underlying all aspects of the writing situation is the **topic.** If you are supposed to choose your own topic or narrow an assigned general topic, you need to keep in mind the constraints of academic writing. If the topic is assigned, you have to write without going off the track. No matter what the topic, *you* are the starting place for your writing. You must draw upon yourself as a source. All writers depend on their accumulated experience and education as they write. Whatever they have seen, heard, read, and even dreamed contributes to their fund of ideas and knowledge. No matter how much you have learned from your reading, going to plays and movies, and watching television, the starting point for your writing is always you, the writer. As you think through and gather ideas (2d) for your topic, your task is to establish a *focus,* or a point of view, about the topic and *support* for that focus.

The writing situation includes the **purpose** for your writing. In college, the major purposes for writing are *to inform* and *to persuade,* as explained fully in 1b. Effective informative and persuasive writing succeed in part because they reflect a clear sense of purpose. Some writing assignments include or clearly imply a statement of purpose. For example, your purpose is informative if you are asked to write about the dangers of smoking. On the other hand, your purpose is persuasive if your assignment calls for an argument against smoking. Many assignments, however, do not stipulate the writing purpose. In such cases, one of your tasks is to choose either an informative or persuasive purpose based on the topic, what you want to say about it (often referred to as the *focus*), and how you develop what you want to say.

The **audience** for your writing is also part of the writing situation. For college writing, your audience is primarily—though not necessarily exclusively—your instructor. Your instructor is both a member of the general reading public and an academic. Your writing needs to be sensitive to such backgrounds, as explained fully in 1c. Sometimes a writing assignment names a very specific audience, such as the head of a major corporation or veterans who have served in Vietnam. These audiences are specialists, people who have more technical knowledge than does the general reading public. You have to write to their level. Sometimes an assignment stipulates that the writing will be read by other students in the class. Students in such situations serve as surrogate instructors, so you are expected to write with the same tone and level of information as you would for your instructor alone.

Special requirements influence every writing situation. These include the time allotted for the assignment, the expected length of the writing, and other practical constraints. If an assignment includes a word count, you have to take it into consideration when you make decisions about topic, purpose, and audience. If an assignment is due in one week, you have to expect that your instructor wants writing that shows more than one day's work. If research is required, you have to build time for it into your schedule.

Throughout this chapter and the next, you will see the work of two students, Tara Foster and Gary Lee Houseman.

Tara Foster was given this assignment: Write an essay of 500 to 700 words that discusses any important problem facing adult men and women today. Your first and second drafts are due in one week. I will read your second draft as an "essay in progress" and will make comments to help you toward a third draft. Your third draft is due one week after I hand back your second draft.

Gary Lee Houseman was given this assignment: Write a 1,000-word essay in which you argue against some aspect of the destruction of our environment. Your final draft is due in two weeks, but bring your earlier drafts to class for possible discussion.

In analyzing her writing situation, Foster saw that the assignment specified the special requirements of length and time. She decided that her audience would be her instructor. She tentatively chose an informative purpose, knowing that as she got further into planning she might change her mind. Her decision process about the topic is discussed in 2c.

In analyzing his writing situation, Houseman saw that the assignment told him about length, time, and purpose. He realized that the due date of two weeks might imply that research was required, so he asked his instructor. He was told not to use outside sources but to draw on his own fund of knowledge and his personal focus—point of view—about the subject. Once Houseman knew that, he decided that his audience would be his instructor. His decision process about his topic is discussed in 2c.

EXERCISE 1

For each assignment listed below, answer these questions: (a) Is its purpose to inform or to persuade? (b) Is the audience the general reading public or specialists? (c) What special requirements of length and time are stated or implied?

1. *Biology:* You have twenty minutes to list and explain three ways that the circulatory system contributes to homeostasis in the human body.

2. *English:* Write a 500- to 700-word essay arguing for or against tougher academic requirements for student athletes. This assignment is due in one week.

3. *Political Science:* Write a 1,000-word essay about television's impact on elections.

4. *English:* Write a 300-word editorial for the student newspaper praising or criticizing the college's library. Draw on your personal experience. Also, interview at least one member of the library staff for his or her reaction to your point of view.

5. *Art:* Write a one-paragraph summary of the difference between a wide-angle lens and a telephoto lens.

▣ 2c
Choose a topic for writing.

Choosing a topic calls for using good judgment and making sound decisions. Experienced writers know that the quality of their writing depends on how they handle a topic. You should, therefore, think through a topic before you rush in and get too deeply involved to pull out within the time allotted. You will write more effectively if your topic is suitable for college writing and if it is one that can be presented and developed well.

Of course, some assignments leave no room for making choices about the topic. You may be given very specific instructions such as "Explain how oxygen is absorbed from the lungs." You may be asked to describe the view from your classroom window or to compare and contrast the personalities of two major characters in a short story. Your job with such assignments is to do precisely what is asked and not go off the topic.

‖ 1
Know how to select a topic on your own.

Some instructors will ask you to write on whatever topic you wish. In such situations, do not assume that all subjects are suitable for informative or persuasive writing in college. Academic settings call for topics that can reflect your ability to think ideas through. For example, the old reliable essay about a summer vacation is probably not safe territory for a college essay if you have nothing extraordinary to report. Your essays need to dive into issues and concepts, and they should demonstrate that you can use specific, concrete details to support what you want to say. The need for specifics should not, however, tempt you to write very technical information, especially for an audience unfamiliar with the particular specialized vocabulary.

When you choose a topic on your own, be careful not to use a very narrow one. You will have little success with topics that give you little to say. For example, for a course in informative and persuasive writing, you might reach a dead end if you tried to write a 500-word essay about what your cat looks like while sleeping, unless you were asked to write an elaborate description of a common sight. Similarly, for the same course, you might find yourself out of ideas if you tried to write 500 words about a single apple. You need to take purpose, audience, and special requirements into account when you make decisions about topics. A cat sleeping might be a fine topic for a zoology course, and an apple might be a suitable topic for a health class.

2
Know how to narrow an assigned topic.

The real challenge in dealing with topics comes when you choose or are assigned a subject that is very broad. You have to *narrow the subject.* This means thinking of subdivisions of the subject, of different areas within the subject. Most very broad subjects can be broken down in hundreds of ways, but you need to think of only a few until you come to one that seems possible for an essay. Think it through before rushing in, however. Think about whether the topic as narrowed can be developed well in writing. **What separates most good writing from bad is the writer's ability to move back and forth between general statements and specific details.** A suitably narrowed topic permits such movement.

For example, if the subject is marriage, you might decide to talk about what makes marriages successful. But you cannot depend merely on generalizations such as "In successful marriages husbands and wives learn to accept each other's faults." You need to explain why accepting faults is important, and you need to give concrete illustrations of what you are talking about.

Whenever you narrow a broad subject to obtain a writing topic, keep in mind the writing situation of each assignment: purpose, audience, and special requirements. Think about what you can handle well according to the conditions of each assignment.

SUBJECT	Music
WRITING SITUATION	Freshman composition class
	Informative purpose
	Instructor as audience
	500 words, one week

POSSIBLE TOPICS	the moods music creates classical music country-western music major classical composers
SUBJECT	Cities
WRITING SITUATION	Sociology Course Persuasive purpose Students and then instructor as audience 500 to 700 words, one week
POSSIBLE TOPICS	comforts of city living discomforts of city living groups that prefer city life how cities develop
SUBJECT	Mythology
WRITING SITUATION	Humanities course Informative purpose Instructor as audience—a specialist in my- thology 1,000 words, two weeks
TOPICS	the purpose of myths mythical views of gods and goddesses myths about the origins of the world

Both Tara Foster and Gary Lee Houseman faced the task of narrowing their topics. Foster's assignment asked for a discussion of "an important problem facing adult men and women today." She knew immediately that "an important problem" was too vague and general, and she realized the assignment implied that she was expected to make it specific and suitably narrow. Being one of today's "adult men and women," she thought of many problems: war, the dangers of nuclear energy, unemployment, divorce. She saw a danger in these topics, however. She knew that she had to avoid what her instructor called *canned rhetoric,* the use of standard statements made commonly by everyone. She wanted to test out what she might say on various topics, so she did some "freewriting" (2d-2). This helped her realize that what interested her most was the problem of divorce. Still, she felt that she did not have enough information to write a 500- to 700-word essay on the subject. She used divorce as a springboard for "brainstorming" (2d-3). She knew people who had gone through divorce, and she was aware that learning to live alone was a major problem for some. This led her to thinking about many types of people who have to face living alone at one time or another in their lives. She began to think about what they needed to know to be able to live alone. She felt that she had found a good topic, but she confirmed this by asking the "journalist's questions" (2d-4) to see if she would have enough to write about.

Houseman's assignment asked for an argument about "some aspect of the destruction of our environment." Houseman's process of narrowing the subject was very different from Foster's. For a number of years, he had been very interested in conservation issues, and so he had a solid fund of knowledge from having read many newspaper and magazine articles. He thought of choosing the topics of acid rain or toxic wastes or pollution. But the topic he cared about most was the destruction of rain forests. To check whether he could remember many details from his reading, he tried "mapping" (2d-5), and he decided that he had made a good choice for himself.

EXERCISE 2
For each general topic, think of three narrowed topics that would be suitable for a 500- to 700-word essay in a writing course. Assume that each essay is due in one week and that the audience is the general reading public, as represented by the course's instructor. List your three narrowed topics and explain briefly why each is suitable for the writing situation.

1. Computers
2. Movies
3. Political campaigns
4. Health
5. Literature

EXERCISE 3
Think of three subjects that interest you. List them. Then pick one and narrow it to three topics suitable for an essay. Assume that the essay is for a writing class, that it should run from 500 to 700 words, that it is due in one week, and that it will be read by both other students in the class as well as the course's instructor. After you finish listing three topics, explain briefly why each is suitable for the writing situation.

 2d

Gather ideas for writing.

Techniques for gathering ideas, sometimes called *prewriting stategies* or *invention techniques,* can help you while you are narrowing your topic. They help you discover what you know and, often, how much you know about a topic before you decide to write on it. As such, techniques for gathering ideas are important aids for thinking of the ideas and of details to use in essays.

Many techniques for gathering ideas have been developed and used by experienced writers. The ones discussed and illustrated in this chapter are summarized in the following chart.

SUMMARY OF WAYS TO GATHER IDEAS FOR WRITING

Keeping an idea book
Writing in a journal
Freewriting
Brainstorming
Using the journalist's questions
Mapping
Knowing when to read for writing

Students sometimes worry that they have nothing to write about. Often, however, students know far more than they give themselves credit for. The challenge is to uncover what is there but seems not to be. Start with the assumption that you know more than you think, and try some of these techniques for discovering what is not coming easily to mind.

No one technique of generating ideas always works for all writers in all situations. Experiment, therefore, with all these methods. If one does not provide enough useful material, try an alternative. Also, even if one strategy produces some good material, you may still want to try another technique to see what additional possibilities it may turn up.

1
Know how to keep an idea book and write in a journal.

Your ease with writing will grow if you get into some of the habits of mind that typify writers. Professional writers are always on the lookout for ideas to write about and for details to develop their ideas. They listen, watch, talk with people, and generally keep their minds open. For this reason, many writers carry an **idea book**—a pocketsize notebook—with them at all times so that they can jot down ideas that spring to mind. They do not trust their memories because they know that good ideas can melt away like snowflakes. If you keep an idea book handy throughout your college

years, you will find that a ready source of ideas is at hand—and
that your powers of observation become increasingly strong.

Like an idea book, a **journal** is a record of your ideas, only
the entries are written daily. Many writers, both amateur and
professional, write journals. Any size notebook *except* pocketsize can
serve well for a journal. Fifteen minutes a day can be enough—
before going to bed, between classes, on a bus. When you write in
your journal, *you* are your audience. The writing is not for publication, so the content and tone can be as personal and informal as you
wish.

When writing in your journal, you can draw on your reading,
your observations, your dreams. You can write down and respond to
quotations that seem particularly meaningful. You can react to
movies, plays, and television programs that are memorable. You
can think on paper about your opinions, beliefs, family, friends.
Writing in a journal gives you the chance to write about whatever
you wish. Unlike a diary, a journal is not merely for listing what
you did that day. In a journal you put down your thoughts. Writing
is a way of thinking, a way of thinking through ideas that need
time to develop, a way of wrestling with problems not given to easy
solution. Equally important, writing is a way of discovering, of allowing thoughts to emerge as the physical act of writing moves
along.

Keeping a journal can help you in three ways. First, writing
every day gives you the habit of productivity. The more you write,
the more you get used to the feeling of words pouring out of you
onto paper, the easier it will become for you to write in all situations. Second, a journal instills the habit of close observation and
thinking. Third, a journal serves as an excellent source of ideas
when you need to write in response to an assignment.

Having served overseas in the armed forces before going to
college, Gary Lee Houseman was attuned to other places and perspectives. He sometimes wrote in his journal about world issues.
When he got the assignment to argue against the destruction of the
environment, he looked in his journal for possible starting points.
Here is a brief excerpt from Houseman's journal.

October 15
Conservation issues always seem to pop up at me when I am reading or watching TV. I get steamed up. What are they doing to our
world? I saw a program on TV last night about rain forests. It
confirmed what I've been reading about for the last few years.
They are destroying the rain forests in the name of progress. They
are robbing *me* of a factory that manufactures oxygen and helps
clean the air. One species of plant or animal a day, many of which

have potential to give us cures for diseases. I read a year ago that a drug from a plant in a South American rain forest is being used to treat Parkinson's disease.

EXERCISE 4
Write a journal entry about one of these subjects. Write to discover what you have to say or to think through what is already on your mind.

1. Your life ten years from now
2. Thanksgiving Day
3. The homeless
4. Learning to play a sport
5. Cartoons
6. Hiroshima
7. Radios
8. Symphony music
9. Politicians
10. VCR's

2
Know how to use freewriting.

Freewriting is writing nonstop. Freewriting means writing down whatever comes into your mind without stopping to worry about whether the ideas are good or the spelling is correct. When you freewrite, you do nothing to interrupt the flow. Let your mind make all kinds of associations. Do not censor any thoughts or flashes of insight. Do not go back and review. Do not cross out. Some days your freewriting might seem mindless, but other days it can reveal interesting ideas to you.

Freewriting gives you the "feel" of pen moving across paper or of fingers in constant motion on the keyboard of a typewriter or computer. This feeling that comes with the physical act of writing serves you well when you draft and revise your writing.

Freewriting works best if you set a goal, such as writing for fifteen minutes or until you have filled one page. Keep going until you reach that goal, even if you must repeat a word over and over until a new word comes to mind.

If you use a word processor, you can avoid the temptation to stop and criticize your writing by doing "invisible writing." Dim the monitor screen so you cannot see your writing. The computer's memory will still be recording your ideas, but will not be able to see them until you brighten the screen again. The same effect is possible for writing by hand if you use worn-out ballpoint pen and a piece of carbon paper between the paper you are writing on and another piece of paper.

Focused freewriting means starting with a set topic. You may focus your freewriting in any way you like—perhaps with a phrase from your journal or a quotation you like. Use the focus as a starting point for writing down as many of your thoughts as you can until you meet the time or page limit you set. Again, do not censor what you say. Keep moving forward.

As with journals, freewriting can be a source for ideas and details to write about. Here is an excerpt from Tara Foster's focused freewriting. She was thinking about narrowing her topic from the subject "an important problem facing today's adult men and women."

> Well, the assignment says a problem. Let's see if I'm going to write a lot of old junk about things. War. War. War is stupid. Unemployment lines and trying to find a job on this campus. Nuclear energy is too frightening to think about. Anyway, I don't know enough to write about it. I really want to think about divorce. The big D. Why bother getting married if I only have a 50–50 chance of making it? I think I'll be in the 50% that makes it. But many of my friends are not making it. Lives ripped apart. Writing like this gets tiring for my hand. Keep moving, keep moving. Sounds like a movie theater usher. My parents had a great marriage. Since my dad died my mother has had a hard time. She has to live alone now that I am out of the house. It isn't easy for her to get used to a new lifestyle.

EXERCISE 5
Freewrite for five minutes on one of these topics.

1. Worrying
2. Procrastinating
3. A famous person, alive or dead
4. Taking tests
5. Loneliness
6. Mark Twain
7. Libraries
8. Spelling
9. Falling in love
10. Peanut butter

3
Know how to use brainstorming.

Brainstorming means making a list of all the ideas that come to mind associated with a topic. The ideas can be listed as words or phrases. Listmaking, like freewriting, produces its best results when you let your mind range freely, generating quantities of ideas before analyzing them.

You may find that brainstorming allows you to generate many ideas quickly because the format does not call for sentences or paragraphs. You can brainstorm in one concentrated session or over several days, depending on how much time is available for the assignment. In courses that use collaborative learning procedures, brainstorming in groups can work especially very well. One person's ideas bounce off the next person's, and collectively more ideas get listed.

Brainstorming is done in two steps. First, you make a list. Then you go back and try to find patterns in the list and ways to group the ideas into categories. The items do not have to be in any particular order within the groups. Set aside any items that do not fit into groups. The areas that have the most items in their lists are likely to be ones you can write about most successfully. If an area interests you but its list is thin, brainstorm on that area alone. If you run out of ideas, ask yourself questions to stimulate your thinking. You might try exploratory questions about the topic, such as: What is it? What is it the same as? How is it different? Why or how does it happen? How is it done? What caused it or results from it? What does it look, smell, sound, feel, or taste like?

Tara Foster used brainstorming while she was narrowing her topic about a problem facing today's adult men and women. She decided to see what she could brainstorm about divorce. The result is shown in her random list. Then she grouped her ideas and discovered that she had more to say about living alone than any other aspect of the topic. She used an asterisk (*) to mark off the items that referred to being alone. A few items did not fit into her grouped list, so she dropped them. She then decided to try writing on the topic of living alone, but first she expanded her ideas by asking the "journalist's questions" (2d-4).

Divorce (random list)
financial problems
many causes of divorce
personality conflicts
shopping alone
pressure from parents
children's reactions
religious laws
hurt and disappointment
having to start over
finding a lawyer

arguments
being on your own again
sexual problems
impact of divorce
buying a car alone
incompatibility
splitting up the money
living alone
fears of loneliness
different tastes

Divorce (grouped list)
causes of divorce
—financial problems
—personality conflicts
—arguments

—sexual problems
—pressure from parents
—financial problems
—incompatability
—different tastes

results of divorce
—living alone*
—being on your own again*
—shopping alone*
—children's reactions

—splitting up the money
—buying a car alone*
—hurt and disappointment
—having to start over
—fears of loneliness*

EXERCISE 6
Here is a brainstormed list for an assignment in political science. The assignment called for a 500-word essay about what makes a good leader. Look over the list and group ideas. Some items might not fit into any group.

personality	roles of leadership	inventive
ambitious	John F. Kennedy	Mahatma Gandhi
presidents	Lee Iacocca	determined
dangers of exposure	family life	gets job done
natural leaders	inspiring	decisive
goal oriented	organized	Golda Meir
Susan B. Anthony	generals	charisma
welcomes new ideas	Martin Luther King	authoritative

EXERCISE 7
Brainstorm on a subject that interests you. First make a random list. Then group ideas within the list. If you cannot think of a subject, use one from Exercise 4 or 5.

4
Know how to use the journalist's questions.

Another common means for generating ideas is using the **journalist's questions:** *Who? What? When? Why? Where? How?* Asking these questions forces you to approach a topic from several different perspectives.

To expand her ideas about living alone, Tara Foster used the journalist's questions. She looked over her answers and decided that she had enough details to write an essay.

WHO lives alone?
—students going off to college
—students finish school and move to get a job
—singles leaving the military
—divorced people (1 out of 2 marriages end in divorce)
—widowed people (8 out of 10 married women will be widows)

WHAT does living alone entail?
—handling practical things
—balancing a checkbook
—opening a checking or savings account
—locating important papers (will, birth certificate, insurance)
—making necessary major purchases
—making new friends
—getting along socially
—dealing with loneliness
—dealing with depression

WHEN do people have problems living alone?
—when they are used to being taken care of
—when they do not know what to expect
—when they try to hide from the statistics

WHY do people live alone?
—want to (May Sarton's essay on the solitary life)
—have no choice
—prefer to live alone than to be unhappily married or to live with
  a roommate they dislike

WHERE do people live alone?
—apartments
—houses
—motel rooms
—cities
—suburbs
—rural areas

HOW do people cope with living alone?
—they learn how to take care of themselves
—self-reliance
—they get out and meet new people
—they fight loneliness by staying busy

EXERCISE 8

Ask the journalist's questions about one of these subjects.

1. Learning foreign languages
2. Making friends
3. Exercising
4. Driving defensively
5. Teaching
6. Reading a novel
7. Playing the drums
8. Joking
9. Voting
10. Going to college

‖ 5
Know how to use mapping.

Mapping, also called *webbing,* is much like brainstorming, but it is more visual and less linear. A "map" looks quite different from sentences, paragraphs, or lists. Many writers find that mapping frees them to think more creatively, to associate ideas more easily.

When you map, start with your subject circled in the middle of a sheet of unlined paper. Next draw a line radiating out from the center and label it with the name of a major division of your subject. Circle it and from that circle move out further to subdivisions. Keep associating to further ideas and to details related to them. When you finish with one major division of your subject, go back to the center and start again with another major division. As you go along, add anything that occurs to you for any section of the map. Continue the process until you run out of ideas.

Gary Lee Houseman used mapping (p. 29) to check what he knew about rain forests, the topic he wanted to write about for his assignment about the destruction of the environment. After mapping, he felt confident that he could begin shaping and drafting his essay.

EXERCISE 9
Think of a topic about which you have some information. Use mapping to chart what you know.

‖ 6
Know when to use reading for writing.

The idea-gathering techniques explained so far in this chapter can help you get onto paper what is stored in your mind as a result of experience, observation, and reading. Reading *after* you receive an assignment is a way to get new information and to confirm what you already know.

But reading is not always part of an assignment. Unless an assignment specifically calls for the use of outside sources, ask your instructor if you can use them. Some instructors want students to use what they know rather than what they learn from new reading at the time of the assignment. Gary Lee Houseman, as explained in 2b, was not sure if research was part of his assignment, so he asked and found out that it was not.

On the other hand, some assignments ask you to read a specific work, such as an essay or short story, and write in reaction to it. Other assignments ask for research writing (see Chapter 32).

28

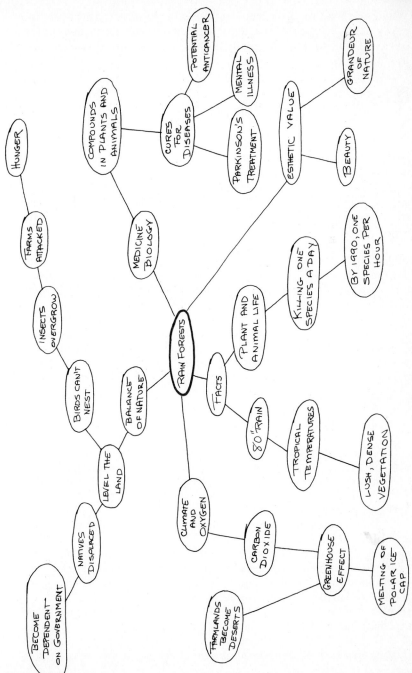

When you read to write, be sure to *read critically*. Critical reading, a key part of critical thinking, is expected of college students. Both critical thinking and its application to reading are discussed fully in Chapter 5.

▊ 2e
Shape ideas for writing.

Shaping is an important step in making the transition from gathering ideas to drafting an essay. Shaping activities are related to the idea that writing is often called *composing,* the putting together of ideas to create a *composition,* one of the synonyms for *essay.* To shape the ideas that you have gathered, you need to group them, decide on your role and tone, draft a thesis statement, and know how to outline.

As you shape ideas, keep in mind that the form of an essay is related to the ancient notion of a story's having a beginning, a middle, and an end. An essay always has an introduction, a body, and a conclusion. The body consists of a number of paragraphs while the introduction and conclusion are usually one paragraph each. The length of each paragraph is in proportion to the overall length of the essay. Introductory and concluding paragraphs are generally shorter than body paragraphs, and no body paragraph should overpower the others by its length. Chapter 4 discusses and illustrates many types of paragraphs for informative and persuasive writing.

‖ 1
Know how to group ideas.

When you group ideas, your task is to make connections and find patterns. You put related ideas into separate groups. If you used brainstorming (2d-3) or mapping (2d-5) when you were gathering ideas for writing, you have had some experience with the underlying principle of grouping.

When you group material for writing, the concept of *levels of generality* helps you make decisions. One idea is more general than another if it is a larger category—less specific—than the next. For example, "cures for diseases" is more general than "Parkinson's treatment." Also "bank account" is more general than "checking account." In turn, "checking account" is more general than "business checking account" or "regular checking account." And those terms are more general than "account number 221222 at the E–Z Come, E–Z Go Bank." Thus, generality is a relative term. Each idea exists in the context of a whole relationship of ideas. An idea may be general in relationship to one set of ideas, but specific in relation to another set.

Thinking about levels of generality can help you remember that effective writing includes both general statements and specific details. In informative and persuasive writing, general statements must be developed with facts, reasons, examples, and illustrations.

To group ideas, review the material you accumulated while gathering ideas. Then look for general ideas. Next group less general ideas under them. If you find that your notes contain only general ideas, or only very specific details, return again to gathering techniques to supply what you need. One of the standard tools for ordering ideas is making a "subject tree." It shows ideas and details in order from most general at the top to most specific at the bottom. The tree Tara Foster made for her essay on living alone is illustrated. As happens with most writers, Foster did not use every item on the tree when she wrote her essay (she dropped the positive outlook section under "Emotional Life," for example). The material did, however, give her a good start for her drafting.

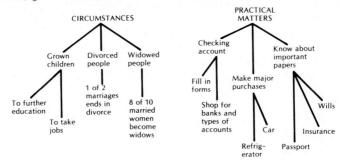

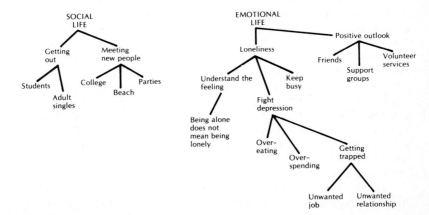

EXERCISE 10

Prepare a subject tree on food, on crime prevention, or on another subject of your choice.

|| 2
|| **Order ideas.**

Shaping ideas for writing also means ordering them into a logical structure. Writing is a social act, so you have to be sure that you are communicating clearly with your audience. You need to decide what should come first, second, third, and so on, until the last.

Within an essay, and within body paragraphs of an essay, you can order ideas in various ways. Common ones are climactic, chronological, and spatial orders.

Climactic order, also called *emphatic order,* moves from least to most important. Ideas are arranged according to degree of impact on your reader or importance to your subject. The order builds to a climax. You can see examples of such arrangements in Chapter 3: Tara Foster's third draft on living alone and Gary Lee Houseman's essay on rain forests.

Climactic order also refers to structures that move from the simplest to most complex idea or from the most familiar to least familiar idea. For example, you might explain how to drive by starting with physical movements such as turning on the ignition, then talking about distance-awareness such as room to brake and make turns, and finally discussing mental alertness. Such strategies of arrangement are useful not only for ordering major groups of ideas within a large framework, but also for ordering supporting details within each major group.

Chronological order presents ideas according to a time sequence. Chronological order is frequently used in narrating a series of events and in showing a process where steps are normally given in the order in which they occur. For example, you might use chronological order to discuss the career of Martin Luther King or to describe the discovery of the sunken *Titanic.*

Spatial order presents ideas arranged according to their physical locations in relation to one another. This can include top to bottom, near to far, left to right. Spatial order is useful for such topics as describing a stage set or a street scene. Similarly, it would work well for moving from the East Coast to the West Coast when comparing historic preservation programs in New York, Chicago, and San Francisco.

These patterns and others are discussed and illustrated with sample paragraphs in Chapter 4.

3
Determine your role and tone.

In all writing situations, you have to play a **role.** Some assignments specify a role, such as being a high school teacher writing to students who have graduated and gone to college. In such cases, you have to imagine what that person would say and would sound like when saying it. Most assignments, however, do not specify a role. You are expected to be yourself.

How you define yourself is important. As an adult writing to an adult audience, you are expected to sound reasonable and moderate. This stance is reflected in your **tone**—*what you say* and *how you say it.* Tone can be broadly described as informal or formal. The tone is informal in the journal entry on page 22 and the freewriting on page 24. As you move from writing for the private you to writing for an audience, you are expected to move toward a more formal tone. This does not mean that you should use overblown language or put on airs that make you sound artificial (see 21d). Most audiences for whom you write expect a tone midway between informal and highly formal. For examples of student writing using a tone appropriate for a general audience, see the third drafts of the essays in Chapter 3; the paragraphs by students in Chapter 4; the research paper in Chapter 33; and various other papers and essays in Chapter 34.

Your tone also has to take into account the writing situation—especially topic, purpose, and audience. For example, if you are supposed to write a humorous piece about current politics, you should inject humor and use a tone that fits what you are saying. On the other hand, if you are asked to discuss how local officials are handling a serious drought or an increase in violent crimes, you should assume that you are supposed to be serious. *Serious* does not mean without spirit, however.

4
Draft a thesis statement.

A **thesis statement** is the central theme of an essay. It is evidence that you have something definite to say about the topic. Because it prepares your reader for the essence of what you discuss in an essay, the thesis statement must accurately reflect the content of the essay. A list of the basic requirements for a thesis statement is on page 34.

Often, instructors ask for more than the basic requirements. For example, you might be required to put your thesis statement at the end of your introductory paragraph. The third draft of the essay

BASIC REQUIREMENTS FOR A THESIS STATEMENT

1. It states the essay's **main idea**—the central point you are making to your readers.
2. It reflects the essay's **purpose**—either to give your readers information or to persuade your readers to agree with you.
3. It includes a **focus**—your assertion that conveys your point of view.
4. It *may* briefly state the major subdivisions of the essay's topic.

on living alone and the essay on rain forests (Chapter 3) are examples. In addition, many instructors require that the thesis statement be contained in one sentence. Others permit two sentences if the material to be covered warrants such length. All requirements, basic and additional, are designed to help you learn to think in structured patterns that communicate clearly with readers.

In most writing situations, you will not be certain that all parts of a thesis statement accurately reflect what you say in the essay until you have written one or more drafts. To start shaping your essay, however, you need a **preliminary thesis statement**. Often a preliminary thesis statement is too broad ("Rain forests must not be destroyed") or too vague ("Rain forests are important to the human race"). Expect to revise a preliminary thesis statement as you write successive drafts of your essay, but an early version helps you find direction in your writing. When you revise into a **final thesis statement**, make sure that it clearly applies to the content of the essay as it has evolved through its drafts.

Consider the final thesis statement in Tara Foster's essay on living alone (in Chapter 3).

> Chances are high that most adult men and women will have to know how to live alone, briefly or longer, at some time in their lives.

Foster's thesis statement reveals that the *topic* is living alone, the *purpose* is to give information, and the *focus* is that chances are high that most people will have to know how to live alone at some time in their lives.

Here are thesis statements written for 500- to 700-word essays with an **informative purpose.** The ineffective versions resemble some types of preliminary thesis statements. The effective versions are final thesis statements written by students after they had gathered and grouped ideas. Note that the good versions contain the first three characteristics listed in the Basic Requirements chart. One of the good versions also includes the major subdivisions of the topic.

TOPIC	houseplants
No	Houseplants can be harmful.
YES	Certain seemingly innocent household plants can cause serious health problems, even death.
TOPIC	science fiction
No	There are many types of science fiction.
YES	Science fiction novels range from stories with scary creatures to stories that make serious comments about modern society.
TOPIC	the history of American architecture
No	The history of American architecture is varied.
YES	American architecture has gone through four major phases: from colonial to federal to victorian to modern.

For a persuasive purpose, Gary Lee Houseman wrote this thesis statement for his essay about rain forests (Chapter 3):

Rain forests must be preserved because they offer the human race many irreplaceable resources.

Houseman's thesis statement reveals that the *topic* is rain forests, the *purpose* is to persuade, and the *focus* is that rain forests must be preserved because they are irreplaceable.

Here are ineffective and effective thesis statements written for 500- to 700-word essays with a **persuasive purpose.** The ineffective versions resemble some types of preliminary thesis statements. The effective versions are final thesis statements written by students after they had gathered and grouped ideas. Note that the good versions contain the first three characteristics listed in the Basic Requirements chart. Two of the good versions also include the major subdivisions of the topic.

TOPIC	industrial pollution
No	Industrial pollution is a serious hazard in modern society.
YES	Unless industrial pollution is controlled more effectively in the near future, this planet will be poisoned beyond repair.

TOPIC	the moods music creates
No	Music can create many moods.
YES	Music can inspire people to feel romantic, patriotic, or nostalgic.
TOPIC	choosing a major in college
No	Choosing a major takes much thinking.
YES	College students should choose their majors according to their interests, their personalities, and their financial goals.

EXERCISE 11

Identify the topic, purpose, and focus of each thesis statement.

1. Emphasizing foreign languages in U.S. schools would benefit U.S. culture, business, and politics.
2. Although programs to eliminate drunk driving have been somewhat effective, additional programs are sorely needed.
3. The earth's surface can be divided into four major landforms: plains, plateaus, hills, and mountains.
4. To be successful, marriages have to adjust to unexpected problems that come along.
5. In the first year of life, babies acquire increasingly sophisticated motor skills as they move from reflexive to nonreflexive activities.

EXERCISE 12

Here are several versions of a thesis statement for the material shown in Exercise 6. Identify the characteristics of the final thesis statement based on the Basic Requirements chart on page 34. Then explain why the student rejected each of the first three versions.

1. Not all leaders are the same.
2. There are two basic styles of leadership.
3. Power leaders are different from personality leaders.
4. Power leaders and personality leaders differ in their sources of authority, their personal qualities, and their leadership skills.

EXERCISE 13

Here are writing assignments, narrowed topics, and tentative thesis statements. Evaluate each thesis statement according to the Basic Requirements chart on page 34.

1. *Nursing class assignment:* 700- to 800-word informative report on one non-traditional form of medicine. Audience: Other students and instructor. Topic: Acupuncture. Thesis: Acupuncture differs from Western medicine in its definition of disease, its diagnostic methods, and its style of treatment.

2. *Writing class assignment for a movie review that might be published in the campus newspaper:* 200 words. Audience: instructor and possibly the whole student body. Topic: *Out of Africa.* Thesis: I really liked *Out of Africa.*

3. *Mass Communications class assignment:* Three-page report on job opportunities available in local media. Audience: classmates and instructor. Topic: The *Evening Times.* Thesis: Working for the *Evening Times* looks like it would be a lot of fun.

4. *Writing class assignment:* Simulation: As part of your work-study job in the college's Public Relations Office, you have been asked to prepare a plan for a day's activities for a visiting group of 10 Chinese high school students, all of whom speak English. Audience: instructor and the college's Director of Public Relations. Topic: Follow a typical college student's day. Thesis: As much as possible, the visiting students should share the experiences of typical American students, including their academic and social activities.

5. *Astronomy class:* One- or two-page explanation of the movement of the planets suitable for elementary school students. Audience: instructor. Thesis: While the stars remain fixed on the celestial sphere, the sun proceeds ponderously on its annual ecliptic journey among them, the wandering planets perform convoluted gyrations within the zodiac.

5
Know how to outline.

Many writers find outlining a useful planning strategy. An outline helps pull together the results of gathering and ordering ideas and preparing a thesis statement. It also provides a visual guide and checklist. Some writers always use outlines; others prefer not to outline. Writers who outline do so at various points in the writing process: for example, before drafting, to arrange and organize material; or while revising, to check the logic of an early draft's arrangement and organization. Especially for informative and persuasive writing, outlines can clearly reveal flaws—missing information, undesirable repetitions, digressions from the thesis.

As a college writer, you will likely find that some instructors require outlines. Understandably, they want you to practice the discipline of planning the arrangement and organization of your writing. The more clearly and sensibly your material is presented, the better chance it has of reaching your audience.

Before the final draft of an essay is complete, an outline is only a projection, an estimate of what the essay will say. Once you start writing, the act of writing might lead you to change your plans somewhat. If you are working from an outline and you make changes, be sure to revise your outline at the end. Then check to make sure that your changes have not upset the logic and arrangement of your essay.

An **informal outline** does not have to follow all the formal conventions of outlining. It lists the main ideas of an essay—the major subdivisions of the thesis statement. It also lists subordinate ideas and details, but without attention to levels of generality (see 2e-2). An informal outline is particularly useful for planning when the order within main ideas is still evolving or when topics imply their own arrangement, such as spatial arrangement for describing a room or chronological order for describing an event.

An informal outline can also be a *working plan,* a layout of the major parts of the material intended for an essay. It can be the next logical step after a brainstormed list (2d-3), a map (2d-5), or a subject tree (2e-2). An informal outline can also serve as an early draft of a formal outline. Here is part of an informal outline that served as a working plan for Gary Lee Houseman when he was writing his essay on rain forests. This excerpt includes the thesis and three of the five body paragraphs.

Thesis statement: Rain forests must be preserved because they offer the human race many irreplaceable resources.
Definition of rain forest
  80 inches rainfall a year
  Tropical regions (warm temperatures)
  Lush, dense vegetation
  Canopy
    Branches overlap
    As high as the trees (I think about 98 feet)
    Evergreens
    Plant and insect life thrive
Biomedical uses
  Over 1,400 plants and animals
  Compounds for medicines
    Parkinson's
    Mental illnesses
    Anticancer

Natural balances
>   Level forests ⟶ birds leave ⟶ insects are no longer eaten
>   by birds ⟶ insects overgrow and eat crops ⟶ hunger
>   Level forests ⟶ natives displaced ⟶ become dependent on
>   government ⟶ more pressure on national debt

A **formal outline** follows conventions concerning content and format. The conventions are designed to display material so that relationships among ideas are clear and so that the content is orderly. A formal outline can be a *topic outline* or a *sentence outline.* Each item in a topic outline is a word or phrase; each item in a sentence outline is a complete sentence. Formal outlines never mix the two. Many experienced writers who use formal outlines find that a sentence outline brings them closer to drafting than does a topic outline. Each item in a sentence outline contains a **predicate.** As a grammatical unit, the predicate includes the sentence's verb. As a unit of communication, the predicate states the focus of the sentence. For example, "compounds for medicines" on a topic outline would carry more information on a sentence outline: "Compounds for medicines come from many plants and animals in the rain forests."

PATTERN FOR FORMAL OUTLINE OF AN ESSAY

Thesis Statement: ....
....

I. First main idea ....
....

   A. First subordinate idea ....
....

      1. First reason or example...
....

      2. Second reason or example ....
....

         a. First supporting detail ....
....

         b. Second supporting detail.....................................
....

   B. Second subordinate idea...
....

II. Second main idea...
....

When writing a formal outline, you are expected to observe the following conventions.

1. **Numbers, letters, and indentations.** All parts of a formal outline are systematically indented and numbered or lettered. Capital roman numerals (I, II, III) signal major subdivisions of the topic. Indented capital letters (A, B) signal the next level of generality. Further indented arabic numbers (1, 2, 3) show the third level of generality. Yet further indented lowercase letters (a, b) show the fourth level, if there is one. The principle here is that within each major subdivision, each succeeding level of the outline shows more specific detail than the one before it. If an outline entry is longer than one line, the second line is indented as far as the first word of the preceding line.

2. **More than one entry at each level.** At all points on an outline, there is no I without a II, no A without a B, and so on. If a category has only one subdivision, you need to either eliminate that subdivision or expand the material to at least two subdivisions.

   No   A. Grown children leaving home
                     1. Moving to other cities
               B. Married people not being together forever

   Yes   A. Grown children moving to other cities
               B. Married people not being together forever

   Yes   A. Grown children moving to other cities
                     1. Going away to school
                     2. Taking jobs
               B. Married people not being together forever

3. **Levels of generality.** All subdivisions are at the same level of generality. A main idea cannot be paired with a supporting detail.

   No   I. Taking care of practical matters
              II. Not overeating

   Yes   I. Taking care of practical matters
              II. Establishing new friendships

4. **Overlap.** Headings do not overlap. What is covered in A, for example, must be quite distinct from what is covered in B.

   No   I. Grown children moving to other cities
                  A. Going away to school

          B. Continuing an education
  Yᴇꜱ   I. Grown children moving to other cities
          A. Going away to school
          B. Taking jobs

5. **Parallelism.** All entries are grammatically parallel. For example, all items start with *-ing* forms of verbs or all items are adjectives and nouns. For more about parallelism in outlines, see
18e.

  Nᴏ   I. Taking care of practical matters
          II. New friends
  Yᴇꜱ   I. Taking care of practical matters
          II. Making new friends
  Yᴇꜱ   I. Practical matters
          II. New friends

6. **Capitalization and punctuation.** Except for proper nouns°,
only the first word of each entry is capitalized. In a sentence outline, end each sentence with a period. Do not punctuate the ends
of entries in a topic outline.

7. **Introductory and concluding paragraphs.** The content of the
introductory and concluding paragraphs is not part of a formal
outline. The thesis statement comes before (above) the roman numeral I entry.

  Here is a topic outline of the final draft of Tara Foster's essay
on living alone (shown in Chapter 3). A sentence outline follows so
that you can compare the two types of outlines.

Thesis Statement: Chances are high that adult men and women
will have to know how to live alone, briefly or longer, at some
time in their lives.

  I. Living alone because of circumstances
      A. Grown children moving to other cities
          1. Going away to school
          2. Taking jobs
      B. Married people not being married forever
          1. One out of two marriages ending in divorce
          2. Eight out of ten married women becoming widowed,
              usually late in life
  II. Taking care of practical matters
      A. Opening a checking account
          1. Comparing bank services

  2. Comparing advantages of different kinds of checking accounts
 B. Making major purchases
  1. Replacing a refrigerator
  2. Buying a car
III. Establishing new friendships
 A. Students getting used to going to classes without old friends
  1. Being able to concentrate better
  2. Being able to meet new friends
 B. Single adults going to the beach or parties
IV. Dealing with loneliness
 A. Understanding the feeling
 B. Avoiding depression
  1. Not overeating
  2. Not overspending
  3. Not getting into unwanted situations
   a. Taking the wrong job
   b. Going into the wrong relationship
 C. Keeping busy

Compare the topic outline you have just read with the following sentence outline of the same material.

Thesis Statement: Chances are high that adult men and women will have to know how to live alone, briefly or longer, at some time in their lives.

 I. Circumstances sometimes force people to live alone.
  A. Grown children leave home.
   1. They go to college or graduate school.
   2. They go to other cities to get jobs.
  B. Many married people do not stay married forever.
   1. One out of two marriages end in divorce.
   2. Eight out of ten married women become widowed, usually late in life.
 II. People living alone have to take care of practical matters.
  A. Students might have to open a checking account.
   1. They can compare bank services.
   2. They can compare advantages of different kinds of checking accounts.
  B. Divorced or widowed people might have to make major purchases.
   1. A refrigerator might have to be replaced.
   2. A car might not be worth fixing.

III. People living alone can establish new friendships.
  A. Students get used to going to classes without old friends.
    1. One advantage is students might concentrate better.
    2. A second advantage is students can meet new friends.
  B. Single adults get used to going to the beach or parties alone.
IV. People living alone sometimes have to deal with loneliness.
  A. First comes the importance of understanding the feeling.
  B. Second comes the importance of avoiding depression.
    1. Overeating can result.
    2. Overspending can result.
    3. Getting into unwanted situations can result.
      a. People might take the wrong job.
      b. People might go into the wrong relationship.
  C. Third comes the importance of keeping busy.

EXERCISE 14

Here is a sentence outline. Revise it into a topic outline. Decide which form you would prefer as a guide to writing. Explain your decision.

Thesis Statement: Common noise pollution, although it causes many problems in our society, can be reduced.
  I. Noise pollution comes from many sources.
    A. Noise pollution occurs in many large cities.
      1. Traffic rumbles and screeches.
      2. Construction work blasts.
      3. Airplanes roar overhead.
    B. Noise pollution occurs in the workplace.
      1. Machines in factories boom.
      2. Machines used for outdoor construction thunder.
    C. Noise pollution occurs during leisure-time activities.
      1. Stereo headphones blare directly into eardrums.
      2. Film soundtracks bombard the ears.
      3. Music in discos assaults the ears.
  II. Noise pollution causes many problems.
    A. Excessive noise damages hearing.
    B. Excessive noise alters moods.
    C. Constant exposure to noise limits learning ability.
  III. Reduction in noise pollution is possible.
    A. Pressure from community groups can support efforts to control excessive noise.
    B. Traffic regulations can help alleviate congestion and noise.
    C. Pressure from workers can force management to reduce noise.
    D. People can wear earplugs to avoid excessive noise.
    E. Reasonable sound levels for headphones, soundtracks, and discos can be required.

3
DRAFTING AND REVISING

In the writing process, drafting and revising follow from planning and shaping, discussed in Chapter 2. **Drafting** means getting ideas onto paper in sentences and paragraphs. In everyday conversation, people usually use the word *writing* when they talk about the activities involved in drafting. In discussing the writing process, however, the word *drafting* is more descriptive. It conveys the idea that the final product of the writing process is the result of a number of versions, each successively closer to what the writer intends and to what will communicate clearly to readers. **Revising** means taking a draft from its preliminary to its final version by evaluating, adding, cutting, moving material, editing, and proofreading.

 ## 3a
Know how to get started.

If ever you have trouble getting started when the time arrives for drafting (or for any other part of the writing process), you are not alone. When experienced writers get temporarily stalled, they recognize what is happening and deal with it.

If you run into a writing block, make sure that you are not being influenced by any of these common myths about writing.

FALSE   Writers are born, not made.

TRUE   Everyone can write. The key to being a good writer is being a patient rewriter. Rough drafts are not final drafts, but they provide useful starting places.

FALSE   Writers have to be "in the mood" to write.

TRUE   If writers always waited for "the mood" to descend, few would write at all. After all, news reporters have to write to meet deadlines for stories, and professional writers often have to meet deadlines set by their contracts.

FALSE   Writers have to know how to spell every word and to recite the rules of grammar perfectly.

TRUE   One useful definition of a good speller is someone who does not ignore the quiet inner voice that says a word looks wrong and has to be checked. The same principle applies to grammar.

FALSE   Writing can be done at the last minute.

TRUE   Writing takes time. Ideas do not leap onto paper in final, polished form. Not only do writers need to go through the various activities of the writing process, but they also need time to get distance from a draft so that they can revise with fresh eyes.

Once you realize the truths behind myths about writing, you are ready to try the time-proven ways experienced writers get started when they are blocked. The key to getting these suggestions to work is to suspend judgment; do not criticize yourself when you are trying to get underway. The time for evaluation comes during revision, but revising too soon can stall some writers. The writing that results from these ideas is most certainly not a final draft, but having something on paper to work with is a comfort—and can serve as a springboard to drafting.

1. Avoid staring at a blank page. Fill up the paper. Relax your mind and allow your hand to move across the page or keyboard. Write words, scribble, or draw while you think about your topic. The movement of filling the paper while thinking can help stimulate your mind to turn to actual drafting.

45

2. Use "focused freewriting" (see 2d-2). Think about your topic, and write sentences about it nonstop for ten or fifteen minutes or until you fill a few pages. Some of the sentences you write can help you begin actual drafting.

3. Picture yourself writing. Before you get up in the morning, when you are waiting for a bus, or as you are walking to classes, get a full visual image of yourself writing. Imagine yourself in the place where you usually write, with the materials you need, busy at work. Many professional writers say that they write more easily if they picture themselves doing it first.

4. Write your material in a letter to a friend. This gives you a chance to relax and chat on paper to someone you like and feel comfortable with. The letter can be a good beginning for a less informal draft.

5. Write your material as if you are someone else. Take your pick: you can be a friend writing to you, an instructor writing to you or a whole class, your parent writing to you, a person in history writing to you or to someone else. Once you take on a role, you will often feel less inhibited about writing.

6. Switch your method of writing. If you usually typewrite or use a word processor, try writing by hand. If you usually use a pen, switch to a pencil. Whenever you write by hand, especially when you are having trouble getting started, try to treat yourself to good quality paper. The pleasure of writing on smooth, strong paper is considerable and helps many experienced writers want to keep going.

7. Start in the middle. If you do not know what you want to write in your introductory paragraph, start with a body paragraph. Write from the center of your essay out, instead of from beginning to end.

▇‖ 3b
Know how to draft.

Once you have your ideas planned and shaped for an essay, you are ready to **compose** them on paper. When you compose, you put together sentences and paragraphs into a unified whole. A *first draft* is a preliminary draft. First drafts are not meant to be perfect; they are meant to give you something to revise. According to your personal preferences and each writing situation, you can use any of these ways (or your own ways) of writing a first draft.

1. Put aside all your notes from planning and shaping. Write a "dis-

covery draft." As you write, be open to discovering ideas and making connections that spring to mind during the physical act of writing. When you finish a discovery draft, you can decide to use it either as a first draft or as part of your notes when you write a structured first draft.

2. Keep your notes from planning and shaping in front of you and use them as you write. Write a structured first draft. Work through all of your material. Depending on the expected length of your essay, draft either the entire essay or blocks of one or two paragraphs at one time.

3. Use a combination of approaches. When you know the shape of your material, write according to that structure. When you feel "stuck" about what to say next, switch to writing as you would for a discovery draft.

The direction of drafting is forward: *keep pressing ahead.* If you are worried about the spelling of a word or a point in grammar, underline the material so that you can come back later and check it—and keep moving ahead. If you cannot think of a word that says precisely what you want, write an easy synonym and circle it so that you will remember to change it later—and move on. If you are worried about your sentence style or the order in which you present the supporting details within a paragraph, write *Style?* or *Order?* in the margin so that you can return to that spot later to revise—and press forward. If you feel that you are running dry, reread what you have written—but only to propel yourself to further writing, not to distract you into rewriting.

As you move into drafting an essay, use the essay's thesis statement as your springboard. A thesis statement has great organizing power. It expresses the central theme that controls and limits what the essay will cover. A thesis statement contains (1) the *topic,* narrowed appropriately for the writing situation; (2) a *focus* which presents what you are saying about the topic; and (3) a *purpose* which is either informative or persuasive as explained in 1b.

As you use your thesis statement, remember that its role is to serve as a connecting thread that unifies the essay. **Unity** is important for communicating clearly to an audience. You achieve unity when all parts of the essay relate to the thesis statement and to each other. Also, an essay is unified when it meets these criteria: (1) The thesis statement clearly ties into all topic sentences. (2) The support for each topic sentence—the paragraph development—contains examples, reasons, facts, and details directly related to the topic and, in turn, to the thesis statement.

Equally important, your essay must be **coherent** to communicate clearly to an audience. An essay is coherent when it supplies guideposts that communicate the relations among ideas. Coherence is achieved through the use of transitional expressions, pronouns, repetition, and parallel structures. These techniques operate within paragraphs and to connect paragraphs; they are discussed and illustrated fully in 4b.

When you write, plan your practical arrangements. For example, try to work in a place where you are comfortable and will not be disturbed. If someone comes along and interrupts, you might lose a train of thought or an idea that has flashed into your mind. Also, have enough paper on hand so that you need to use only one side of each sheet of paper. When you revise, you should be able to spread your full draft in front of you so that you can physically see how the parts relate to one another. As you write, leave large margins and plenty of room between lines so that you have space to enter changes when you revise.

This chapter (and Chapter 2) refers to the writing processes of two students, Tara Foster and Gary Lee Houseman, for illustration. Their writing assignments are shown on page 16. Their work in gathering ideas and shaping their material is shown in Chapter 2. In this chapter, you will see three drafts of Foster's essay and the final draft of Houseman's essay.

The dominant purpose of Foster's essay is *informative*. Here is the thesis statement that serves as Foster's central theme:

> Chances are high that most adult men and women will have to know how to live alone, briefly or longer, at some time in their lives.

Here is how Foster used her thesis statement to help her write the first draft of her essay.

FIRST DRAFT

Lots of people are scared of living alone.
They like to live with others. When the statistics
catch up with you, therefore, you are never prepared.
Chances are high that most adult men and women
will have to know how to live alone, briefly or longer,
at some time in their lives.

Many grown children move away from their hometowns
to get an education or take jobs. Also, married people
think they'll always be together, but many marriages

---

end in divorce. The divorce rate is frightening.
People are not making the right choices, or they are
too immature to work out their differences. Fighting
over money, parents, or religion although the underlying
reason is lack of compatability. Divorce brings the
couple and their children a great deal of pain.

I read recently in the newspaper where estimates
are that in the next twety years, 8 out of 10 married
women end up widows. This will happen to most of
them late in life. This statistic is even sadder
than divorce. I feel sorry for any happily married
person whose spouse dies.

People living alone need to establish new friendships.
When single people feel self-reliant. It's easier
for them to start getting out and meeting new people.
Some students are in the habit of always going to classes
with a friend, and they can be find that they can
concenzrate better on the course. And also have a chance
to make some new friends. Friends can help people take care
of practical by keeping them company and going with them.

One good way to prepare for living alone is to
learn how to take care of practical matters. Many people
don't know how to do something as simple as opening a
checking account. Making major purchases is something
people have to handle. Such as a refrigerator that can't
be repaired or a useless car. Shop around and make price
comparisons. All decisions are much easier than at first.

Feelings of lonliness are the hardest to take.
I think this is what people fear the most. First,
people have to understand what is going on. Being
alone does not mean being lonely. Second, singles
have to fight depression. Third, they have to keep busy.

People living alone have to handle practical,
social, and emotional problems.

3c
Know how to revise.

To **revise** you must evaluate. You assess your first (or subsequent) draft and decide where improvements are needed. Then you make the improvements and evaluate them alone and in the context of the surrounding material. This process continues until you are satisfied that the essay is in final draft.

To revise successfully you need first to expect to revise. Some people think that anyone who revises is not a good writer. Only the opposite is true. Writing is largely revising. Experienced writers know that the final draft of any writing project shows on paper only a fraction of the decisions made from draft to successive draft. Revision means "to see again," to look with fresh eyes. Good writers are rewriters, people who can truly *see* their drafts and rework them into better form.

To revise successfully you need also to distance yourself from each draft. You need to read your writing with objective eyes. A natural reaction of many writers is to want to hold onto their every word, especially if they had trouble getting started with a draft. If you ever have such feelings, resist them and work on distancing yourself from the material. Before revising, give yourself some time for that rosy glow of authorial pride to dim a bit. The classical writer Horace recommended waiting nine years. Given the hectic pace of modern life, you do not have that much time. But wait a few hours, if at all possible, before going back to look anew at your work.

If time does not help you develop an objective perspective, try reading your draft aloud; hearing the material can give you a fresh new sense of an essay's content and organization. Another useful method is to read the paragraphs in your essay in reverse order, starting with the conclusion; eventually, of course, you must read your essay from beginning to end, but to achieve distance you can temporarily depart from that sequence.

1
Know the steps and activities of revision.

Once you understand the attitudes that underlie the revision process, you are ready to move into actual revising.

As you revise, you are working to improve your draft at all levels: whole essay, paragraph, sentence, and word. A revised draft usually looks quite different from its preceding draft. To revise you need to engage in all the activities in the charts on p. 51. As you

1. Shift mentally from suspending judgment (during idea gathering and drafting) to making judgments.
2. Read your draft critically to evaluate it. Be guided by the questions on the Revision Checklist in this chapter or by material supplied by your instructor.
3. Decide whether to write an entirely new draft or to revise the one you have. Do not be overly harsh. While some early drafts serve best as "discovery drafts" rather than first drafts, many early drafts provide sufficient raw material for the revision process to get underway.
4. Be systematic. Do not evaluate at random. You need to pay attention to many different elements of a draft, from overall organization to choice of words. Some writers prefer to consider all elements concurrently, but most writers work better when they concentrate on different elements during separate rounds of revision.

engage in each activity, keep the whole picture in mind. Changes affect more than the place revised. Check that your separate changes operate well in the context of the whole essay or a particular paragraph. Here again, getting distance from your material allows you the chance to be more objective.

MAJOR ACTIVITIES DURING REVISION

Add. Insert needed words, sentences, and paragraphs. If your additions require new content, return to idea-gathering techniques (see 2d).

Cut. Get rid of whatever goes off the topic or repeats what has already been said.

Replace. As needed, substitute new words, sentences, and paragraphs for what you have cut.

Move material around. Change the sequence of paragraphs if the material is not presented in logical order (see 2e-2). Move sentences within paragraphs or to other paragraphs if arrangements seem illogical (see 4c).

Revising is usually separate from editing (3d). During editing you concentrate on important surface features such as correct spelling and punctuation. During revising, you pay attention to the meaning you want your material to deliver effectively.

2
Use the organizing power of your thesis statement and essay title.

When you revise, you need to pay special attention to your essay's thesis statement and title. Both of these features help you stay on the track, and they orient your reader to what to expect.

If your **thesis statement** does not match what you say in your essay, you need to revise either the thesis statement or the essay—and sometimes both. A thesis statement, as explained in 2e-4, must present the topic of the essay, the writer's particular focus on that topic, and the writer's purpose for writing the essay. The first draft of a thesis statement is often merely an estimate of what will be covered in the essay. Early in the revision process, you should check the accuracy of your estimate. You can then use the thesis statement's controlling role to bring it and the essay in line with each other.

Each writer's experience with revising a thesis statement varies from essay to essay. Tara Foster wrote a number of versions of her thesis statement before she started drafting. When she checked her thesis statement after she wrote her first draft, Foster decided that her thesis statement communicated what she wanted to say. But she did decide to change parts of her essay to conform more closely to her thesis statement. (For an example of a thesis statement revised after the first draft, see Chapter 33.)

The **title** of an essay also plays an important organizing role. A good title can set you on your course and tell your reader what to expect. A *direct title* tells exactly what the essay will be about. A direct title contains key words under which the essay would be cataloged in a library or a computerized database system. As a result, a direct title is very efficient. The titles of the two essays in this chapter are direct: Tara Foster's "Knowing How to Live Alone" and Gary Lee Houseman's "Rain Forests Must Not Be Destroyed." Each title is specific and prepares the reader for the topic of the essay.

A direct title should not be too broad. An overly broad title implies that the writer has not thought through the essay's content. For example, an unsatisfactory title for Foster's essay would be "Living Alone." On the other hand, a direct title should not be too narrow. An equally unsatisfactory title for Foster's essay would be "Knowing How to Live Alone Is Important for Practical, Social, and Emotional Reasons." Such a title is closer to a thesis statement.

An *indirect title* is also acceptable in some situations, according to the writer's taste and instructor's requirements. An indirect title hints at the essay's topic. It presents a puzzle that can be solved when the essay is read. This approach can be intriguing for the reader, but the writer has to be sure that the title is not too obscure. "Solitary Strength," for example, would be a satisfactory indirect title for Tara Foster's essay, but "The Test" would be too indirect.

As you write, plan your essay's title carefully. Do not wait until the last minute to tack on a title. You might write a title before you start to draft or after a first draft while you are revising, but always check as you review your essay and make sure that the title clearly relates to the content of the evolving essay.

Whether direct or indirect, a title stands alone. The opening of an essay should never refer to the essay's title as if it were part of a preceding sentence. For example, after the title "Knowing How to Live Alone," a writer should not begin the essay with the words "This skill is very important" or "Everyone should know how to do this." The title sets the stage, but it is not the first sentence of the essay.

3
Know how to use a revision checklist.

A revision checklist can help you focus your attention as you evaluate your writing. Use a checklist provided by your instructor or compile your own based on the Revision Checklist here. This checklist is comprehensive and detailed; do not let it overwhelm you. Feel free to adapt it to the emphases in each course and writing assignment. Also, tailor it to your personal needs. If you know that you are weak in certain areas, spend more time on them and make the questions even more detailed.

This checklist moves from the whole essay to paragraphs to sentences to words. This progression from larger to smaller elements works well for many writers.

Revision Checklist

The answer to each question on this checklist should be "yes." If it is not, you need to revise. If you are unsure of the meaning of any question, look up the material in this book. The reference numbers in parentheses tell you what chapter or section to consult.

53

THE WHOLE ESSAY

1. Is the topic of the essay suitable for college writing and sufficiently narrow? (2c)
2. Does your thesis statement clearly communicate the topic and focus of the essay? (2e-4)
3. Does your thesis clearly reflect the purpose of the essay? (1b)
4. Does the essay reflect an awareness of its audience? (1c)
5. Does the essay take into account the special requirements—the assignment's time limit, word limit, and other factors? (2b)
6. Does your essay have a logical organization pattern? (2e-2)
7. Is the tone of the essay suitable for its audience? Is an appropriate tone consistent throughout? (2e-3)
8. Is your thesis supported well by the main ideas of the paragraphs? (4e-4)
9. Do the paragraphs cover separate but related main ideas? (2e-1 and 2e-5)
10. Have you covered all the material promised by your thesis statement? (2e-4)
11. Are the connections among the paragraphs clear? (4b-1)
12. Does your introduction lead into the thesis statement and the rest of the essay? (4e)
13. Does your conclusion provide a sense of completion? (4e)
14. Have you cut all material that goes off the topic?
15. Is the length of each paragraph in proportion to the whole essay and the length of the other paragraphs? (Remember that an introduction and a conclusion are usually shorter than any of the body paragraphs in an essay.)
16. Does your essay have a title? Does it reflect the content of the essay, directly or indirectly?
17. Is your reasoning sound? (5c–5e)
18. Does your essay avoid logical fallacies? (5f)

PARAGRAPHS

1. Does the introduction help your audience make the transition to the body of your essay? (4e)
2. Does each body paragraph express its main idea in a topic sentence as needed? (4a-1)
3. Are the main ideas—and topic sentences—clearly related to the thesis statement of the essay? (4a)
4. Are your body paragraphs *developed?* Is the development sufficient? (4a-2)

5. Does each body paragraph contain specific and concrete support for its main idea? Do the details provide examples, reasons, facts? (4d)
6. Are your facts, figures, and dates accurate?
7. Is each body paragraph arranged logically? (4c)
8. Does the conclusion give your reader a sense of completion? (4e)
9. Have you cut all material that goes off the topic?
10. Have you used necessary transitions? (4b-1, 4b-6)
11. Do the paragraphs maintain coherence with pronouns (4b-2), selective repetition (4b-3), parallel structures (4b-4 and Chapter 18)?
12. Do you show relationships between paragraphs? (4b-6)

SENTENCES

1. Are your sentences concise? (Chapter 16)
2. Have you eliminated sentence fragments? (Chapter 13)
3. Have you eliminated comma splices and fused sentences? (Chapter 14)
4. Have you eliminated confusing shifts? (15a)
5. Have you eliminated misplaced modifiers? (15b)
6. Have you eliminated dangling modifiers? (15c)
7. Have you eliminated mixed sentences? (15d)
8. Have you eliminated incomplete sentences? (15e)
9. Do your sentences express clear relationships among ideas? (Chapter 17)
10. Do you use coordination correctly? (17a–17c)
11. Do you use subordination correctly? (17d–17g)
12. Do your sentences avoid faulty parallelism? (Chapter 18)
13. Do you use parallelism as needed to help your sentences deliver their meaning? (Chapter 18)
14. Does your writing style reveal a sensitivity to the need for variety and emphasis? (Chapter 19)
15. Do your sentences vary in length? (19a)
16. Does the structure of your sentences help convey the emphasis you intend? (19c–19f)

WORDS

1. Have you used exact words? (20b)
2. Does your word choice reflect your intentions in denotation and connotation? (20b-1)

3. Have you used specific and concrete language to bring life to general and abstract language? (20b-2)

4. Does your word choice reflect a level of formality appropriate for your purpose and audience? (21a-1)

5. Do you avoid sexist language? (21a-3)

6. Do you avoid slang and colloquial or regional language not appropriate to your audience and purpose? (21a-4)

7. Do you avoid slanted language? (21a-5)

8. Do you avoid clichés? (21c)

9. Do you avoid artificial language by eliminating pretentious word choice, unnecessary jargon, unnecessary euphemisms, "doublespeak," and bureaucratic prose? (21d)

10. Is your usage correct? (Usage Glossary)

When Tara Foster revised her first draft, she concentrated first on the overall essay and then on the paragraphs, the sentences, and the words. As many writers do, sometimes she changed words as she looked at the whole essay, and sometimes she made changes in paragraphs as she looked at her word choice. Nevertheless, she proceeded systematically through the elements so that she was sure she had covered everything.

In working with the larger elements, Foster decided that her thesis statement was working well. But she realized that she needed a title and a better topic sentence in her next-to-last paragraph and that the conclusion sounded "tacked on." She also saw that the sequence of her paragraphs was not logical. In order of importance, she felt that taking care of practical matters came before establishing new friendships, so she rearranged the sequence.

In working at the paragraph level, Foster cut some material that went off the topic. She then decided to integrate what remained into the next paragraph. She also saw that she had insufficiently developed two paragraphs, so she added examples and details to them. To help her readers understand the relations among her ideas, Foster saw that some transitional expressions were called for. She felt that the introduction and conclusion were flat, worked on new ones, and then worked to tie her conclusion more closely to the rest of her essay.

At the sentence and word level, Foster combined sentences to be more concise in discussing a statistic. She also worked for sentence variety by using an occasional short sentence and by transforming one statement into a question. She then changed some words to be more exact. For example, she replaced "what is going on" with "the feeling." As often happens with writers, she did some editing as she was revising: she changed two numerals to spelled-out numbers and she got rid of contractions.

FIRST DRAFT REVISED BY STUDENT

(I need a title)

terrified

~~Lots of~~ People are ~~scared~~ of living alone.   (I need a better introduction. check Chapter 4.)

are used to living

They ~~like to live~~ with others. When the statistics

catch up with you, therefore, you are never prepared.

Chances are high that most adult men and women

will have to know how to live alone, briefly or longer,

at some time in their lives.

    Many grown children move away from their hometowns

continue their   s

to ~~get an~~ education, or take jobs. ~~Also,~~ Married people

might feel they will   currently one out of two

~~think they'll~~ always be together, but ~~many~~ marriages

end in divorce. [The divorce rate is frightening. (Cut. I'm off the topic here)

People are not making the right choices, or they are

too immature to work out their differences. Fighting

over money, parents, or religion although the underlying

reason is lack of compatability. Divorce brings the

couple and their children a great deal of pain.]

    ~~I read recently in the newspaper where~~ Estimates

n   eight   ten

are that in the next twenty years, ~~8~~ out of ~~10~~ married

                                        (Change order of these two sentences)

women end up widows, ~~This will happen to most of~~

usually   An

~~them~~ late in life. ~~This~~ (statistic) ~~is~~ even sadder,

~~than divorce.~~ ~~I feel sorry for any happily married~~

~~person whose spouse dies.~~

concerns the death of a spouse.

(Move first paragraph down to come after practical matters paragraph)

People living alone need to establish new friendships.
When single people feel self-reliant, ~~It's~~ they can have an easier ~~time~~ ~~for them to start~~ getting out and meeting new people.
For instance, ~~S~~some students are in the habit of always going to classes with a friend, ~~and~~ but they can be~~,~~ pleasantly surprised to find that they can concentrate better on the course~~s~~. And also have a chance to make some new friends. ~~Friends can help people take care~~ The idea of going places alone can paralyze some people. Once you make the attempt, however, you find that everyone ~~of practical by keeping them company and going with them.~~ welcomes a new friendly face.

One good way to prepare for living alone is to learn how to take care of practical matters. ~~Many people~~ For example, they might not ~~don't~~ know how to do something as simple as opening a checking account. Similarly, ~~M~~making major purchases is something people have to handle. ~~Such as~~ How long can a person manage with a refrigerator that ~~can't~~ cannot be repaired or a useless car? ~~Shop~~ Shopping around and making price comparisons. Most ~~All~~ decisions are much ~~easier~~ less complicated than they seem at first.
Probably the most difficult problem for people living alone is dealing with ~~F~~feelings of lonliness. ~~are the hardest to take.~~

~~I think this is what people fear the most.~~ First, people have to understand the feeling, they confuse ~~what is going on.~~ ~~B~~being alone ~~does not mean~~ with being lonely. Second, ~~singles~~ people living alone have to fight depression. Third, ~~they have to keep busy.~~ everyone needs to get involved with activities such as volunteering their services to help others.
People living alone have to handle practical, social, and emotional problems.

(The last paragraph seems boring to me now. I'll look for a more interesting kind of concluding device in Chapter 4)

(Move this paragraph up)

Foster then typed her second draft neatly and, as required by the assignment, submitted it with the first draft on which she had handwritten her revisions.

SECOND DRAFT

Knowing How to Live Alone

"Alone one is never lonely," says May Sarton. Most people, however, are terrified of living alone. They are used to living with others. When the statistics catch up with you, therefore, you are never prepared. Chances are high that most adult men and women will have to know how to live alone, briefly or longer, at some time in their lives.

Many grown children move away from their hometowns to continue their educations or take jobs. Married people might feel they will always be together, but currently one out of two marriages end in divorce. An even sadder statisitic concerns the death of a spouse. Estimates are that in the next twenty years eight out of ten married women will end up widows, usually late in life.

One good way to prepare for living alone is to learn how to take care of practical matters. For example, they might not know how to do something as simple as opening a checking account. Similarly, making major purchases is something people might have to handle. How long can a person manage with a refrigerator that cannot be repaired or a useless car? After some shopping around and making price comparisons. Most decisions are much less complicated than they seem at first.

People living alone need to establish new friendships. When, single people feel self-reliant they can have an easier

---

time getting out and meeting new people. For instance, some students are in the habit of always going to classes with a friend, but they can be pleasantly surprised to find that they can concentrate better on the course and also have a chance to make some new friends. The idea of going places alone can paralyze some people. Once you make the attempt, however, you find that everyone welcomes a new friendly face.

Probably the most difficult problem for people living alone is dealing with feelings of lonliness. First, people have to understand the feeling, they confuse being alone with being lonely. Second, people living alone have to fight depression. Third, everyone needs to get involved with activities, such as volunteering their services to help others.

People need to ask themselves, "If I had to live alone starting tomorrow morning, would I know how?" This is an important question.

4
Know How to Use Criticism.

When criticism is constructive, you can learn a great deal about your writing through the eyes of others. Still, you have much company among writers if your initial reaction to criticism is defensive. Someone else's reactions to your writing can feel like an intrusion at first. Writing is a personal act, even when a writer is trying to communicate with a reader. The more you write, however, the more you will come to welcome constructive criticism.

The eyes of another person, someone who cares to help you improve, can give you an objective view of your material. Useful criticism helps you move your writing closer to what a reader needs to complete the act of communication. In working with comments, look at each one separately. First, make sure that you understand what the comment says. If you are unsure, ask. Next, be open-minded about the comment. If you resist every comment, you will miss many opportunities to improve. Finally, use the comment to make whatever changes you think will improve your draft.

Tara Foster's assignment, shown on page 16, called for Foster to hand in both a first and second draft. Foster's instructor explained that the second draft would be considered an "essay in progress" and all comments would be geared toward helping students write a final draft. When her second draft was returned, Foster saw two types of comments from her instructor: questions to stimulate further writing and codes referring to places in this handbook for Foster to consult. Here is Foster's second draft with comments from her instructor.

SECOND DRAFT WITH INSTRUCTOR'S COMMENTS

How does this interesting quotation tie into your point? Also, who is Sarton?

Knowing How to Live Alone

Can you be more specific?

(15a) "Alone one is never lonely," says May Sarton. Most people, however, are terrified of living alone. They are used to living with others. When the statistics catch up *Qualify this statement. (See 5c.)* with you, therefore, you are never prepared. Chances are high that most adult men and women will have to know how to live alone, briefly or longer, at some time in their lives.

Can you be more specific?

Many grown children move away from their hometowns to continue their educations or take jobs. Married people might feel they will always be together, but currently (11a) one out of two marriages end in divorce. An even sadder statisitic (sp) concerns the death of a spouse. Estimates are that in the next twenty years eight out of ten married women will end up widows, usually late in life.

What is your main idea in this paragraph? (See 4a-2 informal (See 21a-1) about topic sentences.)

(10b) *unclear pronoun ref.*

One good way to prepare for living alone is to learn how to take care of practical matters. For example, they might not know how to do something as simple as opening a checking account. Similarly, making major purchases is something people might have to handle. How long can a person manage

Can you help your readers tie this information into your thesis?

How do the points about checking accounts and major purchases tie into your thesis?

with a refrigerator that cannot be repaired or a useless car? *(1B) parallelism*

[After some shopping around and making price comparisons.] *(13b) fragment* Most

decisions are much less complicated than they seem at first.

(24b-1) comma error People living alone need to establish new friendships. *How does this main idea relate to the previous one?*

When, single people feel self-reliant, they can have an easier

time getting out and meeting new people. [For instance, some

students are in the habit of always going to classes with a *What is the relationship*

friend, but they can be pleasantly surprised to find that they

can concentrate better on the course and also have a chance to *among these ideas? See Chap. 17 about subordination.*

make some new friends.] The idea of going (places) alone can

paralyze some people. *(15a)* Once you make the attempt, however,

you find that (everyone) welcomes a new friendly face. *(24d) comma error* *Can you be more specific?*

Probably the most difficult problem for people living *Are there no exceptions?*

alone is dealing with feelings of loneliness. *(SP)* First, people

have to understand the feeling, they confuse being alone with *comma splice (14a)*

being lonely. Second, (people) living alone have to fight *What details support your 1st and 2nd*

depression. Third, (everyone) needs to get involved with *points? Develop your paragraph*

activities, such as volunteering (their) services to help *as explained in 4a-2.*

others. *number shift and agreement problem*

People need to ask themselves, "If I had to live alone *How does this*

starting tomorrow morning, would I know how?" This is an *question tie into your thesis?*

important question.

You revised your first draft well, so this second draft shows good progress. Your thesis statement clearly reflects your purpose and focus. Now you are ready to develop your paragraphs more fully. When you revise, think through the questions I ask, and refer to the handbook material I point out. I'm looking forward to reading your final draft. You are writing on a fresh and interesting topic.

In some classes you might be asked to share your writing with other students as you revise. In such cases, you can use the reactions of your peers to look at your material with fresh eyes. As much as possible, seek *specific* advice from your peers. To get concrete reactions, ask questions taken from the Revision Checklist in this chapter or worksheets your instructor prepares.

3d
Know how to edit.

Editing focuses on surface features. When you edit, you check the technical correctness of your writing. You pay attention to correct grammar, spelling, and punctuation, and to correct use of capitals, numbers, italics, and abbreviations.

Editing is a separate part of the writing process because, in contrast to revising (3c), it focuses more on presentation than on meaning. If you edit too soon in the writing process, you might distract yourself from checking to see if your material delivers its meaning effectively. You are ready to edit when you have a final draft that contains suitable content, organization, development, and sentence structure. Your job during editing is not to generate a new draft but to fine-tune the surface features of the draft you have. Once you have polished your work, you are ready to transcribe it into a final copy.

Editing is crucial in writing. No matter how much attention you have paid to planning, shaping, drafting, and revising, slapdash editing will distract your readers and, in writing for assignments, lower your grade.

Editing takes patience. Inexperienced writers sometimes rush editing, especially if they have revised well and feel that they have prepared a good essay. When you edit, resist any impulses to hurry. Matters of grammar and punctuation take concentration—and frequently the time to check yourself by looking up rules and conventions in this handbook. As you edit, be systematic. Use a checklist supplied by your instructor or one you compile from the following Editing Checklist.

Editing checklist

The answer to each question on this checklist should be "yes." If it is not, you need to edit. If you are unsure of the meaning of any question, look up the material in this book. The reference numbers in parentheses tell you what chapter or section to consult.

1. Is the grammar correct? That is, have you used correct verb forms (Chapter 8): have you used the correct case of nouns and pronouns (Chapter 9); do pronouns refer to clear antecedents (Chapter 10); do subjects and verbs agree (Chapter 11); do pronouns agree with their antecedents (Chapter 11); have you distinguished between adjectives and adverbs (Chapter 12)?

2. Is the spelling correct? (Chapter 22)

3. Have you used hyphens correctly both for compound words and for dividing words at the end of a line? (Chapter 22)

4. Have you correctly used commas? (Chapter 24)

5. Have you correctly used semicolons (Chapter 25), colons (Chapter 26), apostrophes (Chapter 27), quotation marks (Chapter 28)?

6. Have you correctly used other marks of punctuation? (Chapter 29)

7. Have you correctly used capital letters, italics, numbers, and abbreviations? (Chapter 30)

8. Have you followed the format requirements of the assignment? (Manuscript Form Appendix)

   Tara Foster revised her work into a final draft based on her instructor's comments and her own sense of what she needed. She then edited it into final form. Here is Foster's final draft.

FINAL DRAFT: ESSAY WITH INFORMATIVE PURPOSE*

Knowing How to Live Alone

Introduction: Identification of situation

"Alone one is never lonely," says the poet and author May Sarton in praise of living alone. Most people, however, are terrified of living alone. They are used to living with others--children with parents, roommates with roommates, friends with friends, husbands with wives. When the statistics catch up

Thesis statement

with them, therefore, they are rarely prepared. Chances are high that most adult men and women will need to know how to live alone, briefly or longer, at some time in their lives.

---

*First draft on pages 48–49; second draft on pages 59–60; second draft with instructor's comments on pages 61–62.

Background:
statistics
and how
they relate
to the
thesis

In the United States, circumstances often force people to live alone. For example, many high school and college graduates move away from their hometowns to continue their educations or take jobs. Most schools assign roommates, but employers usually expect people to take care of their own living arrangements. Also, married people might feel they will always be together, but currently one out of two marriages ends in divorce. An even sadder statistic concerns the death of a spouse. Estimates are that in the next twenty years eight out of ten married women will become widows, usually late in life. These facts show that most people have to live by themselves at least once in their lives whether they want to or not.

Support:
first area

One good way to prepare for living alone is to learn how to take care of practical matters. For example, some students and newly single people might not know how to do something as simple as opening a checking account. When making arrangements alone, they might be too tense to find out that they can compare banks as well as the benefits of various types of accounts. Similarly, making major purchases is something people living alone might have to handle. When divorced or widowed people were married, perhaps the other spouse did the choosing or the couple made the decisions together. But how long can a person manage with a refrigerator that cannot be repaired or a car that will not run? After shopping around and making price comparisons, most people find that these decisions are much less complicated than they seem at first.

Support:
second area

The confidence that single people get from learning to deal with practical matters can boost

65

their chances for establishing new friendships. When
singles feel self-reliant, they can have an easier
time getting out and meeting new people. For
instance, some students are in the habit of always
going to classes with a friend. When they break this
dependency, they can be pleasantly surprised to find
that they can concentrate better on the course and
also have a chance to make some new friends.
Likewise, the idea of going alone to the beach or to
parties can paralyze some singles. Once they make the
attempt, however, people alone usually find that
almost everyone welcomes a new, friendly face.

Support:
third area

Probably the most difficult problem for people
living alone is dealing with feelings of loneliness.
First, they have to understand the feeling. Some
people confuse being alone with feeling lonely. They
need to remember that unhappily married people can
feel very lonely with spouses, and anyone can suffer
from loneliness in a room crowded with friends.
Second, people living alone have to fight any
tendencies to get depressed. Depression can lead to
much unhappiness, including compulsive behavior like
overeating or spending too much money. Depression can
also drive people to fill the feeling of emptiness by
getting into relationships or jobs that they do not
truly want. Third, people living alone need to get
involved in useful and pleasurable activities, such as
volunteering their services to help others.

Conclusion:
call for
awareness

People need to ask themselves, "If I had to live
alone starting tomorrow morning, would I know how?"
If the answer is "No," they need to become conscious
of what living alone calls for. People who face up to
life usually do not have to hide from it later on.

Gary Lee Houseman went through all steps in the writing process as he wrote his essay on rain forests. (See page 16 for the assignment.) His work in gathering ideas is shown in 2d-1 and 2d-5, and his informal outline is shown in 2e-5. The dominant purpose of Houseman's essay is *persuasive*. He used a reliable format for presenting an argument or an opinion. He put his thesis statement at the beginning of the introductory paragraph. Next, he sequenced the body paragraphs by first giving background (along with a definition) of the topic, then supporting his thesis with several main ideas, and then refuting major objections to his position. Finally, he wrote a conclusion that points to the future and calls for awareness. Here is Houseman's final draft.

FINAL DRAFT: ESSAY WITH PERSUASIVE PURPOSE

Rain Forests Must Not Be Destroyed

Introduction:
Identification
of the problem

Developers' bulldozers have been leveling thousands of acres of rain forests every day in recent years. The rain forests of Central and South America, Africa, and the Orient are being destroyed to make way for civilization. As a result, one plant or animal a day is added to the list of extinct species on this planet. By 1990 the number will rise to one life form per hour. Early in the next century,

Thesis
statement

rain forests will disappear forever. This destruction must stop. Rain forests must be preserved because they offer the human race many irreplaceable resources.

Background:
definition
and
description

Rain forests are a special category of forests. They are found only in tropical regions of the world, usually close to the equator. Rainfall averages 80 inches a year, which explains why the forests are identified as <u>rain</u> forests. The rain combined with the warm tropical temperatures creates dense, lush vegetation. The huge evergreen trees are so close together their branches overlap and form an enormous, towering "canopy." Little light gets through to the ground, but on the canopy and immediately below on

---

the trees, plant and insect life are abundant and
rich with benefits for humanity.

Support:
first reason

One major value of rain forests is biomedical.
The plants and animals of rain forests are the source
of many compounds used in today's medicines. A drug
that helps treat Parkinson's disease is manufactured
from a plant that grows only in South American rain
forests. Some plants and insects found in rain
forests contain rare chemicals that relieve certain
mental disorders. Discoveries, however, have only
begun. Scientists say that rain forests contain over a
thousand plants that have great anticancer potential.
To destroy life forms in these forests is to deprive
the human race of further medical advances.

Support:
second reason

Not only for their medical riches but also for
their role in maintaining global natural balances,
rain forests must be saved. Living organisms exist in
check with each other, so when one is destroyed,
another can overgrow and cause terrible problems. For
example, when developers level rain forests, birds
lose their nesting areas and no longer feed on the
insects there. The insects flourish and attack farm
crops. Then the devastation of agriculture causes an
increase in food prices and a resulting increase in
human hunger world wide. Similarly, when thousands of
acres of rain forest are bought up by developers and
stripped of their vegetation, the natives who support
themselves on the land have no means of subsistence.
Deprived of their livelihood, as well as their
dignity, the natives have to look elsewhere to
survive. People who used to be self-sufficient often
become dependent on their already debt-ridden
governments.

Support:
third reason

Most important, rain forests must be protected
because their trees regulate the planet's oxygen
supply and climate. Rain forests help to balance

conditions in the atmosphere by manufacturing oxygen and absorbing carbon dioxide. As the number of trees decreases, the world has less oxygen. Furthermore, deforestation leads to reduced ability to absorb carbon dioxide. Carbon dioxide creates what is called a "greenhouse effect," a process that is gradually warming the planet. By the middle of the next century, the warming of Earth's atmosphere could cause some melting of the polar ice caps. The sea levels would then rise and put some coastal areas and islands under water. Although the melting would be gradual enough to give people a chance to relocate, the rising ocean would cover such landmarks as the Statue of Liberty and such cities as New Orleans. Also, the greenhouse effect would change rainfall patterns. Areas formerly good for agriculture could become deserts.

Major likely objections and responses to them

Some people see no problem in the destruction of rain forests. These people say that developing the land provides needed raw materials. They point to the hungry demand for firewood for natives and people in third-world countries. In most cases, however, synthetic fuels could be used and the trees spared. The extra cost of such measures would be repaid many times in the benefits from rain forests. Another justification for destroying rain forests is the need for land to farm. This plan is extremely shortsighted because the topsoil in leveled rain forests erodes quickly in the rain and becomes useless for crops of any kind. Land cleared of rain forests usually looks like moonscapes within a few years. An equal lack of foresight is shown by greedy investors who argue for modernizing by building roads and cities at the expense of the forests. They fail to recognize that the economy of the entire world is tied to the balanced natural setting which they want to uproot.

Conclusion: point to the future and call for action	The demands on rain forests will get worse, not better, in the future. The pessimist says that nothing can be done. The optimist says that people can work together to slow and even reverse the pace of destruction. Anyone who wants to take part can begin by sending a contribution to an organization like Friends of the Earth, an environmental group based in London. They buy seedlings to reforest stripped areas and publicize the dangers of leveling rain forests. No one can afford any longer to be apathetic about the devastating destruction of the world's precious rain forests.

3e
Know how to proofread.

When you **proofread,** you check a final version carefully before handing it in. You need to make sure your work is an accurate and clean transcription of your final draft. You then need to proofread, after you revise and edit. If you try to proofread while you edit, one process might distract from the other.

DISTINCTIONS AMONG THE LATER PARTS OF THE WRITING PROCESS

Revising ——————→multiple drafts leading to unedited final draft

Editing ——————→final draft with correct surface features

Proofreading ——————→final, edited draft with repaired typographical or handwriting errors

Proofreading involves a careful, line-by-line reading of an essay. You may want to proofread with a ruler so that you can focus on one line at a time. Starting at the end also helps you avoid becoming distracted by the content of your paper.

In proofreading, look for letters inadvertently left out of a word or reversed. If you handwrite your material, make sure that your handwriting is legible. If you type, make sure that you have neatly corrected any typing errors. If a page has numerous errors, retype the page. Do not expect your instructor to make allowances for crude typing; if you cannot type well, arrange to have your paper typed properly. No matter how hard you have worked on other parts of the writing process, if your final copy is inaccurate or messy, you will not reach your audience successfully.

 ## 3f
Understand the impact of a word processor on your writing process.

Word processors are becoming commonplace today. If you do not have one at your disposal, worry not. The usual methods of writing will continue to serve you well. If you can use a word processor, however, you will likely agree with most writers who rejoice over a new-found flexibility. With a good word-processing program, you can add, cut, replace, and move material with great ease.

As much as possible, try to tailor your use of a word processor to your personal needs. Some experienced writers prefer to use word processors only for preparing the final copy. Others like to do activities such as freewriting (2d-2) and brainstorming (2d-3) by hand and to write all drafts on the computer. Still other writers feel more comfortable writing out drafts by hand and then revising with a computer. Yet others like to use a word processor throughout the writing process. See what works best for you in each writing situation.

To use a word processor to greatest benefit, you need to take the time to learn its various operations. Once you can handle word processing with ease, you will not have to interrupt your writing process to figure out how to do something mechanical. Each program is a little different, and many call their functions by different names. Become familiar with your word processor's jargon so that you can learn from a manual or discuss the program's functions with other people. When starting with a word processor, learn how to create and format a "document." Learn what keys to press to activate various functions such as "insert," "delete," and "move." Also, learn how to "call up" pages that you have already written and want to look at or work on again.

As you write on a word processor, be sure to "save" or

"backup" your material frequently. What appears on the computer screen is stored in a temporary memory. If the electric power goes off, your work vanishes forever. Also, at the end of each work session, "print out" your writing. A printout is often called a *hard copy*. Do not assume that your work is safe simply because it is on a computer disk. Disks are highly vulnerable, especially to magnetism. Place a disk too close to a magnetic source and, quick as a cursor's flash, your hours of work can be irretrievably garbled. In general, disks do not survive well when they have to coexist with dust, cigarettes ashes, food, or humidity.

Relieved of the sometimes tedious work of copying and recopying material, many writers feel more creative when they use a word processor. Their ideas seem to flow more freely when each new thought does not lead to a recopying job. Nevertheless, some writers find that recopying by hand helps them think of new ideas. Be careful, therefore, not to ignore what has always served you well when you wrote by hand. Also, do not let yourself be seduced by the wonders of a word processor. It is only a machine.

4
WRITING PARAGRAPHS

A **paragraph** is a group of sentences that work in concert to develop a unit of thought. Without paragraphs, even a brief essay could be unwieldy for you and your reader. Paragraphing permits you to subdivide material into manageable parts and, at the same time, to arrange those parts into a unified whole that effectively communicates its message.

Paragraphing is signaled by indentation. The first line is indented five spaces in a typewritten paper and one inch in a handwritten paper. (Business letters are sometimes typed in a "block" format, with paragraphs separated by a skipped line between them but no paragraph indentations. The "block" format is not appropriate for essays.)

A paragraph's purpose determines its structure. In college, the most common purposes for writing are *to inform* and *to persuade,* as discussed in 1b. Some paragraphs in informative or persuasive essays serve special roles: they introduce, conclude, or provide transitions. Most paragraphs, however, are **topical paragraphs,** which are also called *developmental paragraphs* or *body paragraphs.* They consist of (1) a statement of a main idea and (2) specific, logical support for that main idea. Here is an example of a topical paragraph that seeks to inform.

1 The cockroach lore that has been daunting us for years is mostly true. Roaches can live for twenty days without food, fourteen days without water; they can flatten their bodies and crawl through a crack thinner than a dime; they can eat huge doses of carcinogens and still die of old age. They can even survive "as much radiation as an oak tree can," says William Bell, the University of Kansas entomologist whose cockroaches appeared in the movie *The Day After*. They'll eat almost anything--regular food, leather, glue, hair, paper, even the starch in book bindings. (The New York Public Library has quite a cockroach problem.) They sense the slightest breeze, and they can react and start running in .05 seconds; they can also remain motionless for days. And if all this isn't creepy enough, they can fly too.
—JANE GOLDMAN, "What's Bugging You"

Goldman states her main idea in the first sentence. She then gives concrete examples supporting her claim that there is much truth to the lore about cockroaches. This paragraph relates to the thesis°* of the whole essay: "Roaches cannot be banished from the world, but they can be controlled in people's homes and apartments."

Here is an example of a topical paragraph that seeks to persuade. It, too, consists of a main idea and support.

2 We know very little about pain, and what we don't know makes it hurt all the more. Indeed, no form of illiteracy in the United States is so widespread or costly as ignorance about pain—what it is, what causes it, and how to deal with it without panic. Almost everyone can rattle off the names of at least a dozen drugs that can deaden pain from every conceivable cause—all the way from headaches to hemorrhoids. There is far less knowledge about the fact that about ninety percent of pain is self-limiting, that it is not always an indication of poor health, and that, most frequently, it is the result of tension, stress, idleness, boredom, frustration, suppressed rage, insufficient sleep, overeating, poorly balanced diet, smoking, excessive drinking, inadequate exercise, stale air, or any of the other abuses encountered by the human body in modern society. —NORMAN COUSINS, *Anatomy of an Illness*

Cousins states his main idea in the first two sentences. The second sentence narrows the focus of the first and sets the stage for the

*Throughout this book a degree mark (°) indicates a term that is defined in the Glossary of Grammatical and Selected Compositional Terms.

supporting statements that follow. This paragraph is part of a chapter whose thesis is reflected in the chapter's title: "Pain Is Not the Enemy."

Goldman's and Cousins's paragraphs demonstrate the three major characteristics of a successful paragraph. By having a clear and logical relationship between the paragraph's main idea and the supporting evidence for that main idea, their paragraphs have **unity.** By arranging a smooth progression from one sentence to the next, their paragraphs have **coherence.** By offering detailed, thorough support of the main idea, their paragraphs are **well developed.**

An understanding of paragraph structure can help you at various points during your writing process. Before you start drafting, you might decide to subdivide your material into paragraphs and to develop each in an effective way. If you prefer to plan less at first and instead write a "discovery" or a rough draft that gets all your ideas down on paper, you can later sort out your material and arrange it into manageable paragraphs. When you are revising, you might find that a particular paragraph is weak because it does not clearly state its main idea or it does not develop that idea well. Also, you might notice that although each paragraph is well structured on its own, the paragraphs do not work together very well. This chapter, therefore, offers you paragraphing options to consider as you plan, draft, and revise your writing.

∎‖ 4a
Write unified paragraphs.

A paragraph is **unified** when all its sentences relate to the main idea. Unity is lost if a paragraph goes off the topic by including sentences unrelated to the main idea. Here is a paragraph about data bases, lacking unity because two deliberately added sentences go off the topic.

> No   We have all used physical data bases since our grammar school days. Grammar school was fun, but high school was more challenging. Our class yearbooks, the telephone book, the shoebox full of receipts documenting our deductions for the IRS—these are all data bases in one form or another, for a data base is nothing more than an assemblage of information organized to allow the retrieval of that information in certain ways. The IRS requires that taxpayers have documentation to support all but standard deductions.

In the preceding paragraph, the first sentence states the main idea, and the third sentence expands upon it. But the second and last sentences wander away from the topic of data bases. As a result, unity is lost. A reader quickly loses patience with material that rambles and therefore fails to communicate a clear message. Here is an improved version. All its sentences, including the ones adding interesting details, bear on the subject of data bases.

YES

3

> We have all used physical data bases since our grammar school days. Our class yearbooks, the telephone book, the shoebox full of receipts documenting our deductions for the IRS —these are all data bases in one form or another, for a data base is nothing more than an assemblage of information organized to allow the retrieval of that information in certain ways. A telephone book, for example, assuming that you have the right one for the right city, will enable you to find the telephone number for, say, Alan Smith. Coincidentally it will also give you his address, provided there is only one Alan Smith listed. Where there are several Alan Smiths, you would have to know the address or at least part of it, to find the number of the particular Alan Smith you had in mind. Even without the address, however, you would still save considerable time by the telephone database. The book might list 50,000 names but only 12 Alan Smiths, so at the outset you could eliminate 49,988 telephone calls when trying to contact the elusive Mr. Smith.
>
> —ERIK SANBERG-DIMENT, "Personal Computers"

The sentence that contains the main idea of a paragraph is called the **topic sentence.** Some paragraphs use two sentences to present a main idea. In such cases, the topic sentence is followed by a **limiting or clarifying sentence** which serves to narrow the paragraph's focus. In the paragraph about physical data bases, the second sentence is its topic sentence, and the third sentence is its limiting sentence. The rest of the sentences in the paragraph support the main idea.

1
Know how to use a topic sentence.

Because it contains the main idea of a paragraph, a topic sentence focuses and controls what can be written in the paragraph. The words that create the focus and control usually appear in the sentence's predicate°. To check this, look at the many sample paragraphs in this chapter. Consider, for example, the topic sentence of paragraph 4. The words that create the focus and control for the rest of the paragraph are shown in italics.

> Everyone *must have had at least one personal experience with a computer error by this time.*

The paragraph is developed with examples of computer errors.

Some professional essay writers do not always use topic sentences because they have the skill to carry the reader along without explicit signposts. Understandably, student writers are usually required to use topic sentences so that their essays will be clearly organized and paragraphs will not stray from the controlling power of each main idea.

Topic sentence at the beginning of a paragraph

Most informative and persuasive paragraphs place the topic sentence first so that a reader knows immediately what to expect.

4
> *Everyone must have had at least one personal experience with a computer error by this time.* Bank balances are suddenly reported to have jumped from $379 into the millions, appeals for charitable contributions are mailed over and over to people with crazy-sounding names at your address, department stores send the wrong bills, utility companies write that they're turning everything off, that sort of thing. If you manage to get in touch with someone and complain, you then get instantaneously typed, guilty letters from the same computer, saying, "Our computer was in error, and an adjustment is being made in your account."
> —LEWIS THOMAS, "To Err Is Human"

When the main idea of a paragraph comes first, *deductive reasoning* is being used. Deductive reasoning, as is explained in 5e-2, is a natural thought pattern that starts with a general statement and moves to specific details supporting that general statement (see also 4c).

Sometimes the main idea in the topic sentence starts a paragraph and is then restated at the end of the paragraph.

5
> *Barbie's life is that of the ultimate swinging single.* Although she has no parents to cast shadows into her life of constant boating, skiing, and camping, she also does not seem to have a need for them. Total independence is a central characteristic of Barbie. Although she owns an extensive amount of sporting equipment, Barbie seemingly has no need for employment that allows her to purchase this merchandise. There is no such thing as a Barbie

office in any of the Barbie equipment, nor are there accessories that remotely suggest a job situation for this carefree doll; although Barbie might be in high school or college, there are no accessories that hint at her having to endure the boredom of education. *Life for Barbie appears to be a kind of endless summer vacation, an extended tour of summer homes and resorts, free from school, family, and financial worries.*

         —Don Richard Cox, "Barbie and Her Playmates"

Topic sentence at the end of a paragraph

Some informative and persuasive paragraphs reveal the supporting details before the main idea. The topic sentence, therefore, comes at the end of a paragraph. This arrangement reflects *inductive reasoning,* another natural thought pattern, discussed in 5e-1. It starts with specifics and finishes with the generalization (see also 4c). This approach is particularly effective for building suspense and for dramatic effect. Still, this arrangement forces readers to move through all the details before encountering the organizing effect of a main idea.

The next two paragraphs end with a topic sentence. In the first example, the main idea is fairly easy to predict as the concrete details build upon themselves. The main idea in the second example is less predictable—thus more satisfying for some readers but more difficult for others.

6   A combination of cries from exotic animals and laughter and gasps from children fills the air along with the aroma of popcorn and peanuts. A hungry lion bellows for dinner, his roar breaking through the confusing chatter of other animals. Birds of all kinds chirp endlessly at curious children. Monkeys swing from limb to limb performing gymnastics for gawking onlookers. A comedy routine by orangutans employing old shoes and garments incites squeals of amusement. Reptiles sleep peacefully behind glass windows, yet they send shivers down the spines of those who remember the quick death many of these reptiles can induce. *The sights and sounds and smells of the zoo inform and entertain children of all ages.*

         —Deborah Harris, student

One of the most common observations anyone can make about honeybees is that they are extraordinarily good at finding honey. Furthermore, not long after one bee finds a source of honey, the whole hive seems to show up to carry it off. A young biologist named Karl von Frisch noted this fact and then asked what seemed to be a very simple question: How does the whole

7   hive find out about a source of honey so quickly? To answer this question completely took him the rest of his life and changed the science of biology in ways still not fully appreciated. Without complicated equipment and with very little laboratory work, von Frisch and his co-workers discovered a whole universe of previously unsuspected senses and behaviors in honeybees. For more than five decades they painstakingly explored the perceptual world of the honeybee, and in recognition of his discoveries and his contribution to the founding of the modern science of animal behavior, Karl von Frisch was awarded the Nobel Prize in physiology and medicine in 1973. *It all began with an observation, a question, and application of the scientific method.*
—ALLEN D. MACNEILL AND LORRIE PENFIELD,
"The Scientific Method in Biology"

Topic sentence implied

Some paragraphs make a unified statement without the use of a topic sentence. Writers must carefully construct such paragraphs, so that a reader can easily discern the main idea.

8   Already, in the nation's heartland—Des Moines or Omaha— you'll find widespread use of Oriental and Mexican vegetables. Houston has some of the best Vietnamese restaurants in the world. The Los Angeles area has more than two hundred Thai restaurants. Mexican fast food has become a $1.6 billion industry covering the whole country—even Barrow, Alaska, north of the Arctic Circle, has a Mexican restaurant. And springing up throughout the land are Ethiopian, Afghan, Brazilian and other exotic ethnic eating places. Indeed, it is no longer enough for a restaurant to be just Chinese; it may be Szechuan, Hunan or Shanghai, but also Suzhou, Hangzhou or some other ethnic specialty within an ethnic specialty.
—NOEL VIETMEYER,
"Exotic Edibles Are Altering America's Diet and Agriculture"

Vietmeyer uses many details to communicate the main idea that exotic foods and restaurants are appearing all across the country. A reader of informative and persuasive writing does not expect to puzzle over material, so implied topic sentences must be very clear, even though they are silent.

EXERCISE 1
Identify all topic sentences, limiting sentences, and topic sentences repeated at the ends of paragraphs. If there is no topic sentence, state an implied one.

A.   It's not easy to distinguish between the two species, but there are some fairly obvious differences. The northern flying squirrel, at ten to fifteen inches in length and weighing four to eight ounces, is larger than the southern species, which is ten to fifteen inches long and weighs only two to four ounces. The northern species has a thicker pelage and thus

9 tends to look more robust, the face profile in particular appearing more rounded. The tail accounts for forty percent of the animal's total length in both species, but the northern flying squirrel's tail is thicker, more uniformly colored and often has a dark tip. Northern adults vary in color from light tan to rust brown, whereas southern adults tend more toward charcoal gray.

—Nancy Wells-Gosling,
"This Little Squirrel Keeps a Big Trick Hidden in Its Sleeve"

B.   Most people don't lose ten dollars or one hundred dollars when they trade cars. They lose many hundreds or even a thousand. They buy used cars that won't provide them service through the first payment. They

10 overbuy new cars and jeopardize their credit, only to find themselves "hung," unable even to sell their shiny new toys. The car business is one of the last roundups in America, the great slaughterhouse of wheeling and dealing, where millions of people each year willingly submit to being taken.

—Remar Sutton, *Don't Get Taken Every Time*

C.   Education which involves only the gathering of knowledge for its own sake ignores the need of all people to learn to ask larger questions. People may possess a wealth of individual facts, a pile of unrelated names, dates, formulas, structures, and equations, and yet be unable to apply their knowledge to issues such as justice and dignity. For example, it is a fact that more than half the U.S. population is female. Why has

11 the American woman always played a subordinate role in a society where she is the majority? Also, it is a fact that the rate of infant death in the United States is thirteen in every thousand births, a rate higher than that in twelve other countries. How is it possible in a country as wealthy and as technologically advanced as the United States such a cruel problem can exist?

—Amy Dunbar, student

D.   This July 1, more than 13,000 doctors will invade over 600 hospitals across the country. Within minutes they will be overwhelmed. Last

12 July 1, Dr. John Baumann, then twenty-five, walked into Washington, DC's, Walter Reed Army Medical Center, where he was immediately faced with caring for "eighteen of the sickest people I have ever seen."

—Marilyn Machlowitz, "Never Get Sick in July"

E.   Peanut butter, the pâté of childhood, is the passion of many adults. They eat it in the morning, snack on it at night and, in between, mix it with everything from jellies to exotic spices in recipes that tax a peanut butter lover's inventiveness—and sometimes patience. Some 600 million pounds of peanut butter are eaten annually in what is a $700 million retail market. That's eight pounds of peanut butter per person per year.

13

—FLORENCE FABRICANT,
"Peanut Butter: An Enduring American Passion"

2
Know how to develop a paragraph.

Because a topic sentence contains a main idea, it is usually a generalization—a general statement or idea. In a topical paragraph, the sentences that support the topic sentence by offering specific, concrete details *develop the paragraph*. Without development, a paragraph is flat and fails to make its point or capture a reader's interest. Compare the following paragraph to the first sample paragraph in this chapter.

No   The cockroach lore that has been daunting us for years is mostly true. Almost every tale we have heard about cockroaches is true. These tales have been disheartening people for generations. No one seems to believe that it is possible to control roaches.

Each sentence merely repeats the first sentence in different words. The paragraph is stalled, going around in circles and failing to develop a main idea.

The key to successful development of topical paragraphs is detail. Details bring generalizations to life by providing concrete, specific illustrations. A paragraph developed with good detail often has one or more "RENNS"—an acronym that stands for *r*easons, examples, *n*umbers, *n*ames, and appeals to the five *s*enses. You can use RENNS as a memory device to help you check the development of your paragraphs. RENNS does not mean, however, that the details of development must occur in the order of the letters in the acronym. Nor does RENNS mean that every good paragraph has a complete menu of RENNS. A well-developed paragraph usually has only a selection of RENNS.

To see RENNS in action, compare again the two versions of the paragraph about cockroaches: paragraph 1 and the "No" example above. The next paragraph has three of the fives types of RENNS.

Whether bad or good, in tune or not, whistling has its practical side. Clifford Pratt is working with a group of speech therapists to develop whistling techniques to help children overcome speech problems through improved breath control and tongue flexibility. People who have a piercing whistle have a clear advantage when it comes to hailing cabs, calling the dog or the children, or indicating approval during a sporting event. And if you want to leave the house and can't remember where you put your keys, there's a key chain on the market now with a beep that can be activated by a whistle: You whistle and the key chain tells you where it is. —CASSANDRA TATE, "Whistlers Blow New Life Into a Forgotten Art"

14

Paragraph 14 succeeds because it does more than merely repeat its topic sentence. It develops the topic sentence by offering concrete, specific illustrations to support the generalization that whistling has its practical side. It has Examples, including treatment for children with speech difficulties; convenience for hailing cabs, dogs, and children, and for sounding off at sporting events; and a signaling key chain. It has Names, such as Clifford Pratt, speech therapists, and children (not the general term *people*), and dogs (not the general term *animals*). It appeals to the Senses by including the feeling of tongue flexibility, the piercing sound of a whistle, the roar at a sporting event, and the sound of a key chain beeping for its owner.

Some well-developed paragraphs have a single extended example to support the topic sentence.

15

He was one of the greatest scientists the world has ever known, yet if I had to convey the essence of Albert Einstein in a single word, I would choose *simplicity*. Perhaps an anecdote will help. Once, caught in a downpour, he took off his hat and held it under his coat. Asked why, he explained, with admirable logic, that the rain would damage the hat, but his hair would be none the worse for its wetting. This knack of going instinctively to the heart of the matter was the secret of his major scientific discoveries—this and his extraordinary feeling for beauty.
—BANESH HOFFMAN, "My Friend, Albert Einstein"

EXERCISE 2
Referring to the paragraphs in Exercise 1, identify the words that give each topic sentence focus and control. Then identify the RENNS in each paragraph.

EXERCISE 3

Using your own words to complete the thought, fill in the blanks. The place can be a city, a spot on campus, a room in your home, an outdoor location, or any other you want.

My favorite place is _____ because it is _____.

Then using this as a topic sentence, write a well-developed paragraph. Be guided by the words that focus and control your development. Use as many RENNS as you need to give the topic sentence concrete, specific support.

▌‖ 4b
Write coherent paragraphs.

A paragraph is **coherent** when its sentences are related to each other, not only in content but also in grammatical structures and choice of words. Techniques that help to make paragraphs coherent include using transitional expressions, using pronouns, repeating key words, and using parallel structures. Decisions about coherence are often made during revising, after you have written a first draft and can begin to see how your sentences might more effectively relate to one another.

‖ 1
Use transitional expressions.

Transitional expressions—words and phrases that signal connections among ideas—can help you achieve coherence in your writing. Each expression is a signal to the reader that explains how one idea is connected to the next. The most commonly used transitional expressions are shown in the chart on the next page.

▌‖ COMMA ALERT: Transitional expressions are usually set off with commas. ‖

Notice how the transitional expressions (shown in boldface) help to make this paragraph coherent.

> Jaguars, **for example,** were once found in the United States from southern Louisiana to California. Today they are rare north of the Mexican border, with no confirmed sighting since 1971. They are rare, **too,** in Mexico, where biologist Carl Koford estimated their population at fewer than a thousand in a 1972 survey. Some biologists think the number is even smaller today. **Similarly,** jaguars have disappeared from southern Argentina and Paraguay.
>
> —JEFFREY P. COHN, "Kings of the Wild"

16

TRANSITIONAL EXPRESSIONS

SIGNAL	WORDS
ADDITION	also, in addition, too, moreover, and, besides, further, furthermore, equally important, next, then, finally,
EXAMPLE	for example, for instance, thus, as an illustration, namely, specifically,
CONTRAST	but, yet, however, on the other hand, nevertheless, nonetheless, conversely, in contrast, on the contrary, still, at the same time,
COMPARISON	similarly, likewise, in like manner, in the same way, in comparison,
CONCESSION	of course, to be sure, certainly, naturally, granted,
RESULT	therefore, thus, consequently, so, accordingly, due to this,
SUMMARY	as a result, hence, in short, in brief, in summary, in conclusion, finally, on the whole,
TIME SEQUENCE	first, firstly, second, secondly, third, fourth, next, then, finally, afterwards, before, soon, later, during, meanwhile, subsequently, immediately, at length, eventually, in the future, currently,
PLACE	in the front, in the foreground, in the back, in the background, at the side, adjacent, nearby, in the distance, here, there,

2
Use pronouns.

When you use pronouns that clearly refer to nouns or other pronouns, you help your reader follow the bridges you build from one sentence to the next. For advice on maintaining clear pronoun reference, see Chapter 10. Notice how the pronouns (shown in bold-face) help make this paragraph coherent.

In the morning, before the sun has broken through, the sandpiper begins to look for food. A tiny thing with gray feathers

17 and a white underbelly, the "peep" looks, front to back, like awl and ball and cotton ball. **He** darts along the wave front, probing the sand for buried flecks of nourishment. Each feeding lasts but seconds and is sneaked in between a departing wave and the one soon to follow. With **his** head poked down into the sand, it seems impossible for the sandpiper to notice the water about to overtake **him.** Yet, at the last possible instant—later than the last possible instant, it sometimes seems—**he** turns, body suddenly erect, and races to higher ground. Rejecting flight, **he** races overland, body perfectly still, feet pounding a noiseless rat-tat-tat-tat-tat into the wet sand. The water is never more than a stride behind **him.**

—RICK HOROWITZ, "The Sandpiper's Politics"

3
Use deliberate, selective repetition.

You can achieve coherence by repeating key words in a paragraph. A key word is usually one related to the main idea in the topic sentence or to a major detail in one of the supporting sentences. Repeating a key word now and then helps your reader follow your material. This technique must be used judiciously, however, because you risk being monotonous. The shorter a paragraph, the less likely that repeated words will be effective.

Notice how the careful reuse of the key words *sounds, words, hear,* and *hearing* (shown in boldface) helps make this paragraph coherent.

18 I was then a listening child, careful to **hear** the very different **sounds** of Spanish and English. Wide-eyed with **hearing,** I'd listen to **sounds** more than to **words.** First, there were English (gringo) **sounds.** So many **words** still were unknown to me that when the butcher or the lady at the drugstore said something, exotic polysyllabic **sounds** would bloom in the midst of their sentences. Often the speech of people in public seemed to me very loud, booming with confidence. The man behind the counter would literally ask, "What can I do for you?" But by being so firm and clear, the **sound** of his voice said that he was a gringo; he belonged in public society. There were also the high, nasal notes of middle-class American speech—which I rarely am conscious of **hearing** today because I **hear** them so often, but could not stop **hearing** when I was a boy. Crowds at Safeway or at bus stops were noisy with birdlike **sounds** of *los gringos.* I'd move away from them all—all the chipping chatter above me.

—RICHARD RODRIGUEZ, "Aria: A Memoir of a Bilingual Childhood"

4
Use parallel structures.

Parallel structures—grammatically equivalent forms—can help you achieve coherence, especially when used for occasional dramatic effect. Parallelism is discussed in Chapter 18. Using the same form of phrase or clause several times sets up a rhythm that gives unity to the paragraph. Notice how the parallel structures (shown in boldface) make the paragraph coherent as well as dramatic.

19
> **The world of work** into which Jacinto and the other seven-year-olds were apprenticed was within sight and sound of the pueblo. **It was work** under blazing suns, in rainstorms, in pitch-black nights. **It was work** that you were always walking to or walking from, **work without wages** and **work without end. It was work** that gave you a bone-tired feeling at the end of the day, so you learned **to swing a machete, to tighten a cinch, and to walk without lost motion.** Between seven and twelve you learned all this, each lesson driven home when your *jefe* said with a scowl: "Así no, hombre; así." And he showed you how.
>
> —ERNESTO GALARZA, *Barrio Boy*

5
Combine techniques of coherence.

Often techniques of coherence work in unison, though they are shown separately in this chapter for the sake of clear illustration. Indeed, in most of the sample paragraphs in this chapter, many techniques of unity and coherence work together. Notice in the following paragraph by Loren Eiseley how pronouns and deliberate repetition, in particular, combine. The key words, *flower* and *pollen* and their derivatives, are boxed. The repeated pronouns *it* and *its* are circled, and arrows point to the antecedent. A transitional word is underlined.

20
> When the first simple flower bloomed on some raw upland late in the Dinosaur Age, it was wind pollinated, just like its early pine-cone relatives. It was a very inconspicuous flower because it had not yet evolved the idea of using the surer attraction of birds and insects to achieve the transportation of pollen. It sowed its own pollen and received

the pollen of other flowers by the simple vagaries of

the wind. Many plants in regions where insect life is

scant still follow this principle today. Nevertheless,

the true flower—and the seed that it produced—

was a profound innovation in the world of life.
—LOREN EISELEY, "How Flowers Changed the World"

6
Show relationships among paragraphs.

Paragraphs in an essay do not stand in isolation. You can use the techniques of coherence discussed in this chapter to communicate relationships among paragraphs in an essay. Transitional expressions, pronouns, deliberate repetition, and parallel structures help you link ideas from paragraph to paragraph throughout an essay.

One excellent way to connect paragraphs is to start a new paragraph with a reference to the previous paragraph. The two student essays discussed in Chapter 3 use this technique. In the final draft of "Knowing How to Live Alone" (pages 64–66), Tara Foster has a paragraph about taking care of practical matters. She suggests that learning to make important practical decisions has positive benefits. Foster then knits the next paragraph, about making new friends, into the essay by referring to the idea of gaining confidence from handling practical matters:

> The confidence that single people get from learning to deal with practical matters can boost their chances for establishing new friendships.

Gary Lee Houseman uses a similar bridging technique in his essay "Rain Forests Must Not Be Destroyed" (pages 67–70). Houseman follows a paragraph about the biomedical benefits of rain forests with one about the role of rain forests in maintaining the balance of nature. He starts the paragraph about maintaining natural balances this way:

> Not only for their medical riches but also for their role in maintaining global balances, rain forests must be saved.

Houseman also links the center of the essay—the reasons why rain forests must be preserved—with words that set up a climactic order. The three paragraphs in which Houseman discusses the importance of rain forests begin this way:

PARAGRAPH PRESENTING FIRST REASON
One major value of rain forests is biomedical.

PARAGRAPH PRESENTING SECOND REASON
Not only for their medical riches but also for their role in maintaining global natural balances, rain forests must be saved.

PARAGRAPH PRESENTING LAST REASON
Most important, rain forests must be protected because their trees control the planet's oxygen supply and climate.

With "Most important," Houseman links three paragraphs and establishes the order he wants readers to use as they evaluate his reasons.

EXERCISE 4

Identify the techniques of coherence—words of transition, pronouns, deliberate repetition, and parallel structures—in each paragraph.

A.   Elephant shrews come into the world nose first, and "nose first" they go through the rest of their nervous lives. Ever alert for danger, these
21 tiny mammals depend on their noses as we do our eyes, mapping their twilight world primarily by scent. Their long, flexible noses twitch constantly, probing, sniffing, and exploring every detail of their brushy, dry habitat.   —SUSAN LUMPKIN, "The Elephant Shrew—By a Nose!"

B.   However, we must try even harder to prevent cancer before it starts, since so far it has been difficult to find many biochemical differences between cancer cells and normal cells that can be exploited in therapy. For prevention, we must devise better methods of testing for factors in the environment, including chemicals from industrial processes and possibly food additives, that can cause cancer, and after we find all
22 these factors we must try to remove them. In addition, we must try to understand more of the mechanisms by which chemicals and radiation cause cancer in the hope that such knowledge will make it easier for us to recognize these carcinogens and perhaps to devise means to prevent their action. However, when, as in the case of smoking, we find that a carcinogen exists, we must act to prevent it from entering the environment.
—HOWARD TEMIN, "Editor's Notebook" of the *Wisconsin State Journal*

C.   The January wind has a hundred voices. It can scream, it can bellow, it can whisper, and it can sing a lullaby. It can roar through the leafless oaks and shout down the hillside, and it can murmur in the white

23 pines rooted among the granite ledges where lichen makes strange hier-
oglyphics. It can whistle down a chimney and set the hearth-flames to
dancing. On a sunny day it can pause in a sheltered spot and breathe a
promise of spring and violets. In the cold of a lonely night it can rattle
the sash and stay there muttering of ice and snowbanks and deep-frozen
ponds. —HAL BORLAND, "January Wind"

D. Kathy sat with her legs dangling over the edge of the side of the
hood. The band of her earphones held back strands of straight copper
hair which had come loose from two thick braids that hung down her
back. She swayed with the music that only she could hear. Her shoulders
raised, making circles in the warm air. Her arms reached out to her side;
24 her opened hands reached for the air; her closed hands brought the air
back to her. Her arms reached over her head; her opened hands reached
for a cloud; her closed hands brought the cloud back to her. Her head
moved from side to side; her eyes opened and closed to the tempo of
the tunes. Kathy was motion. —CLAIRE BURKE, student

E. Diving is perhaps one of their more stupendous feats. The sperm
whale is the undoubted master, the only whale that can dive 4,000 feet
down—or more. As he prepares to penetrate the depth, he jackknifes
25 with an utter grace--especially his tail movements, which seem desultory
and almost casual. His grace, however, is deceptive; the power in that
tail is the estimated equivalent of that of a 500-horsepower engine.
—JACQUES-YVES COUSTEAU, "Jonah's Complaint"

EXERCISE 5
Reread the paragraphs in Exercise 1 and identify all techniques of coherence—words of transition, pronouns, deliberate repetition, and parallel
structures.

EXERCISE 6
Develop three of the following topic sentences into unified paragraphs, with
RENNS and techniques of coherence. On a separate sheet of paper, list the
RENNS and the techniques of coherence you built into each paragraph.

1. The family photograph I treasure most is _____.
2. Weather often affects people's moods.
3. Television encourages materialism.
4. _____ is the most serious problem facing humanity today.
5. Medical schools should include in their curriculums courses in literature
   and history.

■ ‖ 4c
Know how to arrange a paragraph.

Arranging a paragraph means putting its sentences into an order logical for communicating that paragraph's message clearly and effectively. The choices for arrangement for topical paragraphs are discussed in this section. Introductions, conclusions, and transitions are discussed in 4e. Decisions about arrangement often come during the revising process, after you have written a first draft and can begin to see how your sentences might be arranged for greatest impact.

In informative and persuasive writing, writers have a variety of options for arranging sentences in topical paragraphs. Choices include moving from general to specific, from specific to general, and from least to most important; progressing from problem to solution; and sequencing according to location and to time.

From general to specific

An arrangement of sentences from the general to the specific is the most common organization for a paragraph. Seen in many of the examples earlier in this chapter, a general-to-specific arrangement begins with a topic sentence (and perhaps is followed by a limiting or clarifying sentence) and ends with specific details. This arrangement is a reflection of **deductive thinking,** a natural thought pattern discussed in 5e-2.

> Unwanted music is privacy's constant enemy. There is hardly an American restaurant, store, railroad station or bus terminal that doesn't gurgle with melody from morning to night, nor is it possible any longer to flee by boarding the train or bus itself, or even by taking a walk in the park. Transistor radios have changed all that. Men, women and children carry them everywhere, hugging them with the desperate attachment that a baby has for its blanket, fearful that they might have to generate an idea of their own or contemplate a blade of grass. Thoughtless themselves, they have no thought for the sufferers within earshot of their portentous news broadcasts and raucous jazz. It is hardly surprising that RCA announced a plan that would pipe canned music and pharmaceutical commercials to 25,000 doctors' offices in eighteen big cities—one place where a decent quietude might be expected. This raises a whole new criterion for choosing a fam-

26

ily physician. Better to have a second-rate healer content with the sounds of his stethoscope than an eminent specialist poking to the rhythms of Gershwin.

—WILLIAM ZINSSER, *The Haircurl Papers*

From specific to general

A less common arrangement than general to specific moves from the specific to the general. Like paragraphs 6 and 7, the paragraph ends with a topic sentence and begins with the details that support the topic sentence. This arrangement reflects **inductive reasoning,** a natural thought pattern discussed in 5e-1.

27 Suddenly we dipped down and landed on a level meadow near a tiny cluster of tents and tarps. As we stepped out of the chopper our boots sank into eight inches of dark water. The meadow was cluttered with leathery-leafed, knee-high plants with tufts bunched at the top of woody stems. Pitcher plants with cup-shaped leaves and delicate terrestrial orchids protruded from the spongy mire. Little palms rose from the higher ground around the meadow. *The overall impression was tropical lushness gone slightly haywire.*

—DONALD DALE JACKSON, "Scientists Zero in on the Strange 'Lost World' of Cerro de la Neblina"

From least to most important

A sentence arrangement that moves from the least to the most important is known as *climatic order* because it saves the climax for the end. This arrangement can be effective in holding the reader's interest because the best part comes at the end. In informative and persuasive writing, this type of arrangement usually calls for the topic sentence at the beginning of the paragraph, although sometimes the topic sentence works well at the end. Here is a climactic paragraph that begins with a topic sentence.

28 But probably the most dumbfounding of nature's extraordinary creations is the horned toad of our Southwest. A herpetologist once invited me to observe one of these lizards right after it had molted. In a sand-filled glass cage I saw a large male. Beside him lay his old skin. The herpetologist began to annoy the beast with mock attacks, and the old man of the desert with his vulnerable new suit became frightened. Suddenly his eyeballs reddened. A final fast lunge from my friend at the beast and I froze in aston-

ishment—a fine spray of blood shot from the lizard's eye, like fire from a dragon! The beast struck back with a weapon so shocking that it terrifies even the fiercest enemy.

—JEAN GEORGE, "That Astonishing Creature—Nature"

From problem to solution

An effective arrangement can be to present a problem and move quickly to a suggested solution. The topic sentence presents the problem and the next sentence—the limiting or clarifying sentence—presents the main idea of the solution. The rest of the sentences give the specifics of the solution.

29

Burnout is a potential problem for any hard working and persevering student. A preliminary step for preventing student burnout is for students to work in moderation. Students can concentrate on school every day, provided that they do not overtax themselves. One method students can use is to avoid concentrating on a single project for an extended period of time. For example, if students have to read two books for a midterm history test, they should do other assignments at intervals so that the two books will not get boring. Another means to moderate a workload is to regulate how many extracurricular projects to take on. When a workload is manageable, a student's immunity to burnout is strengthened.

—BRADLEY HOWARD, student

According to location

A paragraph arranged according to location is put into a *spatial sequence*. It describes the position of objects relative to one another, often from a central point of reference. The topic sentence usually establishes a location that serves as the orientation for all other places mentioned. The other sentences in the paragraph often use transitional expressions (see page 83) that indicate *place*.

30

About two-hundred feet from where I had waded ashore, the coral rose to a high promontory and I decided to start my exploration there. I climbed carefully to the top of the ledge and looked around. Only a narrow strait, about the length of a football field, separated me from the nearest island, which I assumed was one of the bird sanctuaries. A submerged reef seemed to join the two islands together. On the other side of the rock ledge was more coral and no sign of sand. As far as I could see, which was no more than a few hundred feet because the island curved sharply, there was nothing but a forest of coconut palms, coral, and the sea. I turned and went back to my arrival point. My government friend had told me there was a sand beach on the island; I decided the best way to find it would be to go inland and come out on the other side.

—CASKIE STINNETT, *Grand and Private Pleasures*

According to time

A paragraph arranged according to time is put into a *chronological sequence*. It tells what happened or what is happening during a period of time.

31 Her name was Aho, and she belonged to the last culture to evolve in North America. Her forebears came down from the high country in western Montana nearly three centuries ago. They were a mountain people, a mysterious tribe of hunters whose language has never been positively classified in any major group. In the late seventeenth century they began a long migration to the south and east. It was a journey toward the dawn, and it led to a golden age. Along the way the Kiowas were befriended by the Crows, who gave them the culture and religion of the Plains. They acquired horses, and their ancient nomadic spirit was suddenly free of the ground. They acquired Tai-me, the sacred Sun Dance doll, from that moment the object and symbol of their worship, and so shared in the divinity of the sun. Not least, they acquired the sense of destiny, therefore courage and pride. When they entered upon the southern Plains they had been transformed. No longer were they slaves to the simple necessity of survival; they were a lordly and dangerous society of fighters and thieves, hunters and priests of the sun. According to their origin myth, they entered the world through a hollow log. From one point of view, their migration was the fruit of an old prophecy, for indeed they emerged from a sunless world.

—N. SCOTT MOMADAY, *The Way to Rainy Mountain*

EXERCISE 7

For each paragraph, arrange the sentences into a logical sequence. Begin by locating the topic sentence and placing it at the beginning of the paragraph.

PARAGRAPH A

1. Handel, through his use of a major key and a dynamic and melismatic melody in the Hallelujah Chorus of his *Messiah,* gives us a sense of hopeful elation.

2. Although defined as "the art of arranging sounds with reference to rhythm, pitch and tone quality" by Funk and Wagnall, music is, in reality, much, much more.

3. Chopin, on the other hand, through his use of the minor mode, bass register and slow tempo, conveys to us the feeling of sullen despair in the third movement of his Second Piano Sonata.
4. There is no doubt that we experience certain feelings when we fall under its hypnotic influence.
5. For example, music is surely the art of creating emotional responses through the skillful manipulation of sounds.
6. Examples of this power can be found among the works of any of the great composers. —KEVIN KERWOOD, student

PARAGRAPH B
1. Thus, if we only knew how to unlock its secrets, a tree could tell us a great deal about what was happening in its neighborhood from the time of its beginning.
2. The records of past climate that they contain can help us to understand the natural forces that produce our weather, and this, in turn, can help us plan.
3. Trees are living archives, carrying within their structure a record not only of their age but also of precipitation and temperature for each year in which a ring was formed.
4. Trees can tell us what was happening before written records became available.
5. This record might also include the marks of forest fires, early frosts and, incorporated into the wood itself, chemical elements the tree removed from its environment.
6. Trees also have a great deal to tell us about our future.
—JAMES S. TREFIL,
"Concentric Clues from Growth Rings Unlock the Past"

EXERCISE 8
For each paragraph, first identify the topic sentence. Then identify the arrangement or arrangements that organize the sentences in each paragraph. Choose from general to specific, specific to general, least to most important, problem to solution, location, and time.

A.   The dampness clings to the land and everything on the land. In cities like Durham and Richmond and Winston-Salem, it weaves itself into the rich aroma of processed tobacco rising from the cigarette factories. The invisible shroud thus formed drops over the cities, testing the olfactory sense of the natives and reassuring their sense of economic security. In the fields the dampness engulfs the machinery and fertilizes the germ of rust. It bathes and swells the doors of the barn and the privies and the little tenant houses so that the doors will not shut tight, allowing the dampness into the houses. It creeps in on the wind, through cracks

32

94

in the doors and windows and walls. It rises on air currents through the floor. It seeps in with the rain that spatters onto the tin roof and trickles into the nail holes and seam cracks, permeating the tenant houses; and then it attacks the tenants.　　　　—DWAYNE E. WALLS, "The Golden Token"

B.　　　But isn't there a contradiction here? Participation in sports has been increasing since World War II. From 1946 until 1963 the numbers of participants doubled, and a glance at any tennis court or golf course is
33 enough to suggest that the rate of growth since then has accelerated. Unfortunately, only a fraction of the population does most of the participating. The rest of us are spectators. Certainly more than half of all Americans do not exercise enough to do themselves any good, and fifty million adult Americans never exercise at all.

　　　　　　　　—JAMES F. FIXX, *The Complete Book of Running*

C.　　　We walked down the path to the well-house, attracted by the fragrance of the honeysuckle with which it was covered. Someone was drawing water and my teacher placed my hand under the spout. As the cool stream gushed over one hand she spelled into the other the word *water,* first slowly, then rapidly. I stood still, my whole attention fixed
34 upon the motions of her fingers. Suddenly I felt a misty consciousness as of something forgotten—a thrill of returning thought; and somehow the mystery of language was revealed to me. I knew then that "w-a-t-e-r" meant the wonderful cool something that was flowing over my hand. That living word awakened my soul, gave it light, hope, joy, set it free! There were barriers still, it is true, but barriers that could in time be swept away.　　　　—HELEN KELLER, *The Story of My Life*

D.　　　I used the verb *to imagine* a moment ago, and now I have some ground for giving it a meaning. *To imagine* means to make images and to move them about inside one's head in new arrangements. When you and I recall the past, we imagine it in this direct and homely sense. The
35 tool that puts the human mind ahead of the animal is imagery. For us, memory does not demand the preoccupation that it demands in animals, and it lasts immensely longer, because we fix it in images or other substitute symbols. With the same symbolic vocabulary we spell out the future—not one but many futures, which we weigh one against another.

　　　　　　　　—JACOB BRONOWSKI, "The Reach of Imagination"

E.　　　When children begin to play with other children and when they finally go to school, their names take on a public dimension. The child with a "funny" name is usually in for trouble, but most kids are proud of their names and want to write them on their books and pads and home-

36 work. There was a time when older children carved their names or initials on trees. Now that there are so many people and so few trees, the spray can has taken over from the jackknife, but the impulse to put one's identifying mark where all the world can see it is as strong as ever. The popularity of commercially produced name-on objects of every kind, from tee-shirts to miniature license plates, also attests to the importance youngsters (and a lot of grown-ups too) place on claiming and proclaiming their names.   —CASEY MILLER AND KATE SWIFT, "Women and Names"

EXERCISE 9

What arrangement (one or more) would be effective for discussing each of the listed subjects? Choose from general to specific, specific to general, least to most important, problem to solution, location, and time. Explain your choice.

1. ways to make friends
2. automobile accidents
3. how to combine work and college
4. role of the U.S. Supreme Court
5. *Romeo and Juliet* by William Shakespeare
6. the computer industry
7. getting from home to college
8. earthquakes
9. junk food
10. music

 4d

Know patterns for developing a paragraph.

Writing starts with a purpose. In college, most writing is *to inform* and *to persuade*. Patterns for paragraph development in informative and persuasive writing have evolved as writers have sought methods to express their ideas most effectively. By knowing a variety of patterns for paragraph development, you have more choices when you are seeking ways to help your paragraphs deliver their meanings most effectively.

For the purpose of illustration, the patterns shown here are discussed in isolation. In essay writing, however, paragraph patterns often overlap. For example, narrative writing often contains descriptions; explanations of processes often include comparisons and contrasts; and so on. As you write paragraphs of various patterns, you will likely find that many patterns share characteristics. Your goal is to use paragraph patterns in the service of communicating meaning, not for their own sakes.

Narration

Narrative writing tells about what is happening or what happened. In informative and persuasive writing, narration is usually written in chronological sequence. Narrative paragraphs that illustrate other aspects of informative and persuasive writing include paragraphs 15, 18, 19, 28, 30, and 31.

Here is another example of a narrative paragraph. Its main idea appears in the third-from-last sentence when the author asks a question that reveals the focus of her story.

37   When I visited the birthplace of my mother twelve years ago, I was embarrassed by the shiny rented car that took me there. Even in 1974, there were no paved roads in Clonmel, a delicate dot of a mountain village in Jamaica. And despite the breathtaking altitude, you could not get yourself into a decent position for "a view": The vegetation was that dense, that lush, and that chaotic. On or close to the site of my mother's childhood home, I found a neat wood cabin, still without windowpanes or screens, a dirt floor, and a barefoot family of seven, quietly bustling about. I was stunned. There was neither electricity nor running water. How did my parents even hear about America, more than half a century ago? In the middle of the "Roaring Twenties," these eager black immigrants came, by boat. Did they have to borrow shoes for the journey?

—JUNE JORDAN, "Thank You, America!"

Description

Descriptive writing permits you to share your sensual impressions of a person, a place, or an object. Descriptive writing appeals to a reader's senses—sight, sound, smell, taste, and touch. Descriptive paragraphs that illustrate other aspects of informative and persuasive writing include paragraphs 6, 9, 17, 23, 24, 25, 27, and 30.

Here is another example of a descriptive paragraph.

38   Then the bells stopped, and a man with a mandolin stood nearby, and began a quiet rhythmic tune. The master of ceremonies, wearing around his neck a stuffed rabbit clothed in a pink satin jacket, waved the flagging dancers into line, helped the less agile to catch step, and the dancing went on. A jammed and breathless crowd and pilgrims inside the churchyard peered through the iron fence, while the youths and boys scrambled up, over the heads of the others, and watched from a precarious vantage. They reminded one irresistibly of a menagerie cage lined

with young monkeys. They spraddled and sprawled, caught toe-holds and fell, gathered themselves up and shinnied up the railings again. They were almost as busy as the dancers themselves.

—KATHERINE ANNE PORTER, "The Fiesta of Guadalupe"

Process

Process is a term used for writing that describes a sequence of actions by which something is done or made. Usually a process description is developed in chronological order. To be effective, process writing must include all steps. The amount of detail depends on whether you want to instruct the reader about how to do something or you want to offer a general overview of the process. For examples, see paragraphs 17, 20, and 29. Here is a process description written to give the reader a general picture.

39   The new earth, freshly torn from its parent sun, was a ball of whirling gases, intensely hot, rushing through the black spaces of the universe on a path and at a speed controlled by immense forces. Gradually the ball of flaming gases cooled. The gases began to liquefy, and Earth became a molten mass. The materials of this mass eventually became sorted out in a definite pattern: the heaviest in the center, the less heavy surrounding them, and the least heavy forming the outer rim. This is a pattern which persists today—a central sphere of molten iron, very nearly as hot as it was two billion years ago, an intermediate sphere of semi-plastic basalt, and a hard outer shell, relatively quite thin and composed of solid basalt and granite.

—RACHEL CARSON, *The Sea Around Us*

Here is a process description that gives the reader specific, step-by-step instructions.

40   Stand or tread water, until you see the right wave far out, gathering momentum. Then position yourself—swim farther out or farther in if necessary—so that you are ready to plunge toward shore in the trough created in front of the cresting wave. Once you are in the trough, swim as hard as you can. Ideally, you will be sucked down into the trough. Suddenly the cresting water above you lifts you, holds you, and shoots you forward. At the moment, arch, point your body with your arms like tensed wings down at your sides, flat and bulletlike. You become a missile projected by the churning, breaking wave. If it works, you are *in*, if you *catch* the wave, you become part of it, the forward part of the cresting wave, like the prow of a boat made somehow of churning foam, and you can ride all the way home to the sand, and come

home *into* the sand like a wedge, grinding into the shore like the
wave itself.   —RUTH RUDNER, *Forgotten Pleasures*

Example

A paragraph developed by example uses illustrations to provide evidence in support of the main idea. Examples are highly effective for developing topical paragraphs. They supply a reader with
concrete, specific information. Many of the sample paragraphs in
this chapter are developed with examples, among them paragraphs
1, 3, 5, 6, 14, and 26. Here is another paragraph with examples used
to develop the topic sentence.

41
> In fact, mistranslation accounts for a good share of verbal
> errors. The slogan "Come Alive with Pepsi" failed understandably
> in German when it was translated: "Come Alive out of the Grave
> with Pepsi." Elsewhere it was translated with more precision:
> "Pepsi Brings Your Ancestors Back from the Grave." In 1965,
> prior to a reception for Queen Elizabeth II outside Bonn, Germany's
> President Heinrich Lübke, attempting an English translation of
> *Gleich geht es los* ("It will soon begin"), told the Queen: "Equal
> goes it loose." The Queen took the news well, but no better than
> the President of India, who was greeted at the airport in 1962 by
> Lübke, who, intending to ask "How are you?" instead said: "Who
> are you?" To which his guest answered responsibly: "I am the
> President of India."
> —ROGER ROSENBLATT, "Oops! How's That Again?"

Definition

A paragraph of definition develops a topic by explaining the
meaning of a word or a concept. A paragraph of definition is an
extended definition—it is more extensive than a dictionary denotation (although the paragraph may include a dictionary definition).
An effective paragraph of definition does not use abstractions to explain abstractions.

Here is a paragraph that offers an extended definition of the
concept of democracy.

42
> Surely the Board knows what democracy is. It is the line
> that forms on the right. It is the don't in Don't Shove. It is the
> hole in the stuffed shirt through which the sawdust slowly trick-
> les; it is the dent in the high hat. Democracy is the recurrent
> suspicion that more than half of the people are right more than
> half of the time. It is the feeling of privacy in the voting booths,

the feeling of communion in the libraries, the feeling of vitality everywhere. Democracy is the score at the beginning of the ninth. It is an idea which hasn't been disproved yet, a song the words of which have not gone bad. It's the mustard on the hot dog and the cream in the rationed coffee. Democracy is a request from a War Board, in the middle of the morning in the middle of a war, wanting to know what democracy is.   —E. B. WHITE, "Democracy"

Analysis and Classification

Analysis (sometimes called *division*) divides things up. Classification groups things together. A paragraph developed by analysis divides one subject into its component parts. Paragraphs written in this pattern usually start by identifying the one subject and continue by explaining that subject's distinct parts. For example, here is a paragraph that analyzes new roles families and friends play in our mobile society.

43   The trouble with the clans and tribes many of us were born into is not that they consist of meddlesome ogres but that they are too far away. In emergencies we rush across continents, and if need be, oceans to their sides, as they do to ours. Maybe we even make a habit of seeing them, once or twice a year, for the sheer pleasure of it. But blood ties seldom dictate our addresses. Our blood kin are often too remote to ease us from our Tuesdays to our Wednesdays. For this we must rely on our families of friends. If our relatives are not, do not wish to be, or for whatever reasons cannot be our friends, then by some complex alchemy we must try to transform our friends into our relatives. If blood and roots don't do the job, then we must look to water and branches, and sort ourselves into new constellations, new families.
          —JANE HOWARD, "A Peck of Salt"

A paragraph developed by classification groups information according to some scheme. The separate groups must be *from the same class*—they must have some underlying characteristics in common. For example, different types of sports—football, Rugby, and soccer—can be classified together according to their handling of the ball, their playing fields, the placement of their goals, and the like. Here is a paragraph that discusses three classes of sports signals.

    Many different kinds of signals are used by the coaches. There are flash signs, which are just what the name implies: the coach may flash a hand across his face or chest to indicate a bunt or hit-and-run. There are holding signals, which are held in one

44   position for several seconds. These might be the clenched fist, bent elbow, or both hands on knees. Then there are the block signals. These divide the coach's body into different sections, or blocks. Touching a part of his body, rubbing his shirt, or touching his cap, indicates a sign. Different players can be keyed to various parts of the block, so the coach is actually giving several signals with the same sign.   —ROCKWELL STENSRUD, "Who's on Third?"

Comparison and Contrast

Comparison deals with similarities and contrast deals with differences. Paragraphs using comparison and contrast can be structured in two ways. A *point-by-point structure* allows you to move back and forth between the two items being compared. A *block structure* allows you to discuss one item completely before discussing the other.

POINT-BY-POINT STRUCTURE

Student body: college *A,* college *B*
Curriculum: college *A,* college *B*
Location: college *A,* college *B*

BLOCK STRUCTURE

College A: student body, curriculum, location
College B: student body, curriculum, location

Here is a paragraph structured point-by-point for comparison and contrast.

My husband and I constantly marvel at the fact that our two sons, born of the same parents and only two years apart in age, are such completely opposite human beings. The most obvious differences became apparent at their births. Our first born, Mark, was big and bold—his intense, already wise eyes, broad shoulders, huge and heavy hands, and powerful, chunky legs gave us the impression that he could have walked out of the delivery room on his own. Our second son, Wayne, was delightfully different. Rather than having the football physique that Mark was

45   born with, Wayne came into the world with a long, slim, wiry body more suited to running, jumping, and contorting. Wayne's eyes, rather than being intense like Mark's, were impish and innocent. When Mark was delivered, he cried only momentarily, then seemed to settle into a state of intense concentration, as if trying to absorb everything he could about the strange, new environment he found himself in. Conversely, Wayne screamed from the moment he first appeared until the nurse took him to the nursery. There was nothing helpless or pathetic about his cry either—he was damned angry!   —ROSEANNE LABONTE, student

Here is a block-form comparison of the impact of building construction a thousand years ago and now. Notice how the word *today* signals the transition between the two parts of the paragraph.

46

A thousand years ago in Europe, acres of houses and shops were demolished and their inhabitants forced elsewhere so that great cathedrals could be built. For decades, the building process soaked up all available skilled labor; for decades the townspeople stepped around pits in the streets, clambered over ropes and piles of timber, breathed mortar dust, and slept and worked to the crashing noise of construction. The cathedrals, when finished, stood half-empty six days a week, but most of them at least had beauty. Today, the ugly skyscrapers go up, shops and graceful homes are obliterated, their inhabitants forced away, and year after year New Yorkers step around the pits, stumble through wooden catwalks, breathe the fine mist of dust, absorb the hammering noise night and day, and telephone in vain for carpenter or plumber. And the skyscrapers stand empty two days and seven nights a week. This is progress.
    —ERIC SEVAREID, *This Is Eric Sevareid*

Analogy

Analogy is a type of comparison. It compares objects or ideas from different classes—things not normally associated. For example, a fatal disease has certain points in common with war. Analogy is particularly effective when you want to explain the unfamiliar in terms of the familiar. Often a paragraph developed with analogy starts with a simile or metaphor (see 21b) to introduce the comparison. Here is a paragraph developed by analogy that starts with a simile and then explains the effect of casual speech by comparing it to casual dress.

Casual dress, like casual speech, tends to be loose, relaxed and colorful. It often contains what might be called "slang words": blue jeans, sneakers, baseball caps, aprons, flowered cotton housedresses, and the like. These garments could not be worn on a formal occasion without causing disapproval, but in ordinary circumstances they pass without remark. "Vulgar words" in dress, on the other hand, give emphasis and get immediate attention in

47 almost any circumstances, just as they do in speech. Only the skillful can employ them without some loss of face, and even then they must be used in the right way. A torn, unbuttoned shirt, or wildly uncombed hair can signify strong emotions: passion, grief, rage, despair. They are most effective if people already think of you as being neatly dressed, just as the curses of well-spoken persons count for more than those of the customarily foul-mouthed.
—ALISON LURIE, *The Language of Clothes*

Cause-and-effect analysis

Cause-and-effect analysis involves examining outcomes and reasons for those outcomes. Causes lead to an event or an effect; and effects result from causes. Section 5d describes making reasonable connections between causes and effects. Here is a paragraph developed through a discussion of how television (the cause) becomes indispensable (the effect) to parents of young children.

48 Because television is so wonderfully available as child amuser and child defuser, capable of rendering a volatile three-year-old harmless at the flick of a switch, parents grow to depend upon it in the course of their daily lives. And as they continue to utilize television day after day, its importance in their children's lives increases. From a simple source of entertainment provided by parents when they need a break from child care, television gradually changes into a powerful and disruptive presence in family life. But despite their increasing resentment of television's intrusions into their family life, and despite their considerable guilt at not being able to control their children's viewing, parents do not take steps to extricate themselves from television's domination. They can no longer cope without it.
—MARIE WINN, *The Plug-In Drug*

EXERCISE 10
Identify the pattern or patterns each paragraph illustrates. Choose from narration, description, process, example, definition, analysis, classification, comparison and contrast, analogy, and cause and effect.

A. The way in which culture affects language becomes clear by comparing how the English and Hopi languages refer to H_2O in its liquid state. English, like most other European languages, has only one word—"water"—and it pays no attention to what the substance is used for or its quantity. The Hopi of Arizona, on the other hand, use *pahe* to mean the large amounts of water present in natural lakes or rivers, and *keyi* for the small amounts in domestic jugs and canteens. English, though, makes other distinctions that Hopi does not. The speaker of English is careful to

49

103

distinguish between a lake and a stream, between a waterfall and a geyser; but *pahe* makes no distinction among lakes, ponds, rivers, streams, waterfalls, and springs.

—PETER FARB, "Man at the Mercy of His Language"

B.   Two days later we had our first storm. It started by the trade wind dying away completely, and the feathery, white trade wind clouds, which were drifting over our heads up in the topmost blue, being suddenly invaded by a thick black cloud bank which rolled up over the horizon from southward. Then there came gusts of wind from the most unexpected directions, so that it was impossible for the steering watch to keep con-
50 trol. As quickly as we got our stern turned to the new direction of the wind, so that the sail bellied out stiff and safe, just as quickly the gusts came at us from another quarter, squeezed the proud bulge out of the sail, and made it swing round and thrash about to the peril of both crew and cargo. But then the wind suddenly set in to blow straight from the quarter whence the bad weather came, and, as the black clouds rolled over us, the breeze increased to a fresh wind which worked itself up into a real storm.   —THOR HEYERDAHL, *Kon-Tiki*

C.   It is Rimsky-Korsakov's bumblebee in its helter-skelter flight, buzzing its way through a summer breeze. It is Greig's "Morning," with the sun peeking over the horizon, its golden rays projecting like spears which prod a world to life, accompanied by sweet birdsong. It is the tumultuous
51 thunder and growling wind of a Beethoven tempest breaking the great solitude of a pastoral scene, and it is the gallant fierceness and the ethereal mystique of Wagner's Valkyries, riding their powerful steeds to Valhalla. It is Rodrigo's Madrid, at times bustling, at times serene, and it is Gershwin's Paris, always brilliant and boisterous. It is music.

—KEVIN KERWOOD, student

D.   *Hard*, in terms of wood, really means *harder* to cut, but most hardwoods are also fine and even-grained. They are not apt to split, and they take polish well. For these reasons, they are generally better for small wood carving than the softwoods; most sculptors prefer to use hard-
52 woods for large pieces, too. All the fruitwoods, like cherry, apple, pear, and orange, are hard, and so are oak, mahogany, walnut, birch, holly, and maple. Hardwoods range in color from the almost white of holly to the almost black of walnut. Oak and mahogany are the most open-grained, and therefore more apt to split. They are probably less good for small carvings than the other kinds.

—FLORENCE H. PETTIT, *How to Make Whirligigs and Whimmy Doodles*

E.   They were flat round wafers, slightly browned on the edges and butter-yellow in the center. With the cold lemonade they were sufficient

for childhood's lifelong diet. Remembering my manners, I took nice little
53 lady-like bites off the edges. She said she had made them expressly for
me and that she had a few in the kitchen that I could take home to my
brother. So I jammed one whole cake in my mouth and the rough crumbs
scratched the insides of my jaws, and if I hadn't had to swallow, it would
have been a dream come true.

—MAYA ANGELOU, *I Know Why the Caged Bird Sings*

F.   Consider cancer cells and non-cancer cells in the human body. The
normal cells are aimed at reproducing and functioning in a way that is
beneficial to the body. Cancer cells, on the other hand, spread in a way
that threatens and ultimately destroys the whole body. Normal cells work
harmoniously, because they "know," in a sense, that their preservation
54 depends upon the health of the body they inhabit. While they are organisms in themselves, they also act as part of the whole body. We might
say, metaphorically, that cancer cells do not know enough about self-
preservation; they are, biologically, more ignorant than normal cells. The
aim of cancer cells is to spread throughout the body, to conquer all the
normal cells—and when they reach their aim, the body is dead. *And so
are the cancer cells.*   —SYDNEY J. HARRIS, "War Is Cancer of Mankind"

G.   Although Littleman, my eleven-year-old poodle, has never been
separated from his thirteen-year-old mother, Simone, they are remarkably
different. Simone weighs in at about ten pounds with very delicate, sophisticated features and coarse, curly hair. Slightly shorter, Littleman tops
the scale at no more than seven pounds and is quite handsome with his
55 teddy-bear features and soft wavy hair. Simone was the first dog in the
family and is a pedigreed poodle. In many ways she is the picture of a
thoroughbred, with her snobby attitude and nonchalant manners. On the
other hand, Littleman came into the family a year later with four other
puppies of pure breeding, but they were never registered. Unlike his
mother, Littleman is very friendly, almost to the point of being pesty at
times.   —LINDA NEAL, student

EXERCISE 11
Write three of the following paragraphs.

1. A narrative about your first job (or first day in college).
2. A personal definition of success.
3. A classification of teachers.
4. An analogy about building a friendship.
5. A cause-and-effect analysis about the popularity of music videos.

■‖ 4e
Know how to write special paragraphs.

Special paragraphs—**introductory paragraphs, concluding paragraphs,** and **transitional paragraphs**—have special roles in an essay. Introductions prepare a reader for the topical paragraphs that follow; conclusions bring the topical paragraphs to a close for a reader; and transitional paragraphs—usually reserved for longer pieces of writing—help the reader move through complex material. Generally, special paragraphs are proportionately shorter than the topical paragraphs with which they appear.

Effective beginnings and endings are indispensable for successful essays. Good writers know that introductions and conclusions are far from merely "ceremonial," so they expect to plan, draft, and revise them as completely as topical paragraphs.

Introductory paragraphs

In informative and persuasive writing, an introductory paragraph sets the stage and prepares a reader for what lies ahead. Introductions provide a bridge from the reader's mind to yours. For this reason, its introduction must clearly relate to the rest of your essay. If it points in one direction and your essay goes off in another, your reader will be confused—and will likely stop reading.

As you write successive drafts of an essay, you might change your mind about what to say in the introductory paragraph. An early draft might contain an idea that does not belong once your topical paragraphs are written. Indeed, when a subject is new to you, you might decide to write your introduction after having written a "discovery" or first draft of your topical paragraphs. Equally important, once your topical paragraphs are written, you might want to change the *tone* of your introduction. For example, a lighthearted tone would be out of place in an introduction to a serious essay.

In college writing, many instructors require that an introductory paragraph include a statement of the essay's thesis°—the central idea of an essay. Understandably, many instructors want students to demonstrate from the start that all parts of any essay are related. Professional writers do not necessarily include a thesis statement in their introductory paragraphs; with experience comes skill at maintaining a line of thought without overtly stating a central idea. Student writers, however, often need to practice explicitly and demonstrate openly external clues to essay organization.

When instructors require a thesis statement, they often want it to be in the last sentence or two of the introductory paragraph.

Here is an example of a student's introductory paragraph with a thesis statement (shown in italics).

> The age of enlightenment introduced the concept of a free society. What most of us perceive as a free society was first outlined in the seventeenth century by John Locke in "Treatise on Civil Government." *The principles delineated by Locke included freedom of speech, religion, and the press.*
>
> —SYLVIA BERGER, student

56

Berger's essay then discusses Locke's three principles. Other examples of students' introductory paragraphs that include thesis statements appear on pages 64 and 67.

An introductory paragraph often includes an **introductory device** to lead into the thesis. Introductory devices serve to stimulate a reader's interest in the subject of the essay. Some of the most common introductory devices are listed in the chart. Usually the introductory device precedes the thesis statement. For example, Berger's introduction shown above gives useful background information before stating a thesis.

SELECTED DEVICES FOR INTRODUCTORY PARAGRAPHS

1. Provide relevant background information.
2. Tell an interesting brief story or anecdote.
3. Give a pertinent statistic or statistics.
4. Ask a provocative question or questions.
5. Use an appropriate quotation.
6. Make a useful analogy.
7. Define a term used throughout the essay.

Here is an introduction that uses an anecdote before its two-sentence thesis statement (shown in italics).

> Bridget and Dorothy are 39-year-old British housewives, identical twins raised apart who first met each other a little over a year ago. When they met, to take part in Thomas Bouchard's twin study at the University of Minnesota, the manicured hands of each bore seven rings. Each also wore two bracelets on one wrist and a watch and a bracelet on the other. *Investigators in Bouchard's study, the most extensive investigation ever made of identical twins reared apart, are still bewitched by the seven rings. Was it coincidence, the result of similar influences, or is this small*

57

107

sign of affinity a true, even inevitable, manifestation of the myste-
rious and infinitely complex interaction of the genes the two women
have in common?
—CONSTANCE HOLDEN, "Identical Twins Reared Apart"

The key to the effectiveness of an introductory device is how
well it relates to the essay's thesis and to the material in the topical
paragraphs. An introductory device must be well integrated into the
paragraph, not mechanically slotted in for its own sake. Note how
smoothly the message of the quotation in the George Will introduction becomes a dramatic contrast that leads into thesis (shown in
italics).

58   In 1895 Sir William Harcourt said to him: "My dear Winston, the experiences of a long life have convinced me that nothing ever happens." *But some things did happen in the stimulating*
next five decades, in which Winston Churchill was the largest fig-
ure.
—GEORGE F. WILL, "Winston Churchill: In the Region of Mass Effects"

In the following paragraph, the author uses unusual questions
to arouse interest and to set the stage for his thesis statement
(shown in italics).

59   Today, what respectable person would call a candidate for
the highest office in the land a carbuncle-faced old drunkard? A
pot-bellied, mutton-headed cucumber? A pickpocket, thief, traitor,
lecher, drunkard, syphilitic, a gorilla, crook, anarchist, murderer?
Such charges were commonplace in Presidential contests in the
nineteenth century.
—PAUL F. BOLLER, JR., "Election Fizzle-Gigery"

As Sharon R. Curtin shows, statistics can also serve well in
an introduction. The statistical data in the first two sentences help
to create a sense of a huge population whose vulnerability comes
into focus in the sentence shown in italics.

60   Old men, old women, almost 20 million of them. They constitute 10 percent of the total population, and the percentage is
steadily growing. Some of them, like conspirators, walk all bent
over, as if hiding some precious secret, filled with self-protection.
The body seems to gather itself around those vital parts, folding
shoulders, arms, pelvis like a fading rose. *Watch and you see how*
fragile old people come to think they are.
—SHARON R. CURTIN, *Nobody Ever Died of Old Age*

An effective introduction has no room for self-conscious statements or overused expressions. Guidelines on what to avoid in introductory paragraphs are listed in the chart.

WHAT TO AVOID IN INTRODUCTORY PARAGRAPHS

1. Don't be too obvious. Avoid bald statements such as "In this paper I will discuss the causes of falling oil prices" or "My assignment asks me to discuss Hamlet's inability to take action."

2. Don't apologize. Avoid self-critical statements such as "I do not have much background in this subject," "Of course, other people are more expert in this subject than I am," or "I am not sure if I am right, but here is my opinion."

3. Don't use overworn expressions. Avoid statements such as "Haste makes waste," "A penny saved is a penny earned," "Love is what makes the world go around," and "War is hell."

Concluding paragraphs

In informative and persuasive writing, a conclusion serves to bring your discussion to a logical end. Too abrupt an ending leaves your reader suddenly cut off. Also, a conclusion that is merely tacked onto an essay does not give the reader a sense of completion. On the other hand, an ending that flows gracefully and sensibly from what has come before it reinforces your ideas and enhances your essay.

A concluding paragraph often takes one of several forms. The most common ways of concluding an essay are given in the chart.

SELECTED DEVICES FOR CONCLUDING PARAGRAPHS

1. Use the devices for introductory paragraphs (page 107) but avoid using the same device in the introduction and conclusion of an essay.
2. Summarize the main points of the essay.
3. Call for awareness and/or action.
4. Point to the future.

WHAT TO AVOID IN CONCLUDING PARAGRAPHS

1. Don't go off the track. Avoid introducing an entirely new idea or adding a fact that belongs in the body of the essay. Your conclusion should flow from the rest of your essay.
2. Don't reword your introduction. Avoid simply listing the main idea in each topic sentence or restating the thesis. While a summary can refer to those points, it must tie them into what was covered in the essay. A good test is to check if the introduction and conclusion are interchangeable. If they are, you need to revise.
3. Don't announce what you have done. Avoid statements such as "In this paper I have tried to show the main causes for the drop in oil prices."
4. Don't make absolute claims. Avoid statements such as "This proves that . . ." and "If we take this action, the problem will be solved." Always qualify your message with expressions such as "This seems to prove . . ." and "If we take this action, we will begin working toward a solution of the problem."
5. Avoid logical fallacies. Conclusions are particularly vulnerable to errors in reasoning. Logical fallacies are explained and illustrated in 5f.
6. Don't apologize. Avoid casting doubt on your material by making statements such as "I may not have thought of all the arguments, but . . ." and "Even though I am not an expert, I feel that what I have said is correct."

Here is a concluding paragraph that summarizes a persuasive essay about the problem of teenagers getting married for the wrong reasons.

61   Teenagers may contemplate marriage for a variety of reasons—most of them misguided. Before they pledge their lifelong devotion to their "one and only," however, teenagers should secure the counsel of an impartial party, and they should seriously consider their options.

—ADRIAN GONZALEZ, student

The essay for which the following conclusion was written is a condemnation of racism as demonstrated by the existence of urban ghettos. This concluding paragraph reinforces the message of the essay by calling for awareness and, by extension, action.

62 It is a terrible, an inexorable, law that one cannot deny the humanity of another without diminishing one's own: in the face of one's victim, one sees oneself. Walk through Harlem and see what we, this nation, have become.
—JAMES BALDWIN, "Fifth Avenue, Uptown: A Letter from Harlem"

The following conclusion ends an essay that discusses the failure of public schools to educate students well. The author points to the future and calls for action.

63 Our schools provide a key to the future of society. We must take control of them, watch over them, and nurture them if they are to be set right again. To do less is to invite disaster upon ourselves, our children, and our nation.
—JOHN C. SAWHILL, "The Collapse of Public Schools"

An effective conclusion does not detract from the central message of an essay. Refer to the chart for a list of what to avoid when writing concluding paragraphs.

Transitional paragraphs

A transitional paragraph provides one or two sentences to help a reader move from one major point to another. Transitional paragraphs often restate a main idea briefly. Transitional paragraphs are uncommon in short essays.

Swedish director Ingmar Bergman uses a transitional paragraph in a fairly long essay about the art of filmmaking. He leads the reader from a complex discussion of how to create patterns from pictures to an equally complex discussion of how rhythm is created by the relation of one picture to another.

64 This is an almost impossible task.
—INGMAR BERGMAN, "Introduction" to *Four Screenplays*

Other typical one-sentence transitional paragraphs convey ideas such as "Much more is at stake, however, than people's comfort" or "Let us examine individually each malfunction in the system."

Here is a two-sentence transitional paragraph written as a bridge between a discussion of people's gestures and people's eating habits. This paragraph is followed by a number of paragraphs each of which discusses a different type of eater.

Like gestures, eating habits are personality indicators, and even food preferences and attitudes toward food reveal the inner

111

65 self. Food plays an important role in the lives of most people beyond its obvious one as a necessity.

—JEAN ROSENBAUM, M.D., *Is Your Volkswagon a Sex Symbol?*

EXERCISE 12

Write an introduction and conclusion for each essay informally outlined below.

A. Violence on Television
   Thesis: Violence on television is harmful to children.
   Topical paragraph 1: cartoons
   Topical paragraph 2: series
   Topical paragraph 3: made-for-television movies

B. Starting a new job
   Thesis: Starting a new job demands much concentration.
   Topical paragraph 1: learning or adapting skills
   Topical paragraph 2: fitting in with co-workers
   Topical paragraph 3: adjusting to the surroundings

EXERCISE 13

Reread the paragraphs in Exercise 10 and do the following.

1. Referring to Section 4a-1, identify all topic sentences, limiting sentences, and implied topic sentences.
2. Referring to Section 4a-2, identify all RENNS.
3. Referring to Section 4b, identify all techniques of coherence.
4. Referring to Section 4c, identify paragraph arrangements.

5
THINKING
CRITICALLY

Thinking is not something you choose to do, any more than a fish "chooses" to live in water. To be human *is* to think. But while thinking may come naturally, awareness of *how* you think does not. Thinking about thinking is the key to thinking critically. When you think critically, you take control of your conscious thought processes. Without such control, you risk being controlled by the ideas of others. Indeed, critical thinking is at the heart of a liberal (from the Latin word for *free*) education.

The word **critical** here has a neutral meaning. It does not mean taking a negative view or finding fault, as when someone criticizes another person for doing something wrong. The essence of critical thinking is thinking beyond the obvious—beyond the flash of visual images on a television screen, the alluring promises of glossy advertisements, the evasive statements by some people in the news, the half-truths of some propaganda, the manipulations of slanted language and faulty reasoning.

Critical thinking is an attitude as much as an activity. If you face life with curiosity and a desire to dig beneath the surface, you are a critical thinker. If you do not believe everything you read or hear, you are a critical thinker. If you find pleasure in contemplating the puzzle of conflicting ideologies, theories, personalities, and facts, you are a critical thinker.

Activities of the mind and higher-order reasoning—the core of a college education—are processes of contemplation and deliberation. These processes take time. They contrast with the glorification of speed in today's culture: fast foods, instant mixes, self-developing film, short-spurt images in movies and videos. If you are among the people who assume that speed is a measure of intelligence, consider this true anecdote about Albert Einstein. The first time that Banesh Hoffman, a scientist, was expected to talk about his work to Albert Einstein, Hoffman was speechless and overawed. Einstein instantly put Hoffman at ease when he said: "Please go slowly. I don't understand things quickly."

The components of critical thinking differ slightly from discipline to discipline, but all critical thinking is rooted in the principles of **analysis** (taking ideas apart), **synthesis** (making connections among ideas), and **evaluation** (determining the quality of the ideas). These principles apply to reading and writing for your English classes and for all other disciplines.

This chapter first discusses reading as a process that leads to critical thinking, and then looks at reasoning processes so that readers may recognize them and writers may use them critically.

■‖ 5a
Understand the reading process.

Reading, like writing, helps you to come to "know," to compose meaning. In college you get many reading assignments that assume you have the ability to analyze, synthesize, and evaluate. If you understand the reading process, you can use it to fullest advantage to think critically.

Reading is not a passive activity. It involves more than looking at words. Reading is an active process—a dynamic, meaning-making encounter among page, eye, and brain. When you read, your brain actively makes connections between what you know already and what is new to you. You comprehend and learn new material by associating it with material you already know.

Experts who have researched the reading process report that the key activity in reading is *making predictions*. As you read, your brain is always involved in guessing what is coming next. Once it discovers what comes next, it either confirms or revises its prediction and moves on. For example, if you encountered a chapter title "The Heartbeat," your predictions could be diverse, ranging from romance to how the heart pumps blood. As you read on, you would confirm or revise your prediction according to what you found—you would be in the realm of romance if you encountered a paragraph about two lovers and roses, and you would be in the realm of biology if you encountered material that included diagrams of the physiology of the heart. Predicting during reading happens at split-second speed without the reader's being aware of it. Without predictions, the brain would have to consider infinite possibilities for assimilating every new piece of information; with predictions, the brain can narrow its expectations to reasonable proportions. Predicting keeps the reader sane.

1
Know your purpose in reading.

Purposes for reading vary. Most reading in college is for the purpose of learning new information, appreciating literary works, or reviewing notes on classes or readings. These types of reading involve much *rereading;* one encounter with the material rarely suffices. Vladimir Nabokov, a respected novelist and lecturer on literature, observed: "Curiously enough, one cannot *read* a book: one can only reread it. A good reader, a major reader, an active and creative reader is a rereader."

Your purpose in reading determines the speed at which you can expect to read. When you are hunting for a particular fact in an almanac, you can skim the material until you come to what you want. When you read about a subject you know well, your brain is familiar with the material, so you can move somewhat rapidly through most of it, slowing down when you come to new material. When you are unfamiliar with the subject, your brain needs time to absorb the new material, so you have to slow down.

2
Use a system for reading to learn.

Three universals about reading to learn hold for all material. These universals have parallels in the writing process, with slightly different labels, as explained in the chart on the next page. These universals help you use what you know about the reading process to study and think critically. Various structured systems for applying these universals have been suggested by experts in reading. Here is one widely endorsed system, popularly known by its acronym: SQ3R.*

*Originated by Francis P. Robinson in 1946, the system has been adapted by many others since. The version here is adapted for college students.

UNIVERSALS IN READING TO LEARN

SKIM   Like *planning°* in the writing process, skimming means getting ready to read.

READ   Like *drafting°* in the writing process, reading means moving through the material, according to your purpose for reading.

REIN-   Like *revising°* and *editing°* in the writing process,
FORCE   reinforcing means rereading, clarifying, fine tuning, and getting into final form.

S = *Survey:* Surveying is part of *skimming.* You survey to get an overview of the material before you start reading closely. As you survey, your brain begins unconsciously to make predictions about the material.

If you are surveying a textbook, first quickly survey the entire text, and then as you read each chapter, survey it more slowly. If the material has headings, subheadings, words in italics or boldface, or visuals, use them as a road map during your surveying. If you are reading a book that has no headings, (1) read the title; (2) establish a general sense of the length of the material you need to read; (3) read the opening and closing paragraphs—unless you do not want to know the ending—and, if the material is long, glance over some intervening paragraphs.

Q = *Question:* Questioning is part of *skimming.* Asking questions stimulates your brain to prepare for learning. Experiments have shown that college students who actively use structured questioning before reading improve dramatically in comprehension and in recall over both short and long periods of time. Question in small chunks, in contrast to covering large amounts of material during surveying. If you are reading a textbook, it is best to question when you encounter each new subsection. Working in small chunks allows your brain to narrow its focus and to make more accurate predictions about what is coming next.

Ask questions deliberately and consciously. Here are some examples, based on the first three pages of this chapter.

TITLE   Thinking Critically

QUESTION   What is thinking critically?

KEY WORD   critically

QUESTION	What does "critically" mean here?
HEADING	Understand the reading process.
QUESTIONS	What is the reading process? What should I understand about it?

Answers during questioning do not necessarily have to be precise. The goal is to get your thinking started so that your brain will be alerted to focus on key matters as you read.

R = *Read.* Reading is the core activity. The speed at which you read depends on your purpose. Your comprehension—making meaning out of the written word—will be enhanced if you have surveyed and questioned before you start reading. The full meaning of written material emerges on three levels—the literal, inferential, and evaluative (these levels are described in 5b).

Comprehension can break down for a number of reasons: (1) If you are reading about a totally unfamiliar subject, your brain might not be able to associate so much new material to what you already know. In such a situation, take the time to build up your store of information by reading easier material in other sources on the subject; of course, for academic work you must return as quickly as possible to the more difficult material you are required to read. (2) Comprehension can elude you if your mind wanders, thus taking up some of your brain's activity with extraneous material. If this happens, you must be fiercely determined to concentrate and resist the appeal of other thoughts. Do whatever it takes: arrange for silence or music, for being alone or in a crowded library's reading room, for studying at your best time of day—some people concentrate better in the morning, others in the evening. (3) You cannot comprehend new material if you have not allotted sufficient time to work with it. College students are pulled in many different directions and have to discipline themselves to balance their class, study, social, and job—if any—schedules with the unavoidable and time-consuming demands of a reading and studying schedule. Nothing prevents learning so much as lack of time.

R = *Recite.* Reciting is part of *reinforcing.* Reciting calls for you to look away from the page and repeat the main points, aloud or to yourself. For best success, recite in chunks—subsections of textbook chapters, for example. Do not try to cover too much material at once. Knowing ahead of time that when you finish a section you will have to recite stimulates your concentration during reading. If you cannot recite the main points of the material, reread it and try again. If you still have trouble, go back to surveying and questioning and then reread.

R = *Review*. Reviewing is part of *reinforcing*. When you finish reading, survey again. This process refreshes your memory about the initial overview you got during surveying. It also gives you a larger framework into which to fit new material you have just learned. Be honest with yourself about what you cannot recall and need to reread. The next day, and again about a week later, repeat your review—always adding whatever new material you have learned since the previous review. As much as your time permits, review again at set intervals during a course. The more reinforcement, the better.

Collaborative learning can help you reinforce what you learn from reading. Ask a friend or classmate who knows the material well to discuss it with you, even test you. Conversely, offer to teach the material to someone, and you will know quickly whether or not you have mastered it sufficiently to communicate it.

Writing can help you reinforce your learning. There is little that promotes authority over knowledge as does writing about it. Keep a learning log: draw a line down the center of your notebook page; on one side take notes on the reading material, and on the other side list key words, ask questions, make connections among ideas, and have a "conversation on paper" with the material. Also, you can master difficult sections by writing paraphrases, the techniques of which are described in 31b.

EXERCISE 1
(1) List the steps you usually go through when you read a textbook. (2) Next, apply SQ3R to reading a chapter in a textbook. (3) Observe your SQ3R reading process and list the steps you go through. (4) Compare the two lists—note how they are alike and how they are different. (5) Write a brief discussion that compares the two lists and that explains which steps in either or both lists helped you learn most successfully from your reading.

■|| 5b

Read to think critically.

During the reading process, the full meaning of a passage emerges on three levels: the **literal,** the **inferential,** and the **evaluative.** If you are like most readers, you stop reading at the literal level. Unless you move to the next two levels, however, your critical thinking skills will suffer.

1
Read for literal meaning.

Reading for literal meaning, sometimes called *reading on the line,* calls for you to understand what is said. It does not include impressions or opinions about the material. Depending on the discipline in which you are reading, the literal level has to do with (1) the key facts, the central points in a line or argument, or the central details of plot and character; and (2) the minor details that lend texture to the picture. If you do not understand the literal meaning of a passage, you cannot move beyond it to the next levels crucial for critical thinking.

2
Read to make inferences.

Reading to make inferences, sometimes called *reading between the lines,* means understanding what is implied but not stated. Often you have to infer information, or background, or the author's purpose. Consider this passage:

> How to tell the difference between modern art and junk puzzles many people although few are willing to admit it. The owner of an art gallery in Chicago had a prospective buyer for two sculptures made of discarded metal and put them outside his warehouse to clean them up. Unfortunately, some junk dealers, who apparently didn't recognize abstract expressionism when they saw it, hauled the two 300-pound pieces away.
> —ORA GYGI, "Things Are Seldom What They Seem"

The literal meaning is that many people cannot tell the difference between art and junk, so two abstract metal sculptures were carted away as junk when an art dealer left them outside a warehouse to clean them.

Now read the material inferentially. You can begin with the unexplained statement, "few are willing to admit" they do not know the difference between art and junk. Reading between the lines, you realize that people feel embarrassed *not* to know; they feel uneducated, or without good taste, or perhaps left out. With this inference in mind, you can move to the last two sentences, in which the author offers not only the literal irony of the art's being carted away as junk, but also the implied irony that the people who carted it away are not among those who might feel embarrassed. This implied irony suggests that the people either do not care if they know the difference between art and junk (after all, they assumed it was junk and went on their way) or they "apparently" (a good word for inference making) want to give the impression that they do not know the difference. Thus, it is the art dealer who ends up being embarrassed, for it is he who created the problem by leaving the sculptures outdoors unattended.

The process of inferring is a critical thinking skill that adds not only texture but also invaluable background for the interpretation of any passage.

CHECKLIST FOR MAKING INFERENCES DURING READING

1. What is being said beyond the literal level?
2. What alternate interpretation is implied rather than stated?
3. What words suggest more than one interpretation?
4. What information does the author expect me to have before I start to read the material?
5. What does the author seem to assume are my biases?
6. What information does the author expect me to have about his or her background, philosophy, and the like?
7. What do I need to be aware of concerning author bias?

3
Read to evaluate.

Evaluative reading, sometimes called *reading beyond the lines,* is essential for critical thinking. Once you know an author's literal meaning and you have drawn as many inferences as possible from the material, you must evaluate.

Evaluative reading calls for many skills, including knowing how to recognize faulty reasoning (5c-5e), logical fallacies (5f), slanted language (21a-5), and artificial language (21d). Evaluative reading also demands the ability to recognize the impact of an author's tone, to detect prejudice, and to differentiate fact from opinion.

Recognizing an author's tone

An author's tone reveals the author's attitude toward the material and the reader. Tone is communicated by all aspects of a piece of writing, from its choice of words to the content it uses to communicate its message.

120

READING TO THINK CRITICALLY

Most writers use a serious tone, but sometimes they use humor to get their point across; if you read such material exclusively for its literal meaning, you will miss the point. Here is a passage from an argument against the destruction of buildings that house small, friendly neighborhood stores and their replacement by large, impersonal buildings.

> Every time an old building is torn down in this country, and a new building goes up, the ground floor becomes a bank. The reason for this is that banks are the only ones who can afford the rent for the ground floor of the new buildings going up. . . . Most people don't think there is anything wrong with this, and they accept it as part of the American free-enterprise system. But there is a small group of people in this country who are fighting for Bank Birth Control.
> —ART BUCHWALD, "Birth Control for Banks"

Buchwald clearly respects his readers, for he expects that they will realize that (1) although he is talking only of banks, the banks stand for many aspects of urban renewal; (2) the first sentence is an exaggeration intended to elicit a smile—Buchwald is being slightly ridiculous to get across his point; and (3) the group "Bank Birth Control" does not exist—it is Buchwald's creation to advance his argument.

Most readers are wary of a highly emotional tone whose purpose is not to give information but to incite the reader.

> Urban renewal must be stopped! Urban redevelopment is ruining this country. Money-hungry capitalists are robbing treasures from law-abiding citizens! Corrupt politicians are murderers, caring nothing about people being thrown out of their homes into the streets.

Writers of such material do not respect their readers, for such writers assume that readers do not recognize screaming in print when they see it. Discerning readers instantly know the tone here is emotional and unreasonable. The exaggerations (robbing treasures, politicians as murderers) hint at the truth of some cases, but they are generalizations too extreme to be taken seriously.

On the other hand, if a writer's tone sounds reasonable and moderate, readers are more likely to pay attention.

> Urban renewal is revitalizing our cities, but it has caused some serious problems. While investors are trying to replace

121

slums with decent housing, they must also remember that they are displacing people who do not want to leave their familiar neighborhoods. Surely a cooperative effort between government and the private sector can lead to creative solutions.

Detecting prejudice

Writers often express opinions, which readers should expect to be based on sound reasoning (see 5c-5f). **Prejudice** is revealed in negative opinions based on beliefs rather than on facts or evidence. Negative opinions might be expressed in positive language, but the underlying assumptions are negative. Prejudicial statements are like these: *Poor people like living in crowded conditions because they are used to the surroundings, Women are not aggressive enough to succeed in business, Men make good soldiers because they enjoy killing.* Often writers imply their prejudices rather than state them outright. Detecting underlying negative opinions is important for critical reading, because discerning readers must call into question any argument that rests upon a weak foundation. (See also Hasty Generalization in 5f.)

Differentiating fact from opinion

An author sometimes intentionally blurs the difference between fact and opinion, and a discerning reader must be able to tell the difference. Sometimes that difference is quite obvious.

A. A woman can never make a good mathematician.

B. Although fear of math is not purely a female phenomenon, girls tend to drop out of math sooner than boys, and adult women experience an aversion to math and math-related activity that is akin to anxiety.

Because of the word *never,* statement *A* is clearly an opinion, whereas statement *B* at least seems to be factual. Knowing who made these statements helps confirm judgments: Statement *A* is by a male Soviet mathematician living in Russia, as reported by David K. Shipler, a well-respected veteran reporter on Russian affairs for the *New York Times;* statement *B* is in a book called *Overcoming Math Anxiety* by Sheila Tobias, a university professor who has undertaken research studies to find out why many people dislike math.

One aid in differentiating between fact and opinion is to *think beyond the obvious.* For example, is "Strenuous exercise is good for your health" a fact? Although the statement has the ring of truth, it is not a fact. People with severe arthritis or heart trouble could be harmed by some forms of exercise. Also, what does "strenuous" mean—a dozen pushups, jogging, aerobics, or playing singles in tennis?

A second aid in differentiating between fact and opinion is to *remember that facts sometimes masquerade as opinions, and opinions sometimes try to pass for facts.* Evaluative reading demands concentration and a willingness to deal with matters that are relative and sometimes ambiguous. For example, in an essay for or against capital punishment, you would likely evaluate the argument differently if you knew that the author is currently on death row, or a victim of a crime committed by someone on death row, or a disinterested party with a philosophy to discuss.

At times, however, the stance of the author is less obvious. Consider these statements:

C. The common wart usually occurs on the hands, especially on the backs of the fingers, but they may occur on any part of the skin. These dry, elevated lesions have numerous projections on the surface.

D. Warts are wonderful structures. They can appear overnight on any part of the skin, like mushrooms on a damp lawn, full grown and splendid in the complexity of their architecture.

Both statements are about warts. Judging only from the words— often all the evidence available—and without knowing who the authors are, we might say that *C* is fact and *D* is opinion.

Information about the authors, however, can make your judgments more subtle and therefore more reliable. Statement *C* is from a respected medical encyclopedia; thus it can be confirmed as fact. Statement *D* is by Lewis Thomas, a distinguished physician, hospital administrator, researcher, and writer who won the National Book Award for his popular essays revealing the intricacies of biology to laypeople. Given this information and the comparatively benign nature of the material, the words in *D* move into the realm of fact—fact cast in metaphoric language. The author is trying to bring the facts to life by looking at them in a new way and explaining them inventively.

EXERCISE 2
Decide if each statement is a fact or an opinion. When the author and source are provided, explain how that information influences your judgment.

1. Only seven of the poems of Emily Dickinson, a famous and prolific American poet who lived from 1830 to 1886, were published during her lifetime.

2. Emily Dickinson is the best American-born female poet, living or dead.
3. "Beethoven is the supreme architect in music." (Joseph Machlis, professor of music, in *The Enjoyment of Music*)
4. "We are, after all, a resourceful people in a nation that has been blessed with abundance." (Lee Iacocca, President of Chrysler Corporation, in his autobiography *Iacocca*)
5. "Capitalism is an economic system based on private property, free enterprise, self-interest as a motivating force, competition, a price system, and a limited government role." (Robert T. Justis, professor at the University of Nebraska—Lincoln, in *Dynamics of American Business*)

EXERCISE 3
After you read this passage, (1) list all literal information, (2) list all implied information, and (3) list the opinions stated.

EXAMPLE   The study found many complaints against the lawyers were not investigated, seemingly out of a "desire to avoid difficult cases."
—Norman F. Dacey

Literal information: Few complaints against lawyers are investigated. *Implied information:* The words "difficult case" imply a coverup: lawyers, or others in power, hesitate to criticize lawyers for fear of being sued, or for fear of a public outcry if the truth about abuses and errors were revealed. *Opinions:* None—all is factual because it refers to, and contains a quote from, a study.

The kind of constitution and government Gandhi envisaged for an independent India was spelled out at the forty-fifth convention of the All-India Congress, which began at Karachi on March 27, 1931. It was a party political convention the like of which I had not seen before—nor seen since—with its ringing revolutionary proclamations acclaimed by some 350 leaders, men and women, just out of jail, squatting in the heat under a tent in a semicircle at Gandhi's feet, all of them, like Gandhi, spinning away like children playing with toys as they talked. They made up the so-called Subjects Committee, selected from the five thousand delegates to do the real work of the convention, though in reality, it was Gandhi alone who dominated the proceedings, writing most of the resolutions and moving their adoption with his customary eloquence and surprising firmness.
—WILLIAM L. SHIRER, *Gandhi: A Memoir*

■∥ 5c
Use evidence to think critically.

The cornerstone of all reasoning is evidence. Readers expect writers to provide solid evidence for any assertion made or conclusion reached. Writers who successfully communicate their messages use evidence well to support their assertions or conclusions. Evidence consists of facts, statistical information, examples, and opinions of experts. Keep these guidelines in mind as you gather, evaluate, and use evidence.

1. **Evidence should be ample.** In general, the more evidence, the better. A survey that draws upon a hundred respondents is likely to be more reliable than a survey involving only ten. As a writer, you may convince your reader that violence is a serious problem in the high schools on the basis of two specific examples, but you will be more convincing if you can give five examples—or, better still, statistics for the whole school district.

2. **Evidence should be representative.** Readers expect as much objectivity and fairness as possible. People should not trust an assertion or conclusion if it is based on only some members of a group being discussed; it must be based on a truly *representative,* or typical, sample of the group. A political pollster would not get representative evidence by asking questions of the first 1,500 people to walk by a street corner in Austin, Texas, because no such group would truly represent the various regional, racial, political, and ethnic subgroups of the American electorate. Leading political and media pollsters, like those who do the Gallup polls and the Nielsen ratings, use sophisticated sampling techniques to try to ensure that their evidence is representative.

3. **Evidence should be relevant.** Determining relevance can demand subtle thinking. If you heard evidence that one hundred students who had watched television for more than two hours a day throughout their high school years earned significantly lower scores on the Scholastic Aptitude Test than one hundred students who had not, you might conclude that students who watch less television perform better on achievement tests. Yet closer examination of the evidence might reveal other, more important differences between the two groups—differences in geographical region, family background, socioeconomic group, even

quality of schools attended. Your evidence would be both ample and representative, but your conclusion would not be *relevant to* the evidence.

4. **Evidence should be qualified.** Rarely does evidence allow claims that use words such as *all, certainly, always,* or *never.* Conclusions are more reasonable if they are qualified with words such as *some, many, a few, probably, possibly, perhaps, may, usually,* and *often.*

5. **Evidence should be accurate.** Evidence must come from reliable sources, either *primary* or *secondary,* as explained below.

Here is a summary of what to remember when you use evidence.

GUIDELINES FOR USING EVIDENCE EFFECTIVELY
1. Use ample evidence.
2. Use representative evidence.
3. Use relevant evidence.
4. Qualify the claims you make based on the evidence.
5. Use accurate evidence.

Primary evidence, first-hand evidence provided by your own (or someone else's) direct observation, has the greatest impact on a reader. Consider this eyewitness account:

> Poverty is dirt. . . . Let me explain about housekeeping with no money. For breakfast I give my children grits with no oleo or cornbread without eggs and oleo. This does not use up many dishes. What dishes there are, I wash in cold water and with no soap. Even the cheapest soap has to be saved for the baby's diapers. Look at my hands, so cracked and red. Once I saved for two months to buy a jar of Vaseline for my hands and the baby's diaper rash. When I had saved enough, I went to buy it and the price had gone up two cents. The baby and I suffered on. I have to decide every day if I can bear to put my cracked sore hands into the cold water and strong soap. But you ask, why not hot water? Fuel costs money. If you have a wood fire it costs money. If you burn electricity, it costs money. Hot water is a luxury. I do not have luxuries. . . .
>
> —Jo Goodwin Parker, in *America's Other Children*

Remember, both as a reader and as a writer, that not all eyewitness accounts are equally reliable. What is it about Parker's account that makes you trust what she says? She is specific. She is also authoritative. It is doubtful that anyone would have invented the story about being two cents short of the price of a jar of Vaseline. As a writer of personal observations, you need to be as specific as possible—to prove that you truly saw what you say you saw. Use language that appeals to all five senses: describe sights, sounds, and experiences that could have been seen, heard, or experienced only by someone who was there. Show your readers *your* cracked, red hands.

Primary evidence can also come from a reported observation. Few will ever see the surface of the moon or the top of Mt. Everest. People rely, therefore, upon the reports of the astronauts and mountain climbers who have been there. History depends heavily on letters, diaries, and journals—the reports of eyewitnesses. Consider this reported observation:

> The immediate causes of death from nuclear attack are the blast wave, which can flatten heavily reinforced buildings many kilometers away, the firestorm, the gamma rays and the neutrons, which effectively fry the insides of passersby. A school girl who survived the American nuclear attack on Hiroshima, the event that ended the Second World War, wrote this first-hand account:
>
> > Through a darkness like the bottom of hell, I could hear the voices of the other students calling for their mothers. And at the base of the bridge, inside a big cistern that had been dug out there, was a mother weeping, holding above her head a naked baby that was burned bright red all over its body. . . . But every single person who passed was wounded, all of them, and there was no one, there was no one to turn to for help. And the singed hair on the heads of the people was frizzled and whitish and covered with dust. They did not appear to be human, not creatures of this world.
>
> —CARL SAGAN, *Cosmos*

As with the eyewitness account, the strength or value of reported observation hinges on the reliability of the observer. That reliability is a function of how specific, accurate, and authoritative the observations are.

Surveys, polls, and experiments are means by which people extend their powers of observation beyond what can be "seen" in the everyday sense of the word. These surveys, polls, and experiments must be carefully controlled—through weighing, measuring, or quantifying information that would otherwise not be available. Jo Parker could look at her hands, as the Japanese schoolgirl could see the singed hair of passersby, but who can see, for example, the attitude of the American public toward marriage, toward a presidential candidate, toward inflation? For evidence on these matters, polls or surveys are necessary.

Secondary evidence is provided by the opinions of experts. Here the old maxim, "consider the source," becomes crucial. Expertise comes from long familiarity with primary evidence. An expert's reputation must stem from some special experience (as the prisoner of war is an "expert" on prison camps) or training (as the history professor is an authority on the Civil War). To discover who is a reliable source, notice what names keep coming up when you read about your subject.

CHECKLIST FOR EVALUATING A SECONDARY SOURCE

1. Is the source written by an expert on the subject?
2. Is the source mentioned in various other sources when you read about the subject?
3. Is the source's material based on primary evidence?
4. Is the source's language relatively objective (therefore more reliable) or slanted (therefore likely not reliable)?
5. Is the material still current (therefore more reliable) or outdated (therefore likely not reliable)?
6. Do the statements appear in a reputable publication—in a book published by an established publisher or a respected journal or magazine (therefore more reliable)?

EXERCISE 4

(a) Is each passage based on primary or secondary evidence? (b) Is the evidence acceptable? Why or why not?

1. Marriages on the frontier were often made before a girl was half through her adolescent years, and some diaries record a casualness in the manner in which such decisions were reached. [As] Mrs. John Kirkwood recounts:

> The night before Christmas, John Kirkwood . . . the path finder, stayed at our house over night. I had met him before and when he heard the discussion about my brother Jasper's wedding, he suggested that he and I also get married. I was nearly fifteen years old and I thought it was high time that I got married so I consented.
> —LILLIAN SCHLISSEL, *Women's Diaries of the Westward Journey*

2. In the fall of 1982, only 4.7 percent of first-year college students indicated an interest in elementary or secondary teaching as a career. In 1970 that percentage was more than 19 percent. And there are other equally disturbing statistical measures. More than a third of the nation's teachers have told pollsters that if they had to start their own careers over again, they would not select teaching. Thirteen out of every 100 teachers say they *certainly* would not become teachers again, and 30 more maintain they *probably* would not do so.

—MARY HATWOOD FUTRELL, "Towards Excellence"

3. Periods of widespread hunger are not new [to Ethiopia]. Famine was first recorded in the ninth century, and ten major famines occurred within the two centuries following the expulsion of the Muslim invaders in 1540. The great famine of 1888–1889 caused widespread death and devastation. More localized but no less lethal famines occurred in 1916–20, 1927–28, and 1934–35.

—ALLAN HOBEN, "The Origins of Famine"

4. Back in the days when large families were desired for their labor, at least children knew they were really needed. Today's child, overwhelmed with possessions and catered to endlessly by parents, is struggling with feelings of worthlessness. Even with labor-saving devices, big families are a lot of work. My children know they have to pitch in, and they know we appreciate their help. Maybe I don't have time to read to the three-year-old, but the eight-year-old does—to the benefit of them both.

—SARA L. SMITH, "Big Families Can Be Happy, Too"

5. I had read about the giant water bug, but never seen one. "Giant water bug" is really the name of the creature, which is an enormous, heavy-bodied brown beetle. It eats insects, tadpoles, fish, and frogs. Its grasping forelegs are mighty, and hooked inward. It seizes a victim with these legs, hugs it tight, and paralyzes it with enzymes injected during a vicious bite. That one bite is the only bite it ever takes. Through the puncture shoot the poisons that dissolve the victim's muscles and bones and organs—all but the skin—and through it the giant water bug sucks out the victim's body, reduced to a juice. This event is quite common in warm water. The frog I saw was being sucked by a giant water bug. I had been kneeling on the island grass; when the unrecognizable flap of skin settled on the creek bottom, swaying, I stood up and brushed the knees of my pants. I couldn't catch my breath.

—ANNIE DILLARD, *Pilgrim at Tinker Creek*

■‖ 5d

Evaluate cause and effect to think critically.

Cause and effect is a type of thinking that seeks to establish some relationship, or link, between two or more specific pieces of evidence. You may seek to understand the effects of a known cause (say, studying two more hours each night):

More studying ⟶ produces ⟶ ?

Or you may attempt to determine the cause or causes of a known effect (say, your recurrent headaches):

? ⟶ produces ⟶ recurrent headaches

Regardless of whether you begin your thinking with a cause or an effect, you are working with this basic pattern:

Cause A ⟶ produces ⟶ effect B

If you want to use reasoning based on a relationship of cause and effect, evaluate the connections carefully. Keep these guidelines in mind as you evaluate cause-and-effect relationships.

GUIDELINES FOR EVALUATING CAUSE AND EFFECT

1. **Clear relationship.** Causes and effects normally occur in chronological order: *first* a door slams, *then* a pie that is cooling on a shelf falls. But suppose you are walking down the sidewalk when, first, a car backfires, and then the person walking in front of you falls to the ground. Does this mean that the backfire is related to the fall? A cause-and-effect relationship must be linked by more than chronological sequence. The fact that *B* happens after *A* does not prove that it was caused by *A*.

2. **A pattern of repetition.** To establish the relationship of *A* to *B*, there must be proof that every time *A* was present, *B* occurred—or that *B* never occurred unless *A* was present. The need for a pattern of repetition explains why the Food and Drug Administration performs thousands of tests before declaring a new food or medicine safe for human consumption.

3. **No oversimplification.** The basic pattern of cause and effect— single cause, single effect—rarely gives the full picture. Most complex social or political problems have **multiple causes,** not a single cause and a single effect.

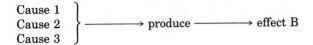

It is oversimplifying to assume that high schools were the only cause of the nationwide decline in scores on the Scholastic Aptitude Test between 1964 and 1984. Not only would it be unfair to high schools, it would also be ignoring a variety of other possible important causes, such as television viewing habits, family life, level of textbooks, and so on. Similarly, one cause can produce **multiple effects:**

Cause A ⟶ produces ⟶ {
effect 1
effect 2
effect 3

Some felt that medical researchers were guilty of this form of oversimplification when they first released an arthritis medicine for public consumption. They had proven that the pill helped control arthritis, but they had not given enough attention to its side effects.

Here is a summary of what to remember when you evaluate cause-and-effect relationships.

GUIDELINES FOR EVALUATING CAUSE-AND-EFFECT RELATIONSHIPS

1. Establish a clear relationship between events.

2. Determine whether the events can be repeated.

3. Avoid oversimplifying: Look for multiple causes and/or effects.

▉‖ 5e

Understand reasoning processes to think critically.

To think critically—to think about thinking—you need to be able to understand reasoning processes so that you can (1) recognize and evaluate them in your reading and (2) use them correctly in your writing. **Induction** and **deduction** are reasoning processes.

They are natural thought patterns that people use every day to think through ideas and to make decisions.

COMPARISON OF INDUCTIVE AND DEDUCTIVE REASONING

	INDUCTION	DEDUCTION
ARGUMENT BEGINS	with specific evidence	with a general claim
ARGUMENT CONCLUDES	with a general claim	with a specific statement
CONCLUSION IS	reliable or unreliable	true or false
USE IT	to discover something new	to apply what is known

1
Recognize and use inductive reasoning.

Induction is the process of arriving at general principles from particular facts or instances. Suppose that you go the Registry of Motor Vehicles to renew your driver's license, and you have to stand

SUMMARY OF INDUCTIVE REASONING

1. Inductive reasoning moves from the specific to the general. It begins with the evidence of specific facts, observations, or experiences and moves to a general conclusion.

2. Inductive conclusions are considered *reliable* or *unreliable,* not true or false. An inductive conclusion indicates probability, the degree to which the conclusion is likely to be true. Frustrating though it may be for those who seek certainty, inductive thinking is, of necessity, based only on a sampling of the facts.

3. An inductive conclusion is held to be reliable or unreliable in relation to the quantity and quality of the evidence supporting it (see 5c).

4. Induction leads to new "truths." Induction allows you to make statements about the unknown on the basis of what is known.

in line for two hours until you get the document. Then a few months later, when you return to the Registry for new license plates, a clerk gives you the wrong advice, and you have to stand in two different lines for three hours. Another time you go there in response to a letter asking for information, and you discover that you should have brought your car registration form, although the letter failed to mention that fact. You conclude that the Registry is inefficient and seems not to care about the convenience of its patrons. You have arrived at this conclusion by means of induction.

2
Recognize and use deductive reasoning.

If several unproductive visits to the Registry of Motor Vehicles have convinced you that the Registry cares little about the convenience of its patrons (as the experiences described in 5e-1 suggest), you will not be happy the next time you are forced to return. Your reasoning might go something like this:

> The Registry wastes people's time.
> I have to go to the Registry tomorrow.
> Therefore, tomorrow my time will be wasted.

You reached the conclusion—"therefore, tomorrow my time will be wasted"—by means of deduction.

Deductive arguments have three parts: two **premises** and a **conclusion.** This structure is known as a **syllogism.**

PREMISE 1	When it snows, the streets get wet.
PREMISE 2	It is snowing.
CONCLUSION	Therefore, the streets are wet.

The first premise of any deductive argument is an assumption. The second premise of any deductive argument can be a statement of fact (It is snowing), or it can be a second assumption that has to be defended with evidence. The conclusion follows logically from the premises.

A deductive argument has to be **valid.** The deductive argument above is valid. Validity has to do with the form, or structure, of the argument. A deductive argument is valid when the conclusion logically follows from the premises. Otherwise it is invalid.

INVALID	When it snows, the streets get wet.
	The streets are wet.
	Therefore, it is snowing.

This invalid argument has two acceptable premises, but its conclusion is wrong because it ignores the fact that streets can get wet from rain, from street-cleaning trucks that spray water, from people using hoses to cool off the pavement or wash off cars, and so on. The first syllogism given above is valid because its conclusion follows logically from the premises.

In any deductive argument, beware of premises that are implied but not stated—called **unstated assumptions.** Often they are wrong. For example, suppose a corporation argued that it should not be required to install pollution control devices because the cost would cut into their profits. This argument rests on the unstated assumption that no corporation should be asked to do something that would lower its profits. That assumption is wrong, and so is the argument. Similarly, if someone says that certain information has to be correct because it was printed in a newspaper, the person's deductive reasoning would be flawed. Here the unstated assumption is that everything in a newspaper is correct—which is not true. Whenever there is an unstated assumption, supply it and then check to make sure it is true.

SUMMARY OF DEDUCTIVE REASONING

1. Deductive reasoning moves from the general to the specific. It begins with a general statement, then moves to a specific instance, and then moves to a conclusion formed from that instance.
2. Deductive conclusions are considered *true* or *false*. This is the strength of deductive reasoning.
3. If deductive reasoning is structured properly—that is, if it is *valid* (see below)—the conclusion must be true.
4. Deductive reasoning applies what you already know. Though it does not yield anything new, it builds stronger arguments than does induction because it offers the certainty of a conclusion's being true or false.

EXERCISE 5

Ignoring for the moment whether the premises seem to you to be true, determine if each conclusion is valid. Explain your answer.

1. Some students are not wealthy.
   Stuart is a student.
   Stuart is not wealthy.

2. All great writers write many drafts of their work.
   E. B. White was a great writer.
   E. B. White wrote many drafts of his work.
3. Some government bureaucracies are inefficient.
   The U.S. Post Office is run by a government bureaucracy.
   The U.S. Post Office is inefficient.
4. Terrorists defy the established order.
   My son defies me.
   My son is a terrorist.
5. When my uncle is hungry, he eats.
   My uncle just finished eating.
   Therefore, he was hungry.

■|| 5f

Recognize and avoid logical fallacies.

Logical fallacies are flaws in reasoning that lead to illogical statements. They tend to occur most often when ideas are being argued, although they can be found in all types of writing. Most logical fallacies masquerade as reasonable statements, but they are in fact attempts to manipulate readers by reaching their emotions instead of their intellects, their hearts rather than their heads. Most logical fallacies are known by labels; all indicate a way that thinking has gone wrong during the reasoning process.

Hasty generalization

A **hasty generalization** occurs when someone generalizes from inadequate evidence. If the statement "My hometown is the best place in the state to live" is supported with only two examples of why it is pleasant, the generalization is hasty. **Stereotyping** is a type of hasty generalization that occurs when someone makes prejudiced, sweeping claims about all of the members of a particular religious, ethnic, racial, or political group: "Everyone from country X is dishonest."

False analogy

A **false analogy** is a comparison in which the differences outweigh the similarities, or the similarities are irrelevant to the claim the analogy is intended to support. "Old Joe Smith would never make a good President because an old dog cannot learn new tricks." Home-spun analogies like this often seem to have an air of wisdom about them, but just as often they fall apart when examined closely.

Learning the role of the President is hardly comparable to a dog's learning new tricks.

Circular argument

A **circular argument,** sometimes called a **circular definition,** is an assertion merely restated in slightly different terms: "Boxing is a dangerous sport because it is unsafe." Here, "unsafe" conveys the same idea as "dangerous" rather than adding something new. This "begs the question" because the conclusion is the same as the premise.

Non sequitur

Non sequitur in Latin translates as "does not follow," meaning a conclusion does not follow from the premises: "Jane Jones is a forceful speaker, so she will make a good mayor." It does not follow that someone's ability to be a forceful speaker means that person would be a good mayor.

Post hoc, ergo propter hoc

Post hoc, ergo propter hoc—which means "after this, therefore because of this"—results when someone assumes that sequence alone proves something. This cause-and-effect fallacy is very common: "Because a new weather satellite was launched last week, it has not stopped raining."

Self-contradiction

Self-contradiction occurs when two premises are used that cannot simultaneously be true: "Only when nuclear weapons have finally destroyed us will we be convinced of the need to control them." This statement is self-contradictory in that no one will be around to be convinced after everyone has been destroyed.

Red herring

A **red herring,** sometimes referred to as **ignoring the question,** sidetracks an issue by bringing up a totally unrelated issue: "Why worry about pandas becoming extinct when we should be concerned about the plight of the homeless?" Someone who introduces an irrelevant issue hopes to distract the audience as a red herring might distract bloodhounds from a scent.

Appeal to the person

An **appeal to the person,** also known as **ad hominem,** attacks the appearance, personal habits, or character of the person involved instead of dealing with the merits of the issue at hand: "We could take her plea for money for the homeless seriously if she were not so nasty to the children who live next door to her."

Bandwagon

Bandwagon, also known as **going along with the crowd,** implies that something is right because everyone is doing it, that truth is determined by majority vote: "Smoking must not be bad for people because millions of people smoke."

False or irrelevant authority

Using **false or irrelevant authority,** sometimes called **ad verecundiam,** means citing the opinion of an "expert" who has no claim to expertise about the subject at hand. This fallacy attempts to transfer prestige from one area to another. Many television commercials rely on this tactic—a famous tennis player praising a brand of motor oil or a popular movie star lauding a brand of cheese.

Card-stacking

Card-stacking, also known as **special pleading,** ignores evidence on the other side of a question. From all the available facts, the person arguing selects only those that will build the best (or worst) possible case. Many television commercials use this strategy. When three slim, happy consumers rave about a new diet plan, they do not mention (a) the plan does not work for everyone and (b) other plans work better for some people. The makers of the commercial selected evidence that helped their cause, ignoring any that did not.

The either–or fallacy

The either–or fallacy, also known as **false dilemma,** offers only two alternatives when more exist: "Either go to college or forget about getting a job." This statement implies that a college education is a prerequisite for all jobs.

Taking something out of context

Taking something out of context separates an idea or fact from the material surrounding it, thus distorting it for special purposes. If a critic writes about a movie saying, "The plot was predictable and boring but the music was sparkling," and an advertisement for the movie says, "Critic calls this movie 'sparkling,'" the critic's words have been taken out of context—and distorted.

Appeal to ignorance

Appeal to ignorance assumes that an argument is valid simply because there is no evidence on the other side of the issue: "Since no one has proven that depression does not cause cancer, we can assume that it does." The absence of opposing evidence, however, proves nothing.

Ambiguity and Equivocation

Ambiguity and **equivocation** describe expressions that are not clear because they have more than one meaning. An ambiguous expression may be taken either way by the reader. A statement such as "They were entertaining guests" is ambiguous. Were the guests amusing to be with or were people giving hospitality to guests? An equivocal expression, by contrast, is one used in two or more ways within a single argument. If someone argued that the President *played an important role* in arms control negotiations and then, two sentences later, accused him of *merely playing a role,* the person would be equivocating.

EXERCISE 6

Identify and explain the fallacy in each item. If the item is correct, circle its number.

EXAMPLE   We cannot use coal for energy because its fumes will pollute our environment. [This is an *either-or fallacy* because it assumes that technology offers us no way to contain or "clean" the fumes.]

1. UFO's must exist because no reputable studies have proven conclusively that they do not.
2. Politics should not interfere with participation in the Olympics because many athletes are not old enough to vote in their countries.
3. I just saw my first Tennessee Williams play, *The Glass Menagerie.* He's the twentieth century's greatest playwright, I'm positive.
4. Water fluoridation affects the brain. Citywide, students' test scores began to drop five months after fluoridation began.
5. (This incident is real.) A 34-year-old female lawyer working in Washington, D.C., for the federal government was denied permission to take the bar examination to practice law in her home state because she was living with a man who was not her husband. What fallacy is working here?
6. Plagiarism is unethical because it is dishonest.
7. Seat belts are the only hope for reducing the death rate from automobile accidents.
8. Medicare is free; the government pays for it from taxes.

II | UNDERSTANDING GRAMMAR

6
PARTS
OF
SPEECH

Knowing grammar helps you understand how language works. Grammar describes the way words deliver meaning. Grammar also describes components of language and standard rules for using language. Still, grammar is only a tool. You need to know more than labels and rules to be able to write. You need to gain control of larger matters as well, all discussed in this handbook: understanding the writing process°; developing and supporting a thesis°; organizing material°; and using words, sentences, and paragraphs to carry out your writing purposes successfully.

When you learn the parts of speech, you gain a basic vocabulary. You can identify words, think about words and the structures they form, and communicate with other people about language. This chapter presents each part of speech—noun, pronoun, verb, adjective, adverb, conjunction, and interjection—to help you identify words and their functions. **Function** is an important aspect of grammar, for the same word can function in more than one way. To identify a word's part of speech, you must see the word functioning in a sentence.

We ate **fish**. [*Fish* is a noun. It names a thing.]

We **fish** on weekends. [*Fish* is a verb. It names an action.]

140

6a

Recognize nouns.

A **noun** names a person, place, thing, or idea.

NOUNS		
PROPER	Names specific people, places, or things (first letter is always capitalized)	John Lennon Paris Buick
COMMON	Names general groups, places, people, or things	singer city car
CONCRETE	Names things that can be seen, touched, heard, smelled, tasted	landscape pizza thunder
ABSTRACT	Names things *not* knowable through the five senses	freedom shyness
COLLECTIVE	Names groups	family team committee
MASS	Names "uncountable" things	water time

Most nouns change form to show number°: *idea, mouse* (singular); *ideas, mice* (plural). Nouns also change form for the possessive case°: *the **pilot's** hometown.* Nouns function as subjects°, objects°, and complements°.

> **Linda** ate **pizza** in **Paris.** [*Linda* = subject, *pizza* = direct object, *Paris* = object of preposition]

> **Linda** is a **singer.** [*Linda* = subject, *singer* = subject complement]

Articles often appear with nouns. These little words—*a, an, the*—are also called **limiting adjectives, noun markers,** or **noun determiners.** *A* and *an* "limit" a noun less than *the* does: a *plan,* the *plan.* Of *a* and *an, a* is the right word to use when the word following it starts with a consonant sound: **a** *carrot,* **a** *broken egg,* **a** *hip. An* is the right word to use when the word following it starts with a vowel sound: **an** *egg,* **an** *old carrot,* **an** *honor.*

6b

Recognize pronouns.

A **pronoun** takes the place of a noun.

David is an accountant. [noun]
He is an accountant. [pronoun]

The word (or words) a pronoun replaces is called its **antecedent.**

Some pronouns have different singular and plural forms: *I, her, himself* (singular) and *we, them, themselves* (plural), for example. Some pronouns change form to show case° changes: *I, me, mine; who, whom, whose,* for example.

PRONOUNS

PERSONAL *I, you, they, we, her, its, ours,* and others	Refers to people or things	I saw **her** take your book to **them.**
RELATIVE *who, which, that, what, whoever,* and others	Introduces certain noun clauses and adjective clauses	**Whoever** took the book **that** I left must return it.
INTERROGATIVE *who, whose, what, which,* and others	Introduces a question	**Who** called?
DEMONSTRATIVE *this, these, that, those*	Points out the antecedent	Is **this** a mistake?
REFLEXIVE; INTENSIVE *myself, yourself, herself, themselves,* and all *-self* or *-selves* words	Reflects back to the antecedent; intensifies the antecedent	They claim to support **themselves.** I **myself** doubt it.
RECIPROCAL *each other, one another*	Refers to individual parts of a plural antecedent	We respect **each other.**
INDEFINITE *all, anyone, each,* and others	Refers to nonspecific persons or things	**Everyone** is welcome here.

EXERCISE 1
Underline and label all nouns (N) and pronouns (P). Circle all articles.

EXAMPLE   Queen Elizabeth II (N) served as (a) driver (N) and mechanic (N) in World War II (N).

1. She joined the Auxiliary Territorial Service in 1944.
2. At the time, she was still a princess.
3. She was treated like all the others, though.
4. When she started, she did not know how to drive.
5. The princess quickly learned to strip and repair many kinds of engines.

■‖ 6c

Recognize verbs.

Main verbs express action, occurrence, or state of being.

I **dance**. [action]

The audience **became** silent. What **happened?** [occurrence]

You **were** wonderful, but the show **seemed** too long. [state of being]

A **linking verb** is a main verb that connects a subject° with a subject complement°—a word (or words) that renames or describes the subject.

> George Washington **was** President. [*George Washington* = subject, *was* = linking verb, *President* = complement; *President* renames *George Washington*.]
>
> George Washington **grew** old at Mount Vernon. [*George Washington* = subject, *grew* = linking verb, *old* = complement; *old* describes *George Washington*.]

Auxiliary, or **helping, verbs** are forms of *be, do, have, can, may, will,* and others; they combine with main verbs to make verb phrases.

> Clothing prices **have soared** recently. [*have* = auxiliary verb, *soared* = main verb, *have soared* = verb phrase]
>
> Leather shoes **can cost** hundreds of dollars. [*can* = auxiliary verb, *cost* = main verb, *can cost* = verb phrase]

WHERE TO FIND INFORMATION RELATED TO VERBS

Verb forms and principal parts	8a
Learning irregular verbs	8b-2
Forms of *be, do, have*	8c
Using *be, do, have* as auxiliaries	8c
Using *can, may, will* (modal auxiliaries)	8c
Using *lie, lay; sit, set; rise, raise*	8d
Showing time with verbs	8e–8h
Making subjects and verbs agree	11a–11k

EXERCISE 2
Underline all verbs.

EXAMPLE   Albert Einstein <u>was offered</u> the presidency of Israel.

1. When Israel's first president died in office, an Israeli newspaper suggested that Einstein become the next president.
2. Many people felt that he could be elected easily.
3. Everyone expected that he would continue his scientific research even if he won the office.
4. Nevertheless, he refused the nomination.
5. He said that he lacked the talent and experience that were needed for politics.

6d

Recognize verbals.

Verbals are verb parts functioning as nouns, adjectives, or adverbs.

VERBALS		
INFINITIVE *to* + simple form of verb	1. Noun: names an action, state, or condition 2. Adjective or adverb: describes or modifies.	**To eat** now is inconvenient. Still, we have far **to go.**
PAST PARTICIPLE *-ed* form of regular verb or equivalent in irregular verb	Adjective: describes or modifies	**Boiled, filtered** water is usually safe to drink.
PRESENT PARTICIPLE *-ing* form of verb	1. Adjective: describes or modifies 2. Noun: see *Gerund,* below	**Running** water may not be safe.
GERUND *-ing* form of verb	Noun: names an action, state, or condition	**Eating** in turnpike restaurants can be an adventure.

■‖ 6e

Recognize adjectives.

Adjectives modify—that is, describe or limit—nouns, pronouns, and word groups functioning as nouns.

I saw a **green** tree. [*Green* modifies noun, *tree.*]

It was **leafy** and **healthy.** [*Leafy* and *healthy* modify pronoun, *it.*]

The flowering trees were **beautiful.** [*Beautiful* modifies noun phrase, *the flowering trees.*]

Descriptive adjectives, like *healthy, leafy,* and *green,* can show levels of intensity: *green, greener, greenest; beautiful, more beautiful, most beautiful.*

Some words quite different from descriptive adjectives still function to limit nouns, so they are classified as adjectives. Articles, one type of these **limiting adjectives,** are discussed in 6a. The chart lists other types.

Because most of these words also function as pronouns, you must see each word functioning in a sentence to identify its part of speech.

That car belongs to Harold. [*that* = demonstrative adjective]

That is Harold's car. [*that* = demonstrative pronoun]

Proper adjectives are formed from proper nouns: *American, Victorian.* See 30e for advice about capitalizing them.

LIMITING ADJECTIVES

DEMONSTRATIVE
this, these, that, those

Those students rent **that** house.

INDEFINITE
any, each, other, some, and others

Few films today have complex plots.

INTERROGATIVE
what, which, whose

What answer did you give?

NUMERICAL
one, first, two, second, and others

The **fifth** question was tricky.

POSSESSIVE
my, your, their, and others

My violin is older than **your** cello.

RELATIVE
what, which, whose, whatever, whichever, whosever

We don't know **which** road to take.

Spelling compound words: e.g., *well-known* or *well known*	22e-3
Using commas with two or more adjectives	24c, 24d
Capitalizing proper adjectives	30e

EXERCISE 3
Underline all adjectives.

EXAMPLE   Thomas H. Holmes was the father of <u>modern</u> embalming.

1. Holmes experimented with embalming while in medical school.
2. Later, he moved to New York and became one of the first professional embalmers in this country.

3. During the Civil War, he received a government contract to embalm dead Union soldiers.

4. He became wealthy because he limited his embalming practice to the officers whose families were rich enough to pay his fee of $100.

5. He gave strict instructions that he was not to be embalmed.

■‖ 6f
Recognize adverbs.

An **adverb** modifies—that is, describes or limits—verbs, adjectives, other adverbs, and entire sentences.

Good cooks plan meals **carefully.** [*Carefully* modifies verb, *plan.*]

They know vegetables provide **very** important vitamins. [*Very* modifies adjective, *important.*]

Potato chips are often **too** highly salted. [*Too* modifies adverb, *highly.*]

Fortunately, people are learning that salt can be harmful. [*Fortunately* modifies the entire sentence.]

Many adverbs are easy to recognize because they are formed by adding *-ly* to adjectives: *sadly, loudly, normally, happily.* Still, some adjectives end in *-ly: brotherly, lovely,* and *silly,* for example. Also, many adverbs do not end in *-ly: very, much, always, not, yesterday, so,* and *well* are just a few that do not. For a complete explanation of how to distinguish between adverbs and adjectives, see Chapter 12.

Conjunctive adverbs modify by creating logical connections in meaning between independent clauses°.

CONJUNCTIVE ADVERBS	
SHOWING ADDITION	*also, furthermore, moreover, besides*
SHOWING CONTRAST	*however, still, nevertheless, conversely, nonetheless, instead*
SHOWING COMPARISON	*similarly, likewise*
SHOWING RESULT OR SUMMARY	*therefore, thus, consequently*
SHOWING TIME	*next, then, meanwhile, finally, subsequently*
SHOWING EMPHASIS	*indeed, certainly*

Descriptive adverbs can show levels of intensity, usually by adding *more* (or *less*) and *most* (or *least*): *more happily, least clearly.*

WHERE TO FIND INFORMATION RELATED TO ADVERBS

Well and *good*	12d
Badly and *bad*	12d
Punctuation with conjunctive adverbs	24f, 25c

EXERCISE 4

Underline all adverbs.

EXAMPLE   Niagara Falls is eroding <u>rapidly</u>.

1. The falls are already 12,000 years old.
2. Erosion has steadily destroyed seven miles of land.
3. Not less than one foot of land disappears annually.
4. In about 35,000 years, the falls will likely merge with Lake Erie, which is now twenty miles away.
5. Recently, the rate of erosion has diminished very slightly, as water has been diverted to hydroelectric plants.

▆‖ 6g

Recognize prepositions.

Prepositions function with other words, in **prepositional phrases.** A prepositional phrase always has a preposition and a noun or pronoun object. It may contain modifying words too. Prepositional phrases often set out relationships in time or space: *in April, under the orange umbrella.*

In the fall, we will hear a concert **by our favorite tenor.**

WHERE TO FIND INFORMATION RELATED TO PREPOSITIONS

Using pronouns as objects: *me, him, whom,* etc.	9b–9h
Recognizing and revising sentence-fragment phrases	13
Placing phrases carefully	15b, 15c
Punctuating introductory phrases	24b
Punctuating nonrestrictive phrases	24e

149

COMMON PREPOSITIONS

about	concerning	onto
above	despite	on top of
according to	down	out
across	during	out of
after	except	outside
against	except for	over
along	excepting	past
along with	for	regarding
among	from	round
apart from	in	since
around	in addition to	through
as	in back of	throughout
as for	in case of	till
at	in front of	to
because of	in place of	toward
before	inside	under
behind	in spite of	underneath
below	instead of	unlike
beneath	into	until
beside	like	up
between	near	upon
beyond	next	up to
but	of	with
by	off	within
by means of	on	without

EXERCISE 5

Circle the prepositions and underline the prepositional phrases.

EXAMPLE   Much (of) New York City's famous skyline was built (by) Mohawk Indians.

1. The first major construction job to employ Mohawks was a bridge across the St. Lawrence River in Canada.
2. Because Mohawks from the Caughnawaga reservation worked skillfully at great heights, builders in the area hired them for additional projects.
3. They did their most famous work during the New York City building boom of the 1920s and 1930s.
4. They traveled by subway from their homes in Brooklyn to work on the Empire State Building and Rockefeller Center.
5. Probably thousands of Mohawks have worked on projects in many North American cities over the years.

6h
Recognize conjunctions.

A **conjunction** connects words, phrases°, or clauses°. **Coordinating conjunctions** join two or more grammatically equivalent structures.

COORDINATING CONJUNCTIONS
and   nor   so
but   or   yet
for

And, but, and *or* can join structures of any kind: two or more nouns, pronouns, verbs, adjectives, adverbs, phrases, or clauses. As a coordinating conjunction, *yet* can do the same.

Oregon and **Washington** are north of California. [nouns]
We **hike** and **camp** there every summer. [verbs]
The air is **fresh** and **clean.** [adjectives]
I love the outdoors, and **my family does too.** [independent clauses]

As coordinating conjunctions, *for* and *so* can connect only independent clauses.

My vacation is in May, so **we will go camping then.** [independent clauses]
We will take warm clothing, for **the outdoors will be cold.** [independent clauses]

Correlative conjunctions function in pairs, joining equivalent grammatical structures.

CORRELATIVE CONJUNCTIONS
both . . . and
either . . . or
neither . . . nor
not only . . . but (also)
whether . . . or

Both English **and** Spanish are spoken in many homes in the United States.

Subordinating conjunctions begin certain dependent (adverb) clauses°.

SUBORDINATING CONJUNCTIONS

after	so that
although	though
as	unless
because	until
before	when
even though	where
if	whether
once	while
since	

Because the floods eroded the shore, the foundations of many buildings along the coast have been weakened.

WHERE TO FIND INFORMATION RELATED TO CONJUNCTIONS

◼‖ 6i
Recognize interjections.

An **interjection** is a word or expression that conveys surprise or another strong emotion. Alone, an interjection is usually punctuated with an exclamation point. As part of a sentence, an interjection is set off with a comma (or commas). In academic writing, use interjections sparingly, if at all.

Alas!
Hooray! I got the promotion.
Oh, they are exasperating.

◼‖ 6j
Recognize expletives.

An **expletive** is not a part of speech, but the term describes a function of the words *there* and *it*. As expletives, *there* and *it* combine with a form of the verb *be* to postpone the subject of a sentence. Used this way, *there* and *it* have no meaning of their own.

There will be a new dean of students next term.
It is the trustees' job to interview final candidates.

Expletives are usually wordy and weak. See 16a-1 for advice on how to revise expletives for conciseness.

The word *expletive* also refers to an oath or exclamation. When you see "Expletive deleted," you can be sure that the words omitted were neither *it* nor *there*.

EXERCISE 6
Identify the part of speech of each word in italics. Choose from noun, pronoun, verb, adjective, adverb, preposition, coordinating conjunction, and subordinating conjunction.

One[1] of the most devastating *natural*[2] *disasters*[3] *of*[4] recorded history *began*[5] on April 5, 1815, *when*[6] Mount Tambora, located *in*[7] present-day Indonesia, erupted. The *volcano*[8] blew off the top 4,000 feet of the mountain, creating a seven-mile-wide crater. Twelve thousand people *were killed*[9] *immediately*,[10] *and*[11] 80,000 died *later*[12] of starvation because the ash *from*[13] the volcano *destroyed*[14] farmland. The *blast*,[15] eighty times stronger than that of Mount St. Helens, was heard over 900 miles away. The cloud of *volcanic*[16] ash *circled*[17] the globe, reaching North America the following summer. The cloud *was*[18] *so*[19] thick that even the sun's rays could not penetrate *it*.[20] *Freezing*[21] temperatures and snow continued through the *entire*[22] summer, resulting in crop failures and death.

7

STRUCTURES
OF THE
SENTENCE

To understand the art of writing, writers often observe how sentences are formed. Although an infinite variety of sentences can be composed, all sentences share a basic structure. This chapter presents the basic structure and explains each of the parts.

The sentence has several definitions, each of which views it from a different perspective. On its most mechanical level, a sentence starts with a capital letter and finishes with a period, question mark, or exclamation point. A sentence can be defined according to its purpose. Most sentences are **declarative;** they make a statement: *Sky diving is dangerous.* Some sentences are **interrogative;** they ask a question: *Is sky diving dangerous?* Some sentences are **imperative;** they give a command: *Be careful.* Some sentences are **exclamatory:** *How I love sky diving!* Grammatically, a sentence contains an independent clause, a group of words that can stand alone as an independent unit: *Sky diving is dangerous.* Sometimes a sentence is described as a "complete thought," but the concept of "complete" is too subjective to be reliable.

The most practical way for you to begin a study of the sentence is to consider its structure.

■ ‖ 7a

Recognize subjects and predicates.

A sentence consists of two basic parts: a subject and a predicate.

‖ 1
Recognize subjects.

The **simple subject** is the word or group of words that acts, is described, or is acted upon.

> The **telephone** rang. [Simple subject, *telephone*, acts.]
> The **telephone** is red. [Simple subject, *telephone*, is described.]
> The **telephone** was being connected. [Simple subject, *telephone*, is acted upon.]

The **complete subject** is the simple subject and its modifiers—all the words that describe or limit it.

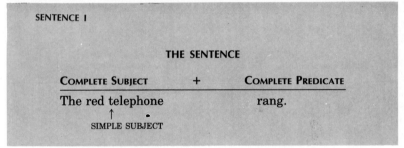

SENTENCE I

THE SENTENCE

COMPLETE SUBJECT   +   COMPLETE PREDICATE

The red telephone   rang.
        ↑ •
    SIMPLE SUBJECT

> The **lawyer** listened. [simple subject = *lawyer*]
> **The wise lawyer** listened. [complete subject = *the wise lawyer*]

A subject can be **compound,** consisting of two or more nouns or pronouns and their modifiers.

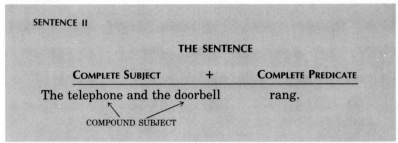

SENTENCE II

THE SENTENCE

COMPLETE SUBJECT   +   COMPLETE PREDICATE

The telephone and the doorbell   rang.
        ↖   ↗
      COMPOUND SUBJECT

The lawyer and her client met. [compound subject = the lawyer, her client]

155

2
Recognize predicates.

The **predicate** is the part of the sentence that contains the verb. The predicate tells what the subject is doing or experiencing or what is being done to the subject.

> The telephone **rang.** [*Rang* tells us what the subject, *telephone,* did.]
> The telephone **is** red. [*Is* tells what the subject experiences—being red.]
> The telephone **was** being connected. [*Was being connected* tells what was being done to the subject.]

The **simple predicate** contains only the verb. The **complete predicate** contains the verb and its modifiers as well as any objects° or complements° and their modifiers.

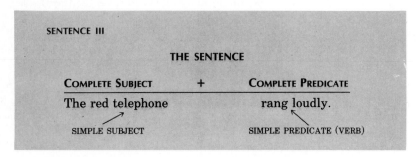

> The lawyer **listened.** [simple predicate = *listened*]
> The lawyer **listened carefully.** [complete predicate = *listened carefully*]

A predicate can be **compound,** consisting of two or more verbs and any objects or modifiers.

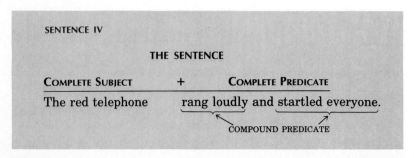

EXERCISE 1

Use a slash to separate the complete subject from the complete predicate.

EXAMPLE   Ordinary water / is essential for all life.

1. Water evaporates constantly.
2. Evaporation alternates with condensation in the water cycle.
3. Water vapor enters the air by evaporation from water surfaces, such as the oceans.
4. Oceans and other bodies of water cover more than seventy percent of our planet.
5. Molecules of water in the air condense and fall as rain or snow.

EXERCISE 2

Draw a single line under the complete subject and a double line under the complete predicate. Circle the verbs.

EXAMPLE   Rain and snow (are) visible stages in a mostly invisible process.

1. The water passes through the ground to evaporation sites.
2. Water also enters the air from the transpiration of plants.
3. In transpiration, water evaporates from leaf surfaces and passes out through leaf openings called *stomata*.
4. Evaporation and transpiration purify the water of its salts.
5. Only water molecules pass into the air.

▉‖ 7b

Recognize objects.

Objects occur in the predicate of a sentence.

‖ 1

Recognize direct objects.

A **direct object** receives the action—completes the meaning—of a transitive verb (see 8d).

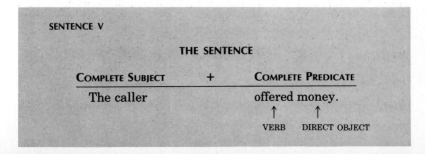

SENTENCE V		
THE SENTENCE		
COMPLETE SUBJECT	+	**COMPLETE PREDICATE**
The caller		offered money.
		↑ ↑
		VERB DIRECT OBJECT

To find a direct object, make up a *whom?* or *what?* question about the verb. The caller offered what? *Money.*

2
Recognize indirect objects.

An **indirect object** answers a *to whom?* or *for whom?* question about the verb.

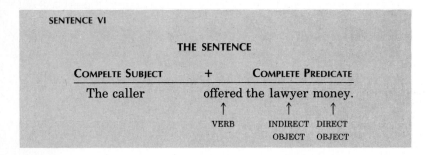

SENTENCE VI

THE SENTENCE

COMPELTE SUBJECT	+	COMPLETE PREDICATE
The caller		offered the lawyer money.

VERB   INDIRECT   DIRECT
          OBJECT   OBJECT

EXERCISE 3
Draw a single line under all direct objects and a double line under all indirect objects.

EXAMPLE   President Woodrow Wilson bought <u>the White House gardeners sheep</u> to serve as lawnmowers during World War I.

1. The government needed the gardeners to serve as soldiers.
2. The sheep attracted tourists.
3. Mrs. Wilson gave the Red Cross money from the sale of their wool.
4. More recently, the U.S. Army gave goats the task of trimming the lawns at ammunition dumps.
5. If you tell people this fact, they may not believe you.

■‖ 7c
Recognize complements, modifiers, and appositives.

1
Recognize complements.

A **complement** occurs in the predicate of a sentence. It renames or describes a subject or an object.

A **subject complement** is a noun or adjective that follows a **linking verb.** (Linking verbs—such as *was* and *seems*—operate like an equal sign, signaling that the subject is being renamed or described.)

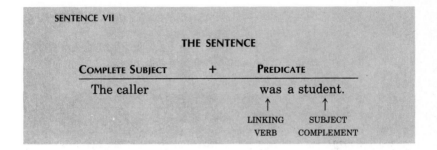

SENTENCE VII

THE SENTENCE

COMPLETE SUBJECT	+	PREDICATE
The caller		was a student.

↑ LINKING VERB   ↑ SUBJECT COMPLEMENT

The caller was **a sophomore.** [noun *sophomore* = subject complement]

The student seemed **nervous.** [adjective *nervous* = subject complement]

Some systems of grammar use the term **predicate nominative** for a noun used as a subject complement and the term **predicate adjective** for an adjective used as a subject complement.

An **object complement** is a noun or an adjective that immediately follows a direct object and either describes or renames it.

SENTENCE VIII

THE SENTENCE

COMPLETE SUBJECT	+	COMPLETE PREDICATE
The student		called himself a victim.

↑ VERB   ↑ DIRECT OBJECT   ↑ OBJECT COMPLEMENT

The student called himself **a pawn.** [noun *pawn* = object complement renaming *student*]

The student considered the situation **hopeless.** [adjective *hopeless* = object complement describing *student*]

159

EXERCISE 4

Underline all complements and identify each as a subject complement or an object complement.

EXAMPLE   The dodo is <u>extinct</u>. (subject complement)

1. The dodo was a native of Mauritius, an island in the Indian Ocean.
2. It was a member of the dove family.
3. It was three feet tall, fat, and clumsy.
4. The dodo was incapable of flight or fight.
5. By 1681, all the dodos were gone.
6. In the eighteenth century, many people thought the dodo a myth.

2
Recognize modifiers.

Modifiers are words or groups of words that describe other words. There are two basic kinds of modifiers, adjectives and adverbs.

Adjectives modify only nouns or words acting as nouns, such as pronouns, noun phrases°, or relative clauses°. Adjectives can appear in the subject or the predicate of a sentence.

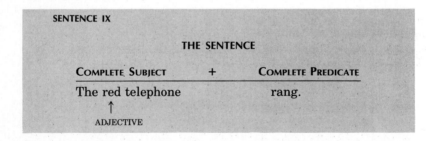

SENTENCE IX

THE SENTENCE

COMPLETE SUBJECT	+	COMPLETE PREDICATE
The red telephone		rang.

↑
ADJECTIVE

The **large red** telephone rang. [adjectives *large* and *red* modifying the noun *telephone*]

The **worried** student needed a **good** lawyer. [adjective *worried* modifying the noun *student;* adjective *good* modifying the noun *lawyer*]

Adverbs modify verbs, adjectives, other adverbs, and independent clauses°. They can appear in the subject or the predicate of a sentence.

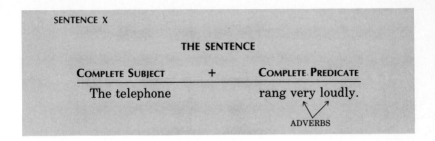

SENTENCE X

THE SENTENCE

COMPLETE SUBJECT	+	COMPLETE PREDICATE
The telephone		rang very loudly.

ADVERBS

The lawyer answered **quickly.** [adverb *quickly* modifying the verb *answered*]

The student was **extremely** upset. [adverb *extremely* modifying adjective *upset*]

The student spoke **very quickly.** [adverb *very* modifying the adverb *quickly*]

Therefore, the lawyer spoke quietly. [adverb *therefore* modifying the independent clause *the lawyer spoke quietly*]

3
Recognize appositives.

An **appositive** is a word (or words) that renames a noun or words functioning as a noun. ▋ PUNCTUATION ALERT: Use a comma to separate a nonrestrictive appositive° from what it renames. ▋

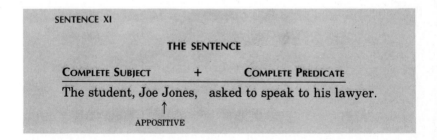

SENTENCE XI

THE SENTENCE

COMPLETE SUBJECT	+	COMPLETE PREDICATE
The student, Joe Jones,		asked to speak to his lawyer.

APPOSITIVE

The student's **story, a tale of broken promises,** was complicated. [*A tale of broken promises* renames the noun *story*.]

161

SENTENCE XII

THE SENTENCE

COMPLETE SUBJECT   +   COMPLETE PREDICATE

The student   asked to speak to his lawyer, Ms. Smythe.

↑

APPOSITIVE

The lawyer consulted an **expert, her law professor.** [*Her law professor* renames the noun *expert*.]

EXERCISE 5

Identify whether each italicized word or group of words is an adjective, adverb, or appositive.

EXAMPLE   William Bligh, *Captain of the H.M.S. Bounty* (appositive), was involved in a total of *three* (adjective) mutinies.

In 1789, *Master's Mate*[1] Fletcher Christian took command and set Bligh and *eighteen*[2] *loyal*[3] crewmen adrift in an *open*[4] boat. Bligh sailed 3,618 miles in *six*[5] weeks, *miraculously*[6] arriving *safely*[7] in the East Indies. In 1797, Bligh, *now commander of the H.M.S. Director,*[8] was involved in the mutiny of the *whole*[9] fleet at The Nore, England. While governor of New South Wales, Australia, Bligh took some unpopular measures, *punishing drunkenness and limiting liquor sales.*[10] *These*[11] actions set off the Rum Rebellion, and Bligh was *again*[12] held in custody by mutineers.

◼||| 7d
Recognize phrases.

A **phrase** is a group of related words that does not contain a subject or a predicate. A phrase cannot stand alone as an independent unit. Phrases function as parts of speech.

A **noun phrase** functions as a noun in a sentence.

The **modern population census** dates back to the **seventeenth century.**

A **verb phrase** functions as a verb in a sentence.

Two military censuses **are mentioned** in the Bible.

The Romans **had been conducting** censuses every five years to establish tax liabilities.

A **prepositional phrase,** which always starts with a preposition, functions as an adjective or an adverb.

After the collapse **of Rome,** the practice was discontinued **until modern times.**

William the Conqueror conducted a census **of landowners in newly conquered England in 1086.** [three prepositional phrases in a row]

An **absolute phrase** consists of a subject and a participle°. It functions as a modifier of the entire sentence to which it is attached.

Census-taking being the fashion, Quebec and Nova Scotia took sixteen counts between 1665 and 1754.

Eighteenth-century Sweden and Denmark had complete records of their populations, **each adult and child having been accounted for.**

EXERCISE 6

Identify whether each italicized word or group of words is a noun phrase, verb phrase, prepositional phrase, or absolute phrase.

PREPOSITIONAL PRHASE

EXAMPLE   In animals, eighty to ninety percent   *of the food*   digested
VERB PHRASE
          is used   to supply energy.

Many specific organic and inorganic substances[1] are necessary *for the growth and maintenance*[2] of the body.[3] Nutritional needs vary from species to species, but *the same general principles*[4] apply *in all cases.*[5] *Body tissue constantly being rebuilt,*[6] proteins, vitamins, and minerals *are always needed.*[7] *The average adult human*[8] requires only 45 to 60 grams, 1½ to 2 *ounces,*[9] *of protein*[10] daily. Protein *is broken down*[11] *during digestion*[12] into *its amino acids,*[13] which *are used*[14] *by the body*[15] to provide the nourishment it needs.

A **verbal phrase** is a word group that contains a verbal. Verbals are infinitives°, past participles°, and present participles°. **Gerund phrases** function as nouns. A gerund is the *-ing* form of a verb—its present participle. **Infinitive phrases** function as nouns or modifiers. An infinitive is the simple form° of a verb, usually preceded by *to,* but not always.

163

In 1624, Virginia began **to count its citizens** in a census. [infinitive phrase = direct object]

The first U.S. census was conducted without **asking anyone's occupation, birthplace, marital status, or exact age.** [gerund phrase = object of preposition *without*]

Understanding the questions on a census is important. [gerund phrase = subject]

Participial phrases function as adjectives or adverbs. Participial phrases can be formed from a verb's present participle—its *-ing* form—as well as from its past participle—the *-ed* form of a regular verb.

Going from door to door, census takers interview millions of people. [participial phrase = adjective modifying *census takers*]

When I was a census taker, I listened **engrossed by people's answers.** [participial phrase = adverb modifying *listened*]

Telling the difference between a gerund phrase and a participial phrase using a present participle can be tricky because both use the *-ing* verb form. The key is to determine how the verbal phrase is functioning: a gerund phrase functions only as a noun, and a participial phrase functions only as a modifier.

Wanting to win the trivia contest was an obsession. [gerund phrase]

Wanting to win the trivia contest, Abby studied the faces of her opponents. [participial phrase]

EXERCISE 7

Identify whether each italicized verbal phrase is an infinitive phrase, a participial phrase, or a gerund phrase.

EXAMPLE $\quad$ The body is not capable of *making vitamins*. (gerund phrase)

To function properly,[1] the human body must take in small amounts of vitamins. *Supplying important amino acids,*[2] vitamins are essential to human growth and natural functioning. *Used to power crucial reactions in humans,*[3] vitamins must be absorbed into the cells. On the other hand, green plants, *manufacturing all the vitamins they need,*[4] are not dependent upon absorbed vitamins. For humans, *eating a wide range of plant and animal foods*[5] is the best way *to ensure good health.*[6]

EXERCISE 8

Combine each set of sentences into a single sentence, converting one sentence in each set into a phrase. Choose from among noun phrases, verb phrases, prepositional phrases, absolute phrases, infinitive phrases, participial phrases, and gerund phrases. You can omit, add, or change words. Most sets can be combined in several equally correct ways, but be sure to check that your combined sentence makes sense.

EXAMPLE   The word *chauvinism* comes from the name of Nicholas Chauvin, a retired French soldier. Chauvin was obsessed with Napoleon's greatness.

The word *chauvinism* comes from the name of Nicholas Chauvin, a retired French soldier obsessed with Napoleon's greatness.

1. Chauvin was wounded in battle at least seventeen times. When he retired he received a medal, a ceremonial sword, and a pension of about $40.
2. Chauvin turned away from bitterness. He became a champion of Napoleon and France.
3. Napoleon was defeated. Chauvin became even more fanatical in his support.
4. Word of his hero worship spread beyond his village. Chauvin was used as a character in a comedy.
5. Other playwrights also used Chauvin as a character. That made his name synonymous with excessive dedication to one's country.
6. Many other words started out as someone's name. These include *sandwich* and *bloomer*.
7. Other words enter the language in other ways. Some words were originally slang. Some words have actually been voted into existence.
8. The number *googol* is a one followed by a hundred zeroes. Milton Sirotta made up the word when he was nine years old.
9. His mathematician uncle used the word in a book in 1940. It caught on.

 7e

Recognize clauses.

A **clause** is a group of words that contains a subject and a predicate. Clauses are divided into two categories: **independent clauses** (also known as **main clauses**) and **dependent clauses** (also known as **subordinate clauses**).

1
Recognize independent clauses.

An **independent** (or **main**) **clause** contains a subject and a predicate. It can stand alone as a sentence because it is an independent grammatical unit.

SENTENCE XIII

THE SENTENCE

INDEPENDENT CLAUSE
COMPLETE SUBJECT	+	COMPLETE PREDICATE
The telephone		rang.

2
Recognize dependent clauses.

A **dependent clause** contains a subject and a predicate and usually starts with a word that makes the clause unable to stand alone as a sentence. A dependent clause must be joined to an independent clause°.

Some dependent clauses start with **subordinating conjunctions.** Each subordinating conjunction implies a relationship

---

SUBORDINATING CONJUNCTIONS AND THE RELATIONSHIPS THEY IMPLY

TIME	*after, before, once, since, until, when, whenever, while*
REASON OR CAUSE	*as, because*
RESULT OR EFFECT	*in order that, so, so that, that*
CONDITION	*if, even if, provided that, unless*
CONCESSION	*although, even though, though, whether*
LOCATION	*where, wherever*
CHOICE	*rather than, than, whether*

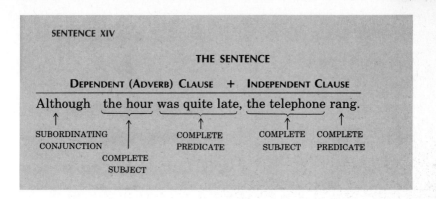

SENTENCE XIV

THE SENTENCE

DEPENDENT (ADVERB) CLAUSE   +   INDEPENDENT CLAUSE

Although   the hour was quite late, the telephone rang.

SUBORDINATING   COMPLETE   COMPLETE   COMPLETE
CONJUNCTION   PREDICATE   SUBJECT   PREDICATE
        COMPLETE
        SUBJECT

between the meaning in the dependent clause and the meaning in the independent clause.

Clauses that start with subordinating conjunctions function as adverbs. **Adverb clauses** modify verbs, adjectives, other adverbs, and entire independent clauses. Adverb clauses may appear in different parts of sentences, but they always begin with subordinating conjunctions. They usually answer some question about the independent clause: *how? why? when?* or *under what conditions?*

> **If the bond issue passes,** the city will install sewers. [The adverb clause modifies the verb *install;* it explains "under what conditions."]
>
> They are drawing up plans as quickly **as they can.** [The adverb clause modifies the adverb *quickly;* it explains "how."]
>
> The homeowners feel happier **because they know the flooding will soon be better controlled.** [The adverb clause modifies the adjective *happier;* it explains "why."]

▌▎ PUNCTUATION ALERT: When an adverb clause comes before its independent clause, separate the clauses with a comma. ▐▌

> **After gold was discovered at Sutter's Mill,** miners flocked to California.

Most **adjective clauses** start with relative pronouns or *when, where,* or *why.* Relative pronouns include *who, that, which, whom, whose, whoever, whomever, whichever, what,* and *whatever.* Another name for these clauses is **relative clauses.**

SENTENCE XV

THE SENTENCE

FIRST PART OF INDEPENDENT CLAUSE	DEPENDENT (ADJECTIVE) CLAUSE	SECOND PART OF INDEPENDENT CLAUSE

The red telephone, **which** belonged to Ms. Smythe, rang loudly.

COMPLETE SUBJECT   RELATIVE   COMPLETE PREDICATE
                  PRONOUN

The word starting an adjective clause refers to something—a specific antecedent°—in the independent clause.

> The car **that Jack bought** is practical. [The adjective clause describes the noun *car; that* refers to *car.*]
>
> The day **when I can buy my own car** is getting closer. [The adjective clause modifies the noun *day; when* refers to *day.*]

■∥ USAGE ALERT: Use *who, whom, whoever, whomever,* and *whose* when the antecedent is a person or a special, intelligent animal. Use *which* or *that* when the antecedent is a thing or an animal. Of *which* and *that,* use *that* or *which* for restrictive° adjective clauses and *which* for nonrestrictive° ones. ∥■

> The Smythes, **who collect cars,** are wealthy.
>
> The Cadillac, **which is very expensive,** is not as costly as some imported cars.
>
> The place **where I will look for my first car** is the want ads.

■∥ PUNCTUATION ALERT: When an adjective clause is nonrestrictive°, use commas to separate it from the independent clause. ∥■

Sometimes, *that* can be omitted from a sentence. For purposes of grammatical analysis, however, the omitted *that* is considered to be implied and therefore present.

> The car [that] **I buy** will have to get good mileage.
>
> The review [that] **he wrote** praised the car's performance well.

EXERCISE 9
Underline the dependent clauses. Write (ADJ) at the end of adjective clauses and (ADV) at the end of adverb clauses.

EXAMPLE The scientists <u>who discovered disease-carrying bacteria</u> (ADJ) did so <u>in the second half of the nineteenth century</u> (ADV).

1. The bacteria that led to typhoid fever and cholera were spread when water was contaminated by solid human waste.
2. Sewers were built so that water supplies could be protected.
3. Waste water pipes from the sewers were connected to storm drainage systems, which took the waste to distant rivers.
4. The people who constructed these systems believed this practice to be safe because a river can purify itself.
5. They were wrong because the rivers cannot renew themselves as quickly as we can pollute them.

EXERCISE 10

Combine each set of sentences into a single sentence by converting some sentences into adjective or adverb clauses. You can add, omit, or change a few words, but do not make major changes. Most sets can be combined in several equally correct ways, but be sure to check that your combined sentences communicate a clear message.

EXAMPLE The detailed workings of sewage treatment plants vary. The basic steps of the operation are the same in most plants.

Although the detailed workings of sewage treatment plants vary, the basic steps of the operation are the same in most plants.

1. A first treatment takes out suspended solids. Second and third treatments remove small particles.
2. Early in the first treatment waste water is screened through a row of iron bars set one inch apart. Large material, such as rags and wood, is filtered immediately.
3. This material must be removed. It could damage the more delicate machinery used later in the process.
4. The water is slowed down. Sand and other suspended particles fall to the bottom. They are removed and used for landfill.
5. The water is allowed to become almost still in the second treatment. Particles settle to the bottom. Oil gathers on top.
6. Chemicals are added at this point. The chemicals cause particles to clump. Clumped particles settle more rapidly.
7. This settled material, along with oil, is considered raw sludge. The settled material is mechanically removed.

8. The third treatment is called the "biological treatment." It uses organisms to eliminate remaining organic contaminants by eating them.

9. No method of treatment can remove all dissolved contaminants. The contaminants include fertilizer chemicals, phosphates from detergents, heavy metals, and synthetic compounds. This is important to realize.

Noun clauses function as subjects°, objects°, or complements°. Noun clauses begin with many of the same words as adjective clauses: *that, who, which,* and their derivatives, as well as *when, where, whether, why,* or *how.* Noun clauses do not *modify.* They replace a noun with a clause.

Promises are not always dependable. [noun]

What politicians promise is not always dependable. [noun clause]

The electorate often cannot figure out the **truth.** [noun]

The electorate often cannot know **what the truth is.** [noun clause]

Because they start with similar words, it is easy to confuse noun clauses and adjective clauses. A noun clause *is* a subject, object, or complement. An adjective clause *modifies* a subject, object, or complement. The word at the start of an adjective clause has a specific antecedent elsewhere in the sentence. The word that starts a noun clause does not.

Politicians understand **whom they must please.** [noun clause = direct object]

Politicians **who make promises** sometimes fail to keep them. [adjective clause modifying *politicians*]

Elliptical clauses are grammatically incomplete for the deliberate purpose of concise prose. The elliptical clause gets its name from the word *ellipsis,* meaning "omission." An elliptical clause delivers its meaning only if the missing elements can be filled in from context. The relative pronouns *that, which,* or *whom* in adjective clauses, the subject and verb in adverb clauses, and the second half of a comparison are common omissions.

Engineering is one of the majors [**that**] **she considered.** [relative pronoun omitted]

After [**he was granted**] **a retrial,** he was released. [subject and verb omitted]

Broiled fish tastes better **than boiled fish** [**tastes**]. [second half of the comparison omitted]

EXERCISE 11

Identify each italicized clause as an adjective clause, an adverb clause, a noun clause, or an elliptical clause.

EXAMPLE   No one knows *how the creative mind works.* (noun clause)

1. In 1964, a freighter was raised in Kuwait harbor *when Karl Kroyer filled the hull with 27 billion polystyrene balls.*
2. *Because lighter than water,* the balls made the ship float.
3. Kroyer, a Danish manufacturer, got his inspiration from an old comic book *in which Donald Duck raised a boat by filling it with Ping-Pong balls.*
4. Until 1959, the world's largest camera was the Mammoth, *which weighed 1400 pounds.*
5. Photographer George R. Lawrence built it for the Chicago and Alton Railway, *whose management wanted pictures of their luxury train, the Alton Limited.*
6. That train must have been very special *since a crew of fifteen was needed to operate the camera.*
7. The Paris Exposition was *where those 4½ by 8 foot pictures were first shown.*
8. In 1959, Rolls-Royce built a larger camera, *which weighed 30 tons.*
9. Which would you prefer to own, the camera by Rolls-Royce *or the car?*

EXERCISE 12

Combine each of the following pairs of sentences using some of the subordinating conjunctions and relative pronouns from this list. Some pairs may be combined in a variety of ways. Create at least one elliptical clause. Subordinators may be used more than once, but try to use as many different ones as possible.

which	because	of which	since	if
while	as	how	that	although

EXAMPLE   Famine occurs. Insects or rodents destroy crops or stored food.
When insects or rodents destroy crops or stored food, famine occurs.

1. Destruction of crops has been a problem for ages. The human race has an equally long history of trying to eliminate pests.
2. The earliest pesticides were not very effective. The earliest pesticides included sulfur, lead, mercury, and arsenic.
3. We now realize something. These original pesticides are poisonous.
4. They accumulate in the soil. They can limit or stop plant growth.

5. Some pests develop immunity to the chemicals. The pests are never completely destroyed.
6. The surviving pests reproduce quickly, passing on resistant genes. A new generation of resistant pests takes the place of those killed.
7. New pesticides are manufactured organic chemicals. The most famous is DDT, dichlorodiphenyltrichloroethane.
8. No one thought about something. DDT would contaminate and threaten the entire planet.

■‖ 7f
Recognize sentence types.

Sentences can be **simple, compound, complex,** and **compound-complex.**

‖ 1
Recognize simple sentences.

A **simple sentence** is composed of a single independent clause° with no dependent° clauses. It has one subject and one predicate (either or both may be compound). It can contain modifying words or phrases.

> Charlie Chaplin was born in London on April 16, 1889. He specialized in pantomime and became famous for his character "The Tramp."

‖ 2
Recognize compound sentences.

A **compound sentence** is composed of two or more independent clauses° joined by a coordinating conjunction *(and, but, for, or, nor, yet,* or *so)* or a semicolon. Compound sentences operate according to principles of **coordination,** a technique of writing style discussed in Chapter 17. ■‖ PUNCTUATION ALERT: Use a comma before any coordinating conjunction that connects two independent clauses. ‖■

> His father died early, **and** his mother often had to spend time in mental hospitals.
> Chaplin lived in orphanages or boarding schools, **but** sometimes he left them to perform in theaters.

3
Recognize complex sentences.

A **complex sentence** is composed of one independent clause°
and one or more dependent clauses°. Many complex sentences operate according to the principles of **subordination,** a technique of
writing style discussed in Chapter 17. ▌▌ PUNCTUATION ALERT:
Always use a comma after a dependent clause when it occurs before
an independent clause. ▌▌

> **When times were bad,** Chaplin lived in the streets. [dependent
> clause starting *when;* independent clause starting *Chaplin*]
>
> **When Chaplin was performing with a troupe which was tour-
> ing the United States,** he was hired by Max Sennett, **who
> owned the Keystone Comedies.** [dependent clause starting
> *when;* dependent clause starting *which;* independent clause start-
> ing *he;* dependent clause starting *who*]

4
Recognize compound-complex sentences.

A **compound-complex sentence** joins a compound sentence
and a complex sentence. It contains two or more independent
clauses° and one or more dependent clause°. ▌▌ PUNCTUATION
ALERT: (1) Use a comma before a coordinating conjunction that
joins two independent clauses. (2) Use a comma after an adverb
clause° that comes before an independent clause. (3) Always use
commas to set off a nonrestrictive clause° from the rest of a
sentence. ▌▌

> Chaplin's comedies were immediately successful, **and** his salaries
> were huge **because of the enormous popularity of his tramp
> character, who was famous for his tiny mustache, baggy
> trousers, big shoes, and trick derby.** [independent clause start-
> ing *Chaplin's;* independent clause starting *his salaries;* dependent
> clause starting *because;* dependent clause starting *who*]
>
> **Once studios could no longer afford him,** Chaplin co-founded
> United Artists, **and** then he was able to produce and distribute
> his own films. [dependent clause starting *Once;* independent
> clause starting *Chaplin;* independent clause starting *then he was
> able*]

EXERCISE 13
Identify each sentence as simple, compound, complex, or compound-complex.

EXAMPLE   The teachings of Voltaire, Montesquieu, and Rousseau contributed to the French Revolution. (simple)

1. Each helped to convince middle-class French intellectuals that the monarchy was corrupt and that they could create a better government.
2. Voltaire considered many social institutions insensitive; his favorite target was the Catholic Church.
3. Voltaire saw the Church as narrow-minded and unsympathetic to the people, so he sought its elimination from politics.
4. The Baron de Montesquieu was a political theorist who traveled all over Europe studying various governments.
5. Montesquieu popularized the English system of checks and balances among the branches of government, and this ideal was adopted as a model by the writers of the American constitution.
6. He also argued that people should select their form of government, an idea of appeal to the French as well as the Americans.
7. Jean Jacques Rousseau saw humanity as pure and good.
8. Rousseau, who was born in Switzerland but lived in France, believed that children are born in a natural and unspoiled state but that civilization corrupts people.
9. Because of private ownership of property, people become selfish, and they must be taught to act for the common good.
10. Rousseau's ideas have had a strong impact on modern socialist and communist thought.

EXERCISE 14
Combine each set of sentences into a sentence of the type given in parentheses.

EXAMPLE   Nine people were killed in London on October 17, 1814. A vat in a brewery burst, releasing 3,500 barrels of beer. (complex)

Nine people were killed in London on October 17, 1814, *when* a vat in a brewery burst, releasing 3,500 barrels of beer.

1. The neighborhood was flat. Run-off accumulated in the basements of local buildings. (complex)
2. Rescuers had to wade through waist-high beer. No one got drunk. (compound)

174

3. A flood of molasses killed 21 people in Boston. This happened in 1919. (simple)

4. The Food and Drug Administration (FDA) allows cola makers to keep "essential ingredients" secret. Rival companies have to rely on chemists to try to duplicate secret formulas. (complex)

5. The original secret ingredient of Coca-Cola was known to fewer than ten people. That ingredient made up less than one percent of the drink. (complex)

6. The original secret ingredient in Seven Up was lithium carbonate. Lithium carbonate is now used to treat severe manic depressive behavior. (complex)

7. Seven Up was a big success during the Depression. Some people suggest something. The suggestion is that Seven Up was popular during the Depression because lithium had a calming effect that people very much needed during those hard times. (compound-complex)

8. In the 1940s lithium was taken out of Seven Up. Lithium was restricted by the FDA. The drink remains a favorite today. (compound-complex)

8
VERBS

Verbs convey information about what is happening, what has happened, and what will happen. In English, a verb tells of an action *(eat, wrestle, argue),* an occurrence *(become, change, happen),* or a state of being *(be, seem, feel, exist).*

> The earth **rotates** on its axis approximately every twenty-four hours. [action]
>
> Mother's Day **falls** on the second Sunday in May. [occurrence]
>
> The cockroach still **exists** after hundreds of millions of years. [state of being]

Verbs do more work than this, however. By means of endings, internal form changes, combinations of main verbs° with other verbs called auxiliary verbs°, and interactions with nouns and pronouns, they also convey the following information:

> **Person:** who or what acts or experiences an action—first (the one speaking), second (the one being spoken to), or third (the person or thing spoken about)
>
> **Number:** how many subjects act or experience an action—one (singular) or more than one (plural)

Tense: when an action occurs—in the past, present, or future

Mood: what attitude the writer or speaker is expressing toward the action—indicative, imperative, or subjunctive

Voice: whether the subject acts (active) or is acted upon (passive)

Understanding verb forms, tense, mood, and voice can give you control of these most important words for delivering meaning.

VERB FORMS

A verb usually changes form by adding an ending *(change, changes, changing, changed)*. Some verbs change forms more extensively *(eat, ate; be, is)*. Changes in form help verbs deliver information about tense and, in a limited way, about person and number.

8a
Recognize the forms of main verbs.

A **main verb** names an action, an occurrence, or a state of being: *earth **rotates**, Mother's Day **fell**, the cockroach **existed**.* Main verbs are distinguished from **auxiliary verbs**. Main and auxiliary verbs together form **verb phrases.**

earth **is rotating** [*is* = auxiliary verb, *rotating* = main verb, *is rotating* = verb phrase]

the cockroach **will have been existing** [*will have been* = auxiliary verbs, *existing* = main verb, *will have been existing* = verb phrase]

Auxiliary verbs help to deliver information about tense, mood, and voice. See 8c for more about auxiliary verbs.

1
Identify a main verb's three principal parts.

Every main verb has three principal parts: a **simple form,** a **past tense,** and a **past participle.**

Other terms for the simple form are **dictionary form** (because it is the form given first in the dictionary entry for a verb) and **base form.** The simple form shows action (or occurrence or state of being) taking place now, in the present, for *I, you, we,* and *they.* That is, the simple form occurs in the first and second person° for a singular subject and in the first, second, and third person for a plural subject: *I learn, they go.* The simple form is also the basis for the future tense, with *will* or *shall* (I will *learn,* they will *go*).

For the present-tense third-person singular, most verbs add a final *-s* or *-es* to the simple form: *she learns, he goes.* ▌▐ VERB ALERT: *Be, have,* and **modal** auxiliary verbs ("helping" verbs like *can* and *would*) are exceptions. ▐ See 8a-2 for more about the *-s* form and 8c for more about *be, have,* and the modal auxiliary verbs.

The **past-tense** form is the second principal part. It indicates an action or occurrence or state of being completed in the past. The past tense of all regular verbs adds final *-ed* or *-d* to the simple form. Many verbs, however, are irregular. That is, their past-tense form, and very often their past participle as well, either change in spelling or make use of different words instead of adding *-ed* or *-d: sing, sang, sung; go, went, gone.* The principal parts of common irregular verbs are listed on pages 183–85.

Except for the past tense of *be* (8c), past-tense forms do not change with changes of person and number:

> We *learned* the way to the library. You *learned* the way too. [*learn* = regular verb]
>
> I *completed* survival training. The cadets *completed* it too. [*complete* = regular verb]
>
> She *swam* three miles. You *swam* three miles. [*swim* = irregular verb]

The **past participle** is the third principal part. In regular verbs, the past participle uses the same form as the past tense. However, these forms differ in many irregular verbs, so you must simply memorize the principal parts of irregular verbs (see pages 183–85).

To function as a verb, a past participle must combine with an auxiliary verb° (see 8c) in a **verb phrase.** Verb phrases formed with past participles make the perfect° tenses (8g) and passive° constructions (page 205).

> I have learned. [*have* = auxiliary verb, *learned* = past participle, *have learned* = verb phrase]
>
> They were startled. [*were* = auxiliary verb, *startled* = past participle, *were startled* = verb phrase]

Used alone, past participles function as adjectives, modifying nouns or pronouns: *crumbled* cookies, *fallen* trees. Alone, a past participle can never function as a verb.

178

Verbs also have a **present participle,** formed by adding -*ing* to the simple form: *eating, falling, learning.* Like the past participle, the present participle needs an auxiliary verb to function as a verb. With the various forms of *be,* present participles make **progressive forms** in all the tenses.

> I **am getting** a headache. [progressive form in the present tense; *am* = auxiliary verb, *getting* = present participle]
>
> The sun **was setting.** [progressive form in the past tense; *was* = auxiliary verb, *setting* = present participle]
>
> The senators **will be meeting.** [progressive form in the future tense; *will* and *be* = auxiliary verbs, *meeting* = present participle]

Used alone, a present participle functions as an adjective (a *diving* board, the *boiling* broth, a *thinking* person) or a noun (*swimming* is fun; *leaving* can be painful). When it functions as a noun, a present participle is called a **gerund.** Alone, a present participle can never function as a verb.

The **infinitive** is another verb form that functions as a noun or an adjective but not as a verb. Infinitives use the simple form and usually, but not always, *to.*

> **To dance** is my dream. [*to dance* = infinitive functioning as noun subject°]
>
> I expected you **to leave.** [*to leave* = infinitive as noun object°]
>
> I heard you **leave.** [*leave* = infinitive, without *to,* as noun object°]

Participles and infinitives functioning as nouns or modifiers are called **verbals.** They are also called **nonfinite verbs,** in contrast to **finite verbs. Finite verbs** are the verb forms that convey information about tense°, mood°, voice°, person°, and number° while they deliver meaning about an action, occurrence, or state of being.

2
Use the -*s* form correctly.

Except for *be* and *have,* all verbs in the present tense—that is, all verbs whose action (or occurrence or state of being) is taking place now—add an -*s* or -*es* ending to the simple form when the subject is third-person singular. (Third-person singular subjects are singular nouns; the pronouns *he, she,* and *it;* and indefinite pronouns—words like *one, everybody,* and *someone.*)

179

The **rabbit travels** faster than the tortoise.

She chooses a rapid pace.

The slow **one,** however, often **wins** the race.

Be and *have*—irregular verbs° (all forms are given on page 187)—do not use their simple forms in third-person singular of the present tense. Instead, *be* uses *is* and *have* uses *has.*

The **rabbit is** unarguably quick.

The **tortoise has** more stamina.

Some dialects of English use forms such as *he be, the rabbit have* for third-person singular in the present tense. Academic writing requires *is* and *has.* Also, if you tend to drop the *-s* or *-es* ending when you speak, you may forget to use it when you write. Be sure to proofread your writing to make sure you have used the *-s* form correctly. (Also see Subject–Verb Agreement, Chapter 11.)

EXERCISE 1

Rewrite each sentence, changing the subject to the word given in parentheses. Change the form of the verb to match this new subject. Keep all sentences in the present tense.

EXAMPLE   In many cultures, shamans heal the sick. (a shaman)
          In many cultures, *a shaman heals* the sick.

1. They also protect the community from danger. (he)
2. They cure patients by calling on supernatural powers. (he)
3. Some shamans are extremely rich. (The shaman)
4. Some shamans have great political power. (The shaman)
5. Shamanism still exists in societies of the far north, such as those in Siberia, Alaska, and Canada. (Shamans)

 8b

Recognize regular and irregular verbs.

A **regular verb** is one that forms its past tense° and past participle° by adding *-ed* or *-d* to the simple form°. Most verbs in English are regular.

SIMPLE FORM	PAST TENSE	PAST PARTICIPLE
enter	entered	entered
smile	smiled	smiled

Some English verbs are **irregular.** They form the past tense and past participle in a number of different ways.

SIMPLE FORM	PAST TENSE	PAST PARTICIPLE
bring	brought	brought
swim	swam	swum

Regular verbs will give you few problems once you understand the use of the *-ed* or *-d* ending and you learn a few spelling guidelines (such as when to change a verb's final *-y* to *-i* with *-ed*, as explained in 8b-1). Irregular verbs are easy to use once you learn the principal parts (see 8b-2).

1
Form the past tense and past participle of a regular verb by adding *-ed* or *-d*.

Adding *-ed* or *-d* to the simple form makes the past tense and past participle of any regular verb. Some verbs that end in a vowel followed by a consonant double the consonant before adding *-ed: occur, occurred; transfer, transferred.* Others do not: *label, labeled; focus, focused.* Many are spelled either way: *travel, traveled, travelled; program, programed, programmed.* You will find advice in 22d-1. You can also confidently follow the preferred spelling shown in an up-to-date college dictionary.

Regular verbs with the simple form ending in *-y* are more consistent. If the final two letters of the simple form are a vowel followed by *y,* simply add *-ed: obey, obeyed; display, displayed.* If the final two letters are a consonant followed by *y,* change the *y* to *i* before you add *-ed: spy, spied; reply, replied.* For more about spelling verbs, see Chapter 22.

Speakers often skip over the *-ed* sound in the past tense, hitting it lightly or not at all. If you are unused to hearing or pronouncing this sound, you may forget to add it when you use the past tense and past participles. Nevertheless, written English requires the *-ed* ending, so be sure to proofread your writing for *-ed* endings.

No	He **promise** to pay me by Tuesday.
Yes	He **promised** to pay me by Tuesday.
No	We were **suppose** to study adverbs for class today.
Yes	We were **supposed** to study adverbs for class today.
No	The conquerors were **prejudice** against the natives.
Yes	The conquerors were **prejudiced** against the natives.

EXERCISE 2
Rewrite each sentence, changing the italicized verb to the past tense.

EXAMPLE   The religious beliefs of many agricultural societies *include* the
           worship of family and tribal ancestors.
           The religious beliefs of many agricultural societies *included* the
           worship of family and tribal ancestors.

1. In these societies, extended family groups often *own* the land.
2. Ancestor worship *stabilizes* social and economic relationships.
3. It *provides* continuity from generation to generation.
4. It *strengthens* family structures.
5. The belief that long-dead family members *participate* in daily life *creates*
   a bond between generations.

2
Memorize the principal parts of irregular verbs.

About two hundred of the most common verbs in English are
irregular: They do not add *-ed* or *-d* to form the past tense and past
participle. Some irregular verbs change an internal vowel to make
past tense and past participle: *sing, sang, sung.* Some change an
internal vowel and add an ending other than *-ed* or *-d; grow, grew,
grown.* Some use the simple form throughout: *read, read, read.*

Unfortunately, a verb's simple form provides no clue about
whether the verb is irregular or regular. If you do not know the
principal parts of a verb you are using, you can find them in a college dictionary. Most college dictionaries use the simple form for the
dictionary entry, listing after it the past-tense form and the past
participle only if the verb is irregular. If only the simple form is
given, you will know the verb is regular and adds *-ed* or *-d.* If the
simple form and only one other form are given, you will know that
both the past-tense form and the past participle use the second form
(buy, bought).

Although you can always look up the principal parts of any
verb, memorizing them is much more convenient in the long run.
The following chart lists most of the common irregular verbs. If you
do not find the verb you need here, look it up in the dictionary and
then add its principal parts to this list.

COMMON IRREGULAR VERBS

SIMPLE FORM	PAST TENSE	PAST PARTICIPLE
arise	arose	arisen
awake	awoke *or* awaked	awaked *or* awoken
be (is, am, are)	was, were	been
bear	bore	borne *or* born
beat	beat	beaten
become	became	become
begin	began	begun
bend	bent	bent
bet	bet	bet
bid (offer)	bid	bid
bid (command)	bade	bidden
bind	bound	bound
bite	bit	bitten *or* bit
blow	blew	blown
break	broke	broken
bring	brought	brought
build	built	built
burst	burst	burst
buy	bought	bought
cast	cast	cast
catch	caught	caught
choose	chose	chosen
cling	clung	clung
come	came	come
cost	cost	cost
creep	crept	crept
cut	cut	cut
deal	dealt	dealt
dig	dug	dug
dive	dived *or* dove	dived
do	did	done
draw	drew	drawn
drink	drank	drunk
drive	drove	driven
eat	ate	eaten
fall	fell	fallen
feed	fed	fed
feel	felt	felt
fight	fought	fought
find	found	found
flee	fled	fled

Simple Form	Past Tense	Past Participle
fling	flung	flung
fly	flew	flown
forbid	forbade *or* forbad	forbidden
forget	forgot	forgotten *or* forgot
forgive	forgave	forgiven
forsake	forsook	forsaken
freeze	froze	frozen
get	got	got *or* gotten
give	gave	given
go	went	gone
grow	grew	grown
hang (suspend)*	hung	hung
have	had	had
hear	heard	heard
hide	hid	hidden
hit	hit	hit
hurt	hurt	hurt
keep	kept	kept
know	knew	known
lay	laid	laid
lead	led	led
leave	left	left
lend	lent	lent
let	let	let
lie	lay	lain
light	lighted *or* lit	lighted *or* lit
lose	lost	lost
make	made	made
mean	meant	meant
pay	paid	paid
prove	proved	proved *or* proven
quit	quit	quit
read	read	read
rid	rid	rid
ride	rode	ridden
ring	rang	rung
rise	rose	risen
run	ran	run
say	said	said
see	saw	seen

*When it means to execute by hanging, *hang* is a regular verb: "In wartime, armies routinely **hanged** deserters."

SIMPLE FORM	PAST TENSE	PAST PARTICIPLE
seek	sought	sought
send	sent	sent
set	set	set
shake	shook	shaken
shine (glow)*	shone	shone
shoot	shot	shot
show	showed	shown *or* showed
shrink	shrank	shrunk
sing	sang	sung
sink	sank	sunk
sit	sat	sat
slay	slew	slain
sleep	slept	slept
sling	slung	slung
speak	spoke	spoken
spend	spent	spent
spin	spun	spun
spring	sprang *or* sprung	sprung
stand	stood	stood
steal	stole	stolen
sting	stung	stung
stink	stank *or* stunk	stunk
stride	strode	stridden
strike	struck	struck
strive	strove	striven
swear	swore	sworn
sweep	swept	swept
swim	swam	swum
swing	swung	swung
take	took	taken
teach	taught	taught
tear	tore	torn
tell	told	told
think	thought	thought
throw	threw	thrown
understand	understood	understood
wake	woke *or* waked	waked *or* woken
wear	wore	worn
wring	wrung	wrung
write	wrote	written

*When it means to polish, *shine* is a regular verb: "We **shined** our shoes."

EXERCISE 3

In each blank, write the correct past-tense form of the verb in parentheses. Use the list of irregular verbs on pages 183–85.

EXAMPLE   The first people in the New World, the Paleo-Indians, (bring) ____ their Old World culture with them.

        The first people in the New World, the Paleo-Indians, *brought* their Old World culture with them.

1. These people (come) _____ mainly from eastern Siberia into the North American territory that is now Alaska.
2. Once across the Aleutian bridge, they (make) _____ their way south.
3. Scientists believe that the Paleo-Indians (spread) _____ rapidly, at least partly because they (be) _____ curious.
4. Each time a group entered an uninhabited area with abundant resources, the number of people (grow) _____.
5. Food, water, and building materials soon (become) _____ scarce, forcing some people to move on.
6. Those who (leave) _____ moved to new territory, where the pattern started over again.
7. In each new place, the settlers (find) _____ different conditions, so they (have) _____ to modify old ways or invent new ones.
8. For example, the mammoth hunters of the western United States (forsake) _____ certain hunting methods as they (keep) _____ traveling eastward into the territory of the smaller bison.
9. Paleo-Indian groups in the eastern United States (build) _____ cultures based on fishing, plant gathering, and small-game hunting.
10. Anthropologists wonder whether the expansion of these peoples (lead) _____ to the extinction of the mammoths, wild horses, camels, and mastodons that roamed the continent.

■|| 8c

Recognize *be, do, have,* and other auxiliary verbs.

The verbs *be, do,* and *have* function both as main verbs° and as auxiliary verbs°. *Be,* the most common verb in English, is the most irregular verb. *Do* and *have* are not as irregular as *be.*

As a main verb°, *be,* along with its forms, is a **linking verb.** These join a subject° to a **subject complement**—a word or group of words that renames or describes the subject.

THE FORMS OF *BE*

SIMPLE FORM	be
PAST TENSE	was, were
PAST PARTICIPLE	been
-s FORM	is
PRESENT PARTICIPLE	being

PERSON	PRESENT TENSE	PAST TENSE
I	am	was
you (singular)	are	were
he, she, it	is	was
we	are	were
you (plural)	are	were
they	are	were

THE FORMS OF *DO* AND *HAVE*

SIMPLE FORM	do	**SIMPLE FORM**	have
PAST TENSE	did	**PAST TENSE**	had
PAST PARTICIPLE	done	**PAST PARTICIPLE**	had
-s FORM	does	**-s FORM**	has
PRESENT PARTICIPLE	doing	**PRESENT PARTICIPLE**	having

High blood pressure **is** a leading cause of chronic illness. [*is* = linking verb, *high blood pressure* = subject, *cause* = subject complement]

A low-salt diet is important for reducing blood pressure. [*low-salt diet* = subject, *is* = linking verb, *important* = subject complement]

▮ USAGE ALERT: Academic writing requires standard forms and uses of *be*. ▮

No	He driving his car to work. [missing *be* form]
No	He **be** driving his car to work. [nonstandard *be* form]
Yes	He **is** driving his car to work. [standard form of *be* supplied]

Used alone, as main verbs, *have* is transitive and *do* can be transitive. **Transitive verbs** must be followed by a direct object° to deliver full meaning, as explained in 8d.

> Most people **have hobbies.** [*have* = main verb, *hobbies* = direct object]
>
> I **do** a crossword **puzzle** every Sunday. [*do* = main verb, *puzzle* = direct object]

Combined with the present or past participle of main verbs, forms of *be* and *have* are **auxiliary verbs** or **helping verbs,** that help the participles to show tense (see page 192) and mood (see page 202).

> I **am listening.** [auxiliary verb *am* + present participle *listening* = progressive present tense]
>
> Several reasons for low birth weight in infants **have been discovered.** [auxiliary verb *have* + auxiliary verb *been* + past participle *discovered* = present perfect tense in the passive voice]

The auxiliary verbs *will* and *shall* help to create two tenses, the **future** *(he will look, you will go)* and, with *have* and past participles of main verbs, the **future perfect** *(we shall have looked, you will have gone). Will* and *shall* never change form. *Shall* is less used than *will.* Formal writing, however, reserves *shall* for the first person *(I, we)* and *will* for all other persons *(you, she, he, it, they).*

> I **shall strive** for excellence.
>
> You **will strive** for excellence.

The verbs *can, could, may, might, should, would, must,* and *ought to* are called **modal auxiliary verbs.** Modal auxiliary verbs have only one form; they do not change, no matter what constructions they appear in.

I, you, he, she, it, we, you, they
{
can
could
may
might
should
would
must
ought to
}

Modal auxiliaries add to the main verb a sense of needing, wanting, or having to do something, a sense of possibility, likelihood, obligation, permission, or ability.

Exercise **can lengthen** lives. [possibility]

The exercise **must occur** regularly. [requirement]

Most of us **should take** better care of our bodies. [obligation]

May I exercise? [permission]

She **can** jog for five miles. [ability]

EXERCISE 4

Using auxiliary verbs from the list below, fill in the blanks. For some sentences, more than one correct answer is possible, but use each auxiliary only once.

      are   can   may   must   should   will

EXAMPLE   When firefighters search the scene of a fire, they _____ first find where the fire originated.

When firefighters search the scene of a fire, they *must* first find where the fire originated.

1. In searching for the point of origin, a keen investigator _____ look for the telltale signs of arson.

2. For example, there _____ be evidence that the fire had multiple points of origin, or *streamers,* trails of gasoline that were used to spread the fire from area to area.

3. The discovery of containers that _____ hold an accelerant is another clue.

4. Ignition devices, from a simple candle to complex electronic mechanisms, _____ convincing evidence of arson.

5. Investigators _____ also look for signs of breaking and entering or theft.

EXERCISE 5

Using each of the auxiliary verbs listed below just once, fill in the blanks. For some sentences, more than one correct answer is possible. Use up all the words by the end of the exercise.

      are   do   may   should   will
      can   have   ought   were

1. The first pet fish were probably goldfish, which _____ kept captive in China over a thousand years ago.

2. You _____ forget the stresses and strains of everyday life as you watch your fish swim about.

3. Fish are unlike any other pets because they _____ not make noise, eat much, or scratch the furniture.

4. Landlords who prohibit other pets _____ permit people to have aquariums.

189

5. Maintaining an aquarium may seem complicated, but if you follow a few simple steps, you _____ find it rather easy.

6. You _____ to buy the largest tank possible, based on your available space and money.

7. Fish thrive when they _____ been placed in a relatively roomy tank.

8. The smallest tank in which you _____ invest is a ten-gallon tank.

9. Rectangular glass tanks with stainless steel frames _____ recommended by most experts.

8d
Use intransitive and transitive verbs correctly, especially *sit* and *set, lie* and *lay, rise* and *raise*.

The difference between *I sing loudly* and *I sing a song* is that the first sentence tells how the subject° does something while the second points to what the subject does. The second sentence points out the goal—or object—of the action the verb tells about. In the first sentence, the verb is **intransitive.** In the second sentence, the verb is **transitive**—the action of the verb carries over to whatever is named in a **direct object°**. Many verbs in English can be either intransitive or transitive.

INTRANSITIVE (NO OBJECT)	TRANSITIVE (WITH AN OBJECT)
The cat **sees** in the dark. [*In the dark* is not a direct object; it is a modifier°.]	The cat **sees** the dog. [*dog* = direct object]
I can **hear** well. [*Well* is not a direct object; it is a modifier°.]	I can **hear** you. [*you* = direct object]
We **teach** tomorrow. [*Tomorrow* is not a direct object; it is a modifier°.]	We **teach** French. [*French* = direct object]

Three important pairs of verbs, which happen to look and sound very much alike, are not so flexible. In these pairs—*sit* and *set, lie* and *lay, rise* and *raise*—one verb is intransitive, the other transitive. If you do not already know the forms of these verbs, memorize them.

To *sit* means to seat oneself; to *set* means to place something else down.

INTRANSITIVE	I **sit** there. I **sat** there. [*there* = modifier, not a direct object]
TRANSITIVE	I **set** the books down. [*books* = direct object]

SUMMARY OF FORMS FOR *SIT, LIE, RISE,* AND *SET, LAY, RAISE*

INTRANSITIVE (NO OBJECT)

SIMPLE FORM	PAST TENSE	PAST PARTICIPLE	-S FORM	PRESENT PARTICIPLE
sit	sat	sat	sits	sitting
lie	lay	lain	lies	lying
rise	rose	risen	rises	rising

TRANSITIVE (WITH AN OBJECT)

SIMPLE FORM	PAST TENSE	PAST PARTICIPLE	-S FORM	PRESENT PARTICIPLE
set	set	set	sets	setting
lay	laid	laid	lays	laying
raise	raised	raised	raises	raising

Set does have one specialized intransitive meaning—the passing of a celestial body below the horizon: *The sun set.*

To *lie* means to recline or place oneself down or to remain; to *lay* means to place something down.

INTRANSITIVE	Vern **lies** down for a nap. Vern **lay** down for a nap. [*down for a nap* = modifier, not a direct object]
TRANSITIVE	Vern **lays** tiles in the kitchen. Vern **laid** tiles in the kitchen. [*tiles* = direct object]

To *rise* means to stand up, get up out of bed, or elevate oneself in some other way or to ascend; to *raise* is to lift up or elevate someone or something else.

INTRANSITIVE	Lee **rises** every morning at 6:00. Lee **rose** every morning at 6:00. [*every morning at 6:00* = modifier, not a direct object]
TRANSITIVE	Lee **raises** the cup high. Lee **raised** the cup high. [*cup* = direct object]

EXERCISE 6

Select the appropriate verb from each pair in parentheses.

EXAMPLE   One day I was (laying, lying) on my towel at the beach.
　　　　　　One day I was *lying* on my towel at the beach.

191

1. When I woke up after a nap, I (raised, rose) my head and saw the sun (sitting, setting) in the east.
2. I was about to (lay, lie) down again when it occurred to me that the sun (rises, raises) in the east and (sets, sits) in the west.
3. So I (lay, laid) my book down and (rose, raised) myself into a (sitting, setting) position.
4. As I (set, sat) there surrounded by sand and the (raising, rising) surf, I thought about this puzzling situation.
5. I had (lain, laid) down for a nap in the late afternoon as the humidity was (raising, rising), but something was now wrong.
6. Then an idea (rose, raised) out of my subconscious.
7. I now (sat, set) with the water in front of me, while before my nap it had (laid, lain) at my back. The sun had not changed positions during my nap: I had.

▪▮ VERB TENSE

Tense conveys when the action, occurrence, or state of being expressed by a verb takes place. Verbs are the only group of words that change form to express time. The time changes are indicated by the addition of final *-ed* or *-d* to the simple form° of the verb; by the use of *be, have,* and *will* and *shall* as auxiliary verbs°; and by other form changes.

English has six verb tenses, divided into simple and perfect groups. The three **simple tenses** divide time into present, past, and future. The **present tense** describes what is happening, what is true at the moment, and what is consistently true.

Rick **wants** to speak Spanish fluently.

Rick **takes** advanced Spanish now.

The **past tense** tells of an action completed or a condition ended. It uses the past-tense form (8a-1 and, for irregular verbs, 8b).

He **wanted** to improve rapidly.

He **took** a language placement test to qualify.

The **future tense** indicates action yet to be taken or a condition not yet experienced. The future tense uses the auxiliary verbs *will* or *shall* and the simple form (8c).

Next year Rick **will want** to progress even further.

Rick **will take** a course in the contemporary South American novel.

SUMMARY OF TENSES—INCLUDING PROGRESSIVE FORMS

SIMPLE TENSES

	REGULAR VERB	**IRREGULAR VERB**	**PROGRESSIVE FORM**
PRESENT	I talk	I eat	I am talking, I am eating
PAST	I talked	I ate	I was talking, I was eating
FUTURE	I will talk	I will eat	I will be talking, I will be eating

PERFECT TENSES

PRESENT PERFECT	I have talked	I have eaten	I have been talking, I have been eating
PAST PERFECT	I had talked	I had eaten	I had been talking, I had been eating
FUTURE PERFECT	I will have talked	I will have eaten	I will have been talking, I will have been eating

The **perfect tenses** also divide time into present, past, and future. They show more complex time relationships than do the simple tenses. The perfect tenses are discussed in 8f.

All six tenses also have **progressive forms.** These forms show an ongoing or continuing dimension to whatever the verb describes. Progressive forms add auxiliary verbs to the *-ing* form (the present participle). Progressive forms are discussed in 8g.

■‖ 8e

Use the simple present tense correctly.

The **simple present tense** describes what is happening or what is true at the moment. It also has special functions, summarized below.

■|| 8f

Use the three perfect tenses correctly.

The **perfect tenses** generally describe actions or occurrences that have already been completed or that will be completed before a more recent point in time. In fact, the name "perfect" comes from the Latin *perfectus,* meaning "completed."

The **present perfect tense** shows that action begun and completed in the past also continues—or its effects continue—into the present.

Eric **has learned** to drive. [action completed but condition still in effect]

Severe drought **has created** terrible hardship for the people of Africa. [condition completed and still prevailing]

I **have** always **believed** in freedom of speech. [condition true once and still true]

The **past perfect tense** indicates that an action was completed before another one took place.

The tornado **had swept** through the town before the warning **could be given.**

Bella **had** barely **mastered** Swedish when her father **was sent** to Greece.

The **future perfect tense** indicates that an action will be complete before some specified or predictable time.

The eggs **will have hatched** before winter comes.

World population **will have reached** 8 billion by the year 2000.

■ 8g

Use the progressive form of each tense correctly.

The **progressive form** uses the present participle° preceded by the various forms of *be* and other auxiliary verbs° appropriate to the tense. It shows that an action or condition is ongoing. This continuing action or state is not infinite, however. The sentence itself often states an explicit time.

The **present progressive** indicates something taking place at the time it is written or spoken about.

The damp weather **is making** her arthritis worse.

Fewer young people **are studying** Latin these days.

The **past progressive** shows the continuing nature of a past action, sometimes within stated or implied limits.

Computers **were selling** well this Christmas season.

The crack in the dam **was getting** larger.

The citizens of Pompeii **were going** about their business when Vesuvius erupted.

The **future progressive** shows that a future action will continue for some time. Often, this future action depends on another action or condition stated in the sentence.

If wholesale prices go down, retail prices **will be falling.**

Now that the first quake is over, we **shall be experiencing** an aftershock.

When he returns from vacation, he **will be looking** more relaxed.

The **present perfect progressive** describes something ongoing in the past that is likely to continue in the future.

The baby **has been crying** ever since his parents brought him home.

Real estate prices **have been rising** steadily.

The **past perfect progressive** describes an ongoing condition in the past that has been ended by something stated in the sentence.

Houses **had been selling** well until home mortgage interest rates went up.

He **had been playing** the saxophone long before he took up the flute.

The **future perfect progressive** describes an action or condition ongoing until some specific future time.

I **shall have been sleeping** for hours by the time you get home.

In May, our college's radio station **will have been operating** for twenty years.

EXERCISE 7

Select the verb in parentheses that best suits the meaning. If there is more than one possible answer, be prepared to explain the differences in meaning among them.

EXAMPLE   In the United States in 1964, only 64.4 percent of eligible voters (turned, had turned, had been turning) out to vote.

In the United States in 1964, only 64.4 percent of eligible voters *turned* out to vote.

1. By the 1970 congressional elections, this figure (fell, had fallen, was falling, had been falling) to about 50 percent.
2. The figure (remained, has remained, had remained) at about 50 percent through the mid-1980s.
3. These low turnouts (compare, have compared, are comparing, have been compared) poorly to the voting records of many other countries.

4. The USSR (leads, has led, has been leading) the world, with an impressive 99.6 percent reported voter turnout.

5. Many other countries (had, have had, were having, have been having) voter turnouts of over 95 percent, including Czechoslovakia, East Germany, and Hungary.

6. Many countries (require, have required, have been requiring) their citizens to vote.

7. Of the countries that require their citizens to vote, however, only the Netherlands (ranks, has ranked, is ranking, has been ranked) in the top twenty countries, at 92.1 percent.

8. In Argentina, despite mandatory voting, fewer people (vote, have voted, are voting, have been voting) than in the United States.

9. Some authorities say that Americans cannot vote because they are at work, and these people (are suggesting, have suggested, had suggested, suggest) that voting take place on Sundays.

10. Other authorities (have said, have been saying) that complicated residency laws are the problem.

11. In 1855, despite only 2,000 registered voters in Kansas, 6,000 ballots were cast in an election when people from neighboring Missouri (crossed, had crossed, were crossing, had been crossing) the state line to vote for candidates in sympathy with Missouri's policies.

12. Episodes like this (have led, were leading, have been leading) to the enactment of strict residency laws.

 8h

Use verbs in accurate tense sequences.

Sentences often have more than one verb, and these verbs often refer to actions taking place at different times. Showing the right time relationships—that is, using accurate tense sequences—is important. Always check tense sequences carefully in your writing to be sure that your sentences are delivering accurate meaning about the actions, occurrences, and states you intend those verbs to express.

1
Use accurate tense sequences in complex sentences.

Complex sentences use dependent clauses° as well as independent clauses°. The tense of the verb in an independent clause determines the possibilities for verb tense in that sentence's dependent clauses.

SUMMARY OF SEQUENCE OF TENSES

WHEN INDEPENDENT-CLAUSE VERB IS IN THE SIMPLE PRESENT TENSE,
FOR THE DEPENDENT-CLAUSE VERB:

■ Use the present tense to show same-time action.

The director **says** that the movie **is** a tribute to Chaplin.
I **avoid** shellfish because I **am** allergic to it.

■ Use the past tense to show earlier action.

I **am** sure that I **deposited** the check.

■ Use the present perfect tense to show a period of time extending from some point in the past to the present.

They **claim** that they **have visited** the planet Venus.

■ Use the future tense for action to come.

The book **is** open because I **will be reading** it later.

WHEN INDEPENDENT-CLAUSE VERB IS IN THE PAST TENSE,
FOR THE DEPENDENT-CLAUSE VERB:

■ Use the past tense to show earlier action.

I **ate** dinner before you **offered** to take me out for pizza.

■ Use the past perfect tense to show earlier action.

The sprinter **knew** she **had broken** the record.

■ Use the present tense to state a general truth.

Christopher Columbus discovered that the world **is** round.

WHEN INDEPENDENT-CLAUSE VERB IS IN THE PRESENT PERFECT OR
PAST PERFECT TENSE, FOR THE DEPENDENT-CLAUSE VERB:

■ Use the past tense.

The agar plate **has become** moldy since I **poured** it last week.
Sugar prices **had** already **declined** when artificial sweeteners first **appeared**.

**WHEN THE INDEPENDENT-CLAUSE VERB IS IN THE FUTURE TENSE,
FOR THE DEPENDENT-CLAUSE VERB:**

- Use the present tense to show action happening at the same time.

    You **will be** rich if you **win** the prize.

- Use the past tense to show earlier action.

    You **will** surely **win** the prize if you **remembered** to mail the entry form.

- Use the present perfect tense to show future action earlier than the action of the independent-clause verb.

    The river **will flood** again next year unless we **have built** a better dam by then.

**WHEN THE INDEPENDENT-CLAUSE VERB IS IN THE FUTURE PERFECT TENSE,
FOR THE DEPENDENT-CLAUSE VERB:**

- Use either the present tense or the present perfect tense.

    Dr. Chang **will have delivered** 5,000 babies by the time she **retires**.
    Dr. Chang **will have delivered** 5,000 babies by the time she **has retired**.

▌ USAGE ALERT: When an independent-clause verb is in the future tense, using a future-tense verb in the dependent clause is redundant. ▐

No   You **will be** rich if you **will** win the lottery.

Yes   You **will be** rich if you **win** the lottery.

No   The river **will flood** again next year unless we **will build** a better dam.

Yes   The river **will flood** again next year unless we **build** a better dam.

199

2
Use correct tense sequences with infinitives and participles.

The present infinitive—*to* and the simple form of the verb—names or describes an activity or an occurrence simultaneous with or coming after the time expressed in the main verb.

> I **hope to buy** a second-hand car. [*To buy* comes later than the hoping.]
>
> I **hoped to buy** a second-hand car. [*To buy* comes at the same time as the hoping.]
>
> I **had hoped to buy** a second-hand car. [The hoping came before the attempt to buy.]

The present participle—a verb's *-ing* form—describes simultaneous action.

> **Walking** into his office, the detective **saw** his car keys on his desk. [The walking and the seeing happen at the same time.]

To describe an action that occurs before the action in the main verb, use the perfect infinitive *(to have eaten, to have worried);* the past participle° (a regular verb's *-ed* form); or the present perfect participle *(having eaten, having worried).*

> Raoul Wallenberg **is said to have saved** a hundred thousand people from the Nazis. [The perfect infinitive, *to have saved,* comes earlier in time than the saying.]
>
> **Pleased** with the short story, Candida **sent** it off to several magazines. [Candida was pleased before she mailed the story.]
>
> **Having sold** one short story, Candida **invested** in a word processor. [Candida sold the story before she bought the machine.]

EXERCISE 8
Select the verb form in parentheses that best suits the sequence of tenses. Be prepared to explain your choices.

EXAMPLE Count Dracula, the subject of so many books and movies, (was, is) based on a real Transylvanian noble named Vlad II.

Count Dracula, the subject of so many books and movies, *is* based on a real Transylvanian noble named Vlad II.

1. Vlad's family name (had been, was) *Dracul,* which (means, was meaning) "devil," "son of devil," or "dragon" in Romanian.
2. Also known as Vlad Tepesh (or Vlad the Impaler), he (earned, had earned) this nickname because he (had, had had) a policy of impaling everyone who offended him.
3. Vlad (impaled, will have been impaling) anyone he suspected of any crime, from treason to rudeness.
4. Throughout his life, Vlad (received, had received) respect because he (defended, had defended) Christianity against the Turks.
5. Nevertheless, he (was, had been) a Turkish ally at one time.
6. Although most of his victims (were, having been) Turkish soldiers, he also impaled many of his own people simply for saying the wrong thing.
7. One man was impaled when he (commented, had commented) on the stench of the bodies rotting on stakes around the outdoor banquet he was attending.
8. It (is, was) also reported that when Turkish ambassadors (refused, were refusing) to remove their turbans in his presence, Vlad had the turbans nailed to their heads.
9. Local peasants also (tell, having told) of an exquisite gold cup that Dracula (placed, had placed) near a mountain spring.
10. As long as Dracula (lived, had been living), people were allowed to use the cup if they replaced it.
11. No one (dared, had dared) to steal the cup since impalement would have been swift and certain.
12. Although Vlad's bloodthirsty reputation (has been documented, was documented), there (is, was) no evidence that he was ever a vampire.

EXERCISE 9

The verbs in each of the following sentences are in correct sequence. For each sentence, change the main verb as directed in the parentheses. Then adjust dependent verbs, infinitives, or participles if necessary to maintain correct verb sequence. Some sentences may have several correct answers.

EXAMPLE　　The resemblance of electric sparks and lightning flashes led some people to believe they were the same. (Change *led* to *leads*.)

The resemblance of electric sparks and lightning flashes *leads* some people to believe they *are* the same.

1. For lightning to occur, there must be a great electrical pressure caused by large opposite charges on the clouds and the earth. (Change *to occur* to *to have occurred*.)

2. In most storms, the earth has a positive charge and the low-lying clouds have a negative charge. (Change *has* to *will have*.)

3. The electrical charges involved are so tremendous that lightning flashes of five miles from cloud to earth, or of ten miles from cloud to cloud, occur frequently. (Change *are* to *can be*.)

4. The thunderclap that followed the flash was caused by inrushing air when the air that had been expanded by the hot lightning bolt had cooled and contracted, creating a partial vacuum that sucked in the surrounding air. (Change *followed* to *follows*.)

5. Ben Franklin's lightning rod worked by providing an easy way for the lightning's charge to reach the ground, bypassing the building itself. (Change *worked* to *works*.)

▚‖ MOOD

Mood refers to the ability of verbs to convey a writer's attitude toward a statement.

By far the most common mood in English is the **indicative mood.** It is used for statements about real things, or highly likely ones, and for questions about fact.

> INDICATIVE   The door opened.
>
>   In walked the student.
>
>   Do you need a tutor?

The **imperative mood,** which always uses the simple form° of the verb, expresses commands and direct requests. When the subject is omitted in an imperative sentence—and it often is—the subject is assumed to be either the singular or plural *you* or the indefinite pronouns *anybody, somebody,* or *everybody.*

> IMPERATIVE   Please shut the door.
>
>   Fasten your seatbelts.
>
>   Watch out!

‖ PUNCTUATION ALERT: A strong command is followed by an exclamation point; a mild command is followed by a period. ▐

The **subjunctive mood** expresses conditions including wishes, recommendations, indirect requests, and speculations. The subjunctive mood is used less often in English than it once was. For example, the subjunctive in the following sentence is correct.

SUBJUNCTIVE   Whether it be now or later, he must eventually pay his tax bill.

But many people now use the indicative to express the same idea:

INDICATIVE   Whether he does it now or later, he must eventually pay his tax bill.

Sooner or later, he must pay his tax bill.

■‖ 8i
Use correct subjunctive forms.

The present subjunctive uses the simple form° for all persons° and numbers°.

The grand jury asks that **she testify** [not *testifies*] again.

When she does, it is important that **her lawyer be** [not *is*] with her.

Except for the verb *be,* the past subjunctive uses the same form as the simple past tense in the indicative mood: *I wish that* **I had** a car. The past subjunctive of *be* is *were* for all persons and numbers.

I wish that **I were** [not *was*] taller.

They asked if **she were** [not *was*] leaving.

1
Use the subjunctive in *if* clauses and some *unless* clauses for speculations or conditions contrary to fact.

In dependent clauses introduced by *if* and sometimes *unless,* the subjunctive describes speculations or conditions contrary to fact.

If **my party were** [not *was*] in power, we would run the city well.

If **it were** [not *was*] to rain, voter turnout would be low.

In an *unless* clause, the subjunctive signals that what the clause says is very unlikely.

Unless **war were** [not *was*] to break out, the elections will be held on Tuesday.

2
Use the subjunctive for conjectures introduced by *as if* or *as though*.

The subjunctive expresses conditions that are possible but cannot be confirmed.

This refrigerator sounds as if **it were** [not *was*] broken, but it is still running.

If the **telephone were** [not *was*] to have rung, we would have heard it.

3
Use the subjunctive in *that* clauses for wishes, indirect requests, recommendations, and demands.

Things that people wish for, ask for, or demand have not yet become reality. Use the subjunctive to express these unrealized goals.

I wish that this **week were** [not *was*] over.

It is important that the **doctor finish** [not *finishes*] the examination because someone is demanding that **she go** [not *goes*] to the clinic.

4
Use the subjunctive in certain standard expressions. Some subjunctive constructions appear in everyday language.

If I **were** you . . .   **Come** what may . . .
Please let me **be.**   If only I **were** there . . .
Be that as it may . . .   Far **be** it from me . . .

EXERCISE 10
Fill in the blanks with the appropriate subjunctive form of the verb in parentheses.

EXAMPLE   It is important that something (to be) _____ done about the rising rate of arson in America.

It is important that something *be* done about the rising rate of arson in America.

1. Criminologists insist that arsonists (to be) _____ caught and punished as a deterrent to others.

2. It is crucial that the arson investigator (to examine) _____ the fire scene for signs of arson immediately, because gasoline and kerosene can evaporate within hours.
3. Also public safety may require that cleanup (to begin) _____ almost immediately.
4. Once evidence evaporates or is moved, it is as if it never (to exist) _____.
5. The United States Supreme Court has ordered that arson investigations (to take) _____ precedence over any search warrant requirements.
6. If all arsonists (to be) _____ caught, our fire insurance rates might come down.

■|| VOICE

   Voice refers to verbs' ability to show whether a subject° acts or receives the action named by the verb. English has two voices: active and passive. In the **active voice,** the subject performs the action.

   Most clams live in salt water.
   They burrow into the sandy bottoms of shallow waters.

   In the **passive voice,** the subject is acted upon, and the person or thing doing the acting often appears as the object° of the preposition *by.*

   Clams have long been considered a delicacy by many people. [*people* = object of the preposition]
   They are also admired by crabs and starfish. [*crabs and starfish* = object]

   The passive voice uses a past participle° to name the action and a form of *be* to specify person°, number°, and tense°.

   He **is respected** by his co-workers. [present tense of *be* + past participle = present passive]
   She **was insulted** by their ignorance of her work. [past tense of *be* + past participle = past passive]
   We **were being photographed** as we walked along the beach. [past progressive of *be* + past participle = past progressive passive]

   Misusing voice usually creates problems of writing style rather than problems of incorrect grammar. To make your writing clear, use voice consistently in sentences on the same topic. (See 15a-2 for ways to identify and correct confusing shifts in voice.)

∎∥ 8j
Write in the active rather than the passive voice except to convey special types of emphasis.

Because the active voice emphasizes the doer of an action, active constructions have a more direct and dramatic effect. Active constructions also use fewer words than passive constructions. It makes sense, therefore, to use the active voice wherever you can. Most sentences in the passive voice can easily be converted to the active voice.

PASSIVE   African tribal masks are often imitated by Western sculptors.

ACTIVE   Western sculptors often imitate African tribal masks.

The passive voice does have some uses. If you learn what they are, you can use the passive to advantage.

1
Use the passive voice when the doer of the action is unknown or unimportant.

When no one knows who or what did something, you have to use the passive voice.

The lock **was broken** sometime after four o'clock. [Who broke the lock is unknown.]

When the doer of an action is unimportant, writers often use the passive voice.

In 1899, the year I was born, **a peace conference was held** at The Hague. [The doers of the action—holders of the conference—are unimportant to White's point.]
—E. B. WHITE, "Unity"

2
Use the passive voice to focus attention on the action rather than on the doer of the action.

The passive voice emphasizes the action, while the active voice focuses on the doer of the action. For example, in a passage about

206

important contributions to the history of science, you might want to emphasize a doer by using the active voice.

> ACTIVE   **Joseph Priestley discovered** oxygen in 1774.

But in a passage summarizing what is known about oxygen, you may want to emphasize what was done.

> PASSIVE   **Oxygen was discovered** in 1774 by Joseph Priestley.

The passive voice is an important feature of some writing in the sciences. (For more about writing in the sciences, see Chapter 34.)

> Most of the oxygen in the blood is carried by the red blood cells. The amount of oxygen that can be transported is directly related to the number of red blood cells and the hemoglobin level within them.
>
> —MALINDA MURRAY, *Fundamentals of Nursing*

Your choices about audience° and purpose° greatly influence the voice you should choose for a sentence.

> PASSIVE   The news that the dictator had fled was received before the order to attack the palace could be given. [Here the emphasis is on events, not on the doers of the action.]

> ACTIVE   Before he could give the order to attack, the commander received the news that the dictator had fled the palace. [Here the emphasis is on the people rather than the actions.]

EXERCISE 11

First, determine whether each of these sentences is in the active or the passive voice. Second, rewrite the sentence in the other voice. Some sentences will require two changes.

> EXAMPLE   The justices of the Supreme Court consider cases that raise questions of constitutional interpretation. [*active voice*]
>
> Cases that raise questions of constitutional interpretation are considered by the justices of the Supreme Court.

1. The Supreme Court's decisions establish a basis for public policy until changing circumstances require new interpretations.
2. The Supreme Court's decisions have always been based on the justices' reading of the Constitution or interpretations of it.

3. Before he or she can interpret the Constitution, however, each member of the Court must understand just what the writers of the Constitution meant by what they wrote.

4. Any question of what the framers of the Constitution intended—or would have intended—is made difficult to answer by several problems.

5. Vague or open-ended language was chosen by the authors in many places.

6. Theoretical principles rather than concrete applications seem to have been focused on by the Constitution's framers.

7. The private thoughts that motivated each person involved in drafting, rewriting, amending, and ratifying the document two hundred years ago cannot be guessed at by anyone.

8. The uncertainties that prevent any court from making absolute decisions also prevent it from imposing its will on other branches of government.

9. That judicial powers will remain limited is guaranteed by the margin for flexibility of interpretation.

10. Although no court will interpret the Constitution with certainty, this very uncertainty encourages a balance between democratic processes and the authority of law.

9
CASE OF NOUNS AND PRONOUNS

Case refers to word form changes to deliver information. The case of a noun or a pronoun communicates how that word relates to other words in a sentence. For example, *I, me,* and *mine* are three different cases of the singular first-person pronoun (Although *I* wanted a small wedding like my sister's, my parents asked *me* to invite all their friends to *mine*).

English has three cases: *subjective, objective,* and *possessive.* This chapter presents the cases of pronouns and nouns and explains how case operates, with special emphasis on the pronouns that writers sometimes find troublesome. See Chapter 27 for using -s and apostrophes to form the possessive case of nouns.

Personal pronouns, the most common type of pronouns, have a full range of cases that show changes in **person** (first, second, and third person) and **number** (singular and plural).

A pronoun in the **subjective case** functions as a subject°.

We were going to get married. [*We* is the subject.]

John and **I** wanted an inexpensive band to play at our wedding. [*I* is part of a compound° subject.]

A resourceful couple, **he** and **I** found a one-person band we could afford. [*He* and *I* are compound° subjects.]

CASES OF PERSONAL PRONOUNS						
	SUBJECTIVE		OBJECTIVE		POSSESSIVE	
PERSON	SING.	PLUR.	SING.	PLUR.	SING.	PLUR.
First	I	we	me	us	my/mine	our/ours
Second	you	you	you	you	your/yours	your/yours
Third	he she it	they	him her it	them	his her/hers its	their/theirs

A pronoun in the **objective case** functions as a direct object°
or an indirect object°.

> We saw **him** perform in a public park. [*Him* is the direct object.]
>
> We showed **him** our budget. [*Him* is the indirect object.]
>
> He understood and shook hands with a very happy bride, **me.** [*Me*
> is an appositive° that renames *bride,* the object of the preposition
> *with.*]

A pronoun in the **possessive case** indicates possession or
ownership. ▮‖ PUNCTUATION ALERT: Do not use an apostrophe for
a personal pronoun in the possessive case, as is explained in Chapter 27. ‖▮

> The signatures appearing quickly on the written agreement were
> **ours.** [*Ours* indicates possession.]
>
> **His** followed. [*His,* which indicates possession, also implies the
> inclusion of the noun *signature.*]

The pronouns *who* and *whoever* also change form for case
changes. Using *who* and *whoever* is discussed in 9d.

■‖ 9a

For pronouns in compound constructions, use the same cases as for single constructions.

A compound construction contains more than one subject or
object.

> **He** saw the eclipse of the sun. [single subject]
>
> **He and I** saw the eclipse of the sun. [compound subject]

That eclipse astonished **us.** [single object]

That eclipse astonished **him and me.** (compound object]

A compound construction has no effect on the choice of pronoun case. A compound subject uses the subjective case, and a compound object uses the objective case. Sometimes, however, people make the mistake of switching cases for compounds. If you sometimes are unsure which case to use, try the "drop test."

Here is a three-step drop test for compound constructions to help you stay in the appropriate case: Temporarily drop *all of the compound element except the pronoun in question,* and then you will be able to tell which pronoun case is needed. Here is how the method works for compound subjects.

EXAMPLE   **Janet and (me, I)** read that the moon has one-eightieth the mass of the earth.

STEP 1   Drop "Janet and."

STEP 2   Which reads correctly: "**Me** read that the moon has one-eightieth the mass of the earth" or "**I** read that the moon has one-eightieth the mass of the earth"?

STEP 3   Answer: Janet and **I** read that the moon has one-eightieth the mass of the earth.

This "drop test" works also when both parts of the compound subject are pronouns: ***She*** *and* ***I*** [not *Her* and *me*] *read that the moon has one-eightieth the mass of the earth.*

The same "drop test" works for compound objects:

EXAMPLE   The instructor told **Janet and (I, me)** that the moon has one-fiftieth the volume of the earth.

STEP 1   Drop "Janet and."

STEP 2   Which reads correctly: "The instructor told **I** that the moon has one-fiftieth the volume of the earth" or "The instructor told **me** that the moon has one-fiftieth the volume of the earth"?

STEP 3   Answer: The instructor told Janet and **me** that the moon has one-fiftieth the volume of the earth.

This "drop test" works also when both parts of the compound object are pronouns: *The instructor told* ***her*** *and* **me** [not *she* and *I*] *that the moon has one-fiftieth the volume of the earth.*

211

When pronouns in a prepositional phrase° occur in compound constructions, inexperienced writers sometimes allow pronouns to slip into the wrong case. A prepositional phrase always has an object°, so any pronouns that follow words such as *with, to, from, for, after,* and *between* must be in the objective case.

No	The instructor gave an assignment **to Sam and I.** [*I* is in the subjective case and cannot follow a preposition.]
Yes	The instructor gave an assignment **to Sam and me.** [*Me* is in the objective case, so it is correct.]
No	The instructor spoke **with he and I.**
No	The instructor spoke **with him and I.**
Yes	The instructor spoke **with him and me.**

Between is a preposition that frequently leads people to pronoun error; a pronoun after *between,* like other prepositions, must always be in the objective case.

No	The instructor divided the work **between Sam and I.** [*I* is in the subjective case and cannot follow a preposition.]
Yes	The instructor divided the work **between Sam and me.** [*Me* is in the objective case, so it is correct.]

If you are in doubt when you use pronouns in prepositional phrases, use the "drop test" shown on page 211.

EXERCISE 1
From each pair of pronouns in parentheses select the correct one and circle it.

EXAMPLE   My sister and ((I,) me) decided to buy our brother a lizard for his birthday.

(We, Us)[1] went to an exotic pet store where the owner showed my sister and (I, me)[2] a variety of lizards. The owner kept trying to give (we, us)[3] lizards to hold, but (she, her)[4] and (I, me)[5] refused. Then across from (we, us)[6] (we, us)[7] spotted a Gila monster. Although it did not appeal to (we, us)[8], (we, us)[9] were sure it would make an unusual pet. My sister and (I, me)[10] asked about buying it, but the owner said, "Between you and (I, me),[11] I don't advise you to get it for your brother—its bite can be fatal."

9b

Match noun and pronoun cases.

When *we* (subjective) occurs with a noun, the noun must be functioning as a subject°; when *us* (objective) occurs with a noun, the noun must be functioning as an object°. The drop test shown in Section 9a can be adapted here. Temporarily drop the noun following the pronoun and see which pronoun reads correctly.

> **(We, Us)** tennis players practice hard.

No   **Us** practice hard.

Yes   **We** practice hard.

Yes   **We** tennis players practice hard. [*Tennis players* functions as a subject, so the pronoun must be in the subjective case.]

> Our coach tells **(we, us)** tennis players to practice hard.

No   Our coach tells **we** to practice hard.

Yes   Our coach tells **us** to practice hard.

Yes   Our coach tells **us** tennis players to practice hard. [*Tennis players* functions as an object, so the pronoun must be in the objective case.]

The same principles hold when pronouns occur in an **appositive**—a word or group of words that renames the noun or noun phrase° preceding it. The drop test shown in Section 9a can be adapted here. Drop the noun and test each pronoun separately to see if it is correct.

No   The winners, **her** and **me,** advanced to the finals. [*Her* and *me* rename the subject, *the winners,* so objective pronouns are incorrect.]

Yes   The winners, **she** and **I,** advanced to the finals. [*She* and *I* rename the subject, *the winners,* so subjective pronouns are correct.]

No   The crowd cheered the winners, **she** and **I.** [*She* and *I* rename the object, *the winners,* so subjective pronouns are incorrect.]

Yes   The crowd cheered the winners, **her** and **me.** [*Her* and *me* rename the object, *the winners,* so objective pronouns are correct.]

213

9c

After linking verbs, use the subjective case.

A **linking verb** connects a subject° to a word that renames it. Linking verbs indicate a state of being (*am, is, are, was, were,* etc.), relate to the senses *(look, smell, taste, sound, feel)*, or indicate a condition *(appear, seem, become, grow, turn, remain,* and *prove).*

Because a pronoun coming after any linking verb renames the subject, the pronoun must be in the subjective case.

> The contest winner was **I**. [*I* renames *the contest winner,* the subject, so the subjective case is required.]
>
> The ones who will benefit are **they** and **I**. [*They* and *I* rename *the ones who will benefit,* the subject, so the subjective case is required.]
>
> May I please speak to Guy? This is **he**. [*He* renames *this,* the subject, so the subjective case is required.]
>
> Who is there? It is **I**. [*I* renames *it,* the subject, so the subjective case is required.]

In speech and informal writing, the objective case is sometimes substituted in the two constructions shown in the last two examples above, but avoid these usages in academic writing.

EXERCISE 2
Circle the correct pronoun in each pair in parentheses.

EXAMPLES   Bob Soak, Jr.: Sally and ((I,) me) lent a friend five hundred dollars, but we have no proof.

             Bob Soak, Sr.: Between you and (I, (me).), son, you are in an awkward situation.

Jr.: The two of us, Sally and (I, me),[1] know. To make matters worse, another friend told Sally and (I, me)[2] today that our friend has moved to another city.

Sr.: Don't you know better, you and (she, her)[3], not to give someone cash and forget to ask for a receipt?

Jr.: It was (we, us)[4] who did exactly that.

Sr.: (Us, We)[5] Soaks are usually more careful, but I think that together you and (I, me)[6] can work out a solution.

Jr.: Sally and (I, me)[7] would truly appreciate your help, and I will not forget that one of the people who created this problem is (I, me).[8]

Sr.: Here is what to do. You and Sally write your friend a letter saying that you and (she, her)[9] have an emergency and need the one thousand dollars back right away.

Jr.: Between you and (I, me),[10] Dad, he will think I am crazy because Sally and (I, me)[11] lent him only five hundred dollars.

Sr.: Give (we, us)[12] experienced folks a little credit. When your friend reads that you expect one thousand dollars from (he, him),[13] he will write quickly to say that (he, him)[14] is the person who owes you five hundred dollars. Then you will have your proof in writing.

9d

Use *who* and *whoever* when the subjective case is needed; use *whom* and *whomever* when the objective case is needed.

The pronouns *who* and *whoever* are in the subjective case, and *whom* and *whomever* are in the objective case. Within each case, the pronouns do not change form for singular or plural or for first, second, or third person.

CASES OF RELATIVE AND INTERROGATIVE PRONOUNS

SUBJECTIVE	OBJECTIVE	POSSESSIVE
who whoever	whom whomever	whose -----

1
Know how to use *who, whoever, whom,* and *whomever* in dependent clauses.

A **dependent clause** (also called a **subordinate clause**) contains a subject° and predicate° and starts with a word that makes the clause unable to stand alone as a sentence. Pronouns such as *who, whoever, whom,* or *whomever* start many dependent clauses.

To determine what pronoun case° is correct in a dependent clause, it is not necessary to determine whether the entire clause is functioning as a subject or an object in the sentence. All that matters is how the pronoun functions in its own clause. Making this determination can sometimes be prickly for inexperienced writers, especially because informal, spoken English tends to blur distinctions between *who* and *whom*.

215

A variation of the drop test shown in Section 9a can be adapted here to a four-step method. Temporarily drop everything in the sentence up to the pronoun in question, and then make substitutions—remembering that *he, she, they, who,* and *whoever* are subjects, and *him, her, them, whom,* and *whomever* (the *-m* forms and *her*) are objects. Here is how the method works for the subjective case:

EXAMPLE	**I wondered (who, whom) would vote.**
STEP 1	Omit "I wondered."
STEP 2	Test the sentence with *he* and *him* (or *she* and *her*): "**He** would vote" or "**Him** would vote."
STEP 3	Answer: "**He** would vote."
STEP 4	Therefore, because *he* is subjective, *who,* which is also the subjective, is correct: "I wondered **who** would vote."

This four-step drop test works also for *whoever.*

Voter registration drives attempt to enroll **whoever** is eligible to vote. ["*He* (not *him*) is eligible to vote" proves that the subjective case of *whoever* is needed.]

The subjective case is called for even when expressions such as *I think* or *he says* come between the subject and verb. Ignore these expressions when you are trying to determine the correct pronoun.

She is the candidate who [I think] will get my vote.

The same four-step drop test works for the objective case:

EXAMPLE	**Volunteers go to senior citizen centers hoping to enroll people (who, whom) others have ignored.**
STEP 1	Omit "Volunteers . . . people."
STEP 2	Test the sentence with *they* and *them:* "Others have ignored **they**" or "Others have ignored **them**."
STEP 3	Answer: "Others have ignored **them**."
STEP 4	Therefore, because *them* is objective, *whom,* which is also objective, is correct: "Volunteers go to senior citizen centers hoping to enroll people **whom** others have ignored."

This four-step drop test works also for *whomever:*

Such transportation means that the senior citizens can vote for **whomever** they wish. ["The senior citizens can vote for *him*" proves that the objective case of *whomever* is needed.]

2
Know how to use *who* and *whom* in questions.

At the beginning of questions, use *who* if the question is about the subject° and *whom* if the question is about the object°. To determine if the case is subjective or objective, recast the question as a statement.

Who watched the space shuttle lift-off? ["*I* watched the space shuttle lift-off" uses the subjective pronoun *I,* so *who* is correct.]

Ann admires **whom?** ["Ann admires *her*" uses the objective pronoun *her,* so *whom* is correct]

Whom does Ann admire? [Same as above.]

To **whom** does Ann speak about becoming an astronaut? ["Ann speaks to *them* about becoming an astronaut" uses the objective pronoun *them,* so *whom* is correct.]

EXERCISE 3
Circle the correct pronoun in each pair in parentheses.

EXAMPLE   Experts say that our personal philosophies depend largely upon ((who) , whom) or what has been important in our lives.

1. For example, many people vote for (whoever, whomever) their parents prefer.
2. Parents transmit to us their ideas about politics and (who, whom) to respect in government.
3. In general, adults treat the world as they were treated by (whoever, whomever) raised them.
4. Research shows that children (who, whom) have been overprotected often become adults for (who, whom) life is difficult beyond the protective family circle.
5. Adults (who, whom) were consulted as children about some family decisions, such as (who, whom) to invite to dinner or what to name the dog, usually are more active politically than people (who, whom) had no voice in family matters.
6. In totalitarian countries, schools indoctrinate youngsters (who, whom) have learned never to question authority, so adults believe that trouble waits for (whoever, whomever) challenges the system.

■‖ 9e

After *than* or *as,* use the pronoun case that reflects your intended meaning.

A sentence of comparison often can be clear even though some of the words following *than* or *as* are implied but not directly stated. For example, the word *are* does not have to be expressed at the end of this sentence: *My two-month-old Saint Bernard is larger* **than** *most full-grown dogs.*

When a pronoun follows *than* or *as,* the pronoun case carries essential information about what is being said. For example, these two sentences convey two very different messages, simply because of the choice between the words *me* and *I* after *than.*

1. My sister loved that dog more **than me.**
2. My sister loved that dog more **than I.**

Sentence 1 means "My sister loved that dog more *than she loved me.*" On the other hand, sentence 2 means "My sister loved that dog more *than I loved it.*" To make sure that any sentence of comparison delivers its message clearly, either include all words in the second half of a comparison or mentally fill in the words to check that you have chosen the correct pronoun case.

■‖ 9f

When a pronoun is the subject or the object of an infinitive, use the objective case.

An **infinitive** is the simple form° of a verb usually, but not always, following *to: to laugh, to dance.* Objective pronouns occur as both subjects and objects of infinitives.

Our tennis coach expected John and **me** *to beat* Jimmy and **her.** [*Me* is the subject of the infinitive *to beat,* and *her* is the object of the infinitive; both are in the objective case.]

■‖ 9g

Before gerunds, use the possessive case.

A **gerund** is a verb's *-ing* form functioning as a noun. (**Brisk walking** *is excellent exercise.*) When a noun or pronoun precedes a gerund, the possessive case is called for. (**Kim's brisk walking** *built up her stamina.* **Her brisk walking** *built up her stamina.*) In contrast, a present participle—a form that also ends in *-ing*—functions as a modifier. It does not take the possessive case. *(Kim,* **walking briskly,** *caught up to me.)*

The possessive case, therefore, communicates important information. Consider these two sentences which convey two different messages, entirely as a result of the possessive:

1. The detective noticed the **man staggering.**
2. The detective noticed the **man's staggering.**

Sentence 1 means that the detective noticed the man; sentence 2 means that the detective noticed the staggering.

The same distinction applies to pronouns:

1. The detective noticed **him** staggering.
2. The detective noticed **his** staggering.

In conversation, the distinction is often ignored, but readers of academic writing expect that information will be precise. Consider the difference in the following two examples:

GERUND (AS A SUBJECT)	The **governor's calling for a tax increase** surprised her supporters.
PARTICIPLE (MODIFIER)	The governor, **calling for a tax increase,** surprised her supporters.

EXERCISE 4
Circle the correct pronoun in each pair in parentheses.

EXAMPLE   Sam Houston, leader of the drive for Texas's independence, is less well-known for ((his) him) championing of the rights of the Cherokees.

1. Houston's concern grew out of (him, his) living with the Cherokees for three years in his late teens.
2. From 1817 to 1818 he served as a government subagent helping to settle some Cherokees on a reservation, but a reprimand from Secretary of War John C. Calhoun persuaded (he, him) to resign.
3. Calhoun was angry about (Houston, Houston's) wearing Indian clothing to meet (he, him).
4. Not only as tall and energetic as Andrew Jackson, Houston was also as popular as (he, him).
5. Houston served as congressman and later governor of Tennessee until his wife of three months left (he, him).
6. (She, Her) leaving prompted (he, him) to resign the governorship.

219

7. He lived again with the Cherokees, who decided to adopt (he, him) as a member of their nation.

8. Later, he went to Washington on behalf of the Cherokees to help (them, they) protest the fraud of some government agents.

◼‖ 9h

Reserve *-self* forms of pronouns for reflexive or intensive use.

Reflexive pronouns reflect back on the subject° or object°.

The detective disguised **himself.**
He had to rely on **himself** to solve the mystery.

Reflexive pronouns should not be used as substitutes for subjects or objects.

The detective and **I** (not *myself*) had a long talk.
He wanted my partner and **me** (not *myself*) to help him.

Intensive pronouns provide emphasis by making another word more intense in meaning.

The detective felt that his career **itself** was at stake.

Avoid these nonstandard forms of reflexive and intensive pronouns in academic writing: *hisself,* nonstandard for *himself; theirself, theirselves, themself,* and *themselfs,* nonstandard for *themselves.*

10
PRONOUN
REFERENCE

The term **pronoun reference** refers to the fact that the meaning of a pronoun comes from its **antecedent,** the noun or pronoun to which the pronoun refers. For your writing to communicate its message clearly, each pronoun must relate directly to an antecedent. This chapter describes clear pronoun reference and alerts you to ways in which unclear pronoun reference can occur.

Consider these sentences in which each pronoun has a clear referent.

> **Facts** do not cease to exist just because **they** are ignored.
> —ALDOUS HUXLEY

> **Martyrdom** does not end something; **it** is only the beginning.
> —INDIRA GANDHI

When pronoun reference is unclear, meaning gets muddled. For example, consider this passage, which contains unclear pronoun reference.

> In 1911, **Roald Amundsen** reached the South Pole just thirty-five days before **Robert F. Scott** arrived. **He** [who? Amundsen or Scott?] had told people that **he** was going to sail for the Arctic, but **he** turned south for the Antarctic. Then on the journey home, **he** [who? Amundsen or Scott?] and **his** party froze to death just a few miles from safety.

■|| 10a

Make a pronoun refer clearly to a single antecedent.

To be understood, a pronoun must refer clearly to a single nearby antecedent. Often the same pronoun is used to serve as a referent to more than one antecedent. For example, in the paragraph above, *he* in different places refers to two different men, thus creating confusion for the reader. You can clarify such a passage by replacing some pronouns with nouns so that all the remaining pronouns clearly refer to a single antecedent.

In 1911, **Roald Amundsen** discovered the South Pole just thirty-five days before **Robert F. Scott** arrived. **Amundsen** had told people that **he** was going to sail for the Arctic but then **he** turned south for the Antarctic. On the journey home, **Scott** and **his** party froze to death just a few miles from safety.

More than one pronoun can appear in a sentence, but each must have a clear antecedent.

Robert F. Scott used **horses** for **his** assault on the Pole, but **they** perished quickly because **they** were unsuited for travel over ice and snow.

Said and *told,* when used with pronouns that refer to more than one person, are particularly prone to creating confusion for readers. Quotation marks and slight rewording can clarify meaning.

No   Her mother told her she was going to visit Alaska.

Yes   Her mother told her, "You are going to visit Alaska."

Yes   Her mother told her, "I am going to visit Alaska."

■|| 10b

For clarity, place pronouns close to their antecedents.

If too much material comes between a pronoun and its antecedent, even though they may be logically related, unclear pronoun reference results. Readers lose track of the meaning of a passage if they have to trace back too far to find the antecedent of a pronoun.

No   **Alfred Wegener,** a highly trained German meteorologist and professor of geophysics and meteorology at the University of Graz in Austria, was the first person to suggest that all the continents on earth were originally part of one large land mass. According to this theory, the supercontinent broke up long ago and the fragments drifted apart. **He** named this supercontinent Pangaea. [Although *he* can refer only to *Wegener,* too much material intervenes between the pronoun and its antecedent.]

Yes   **Alfred Wegener,** a highly trained German meteorologist and professor of geophysics and meteorology at the University of Graz in Austria, was the first person to suggest that all the continents on earth were originally part of one large land mass. According to **his** theory, the supercontinent broke up long ago and the fragments drifted apart. **Wegener** named this supercontinent Pangaea.

EXERCISE 1
Rewrite each passage so that each pronoun has a single, nearby antecedent. Either replace pronouns with nouns or restructure a sentence to clarify pronoun reference. If you consider a passage correct as written, circle its number.

EXAMPLE   Dag Hammarskjold was born in Jonkopin, Sweden, on July 29, 1905. He became a diplomat, economist, and United Nations official. People considered him a tactful and energetic leader. After his death, he was awarded the Nobel Peace Prize.

(To correct, replace the last *he* with *Hammarskjold.*)

1. He was given the Nobel Peace Prize in 1961. His father, Hjalmar Hammarskjold, a former Swedish prime minister, had been head of the Nobel Prize Foundation from 1929 to 1947. He died eight years before his son was awarded the prize, so no family influence could have been involved.

2. In 1952 Dag Hammarskjold was appointed head of Sweden's delegation to the United Nations General Assembly. In April 1953 he was elected Secretary-General of the United Nations, succeeding the popular Trygve Lie, a Norwegian diplomat. He had served as Secretary-General since 1946.

3. Around the time of his unanimous reelection for a second five-year term in 1957, Hammarskjold became deeply involved in the Middle East, especially the Suez Canal crisis. He made several trips to confer with Arab and Israeli leaders.

223

4. Hammarskjold met with Soviet Premier Nikita Khrushchev on March 27, 1959, to discuss world peace. He found the meeting productive for furthering his goals as leader of the United Nations.

5. In 1960, war broke out in what was then called the Belgian Congo. Hammarskjold sent United Nations troops in an effort to restore peace and unity. Khrushchev denounced this move and demanded Hammarskjold's resignation. He maintained that he was justified, and he refused to resign.

6. Tragically, he was killed soon after when his plane crashed while he was on a peace mission for the United Nations to the new Republic of the Congo.

10c
Make a pronoun refer to a definite antecedent.

The antecedent of a pronoun must be clear or your writing will not succeed in delivering its intended message.

1
Do not let a pronoun refer to a noun's possessive form.

A pronoun cannot have as an antecedent a noun's possessive form.

No   Geologists think that about one hundred of the **earth's** biggest craters are the result of large asteroids colliding with **it.** [*It* cannot refer to the possessive *earth's.*]

Yes   Geologists think that about one hundred of the **earth's** biggest craters are the result of large asteroids colliding with **our planet.**

2
Do not let a pronoun refer to an adjective.

An adjective° serves as a modifier and cannot therefore serve double duty as a noun to which a pronoun can refer.

No   Avery likes to study **geological** records. **That** will be her major. [*That* cannot refer to the adjective *geological.*]

Yes   Avery likes to study **geological** records. **Geology** will be her major.

3
Make *it, that, this,* and *which* refer to only one antecedent.

Pronouns such as *it, that, this,* and *which* are particularly prone to creating unclear pronoun reference. As you write and revise, check carefully to see that the referent of these pronouns can be determined easily by your readers.

No   Comets usually fly by the earth at 100,000 m.p.h., whereas asteroids sometimes collide with the earth. **This** interests scientists. [What does *this* refer to? . . . the speed of the comets? . . . comets flying by the earth? . . . asteroids colliding with the earth?]

Yes   Comets usually fly by the earth at 100,000 m.p.h., whereas asteroids sometimes collide with the earth. **This difference** interests scientists.

No   A fireball, caused by the impact of either a comet or an asteroid, rose twelve miles above central Siberia in 1908, but **it** is still unknown. [What does *it* refer to?]

Yes   A fireball, caused by the impact of either a comet or an asteroid, rose twelve miles above central Siberia in 1908, but **the source of the explosion** is still unknown.

No   According to some scientists, a rain of comets lasting hundreds of centuries hits the earth every 26 million years. Maybe **that** is how the dinosaurs perished in a mass extinction 65 million years ago. [What does *that* refer to?]

Yes   According to some scientists, a rain of comets lasting hundreds of centuries hits the earth every 26 million years. Maybe **such a bombardment of comets killed the dinosaurs** in a mass extinction 65 million years ago.

No   I told my friends that I was going to major in geology, **which** annoyed my parents. [What does *which* refer to?]

Yes   My parents were annoyed because I discussed my major with my friends.

Yes   My parents were annoyed because I chose to major in geology.

4
Use *it* and *they* precisely.

In speech, common statements are *It said on the radio* or *In Washington they say,* but such expressions are inexact and wordy. They should be avoided in academic writing.

The newspaper reports [not *It said in the newspaper*] that minor earthquakes occur almost daily in California.

Californians say [not *In California they say*] that no one feels a minor earthquake.

5
Do not use a pronoun in the first sentence of a work to refer to the work's title.

A piece of writing has to stand on its own, so when referring to a title, be sure to repeat or reword whatever part of the title you want to use.

TITLE   Geophysics as a Major

No   It unites the sciences of physics, biology, and ancient life.

YES   Geophysics unites the sciences of physics, biology, and ancient life.

10d
Avoid overusing *it.*

It has three different uses in English.

1. *It* is a personal pronoun: *Doug wants to visit the 18-inch Schmidt telescope, but* **it** *is on Mount Palomar.*
2. *It* is an expletive, a word that postpones the subject: **It** *is interesting to observe the stars.*
3. *It* is part of idiomatic expressions of weather, time, or distance: **It** *is sunny.* **It** *is midnight.* **It** *is not far to the hotel.*

All of these uses are acceptable, but combining them in the same sentence can create confusion.

No   Because our car was overheating, **it** came as no surprise that **it** broke down just as **it** began to rain. [*It* is overused here even though all three uses—2, 1, and 3 above, respectively—are acceptable.]

Yes   **It** came as no surprise that our overheating car broke down just as the rain began to fall.

◼‖ 10e
Use *you* only for direct address.

In academic writing, *you* is not a suitable substitute for specific words that refer to people, situations, and occurrences. Exact language is always preferable. Also, *you* used for other than direct address tends to lead to wordiness.

No   Uprisings in prison often occur when **you allow** overcrowded conditions to continue. [Are you, the reader, allowing the conditions to continue?]

Yes   Uprisings in prison often occur when **the authorities allow** overcrowded conditions to occur.

No   In many states, **you have prisons** with few rehabilitation programs. [Do you, the reader, have few programs?]

Yes   In many states, **prisons have** few rehabilitation programs.

No   In the Soviet Union **you** usually have to stand in long lines to buy groceries. [Are you, the reader of this handbook, planning to do your grocery shopping in the Soviet Union?]

Yes   **Soviet consumers** usually have to stand in long lines to buy groceries.

227

EXERCISE 2

Rewrite each sentence so that all pronoun references are clear. If you consider a passage correct as written, circle its number.

EXAMPLE It says the term "memory storage" refers to a not-yet-understood process that helps memory work. (Replace *It* with *My psychology text.*)

1. No one is certain how the brain stores information, but they claim the particular way you organize material affects the way you store and recall it.
2. It is clear that it is a complicated process to store material.
3. Sir Frederick Bartlett, an early student of memory, suggested that your prior knowledge makes it possible for new material to be learned.
4. Bartlett claimed that each person's memory has its own unique features.
5. Endel Tulving, another expert, found that no matter how a given list of words was arranged, people participating in experiments always learned the words by regrouping them into the same categories.
6. It proves that this means you can use patterns in sets of information to help you remember them.
7. It is very interesting.
8. In this way, students' beliefs that they can cram large amounts of material just before a test have been proven wrong.
9. Cramming does not work because no time is available for your brain to find patterns into which to fit new information.

◼‖ 10f

Use *who*, *which*, and *that* correctly.

Who refers to people or animals with names or special talents.

Theodore Roosevelt, who served from 1901 to 1909 as the twenty-sixth President of the United States, inspired the creation of the stuffed animal, the "teddy bear."

Lassie, the famous movie and TV collie, **who** was known for her intelligence and courage, was actually played by a series of male collies.

Which and *that* refer to animals, things, and sometimes anonymous or collective groups of people. The choice between *which* and *that* depends on whether the clause introduced by the pronoun is restrictive° or nonrestrictive°. (A restrictive clause is essential to limit meaning; a nonrestrictive clause is nonessential. See 24e for a full discussion.) Use *that* or *which* with restrictive clauses and *which* with nonrestrictive clauses. Use *who,* for people, in both kinds of clauses. ▮ COMMA CAUTION: Set off nonrestrictive clauses with commas. ▮

> In modern zoos, **animals that** are dangerous are exhibited so that the public can observe them from monorails or other types of moving cages for humans.
>
> Modern **zoos that** are being built or renovated today provide natural habitats for their animals.
>
> **Giant pandas, which** are native to China, are in danger of extinction.
>
> **Bamboo, which** is their primary food source, recently has become scarce in many areas of China.
>
> **Children, who** virtually all enjoy zoos, especially enjoy "petting zoos," where they can touch animals safely.
>
> **Children who** like animals usually grow up to be affectionate adults.

EXERCISE 3

Fill in the blanks with *who, which,* or *that.*

EXAMPLE   Sometimes words __that__ [*or* which] look alike may have several different meanings.

1. One such word is *hydra,* _____ refers to a monster, an island, and a group of animals.
2. In Greek legend, Hydra was a gigantic monster _____ had nine heads, each of _____ grew back two new heads as soon as one was cut off.
3. Hercules was given twelve supposedly impossible tasks, one of _____ was to destroy the monster.
4. Hercules, _____ found killing the creature difficult, was finally successful when he burned out the roots as he cut off each head.
5. Hydra was also the old name of the Greek island now called Idhra, _____ is located in the Aegean Sea.
6. This is an island _____ was largely settled in the seventeenth century by Albanians _____ were fleeing the Turks.
7. In zoology, hydras, _____ are small, tentacled polyps, are found in fresh water throughout the world.
8. They capture food by means of stingers located in tentacles _____ carry the food to a centrally located mouth.

11
AGREEMENT

The concept of *agreement* in human affairs rests on matching knowledge and opinions. Grammatical agreement is also based on matching. Before language can work properly, certain parts of speech that change number°, person°, and, less often, gender° must match each other in form when they work together. Although the rules governing agreement are not difficult, their applications can seem tricky. Indeed, almost everyone has to consult a handbook once in a while to check one or another of the rules for agreement. This chapter discusses agreement in (1) subjects and verbs and (2) pronouns and antecedents—the only two combinations in which questions of matching forms arise.

▣‖ SUBJECT–VERB AGREEMENT

Subject–verb agreement occurs at least once per sentence. To be grammatically correct, subjects and verbs must match in number (singular or plural) and in person (first, second, or third).

The **firefly glows** with luminescent light. [*firefly* = singular subject in the third person; *glows* = singular verb in the third person]

Fireflies glow with luminescent light. [*fireflies* = plural subject in the third person; *glow* = plural verb in the third person]

This **insect is** nocturnal.

These **insects are** nocturnal.

A QUICK REVIEW OF "PERSON" FOR AGREEMENT

The **first person** is the speaker or writer. *I* (singular) and *we* (plural) are the only subjects that occur in the first person.

SINGULAR   **I** see a field of fireflies.

PLURAL   **We** see a field of fireflies.

The **second person** is the person spoken or written to. *You* (both singular and plural) is the only subject that occurs in the second person.

SINGULAR   **You** see a shower of sparks.

PLURAL   **You** see a shower of sparks.

The **third person** is the person or thing being spoken or written of. Most rules for subject–verb agreement involve the third person. A subject in the third person can vary widely—for example, *student* and *students* (singular and plural people), *table* and *tables* (singular and plural things), and *it* and *they* (singular and plural pronouns).

SINGULAR   The **scientist sees** a cloud of cosmic dust.

            She (he, it) sees a cloud of cosmic dust.

PLURAL   The **scientists see** a cloud of cosmic dust.

            They see a cloud of cosmic dust.

■‖ 11a
Use the final *-s* or *-es* for plural subjects or for singular verbs.

Subject–verb agreement often involves one letter: *s*. The key is the distinction between the *-s* added to subjects and the *-s* added to verbs.

We form most **plural subjects** by adding an *-s* or *-es* *(lip, lips; princess, princesses)*. Exceptions include most pronouns *(they, who);* a few nouns that do not change form *(deer, deer);* and a few nouns that change in other ways *(mouse, mice; child, children)*. We form **singular verbs** in the present tense of the third person by adding *-s* or *-es* to the simple form°— *(laugh* becomes *laughs, kiss* becomes *kisses)*—with the exceptions of *be (is)* and *have (has)*. (*Is* and *has* have an *-s* ending, but they are not formed from the simple form.)

Here is a memory device to help you to visualize how, in most cases, the *s* works in agreement. The *-s* (or *-es* when the word ends in *s*) can take only one path at a time, either the top or bottom.

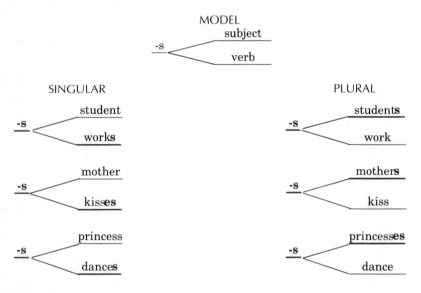

MODEL

subject

-s

verb

SINGULAR	PLURAL
student	students
-s	-s
works	work
mother	mothers
-s	-s
kisses	kiss
princess	princesses
-s	-s
dances	dance

Even though some plural subjects do not have a final *s*, the principle of the memory device holds. The final *s* does not appear in some plural nouns (such as *people, children*), in plural personal pronouns *(we, you, they)*, in the plural demonstrative pronouns *(these* and *those)*, or in certain indefinite pronouns when they are used as plurals *(few, some, more, many, most,* and *all)*.

The **child enjoys** watching cartoons.

Children enjoy watching cartoons.

We watch cartoons every Saturday morning.

They reflect rudimentary human impulses.

Most involve a startling amount of violence.

▐▌ USAGE ALERT: Do not add -*s* to the third person singular main verb after a modal auxiliary verb—a helping verb like *can, might, must, would*—see 8c. ▐▌

No   The coach **must thinks** every student likes swimming.

Yes   The coach **must think** every student likes swimming.

EXERCISE 1

Using the subject and verb in each set shown, write two complete sentences—one with the subject as a singular and one with the subject as a plural. Keep all verbs in the present tense.

1. boat
   race
	2. flag
	   fly
		3. man
		   applaud
			4. woman
			   cheer

5. chorus
   sing
	6. baby
	   burp
		7. judge
		   might decide
			8. winner
			   kiss

▊▌ 11b

For the purposes of agreement, ignore words that come between a subject and verb.

Words that separate the subject from the verb can cause confusion about what a verb should agree with. This intervening material often appears as a prepositional phrase°. To locate the subject of a sentence, eliminate any prepositional phrases from consideration.

No   The **winners** in the state competition **goes** to the national finals. [*Winners* is the subject with which the verb must agree; *in the state competition* is a prepositional phrase.]

Yes   The **winners** in the state competition **go** to the national finals.

No   The **sponsor** of the concerts **pay** all expenses. [*Sponsor* is the subject with which the verb must agree; *of the concerts* is a prepositional phrase.]

Yes   The **sponsor** of the concerts **pays** all expenses.

Also, to locate the subject of a sentence, eliminate any phrases that start with *including, together with, along with, accompanied by, in addition to, except,* and *as well as.*

No   **The moon,** as well as Venus, **are** visible in the night sky. [*The moon* is the subject with which the verb must agree; ignore *as well as Venus.*]

Yes   **The moon,** as well as Venus, **is** visible in the night sky.

No   **The Big Dipper,** along with many other constellations, **are** easy to learn to find. [*The Big Dipper* is the subject with which the verb must agree; ignore *along with many other constellations.*]

Yes   **The Big Dipper,** along with many other constellations, **is** easy to learn to find.

11c
Use a plural verb for subjects connected by *and.*

When two or more subjects are joined by *and,* they become plural as a group; therefore, they need a plural verb.

The moon and Venus are visible in the night sky.
The Big Dipper and the constellation Orion are easy to learn to find.
Herb and Phyllis like to gaze at the stars.

However, if the word *each* or *every* precedes a singular subject, use a singular verb.

Each human hand and foot leaves a distinctive print.
Every police chief, sheriff, and federal marshall in the country has used these prints to identify people.

But when *each* or *every* follows subjects joined by *and,* they do not affect the basic rule: use a plural verb for subjects joined by *and.*

The Splitting Devil and the Masked Madman each claim to be the meanest wrestler alive.
Memphis and St. Louis each claim to be the birthplace of the blues.

The one exception to the *and* rule occurs when the parts combine to form a single thing or person.

> **Ham and cheese is** our best-selling sandwich.
>
> **My best friend and neighbor feeds** my cat when I go away.

EXERCISE 2

Supply the correct present-tense form of the verb in parentheses.

EXAMPLE   Increased heartbeat, rapid breathing, muscular tension, and sweaty palms (to be) _____ physical signs of fear.

Increased heartbeat, rapid breathing, muscular tension, and sweaty palms *are* physical signs of fear.

1. Every man, woman, and child in every culture (to experience) _____ fear from time to time.
2. An internal state of tension and generalized nameless worry accompanied by physical changes and irrational behavior (to be) _____ called *anxiety*.
3. A person who (to feel) _____ anxiety, as well as fear, often (to feel) _____ a need to escape from some imagined danger.
4. Anxiety, as it is expressed in disordered behaviors, (to take) _____ several forms.
5. Sigmund Freud, one of the founders of modern psychoanalysis, (to be) _____ said to have been the first to call these disorders *neuroses*.
6. Anxiety can (to make) _____ a sufferer very uncomfortable.

▌▌ 11d

When subjects are joined by *or, nor,* or *not only . . . but (also),* the verb should agree with the subject closest to it.

When you join subjects with *or* or *nor* or correlative conjunctions°, *either . . . or, neither . . . nor, not only . . . but (also),* make the verb agree with the subject closest to it. Unlike *and,* these conjunctions do not automatically create plurals. For the purposes of agreement, ignore everything before the final subject.

> ~~Either a spider or~~ a **fly makes** a nice treat for a frog.
>
> ~~Either my sisters or~~ my **brother plans** to get a pet frog.

~~Not only the spider but also all other~~ **arachnids have** four pairs of legs.

~~Neither spiders nor~~ **flies tempt** my appetite.

~~Six clam fritters, four blue crabs, or one steamed~~ **lobster tempts** my appetite.

If the final example sounds awkward, rearrange the items so that the plural subject is next to the verb: *One steamed lobster, four blue crabs, or six clam fritters tempt my appetite.*

■‖ 11e
With inverted word order, make sure the verb agrees with its subject.

In English, the subject of a sentence normally precedes its verb: *Astronomy is interesting.* Inverted word order occurs primarily in two situations: in questions, and in sentences using *there* or *it* in expletive° constructions.

In questions, the auxiliary verb that has to agree with the subject often comes before the subject. Be sure to look ahead to check that the subject and verb agree.

Is astronomy interesting?

What **are** the **requirements** for the major?

Do John and Mary study astronomy?

Expletive constructions postpone the subject. Expletives using *there* or *it* plus a form of the verb *be* can be tricky because the form of *be* must agree with the sentence subject. Check ahead in such sentences to identify the subject, and make the form of *be—is, are, was, were,* for example—agree with the subject.

There are nine **planets** in our solar system. [The verb *are* agrees with the subject, *planets.*]

There is probably no **life** on eight of them. [*Is* agrees with *life.*]

The introductory *it* plus a form of the verb *be* can be an expletive construction as well, but one that always takes a singular verb.

It is astronomers who want to talk about the possibility of life in other galaxies.

It was the Viking mission to Mars ten years ago that ruled out any possibility of life on Mars.

For advice on making sentences more direct and concise by eliminating expletives, see 16a-1.

You may occasionally want to write a statement in inverted word order for special effect (see 19e). Be sure to locate the subject and make the verb agree with it.

> Into deep space **shoot** probing **satellites.** [*Shoot* agrees with the inverted subject, *satellites.*]
>
> On the television screen **appears** an **image** of Saturn. [*Appears* agrees with the inverted subject, *image.*]

EXERCISE 3

Supply the correct present-tense form of the verb in parentheses.

EXAMPLE   Either sales and marketing or finance (to provide) _____ the basic training for most top corporate executives.

Either sales and marketing or finance *provides* the basic training for most corporate executives.

1. To an outsider, the chief executive officer (CEO) of a company or conglomerate of companies (to seem) _____ to be an independent decision-maker.
2. Neither the economic climate nor a business's social responsibilities (to permit) _____ independence today, however.
3. There (to be) _____ many conflicting demands to reconcile from both stockholders and consumers.
4. Not only daily operations but also the public image of the corporation (to set) _____ the environment for a CEO.
5. The finance people, along with the public relations department, (to decide) _____ on the corporation's short-term goals.
6. Either the members of the board of directors or the CEO (to attempt) _____ to influence the government agencies that regulate business.

■‖ 11f

Use singular verbs for most indefinite pronouns.

Indefinite pronouns do not refer to any particular person, thing, or idea. In context, however, they take on very clear meanings. Most indefinite pronouns are singular and therefore take singular verbs. (See 11n for a discussion of masculine pronouns with indefinite pronouns as antecedents.) Following is a list of indefinite pronouns.

237

another	either	neither	somebody
anybody	every	nobody	someone
anyone	everybody	no one	something
anything	everyone	nothing	
each	everything	one	

Everything about that intersection **is** dangerous.

But whenever **anyone says** anything, **nothing is** done.

Everyone knows that **something** terrible **is** likely to happen.

A few indefinite pronouns—*none, some, more, most, any,* and *all*—may be either singular or plural, depending on the meaning of the sentence.

Some of our streams **are** polluted. [*Some* refers to more than one stream.]

Pollution is always a threat, but **some is** easy to reverse. [*Some* refers to a portion of *pollution,* so it is singular and the verb *is* is used.]

All he asks **is** a chance. [*Chance* is singular; therefore, *all* is singular, and *is* is a singular verb.]

All are gone. [*All* here refers to more than one, so the verb *are* is correct.]

11g
With collective nouns, use singular or plural verbs according to context.

A **collective noun** names a group of people or things: *family, group, audience, class, number, committee, team,* and the like. When the group acts as one unit, use a singular verb. When the members of the group act individually, thus creating more than one action, use a plural verb.

The senior class nervously **awaits** final exams. [*Class* is acting as a single unit, so the verb is singular.]

The senior class were fitted for their graduation robes today. [Each member was fitted individually, and because there is more than one action, the verb is plural.]

The couple in red **is** invited. [*Couple* refers to a single unit, so the verb is singular.]

The couple say their vows tomorrow. [The two people will take a separate action, so there will be more than one action, and the verb is plural.]

■‖ 11h
Make sure a linking verb agrees with the subject—not the subject complement.

A **linking verb°** acts like an equal sign between a subject and a word that renames the subject—its **subject complement°**.

You **seem** angry. [*you* = *angry; you* is the subject and *angry* is the subject complement]

The subject complement that follows a linking verb may differ in number° from the subject. When it does, the verb agrees with the subject, regardless of the number of the complement.

No   **The worst part** of owning a car **are** the bills.

Yes   **The worst part** of owning a car **is** the bills.

However, notice what happens when the subjects and complements are reversed:

No   **Bills is** the worst part of owning a car.

Yes   **Bills are** the worst part of owning a car.

■‖ 11i
With *who, which,* and *that* as subjects, use verbs that agree with the antecedents of these pronouns.

Who, which, and *that* have the same form in singular and plural. Find their antecedents—words to which the pronouns refer—before deciding whether the verb is singular or plural.

The scientist will share the income from her new patent with the graduate **students who work** with her. [*Who* refers to *students,* so the verb *work* is plural.]

George Jones is **the student who works** in the science lab. [*Who* refers to *student,* so the verb *works* is singular.]

Be especially careful to identify the antecedent of *who, which,* or *that* when you see *one of the* or *the only one of the* in a sentence.

George Jones is one of the lab assistants **who deserve** recognition. [*Who* refers to *lab assistants,* so *deserve* is plural.]

George Jones is the only one of the lab assistants **who deserves** recognition. [*Who* refers to *one,* so *deserve* is singular.]

239

When you write a sentence with *one . . . who, one . . . which,* or *one . . . that,* decide whether the relative pronoun° refers to *one* or to the group named after *one of the.* If the pronoun refers to *one,* use a singular verb. If the pronoun refers to what comes after *one of the,* use a plural verb.

EXERCISE 4

Supply the correct present-tense form of the verb in parentheses.

EXAMPLE   Everyone (to experience) _____ anxiety from time to time, but some people (to have) _____ difficulty controlling their feelings.

Everyone *experiences* anxiety from time to time, but some people *have* difficulty controlling their feelings.

1. In free-floating anxiety, often someone (to feel) _____ as if an inescapable danger were imminent.
2. The family (to watch) _____ the victim go through attacks of sweating, dizziness, heart palpitations, and shortness of breath.
3. Of all the anxieties, none (to be) _____ as startling as a sudden panic attack.
4. A severe group of symptoms (to affect) _____ anxiety-ridden people when they (to have) _____ to appear in public or to be in large open spaces.
5. Psychiatrists are medical doctors who (to have) _____ completed at least three years of clinical training beyond the M.D. degree.
6. The program for psychoanalysts is one that (to require) _____ the psychoanalysis of the doctor in training.
7. Social workers who (to have) _____ taken advanced studies may become psychiatric social workers.

◼‖ 11j

Use singular verbs with subjects that specify amounts and with singular subjects that are in plural form.

Subjects that refer to sums of money, distance, or measurement are considered singular and take singular verbs.

Ninety cents is the current bus fare.
Three hundred dollars is the price.
Three-quarters of an inch is all we need.
Two miles is a short sprint for a serious jogger.

Many words that end in *-s* or *-ics* are singular in meaning despite their plural appearance. They include *news, ethics, economics*, mathematics, physics (as a course of study), *politics, sports, measles,* and *statistics* (as a group of data).

The **news gets** better each day.

Experts say that **sports builds** character.

Statistics is required of math and science majors. [Here *statistics* is a source of study.]

Statistics indicate a coming shortage of teachers. [Here *statistics* refers to a body of data, not a discipline or course.]

There are also some words treated as plural, even though they refer to one thing; they include *jeans, pants, scissors, clippers, tweezers, eyeglasses, thanks,* and *riches.*

Eyeglasses fog up in damp weather, so **my thanks go** to the inventor of contact lenses.

My **slacks need** pressing. [But: My *pair* of slacks *needs* pressing.]

Series and *means* have the same form in singular and plural, so the meaning determines whether the verb is singular or plural.

The new series begins on Sunday night.

A series of disasters are plaguing our production.

◼‖ 11k

Use singular verbs for titles of written works, companies, and words as terms.

Even though plural and compound nouns occur in a title, the title itself signifies one work or entity. Therefore, these subjects are singular and always take singular verbs.

Cider House Rules by John Irving **is** a popular novel.

***Dreamgirls* was** a major Broadway hit.

Even if a word is plural, when you refer to it as a term, it takes a singular verb.

Our implies that I am included.

During the Vietnam War, ***protective reaction strikes* was** a euphemism used by the United States government to mean *bombing.*

241

EXERCISE 5
Supply the correct present-tense form of the verb in parentheses.

EXAMPLE   Palmistry, also known as hand reading, (to go) _____ back to the ancient Chinese and Egyptians.

Palmistry, also known as hand reading, *goes* back to the ancient Chinese and Egyptians.

1. Advocates believe that if they (to study) _____ the weaknesses revealed in their palms and (to strive) _____ to correct them, then they (to give) _____ new meaning to the expression "Your fate is in your hands."
2. Contrary to popular belief, people who read palms (to say) _____ that nothing revealed in palms (to be) _____ irreversible.
3. Believers in palmistry also claim that people's hands (to change) _____ to reflect their lives.
4. Everybody who is curious about palmistry (to ask) _____ which hand is read; both (to be) _____.
5. According to believers, if someone (to be) _____ right-handed, the left hand (to show) _____ inherited characteristics and potential.
6. The other hand (to reveal) _____ how the person (to be) _____ using what is given to him or her.
7. Supposedly, either the right hand or the left hand alone (to do) _____ not give a complete reading.
8. Palm readers claim that there (to be) _____ a "poison line" that (to appear) _____ in the hands of chronic drug users.
9. Five dollars (to be) _____ is the usual fee for a basic reading; even fifteen minutes at lunch hour (to give) _____ a person enough time to get a quick reading.
10. I would think that eyeglasses (to be) _____ a necessity for a nearsighted palm reader.

∥ PRONOUN-ANTECEDENT AGREEMENT

The form of most pronouns depends on **antecedents**—nouns, noun phrases, or other pronouns to which the pronouns refer. The connection between a pronoun and its antecedent must be clear if writing is to be clear and coherent (see Chapter 10 for advice on pronoun reference). These connections are achieved by agreement in number (singular or plural), person (first, second, or third), and gender (male or female).

Pronouns must match their antecedents in number (singular pronouns refer to singular antecedents, and plural pronouns to plural antecedents).

Loud music has **its** harmful side effects.

Many musicians suffer damage to **their** auditory nerves.

■‖ 11l

Use a plural pronoun when its antecedents are joined by *and*.

Two or more antecedents joined by *and* require a plural pronoun, even if the antecedents are singular.

The United States and Canada maintain **their** border as the longest open frontier in the world.

Although **France and Spain are** friendly nations, **they** control access across **their** common border.

When *each* or *every* precedes singular nouns joined by *and,* use a singular pronoun.

Every American and Canadian may cross the border without showing **his or her** passport.

Each car and truck that comes through the border station has **its** contents inspected.

When the singular nouns joined by *and* refer to a single person or thing, use a singular pronoun.

Our guide and translator told us to watch out for scorpions as she took us into the tomb.

■‖ 11m

When antecedents are joined by *or* or *nor,* make the pronoun agree with the antecedent closest to it.

Antecedents joined by the conjunction° *or, nor,* or correlative conjunctions° (such as *either . . . or, neither . . . nor),* often mix the masculine and feminine or singular and plural. For the purposes of agreement, ignore everything before the final antecedent.

243

~~Either the waitress or~~ **the waiter** will seat you in **his** section.
~~Either the waiter or~~ **the waitress** will seat you in **her** section.
~~Neither Chef Jacques nor~~ **the waiters** eat **their** dinners early.
~~Neither the waiters nor~~ **Chef Jacques** eats **his** dinner early.

■‖ 11n
Use a singular pronoun to refer to most indefinite-pronoun antecedents.

Indefinite pronouns (see 11f for a list) do not refer to any particular person, thing, or idea. In context, however, they take on very clear meanings. Indefinite pronouns are usually singular, so the pronouns that refer to them should also be singular.

Anyone who knows the answer should raise **his or her** hand.
Everybody hopes **he or she** will find it.

‖ 1
Use a plural pronoun when an indefinite-pronoun antecedent is plural.

Some indefinite pronouns can be singular or plural *(none, some, more, most, any, all)*, depending on the meaning of the sentence. When an indefinite pronoun is plural, the pronouns that refer to it should be plural.

‖ 2
Use masculine pronouns appropriately.

Until the 1960s, grammatical convention specified using masculine pronouns to refer back to indefinite pronouns and nouns and pronouns naming general categories to which any person might belong: *"Everyone* **should** admit *his* mistakes." Today people are more conscious that *he, his, him,* and *himself* exclude women, who make up over half the population. Experienced writers try to avoid using masculine pronouns to refer to the entire population. The chart shows three ways to avoid using masculine pronouns to refer to males and females together. For advice on how to avoid other types of sexist language, see 21a-3.

244

HOW TO AVOID USING ONLY THE MASCULINE PRONOUN TO REFER TO MALES AND FEMALES TOGETHER

Solution 1: Use a pair—but try to avoid a pair more than once in a sentence or in many sentences in a row.

> **Everyone** hopes that **he or she** will win the scholarship.
> **A successful doctor** knows that **he or she** has to work long hours.
> With the explosion of knowledge, no **doctor** can read much outside **his or her** specialty.

Solution 2: Revise into the plural.

> **Many people** hope that **they** will win the scholarship.
> **Successful doctors** know that **they** have to work long hours.
> With the explosion of knowledge, few **doctors** can read much outside **their** specialties.

Solution 3: Recast the sentence.

> Everyone hopes to win the scholarship.
> Successful doctors should expect to work long hours.

▮‖ 11o
Use singular or plural pronouns according to context to match collective-noun antecedents.

A **collective noun** names a group of people or things: *family, group, audience, class, number, committee, team,* and the like. When the group acts as one unit, use a singular pronoun to refer to it. When the members of the group act individually, thus creating more than one action, use a plural pronoun.

> **The audience** is cheering as **it** stands to applaud the performers. [The audience is acting as one unit, so the pronoun is singular.]
>
> **The audience** put on **their** coats and walk out. [Here the audience is acting as individuals, so all the actions collect to become plural. The verbs *put* and *walk* must be plural as well as the pronoun *their*.]
>
> The **family is** spending **its** vacation in Maine. [All the family members went to one place together.]
>
> The **family are** spending **their** vacations in Maine, Hawaii, and Rome. [Each family member went to a different place.]

EXERCISE 6

Revise each sentence so that all pronouns agree with their antecedents. When necessary, change verbs and other words to maintain subject–verb agreement. Most sentences have more than one solution.

EXAMPLE   All political interest groups aim to advance the interests of its members while affecting public policy.
All political interest groups aim to advance the interests of *their* members while affecting public policy.

1. Interest groups differ from political parties in its aims, structure, and number.
2. Unlike political parties, each group selects their leaders without elections.
3. The interest group is concerned only with one or two issues, such as gun control or crop subsidies, and they seek no official representative in government.
4. For example, the American Tobacco Institute tries to gain support for their claim that cigarette smoking is not dangerous.
5. Even the membership of a diverse special interest group, such as the Sierra Club, are more focused on their specific goals than are members of the large political parties.
6. Many fast-food chains have pushed hard for its goal of a reduced minimum wage for teenagers.
7. The United States Senate and House of Representatives in its meetings is constantly hearing pleas from these thousands of groups.

12

DISTINGUISHING BETWEEN ADJECTIVES AND ADVERBS

Both adjectives and adverbs are **modifiers**—words or groups of words that describe other words. Distinguishing between adjectives and adverbs is sometimes troublesome for writers.

ADJECTIVE   *The* **brisk** wind blew.

ADVERB   *The wind blew* **briskly.**

This chapter explains that the key to distinguishing between adjectives and adverbs is understanding that they modify different words or groups of words. The chart on the next page will help you to remember these distinctions.

In spite of these essential differences, inexperienced writers sometimes interchange adjectives and adverbs because of the *-ly* ending. In many cases, an adverb is formed by adding *-ly* to an adjective: *smooth* and *smoothly, beautiful* and *beautifully, busy* and *busily.* Even though many adverbs end in *-ly* (eat *swiftly,* eat *frequently,* eat *hungrily*), some do not (eat *fast,* eat *often,* eat *little*). To complicate matters further, some adjectives end in *-ly* (*lovely* flower, *friendly* dog). The *-ly* ending, therefore, is not a reliable way to identify adverbs.

SUMMARY OF DIFFERENCES BETWEEN ADJECTIVES AND ADVERBS

WHAT ADJECTIVES MODIFY	EXAMPLE
nouns°	The **busy** *lawyer* rested.
pronouns°	*She* felt **triumphant.**

WHAT ADVERBS MODIFY	EXAMPLE
verbs°	The lawyer *spoke* **quickly.**
adverbs°	The lawyer spoke **very** *quickly.*
adjectives°	The lawyer was **extremely** *busy.*
independent clauses°	**Therefore,** the lawyer rested.

To determine whether a specific occasion calls for an adjective or an adverb, see how the word functions in its sentence. If a noun or pronoun is being modified, use an adjective; if a verb, adjective, or other adverb is being modified, use an adverb. Also, you can consult your dictionary for the word's part of speech.

EXERCISE 1

First underline and label all adjectives (ADJ) and adverbs (ADV). Then go back and draw an arrow from each adjective and adverb to the word or words it modifies.

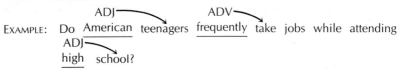

EXAMPLE: Do American teenagers frequently take jobs while attending high school?

1. Many American teenagers have always worked very hard at part-time jobs while going to high school, but a greater percentage of teenage students work today than ever before.
2. Reliable statistics reveal that almost one-third of all ninth and tenth graders and almost one-half of all eleventh and twelfth graders are employed.
3. Interestingly, they are working longer hours than the high school students of twenty-five years ago.
4. Some determined students earn more than two hundred dollars a month.
5. Not surprisingly, the number of hours worked greatly influences school performance.
6. An important study conducted recently at the University of California disclosed that most eleventh and twelfth graders can manage a weekly work schedule of twenty hours without damaging their grades.

248

■|| 12a
Use adverbs—not adjectives—to modify verbs.

Only adverbs modify verbs. Using adjectives as adverbs is nonstandard.

> No   He drove **careless.** [Adjective *careless* cannot modify verb *drove.*]

> Yes   He drove **carelessly.** [Adverb *carelessly* modifies verb *drove.*]

■|| 12b
Use adverbs—not adjectives—to modify adjectives and other adverbs.

Only adverbs can modify adjectives and other adverbs. Here again, using adjectives as adverbs is nonstandard.

> No   The candidate felt **unusual** energetic today. [Adjective *unusual* cannot modify adjective *energetic.*]

> Yes   The candidate felt **unusually energetic** today. [Adverb *unusually* modifies adjective *energetic.*]

> No   The candidate spoke **exceptional forcefully** today. [Adjective *exceptional* cannot modify adverb *forcefully.*]

> Yes   The candidate spoke **exceptionally forcefully** today. [Adverb *exceptionally* modifies adverb *forcefully.*]

■|| 12c
Do not use double negatives.

A **double negative** is a statement that contains two negative modifiers, the second of which repeats the message of the first. (This form, nonstandard today, was standard in the days of Chaucer and Shakespeare.) Negative modifiers include *no, neither, not, none, nothing, never, hardly, scarcely,* and *barely.*

> No   The union members did **not** have **no** money in reserve.

> Yes   The union members did **not** have **any** money in reserve.

249

No	The factory workers will **never** vote for **no** strike.
Yes	The factory workers will **never** vote for a strike.
No	The factory workers will **not never** vote for a strike.
Yes	The factory workers will **not ever** vote for a strike.
Yes	The factory workers will **not** vote for a strike.
No	The office workers will **not** be hurt **none** by a strike.
Yes	The office workers will **not** be hurt by a strike.

Not—No—Nothing

The words *not, no,* and *nothing* are particularly prone to creating double negatives.

No	He did **not** hear **nothing.**
Yes	He did **not** hear **anything.**
No	The trees do **not** have **no** leaves.
Yes	The trees do **not** have **any** leaves.
Yes	The trees have **no** leaves.

When the word *not* is used in a contraction°, such as *isn't, don't,* or *haven't,* the negative message carried by *not* tends to slip by some inexperienced writers. They add a second—incorrect—negative. If you use contractions, which many writers prefer to avoid in their academic writing, be especially careful not to use double negatives.

No	He did**n't** hear **nothing.**
Yes	He did**n't** hear **anything.**
No	She **couldn't scarcely** hear the music.
Yes	She **could scarcely** hear the music.
No	She **couldn't hardly** hear the music.
Yes	She **could hardly** hear the music.

◼‖ 12d

After linking verbs, use adjectives—not adverbs—as complements.

Linking verbs indicate a state of being or a condition. They include *be (am, is, are, was, were)*; verbs related to the senses, including *look, smell, taste, sound,* and *feel*; and verbs such as *appear, seem, become, grow, turn, remain,* and *prove.* Linking verbs connect the subject° to a complement, a word that renames or describes the subject. You can think of a linking verb as an equal sign between a subject and its complement.

The guests looked **happy.** [subject *guests* = adjective *happy*]

The party was **successful.** [subject *party* = adjective *successful*]

Problems can arise with verbs that are sometimes linking verbs and sometimes action verbs, depending on the sentence. As linking verbs, these verbs use adjectives in complements. As action verbs, they use adverbs.

Anne **looks** happy. [*looks* = linking verb]

Anne **looks** happily at the sunset. [*looks* = action verb]

He **grows happy** when he sees Emily. [*grows* = linking verb]

He **grows** flowers **happily.** [*grows* = action verb]

Bad—Badly

The words *bad* (adjective) and *badly* (adverb) are particularly prone to misuse with verbs such as *feel, grow, smell, sound, taste.* Only the adjective *bad* is correct when a verb is functioning as a linking verb.

FOR DESCRIBING A FEELING

No   The student felt **badly.**

YES   The student felt **bad.**

FOR DESCRIBING A SMELL

No   The food smelled **badly.**

YES   The food smelled **bad.**

Good—Well

Good and *well* can be especially tricky, for *well* functions both as an adverb and as an adjective. *Good* is always an adjective. *Well* is an adjective referring to good health. When it is describing anything other than good health, *well* is an adverb.

You look **well** = You look in good health. [*well* = adjective]

You write **well** = You write skillfully. [*well* = adverb]

Except when *well* is an adjective referring to health, use *good* only as an adjective and *well* only as an adverb.

No   She sings **good.** [*sings* = action verb; adverb, not adjective, required]

Yes   She sings **well.** [*well* = adverb]

EXERCISE 2

Revise these sentences to eliminate double negatives and to make the use of all adjectives and adverbs suitable for academic writing.

Example   Does love come natural?

          Does love come *naturally?*

1. Is romance thriving good in America?
2. If sales of Valentine's Day cards are any indication, many Americans do not never want to forget to say "I love you" on February 14.
3. Sure people think the Valentine's Day idea is good because every year the cards sell brisk.
4. Americans buy from 900 million to 1.1 billion Valentine's Day cards yearly, proving that people are powerful eager to express affection.
5. Interestingly, adults frequent send and receive only 20 percent of all the cards; children buy enormous numbers of them for any good friends or teachers they consider unusual fine.
6. Even though many spouses and sweethearts feel strong about their mutual love, they easy send more Valentine's Day cards to their mothers than to each other.
7. For many centuries, people have reacted positive to a day that honors love.
8. The ancient Romans honored careful their clear popular tradition of holding a "love lottery" in mid-February.
9. An unmarried man would draw random the name of an unmarried woman from a secure guarded box, and then the couple would court polite to see if they liked each other good enough to get married.

ad

■‖ **12e**

Use correct comparative and superlative forms of adjectives and adverbs.

When comparisons are made, descriptive adjectives and adverbs often carry the message. Adjectives and adverbs, therefore, have forms that communicate relative degrees of intensity.

‖ **1**

Use correct forms of comparison for regular adjectives and adverbs.

Most adjectives and adverbs show degrees of intensity by adding *-er* and *-est* endings or by combining with the words *more* and *most*. (All adjectives and adverbs show diminishing or negative comparison by combining with the words *less* and *least: less jumpy, least jumpy; less surely, least surely*.) A few adjectives and adverbs are irregular; see 12e-2.

FORMS OF COMPARISON FOR REGULAR ADJECTIVES AND ADVERBS	
FORM	**FUNCTION**
Positive	Used for a statement when nothing is being compared
Comparative	Used when only two things are being compared—with *-er* ending or *more* (or *less*)
Superlative	Used when three or more things are being compared—with *-est* ending or *most* (or *least*)

Here is a list that contrasts the three forms. Consider the messages of comparison in the sentences after the list.

POSITIVE	COMPARATIVE	SUPERLATIVE
green	greener	greenest
happy	happier	happiest
selfish	less selfish	least selfish
beautiful	more beautiful	most beautiful

Her tree is **green.**
Her tree is **greener** than his tree.
Her tree is the **greenest** tree on the block.

His flower garden is **beautiful.**

His flower garden is **more beautiful** than her flower garden.

His flower garden is the **most beautiful** on the block.

The choice of whether to use *-er, -est* or *more, most* depends largely on the number of syllables in the adjective or adverb. With **one-syllable words,** the *-er, -est* endings are most common: *large, larger, largest* (adjective); *far, farther, farthest* (adverb). With **three-syllable words,** *more, most* are used. With **adverbs of two or more syllables,** *more, most* are used: *easily, more easily, most easily.* With **adjectives of two syllables,** practice varies: some take the *-er, -est* endings; others combine with *more* and *most.* One general rule covers two-syllable adjectives ending in *-y:* use the *-er, -est* endings after changing the *-y* to *i.* For other two-syllable adjectives, often you will form comparatives and superlatives intuitively, based on what you have heard or read for a particular adjective. If neither form "sounds" natural for a given adjective, use whichever form your dictionary advises.

Be careful not to use a **double comparative** or **double superlative.** The words *more* or *most* cannot be used if the *-er* or *-est* ending has been used.

No   He was **more younger** than his brother.

Yes   He was **younger** than his brother.

No   Her music was the **most snappiest** on the radio.

Yes   Her music was the **snappiest** on the radio.

No   People danced **more easier** [or **more easilier**] to her music.

Yes   People danced **more easily** to her music.

2
Use correct forms of comparison for irregular adjectives and adverbs.

Some comparative and superlative forms are irregular. Learn the short list in the chart on the opposite page.

The Perkinses saw a **good** movie.

The Perkinses saw a **better** movie than the Smiths did.

The Perkinses saw **the best** movie that they had ever seen.

The Millers had **little** trouble finding jobs.
The Millers had **less** trouble finding jobs than the Smiths did.
The Millers had **the least** trouble finding jobs of everyone.

IRREGULAR COMPARATIVES AND SUPERLATIVES

POSITIVE (1)	COMPARATIVE (2)	SUPERLATIVE (3+)
good (adjective)	better	best
well (adjective and adverb)	better	best
bad (adjective)	worse	worst
badly (adverb)	worse	worst
many	more	most
much	more	most
some	more	most
little	less	least

▌ USAGE ALERT: Do not use *less* and *fewer* interchangeably. *Less* refers to amounts or values that form one whole. *Fewer* refers to numbers or anything that can be counted. *They consumed fewer calories; the sugar substitute had less aftertaste.* ▐

EXERCISE 3
First complete this chart. Next, write sentences that set a context for each word in the completed chart.

EXAMPLE Weighing 270 pounds and standing seven feet tall, he is big, even for a football player.

POSITIVE (1)	COMPARATIVE (2)	SUPERLATIVE (3+)
big	_____	_____
_____	_____	hungriest
_____	more hungry	_____
quickly	_____	_____
important	_____	_____
_____	thicker	_____
_____	_____	most thirsty

EXERCISE 4

Revise these sentences so that all comparative and superlative forms are suitable for academic writing.

EXAMPLE   Most people say that airlines serve the worse food they have ever tasted.

Most people say that airlines serve the *worst* food they have ever tasted.

1. Passengers say that often the chicken sauce is more thick than glue, the beef is best suited to feeding dogs than humans, and the pasta is soggier than a wet sponge.
2. The more popular joke seems to be about a cabin attendant who announced, "You can choose chicken, beef, or pasta for dinner tonight. But please don't get upset if we run out of your choice because one is no more better than the other."
3. Of the more than a dozen caterers who supply airline food, the larger prepares 90 million meals a year.
4. Controlling quality might be more easier if the numbers were less larger.
5. Still, some airlines are trying hardest: One large American airline offers the choice of a low-cholesterol meal with a least fatty grade of meat.
6. A recent survey, however, revealed that frequent flyers consider food least important compared to on-time records.
7. Airline executives are less motivated to upgrade food if passengers are willing to settle for the most cheapest meals an airline can serve.

■‖ 12f

Avoid using too many nouns as modifiers.

Sometimes nouns can modify other nouns: *truck driver, train track, security system.* These very familiar terms create no problems. However, when nouns pile up in a sequence of modifiers, it can be difficult to know which nouns are being modified and which nouns are doing the modifying. As a result, the style puts too much burden on the reader to decipher the writer's message. Depending on the particular sentence, writers have several routes to revision: (1) rewrite the sentence, (2) change a noun to an adjective, (3) change a noun to the possessive case°, or (4) change a noun to a modifying phrase.

(1) SENTENCE REWRITTEN

No   I asked my advisor to write **two college recommendation** letters for me.

YES   I asked my advisor to write **letters of recommendation** to **two colleges** for me.

(2) AND (3) ONE NOUN CHANGED TO POSSESSIVE CASE AND ANOTHER TO ITS ADJECTIVE FORM

No   Some students might take the **United States Navy examination** for **navy engineer training.**

YES   Some students might take the **United States Navy's examination** for **naval engineer training.**

(4) NOUN CHANGED TO PREPOSITIONAL PHRASE

No   Our **student advisement program** has won awards for excellence.

YES   Our **program in student advisement** has won awards for excellence.

EXERCISE 5

Revise the following sentences so that they are suitable for academic writing. Apply all the material covered in this chapter.

EXAMPLE Increasing in recent years, bankrupt businesses are being rescued by their employees who think creative.
Increasingly in recent years, bankrupt businesses are being rescued by their employees who think *creatively*.

1. Workers who want bad to keep their jobs pool their money careful and become worker-owners.
2. Typical each worker-owner buys a share in the business and participates democratic in its operations.
3. The resulting "cooperative" often has unusual enthusiastic workers and the most happiest customers.
4. Cooperatives most frequent run supermarkets, but they have also taken over sewing factories, tool manufacturing plants, and even a steel mill.
5. Worker-owner rescue actions can be exciting when new.
6. The worker-owners, however, work the hardest than they ever did because they must do their original jobs good and spend extra time on management.
7. Because collective decision-making does not never work well if the worker-owners number over 400, most larger cooperatives hold democratic run elections to choose managers.

8. Unless all goes well, there are not no profits to share, and sometimes the workers cannot be paid no salary until the business gets on its feet.

9. Wide publicized examples of successfully run cooperatives, many in severe economically depressed areas, give encouragement to groups having little success than others.

10. Cooperative managed businesses are seen by some experts as the better hope for the future of small, local owned businesses in America.

III WRITING CORRECT SENTENCES

13
SENTENCE FRAGMENTS

A **sentence fragment** is a portion of a sentence that is punctuated as though it were a complete sentence. Most sentence fragments are phrases° or dependent clauses°. You can avoid writing sentence fragments if you recognize the difference between a fragment and a complete sentence.

FRAGMENT	The telephone with two outside lines. [no verb]
REVISED	The telephone has two outside lines.
FRAGMENT	Rang loudly for ten minutes. [no subject]
REVISED	The telephone rang loudly for ten minutes.
FRAGMENT	At midnight. [no verb or subject]
REVISED	The telephone rang at midnight.
FRAGMENT	**Because** the telephone rang loudly. [dependent clause with subordinating conjunction]
REVISED	Because the telephone rang loudly, the family was awakened.

FRAGMENT	The telephone **that** I answered. [dependent clause with relative pronoun]
REVISED	The telephone that I answered woke the family.

▮‖ 13a
Know how to test for sentence completeness.

If you write sentence fragments frequently, you need a system to check that your sentences are complete. Here is a test to use if you suspect that you have written a sentence fragment.

TEST FOR SENTENCE COMPLETENESS

1. **Is there a verb?** If no, there is a sentence fragment.
2. **Is there a subject?** If no, there is a sentence fragment.
3. **Do the subject and verb start with a subordinating word—and lack an independent clause to complete the thought?** If yes, there is a sentence fragment.

QUESTION 1: Is there a verb?

If there is no verb, you are looking at a sentence fragment. Verbs convey information about what is happening, what has happened, or what will happen. In testing for sentence completeness, you need to find a verb that can change form to communicate a change in time.

> Yesterday, the telephone **rang.**
> Now the telephone **rings.**

Verbals° do not function as verbs. Do not, therefore, mistake a verbal for a verb. Verbals are present participles°, past participles°, and infinitives°.

FRAGMENT	Yesterday, the students registering for classes.
REVISED	Yesterday, the students **were** registering for classes.

261

FRAGMENT	Now the students registering for classes.
REVISED	Now the students **are** registering for classes.
FRAGMENT	Yesterday, told about an excellent teacher.
REVISED	Yesterday, I **was** told about an excellent teacher.
FRAGMENT	Yesterday, the students to register for classes.
REVISED	Yesterday, the students **wanted** to register for classes.
FRAGMENT	Now the students to register for classes.
REVISED	Now the students **want** to register for classes.

In the sentences above, _were, are, was, wanted,_ and _want_ are verbs that change form to indicate time. They are examples of complete-sentence verbs.

QUESTION 2: Is there a subject?

If there is no subject, you are looking at a sentence fragment. To find a subject, ask the verb "who?" or "what?"

FRAGMENT	Studied hard for the test. [Who studied? unknown]
REVISED	The students studied hard for the test. [Who studied? students]
FRAGMENT	Contained some difficult questions. [What contained? unknown]
REVISED	The test contained some difficult questions. [What contained? the test]

Every sentence must have its own subject. A sentence fragment without a subject often occurs when the missing subject is the same as the subject in the preceding sentence.

No	World War II ended in 1945 for most people. **Continued for others, however, until the end of their lives.**
YES	World War II ended in 1945 for most people. **It continued for others, however, until the end of their lives.**

Imperative statements—commands and some requests—are an exception. Imperative statements imply the word "you" as the subject.

    Run! = (You) run!
    Think fast. = (You) think fast.
    Please return my books. = (You) please return my books.

QUESTION 3: Do the subject and verb start with a subordinating word—and lack an independent clause to complete the thought?

If the answer is "yes," you are looking at a sentence fragment. Clauses that begin with subordinating words are called **dependent clauses,** and they cannot stand alone as independent units. A dependent clause must be joined to an independent clause to be part of a complete sentence. One type of subordinating word is a **subordinating conjunction.** The most frequently used are:

after	even though	until
although	if	when
as	since	whenever
because	though	where
before	unless	wherever

FRAGMENT   **Because** she returned my books.

REVISED   **Because** she returned my books, I can study.

FRAGMENT   **When** I study.

REVISED   I have to concentrate **when** I study.

▋ PUNCTUATION ALERT: When a dependent clause starting with a subordinating conjunction comes before an independent clause, a comma always separates the clauses. ▋

Another type of subordinating word is a **relative pronoun.** The most frequently used relative pronouns are *who, which, that, what, whoever,* and *whatever.*

FRAGMENT   The test **that** we studied for.

REVISED   The test **that** we studied for was cancelled.

FRAGMENT   The professor **who** taught the course.

REVISED   The professor **who** taught the course was ill.

FRAGMENT   **Whoever** registered early.

REVISED   **Whoever** registered early got a good schedule.

Questions are an exception—they can begin with words such as *when, where, who,* and *which* without being sentence fragments: *When do you want to study? Where is the library? Who is your professor? Which class are you taking?*

EXERCISE 1
Check each word group according to the Test for Sentence Completeness on page 261. If a word group is a sentence fragment, explain what makes it incomplete. If a word group is a complete sentence, circle its number.

EXAMPLE   The rescue of thousands of whales. [no verb; Question 1 on the Test]

1. A Soviet icebreaker trying to rescue the whales.
2. Thousands of ten-foot-long whales struggling for air in the thick ice.
3. In the Arctic Ocean in the winter of 1983.
4. Raced to reach the whales.
5. The icebreaker arrived in time.
6. Because the whales were afraid of the ship.
7. Although the ship wanted to cut a path through the ice.
8. A crew member who found a solution.
9. Classical music which he played over the ship's loudspeaker.
10. The whales then followed the ship to the open sea.

▪▮ 13b

Revise dependent clauses punctuated as sentences.

A **dependent clause** contains both a subject and verb but starts with a subordinating word and is thus unable to stand on its own as a sentence. Subordinating words include subordinating conjunctions and relative pronouns (listed on page 263).

To correct a dependent clause punctuated as a sentence, you can do one, or sometimes either, of two things. (1) You can join the dependent clause to an independent clause that comes directly before or after; sometimes you will need to add words so that the combined sentence makes sense. (2) You can drop the subordinating word and, if necessary, add words to create an independent clause.

FRAGMENT	Many people over twenty-five years of age are deciding to get college degrees. **Because they want the benefits of an advanced education.**
REVISED	Many people over twenty-five years of age are deciding to get college degrees because they want the benefits of an advanced education. [joined into one sentence]
REVISED	Many people over twenty-five years of age are deciding to get college degrees. They want the benefits of an advanced education. [subordinating conjunction dropped to create an independent clause]
FRAGMENT	College is an attraction for many older people. **Who could not attend upon graduation from high school.**
REVISED	College is an attraction for many older people who could not attend upon graduation from high school. [joined into one sentence]
REVISED	College is an attraction for many older people. They could not attend upon graduation from high school. [relative pronoun dropped and *they* added to create an independent clause]

When trying to identify dependent clauses, be especially careful with words that indicate time – such as *after, before, since,* and *until.* In some sentences they function as subordinating conjunctions, but in other sentences they function as adverbs° and prepositions°. Do not automatically assume when you see these words that you are looking at a dependent clause.

Before, the class was never full. Now it is overfilled. [These are two complete sentences. In the first sentence, *before* is an adverb modifying the independent clause *the class was never full*.]

Before this semester, the class was never full. [This is a complete sentence. *Before* is the preposition in the prepositional phrase° *before this semester*.]

Before the professor arrived. [This is a sentence fragment. *Before* is a subordinating conjunction.]

Before the professor arrived, the room was empty. [This is a complete sentence. The dependent clause precedes an independent clause.]

265

When you use time-indicator words such as *before,* consider the context of the sentence before you decide if you are looking at a sentence fragment.

EXERCISE 2
Find and correct any sentence fragments.

EXAMPLE   Headlights help drivers see and be seen. When it rains, sleets, or snows, no matter what time of day. Drivers should always turn on their headlights.

Headlights help drivers see and be seen. When it rains, sleets, or snows, no matter what time of day, drivers should always turn on their headlights.

1. The ancient Egyptians valued silver more than gold. Because silver was easier to mine and work with.

2. Greyhounds which are the fastest dogs. They have been clocked running 42 miles per hour.

3. Although it consumes 25 percent of the blood's oxygen supply, the human brain is motionless. If it is deprived of oxygen for four to five minutes. It will die.

4. In 1911 Bobby Leech went on a worldwide lecture tour. After surviving a barrel ride over Niagara Falls. Which broke many of his bones. He slipped on a banana peel in New Zealand and died of his injuries.

5. Many Vietnamese immigrants to the United States have been high school valedictorians in recent years. Because education is important in their culture. Vietnamese families expect their children to study hard.

6. People who refuse to wear seat belts in spite of the evidence about safety. They should realize that fatalities involving nonbelted occupants have been recorded at 12 miles per hour. That is the approximate speed in a large parking lot.

7. Even though everyone knows that confronting the unpleasant is inevitable. Procrastination affects nearly everyone at some time. Many people are expert at knowing how to postpone cleaning, paying bills, and other chores.

8. The world's largest diamond which was found in 1905. After, it was cut into 105 stones. Each was considered especially valuable.

9. Whoever refuses to walk under a ladder in fear of bad luck. The person is perpetuating an ancient superstition.

10. Selling and buying babies has become a big business in the United States. Although this route to adopting a child is illegal. Unfortunately, many people who lose their life savings hoping to get a baby. They pay their money and never see the "agency representative" again.

13c
Revise phrases punctuated as sentences.

A phrase is a group of words that lacks a subject, a verb, or both. A phrase, therefore, is not a sentence. To revise a phrase into a complete sentence, you can either rewrite it to become an independent clause, or you can join it to an independent clause that comes directly before or after.

A **verbal phrase** contains a verbal. Verbals are present participles°, past participles°, and infinitives°.

FRAGMENT   The mayor called a news conference last week. **To announce new programs for crime prevention and care for the homeless.**

REVISED   The mayor called a news conference last week to announce new programs for crime prevention and care for the homeless. [joined into one sentence]

REVISED   The mayor called a news conference last week. She wanted to announce new programs for crime prevention and care for the homeless. [rewritten]

FRAGMENT   **Introduced by her assistant.** The mayor began with an opening statement.

REVISED   Introduced by her assistant, the mayor began with an opening statement. [joined into one sentence]

REVISED   The mayor **was** introduced by her assistant. She then began with an opening statement. [rewritten]

FRAGMENT   **Hoping for strong public support.** She gave many examples of problems everywhere in the city.

REVISED   Hoping for strong public support, she gave many examples of problems everywhere in the city. [joined into one sentence]

REVISED   She hoped for strong public support. She gave many examples of problems everywhere in the city. [rewritten]

A **prepositional phrase** contains a preposition° (for a complete list, see 6g), its object°, and any modifiers°.

FRAGMENT   Cigarette smoke made the conference room seem airless. **During the long news conference.**

REVISED   Cigarette smoke made the conference room seem airless during the long news conference. [joined into one sentence]

REVISED   Cigarette smoke made the conference room seem airless. It was hard to breathe during the long news conference. [rewritten]

An **appositive** is a word or word group that renames a noun or a group of words functioning as a noun.

FRAGMENT   Most people respected the mayor. **A politician with fresh ideas and practical solutions.**

REVISED   Most people respected the mayor, a politician with fresh ideas and practical solutions. [joined into one sentence]

REVISED   Most people respected the mayor. She seemed to be a politician with fresh ideas and practical solutions. [rewritten]

Compound predicates contain two or more verbs along with any objects and modifiers. To be part of a complete sentence, a predicate must have a subject. If the second half of a compound predicate is punctuated as a separate sentence, it is a sentence fragment.

FRAGMENT   The reporters asked the mayor many questions about the details of her program. **And then discussed her answers at length among themselves.**

REVISED   The reporters asked the mayor many questions about the details of her program and discussed her answers at length among themselves. [joined into one sentence]

REVISED   The reporters asked the mayor many questions about the details of her program. Then the reporters discussed her answers at length among themselves. [rewritten]

EXERCISE 3
Go back to Exercise 1 and revise any sentence fragments into complete sentences.

EXERCISE 4
Correct all sentence fragments.

New words coming into American English constantly. Many start out as slang. For example, *preemie* meaning "a prematurely born infant." Unknown until a few years ago. Another word rarely heard was "humongous." Indicating something of enormous size. Other words fade from the language. And disappear from use. Rudolph Flesch, the author of *Lite English: Popular Words That Are O.K. to Use.* A book explaining that the American language is changing every day. Just like the American people.

 13d
Recognize intentional fragments.

Professional writers sometimes intentionally use fragments, sparingly, for emphasis and effect.

> The cars were jammed for 30 miles along the Karagatch road. Water buffalo and cattle were hauling carts through the mud. **No end and no beginning. Just carts loaded with everything they owned.** The old men and women, soaked through, walked along keeping the cattle moving.
> —ERNEST HEMINGWAY, *In Our Time*

The ability to judge the difference between an acceptable and unacceptable sentence fragment comes from much exposure to reading the work of skilled writers. Many instructors, therefore, often do not accept sentence fragments in student writing until a student can demonstrate the firm ability to write well-constructed complete sentences.

EXERCISE 5
Revise this paragraph to eliminate any sentence fragments. In some cases, you can join word groups to create complete sentences; in other cases, you have to revise the word groups into complete sentences. In the final version, check not only the individual sentences but also the clarity of the whole paragraph.

Students looking for jobs need more than the "Help Wanted" section of a newspaper. One major tool, a carefully written resumé. A resumé should be written in a standard form (see Chapter 35). And proofread carefully to eliminate errors in spelling, punctuation, or grammar. For the content of the resumé. Students should analyze all types of experiences. A resumé including not only paid jobs but also volunteer positions and extracurricular activities. Students have a better chance of getting a job. If they have supervised other people, handled money, or taken on highly responsible tasks. Such as participating in political campaigns or chairing major committees at school. Many employers will consider student resumés. Especially when the resumés include names of the students' supervisors.

EXERCISE 6

Revise this paragraph to eliminate any sentence fragments. In some cases, you can join word groups to create complete sentences; in other cases, you have to write new sentences. In the final version, check not only the individual sentences but also the clarity of the whole paragraph.

When most people need to earn a living. They look for a job. Interviewing for a job. Punctuality, a very important trait. Although arriving too early is not wise. Job candidates should greet the interviewer pleasantly. And use a firm handshake. To refrain from smoking. Called upon to discuss their backgrounds and experience. Job applicants should, above all, emphasize their strengths. To appear self-confident, without a trace of conceit. Interviewers appreciate people who answer questions directly and specifically. Job candidates who know when to leave. And thank the interviewer for his or her time. When the choice is between two candidates with similar credentials. A follow-up letter which can sometimes make the difference between getting a job or not.

14
COMMA SPLICES AND FUSED SENTENCES

A **comma splice,** also known as a **comma fault,** occurs when a comma by itself joins independent clauses°. The only time that a comma is correct between two independent clauses is when the comma is followed by a coordinating conjunction (*and, but, for, or, nor, yet,* and *so*). The word *splice* means "to fasten ends together." The end of one independent clause and the beginning of another cannot be fastened together with a comma alone.

> COMMA SPLICE   The hurricane intensified, it turned toward land.

A **fused sentence** occurs when two independent clauses are not separated by punctuation or joined by a comma with a coordinating conjunction. The word *fused* means "to unite as if by melting together." Two independent clauses cannot be united as if melted together. A fused sentence is also known as a **run-on sentence** or a **run-together** sentence.

> FUSED SENTENCE   The hurricane intensified it turned toward land.

Comma splices and fused sentences are two versions of the same problem: incorrect joining of two independent clauses. A fused sentence, however, reveals less awareness of the need for a separation between the independent clauses. Comma splices and fused sentences can be corrected in a variety of ways.

> The hurricane intensified. It turned toward land. [period]
>
> The hurricane intensified; it turned toward land. [semicolon]
>
> The hurricane intensified, and it turned toward land. [comma and coordinating conjunction]
>
> As the hurricane intensified, it turned toward land. [the first independent clause revised into a dependent clause°]
>
> The hurricane intensified as it turned toward land. [the second independent clause revised into a dependent clause°]
>
> The hurricane intensified; then it turned toward land. [semicolon and conjunctive adverb]

■|| 14a

Know how to recognize comma splices and fused sentences.

To recognize comma splices and fused sentences, you need to be able to recognize an independent clause. As was explained in 7e-1, an independent clause contains a subject° and predicate°. Also, an independent clause can stand alone as a sentence because it is an independent grammatical unit.

SUBJECT   PREDICATE

Thomas Edison   was an American inventor.

If you tend to write comma splices, here is a useful technique for proofreading your work. Cover all the words on one side of the comma and see if the words remaining constitute an independent clause. If they do, cover that clause and uncover all the words on the other side of the comma. If the second side of the comma is also an independent clause, you have written a comma splice. To further help yourself avoid writing comma splices, become familiar with correct uses for commas, explained in Chapter 24. Experienced writers sometimes use a comma to join very brief parallel° independent clauses: *Mosquitos do not bite, they stab.* Many readers, including most instructors, consider this form an error; therefore, use a semicolon or period instead of the comma.

If you tend to write fused sentences, you are ignoring the need to signal the end of one sentence before another one starts. If you

LEADING CAUSES OF COMMA SPLICES AND FUSED SENTENCES

1. **Pronouns.** A comma splice or fused sentence often occurs when the second independent clause starts with a pronoun.

> No   Thomas Edison was a productive inventor, **he** held over 1,300 U.S. and foreign patents.

> Yes   Thomas Edison was a productive inventor. **He** held over 1,300 U.S. and foreign patents.

2. **Conjunctive adverbs and other transitional expressions.** A comma splice or fused sentence often occurs when the second independent clause starts with a conjunctive adverb° (see page 148 for a list) or other transitional expression° (see page 84 for a list). Remember that these words are *not* coordinating conjunctions, so they cannot work in concert with a comma to join two independent clauses.

> No   Thomas Edison was a brilliant scientist, **however,** his schooling was limited to only three months of his life.

> Yes   Thomas Edison was a brilliant scientist. **However,** his schooling was limited to only three months of his life.

3. **Explanations or examples.** A comma splice or fused sentence often occurs when the second independent clause explains or gives an example of the information in the first independent clause.

> No   Thomas Edison was the genius behind many inventions, the phonograph and the incandescent lamp are among the best known.

> Yes   Thomas Edison was the genius behind many inventions. The phonograph and the incandescent lamp are among the best known.

are making this error because you are unsure about how to identify a complete sentence, use the Test for Sentence Completeness given in 13a.

You will also learn to avoid writing comma splices and fused sentences if you become aware that the majority of such errors occur for one of the three reasons listed on page 273.

▌▌ 14b
Use a period or semicolon to correct comma splices and fused sentences.

You can use a period or semicolon to correct comma splices and fused sentences. For the sake of sentence variety and emphasis, however, do not always choose punctuation to correct this type of error. Other methods are discussed in 14c and 14d. Strings of too many short sentences rarely establish relationships and levels of importance among ideas.

A **period** can separate the independent clauses in a comma splice or fused sentence.

COMMA SPLICE	The Muir Woods National Monument is located in central California, its dominant tree is the coast redwood.
FUSED SENTENCE	The Muir Woods National Monument is located in central California its dominant tree is the coast redwood.
CORRECTED	The Muir Woods National Monument is located in central California. Its dominant tree is the coast redwood.

A **semicolon** can separate independent clauses that are closely related in meaning. See also 25a.

COMMA SPLICE	The coast redwood is named "Sequoia" after a Cherokee Indian, he developed the first alphabet used by that tribe.
FUSED SENTENCE	The coast redwood is named "Sequoia" after a Cherokee Indian he developed the first alphabet used by that tribe.
CORRECTED	The coast redwood is named "Sequoia" after a Cherokee Indian; he developed the first alphabet used by that tribe.

The question mark and exclamation point also signal the ends of independent clauses.

▉‖ 14c

Use coordinating conjunctions to correct comma splices and fused sentences.

When ideas in independent clauses are closely related and grammatically equivalent, you might decide to connect them with a coordinating conjunction. If you are correcting a comma splice, you can insert a coordinating conjunction and retain the comma. In correcting a fused sentence, you must insert a comma if you use a coordinating conjunction.

When using a coordinating conjunction, you need to be sure that it fits the meaning of the material. *And* signals addition; *but* and *yet* signal contrast; *for* and *so* signal cause; and *or* and *nor* signal alternatives. A sentence consisting of two independent clauses joined by a coordinating conjunction and a comma is called a **compound sentence** (7f-2). ▉ PUNCTUATION ALERT: Use a comma before a coordinating conjunction that links independent clauses (see 24a). ▉

COMMA SPLICE	Redwood trees can grow to over 300 feet in height and up to 16 feet in diameter, their seeds are only a sixteenth of an inch long.
FUSED SENTENCE	Redwood trees can grow to over 300 feet in height and up to 16 feet in diameter their seeds are only a sixteenth of an inch long.
CORRECTED	Redwood trees can grow to over 300 feet in height and up to 16 feet in diameter, **but** their seeds are only a sixteenth of an inch long.
COMMA SPLICE	The foot-thick bark of the redwood tree is a barrier to destructive insects, the bitter chemicals and tannins in the bark further discourage insects and fungi.
FUSED SENTENCE	The foot-thick bark of the redwood tree is a barrier to destructive insects the bitter chemicals and tannins in the bark further discourage insects and fungi.
CORRECTED	The foot-thick bark of the redwood tree is a barrier to destructive insects, **and** the bitter chemicals and tannins in the bark further discourage insects and fungi.

EXERCISE 1

Revise any comma splices or fused sentences by using a period, a semicolon, or a coordinating conjunction (and a comma, if the sentence is fused). If an item is correct, circle its number.

EXAMPLE   Cattle rustlers were common figures in the Old West, they wore eye masks and rode dark horses.

Cattle rustlers were common figures in the Old West. They wore eye masks and rode dark horses.

1. Today cattle rustling remains a thriving business, it does not depend on horses and cowboys.

2. Modern rustlers are a far cry from their Old West predecessors they use helicopters instead of horses.

3. Some cattle thieves even use computers, this modern technology helps them to steal more than $30 million worth of livestock per year.

4. Ranchers try to fight back, often by offering money for information, they also hire guards to patrol grazing land from airplanes.

5. Like the rustlers, ranchers take advantage of modern technology, some of them "brand" their cattle by implanting electronic computer chips which can be detected by portable sensors.

■‖ 14d

Revise one of two independent clauses into a dependent clause to correct a comma splice or fused sentence.

You can revise a comma splice or fused sentence by changing one of two independent clauses into a dependent clause. This method is suitable when one idea can be logically subordinated to the other. Sentences composed of one independent clause and one or more dependent clauses are called **complex sentences** (see 7f-3). ▮ PUNCTUATION ALERT: If you put a period after a dependent clause that is not attached to an independent clause, you will create the error called a sentence fragment (see Chapter 13). ▮

One way to create a dependent clause is to insert a subordinating conjunction in front of the subject and verb. When using a subordinating conjunction, be sure that it fits the meaning of the material. For example, *as* and *because* signal reason, *although* signals concession, *if* signals condition, and *when* signals time (see page 166 for a fuller list. ▮ PUNCTUATION ALERT: Always use a comma after an introductory dependent clause that starts with a subordinating conjunction. (see 24b-1). ▮

COMMA SPLICE   Gertrude Stein wanted to support struggling artists in the 1920s, she bought many paintings by Picasso and others.

FUSED SENTENCE   Gertrude Stein wanted to support struggling artists in the 1920s she bought many paintings by Picasso and others.

CORRECTED   **Because Gertrude Stein wanted to support struggling artists in the 1920s,** she bought many paintings by Picasso and others.

COMMA SPLICE   Gertrude Stein wrote many novels, short stories, essays, poems, plays, and one opera, she is better known for her art collection.

FUSED SENTENCE   Gertrude Stein wrote many novels, short stories, essays, poems, plays, and one opera she is better known for her art collection.

CORRECTED   Gertrude Stein wrote many novels, short stories, essays, poems, plays, and one opera **although she is better known for her art collection.**

A relative pronoun can also create a dependent clause. Commonly used relative pronouns are *who, which,* and *that.* ▋ PUNCTUATION ALERT: Use commas to set off nonrestrictive—nonessential—elements (see 24e). ▋

COMMA SPLICE   Gertrude Stein moved from America to Paris in 1902, she quickly became fascinated by impressionist painting.

FUSED SENTENCE   Gertrude Stein moved from America to Paris in 1902 she quickly became fascinated by impressionist painting.

CORRECTED   Gertrude Stein, **who moved from America to Paris in 1902,** quickly became fascinated by impressionist painting.

EXERCISE 2
Revise any comma splices or fused sentences.

Some legendary creatures such as leprechauns and vampires are strictly imaginary they cannot be accounted for by science. One fabled creature likely can be explained by reality, however, the facts have been distorted through the centuries. Unicorns are probably based on mountain goats viewed from far away. Goats sometimes lose a horn during a fight or in an accident, from a distance, the remaining horn appears to be centered on the goat's head. Another creature, the zombie, has origins in old West Indian superstitions, it can be explained by recent research on a fish common to West Indian waters. A zombie is supposedly a human corpse it roams around in a trance-like state ready to do the will of someone who has power over it. Pufferfish, also known as blowfish, contain a potent toxin that paralyzes nerves if the fish is cooked improperly, then a person who eats the fish will act like the traditional "living dead."

■‖ 14e

Use a semicolon or a period before a conjunctive adverb or other transitional expression between two independent clauses.

Conjunctive adverbs and other transitional expressions link ideas between sentences. Remember, however, that these words are *not* coordinating conjunctions, so they cannot work in concert with commas to join independent clauses. Conjunctive adverbs and other transitional expressions require that the previous sentence end in a period or semicolon.

Conjunctive adverbs include such words as *however, therefore, also, next, then, thus, furthermore,* and *nevertheless* (see page 148 for a fuller list). ‖ PUNCTUATION ALERT: Use a comma after a conjunctive adverb at the beginning of a sentence. ‖

COMMA SPLICE	Car theft has increased alarmingly in most major cities**, however,** one city has decided to fight back.
FUSED SENTENCE	Car theft has increased alarmingly in most major cities **however,** one city has decided to fight back.
CORRECTED	Car theft has increased alarmingly in most major cities. **However,** one city has decided to fight back.

Transitional expressions include *for example, for instance, in addition, in fact, of course,* and *on the other hand* (see page 84 for a fuller list). ‖ PUNCTUATION ALERT: Use a comma after transitional words at the beginning of a sentence. ‖

COMMA SPLICE	In Boston stolen car reports are broadcast over the radio**, in fact,** a police officer "deputizes" about 500,000 listeners to be on the alert for stolen vehicles.

FUSED SENTENCE	In Boston stolen car reports are broadcast over the radio **in fact,** a police officer "deputizes" about 500,000 listeners to be on the alert for stolen vehicles.
CORRECTED	In Boston stolen car reports are broadcast over the radio. **In fact,** a police officer "deputizes" about 500,000 listeners to be on the alert for stolen vehicles.

A conjunctive adverb or other transitional expression can appear in more than one location within an independent clause. In contrast, a coordinating conjunction can appear only between the independent clauses it joins.

Car theft has increased alarmingly in most major cities.
  One city, **however,** has decided to fight back.
Car theft has increased alarmingly in most major cities.
  One city has decided, **however,** to fight back.
Car theft has increased alarmingly in most major cities.
  One city has decided to fight back, **however.**
Car theft has increased alarmingly in most major cities, **but** one city has decided to fight back.

EXERCISE 3
Revise any comma splices or fused sentences caused by a conjunctive adverb or other transitional expression. If an item is correct, circle its number.

EXAMPLE   Old comic books can be very valuable, therefore, many people collect them.
Old comic books can be very valuable. Therefore, many people collect them.

1. Comic strips and comic books have been loved by some, however, others have viewed them as dangerous and degrading.
2. In recent years, television has been named as a bad influence on children; consequently, comics have not gotten as much attention.
3. In the 1950s, however, many parents believed that reading "Superman" and "Tales from the Crypt" would cause their children to grow up with distorted minds therefore, comic books were forbidden in many homes.
4. Some communities banned the sale of comic books, teachers and clergy, in addition, complained about the negative effects of comic books.
5. Comic books, nevertheless, have continued to be popular in fact, people are often amazed to discover that comic books were once objected to so fiercely.

EXERCISE 4
Revise all comma splices or fused sentences, using a different method of correction for each one. If an item is correct, circle its number.

EXAMPLE No two adults have exactly the same handwriting therefore, handwriting analysis can help solve crimes.
No two adults have exactly the same handwriting. Therefore, handwriting analysis can help solve crimes.

1. Children learn penmanship by consciously practicing how to form each letter, in a few years, however, their handwriting becomes automatic.
2. As people mature, their handwriting takes on unique traits, the slight variations in angles, slope, speed, and pressure become enormous.
3. Handwriting experts know how to recognize minute differences in letter and word spacing, in comparative sizes of letters, and in finger dexterity, furthermore, experts can see patterns in how people spell, punctuate, and use certain phrases.
4. Handwriting specialists working on criminal cases prefer not to make judgments based on a short sample they know that it gets harder to maintain a forged handwriting with each successive word.
5. Clifford Irving tried to forge the signature of Howard Hughes, and although the signatures look alike to most untrained eyes, trained investigators found many of Irving's personal handwriting traits in his forgery.

EXERCISE 5
Revise any comma splices and fused sentences, using as many different methods explained in this chapter as you can.

Most baseball fans know many amusing stories and wild tales about Casey Stengel, he could be a clown on the ball field but a great strategist behind the scenes. Stengel was born in Kansas City, Missouri, in 1890 he died in Glendale, California, in 1975, he had eighty-five years in between to devote to baseball. He claimed that he did not play golf or go to the movies, baseball was all that was left. In 1929 he was managing a last-place team called the Toledo Mud Hens, he was not, of course, very happy with their performance. He told the players that they should all get interested in the stock market; in fact, he told them to invest in Pennsylvania Railroad stock. He told the team that they had to improve, otherwise they would be riding trains out of town. The railroad would get many new customers, therefore, Stengel reasoned, the stock would go up. Baseball history does not reveal whether the players bought the stock, they did start playing better.

15
SENTENCES THAT SEND UNCLEAR MESSAGES

A sentence can seem structurally correct at first glance—as if no grammatical principles of English have been violated—but still have internal flaws that keep it from delivering a sensible message. To help you sort through the various ways that sentences can send unclear messages, here is a summary of the material covered in this chapter:

Section 15a	Shifts in person and number, subject and voice, tense and mood, and direct and indirect discourse
Section 15b	Misplaced modifiers
Section 15c	Dangling modifiers
Section 15d	Mixed sentences
Section 15e	Incomplete sentences

Most sentence flaws can be hard to spot because of the way the human brain works. When writers know what they mean to say, they sometimes misread what is on the paper for what they intend. The brain unconsciously "adjusts" an error or "fills in" missing material. Readers, on the other hand, see only what is on paper.

No	Heated for 30 seconds, you get bubbles on the surface of the mixture. [This sentence says *you* are heated for 30 seconds.]
Yes	After the mixture is heated for 30 seconds, bubbles form on the surface.
No	After you boil the mixture for two minutes, it is cooled in a test tube. [This sentence shifts from *you* to *it* and from the active to the passive voice.]
Yes	After you boil the mixture for two minutes, you cool it in a test tube.
Yes	After the mixture is boiled for two minutes, it is cooled in a test tube.
No	The chemical reaction taking place rapidly creates a salt. [Does *rapidly* refer to the pace of the reaction or to the speed at which the salt is created?]
Yes	The chemical reaction takes place rapidly and creates a salt.
Yes	The chemical reaction rapidly creates a salt.

If you make such errors and have trouble noticing them, what can you do to get yourself to "see" the flaws? Here are some suggestions.

1. Finish your revision well before its deadline so that you can put it aside and go back to it with fresh eyes that will pick up flaws more easily as you proofread.
2. Proofread by working backwards, from your last sentence to your first; this can help you see each sentence as a separate unit free of context that might trick your brain into overlooking flaws.
3. Ask your instructor or other experienced readers to check you, and then look over their findings and try to raise your consciousness about what went wrong.
4. Proofread an extra time exclusively for any error that you tend to make more than any other.

▆‖ 15a
Avoid unnecessary shifts.

Shifts within sentences blur meaning quickly. Readers expect to stay on the track you started them on. If you switch to another track, your readers become confused. Few readers have the patience to read material that seems garbled.

Unless the meaning or grammatical structure of a sentence requires it, always avoid shifting between person and number, subject and voice, and tense and mood. Also do not shift from indirect to direct discourse within a sentence without using punctuation and grammar to make the changes clear.

1
Stay consistent in person and number.

Person in English consists of the *first person* (I, we), who is the speaker; the *second person* (you), who is the person spoken to; and the *third person* (he, she, it, they), who is the person or thing being spoken about. Do not shift person within a sentence or a longer passage unless the meaning calls for a shift.

No   **They** enjoy feeling productive, but when a job is unsatisfying **you** usually become depressed. [*They* switches to *you*.]

Yes   **They** enjoy feeling productive, but when a job is unsatisfying **they** usually become depressed.

Number refers to one (singular) and more than one (plural). Do not start to write in one number and then shift suddenly to the other. Such shifting gives your sentences an unstable quality and your message becomes fuzzy.

No   By the year 2000, most **people** will live longer, and **an employed person** will retire later. [The plural *people* shifts to the singular *person*.]

Yes   By the year 2000, most **people** will live longer, and **employed people** will retire later.

A common cause of inconsistency in person and number is shifts to the second-person *you* from the first-person *I* or a third-person noun such as *person, the public,* or *people.* You will avoid this error in academic writing if you remember to reserve *you* for sentences that directly address the reader and to use third-person pronouns for general statements.

No   **I** enjoy reading forecasts of the future, but **you** wonder which will turn out to be correct. [*I*, first person, shifts to *you*, second person.]

Yes   **I** enjoy reading forecasts of the future, but **I** wonder which will turn out to be correct.

No   By the year 2000, **Americans** will pay twice today's price for a car, and **you** will get twice the gas mileage. [*Americans,* third person, shifts to *you,* second person.]

Yes   In 2000, **Americans** will pay twice today's price for a car, and **they** will get twice the gas mileage.

EXERCISE 1

Eliminate shifts in person and number. Be alert to shifts between, as well as within, sentences.

(1) Hyperactivity in children is a problem that affects up to 6 percent of young boys and girls, although a boy is more likely to be affected than a girl. (2) Teachers can find teaching hyperactive children difficult, especially if you do not know how to recognize the characteristics of such a child. (3) In one study, teachers called as many as 30 percent of their students hyperactive. (4) In school, these children may daydream excessively, fidget a great deal, or talk. (5) He shows other traits including tactlessly blurting out whatever is on their minds or racing around charging into people. (6) A hyperactive child is often impatient, cannot wait your turn, and are unable to follow directions. (7) New studies recently have been published. (8) It indicates that a key element in hyperactivity is a short attention span, possibly because we eat too much sugar.

‖ 2
‖ Stay consistent in subject and voice.

The **subject** of a sentence is the word or group of words that acts, is acted upon, or is described: *People laugh, people were entertained, people are nice.* A subject can shift within a sentence only if the meaning justifies the shift.

People look forward to the future, but **the future** holds many secrets.

Shifts in subjects, however, are rarely justified when they are accompanied by a shift in voice. The **voice** of a sentence is either **active** *(People expect changes in the future)* or **passive** *(Changes are expected in the future).* The active voice emphasizes the doer of an action, and the passive voice does not. Unnecessary shifts in subject and voice reflect a lack of planning that causes a sentence or longer stretch of writing to drift out of focus.

No   Most of **the people polled expect** major improvements by the year 2000, but some **hardships are anticipated.** [The subject shifts from *people* to *hardships,* and the voice shifts from active to passive.]

YES   Most of **the people polled expect** major improvements by the year 2000, but **they anticipate** some hardships.

No   When some **respondents consider** the year 2000, very optimistic **predictions are made.** [The subject shifts from *respondents* to *predictions,* and the voice shifts from active to passive.]

YES   When some **respondents consider** the year 2000, **they make** very optimistic predictions.

YES   Some **respondents consider** the year 2000 very optimistically.

3
Stay consistent in tense and mood.

Tense refers to the ability of verbs to show time. Tense changes are required when time movement is described: *We will go to the movies after we finish dinner.* If tense changes are illogical, sentence clarity suffers. (See 8h for guidance about correct sequences of tenses.)

No   The campaign in the United States to clean up the movies **began** in the 1920s as civic and religious groups **try** to ban sex and violence from the screen. [The tense shifts from the past *began* to the present *try.*]

YES   The campaign in the United States to clean up the movies **began** in the 1920s as civic and religious groups **tried** to ban sex and violence from the screen.

No   Producers and distributors **created** a film Production Code in the 1930s. At first, violating its guidelines **carried** no penalty. Eventually, however, films that **fail** to get the board's Seal of Approval **are not distributed** widely. [This shift occurs between sentences: the past tense *created* and *carried* shift to the present tense *fail* and *are not distributed.*]

YES   Producers and distributors **created** a film Production Code in the 1930s. At first, violating its guidelines **carried** no penalty. Eventually, however, films that **failed** to get the board's Seal of Approval **were not distributed** widely.

Mood refers to whether a sentence is a statement or question (indicative° mood), a command or request (imperative° mood), or a conditional or other-than-real statement (subjunctive° mood). Shifts among moods blur your message. The most common error in shifts is between the imperative and indicative, though other types sometimes occur.

NO   The Production code included two guidelines about violence. **Do not show** the details of brutal killings, and **movies should not be** explicit about how to commit crimes. [The verbs shift from the imperative mood *do not show* to the indicative mood *movies should not be.*]

YES   The Production code included two guidelines about violence. **Do not show** the details of brutal killings, and **do not be** explicit about how to commit crimes.

YES   The Production code included two guidelines about violence. **Movies should not show** the details of brutal killings, and **should not be** explicit about how to commit crimes.

NO   **If a movie were going to be shown** outside the United States, the **guidelines are** less strict. [The verbs shift from the subjunctive mood *if a movie were going to be shown* to the indicative mood *guidelines are.*]

YES   **If a movie were going to be shown** outside the United States, the **guidelines would be** less strict.

4
Avoid unmarked shifts between indirect and direct discourse within the same sentence.

Indirect discourse reports speech or conversation and is not enclosed in quotation marks. **Direct discourse** repeats speech or conversation exactly and encloses the spoken words in quotation marks. Sentences that merge indirect and direct discourse without quotation marks and other markers, confuse readers and distort the message.

No   Professor Anderson attributed acid rain specifically to carbon fuels but **are we ready to give them up?** [The first clause is indirect discourse; the second shifts to unmarked direct discourse.]

Yes   Professor Anderson attributed acid rain specifically to carbon fuels but **asked whether we are ready to give them up.** [This revision sustains indirect discourse.]

Yes   Professor Anderson attributed acid rain specifically to carbon fuels but **asked, "Do we really want to give them up?"** [This revision uses direct and indirect discourse correctly because the quotation marks and grammatical structures clearly signal which is which.]

EXERCISE 2

Revise these sentences to eliminate all incorrect shifts discussed so far in this chapter. Some sentences have several possible revisions.

EXAMPLE   British physicist J. H. Fremlin speculated that some day the world might be housed in a continuous 2,000-story building and did we understand that the building would cover our entire planet?

British physicist J. H. Fremlin speculated that some day the world might be housed in a continuous 2,000-story building *and asked whether we understood that the building would cover our entire planet.*

1. In 8000 B.C., five million people lived on earth, but about 10,000 years later the population grows to 500 million.
2. One expert pointed out that the population doubled only once every thousand years between 8000 B.C. and A.D. 1650 and did we realize that such a rate presented no problem in those days?
3. In 1850 the earth's population reaches one billion; it had doubled in 200 years.
4. The world needed only 80 years to double again by 1930, and you saw the next doubling 35 years later in 1965.
5. Some people think that space colonies will eventually relieve crowding on earth, but that possibility is doubted by me.

EXERCISE 3

Revise this paragraph to eliminate incorrect shifts. Be alert to shifts between, as well as within, sentences.

(1) The twentieth-century intercontinental traveler faces different challenges than their ancestors a hundred years ago. (2) The traveler a hundred

years ago crossed oceans on a slow ship that takes weeks to arrive at their destination. (3) Today's traveler, on the other hand, rides on a jet airliner that took only hours. (4) Nineteenth-century voyagers often encountered delays because of ocean storms, but today problems are caused for travelers by the speed of jet planes. (5) If travelers cross through several time zones in a few hours, jet lag may be experienced. (6) Victims of jet lag often feel weak, and sometimes you may be disoriented for days following the trip. (7) To help prevent jet lag, avoid alcoholic beverages while in flight. (8) Also you should get plenty of sleep the day before your intercontinental trip.

■‖ 15b
Avoid misplaced modifiers.

A **modifier** is a word, phrase°, or clause° that describes other words, phrases, or clauses. A **misplaced modifier** is a description incorrectly positioned in a sentence, thus distorting your meaning. As you write and revise, always check to see that your modifiers are placed as close as possible to what they describe so that your reader will attach the meaning where you intend it to be.

1
Avoid ambiguous placements.

With **ambiguous placement,** a modifier can refer to two or more words in a sentence.

Little limiting words (such as *only, just, almost, hardly, nearly, even, exactly, merely, scarcely, simply*) can change meaning according to where they are placed. When you use such words, position them precisely. Consider how the placement of *only* changes the meaning of this sentence: *Professional coaches say that high salaries motivate players.*

> **Only** professional coaches say that high salaries motivate players. [No one else says this.]
>
> Professional coaches **only** say that high salaries motivate players. [The coaches probably do not mean what they say.]
>
> Professional coaches say **only** that high salaries motivate players. [The coaches say nothing else.]
>
> Professional coaches say that **only** high salaries motivate players. [Nothing except high salaries motivates players.]
>
> Professional coaches say that high salaries **only** motivate players. [High salaries do nothing other than motivate players.]

Professional coaches say that high salaries motivate **only** players. [No others on the team, such as coaches and managers, are motivated by high salaries.]

Squinting modifiers also cause ambiguity. A squinting modifier can describe both what precedes and what follows it. Since a modifier cannot do double duty, either move the modifier to a position where its meaning will be precise or revise the sentence.

No   The high school star being recruited **actively** believed each successive offer would be better. [What was active— the recruitment or the star's belief?]

Yes   The high school star being recruited believed **actively** that each successive offer would be better.

Yes   The **actively** recruited high school star believed each successive offer would be better.

2
Avoid wrong placements.

With **wrong placement,** modifying words are misplaced in a sentence, thus garbling the meaning.

No   The history of college athletics sheds light on current policies and practices of college football **beginning in the nineteenth century.** [This sentence says that current policies and practices, not the history, started in the nineteenth century.]

Yes   The history of college athletics, **beginning in the nineteeth century,** sheds light on current policies and practices of college football.

No   Most college athletic departments in the 1920s evolved from academic divisions, **especially those with large football programs.** [This sentence says that academic divisions, not athletic departments, had football programs.]

Yes   Most college athletic departments in the 1920s, **especially those with large football programs,** evolved from academic divisions.

3
Avoid awkward placements.

Awkward placements are interruptions that seriously break the flow of a message.

A **split infinitive** is one type of awkward placement. An **infinitive** is a verb form that starts with *to: to convince, to create*. When material comes between the *to* and its verb, it can interrupt meaning, particularly when the intervening material could easily go before or after the infinitive.

> **No**   Orson Welles's radio drama "War of the Worlds" managed **to,** on October 30, 1938, **convince** listeners that they were hearing an invasion by Martians.
>
> **Yes**   On October 30, 1938, Orson Welles's radio drama "War of the Worlds" managed **to convince** listeners that they were hearing an invasion by Martians.

Often the intervening word that splits an infinitive is an adverb ending in -*ly*. Many such adverbs sound awkward unless they are placed either before or after the infinitive.

> **No**   People feared they would no longer be able **to happily live** in peace.
>
> **Yes**   People feared they would no longer be able **to live happily** in peace.

Nevertheless, sometimes an adverb seems awkward in any position except between *to* and the verb. Many readers, therefore, accept split infinitives like these:

> The starship Enterprise on "Star Tek" was charged **"to boldly go. . . ."**
>
> Welles wanted **to realistically portray** a Martian invasion for the radio audience.

If you think your readers prefer that infinitives never be split, you can usually revise the sentence to avoid the split:

> Welles wanted his "Martian invasion" to sound realistic to the radio audience.

Interruptions of **subjects and verbs** by highly complex phrases° or clauses° disturb the smooth flow of a sentence.

> **No**   **The announcer,** because the script, which Welles wrote himself, called for perfect imitations of emergency announcements, **opened** with a warning that included a description of the "invasion."
>
> **Yes**   Because the script, which Welles wrote himself, called for perfect imitations of emergency announcements, **the announcer opened** with a warning that included a description of the "invasion."

When a **verb phrase** (a group of words that functions as verb in a sentence: *was kissed, had been kissed*) is interrupted by words unrelated to the time sequence of the verb, the sentence lurches instead of flows.

No   People who tuned in late to "The War of the Worlds" believed that New Jersey **had,** by Martians bent on destruction, **been invaded.**

Yes People who tuned in late to "The War of the Worlds" believed that New Jersey **had been invaded** by Martians bent on destruction.

No   Police switchboards **were,** not surprisingly, **jammed** with frantic phone calls.

Yes Not surprisingly, police switchboards **were jammed** with frantic phone calls.

When a verb and its object are interrupted by words that should modify both those elements, clarity often suffers.

No   Many churches **held** for their frightened communities **"end of the world" prayer services.**

Yes Many churches **held "end of the world" prayer services** for their frightened communities.

EXERCISE 4
Revise these sentences to correct any ambiguous, wrong, or awkward placements. If a sentence is correct, circle its number.

EXAMPLE   Experience makes only college registration easier.
          Only experience makes college registration easier.

1. Many students have, before they begin college, an ideal image of college life.
2. The first challenge is to, without feeling hesitant or losing your temper, enroll in required classes.
3. At some colleges, freshman courses because of overenrollment fill up very quickly.
4. If a course you want has, in spite of your having planned to take it, been closed, you have to think of alternatives.
5. You might consider bringing your problem, even though it is unlikely to be solved unless you are an isolated case, to the registrar.
6. The registrar, in consultation with each department, plans the number of sections that will be offered for each class in advance.

7. Therefore, you should, as much as prerequisites will permit, go to registration with alternate plans for your schedule.

8. Colleges that use on-line computer registration regularly have easier procedures for students.

9. Upper-class students have to, because they must take courses in their majors, be sure to get into the classes they need.

10. Once classes begin, registration, with its long lines, frustrations, and disappointments, often fades into memory.

EXERCISE 5
Combine each list of words or word groups to create all the possible logical sentences. Each list offers more than one possibility. Explain any differences in meaning among the alternatives you create.

EXAMPLE   college graduates
             on the average
             than do high school graduates
             earn more money

a. On the average, college graduates earn more money than do high school graduates.

b. College graduates earn more money, on the average, than do high school graduates.

c. College graduates, on the average, earn more money than do high school graduates.

1. the microbiologist
   frequently
   new
   to explore
   old
   used
   problems
   methods

2. to become
   engineering
   medicine
   the student
   a biomedical engineer
   studied
   successfully
   and

3. eagerly
   the computer specialists
   to solve problems
   worked
   artificial intelligence
   in
   only

4. know
   scientists
   that
   smoking
   lung
   not
   causes
   only
   cancer

15c

Avoid dangling modifiers.

A **dangling modifier** modifies what is implied but not stated in a sentence. Dangling modifiers can be hard for a writer to spot, because the writer's brain tends to supply the missing material, thereby allowing the error to go unnoticed.

No Reading Faulkner's short story "A Rose for Emily," the ending surprised us.

This sentence says that the ending is doing the reading. The implied subject of the modifier is *we,* but nowhere is that subject stated—thus the modifier dangles. You can correct a dangling modifier by revising the sentence so that the intended subject is expressed.

Yes Having read Faulkner's short story "A Rose for Emily," we were surprised by the ending.

Yes We read Faulkner's short story "A Rose for Emily" and were surprised by the ending.

No Shocked by her father's death, the family home became a refuge for Emily. [*The family home* cannot be shocked.]

Yes Shocked by her father's death, Emily took refuge in the family home.

No When courting Emily, the townspeople gossiped about her. [*The townspeople* were not courting Emily.]

Yes When Emily and Homer Barron were courting, the townspeople gossiped about her.

Dangling modifiers sometimes result from unnecessary use of the passive voice°.

No To earn money, china-painting lessons were offered by Emily to wealthy young women. [*China-painting lessons* cannot earn money.]

Yes To earn money, Emily offered china-painting lessons to wealthy young women.

293

EXERCISE 6

Identify and correct any dangling modifiers in these sentences. If a sentence is correct, circle its number.

EXAMPLE Assigned to interview an unfriendly person, the experience can be instructive to a student journalist.
Assigned to interview an unfriendly person, *a student journalist can find the experience instructive.*

1. To be successful, careful plans must be made by the student journalist.
2. Being tense, the interview might begin on the wrong note for an inexperienced journalist.
3. Until relaxed, questions should mention only neutral topics.
4. After the journalist is more at ease, the person being interviewed might also relax.
5. With a list of questions, the interview process goes more smoothly for everyone involved.
6. Although easy to answer, mistakes are sometimes made on factual questions by a hostile interviewee.
7. By being analytic and evaluative, those mistakes can reveal a great deal to an experienced journalist.
8. Knowing how to pace an interview, the hard questions are more likely to be answered honestly after the interviewee has been caught off guard.
9. Until an interview is complete, the seasoned journalist always remains alert.
10. Essential information might be revealed when leaving.

■∥ 15d
Avoid mixed sentences.

A **mixed sentence** has two or more parts that do not make sense together.

∥ 1
Revise mixed constructions.

A **mixed construction** starts out taking one grammatical form and then changes, derailing the meaning of the sentence.

No   Because television's first transmissions in the 1920s included news programs became popular with the public. [The opening subordinate clause is fused with the independent clause that follows. What does the writer want to emphasize—the first transmissions or the popularity of news programs?]

Yes   Television's first transmissions in the 1920s included news programs, which quickly became popular with the public. [The idea of the first transmissions is now emphasized. *Because* has been dropped, making the first clause independent; and *which* has been added, making the second clause subordinate and logically related to the first.]

No   By doubling the time allotment for network news to thirty minutes increased the prestige of network news programs. [A prepositional phrase, such as *by doubling,* cannot be the subject of a sentence.]

Yes   Doubling the time allotment for network news to thirty minutes increased the prestige of network news programs. [Dropping the preposition *by* clears up the problem.]

Yes   By doubling the time allotment for network news to thirty minutes, the network executives increased the prestige of network news programs. [Inserting a logical subject, *the network executives,* clears up the problem; an independent clause is now preceded by a modifying prepositional phrase.]

The phrase *the fact that* is sometimes the cause of a mixed sentence. Most writers prefer to avoid the expression.

No   The fact that quiz show scandals in the 1950s prompted the networks to produce even more news shows.

Yes   The fact is that quiz show scandals in the 1950s prompted the networks to produce even more news shows.

Yes   Quiz show scandals in the 1950s prompted the networks to produce even more news shows.

2
Revise faulty predication.

Faulty predication, sometimes called **illogical predication,** occurs when a subject and its predicate (the part of the sentence that says something about the subject) do not make sense together.

295

No	The **purpose** of television **was invented** to entertain people.
Yes	The **purpose** of television **was** to entertain people.
Yes	**Television was invented** to entertain people.

One key cause of illogical predication is a breakdown in the connection between a subject and its complement. A **complement** renames or describes the subject; it follows a form of a verb such as _be,_ which acts like an equal sign: _The student is happy_ (student = happy).

No	Walter Cronkite's outstanding characteristic as a newscaster was credible.

The subject of this sentence is _characteristic_. While _credible_ can rename (and would complement) a person, it cannot rename (or complement) a characteristic. A suitable renaming of a characteristic is _credibility._

Yes	Walter Cronkite's outstanding characteristic as a newscaster was credibility.

Illogical predication is the problem in most constructions that begin **is when** or **is where.** Avoid these constructions in academic writing.

No	A disaster **is when** television news shows get some of their highest ratings.
Yes	Television news shows get some of their highest ratings during a disaster.

Similarly, avoid **reason . . . is because** in academic writing.

No	**One reason** television news captured national attention **is because** it covered the Vietnam War thoroughly.
Yes	**One reason** television news captured national attention **is that** it covered the Vietnam War thoroughly.
Yes	Television news captured national attention **because** it covered the Vietnam War thoroughly.

EXERCISE 7
Revise the mixed sentences below so that the beginning of each sentence fits logically with its end. If a sentence is correct, circle its number.

EXAMPLE   As a result of an archaeologist's discovery of an ancient grave site often provides important physical evidence of a past society.
An archaeologist's discovery of an ancient grave site often provides important physical evidence of a past society.

1. Archaeology is when you study the material remains, relics, artifacts, and monuments of past human life.
2. The reason that grave sites are important is because archaeologists can infer a great deal about a society from the way it buried its dead.
3. By comparing grave sites of other civilizations with burial places of North American civilization suggests interesting hypotheses about our society.
4. Among the conclusions such a study will produce include noting how democratic modern-day burials have become.
5. In an Egyptian pharaoh's desire to please the gods might demand as much as 40 percent of his country's gross national product to be spent on his burial.
6. By contrast, less that 0.2 percent of the gross national product of the United States is spent each year for all funerals.
7. The fact that China's first emperor, Qin Shihuangdi, was buried surrounded by an army of 7,500 terra cotta figures the extravagant interments favored by the ancient Chinese.
8. When George Washington, America's first president, was buried a simple ivy-covered tomb is a symbol of his country's values.
9. The fact that the Duke of Wellington was buried inside four nested coffins in a manner that the British felt would honor their beloved military hero.
10. Future archaeologists might compare Wellington's burial with burials in Arlington National Cemetery is where American military heroes are interred.

▮‖ 15e
Avoid incomplete sentences.

An **incomplete sentence** has missing words, phrases°, or clauses° necessary for grammatical correctness or sensible meaning. Such omissions quickly blur meaning.

1
Use elliptical constructions carefully.

An **elliptical construction** deliberately leaves out words that have already appeared in the sentence: *I have my book and Joan's [book]*. The paramount rule for an elliptical construction is that the words that are left out must be exactly the same as the words that do appear in the sentence.

No
> The first important jazz **period belongs** to Dixieland, and the later **periods** to diverse styles ranging from ragtime to classical. [The word *belongs* cannot take the place of *belong,* needed in the second clause.]

Yes
> The first important jazz **period belongs** to Dixieland, and the later **periods belong** to diverse styles ranging from ragtime to classical.

No
> During the 1920s in Chicago, the cornetist Manuel Perez **was leading** one outstanding jazz group, Tommy and Jimmy Dorsey another. [The words *was leading* cannot take the place of *were leading,* needed in the second clause.]

Yes
> During the 1920s in Chicago, the cornetist Manuel Perez **was leading** one outstanding jazz group; Tommy and Jimmy Dorsey **were leading** another.

Yes
> During the 1920s in Chicago, the cornetist Manuel Perez **led** one outstanding jazz group; Tommy and Jimmy Dorsey another. [The verb *led* works in both clauses, so it can be omitted from the second clause.]

No
> The period of the big jazz dance bands **began** and **lasted through** World War II. [This construction implies *began through* in the first clause, but *began* requires *in,* not *through.*]

Yes
> The period of the big jazz dance bands **began in** and **lasted through** World War II.

2
Make comparisons complete, unambiguous, and logical.

In writing a comparison, be sure to include all words needed to make clear the relationship between the items or ideas being compared.

No	Individuals with high concern for achievement make better business executives. [*Better* indicates a comparison, but none is stated.]
Yes	Individuals with high concern for personal achievement make better business executives than do people with little interest in getting ahead.
No	Most personnel officers value high achievers more than risk takers. [Not clear: more than risk takers value high achievers, or more than personnel officers value high achievers?]
Yes	Most personnel officers value high achievers more than they value risk takers.
Yes	Most personnel officers value high achievers more than risk takers do.
No	An achiever's chance of success in business is greater than a gambler. [*Chance* is compared to *a gambler;* a thing cannot be compared logically to a person.]
Yes	An achiever's chance of success in business is greater than a gambler's. [A correct elliptical construction, with the word *chance* omitted]
No	Achievers value success as much, if not more than, a high salary. [Comparisons using *as . . . as* require the second *as.*]
Yes	Achievers value success as much as, if not more than, a high salary.
No	Achievers have such a reputation for success. [In academic writing, intensifiers such as *such, so,* and *too* must be completed.]
Yes	Achievers have such a reputation for success that often they are offered jobs before they complete their formal educations.

3
Proofread carefully to catch inadvertently omitted articles, pronouns, conjunctions, and prepositions.

Small words—articles, pronouns, conjunctions, and prepositions—that are needed to make sentences complete, sometimes slip into the cracks. If you tend inadvertently to omit words, proofread your work an extra time solely to find them.

No   On May 2, 1808, citizens Madrid rioted against French soldiers.

Yes   On May 2, 1808, **the** citizens **of** Madrid rioted against French soldiers.

No   On following day, captured rioters were taken into country and shot.

Yes   On **the** following day, captured rioters were taken into **the** country and shot.

No   The Spanish painter Francisco Goya recorded both the riot the execution in a pair of pictures painted 1814.

Yes   The Spanish painter Francisco Goya recorded both the riot **and** the execution in a pair of pictures painted **in** 1814.

EXERCISE 8
Revise this paragraph for correct elliptical constructions and complete comparisons. Also, insert any missing small words.

(1) Trained criminal investigators often value bits of glass as evidence more than eyewitness reports about crimes. (2) Information about the force and direction the impact that broke the glass creates a unique identification. (3) The chances of finding useful fingerprints at the scene of a robbery are less than glass from a broken window or glassware. (4) Often, glass fragments cling to robbers' clothes or a shard of glass to their shoes. (5) In many hit-and-run accidents, investigators use pieces of headlights or windshields evidence. (6) Because glass is so common in our society, being able to physically fit together pieces of glass offers best possibility of useful evidence, while making chemical matches the least.

IV ‖ WRITING EFFECTIVE SENTENCES

16
CONCISENESS

Conciseness describes writing that is direct and to the point. Writing that is not concise is wordy. It forces readers to clear away excess words before sentences can deliver their messages.

WORDY PARAGRAPH

Every once in a while you will find that there is a day when everything seems to run very smoothly and even the riskiest of ventures seems to have come out exactly right. You may exclaim as a result of this, "This seems to be a lucky day for me!" Then, as an afterthought after such an utterance, you may say to yourself, "Knock on wood!" Of course, it is not really a situation where you believe that danger would actually be warded off if you happen to knock on wood. Still, you can be given a slight uneasy feeling because of boasting about your own luck, and so you go ahead and see that the little protective ritual is carried out. If someone were to challenge you at that moment, probably you would quickly rush to say, "Oh, that's nothing. Just an old superstition."

Wordy, indirect writing irritates readers. In contrast, concise writing, appeals to readers because it is direct.

CONCISE ORIGINAL PARAGRAPH

Once in a while there is a day when everything seems to run smoothly and even the riskiest venture comes out exactly right. You exclaim, "This is my lucky day!" Then as an afterthought you say, "Knock on wood!" Of course, you do not really believe that knocking on wood will ward off danger. Still, boasting about your own good luck gives you a slightly uneasy feeling—and you carry out the little protective ritual. If someone challenged you at that moment, you would probably say, "Oh, that's nothing. Just an old superstition."

—MARGARET MEAD AND RHODA METRAUX, "New Superstitions for Old"

Good writers stand behind the principle of conciseness—and illustrate it as well.

If it is possible to cut out a word, then always cut it out.
—GEORGE ORWELL, "Politics and the English Language"

Omit unnecessary words.
—WILLIAM STRUNK JR. AND E. B. WHITE, *The Elements of Style*

16a
Eliminate wordy sentence structures.

Wordy sentence structures, including expletive and passive constructions, can make writing seem abstract and uninteresting.

1
Revise unnecessary expletive constructions.

An **expletive** postpones the subject and diminishes its effect by putting *it* or *there* plus a form of the verb *be* before the subject. If you remove the expletive and revise slightly, you give the subject—and the entire sentence—greater power.

No   It is necessary for students to fill out both registration forms.

YES   Students must fill out both registration forms.

No   There are three majors offered by the computer science department.

Yes   Three majors are offered by the computer science department.

Yes   The computer science department offers three majors.

2
Revise unnecessary passive constructions.

In the **active voice,** the subject of a sentence *does* the action named by the verb.

Active   In *My Fair Lady,* **Professor Higgins teaches** Eliza to speak "proper" English. [*Professor Higgins* is the subject, and he does the action: he *teaches.*]

In the **passive voice,** the subject of a sentence *receives* the action named by the verb.

Passive   In *My Fair Lady,* **Eliza is taught** to speak "proper" English by Professor Higgins. [*Eliza* is the subject, and she receives the action: she *is taught.*]

For most writing, the active voice adds liveliness as well as conciseness. One way to revise from the passive to the active voice is to make the doer of the action the subject of the sentence. For example, when a passive construction names the doer of an action, it does so in a phrase starting with *by.* Therefore, make the noun or pronoun in the *by* phrase the sentence subject.

No   Volunteer work **was done by the students** for credit in sociology. [The students are doers of the action, but they are not the subject of the sentence.]

Yes   The **students did** volunteer work for credit in sociology.

No   The new spending bill **was vetoed by the governor.** [The governor is the doer of the action, but he is not the subject of the sentence.]

Yes   The **governor vetoed** the new spending bill.

Sometimes you can revise a sentence from passive to active by finding a new verb, especially when you want to keep the same subject.

PASSIVE	Britain **was defeated** by the United States in the war of 1812.
ACTIVE	Britain **lost** the war of 1812 to the United States.
PASSIVE	Hundreds of soldiers **were stricken** with yellow fever.
ACTIVE	Hundreds of soldiers **caught** yellow fever.

Writers use the passive voice when the doer of an action is unknown or when naming the doer would disrupt the focus they want a sentence to have. (The passive voice occurs often in science writing, as is discussed in Chapter 34d.) In situations that do not call for the passive voice, writers sometimes deliberately use it for sentence after sentence in the mistaken belief that it sounds "mature" or "academic." When the doers of the action are important, as in the following example, you should use the active voice.

No	One very important quality developed by an individual during a first job is self-reliance. This strength was gained by me when I was allowed by my supervisor to set up and conduct my own survey project.
YES	During their first job, many individuals develop the very important quality of self-reliance. I gained this strength when my supervisor allowed me to set up and conduct my own survey project.
YES	During a first job, many people develop self-reliance, as I did when my supervisor let me set up and conduct my own survey project.

One important caution about the passive voice: Do not use it to hide information about who acts. For example, a report might say this:

> Cracks in the foundation of the structure had been found in 1984, but these problems were not considered serious.

Left out of this sentence is possibly important information about who found cracks and who decided the cracks were not serious. Such omissions may be intentional; writers may choose the passive voice to sound impersonal or objective. In most cases, however, use of the passive voice creates distorting omissions of information. For more advice on acceptable uses of the passive voice, see Voice, page 205.

3
When possible, combine sentences, reduce clauses to phrases, and reduce phrases to words.

Clarity is among your main concerns during revision. Often when you see the need for conciseness, you can combine sentences or reduce a clause to a phrase or reduce a phrase to a single word. When you aim for conciseness, often you also achieve better clarity.

Combining sentences

When you revise, look carefully at sets of sentences in your draft. You may be able to reduce the information in one sentence to a group of words that you can include in another sentence.

TWO SENTENCES
The *Titanic* was discovered seventy-three years after being sunk by an iceberg. The wreck was located in the Atlantic by a team of French and American scientists.

COMBINED SENTENCE
Seventy-three years after being sunk by an iceberg, the *Titanic* was located in the Atlantic by a team of French and American scientists.

TWO SENTENCES
These scientists used several million dollars worth of equipment to locate the wreck. This electronic equipment included sonar devices.

COMBINED SENTENCE
These scientists used several million dollars worth of electronic equipment, including sonar devices, to locate the wreck.

TWO SENTENCES
The stern of the ship was missing and there was some external damage to the hull. Otherwise, the Titanic seemed to be in excellent condition.

COMBINED SENTENCE
Aside from its missing stern and external damage to its hull, the *Titanic* seemed to be in excellent condition.

You will find more advice about reducing sentence structures and combining and subordinating information in Chapter 17.

Reducing clauses

You can often reduce adjective clauses (7e-2) to phrases, sometimes just by dropping the opening relative pronoun° and its verb.

The *Titanic,* **which was a huge ocean liner,** sank in 1912.
The *Titanic,* **a huge ocean liner,** sank in 1912.

Sometimes you can reduce the clause to a single word.

The scientists held a memorial service for the passengers and crew members **who had died.**
The scientists held a memorial service for the **dead** passengers and crew members.

Creating elliptical constructions° is another way to reduce clauses, but be sure to omit only clearly implied words.

When they were confronted with disaster, some passengers behaved heroically, **while others behaved selfishly.**
Confronted with disaster, some passengers behaved heroically, **others selfishly.**

Keep your meaning clear when you reduce clauses. Making your writing concise should never make it hard to understand.

Reducing phrases

Sometimes you will be able to reduce phrases to shorter phrases or to single words.

Although loaded with luxuries, the liner was thought to be unsinkable.
The **luxury** liner was thought to be unsinkable.

Over fifteen hundred **travelers on that voyage** died in the shipwreck.
Over fifteen hundred **passengers** died in the shipwreck.

Objects found inside the ship **included unbroken** bottles of wine and expensive **undamaged** china.
Found undamaged inside the ship were bottles of wine and expensive china.

4
Use strong verbs and avoid nouns formed from verbs.

Your writing will have more impact when you choose strong verbs—verbs that directly convey an action. *Be* and *have* are not strong verbs. When you revise weak verbs to strong ones, you will often reduce the number of words in your sentences.

WEAK VERB
The proposal before the city council **has to do with** locating the sewage treatment plant outside city limits.

STRONGER VERB
The proposal before the city council **suggests** locating the sewage treatment plant outside city limits.

WEAK VERBS
The board members **were of the opinion** that the revisions in the code **were not** changes they could accept.

STRONGER VERBS
The board members **said** they **could not accept** the revisions in the code.

When you look for weak verbs to revise, look too for nominals—nouns derived from verbs, often by adding suffixes° such as *-ance, -ment,* or *-tion.* To achieve conciseness, try turning a nominal back into a verb, thus reducing words and gaining impact.

No   We **oversaw the establishment of** a student advisory committee.

Yes   We **established** a student advisory committee.

No   The building **had the appearance of** being renovated.

Yes   The building **appeared** to be renovated.

EXERCISE 1
Combine each set of sentences. Eliminate wordy constructions, such as expletives and unnecessary passives, and condense clauses and phrases.

EXAMPLE   An occurrence in the nineteenth century in America was the springing up of various mining towns across the United States. These towns were noted by all as being usually both flamboyant and short-lived.

A variety of flamboyant, short-lived mining towns sprang up in nineteenth-century America.

1. It was in the late 1800s that a town which was known as Leadville developed in Colorado. The town developed as the result of the discovery of silver.

2. Other towns in various areas of the country grew rapidly as the result of gold and silver mines. It can be seen that Leadville was no exception to this general rule.

3. There were thousands of people flocking into Leadville. As was the case in many other mining towns, a large variety of colorful characters were soon to be seen.

4. One of the most famous citizens to be found in Leadville was H. A. W. Tabor. He was originally a citizen of Vermont. He and two other men all owned a mine called the Little Pittsburg. The mine brought fortunes to all three men.

5. It was because of the Little Pittsburg that Tabor grew very wealthy. After that he continued to prosper in other investments. He was eventually elected by the citizens of Colorado to be their Lieutenant Governor.

6. But eventually Tabor, like many other men, was made bankrupt by a silver panic in the 1980s. Before he died, he warned his second wife, Elizabeth, not to sell a mine they still owned called the Matchless Mine. He told her that someday it would make her another fortune.

7. But Tabor was wrong. When the formerly wealthy Elizabeth McCourt Doe Tabor died, she was living in great poverty in a cabin by the Matchless Mine. She died in her eighties.

8. The life story of the Tabors was colorful enough that it was captured in an opera. The opera was called *The Ballad of Baby Doe,* and it was composed by Douglas Moore.

9. Many well-known names are associated with Leadville, which seems to have been visited by a wide range of people in the nineteenth century. They included the poet and playwright Oscar Wilde, suffragette Susan B. Anthony, and the well-known western figure Doc Holliday.

10. Leadville was, however, a typical mining town in what happened to it. It sprang up suddenly, it had for a short time a vivid and exciting history, and then it faded away. Now the town of Leadville can be seen as being a shadow of its former self, but there is still the memory of its former more colorful days.

■|| 16b
Eliminate unneeded words.

Unneeded words clutter your writing. Always eliminate them to achieve conciseness. Also, imprecise language creates wordiness.

A writer may use six inexact words when one precise word would work better.

When a writer tries to write very formally or tries to reach an assigned word limit, **padding** usually results. Sentences are loaded down with **deadwood**—empty words and phrases that increase the word count but lack meaning. Deadwood never substitutes for more ideas or more evidence. If you find deadwood, clear it away.

PADDED	~~In fact~~, the television station ~~which was situated in the local area~~ had won ~~a great~~ many awards ~~as a result of its having been involved in the~~ coverage of ~~all kinds of~~ controversial issues.
CONCISE	The local television station had won many awards for its coverage of controversial issues.
PADDED	~~In a manner of speaking,~~ the PTA ~~could be seen as having~~ cancelled the play ~~due to the pressure~~ of financial problems.
CONCISE	The PTA cancelled the play because of financial problems.
PADDED	The bookstore ~~entered the order for~~ the books ~~that the instructor has said will be utilized in~~ the course ~~sequence~~.
CONCISE	The bookstore ordered the books for the course.

Clearing out deadwood may require a few structural changes in sentences, such as the addition of *because* in the example about the PTA. Still, the final version is shorter than the original.

Sentences loaded with empty words can damage an entire paragraph by hiding the message in distracting language.

WORDY VERSION

Computers are good at some things, and people are good at some things, but as a matter of fact, the things people and computers are good at tend to be rather different. It is clear that computers have good memories. It is also true that computers are fast, consistent, and reliable. However, as of yet, it appears that computers are not creative and they are also not able to adapt readily to novel and unusual situations. It can be seen that people have memories that are poor. People are also slow, seldom do something in the same manner twice, and are unreliable in nature, but they can also be viewed as adaptable and full of creativity. Computers seem on the whole to belong to a totally different race when considered in comparison with people. It would be a wonderful ideal to consider the possibility of designing and creating systems wherein these two groups can complement and wed together the talents which each one of them has.

CONCISE ORIGINAL VERSION

What computers are good at and what people are good at tend to be different. Computers have good memories and are fast, consistent, and reliable but as yet are not creative or readily able to adapt to novel situations. People have poor memories, are slow, seldom do things the same way twice, and are unreliable, but they are adaptable and creative. Computers are a different race from people. It is a wonderful ideal to design systems wherein these two can complement and wed their talents.

—THOMAS B. SHERIDAN, "Computer Control
and Human Alienation"

Here is a list of worst-offender empty words, showing how they are often used and how they can be revised.

GUIDE FOR ELIMINATING EMPTY WORDS AND PHRASES

EMPTY WORD OR PHRASE	WORDY EXAMPLE	REVISION
as a matter of fact	*As a matter of fact*, statistics show that many marriages end in divorce.	Statistics show that many marriages end in divorce.
because of the fact that	*Because of the fact that* a special exhibit is scheduled, the museum will be open until ten o'clock.	Because of a special exhibit, the museum will be open until ten o'clock.
case	*In the case of* the proposed water tax, residents were very angry.	Residents were very angry about the proposed water tax.

16b

EMPTY WORD OR PHRASE	WORDY EXAMPLE	REVISION
exist	The crime rate that *exists* is unacceptable.	The crime rate is unacceptable.
factor	The project's final cost was an essential *factor* to consider.	The project's final cost was essential to consider.
for the purpose of	Work crews were dispatched *for the purpose of* fixing the potholes.	Work crews were dispatched to fix the potholes.
in a very real sense	*In a very real sense,* the drainage problems caused the house to collapse.	The drainage problems caused the house to collapse.
in fact	*In fact,* the physicist published her results yesterday.	The physicist published her results yesterday.
in view of the fact that	*In view of the fact that* the rainfall was so heavy, we had flooding.	Because the rainfall was so heavy, we had flooding.
manner	The child touched the snake in a reluctant *manner*.	The child touched the snake reluctantly.
nature	His comment was of an offensive *nature*.	His comment was offensive.
seems	It *seems* that the union called a strike over health benefits.	The union called a strike over health benefits.
tendency	The team had a *tendency* to lose home games.	The team often lost home games.
that is to say	*That is to say* that we cannot afford a strike.	We cannot afford a strike.

the point I am trying to make	*The point I am trying to make* is that news reporters should not invade people's privacy.	News reporters should not invade people's privacy.
to get to the point	*To get to the point,* the crime rate is going up.	The crime rate is going up.
type of	Gordon took a relaxing *type of* vacation.	Gordon took a relaxing vacation.
what I mean to say	*What I mean to say* is that I expect a bonus.	I expect a bonus.

EXERCISE 2

Eliminate unnecessary words or phrases. Be especially alert for empty words that add nothing to meaning.

EXAMPLE   If in fact it seemed that you had to be the one to award a prize to the most famous detective in the world, which one would you choose?

If you had to award a prize to the world's most famous detective, which one would you choose?

In a very real sense, Sherlock Holmes is probably the best known fictional detective in all the world. Readers and moviegoers alike are in fact likely to feel a sense of recognition when they hear the phrase "Elementary, my dear Watson," or see a pipe and deerstalker cap. Sherlock Holmes, of course, is widely noted for his ability to combine a variety of obscure clues and come to a correct conclusion which is of such a nature as to totally astound his readers. His companion, Dr. Watson, is unfortunately remembered for his tendency to jump to conclusions and the situation of his complete inability to understand what Holmes is doing. Sherlock Holmes was born, that is to say he was created by the pen of Sir Arthur Conan Doyle, in 1887 with the publication of A Study in Scarlet. It seems that Holmes's popularity with his readers grew very quickly. Doyle tried to kill off his creation by a type of a situation in which it seemed that Holmes had been killed by his chief foe, Professor Moriarty, but fans in several countries protested. Eventually Sherlock Holmes was brought back by his creator. In fact, Doyle himself is now long since dead, but Holmes continues to capture the hearts of readers with his exploits.

313

▇‖ 16c
Revise redundancies.

Planned repetition can create a powerful rhythmic effect (see 19f), but the dull drone of unplanned repetition can undermine writing. Unplanned repetition is called **redundancy.** A redundant phrase gives your message at least twice.

No   Bringing the project to **final completion** three weeks early, the new manager earned our **respectful regard.**

Yes   **Completing** the project three weeks early, the new manager earned our **respect.**

No   **Astonished,** the architect **circled around** the building in **amazement.**

Yes   **Astonished,** the architect **circled** the building.

Yes   The architect **walked around** the building **in amazement.**

Notice how redundancies deaden a sentence's impact.

No   The council members **proposed a discussion** of the amendment, but that **proposal for a discussion** was voted down after they had **discussed** it for a while.

Yes   The council members' proposal to discuss the amendment was eventually voted down.

No   The package, **rectangular in shape,** lay on the counter.

Yes   The rectangular package lay on the counter.

No   We need **an addition** on the math building for **additional space.**

Yes   The math building needs an addition.

EXERCISE 3
Eliminate redundant words and phrases. Then revise the paragraph so that it is concise.

EXAMPLE   The possibility that brain development continues into adulthood has fascinated and intrigued many scientists, but yet clear proof has continued to be difficult to find.

The possibility that brain development continues into adulthood has intrigued many scientists, but proof is difficult to find.

For a long period of many years, many people have believed that the brain reaches its height and peak of development and growth sometime in late childhood. But recent studies with rats, however, suggest the implication that a stimulating environment can cause positive changes and transformations in brain cells. This is to an extent due to experiments in California involving rats. These experiments used rats which were in terms of rat age equivalent to humans in their seventies in age. Some of the rats were placed in bare, lonely cages, while the other rats were placed in cages where there were also to be found other rats and a variety of toys. The rats living in the stimulating environment with toys and other rats were the ones whose brains showed positive changes. It still does seem nevertheless to be true that the effect of a challenging environment on the brain decreases as the brain gets older. But these new and innovative theories about later brain development suggest that the brain is far more flexible than was usually thought by most people.

EXERCISE 4
Rewrite this paragraph, making it clear and concise.

Among the authors of detective fiction who are popular and well-known is the British writer Agatha Christie. In Christie's books, she generally writes about one of her two major detectives, Hercule Poirot and Jane Marple. These two detectives both have their own fans among detective fiction readers, but the two of them are actually quite different as far as personality and temperament are concerned. Poirot it seems does his detective work as a private detective who sees as the basis and foundation of his investigations the use of method, order, and mental kinds of activity—what he calls the "little grey cells." The other detective, Jane Marple, on the other hand, is quite different. She is a seemingly fragile elderly woman who is shown as living alone in the small English village of St. Mary Mead. Whereas Poirot is the type of person who is hired by clients to investigate specific cases, murder seems to be inevitably drawn toward the person of Jane Marple. Her assistance is sought by friends, relatives, and some police detectives, and she always manages as a matter of fact to provide the answer to the puzzle. It often happens in the novels that she is able to see through the confusion of tricky and misleading clues because of the fact that she compares events and people linked to the crime to events and people she is familiar with in St. Mary Mead.

17
COORDINATION AND SUBORDINATION

Coordination and subordination help writers communicate relationships between two or more ideas. **Coordination** uses grammatical equivalency to communicate a balance or sequence in ideas. **Subordination** puts an idea to which the writer wants to give less importance in a dependent clause° and puts the more important idea in an independent clause°.

TWO IDEAS	The sky became dark gray. The air stilled ominously.
COORDINATED VERSION	The sky turned dark gray, and the air stilled ominously.
SUBORDINATED VERSION	As the sky turned dark gray, the air stilled ominously. [The *air* is the focus.]
SUBORDINATED VERSION	As the air stilled ominously, the sky turned dark gray. [The *sky* is the focus.]

This chapter explains how coordination and subordination make it possible for your writing style to work in concert with the meaning that you want to deliver.

▮‖ COORDINATION

A **coordinate sentence** is also known as a **compound sentence.** It consists of grammatically equivalent independent clauses° joined by a semicolon or a coordinating conjunction *(and, but, for, or, nor, yet,* or *so).* Coordination can produce harmony by bringing together related but separate elements to function smoothly in unison. The compounding of a sentence must be justified by its meaning, for coordinate sentences communicate balance or sequence in ideas they contain.

COORDINATE (COMPOUND) SENTENCE

	, **and**	
	, **but**	
	, **for**	
Independent clause	, **nor**	independent clause.
	, **or**	
	, **so**	
	, **yet**	
	;	

MEANING OF THE COORDINATING CONJUNCTIONS

Conjunction	Meaning	Function
and	also, in addition to	to join
but	however	to contrast
for	because	to show cause
nor	an additional negative	to make the second element negative
or	an alternative	to show more than one possibility
so	therefore	to show result
yet	nevertheless	to contrast

Each coordinating conjunction has a specific meaning that establishes the relationship between the ideas in a coordinate sentence.

The sky became dark gray, **and** the air stilled ominously.

The November morning had just begun, **but** it looked like dusk.

Shopkeepers closed their stores early, **for** they wanted to get home.

■‖ PUNCTUATION ALERT: Always use a comma before a coordinating conjunction that joins two independent clauses. ‖■

■‖ 17a
Use coordinate sentences to show relationships.

Coordination communicates relationships among ideas more effectively than does a group of separate sentences—except when you want occasionally to use a string of short sentences for impact. (For advice on how to handle such a technique well, see 19a.)

UNCLEAR RELATIONSHIPS
We decided not to go to class. We planned to get the notes. Everyone else had the same plan. Most of us ended up failing the quiz.

CLEAR RELATIONSHIPS
We decided not to go to class, **but** we planned to get the notes. Everyone else had the same plan, **so** most of us ended up failing the quiz.

Be sure to employ coordination sparingly so that you do not bore your reader with an unbroken rhythm. Also use subordination.

■‖ 17b
Use coordinate sentences for occasional effect.

Consider the following passage in which the writers use coordinate sentences to communicate an unfolding of events.

The first semester of my junior year at Princeton University is a disaster, **and** my grades show it. D's and F's predominate, **and** a note from the dean puts me on academic probation. Flunk one more course, **and** I'm out.

—JOHN A. PHILLIPS and DAVID MICHAELS, "Mushroom: The Story of an A-Bomb Kid"

Coordinate structures can be effective for joining ideas not ordinarily associated, thus surprising or amusing the reader. Consider the irony communicated through coordination in this passage.

> On August 27, 1947, a multimillionaire and a bull killed each other in Linares, Spain, and plunged an entire nation into deep mourning. The bull's name was Islero, **and** he was of the miura strain. The man's name was Manolete, **and** he was the essence of everything Spanish.
>
> —BARNABY CONRAD, *La Fiesta Brava*

F. Scott Fitzgerald (as well as Ernest Hemingway) often used coordination in his fiction to achieve dramatic effect. Consider this passage by Fitzgerald in which coordination underlines the contrasts in the scene.

> It was a hidden Broadway restaurant in the dead of night, **and** a brilliant and mysterious group of society people, diplomats, and members of the underworld were there. A few minutes ago the sparkling wine had been flowing, **and** a girl had been dancing gaily upon a table, **but** now the whole crowd were hushed and breathless.
>
> —F. SCOTT FITZGERALD, "The Freshest Boy"

■■ ‖ 17c
Avoid misusing coordination.

‖ 1
‖ **Avoid illogically coordinated sentences.**

Coordination is illogical when ideas in the compounded independent clauses are not related. Your reader expects one part of a coordinate construction to lead logically to the other.

No   Computers came into common use in the 1970s, and they sometimes make costly errors.

The statement in each independent clause is true, but the ideas are not related. The date computers became commonly used is unrelated to their making errors. The two ideas should not be coordinated.

YES   Computers came into common use in the 1970s, but they have not been improved sufficiently to prevent occasional costly errors.

2
Avoid overusing coordination.

Like all good techniques, coordination can be used too often. Overused coordination can create "babble"—the writing that results from putting down whatever comes into a writer's head, without later revision to ensure that the meaning justifies the compounding. Readers become impatient with "babble." They quickly lose interest when they have to figure out what the writer meant, or indeed if the writer had a clear idea in mind in the first place.

> **No**   Dinosaurs could have disappeared for many reasons, and one theory holds that the climate suddenly became cold, and another theory suggests that a sudden shower of meteors and asteroids hit the earth, so the impact created a huge dust cloud that caused a false winter. The winter lasted for years, and the dinosaurs died, for most of the vegetation they lived on died out.

> **Yes**   Dinosaurs could have disappeared for many reasons. One theory holds that the climate suddenly became cold, and another suggests that a sudden shower of meteors and asteroids hit the earth. The impact created a huge dust cloud that caused a false winter. The winter lasted for years, killing most of the vegetation that dinosaurs used for food.

In the corrected version, the sentences deliver their meanings clearly.

Writers also overuse coordination if they fail to feature some ideas more prominently than others. Such undifferentiated writing tends to drone monotonously.

> **No**   Laughter seems to help healing, so many doctors are prescribing humor for their patients, and some hospitals are doing the same. Comedians have donated their time to several California hospitals, and the nurses in one large hospital in Texas have been trained to tell each patient a joke a day.

> **Yes**   Laughter seems to help healing. Many doctors and hospitals are prescribing humor for their patients. Comedians have donated their time to several California hospitals, and the nurses in one large hospital in Texas have been asked to tell each patient a joke a day.

In the corrected version, some ideas are kept separate and some are put into a coordinate sentence.

320

EXERCISE 1

Revise these sentences to eliminate illogical or overused coordination. If you think a sentence needs no revision, circle its number.

EXAMPLE   Automation has come to many American factories, so computer-driven robots do the work, and the job gets done quickly, but fewer people are needed in those factories.

Automation has come to many American factories. Computer-driven robots do the work. The job gets done quickly, but fewer people are needed in those factories.

1. General Electric has a new automated locomotive plant, and it is located in Erie, Pennsylvania, and it is an example of what American factories will look like in the twenty-first century.
2. Tools are selected for machining, and they are inserted into machines, and then 2,500-pound castings are made, but no employees work in this section of the factory.
3. General Electric employs 8,000 workers, but the machining operation at the locomotive plant requires only a computer technician and two semi-skilled workers.
4. To do the same work, the factory used to employ seventy workers, and they had to work sixteen days to do each casting, but now computers and robots do all the work, and the company produces the same item in just sixteen hours.
5. American factories use robots, and as of 1985 they had about 13,000 robots in operation, but the Japanese were leading the world in robot production, for they already had more than 40,000 in use.

EXERCISE 2

Revise this paragraph. Choose which ideas seem to have equal weight and could therefore be contained in compound sentences. Your final version should have no more than two compound sentences—all other sentences should be left as they are.

Many modern couples choose traditional weddings. Some do not. Some couples are very sentimental about how they met. They decide to have unique marriage ceremonies. For example, a firefighter and his fiancée exchanged vows in a burning building. Two marathon runners got married while participating in a race. An adventurous couple said "I do" as they parachuted from an airplane. One modern wedding reportedly took place in a California hot tub. The guests and the Justice of the Peace got into the water with the bride and groom. Perhaps the next unusual wedding will be in outer space.

▮‖ SUBORDINATION

A sentence with some information **subordinated** contains (1) an **independent clause,** which stands on its own as a complete grammatical unit and (2) one or more phrases or clauses that cannot stand alone as a sentence. (When a sentence contains one independent and at least one **dependent clause,** it is called a **complex sentence.**)

Subordination weaves elements together so that one idea is featured, in the independent clause, and others are subordinated. What information you choose to subordinate depends on what meaning you want a sentence to deliver.

Adverb clauses are dependent clauses that start with **subordinating conjunctions,** such words as *after, before, until, when, so that,* and *although.* An adverb clause usually occurs before or after the independent clause.

SENTENCES WITH ADVERB CLAUSES

Adverb clause, independent clause.
Independent clause, **adverb clause.**
Independent clause **adverb clause.**

After the sky grew dark, the air stilled ominously.

Birds stopped singing, **as they do during an eclipse.**

The shopkeepers closed early **because they wanted to get home before the storm began.**

▮‖ PUNCTUATION ALERTS: (1) When a dependent clause that starts with a subordinating conjunction occurs before the independent clause, separate the clauses with a comma. (2) When an adverb clause follows the independent clause, separate these clauses with a comma *unless* the adverb clause is essential to the meaning of the independent clause. (See 24e.) ▮‖

Each subordinating conjunction has a specific meaning that establishes a relationship between the clause and the independent clauses.

Another pattern of subordination is created by **relative pronouns°,** such as *who, which,* and *that. Who* refers to people (and

SUBORDINATING CONJUNCTIONS AND THE RELATIONSHIPS THEY IMPLY

TIME	*after, before, once, since, until, when, whenever, while*
REASON OR CAUSE	*as, because*
RESULT OR EFFECT	*in order that, so, so that, that*
CONDITION	*if, even if, provided that, unless*
CONCESSION	*although, even though, though, whether*
LOCATION	*where, wherever*
CHOICE	*rather than, than, whether*

sometimes to animals with names or special talents); *which* refers to animals or things; *that* refers to animals, things, and sometimes to a collective or anonymous group of people. **Adjective clauses** start with relative pronouns. Adjective clauses are dependent clauses. They either follow or interrupt the independent clauses they modify.

SENTENCES WITH ADJECTIVE CLAUSES

Independent clause **restrictive adjective clause.**

Independent clause, **nonrestrictive adjective clause.**

Beginning of independent clause **restrictive adjective clause** end of independent clause.

Beginning of independent clause, **nonrestrictive adjective clause,** end of independent clause.

The weather forecasts warned of a storm **that might bring a thirty-inch snowfall.**

Spring is the season for tornados, **which terrify me.**

Anyone **who lives through a tornado** recalls the experience.

The sky, **which had been clear,** was turning gray.

▮▮ PUNCTUATION ALERT: When an adjective clause is nonrestrictive—that is, when the clause is not essential to the meaning of the sentence—separate it from the independent clause with commas. ▮▮

■‖ 17d

Use subordination to show relationships.

Subordination directs your readers' attention to the idea in the independent clause while at the same time using the idea in the dependent clause to provide context and support. Consider these examples (the dependent clauses are in boldface).

> **As soon as I saw the elephant,** I knew with perfect certainty that I ought not to shoot it.
> —GEORGE ORWELL, "Shooting an Elephant"

> **When I think of hills,** I think of the upward strength I tread upon. **When water is the object of my thought,** I feel the cool shock of the plunge and the quick yielding of the waves that crisp and curl and ripple above my body.
> —HELEN KELLER, *The World I Live In*

Subordination usually communicates relationships among ideas more effectively than does a group of separate sentences. (You may want to use an occasional string of short sentences for impact. For advice on how to handle short sentences well, see 19a.)

UNCLEAR RELATIONSHIPS

In 1888, two cowboys had to fight a dangerous Colorado snowstorm. They were looking for cattle. They came to a canyon. They saw outlines of buildings through the snow. Survival then seemed certain.

CLEAR RELATIONSHIPS

In 1888, two cowboys had to fight a dangerous Colorado snowstorm **while they were looking for cattle. When they came to a canyon,** they saw outlines of buildings through the snow. Survival then seemed certain.

In the clearer version the first four short sentences have been combined into two subordinate sentences. The last sentence is left short for dramatic impact.

■‖ 17e

Choose the subordinate conjunction appropriate to your meaning.

Subordinating conjunctions are your allies in communicating the relationship between major and minor ideas in sentences. Refer to the chart on page 323 for the relationship implied by various subordinating conjunctions. Each of the following sentences, deals with a similar idea. However, each has a different meaning because of the influence of the subordinating conjunction.

> **After you have handed it in,** you cannot make any changes in your report. [time limit]
>
> **Because you have handed it in,** you cannot make any changes in your report. [reason]
>
> **Unless you have handed it in,** you cannot make any changes in your report. [condition]
>
> **Although you have handed it in,** you can make changes in your report. [concession]
>
> I want to read your report **so that I can evaluate it.** [purpose]
>
> **Since you handed in your report,** three more people have handed in theirs. [time]
>
> **Since I have not seen the report,** I cannot comment on it. [condition]

EXERCISE 3

Combine each pair of sentences, using an adverb clause to subordinate one idea. Then revise each sentence so that the adverb clause becomes the independent clause. Refer to the list of subordinating conjunctions on page 323.

EXAMPLE   The days of Captain Hook are gone forever. Pirates still sail the oceans.

   a: *Although the days of Captain Hook are gone forever, pirates still sail the oceans.*

   b: *Although pirates still sail the oceans, the days of Captain Hook are gone forever.*

1. Blackbeard has been dead for over a hundred years. His modern counterparts tyrannize today's shipping companies.
2. Modern pirates feel free to use commando tactics. No ship is safe from these buccaneers.
3. Pirates of yesteryear looked for gold. Modern buccaneers often look for drugs as their treasure.
4. People thought that government ships were safe from pirate raids. A Navy cargo ship was robbed of nearly $20,000.
5. The raiders were silent and stealthy. None of the crew ever saw them.

325

EXERCISE 4

Combine each pair of sentences, using an adjective clause to make one idea subordinate to the other. Then revise each sentence so that the adjective clause becomes the independent clause. Use the relative pronoun given in parentheses.

EXAMPLE   Rembrandt was a seventeenth-century Dutch painter. Rembrandt is probably the most widely known artist of the baroque period. (who)

    a: *Rembrandt, who was a seventeenth-century Dutch painter, is probably the most widely known artist of the baroque period.*

    b: *Rembrandt, who is probably the most widely known artist of the baroque period, was a seventeenth-century Dutch painter.*

1. Rembrandt had a vibrant talent. Rembrandt's talent was demonstrated early in his life. (that)
2. Rembrandt was happily married. Rembrandt was financially successful and creatively vigorous. (who)
3. "The Night Watch" became one of Rembrandt's most famous canvases. "The Night Watch" was commissioned in 1642. (which)
4. For centuries "The Night Watch" was a misunderstood and neglected painting. "The Night Watch" became covered with yellowish varnish and layers of dirt. (which)
5. Experts finally came into possession of the painting after World War II. The experts thoroughly cleaned and restored the huge thirteen-foot canvas to its original brilliance and detail. (who)

17f

Avoid misusing subordination.

1

Avoid illogical subordination.

Subordination is illogical when the subordinating conjunction does not make clear the relationship between the independent and dependent clause.

No   Because he was deaf when he wrote them, Beethoven's final symphonies were masterpieces.

The above sentence is illogical because it was not Beethoven's deafness that led to his writing symphonic masterpieces.

YES   Although Beethoven was deaf when he wrote his final symphonies, they are musical masterpieces.

‖ 2
‖ **Avoid overusing subordination.**

Like all good writing techniques, subordination can be over-used. Too many images or ideas may crowd together, confusing readers and making them lose track of the message. If you have used more than two subordinating conjunctions or relative pronouns in a sentence, check carefully to see if your meaning is clear.

> **No** A new technique for eye surgery, which is supposed to correct nearsightedness, which previously could be corrected only by glasses, has been developed, although many doctors do not approve of it because it can create unstable eyesight.

> **Yes** A new technique for eye surgery, which is supposed to correct nearsightedness, has been developed. Previously, nearsightedness could be corrected only by glasses. Because it can create unstable eyesight, many doctors do not approve of it, however.

In the revised version the first sentence has a relative clause, the second is a simple sentence°, and the third has a dependent clause starting *Because*. Some words have been moved to new positions. The revision communicates its message more clearly because it provides a variety of sentence structures (see 19a) while avoiding the density of overused subordination.

EXERCISE 5
Correct illogical or excessive subordination in this paragraph. As you revise, use not only some short sentences but also some correctly constructed adverb clauses. Also, you can apply the principles of coordination discussed in 17a–17c.

Although some experts question the value of traditional fairy tales, most parents continue to read their old favorites to their children. For instance, some experts think that fairy tales are too scary because they have characters like witches and dragons which often frighten little children who are not yet mature enough to understand the difference between fantasy and reality, while other experts object to the theme of the "handsome prince and beautiful princess" theme which many fairy tales feature because the princess is always shown as weak while the prince is always depicted as infallibly strong so that children get a distorted impression about what they should expect of themselves and the opposite sex.

327

■‖ 17g
Achieve a balance between subordination and coordination.

Coordination and subordination are not always used in separate sentences. Compound-complex sentences°, for example, combine coordination with subordination.

> **When two Americans look searchingly into each other's eyes,** emotions are heightened, and the relationship tipped toward greater intimacy.
> —FLORA DAVIS, "How to Read Body Language"

Varying sentence types improves your ability to emphasize key points in your writing. Consider the following paragraph which demonstrates a good balance between simple sentences, compound sentences°, and sentences with dependent, as well as independent, clauses:

> As a paleoanthropologist—one who studies the fossils of human ancestors—I am superstitious. Many of us are because the work we do depends a great deal on luck. The fossils we study are extremely rare, and quite a few distinguished paleoanthropologists have gone a lifetime without finding a single one. I am one of the more fortunate. This was only my third year in the field at Hadar, and I had already found several. I know I am lucky, and I don't try to hide it. That is why I wrote "feel good" in my diary. When I got up that morning, I felt it was one of those days when you should press your luck.
> —DONALD JOHANSON, *Lucy: The Beginnings of Humankind*

EXERCISE 6

Using subordination and coordination, combine these sets of short, choppy sentences.

EXAMPLE   Some people love their cars. Some people give their cars pet names.

Because some people love their cars, they like to give them pet names.

1. Five-figure prices are for new cars. The prices are shocking. The prices may keep you away from the showrooms.
2. Perhaps you should lease your next car. You may pay less as a down payment. You may pay less each month.

328

3. You are a potential customer. Potential customers should shop carefully. You may find a particularly good arrangement. The arrangement might save you money.

4. Ten years ago only one in every ten private cars was leased. In 1984, one of every six private cars was leased. By now many more drivers favor car leasing.

5. Leasing has become popular with many drivers. It is particularly popular with young professionals. They want to save their money for necessities or other luxuries.

6. You may want a particular make of car. You can lease it from a new car dealer. You can lease it from a company. The company specializes in leasing.

EXERCISE 7
Using topics of your choosing, imitate the style of two different examples shown in this chapter. Choose from Fitzgerald, Keller, or Johanson.

18
PARALLELISM

Parallelism, related to the concept of parallel lines in geometry, calls for the use of equivalent grammatical forms to express equivalent ideas.

To line up a putt correctly, **examine** the grain of the grass, **observe** the contours of the green, and **gauge** the slope between the ball and the cup. [The same part of speech—all verbs in the present tense—introduces each parallel word group.]

An **equivalent grammatical form** is a word or group of words that matches—is parallel to—the structure of a corresponding word or group of words. When you are expressing similar information or ideas in your writing, parallel sentence structures echo that fact.

PARALLEL WORDS

Recommended exercise includes

running,	The *ing* words are parallel
swimming,	in structure and equal in
and	importance.
cycling.	

PARALLEL PHRASES

Exercise helps people
to maintain healthy bodies
and
to handle mental pressures. ||| The phrases are parallel in structure and equal in importance.

PARALLEL CLAUSES

Many people begin to exercise
because they want to look healthy,
because they need to have
stamina,
and
because they hope to live longer. ||| The clauses starting with *because they* are parallel in structure and equal in importance.

This chapter explains how parallelism helps you avoid the error of **faulty parallelism**—using nonequivalent grammatical patterns—and lets you strengthen your writing with the style and grace of parallel forms.

■|| 18a
Use words in parallel form.

Words in parallel structures must occur in the same grammatical form. Be sure to use matching forms for parallel items.

No   The strikers had tried **pleading, threats,** and **shouting.**

Yes   The strikers had tried **pleading, threatening,** and **shouting.**

Yes   The strikers had tried **pleas, threats,** and **shouts.**

Parallelism offers you a writing style that uses rhythm to help deliver the meaning of a sentence.

Briefly, solemnly, and **sternly,** they delivered their awful message.
——JAMES ANTHONY FROUDE, "The Execution of Queen Mary"

If Froude had expressed the same idea without using parallelism, his message would have been weaker. If he had used an ordinary sentence such as "They were stern and solemn as they delivered their awful message," his words would have lost their opportunity

331

to unfold ominously to the reader—just as surely as did the "awful message" to Queen Mary. Froude's placing the three parallel words first in his sentence also contributed to their impact.

■ ‖ 18b
Use phrases and clauses in parallel form.

Phrases and clauses in parallel structures must occur in the same grammatical form. Be sure to use matching forms for parallel items.

> No   The committee members **read the petition, were discussing its arguments,** and **the unanimous decision was to ignore it.**

> Yes   The committee members **read the petition, discussed its arguments,** and unanimously **decided to ignore it.**

‖ 1
Use the rhythm of parallel phrases and clauses for impact.

Deliberate repetition of word forms, word groups, and sounds creates a rhythm that underlines the message your sentence delivers. This technique can be highly effective as long as you do not overuse it.

> Go back to Mississippi, go back to Alabama, go back to South Carolina, go back to Georgia, go back to Louisiana, go back to the slums and ghettos of our northern cities, knowing that somehow this situation can and will be changed.
> —MARTIN LUTHER KING, JR., "I Have a Dream"

If King had expressed the same idea without parallelism, his message would have been weaker. His words reinforce the power of his message. An ordinary sentence would have been less effective: "Return to your homes in Mississippi, Alabama, South Carolina, Georgia, Louisiana, or the cities, and know that the situation will be changed."

2
Arrange parallel elements from least to most important.

Arranging elements from least to most important is called **climactic order** because the material builds to a climax. Parallel structures in climactic order are particularly effective.

> You can fool some of the people all of the time, and all of the people some of the time, but you cannot fool all of the people all of the time.   —ABRAHAM LINCOLN

3
Use parallel forms in balanced sentences.

Balanced sentences use parallel structures to enhance the message of compared or contrasted ideas.

> The limits of my language stand for the limits of my world.
> —LUDWIG WITTGENSTEIN

> Ask not what your country can do for you, but what you can do for your country.   —JOHN F. KENNEDY

■‖ 18c
Be aware that certain words call for parallel structures.

1
Use parallel forms with coordinating conjunctions.

Whenever you join words, phrases, or clauses with coordinating conjunctions *(and, but, for, or, nor, yet, so),* be sure that they occur in parallel form.

> You come to understand what to expect when you **tease a cat, or toss a pebble** in a pool, **or touch a hot stove.**
> —ANN E. BERTHOFF, *Forming, Thinking, and Writing*

2
Use parallel forms with paired words (correlative conjunctions).

Be sure to use parallel form when you link elements of a sentence with pairs of words known as **correlative conjunctions,** such as *both . . . and, not only . . . but also, either . . . or, neither . . . nor.*

> Writing permits us to understand **not only** the world **but also** the self.
> —ERIKA LINDEMANN, *A Rhetoric for Writing Teachers*

3
Repeat certain words to begin parallel elements.

To enhance the effect of parallelism, you can intentionally repeat certain words that begin parallel phrases or clauses. Such words include prepositions°, articles *(a, an, the),* and the *to* of the infinitive°.

> **To assign** unanswered letters their proper weight, **to free us** from the expectations of others, **to give us** back to ourselves— here lies **the great, the singular** power of self-respect.
> —JOAN DIDION, "On Self-Respect"

Because repetition can create dull prose, the technique has to be used carefully. The Didion passage avoids monotony by mixing parallel repetition with much variety in her other word choices. Consider the rich combination in this famous passage:

> It was the best of times, it was the worst of times, it was the age of wisdom, it was the age of foolishness, it was the epoch of belief, it was the epoch of incredulity, it was the season of Light, it was the season of Darkness, it was the spring of hope, it was the winter of despair, we had everything before us, we had nothing before us, we were all going direct to Heaven, we were all going direct the other way.
> —CHARLES DICKENS, *A Tale of Two Cities*

Dickens mixes repetition *(it was the)* with variety *(times, age, epoch, season)* and with contrasts *(best* and *worst, wisdom* and *foolishness, belief* and *incredulity, Light* and *Darkness, spring* and *winter, hope* and *despair, everything* and *nothing, Heaven* and *the other way).*

4

Use parallel clauses beginning with *and who, and whom,* or *and which* when they follow clauses beginning with *who, whom* or *which.*

I have in my own life a precious friend, a woman of 65 **who has** lived very hard, **who is** wise, **who listens** well, **who has** been where I am and can help me understand it; **and who represents** not only an ultimate ideal mother to me but also the person I'd like to be when I grow up.

—JUDITH VIORST, "Friends, Good Friends—and Such Good Friends"

■|| 18d

Use parallel sentences in longer passages for impact.

Parallel sentences in longer passages create a dramatic unity through carefully controlled repetition of words and word forms. Consider this rich passage of repeated words, concepts, and rhythms.

You ask me what is **poverty? Listen** to me. Here I am, dirty, **smelly,** and with no "proper" underwear on and with the **stench** of my rotting teeth near you. I will tell you. **Listen** to me. **Listen** without pity. I cannot use your pity. **Listen** with understanding. Put yourself in my dirty, worn-out, ill-fitting shoes, and hear me.

Poverty is getting up every morning from a dirt- and illness-stained mattress. The sheets have long since been used for diapers. **Poverty** is living in a **smell** that never leaves. **This is a smell** of urine, sour milk, and spoiling food sometimes joined with the strong **smell** of long-cooked onions. Onions are cheap. If you have **smelled** this **smell,** you did not know how it came. **It is the smell** of the out-door privy. **It is the smell** of young children who cannot walk the long dark way in the night. **It is the smell** of the mattresses where years of "accidents" have happened. **It is the smell** of the milk which has gone sour because the refrigerator long has not worked, and it costs money to get it fixed. **It is the smell** of rotting garbage. I could bury it, but where is the shovel? Shovels cost money.

—JO GOODWIN PARKER, "What Is Poverty?"

EXERCISE 1

Reread the Jo Goodwin Parker passage above. Discover all parallel elements in addition to those shown in boldface.

EXERCISE 2

Using topics of your choosing, imitate the writing style of three different passages shown in this chapter. Choose from King, Lincoln, Didion, Dickens, Viorst, or Parker.

EXERCISE 3

Revise these sentences to eliminate any errors in parallel structure.

EXAMPLE The Alabama Space and Rocket Center offers a Space Camp where participants hear lectures, are sampling astronaut training, and fly simulated missions.

The Alabama Space and Rocket Center offers a Space Camp where participants hear lectures, *sample* astronaut training, and fly simulated missions.

1. The Space Camp is open to adults, and children over ten years can attend.
2. The "campers" are people who want to experience a three-day educational fantasy, who can pay the $350 tuition, and they are willing to take part in serious role-playing.
3. Jerry Hill, the camp director, says that many participants always wanted to be astronauts, or learning about science and space is another reason many attend.
4. On the first day, participants take tests that determine what roles they will play and whether work in mission control or in the shuttle simulator will be their assignment.
5. The people assigned to the shuttle simulator perform scientific experiments, and then there is the Five Degrees of Freedom Chair and the Manned Maneuvering Unit in which they have to complete tasks as part of the extravehicular work.
6. Everyone agrees that the adults take their roles seriously and professionally, but liking to joke around is more of what the children do.

EXERCISE 4

Combine these sentences using techniques of parallelism.

EXAMPLE Many United States Presidents are famous for their political skill. Some of their unusual ways are not well known.

Many United States Presidents are famous *for* their political skill *but not for* their unusual ways.

1. John Quincy Adams, sixth U.S. President, read his Bible to start each day. Swimming in the nude each morning was also a daily routine.
2. William McKinley, twenty-fifth U.S. President, thought the red carnation he wore each day would bring him luck. It was also supposed to protect him from harm.
3. On September 6, 1901, after McKinley gave his lucky carnation to a little girl, an assassin stalked him. The assassin's shot wounded the President. He was killed.
4. The glare from a portrait of John Quincy Adams was annoying to Calvin Coolidge, thirtieth U.S. President. Coolidge called in an artist to paint hairs on Adams's shiny head.
5. William Henry Harrison, ninth U.S. President, gave the longest inaugural speech on record. It contained 8,500 words. Delivering it took two hours.
6. During Harrison's inauguration ceremonies it snowed. Harrison spoke without a coat. He was also hatless. He died one month later from pneumonia.

■‖ 18e
Use parallel structure for formal outlines and lists.

Items in formal outlines and lists must be parallel in structure. If the parallelism is faulty, the information fails to be clear to the reader and fails to communicate that the items are equally important. (For information about developing outlines, see pages 37–43.)

OUTLINE NOT IN PARALLEL FORM

Reducing Traffic Fatalities

I. Stricter laws
   A. Top speed on any highway should be 50 m.p.h.
   B. Higher fines
   C. Repeat offenders sentenced to jail
II. Legislating installation of safety devices
   A. All automobiles should be required to have safety belts in both front and back seats
   B. Making seat belt use mandatory for all drivers
   C. We should force auto manufacturers to offer airbags as an option in all cars

OUTLINE IN PARALLEL FORM

Reducing Traffic Fatalities

I. **Passing** stricter speed laws
  A. **Making** 50 m.p.h. top speed on any highway
  B. **Raising** fine for first-time speeding offenders
  C. **Requiring** jail sentences for repeat offenders
II. **Legislating** installation and use of safety devices
  A. **Requiring** all automobiles to have safety belts in front and back seats
  B. **Making** seat belt use mandatory for all drivers
  C. **Forcing** auto manufacturers to offer airbags as an option in all cars

Although the faulty outline might be useful as a scratch outline for a writer's private purposes in the early stages of the writing process, only the parallel outline communicates clearly to a reader. The parallel outline fills in the gaps of information and communicates equivalencies. The same principles apply to lists.

LIST NOT IN PARALLEL FORM

Workaholics share the following characteristics:

1. They are intense, energetic, competitive, and driven.
2. Strong self-doubters.
3. Labor is preferred to leisure by workaholics.
4. Workaholics: work any time and anywhere.
5. Making the most of their time.
6. Workaholics will blur the distinction between business and pleasure.

LIST IN PARALLEL FORM

Workaholics share the following characteristics:

1. **They are** intense, energetic, competitive, and driven.
2. **They have** strong self-doubts.
3. **They prefer** labor to leisure.
4. **They can—and do—work** any time and anywhere.
5. **They make** the most of their time.
6. **They blur** the distinction between business and pleasure.

The list not in parallel format appears disorganized and is more difficult and unpleasant to read. The list in parallel format carries the unspoken message that all these items are equivalent and contribute equally to the definition of a workaholic.

EXERCISE 5

Revise this outline into parallel form.

Problems in Weather Forecasting

I. Information unavailable from some areas
   A. Politics leads some countries not to cooperate.
   B. If war breaks out, no one communicates about the weather.
   C. Cost
II. Computer problems
   A. Computer repairs not easily available in remote areas.
   B. Unreliable computers send garbled messages.
III. Unstable atmosphere
   A. The weather is harsh.
      1. South Pole
      2. The North Pole is extremely cold and windy.
   B. Conditions shift suddenly.
   C. There is a lack of reliability over time.

EXERCISE 6

Find the parallel elements in the following examples. Next, using your own topics, imitate the style of two of the examples.

1. Our earth is but a small star in a great universe. Yet of it we can make, if we choose, a plane unvexed by war, untroubled by hunger or fear, undivided by senseless distinctions of race, color, or theory.

   —Stephen Vincent Benét

2. Difficult choices arise for all those who have promised to keep secret what they have learned from a client, a patient, or a penitent. How to deflect irate fathers asking whether their daughters are pregnant and by whom; how to answer an employer inquiring about the psychiatric record of someone on his staff; how to cope with questions from the press about the health of a Congressional candidate: such predicaments grow more common than ever.

   —Sissela Bok, *Lying*

3. I think I learned more from the town dump than I learned from school: more about people, more about how life is lived, not elsewhere but here, not in other times but now.

   —Wallace Stegner, "The Town Dump"

4. I have never been lonely in a cemetery. They are perfect places to observe the slow changing of the seasons, and to absorb human history—the tragedies and anguishes, the violences and treacheries, and always the guilts and sorrows of vanished people.

   —Willie Morris, "A Love That Transcends Sadness"

339

19
VARIETY
AND
EMPHASIS

Your writing style has **variety** when your sentence lengths and patterns vary. Your writing style is characterized by **emphasis** when your sentences are constructed to communicate the relative importance of the ideas. This chapter discusses both variety and emphasis. Together they affect how form and meaning are unified.

Consider the following passage, which successfully employs key techniques of variety and emphasis. The authors vary their sentence length (19a), include a variety of structures (19b), and use different kinds of modifiers in various positions (19d).

> Henri Poincaré, a famous mathematician who lived in the nineteenth century, devised an exercise in imagination to help people understand the relativity of measures. Imagine that one night while you were asleep everything in the universe became a thousand times larger than before. Remember this would include electrons, planets, all living creatures, your own body, and all the rulers and other measuring devices in the world. When you awoke, could you tell that anything had changed? Is there any experiment you could make to prove that some change had occurred? According to Poincaré there is no such experiment.

> —Judith and Herbert Kohl, *The View from the Oak*

The techniques of variety and emphasis rarely emerge from a writer's pen (or fingers on a keyboard) in final form. Most writers attend to such matters during the revision process.

■‖ 19a
Vary sentence length.

If you vary your sentence length, you communicate clear distinctions among ideas so that your readers can understand the focus of your material. Also, you avoid the unbroken rhythm of monotonous sentence length—a trait that eventually lulls a reader into losing attention.

‖ 1
Revise strings of too many short sentences.

Strings of too many short sentences rarely establish relationships and levels of importance among ideas. Readers cannot discern distinctions between major and minor points. Such strings, unless deliberately planned in a longer piece of writing for occasional impact, suggest that the writer has not thought through the material and decided what to emphasize. The style tends to read like that of young children.

No   There is a legend. This legend is about a seventeenth-century Algonquin Indian. It says that he was inspired. He had an idea about popcorn. He transformed it into a gift. It was the first gift to a hostess in American history. He was invited to the Pilgrims' harvest meal. He brought along a bag of popcorn. This was a demonstration of good will. The occasion is honored to this day with Thanksgiving dinner.

The ten short sentences above range from four to eleven words. The sentence structures do not feature significant ideas over unimportant ones.

Yes   According to legend, in the seventeenth century an inspired Algonquin transformed popcorn into the first hostess gift in history. Invited to the Pilgrims' harvest meal, the Indian brought along a bag of popcorn as a demonstration of good will. The occasion is honored today with Thanksgiving dinner.

—Patricia Linden, "Popcorn"

341

In the revised version above, the sentence structures permit the key ideas to be featured. (In addition, this version employs techniques of conciseness discussed in Chapter 16: ten sentences reduce to three and 73 words reduce to 47.) The two versions use almost the same short last sentence, but because the improved version leads up to it with longer, carefully textured sentences, the message in the last sentence is emphasized.

‖ 2
Revise a string of too many compound sentences.

A **compound sentence**° consists of independent clauses° which present closely related and equally important ideas. The compounding of a sentence must be justified by its meaning. Too often, compound sentences are only short sentences strung together with *and* or *but,* without consideration of the relationships among the ideas.

> **No** Science fiction writers are often thinkers, and they are often dreamers, so they let their imaginations wander. Jules Verne was such a writer, and he predicted space ships and atomic submarines, but most people did not believe airplanes were possible.

> **Yes** Science fiction writers are often thinkers and dreamers who let their imaginations wander. Jules Verne was one such writer. He predicted space ships and atomic submarines before most people believed airplanes were possible.

In the revised version the relationships among the ideas are clear and key ideas are featured. In the last sentence a particularly obscure connection is clarified. (In addition, this version employs techniques of conciseness discussed in Chapter 16: one independent clause is reduced to a word, *dreamers;* another is reduced to a relative clause, *who let their imaginations wander;* another starts a new sentence, *He predicted . . .;* and another is reduced to a subordinate clause, *before most people . . . possible.)*

‖ 3
Revise for a suitable mix of sentence lengths.

You can emphasize one idea among many others by expressing it in a sentence noticeably different in length or structure from the

342

sentences surrounding it. Consider this passage, which carries its emphasis in one short sentence among longer ones:

> Today is one of those excellent January partly cloudies in which light chooses an unexpected landscape to trick out in gilt, and then shadow sweeps it away. **You know you are alive.** You take huge steps, trying to feel the planet's roundness arc between your feet. Kazantzakis says that when he was young he had a canary and a globe. When he freed the canary, it would perch on the globe and sing. All his life, wandering the earth, he felt as though he had a canary on top of his mind, singing.
>
> —ANNIE DILLARD, *Pilgrim at Tinker Creek*

A long sentence among shorter ones is equally effective.

> Mistakes are not believed to be part of the normal behavior of a good machine. **If things go wrong, it must be a personal, human error, the result of fingering, tampering, a button getting stuck, someone hitting the wrong key.** The computer, at its normal best, is infallible. I wonder whether this can be true.
>
> —LEWIS THOMAS, "To Err Is Human"

EXERCISE 1
Revise these sets of sentences to vary the sentence lengths effectively.

1. Horror tales are not new. *Frankenstein* was written in the nineteenth century. It was written by Mary Shelley. She was the wife of the poet Percy Bysshe Shelley. *Frankenstein* tells the story of a scientist. He makes a monster. He makes it from a human corpse.

2. Another famous horror tale of the nineteenth century is "The Monkey's Paw," by W. W. Jacobs, and it tells about an old English couple with a teenage son, and they get a monkey's paw. It has the power to grant three wishes, so the father wishes for 200 pounds, but the money comes because their son is killed in an accident at work. The mother uses the second wish to bring her son back, and soon there is a knocking at their door, and the mother rushes to unbolt it, but the father is terrified of seeing a walking, rotting corpse, so he uses the last wish, and the knocking stops.

3. After radios became common, horror programs broadcast their tales of terror into the living rooms of America which were filled with families that included children of all ages who were grouped around the radio while they listened for the latest story of monsters and strange events. The many programs, which included *The Inner Sanctum*, which featured a creaking door, and *The Fat Man* who had a madman's laugh, scared and delighted the audience who came from different parts of the country, from different occupations, and from different economic and social groups.

343

19b

Use an occasional question, mild command, or exclamation.

To vary your sentence structure and to emphasize material, you can call on four basic sentence types. The most typical English sentence is **declarative:** it makes a statement—it declares something. Declarative sentences offer an almost infinite variety of structures and patterns, as described in other sections of this chapter.

A sentence that asks a question is called **interrogative.** Occasional questions help you involve your reader.

A sentence that issues a mild or strong command is called **imperative.** Occasional mild commands are particularly helpful for gently urging your reader to think along with you. A sentence that makes an exclamation is called **exclamatory.** ▮ PUNCTUATION ALERT: A mild command ends with a period, whereas a strong command or an exclamation ends with an exclamation mark. ▮

Consider the following examples from *Change!* by Isaac Asimov, a writer who often uses different sentence types to keep his material lively and to focus attention on what he wants to emphasize.

QUESTION

The colonization of space may introduce some unexpected changes into human society. **For instance, what effect will it have on the way we keep time?** Our present system of time-keeping is a complicated mess that depends on accidents of astronomy and on 5,000 years of primitive habit.

MILD COMMAND

Consider the bacteria. These are tiny living things made up of single cells far smaller than the cells in plants and animals.

EXCLAMATION

The amazing thing about the netting of the coelanth was that till then zoologists had been convinced the fish had been extinct for 60 million years! Finding a living dinosaur would not have been more surprising.

EXERCISE 2

The paragraph below effectively varies sentence lengths and uses a question and a command. The result emphasizes the key points. Write an imitation of this paragraph, closely following all aspects except the topic. Choose your own topic.

EXAMPLE   If your topic were pets, your first sentence might be: *Why do most people buy expensive pure-bred dogs or cats when they want pets?*

Why do most people imagine hurricanes or bombs when they think of disasters? Consider the worst disaster in history. In 1347–1351, the black death killed over 75 million victims. A snow avalanche in Peru killed 25,000 in 1970, and a panic in an air raid shelter in Chungking, China, claimed 4,000 in 1941. Yet, the strangest disaster of all happened at the coronation of Czar Nicholas II when 5,000 were trampled to death in the stampede for free beer that was part of the celebration.

EXERCISE 3

In each passage, change one sentence to a question, a command, or an exclamation. Choose the sentence to change according to what you think should be emphasized.

EXAMPLE   You can think about race horses. They have become some of the most valuable animals in the world.

Think about race horses. They have become some of the most valuable animals in the world.

1. In October 1980, Easy Jet, a multi-race winner, was sold for 30 million dollars. That is more than the average combined yearly income of a town of 2,000 people.
2. We may wonder what the popularity of horse racing might suggest about the American national character. We may be a nation of gamblers. On the other hand, we may simply want the chance to become financially independent.
3. Lotteries have become as popular as horse racing. Many states run lotteries to raise money for services that used to be provided from taxes. You may not know that in many states school books are purchased with funds gambled on lottery tickets.
4. Some television commercials for lotteries show winners riding in limousines and dressed in expensive clothing. Most lottery ticket holders lose, though. That tempting chance to win a million dollars has odds worse than a million to one.

■|| 19c

Choose the subject of your sentence according to your intended emphasis.

The subject° of a sentence establishes the focus for that sentence. The subject you choose should therefore correspond to the emphasis you want to communicate to your reader.

The following sentences, each of which is correct grammatically, contain the same information. Consider, however, how changes of the subject (and its verb) influence meaning and impact.

1. **Our study showed** that 25 percent of college students' time is spent eating or sleeping.
2. **College students eat or sleep** 25 percent of the time, according to our study.
3. **Eating or sleeping occupies** 25 percent of college students' time, according to our study.
4. **Twenty-five percent** of college students' time **is spent** eating or sleeping, according to our study.

Sentence 1 focuses on the study, 2 on the students, 3 on eating and sleeping, and 4 on percentage of time. Each sentence provides a different emphasis. You would use whichever version most effectively delivers your message in relation to your purpose: for example, sentence 4 seems more suitable for a statistical report while sentence 2 might work well in an article for a college newspaper.

■|| 19d

Add modifiers to basic sentences for variety and emphasis.

A **modifier** is a word, phrase°, or clause° that describes other words, phrases, or clauses. A basic message is delivered by the subject and verb of a simple declarative sentence°—a sentence that consists of a single independent clause°: *The river rose.* Adding modifiers to basic sentences permits you to expand a simple subject and verb into a rich variety of sentence patterns.

1
Expand basic sentences with modifiers.

Sentences that consist only of a subject and verb usually seem very thin. Except when you choose to use a very short sentence for its dramatic effect in emphasizing an idea, you can expand basic sentences with modifying words, phrases, and clauses, as shown in boldface below.

BASIC SENTENCE	The river rose.
ADJECTIVE	The **swollen** river rose.
ADVERB	The river rose **dangerously.**
PREPOSITIONAL PHRASE	**In April,** the river rose **above its banks.**
PARTICIPIAL PHRASES	**Swollen by melting snow,** the river rose, **flooding the farmland.**
ABSOLUTE PHRASE	**Trees swirling away in the current,** the river rose.
ADVERB CLAUSE	**Because the snows had been heavy that winter,** the river rose.
ADJECTIVE CLAUSE	The river, **which runs through vital farmland,** rose.

Your decision to expand a basic sentence or to add information to any sentence will depend on the focus of each sentence and how it works in concert with its surrounding sentences.

EXERCISE 4

Expand each sentence by adding (a) an adjective, (b) an adverb, (c) a prepositional phrase, (d) a participial phrase, (e) an absolute phrase, (f) an adverb clause, and (g) an adjective clause. For guidance, refer to the expansion list above.

1. We went to register for classes.
2. The lines were long.
3. The students seemed edgy.
4. The staff remained calm.
5. Both of us got the schedules we wanted.

2
Position modifiers to create variety and emphasis.

Brain research suggests that readers are more likely to retain the message at the very beginning or the very end of a sentence. Although you do not have unlimited choices about where to place modifiers, you do have some. Try to place them according to the emphasis you want to achieve. At the same time, you must place your modifiers precisely within sentences so that you avoid the error of misplaced modifiers°.

A sentence that starts with a subject and verb is called a **cumulative sentence.** You add information by placing modifiers after the subject and verb. This is the most common sentence structure. Its name derives from the notion that information accumulates. Sometimes it is referred to as a **loose sentence** because it lacks the tightly planned structure of other sentence varieties. Although such sentences are easy to read because they reflect how humans receive and pass on information, cumulative sentences often do not provide impact.

In contrast, a **periodic sentence** (sometimes called a **climactic sentence**) is highly emphatic. It builds up to the period of the sentence, reserving the main idea for the end. It draws the reader in as it builds to its climax.

PERIODIC	At midnight last night, on the road from Las Vegas to Death Valley Junction, **a car hit a shoulder and turned over.**
	—JOAN DIDION, "On Morality"
CUMULATIVE	**A car hit a shoulder and turned over** at midnight last night on the road from Las Vegas to Death Valley Junction.
PERIODIC	**The driver,** very young and apparently drunk, **was killed instantly.**
	—JOAN DIDION, "On Morality"
CUMULATIVE	**The driver, killed instantly,** was very young and apparently drunk.

Periodic sentences can be very effective, but if you overuse them they lose their punch. For this reason, Joan Didion follows the two periodic sentences presented above with a cumulative sentence: *His girl was found alive but bleeding internally, deep in shock.*

Another way to vary your sentence structures is to start sentences with introductory words, phrases, or clauses.

WORD   **Indeed,** Henry Wallace once said, "Certain books are more powerful by far than any battle."

PHRASE   **Along with cereal boxes and ketchup labels,** comic books were the primers that taught me how to read.

                                                      —GLORIA STEINEM

CLAUSE   **Long before I wrote stories,** I listened for stories.

                         —EUDORA WELTY, *One Writer's Beginnings*

Positioning modifiers in two or more places can also lend your writing style both variety and emphasis—as long as you avoid overly complicated sentences.

On our half-acre or three-quarters we can raise enough tomatoes **for our salads** and assassinate enough beetles **to satisfy the gardening urge.**

                    —PHYLLIS MCGINLEY, "Suburbia, Of Thee I Sing"

Television, **by its emphasis on movement and activity, by its appetite for incident,** has become **by far** the most potent instrument **in creating this overexcited atmosphere, this barely recognizable world.**

                    —HENRY FAIRLIE, "Can You Believe Your Eyes?"

EXERCISE 5

Combine each set of sentences by changing one sentence to a clause, phrase, or word that will modify the other sentence.

EXAMPLE   Computer fraud has been rapidly increasing. This increase has been since 1964.

            Since 1964, computer fraud has been rapidly increasing.

1. Students have found the code to college computers. This happened even at large universities with sophisticated technology.
2. Students at one college changed their grades to all "A's." They did this without going to any classes.
3. Computer fraud happens more often than robberies. This happens when banks have weak security.
4. A man was arrested by the FBI in 1978. He was charged with defrauding a Los Angeles bank of $10.2 million.

5. Over 64,000 fake insurance policies were created on the Equity Funding Corporation computer. It happened between 1964 and 1973.

6. The Equity Funding Corporation lost over $2 million. This happened gradually.

7. Fraudulent use of computers in education and in business is serious. Even more terrifying possibilities exist.

8. Teenagers seriously endangered the lives of many patients. They invaded vital health records at a hospital.

9. The film *War Games* suggests a problem. The problem could result from the misuse of military computers.

10. There is a computer in the film. The computer gets the wrong message and almost starts a nuclear war.

EXERCISE 6
Revise each set of sentences—a new set starts at each number in parentheses—by combining them. Choose one sentence in each set to be the main focus, and reduce the other(s) to modifying clauses, phrases, or words.

EXAMPLE   Characters in folklore are usually strong. Many of them perform daring acts. They are often described as bigger than people in real life.

Characters in folklore are usually described as strong, daring, and bigger than people in real life.

(1) Molly Brown was a tough settler of the American Frontier. She is remembered for bravery because she saved some of the *Titanic* passengers. (2) Don Diego was a hero who lived on a hacienda in Southern California. He opposed a cruel governor. (3) He wore a mask and assumed the name *Zorro*. He would take unfairly gained riches from the Governor's friends. Then he would return the goods to the poor. (4) Then there was John Henry. He was a man. He worked building the railroads. He could drive steel spikes very fast. He could drive them faster than anybody else. (5) Sacajawea was a Native American. She knew how to find mountain passages. No one else could find these passages. Because of this skill, she was chosen to guide an expedition. The expedition was important. The expedition was led by Lewis and Clark.

19e
Invert standard word order.

Standard word order in the English sentence calls for the subject to be followed by the verb: *The mayor walked into the room.* Because this pattern is so common, it is set in people's minds, and any variation automatically creates emphasis. Used too often, inverted word order can be distracting, but used sparingly, it can be very effective.

STANDARD   **The mayor walked** in. **The governor walked** out.

INVERTED   In **walked the mayor.** Out **walked the governor.**

STANDARD   **The house** that shelters a friend **is happy.**

INVERTED   **Happy is the house** that shelters a friend.
                                              —RALPH WALDO EMERSON

 19f

Repeat important words or ideas to achieve emphasis.

Repeating carefully chosen words can help you emphasize your meaning. Choose for repetition only words that contain a main idea or that use rhythm to focus attention on a main idea. Consider this passage, which uses deliberate repetition along with a variety of sentence lengths to deliver its meaning.

Coal is **black** and it warms your house and cooks your food. The night is **black,** which has a moon, and a million stars, and is beautiful. Sleep is **black** which gives you rest, so you wake up **feeling good.** I am **black.** I **feel** very **good** this evening.
                                    —LANGSTON HUGHES, "That Word *Black*"

Hughes repeats the word *black,* each time linking it to something related to joy and beauty. The incantation that results from the rhythm of deliberate repetition of *black* and *good* emphasizes Hughes's message and helps the reader remember it.

While deliberate repetition is a good ally when you use it occasionally to achieve variety and emphasize selected ideas, it can be misused. Be sure to use deliberate repetition sparingly, with central words, and only when your meaning justifies such a technique. Consider this passage, which misuses repetition:

No   **An insurance agent** can be an excellent adviser when you want to buy a **car. An insurance agent** has records on most **cars. An insurance agent** knows which **models** tend to have most accidents. **An insurance agent** can tell you which **models** are the most expensive to repair if they are in a collision. **An insurance agent can** tell you which **models** are most likely to be stolen.

The repetition in this passage seems merely the result of a limited vocabulary and a dull, unvaried style. Although there are few synonyms for the words *an insurance agent, car,* and *model,* there are some. Also, the writer could have achieved variety in sentence structure. The passage's content does seem to call for the rhythmic effect of deliberate repetition.

> **YES** If you are thinking of buying a new car, an insurance agent can be an excellent adviser. An insurance broker has complete records on most automobiles. For example, he or she knows which models are accident prone. Did you know that some car designs suffer more damage than others in a collision? If you want to know which automobiles crumple more than others and which are least expensive to repair, ask an insurance agent. Similarly, some models are more likely to be stolen, so find out from the person who specializes in dealing with claims.

EXERCISE 7

Revise this paragraph to achieve emphasis through varied sentence length and deliberate repetition. You can reduce or increase the number of sentences.

Dreams come in many forms. Some are pleasing. They also can be distressing. They can be about the future. They can be about past successes or joys. Sometimes, they are bizarre. According to researchers, some visions during sleep recur over and over again. Typical ones are about flying or falling. Many people see themselves failing tests. Being unable to make an important telephone call is also common. Experts have suggested various explanations for some dreams. This makes a person's dreams seem objective and impersonal, but they are not. No matter how common, a dream is special to the dreamer.

EXERCISE 8

Using topics of your choosing, imitate the variety and emphasis of two different passages shown in this chapter: choose from Kohl, Dillard, Thomas, or Hughes.

EXERCISE 9

Using the techniques of variety and emphasis discussed in this chapter, revise the following paragraph.

Many amazing events in bathtubs have taken place. Three different women died by drowning in the bathtub while they were married to George Joseph Smith of England. There was great surprise at Mr. Smith's trial when the fact that he now had a fourth wife, Edith, was revealed. Edith testified at the trial that she remembered George's taking only one bath during the whole time they were married. Other things besides gory murders, however, happen in the bathtub. For example, French author Edmond Rostand took baths while he was writing plays like *Cyrano de Bergerac* to escape interruptions from friends. Also, many people know that the discovery of the scientific theory of displacement by Archimedes took place in the bathtub. Archimedes shouted "Eureka!" jumped out of his bath, and ran through the streets in the nude because he was so excited by his discovery. A modern example of the importance of the bathtub is illustrated by what happened to astronaut John Glenn. There was going to be an election for senator in Ohio, but Glenn had to withdraw from the race because he hurt himself when he fell in a bathtub.

V | USING EFFECTIVE WORDS

20
UNDERSTANDING THE MEANING OF WORDS

American English, evolving over centuries into a rich language, reflects the many cultures that have merged in our melting-pot society. The earliest varieties of American English can be traced from sixteenth-century Elizabethan English—the language of Shakespeare. As the United States expanded, so did American English. Changes from Elizabethan forms occurred in vocabulary, spelling, and syntactic patterns. Distinctly American words originated colloquially—in spoken language—and words from all the cultures settling the United States became part of the language. Food names, for example, show how other languages and cultures loaned words to English. Africans brought the words *ham, okra, gumbo,* and *goober* (peanut). Spanish and Latin American peoples contributed *tortilla, taco, burrito,* and *enchilada.* From German we got *hamburger, wiener,* and *pretzel;* Italian supplied *spaghetti, pasta, pizza,* and *antipasto;* and Yiddish is responsible for *gefilte fish, tsimmes,* and *bagel.* American English creates a truly international *smorgasbord,* a Scandinavian word meaning "a wide variety of appetizers and other tasty foods."

Etymology is the study of a word's origins and historical development—its changes in form and meaning. For example, *alphabet* originates from the names of the first two letters in Greek: *a* =

alpha, b = *beta. Nice* shows how a word's meaning can change with time. As W. Nelson Francis points out in *The English Language,* *nice* "has been used at one time or another in its 700-year history to mean . . . foolish, wanton, strange, lazy, coy, modest, fastidious, refined, precise, subtle, slender, critical, attentive, minutely accurate, dainty, appetizing, agreeable."

The fact that American English is a growing, changing language affects you as a writer. To write well, you need to use words accurately. Three important steps toward using American English effectively are knowing what kinds of information dictionaries hold (20a), understanding denotation *and* connotation of words (20b), and actively building your own vocabulary (20c).

■‖ 20a
Learn to use dictionaries.

Good dictionaries show how language has been used and is currently being used. Such dictionaries give at each entry not only the word's meaning but also much additional important information. Many dictionaries also include essays on the history and use of language.

‖ 1
Understand the information in a dictionary entry.

A good dictionary entry includes items 1 through 8 listed below, and sometimes items 9 through 12.

1. Spelling
2. Word division into syllables (syllabication)
3. Pronunciation
4. Functions (parts of speech)
5. Grammatical forms (plural, parts of verb including irregular forms, etc.)
6. Etymology
7. Meanings
8. Related words (nouns, adjectives)
9. Synonyms (and often antonyms)
10. Word used in context
11. Usage label
12. Idioms that include the word

Spelling and syllabication

Pronunciation

Part of speech

Grammatical forms

Etymology

Meanings

Related words

Synonyms

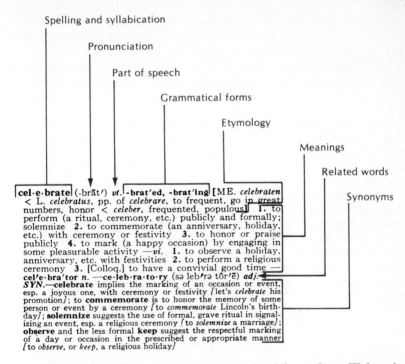

cel·e·brate (-brāt′) *vt.* **-brat′ed, -brat′ing** [ME. *celebraten* < L. *celebratus*, pp. of *celebrare*, to frequent, go in great numbers, honor < *celeber*, frequented, populous] **1.** to perform (a ritual, ceremony, etc.) publicly and formally; solemnize **2.** to commemorate (an anniversary, holiday, etc.) with ceremony or festivity **3.** to honor or praise publicly **4.** to mark (a happy occasion) by engaging in some pleasurable activity —*vi.* **1.** to observe a holiday, anniversary, etc. with festivities **2.** to perform a religious ceremony **3.** [Colloq.] to have a convivial good time — **cel′e·bra′tor** *n.* —**ce·leb·ra·to·ry** (sə leb′rə tôr′ē) *adj.* **SYN.**—**celebrate** implies the marking of an occasion or event, esp. a joyous one, with ceremony or festivity [let's *celebrate* his promotion]; to **commemorate** is to honor the memory of some person or event by a ceremony [to *commemorate* Lincoln's birthday]; **solemnize** suggests the use of formal, grave ritual in signalizing an event, esp. a religious ceremony [to *solemnize* a marriage]; **observe** and the less formal **keep** suggest the respectful marking of a day or occasion in the prescribed or appropriate manner [to *observe*, or *keep*, a religious holiday]

Look at the entry above for the word *celebrate* from *Webster's New World Dictionary, Second College Edition.* The spelling is given first, with the word divided into syllables by a centered dot. The pronunciation follows, in parentheses. Here you will sometimes see unusual symbols, such as /ə/, the *schwa* or "uh" sound. Pronunciation symbols are explained in a pronunciation key in the dictionary's introductory pages. Some dictionaries also include a shortened version of the key at the bottom of each right-hand page. The accented syllable is shown by the stress mark /′/. Next you see the part of speech: *vt.* in the entry for *celebrate,* standing for *transitive verb.* Inflected forms (in regular verbs, the *-ed* form for past tense and past participle, the *-ing* form for the present participle) come before the bracketed etymology (word history). Definitions and related forms of the word are then given. Also note these features:

> *Celebrate* comes from a Middle English (ME) word, which is derived from the Latin *celeber,* meaning "populous"; one celebrates with numbers of other people at the same ceremony or festivity, according to the original meaning of the word.

> The numbered definitions reflect current usage by educated speakers and writers of English.

Following the four meanings of the transitive verb are three meanings of the intransitive verb, and then noun and adjective forms with their pronunciations.

A discussion of synonyms starts at *SYN*. Here the differences among four words close in meaning to *celebrate* are pointed out; each word is defined and used in context.

Usage labels in a dictionary give much important information. See [Colloq.] at the third definition of *celebrate* as an intransitive verb. The most common usage labels are shown in the chart below. All labels and their abbreviations used in your dictionary are identified in its opening pages.

Besides usage labels, meanings specific to a particular field of knowledge or activity are so labeled. For example, one meaning of *carrier* is specific to chemistry ("a catalytic agent that causes an element or radical to be transferred from one compound to another") and is preceded by the label *Chem.* Another meaning of *carrier* is specific to electronics ("a steady transmitted wave whose amplitudes, frequency, or phase is modulated by the signal") and is labeled *Elec.*

USAGE LABELS

LABEL	DEFINITION	EXAMPLE
Colloquial	Characteristic of conversation and informal writing	**pa** [father] **ma** [mother]
Slang	Not considered part of standard language, but sometimes used in informal conversation	**whirlybird** [helicopter]
Archaic or *Obsolete*	No longer used; occurred in earlier writing	**betimes** [promptly, quickly]
Poetic	Found in poetry or poetic prose	**o'er** [for *over*]
Dialect	Used only in some geographical areas	**poke** [Southern: a bag or sack]

EXERCISE 1
Use a dictionary that has entries which include a list of synonyms and some labels, as in the entry for *celebrate* on page 357. Then, assuming as your audience a student unfamiliar with such entries, write an explanation of each part.

EXERCISE 2
Consult a dictionary that gives usage labels. First, for each word below, give the usage label or labels: colloquial, slang, archaic or obsolete, poetic, or dialect. Then use the word in a sentence to show the meaning clearly.

1. *cool* (adj.) not referring to temperature
2. *mutt*
3. *yore*
4. *bread* (noun) not referring to food
5. *a wrapup*
6. *nigh*
7. *sure* (adv.)
8. *nerd*
9. *yon*
10. *flunk*
11. *jive* (verb)
12. *lea* (noun) not referring to yarn
13. *offbeat* (noun) not referring to music
14. *varmint*
15. *fixings*

EXERCISE 3
Consult a college dictionary for the etymology of the following words.

1. *current*
2. *pasteurize*
3. *mausoleum*
4. *nicotine*
5. *boycott*
6. *Taoism*
7. *erotic*
8. *olympic*
9. *popular*
10. *chauvinism*

2
Know about unabridged dictionaries.

Unabridged means "not shortened." Unabridged dictionaries have the most in-depth, accurate, complete, and scholarly entries of the various kinds of dictionaries. They give many examples of a word's current uses and changes in meanings over time. They include infrequently used words that abridged (shortened) dictionaries may omit. The most important and comprehensive unabridged dictionary of English is the *Oxford English Dictionary (OED)*. The *OED* has fifteen volumes plus supplements with more than 500,000 entries. These volumes comprise the definitive dictionary of the English language. The *OED* traces the history of each word and gives dated quotations to illustrate changes in meaning and spelling. The 1986 supplement to the *OED* shows that American words are the greatest source of new words in the English language. The *OED* is particularly useful for people with an intense or scholarly interest in language.

For most college students *Webster's Third New International Dictionary of the English Language* will provide any needed information. This highly respected, one-volume work has more than 450,000 entries and is especially strong in new scientific and technical terms. It uses quotations to show various meanings, and its definitions are given in order of their appearance in the language.

Random House Dictionary of the English Language is another one-volume work. The newest unabridged dictionary, it has more than 260,000 entries. It is the least expansive and least expensive of the three unabridged dictionaries and has an atlas with color maps as well as a list of reference books in appendixes.

3
Know about abridged dictionaries.

Abridged means "shortened." Abridged dictionaries contain the most commonly used words. They are convenient in size and economical to buy. They serve as the most practical reference books for writers and readers. Many good abridged dictionaries are referred to as "college" editions because they serve the needs of most college students.

Webster's New World Dictionary of the American Language, 2nd edition, has more than 158,000 entries and gives detailed etymologies. It lists all entries in alphabetical order, with names of people, places, abbreviations, and foreign expressions in the main body of the work (rather than in appendixes). Its precise, easy-to-read definitions appear in chronological order of their acceptance into the language. *Webster's New World Dictionary* has a contemporary American emphasis. It uses a star symbol (☆) for Americanisms—words that first became part of the language in the United States. It gives the origins of American place names (cities, states, rivers, and so on). It supplies usage labels for many words and gives thorough synonymies. Its appendixes cover punctuation, mechanics, and manuscript form (footnotes, bibliography, proofreading marks, scholarly terms). Its introductory material includes essays on language, etymology, and Americanisms.

Although not itself a "college edition," *Webster's New World Compact School and Office Dictionary* is based on *Webster's New World Dictionary, Second College Edition.* Far more complete than "pocket" dictionaries, this compact version of *Webster's New World Dictionary* has 56,000 entries, clearly and precisely defined. Its coverage of frequently encountered terms from the sciences, arts, business, technical, and professional fields is thorough and up-to-date. It contains pronunciation and spelling guidance, common abbreviations, foreign words and phrases often used in English writing, and etymologies. *Webster's New World Compact* gives tables of weights and measures, a dictionary of geography, a list of Presidents and Vice-Presidents of the United States, and lists of principal cities in the United States and in the rest of the world.

The American Heritage Dictionary of the English Language has more than 200,000 entries and 3,000 photographs, illustrations, and maps. This dictionary lists a word's most common meaning first, departing from the traditional practice of listing the oldest meaning first. *The American Heritage Dictionary* has especially thorough guidance on usage and extensive notes in its synonymies to distinguish subtle differences among words of similar meaning. Its introductory material contains essays on language, culture, and usage, as well as sections on grammar, spelling, and pronunciation. Biographical and geographic-name entries are in separate sections, and a list of Indo-European roots appears in an appendix.

Random House Dictionary of the English Language, based on the unabridged *Random House Dictionary,* has more than 155,000 entries. It gives a word's most common definition first and has full synonymies. It includes recent technical words and is generously illustrated. *The Random House Dictionary of the English Language* does not separate biographical and geographic entries from other entries. Its introductory section presents essays on usage, dialects, and functional varieties of English; its appendixes include a style manual.

4
Know about specialized dictionaries of English.

A specialized dictionary focuses on a single area, such as slang, word origins, synonyms, usage, or almost any other aspect of language.

SYNONYMS
New Roget's Thesaurus of the English Language in Dictionary Form

SLANG
Dictionary of Slang and Unconventional English, ed. Eric Partridge

Dictionary of American Slang, ed. Harold Wentworth and
   Stuart Berg Flexner

ETYMOLOGIES
Dictionary of Word and Phrase Origins, ed. William Morris
   and Mary Morris
*Origins: A Short Etymological Dictionary of Modern
   English,* ed. Eric Partridge

USAGE
Modern American Usage, ed. Jacques Barzun

REGIONALISMS
Dictionary of American Regional English, ed. Frederic
   Cassidy

■‖ 20b
Choose exact words.

Experienced writers pay close attention to **diction**—word
choice. To choose the most appropriate and accurate word, a writer
must understand the word's *denotation* and *connotation.*

‖ 1
Understand denotation and connotation.

Denotation is the explicit dictionary meaning of a word—its
definition. When you look up a new word in the dictionary to find
out what it means, you are looking for its denotation. For example,
the denotation of the word *semester* is "a period of time of about
eighteen weeks that makes up part of a school or college year."
   Readers expect words to be used according to their established
meanings for their established functions. Exactness is essential.
Thus dangers, as well as benefits and pleasures, arise when you use
a thesaurus or dictionary of synonyms. Be aware that subtle shades
of meaning differentiate words with the same general definitions.
These subtle differences in meaning allow you to be very precise in
choosing just the right word, but they also oblige you to make sure
you know what meanings your words convey. For instance, describing a person famous for praiseworthy achievements in public life as
notorious would be wrong. Although *notorious* means "well-known"
and "publicly discussed"—which renowned people are likely to be—
notorious means "unfavorably known or talked about." George

Washington is *famous,* not *notorious.* Al Capone, on the other hand, is *notorious.*

Here is another example. *Obdurate* means "not easily moved to pity or sympathy," and its synonyms include "inflexible, obstinate, stubborn, hardened." You could correctly use *obdurate* in sentences like the following:

YES   The supervisor remained *obdurate* in refusing to accept excuses.

YES   My roomates, *obdurate* people who are unwilling to compromise, want me to get rid of my pet boa constrictor, Alphonse.

However, the synonym *hardened* may prompt someone unfamiliar with *obdurate* to use the word incorrectly.

NO   Footprints showed in the *obdurate* concrete.

As a final example of the importance of explicit meaning, suppose a writer who is describing the location of a mine shaft has used the word *deep* several times. Searching for a synonym, the writer consults a thesaurus and finds, among other alternatives, the word *profound.* The writer then states: "Shaft 4, outside Woodville, is the most profound in the state." Because *profound* means "deep" in reference to thoughts or ideas, it cannot be used in reference to a mine shaft.

Connotation refers to the ideas implied, but not directly indicated, by a word. Connotations convey associations as emotional overtones beyond a word's direct, explicit definition. What first comes to mind when you see the word *home?* Probably *home* evokes more emotion than does its denotation, "a dwelling place," and its synonym *house. Home* may have very pleasant connotations of warmth, security, the love of family. Or *home* may have unpleasant connotations of an institution for elderly or disabled people. Good writers understand the additional layer of meaning connotations deliver. Connotations are never completely fixed, for the associations to a word often are individual. Still, people can communicate effectively because most words have relatively stable connotations and denotations in most contexts.

Being sensitive to the differences between a word's denotation and connotation is essential for critical thinking. Critical thinkers must first consider material at its literal level (5b-1). Doing so calls for dealing with the denotation of words. Next, critical thinkers must move to the inferential level (5b-2)—to what is implied, although not explicitly stated. Here the connotations of words often

363

carry the message. Consider these comparisons of denotation and connotation:

Word	Denotation	Connotation
additive	an added substance	in food, a preservative, but perhaps also harmful to health
cheap	inexpensive	of products, low quality; of people, stingy
nuclear accident	unintentional meltdown of fuel rods in nuclear reactor	release of dangerous radiation; possibility of imminent death or eventual cancer; poisoning of food chain

EXERCISE 4

Separate the words in each set of words into one of three columns: *Neutral* if you think the word has no connotations; *Positive* if you think it has good connotations; *Negative* if you think it has bad connotations.

EXAMPLE   alibi, excuse, pretext, reason, explanation

Positive	Neutral	Negative
explanation	reason	alibi
		pretext
		excuse

1. fat, fleshy, stout, portly, rotund, chubby, plump, obese, corpulent, heavy, paunchy, overweight, rolypoly, large-sized.
2. thin, lean, lanky, skinny, gaunt, scrawny, rawboned, slender, slim, slight, skin and bones.
3. teacher, lecturer, instructor, professor, pedant, pedagogue, mentor, scholar, educator.
4. politician, lawmaker, senator, representative, leader, demagogue, rabble-rouser.
5. loyal, dedicated, devoted, determined, stubborn, firm, unyielding.

2
Use specific and concrete language to bring life to general and abstract language.

Specific words identify individual items in a group *(Oldsmobile, Honda, Ford).* **General** words relate to an overall group *(car).*

Concrete words identify persons and things that can be perceived by the senses—seen, heard, tasted, felt, smelled (the *black padded vinyl dashboard* of my car). **Abstract** words denote qualities, concepts, relationships, acts, conditions, ideas *(transportation)*. Writers must use all these types of words: specific and concrete as well as general and abstract. Effective writers, however, make sure to supply enough specific details and examples to substantiate and illustrate generalizations and abstractions. For example, compare the general sentences with the more specific versions:

GENERAL	My car has a great deal of power, and it is very quick.
SPECIFIC	My Trans Am with 135 horsepower can go from zero to fifty in six seconds.
GENERAL	The car gets good gas mileage.
SPECIFIC	The Dodge Lancer gets about 35 mpg on the highway and 30 mpg in the city.
GENERAL	Her car is comfortable and easy to drive.
SPECIFIC	Her Buick Regal has an 8-way adjustable leather seat, cruise control, tilt steering wheel, and automatic transmission.
GENERAL	His car has the latest technology for a smooth ride.
SPECIFIC	His Toyota Celica has four-wheel independent suspension, stabilizer bars, and rack-and-pinion steering for stability and controllability.

Usually, good writing combines general and abstract words and ideas with specific and concrete words and ideas. In the following sentences from a paper comparing American-made and imported cars, the combination works effectively.

GENERAL   SPECIFIC   SPECIFIC   ABSTRACT
My car, a **135-horsepower Trans Am,** is **quick.** It accelerates from

SPECIFIC   SPECIFIC   SPECIFIC
0 to 50 miles per hour in **6 seconds**—but it gets only **18 miles** per gallon. The

SPECIFIC   ABSTRACT   GENERAL
Dodge Lancer, on the other hand, gets **very good** gas **mileage:** about

SPECIFIC   GENERAL   SPECIFIC   SPECIFIC   GENERAL
35 mpg in **highway driving** and **30 mpg** in **stop-and-go driving conditions.**

Note that specific language is not always preferable to general language, and concrete language is not always preferable to abstract language. For example, in a paper about how to change a washer in a faucet, readers who are looking for information do not care that the faucet is a 1984 model Kohler stainless steel flange handle with lucite ribs. All those readers need to know is how to put the washer in the faucet so that the faucet works driplessly. Although the directions must include specific details about installing the washer, using ultraspecific language to describe the faucet would create an annoying distraction for do-it-yourself plumbers.

EXERCISE 5
Revise the following paragraph by providing specific and concrete words to explain and enliven the general and abstract words.

I enjoy good food. I do not like to eat greasy foods or foods made with more artificial ingredients than real ones. To me, good food starts with sweet, delicious desserts. I am also fond of many ethnic dishes. Bread is one of my other favorites. As long as I watch my weight, I can look forward to years of pleasure from good food.

20c
Increase your vocabulary.

A larger and richer vocabulary is one of the most rewarding outcomes of a college education. Dictionaries, of course, are a logical source of new words, as well as of new meanings for familiar words. In addition, you can use a few routine practices to build into your vocabulary new words you encounter.

1
Know prefixes and suffixes.

Prefixes are syllables in front of a **root** word that modify its meaning. *Ante-* (before) placed before the root *bellum* (war) gives *antebellum,* which means "before the war." *Antebellum* refers to the time before the Civil War. **Suffixes** are syllables added to the end of a root word that modify its meaning. For example, *excite* (formed by adding the prefix *ex,* "out," to the past participle of *cierce,* "to summon," has the various forms of adjective, adverb, and noun when suffixes are added: *excited, exciting, excitedly, excitement.* A word's part of speech is often signaled by the suffix.

TECHNIQUES FOR BUILDING YOUR VOCABULARY

1. Using a highlighter pen, mark all unfamiliar words in your textbooks and other reading material you own. Then define the words in the margin so you can study the meaning in context. Copy new words onto index cards or into a special notebook.
2. Listen carefully to learn how speakers use the language. Jot down new words and later look them up and write each word and its definitions on an index card or in a special notebook.
3. Set aside time each day to study the new words. You can carry your cards or notebook in your pocket to study in spare moments during the day.
4. Use mnemonics to memorize words (see 22b-2). Set a goal of learning *and using* 8 to 10 new words a week.
5. Every few weeks go back to the words from the previous weeks. Make a list of any words you still do not remember and study them again.

Roots are the central parts of words to which prefixes and suffixes are added. Once you know, for example, the Latin root *bene* ("well, good"), you can decipher various forms: **bene**gign, **bene**factor, **bene**diction, **bene**ficial, **bene**ficiary, **bene**volent, **bene**fit.

Knowing common prefixes and suffixes is an excellent way to learn to decode unfamiliar words and increase your vocabulary.

PREFIXES

Prefix	Meaning	Example
anti-	against	antiballistic
contra-	against	contradict
extra-	more	extraordinary
hyper-	more	hyperactive
super-	more	supernatural
ultra-	more	ultraconservative
dis-	not	disagree
il-	not	illegal
im-	not	immoral
in-	not	inadequate
ir-	not	irresponsible
mis-	not	misunderstood

367

PREFIXES

Prefix	Meaning	Example
non-	not	noninvolvement
un-	not	unhappy
semi-	half	semicircle
mono-	one	monopoly
uni-	one	uniform
poly-	many	polygamy
ante-	before	antebellum
pre-	before	prehistoric
post-	after	postscript
re-	back	return
retro-	back	retroactive
sub-	under	submissive
trans-	across	transportation
inter-	between	interpersonal
intra-	inside	intravenous
auto-	self	autobiography
mal-	poor	malnutrition

SUFFIXES

NOUNS

Suffix	Meaning	Example
-tion	act of	integration
-hood	state of	childhood
-ness	state of	kindness
-ship	state of	friendship
-tude	state of	solitude
-dom	state of	freedom

VERBS

Suffix	Meaning	Example
-ate	to make	integrate
-ify	to make	unify
-ize	to make	computerize

SUFFIXES

ADJECTIVES

Suffix	Meaning	Example
-able	able to be	comfortable
-ible	able to be	compatible
-ate	full of	fortunate
-ful	full of	tactful
-ous	full of	pompous
-y	full of	gloomy
-less	without	penniless

EXERCISE 6

Add a prefix to each italicized word to match the definition given. Consult a dictionary if necessary.

EXAMPLE   not *happy* = unhappy

1. not *logical*
2. not *athletic*
3. not *decent*
4. excessively *sensitive*
5. below the *conscious*
6. against the *freeze*
7. *dated* after
8. one *rail*
9. *existing* before
10. *consider* again

EXERCISE 7

Add a suffix to each italicized word to match the definition given. Notice that you will be changing the form of the word to match the exact definition.

EXAMPLE   state of being *lazy* = laziness

1. state of being *happy*
2. act of *flirting*
3. full of *room*
4. able to *agree*
5. to make *beautiful*
6. to make *ideal*
7. state of being *grateful*
8. full of *courage*
9. to make *original*
10. state of being *contented*

2
Use context clues to deduce word meanings.

The familiar words that surround an unknown word can give you hints about the new word's meaning. Such **context clues** include four main types.

1. **Restatement context clue:**   You can figure out an unknown word when a word you know repeats the meaning. *He jumped into the* fray *and enjoyed every minute of the fight. Fray* means "fight." The restatement may be set off with punctuation, such as commas, dashes, or parentheses: Et al. *("and others") is used in a bibliography to indicate other authors of a work.* But often a restatement is not set off: Et al. *indicates that other authors' names have been omitted.*

2. **Contrast context clue:**   You can figure out an unknown word when an opposite or contrast is presented: *We feared that the new prime minister would be a* menace *to society, but she turned out to be a great peacemaker. Menace* means "threat." The explanatory contrast is *but she turned out to be a great peacemaker.*

3. **Example context clue:**   You can figure out an unfamiliar word when an example or illustration relating to the word is given: *They were* conscientious *workers, making sure that everything was done correctly and precisely. Conscientious* means "motivated by a desire to do what is right." You get close to that definition with "done correctly and precisely."

4. **General sense context clue:**   An entire passage can convey a general sense of particular difficult words. For example, in *Nearly forty million Americans are overweight; obesity has become an* epidemic. You can deduce that *epidemic* refers to something happening to many people.

Sometimes a "general sense context clue" may fail to make clear a word's exact denotation. In the example in clue 4 above, for instance, you might guess that *epidemic* indicates a widespread threat, but you might miss the connection of the word *epidemic* with the concept of disease. Interpreting a word's meaning from the general sense of a passage can nevertheless make you miss the subtle variations that distinguish one word from another. When you believe you have deciphered a meaning from any of these context clues, check the exact definition in a dictionary. Then add the word to your vocabulary.

21

UNDERSTANDING
THE EFFECT
OF WORDS

Words do not exist in a vacuum. They communicate meaning and so have an effect on the people reading or hearing them. As a writer, therefore, use words carefully both for their correct meaning (Chapter 20) and for their effect.

Using words well depends on making good choices. Sometimes the choices are either right or wrong, but sometimes the choices are subtler. Your awareness of your purpose in writing, your audience, and the situation in which you are writing should influence your choice of words. Your choice of words affects the *tone* of your writing. A chummy tone is fine for a letter to a friend but inappropriate for an essay written for a college course. A humorous tone might be fine for an essay about the time you wore an unmatched pair of shoes to an interview, but a serious tone would be needed in your letter of application for a job. This chapter discusses the many options available when you choose words for the effect they will have on your audiences.

■‖ 21a
Use appropriate language.

Good writers pay special attention to **diction**—word choice—making certain that the words they use will communicate their meaning as clearly and convincingly as possible.

1
Be aware of levels of formality in language use.

Informal and highly formal levels of writing use different vocabulary and sentence structures, and they differ clearly in **tone.** Tone in writing means the attitude of the writer toward the subject and toward the audience. Tone may be highly formal, informal, or somewhere in between. Different tones are appropriate for different audiences, different subjects, and different purposes. An informal tone occurs in casual conversation or letters to friends. A highly formal tone, in contrast, occurs in sermons and proclamations, treatises and treaties.

Informal language, which creates an informal tone, may include slang, colloquialisms, and regionalisms. In addition, informal writing may include sentence fragments, contractions, and other forms that approximate casual speech. **Medium** language level uses general English—not too casual, not too scholarly. Unlike informal language, medium-level language is acceptable for academic writing. This level uses standard vocabulary (for example, *learn* instead of *wise-up*), conventional sentence structure, and few or no contractions. A **highly formal** language level uses a multisyllabic Latinate vocabulary (*edify* instead of *learn*) and often stylistic flourishes such as extended or complex figures of speech. Academic writing and most writing for general audiences should range from medium to somewhat formal levels of language.

INFORMAL	Ya know stars? They're a gas!
MEDIUM	Gas clouds slowly changed into stars.
FORMAL	The condensations of gas spun their slow gravitational pirouettes, slowly transmogrifying gas cloud into star.

—CARL SAGAN, "Starfolk: A Fable"

INFORMAL	Basically, we're ex-chimps.
MEDIUM	The human race's genes evolved in a manner similar to that of other reproducing things on earth.
FORMAL	And then one day there came to be a creature whose genetic material was in no major way different from the self-replicating molecular collectives of any of the other organisms on his planet, which he called Earth.

—CARL SAGAN, "Starfolk: A Fable"

As these examples show, the choice of informal, medium, or formal language establishes the *tone,* the way the writer regards the audience and the subject. The informal examples would be appropriate in a letter to a close friend or in a journal; the writer's attitude toward the subject is playful and humorous. Word choice and sentence structure assume great familiarity between writer and audience. The medium examples would be appropriate in most academic and professional situations. It is easy to see an instructor as the audience for these sentences; the writer's attitude toward the subject is serious and straightforward. The formal examples are addressed to an audience with considerable interest in and knowledge of scientific phenomena—perhaps readers of a science journal or magazine.

‖ 2
‖ Use edited American English for most writing.

The language standards you are expected to use in academic writing are those of **edited American English**—the accepted written language of a book like this handbook or a magazine like *Newsweek* or *Harper's.* Such language is called *standard English* because it conforms to established rules of grammar, sentence structure, punctuation, and spelling. When referring to writing, this language is also called *edited American English* because it is often the result of careful revision into standard forms from quickly drafted informal writing. Because advertising language and other language intended to reach and sway a large audience often ignores conventional usage, readers *do* encounter English that varies from the standard. However, do not let these published departures from edited English influence you into believing they are acceptable in academic writing. Edited English is not a fancy dialect for the elite; it is a practical form of the language that most educated people use. When you use edited American English in your academic writing, you will not risk distracting your readers from the message you want to communicate.

‖ 3
‖ Do not use sexist language.

Sexist language assigns roles or characteristics to people on the basis of sex. Such practices unfairly limit or discriminate against both sexes. Sexist language inaccurately assumes all nurses and homemakers are female (and therefore refers to them as "she") and all physicians and wage earners are male (and therefore refers to them as "he"). One of the most widespread occurrences of sexist language is the use of the pronoun *he* to refer to someone of unidentified sex. Although tradition holds that *he* is correct in such situations, using only masculine pronouns to represent the human species excludes females—a distortion of reality. You can avoid this problem by following the suggestions in the chart below.

HOW TO AVOID SEXIST LANGUAGE

1. Avoid using only the masculine pronoun to refer to males and females together by using a pair of pronouns, but try to avoid strings of pairs in a sentence or in several consecutive sentences.

   No   A doctor cannot read much outside **his** specialty

   Yes   A doctor cannot read much outside **his or her** specialty.

   Revise into the plural.

   No   A successful doctor knows that **he** has to work long hours.

   Yes   Successful doctors know that **they** have to work long hours.

   Recast the sentence to omit the gender-specific pronoun.

   No   Everyone hopes that **he** will win the scholarship.

   Yes   Everyone hopes to win the scholarship.

2. Avoid the use of *man* when men and women are clearly intended in the meaning.

   No   **Man** is a social animal.

   Yes   **People** are social animals.

   No   A **man's** best friend is a dog.

   Yes   A **person's** best friend is a dog.

3. Avoid stereotyping jobs and roles by gender when men and women are included.

No	chairman; policeman; businessman; statesman
Yes	chair, chairperson; police officer; businessperson, business executive; diplomat, prime minister, statesperson

No	teacher . . . **she;** principal . . . **he**
Yes	teachers . . . **they;** principals . . . **they**

4. Avoid expressions that exclude one sex.

No	mankind; the common man; man-sized sandwich; old wives' tale
Yes	humanity; the average person; huge sandwich; superstition

5. Avoid using demeaning and patronizing labels.

No	lady lawyer; gal Friday; career girl; coed
Yes	lawyer; assistant; professional woman; student

No	My girl will help you.
Yes	My secretary will help you. Jane Baumann will help you.

EXERCISE 1
Revise the following sentences using a medium level of formality consistently and changing sexist language to nonsexist language.

1. After Professor John Smith lectured brilliantly for ninety minutes on the urbanization of the South, he was too pooped to answer questions.
2. I told my friend, "You know, that was the most sagacious blab I've ever heard."
3. That professor learned me a lesson about stereotyping Southerners.
4. Some Northerners think that a Southerner don't know nothing because of his Southern drawl—slow talking gotta mean slow thinking.
5. The Northerner may claim that he is right smarter than the Southerner.
6. When a Northerner runs into people with southern accents, he often forgets the lowdown about Southerners.
7. Some of America's brightest businessmen and statesmen have come from the South.

4
Avoid slang, colloquial, or regional language for most expository writing.

Slang consists of coined words and new or extended meanings attached to established terms. Slang words and phrases usually pass out of use quickly. Occasionally slang terms become accepted into standard usage. **Colloquial** language is characteristic of casual conversation and informal writing: *The student flunked chemistry* instead of *the student failed chemistry*. **Regional (dialectal) language** is specific to some geographic areas: *They have nary a cent.*

Although slang and colloquial words and regional language are neither substandard nor illiterate, they are not appropriate for academic writing. Replacing slang, colloquial, and regional language with general English in your college writing allows you to communicate clearly with the large number of people who speak and write in medium or somewhat formal levels of langauge. Slang, colloquial, and regional expressions can have a place in narratives in which you describe the exact speech of individuals, however.

Slang words are used only in very informal situations. Sometimes slang terms are inventions: *hippie* from the 1960s and its 1980 counterpart *yuppie* are examples. Sometimes slang terms are redefinitions of existing words: *psyched* or *wired* to mean "enthusiastic" are examples. Slang varies according to time and place. Consider, for instance, these expressions defined in a 1983 *New York Times* article, "City Teenagers Talking Up a 'Say What?' Storm": *chill out* meaning "relax, be cool"; *say what?* for "excuse me?"; *box* for "radio"; *gear* for "stylish clothing." These expressions communicated their meanings colorfully and accurately among teenagers in New York in 1983. They might not have communicated the same meanings to teenagers in California in 1983 or to teenagers anywhere in 1987. And they certainly would not communicate accurate meanings in an academic paper or business report in New York in 1983 nor in any other time or place. Slang is fun, informal, and personal; it rarely has a place in writing for college.

Dialects are different from slang because dialectic differences correlate with both geographical regions and socioeconomic status. Although no regional or social dialect can be designated as the one "correct" form of a language, dialects spoken by educated people usually hold the attention of educated people more than do the speech patterns of others. Using a dialect when writing for the general reading public tends to shut some people out of the communication. One way to assess the appropriateness of dialect is to remember that the best form of language is whatever language most clearly communicates to a given audience.

5
Avoid slanted language.

To communicate clearly, you need to choose words that convince your audience of your fairness as a writer. When you are writing about a subject on which you hold strong opinions, it is easy to slip into biased or emotionally loaded language. Such **slanted language** usually does not convince a careful reader to agree with your point. Instead, it makes the reader wary or hostile. For example, suppose you are arguing against the practice of scientific experimentation on animals. If you use language such as "laboratory Frankensteins" who "routinely and viciously maim helpless kittens and puppies," you are using slanted language. A neutral audience will doubt your ability to write fairly about the subject. Especially in persuasive writing, you want to use words that make your side of an issue the more convincing one. Once you start using slanted, biased language, however, readers feel manipulated rather than reasoned with. Only those who already agree with you will be convinced. Those who disagree will be annoyed. And those who might have been persuaded will start to think of rebuttals to your unfair, slanted presentation.

◼‖ 21b
Use figurative language.

Figures of speech use words for more than their literal meanings. Figurative language creates comparisons and connections that use one idea or image to enhance or explain another. The most common figures of speech are similes and metaphors.

A **simile** states a direct comparison between otherwise dissimilar things. It sets up the comparison by using the words *like* or *as*. The famous black poet Langston Hughes says that a deferred dream dries up *like a raisin in the sun*.

A **metaphor** implies a comparison between otherwise dissimilar things without using *like* or *as: the soldier tulips march in even rows*. Many words are used metaphorically almost as often as they are used literally. With common metaphoric words, writers must be especially careful not to create an unintentionally impossible image. Consider this sentence for example: *The rush-hour traffic bled out of all the city's major arteries.* Cars are not at all like blood and their movement is not similar to the flow of blood, so the metaphor ends up being confusing rather than clarifying. Words with metaphorical meanings can also create **mixed metaphors,** incongruously combined images: *Milking the migrant workers for all they were worth, the supervisors bled them dry.* Here the initial image is of taking milk from a cow; but the final image has blood, not milk, as the result of the supervisors' evil actions.

Other types of figurative language include:

Understatement, or using a very restrained style
It gets warm when the temperature goes above 101 degrees.

Personification, or giving human traits to nonhuman things
The *book begged* to be read.

Irony, or suggesting the opposite of the usual sense
Told that the car repair would cost $1,000 and take at least two weeks, she muttered, "A bargain!"

Onomatopoeia, or using words to imitate the sound they denote
I heard a *hiss* of steam

Metonymy, or using a name associated with something to refer to anything in that class
The White House [the President] had no comment.

Synecdoche, or substituting a part for the whole (or vice versa)
The *pen* [discourse] is mightier than the *sword* [warfare].

Oxymoron, or combining opposites for a seeming contradiction or paradox
The *silence* was *thunderous.*

EXERCISE 2
Identify each figure of speech. Revise any mixed metaphors.

1. The challenger, another Goliath, fell with the first blow.
2. She went inside the house, shutting the door like a clam snapping shut its shell.
3. The ocean screamed its fury.
4. Triple bypass heart surgery is no tea party.
5. In tilling his land, Henry David Thoreau wanted the earth to say "beans" instead of "grass."
6. The beaver buzz-sawed through the tree trunk.
7. The world ended when his parents divorced.
8. The champion was like a cobra ready to strike.

9. The soft mountains shone in the sun.
10. Changing a flat tire is exactly how I love to spend my time.

■‖ 21c
Avoid clichés.

A **cliché** is an overused, worn-out expression that has lost its capacity to communicate effectively. Some comparisons, once clever, have grown trite: *dead as a doornail, gentle as a lamb, straight as an arrow*. If you have heard words over and over again, so has your reader. If you cannot think of a way to rephrase a cliché, delete the phrase entirely.

The word *cliché* is often used to describe both overused expressions and overused words. But a single word cannot really be a cliché, although it can become tiresome and trite. Such words are called **vogue words** by linguists. For a while you hear and see them everywhere; their use is a kind of fad. Like fads, vogue words soon lose their popularity, and then they once again take their place as useful, but not overused, terms. Examples of vogue words are *relevant* which in the early 1970s was used to describe everything from school curricula to political party platforms. Occasionally a perfectly useful phrase will also enjoy a span of overpopularity and become a vogue phrase. For example, during the period following World War II "in our time"—perhaps echoing Churchill's ringing conviction that there would be "peace in our time"—became popular and was overused by the journalists and newscasters of that period. Now the phrase has receded to its former status, and a writer can use it without fear of being thought unoriginal.

The difference between a vogue phrase and a cliché is that although a vogue phrase can return to being a useful part of the language, a cliché cannot. The language loses its punch *(happily ever after, face the music, ripe old age)* and new ways of expressing the ideas are needed. Nevertheless, clichés are not created simply by being repeated or by becoming overly familiar. English is full of word groups that are very common and are frequently used, yet they do not become clichés: We can always say "up and down" and "in and out." Adjectives also fall into certain patterns. We usually say "a tiny blue book" or "a gigantic yellow moon" rather than "a blue, tiny book" or a "yellow, gigantic moon." Such common patterns are not clichés and you should not try to alter them in the search for fresh language.

Like vogue phrases, **proverbs** are also often confused with clichés. However, although both proverbs and clichés are used frequently, they are very different. Proverbs are lean and economical phrases that express a great deal with a few words. A true proverb cannot be shortened or edited. For example, "Don't count your chickens before they hatch" or "a stitch in time saves nine" communicates its message in the most economical way possible. A cliché, on the other hand, can easily be turned into a more direct expression. For instance, "hit the books" translates to "study" and "keep your nose to the grindstone" becomes "work hard." A proverb sums up accumulated experience and observation; a cliché lacks the permanent power of a proverb.

EXERCISE 3

Revise these clichés. Use the idea in each cliché for a sentence of your own in plain English.

1. If you want a sale, you have to take the bull by the horns.
2. You can't be shrinking violets when it comes to getting a sale.
3. Being aggressive means knocking the socks off prospective buyers with an impressive sales pitch.
4. To stay cool as a cucumber, you have to know your onions.
5. To make customers as happy as a lark, give them a good product and good service.
6. Slowly but surely they realize that you are there to help them.
7. Last but not least, be sure to get the buyers to put their John Hancocks on the dotted line.
8. Her sales pitch hit the nail on the head.
9. She felt ready to climb the ladder of success.
10. Nevertheless, she knew that was easier said than done.

21d
Avoid artificial language.

Sometimes a beginning writer thinks that using ornate words and complicated sentence structures makes writing impressive. Most experienced writers, on the other hand, work hard to communicate as clearly and directly as they can. These writers do not spend time looking for long, fancy words to explain a point. Instead, they try to make what they are saying as accessible as possible to their readers. Extremely complex ideas or subject areas may require complex terms or phrases to explain them, but in general the simpler the language, the more likely it is to be understood.

‖ 1
‖ Avoid pretentious language.

Pretentious language is too showy, calling undue attention to itself with complex sentences and polysyllabic words. College writing does not call for big words used for their own sake. Plain English that communicates clearly is far better than embellished English that makes the reader aware that you are trying to be "fancy" for no reason. "The clearer, the better" is good advice. Overblown words are likely to obscure your message.

> I hate it when he tries ostentatiously to flaunt his accoutrements recently acquired in the haberdashery shop. [*Translation: I hate it when he tries to show off his new clothes.*]
>
> The raison d'être for my matriculation in this institution of higher learning is the acquisition of a better education. [*Translation: The reason I am in college is to get a better education.*]

‖ 2
‖ Avoid unnecessary jargon.

Jargon is specialized vocabulary of a particular group—words that an outsider unfamiliar with this field would not understand. Whether or not a word is considered jargon depends on purpose and audience. For example, when a sportswriter uses words such as *gridiron, sacked, TD,* and *safety,* a football fan understands them with no difficulty. Specialized language evolves in every field: professions, academic disciplines, commerce, even hobbies. However, using jargon unnecessarily is pretentious, showy, and artificial. Instead of communicating, jargon may shut readers out. Whenever you must use jargon for a general audience, be sure to explain the specialized meanings.

ACCEPTABLE SPECIALIZED LANGUAGE

As the lake eutrophicates, it gradually fills until the entire lake will be converted into a terrestrial community. Eutrophic changes (or eutrophication) is the nutritional enrichment of the water, promoting the growth of aquatic plants.

—DAVIS AND SOLOMON, *The World of Biology*

Subroutines may call other subroutines. That is, subroutines may be "nested." Nesting can be carried out to any desired depth. You must remember, though, that the RETURN statement in a subroutine will cause the program to return to the statement immediately following the GOSUB statement which the computer executed last.

—Mario V. Farina, *Programming in Basic*

These examples show acceptable specialized language. They are from college textbooks which expect that students either know or can decipher the meaning of *eutrophication, eutrophic, subroutines,* and *nesting.*

3
Avoid euphemisms.

The word *euphemism* comes from the Greek meaning "words of good omen" (*eu-,* "good" + *pheme,* "voice"). Euphemisms attempt to avoid the harsh reality of truth by using more pleasant-sounding, "tactful" words. Although they are sometimes necessary for tact in social situations, euphemisms can drain meaning from truthful writing. People use unnecessary euphemisms to describe socially unacceptable behavior: "Johnny has a wonderfully vivid imagination" instead of "Johnny lies." They use euphemisms to hide unpleasant facts: "She is between assignments" instead of "She lost her job." Euphemisms like these fool no one, and they are unlikely to spare feelings.

EXERCISE 4
Revise each example of pretentious language, jargon, or euphemism.

1. It is of utmost importance that students prioritize their hours in the day in a type of apportionment to fulfill all their academic obligations.
2. She came within the venue of the law enforcement establishment.
3. It is with grave misgivings that I undertake this endeavor to instruct myself in the intricacies of computer programming.
4. Her occupation is domestic engineering.
5. His conversation was full of amusing thoughts concisely expressed with humor.
6. She announced herself to be in favor of terminating the employment of the sales representative.
7. The administrative assistant typed an epistle for his superior.

8. She is awaiting a little bundle of joy from heaven.

9. I recall the time in my past when the school I matriculated at was razed by an incendiary event.

10. Their cat passed away and is now reposing in the Slumber Haven Pet Cemetery.

4
Avoid "doublespeak."

Doublespeak is artificial, evasive language. Moreover, it can be grossly unfactual, deceptive, confusing, and self-contradictory. For example, people who strip and sell stolen cars might call themselves "auto dismantlers and recyclers" selling "predismantled, previously owned parts." A toothpick has been called a "wood interdental stimulator," and a bribe was once described as a "rebate . . . one of the clearest instances of the free market at work." Such language is distorting and dishonest. To use doublespeak is to use words to hide the truth, a highly unethical practice that tries to control people's thoughts. So severe is the doublespeak problem today that the National Council of Teachers of English yearly awards a "Doublespeak Award" for the "best" example of language that is purposely deceptive or grossly unfactual. In so doing, the Council wants to call attention to distorting language. In 1984 the award went to the U.S. State Department for announcing it will no longer use the word *killing* in its official reports about human rights in other countries. *Killing* was replaced with *unlawful or arbitrary deprivation of life*. Such misuses of language have devastating social and political consequences for a free society that seeks truth, rather than evasion, distortion, self-contradiction, and confusion.

5
Avoid bureaucratic language.

Like doublespeak, **bureaucratic language** is distorting. Unlike doublespeak, it is not intended to mislead. Rather, it is carelessly written, stuffy, overblown language.

> You can include a page that also contains an Include instruction. The page including the Include instruction is included when you paginate the document but the included text referred to in its Include instruction is not included.

The irony here is that the writer seems to be trying to communicate very precisely. Bureaucratic language (or *bureaucratese*, the coined word to describe the style) is marked by jargon, euphemism, and unnecessary complexity. Such writing becomes meaningless because it is evasive, ambiguous, and wordy.

EXERCISE 5
Rewrite into plain English these examples of doublespeak and bureaucratic language.

1. The government will add a user fee to the cost of gasoline.
2. In 1983 when the Soviets shot down Korean Airlines Flight 007, killing all aboard, they said, "The interceptor fight plane of the anti-aircraft defenses fulfilled the order of the command post to stop the flight."
3. For fire safety, all homes must have a "combustion enunciator" to warn people of smoke.
4. At a commercial postal delivery service, the "least-best" drivers are the ones who have poor driving and/or delivery records.
5. That explanation is no longer operative.

22
SPELLING AND HYPHENATION

One reason English spelling can be difficult is that English words originate from several sources. Some come from Latin, some from Greek, some from French (the French invaded Britain in the eleventh century). Many words have come into the language recently from technical jargon; nobody spoke of *lasers* or *bytes* thirty years ago. These various origins and the various ways English-speaking people pronounce words make it almost impossible to rely on pronunciation in spelling a word. What you *can* rely on, however, is a system of proofreading, studying, and learning spelling rules. With a little time and effort, English spelling can be mastered.

■‖ 22a
Eliminate careless errors.

Many spelling errors are not *spelling* errors at all. They are the result of illegible handwriting, slips of the pen, or typographical errors. Although you may not be able to change your handwriting, you can make it legible enough so that readers know what words you are writing. Catching "typos" requires careful proofreading. Try these techniques:

1. Read the page *backwards,* from the last sentence to the first. This method forces you to look at the words themselves by depriving you of the sense of a paragraph or sentence.
2. Use a ruler or other device to focus on only one line at a time.

See Appendix B, Using Correct Manuscript Format, for advice on correcting typos with proofreaders' marks.

EXERCISE 1
Proofread this paragraph, using one or both of the methods described above. Eight typos of various sorts occur. Underline each typo and write the correction above it.

I'll never forget the day I thought my car had been stollen. I had just finished an hour-long ordeal in the super market after haveing spend three hours studying. As I stepped out of the 68° air-conditioned store in the 97° Kansas sunshine, I headed for the car as quickly as I could. Not only was I about to mealt, but the two bowls of low-calorie non-dairy whipped topping and the four cans of frozen lemonad were already dripping in the bag. When I reached the spot where I knew I had parked the car, all I saw were three cricles of motor oil, a discarded popsicle stick oozing orange-red goo, and a crumpled ticket from the prevous week's lottery. Not an orange Vega in sight. Do you know what my first thought was? "Who could be fool enogh to steal a '76 Vega?"

 # 22b
Train yourself to improve your spelling.

1
Use the dictionary and be alert for new words.

Not all good spellers automatically know how to spell every word, but most good spellers know when to consult the dictionary for help. If you are unsure of how to spell a word but you know how it starts, look it up in the dictionary. The first spelling listed in most college dictionaries is the *preferred* spelling; use it. (The dictionary will also tell you whether the word can be divided, and if it can be, where to hyphenate it.) If you have no idea of how a word is spelled or if you do not know how to spell the beginning of a word, think of a synonym you can spell and look that word up in a thesaurus. Chances are you will find the original word listed.

Unfamiliar words often cause problems. When you come across key terms in a textbook, highlight or underline them as you read. (Do not underline *all* unfamiliar words; stick to the terms that are essential to the subject.) Then, *after you have finished reading,* memorize the spelling of those words. Writing unfamiliar words on 3 × 5″ cards can be especially helpful, because an isolated word on a card stands out far more clearly than one item in a long list. You may wish to write the word twice on the card, once regularly and once dividing it into parts that will simplify your learning. For example, you may find it easier to spell *perseverate* if you isolate the *sever: per sever ate.*

‖ 2

Use visuals and mnemonic devices to help you spell.

The 3 × 5″ card system described in 22b-1 can also help you learn how to spell familiar words. As you discover words you frequently misspell, print each carefully on a card, highlighting the problem area by using larger print, a different-colored ink, or a pastel highlighter.

democRACY   neCESSary

Mnemonic devices—techniques to improve memory—can also help you to remember the spelling of difficult words. Remember "the principal is your pal" line from high school? That mnemonic has helped many students distinguish between *principle* and *principal* by associating the latter word with a simple, familiar word. Memory techniques allow your brain to do more than simply memorize letters. For example, if you have trouble with the homonyms *stationary* and *stationery* try this: *Stationary* means standing still, while *stationery* is used to writ**e** on." The *a* and the *e* are the problem letters here, so by associating the *a* in *stationary* with the *a* in the word *stand*, you can remember more easily. The same principle holds for the *e* in *stationery*. Here are two more examples: *an emigrant leaves, and an immigrant comes in; the weather is clear, and whether is what.* Try to make up similar mnemonics for words you misspell.

‖ 3

‖ Look for patterns in your misspelled words and keep ‖ a spelling chart.

Misspellings usually occur in patterns. Many people, for example, are confused by words containing *ei* or *ie*. You will find it easier to learn the rule for these words than to try to memorize each word separately. Here are some of the many patterns of misspellings:

DOUBLING CONSONANTS	**coming** not *comming* (22d-1)
ADDING SYLLABLES	**athletic** not *atheletic*
DELETING SYLLABLES	**mathematics** not *mathmatics*
USING APOSTROPHES FOR PLURALS	ten **boys** not ten *boy's*
DROPPING FINAL e	**management** not *managment* (22d-1)
RETAINING FINAL e	**debatable** not *debateable* (22d-1)
RETAINING FINAL y	**merriment** not *merryment* (22d-1)
BLENDING SOUNDS	**length** not *lenth*
OMITTING SILENT LETTERS	**wealthy** not *welthy*
TRANSPOSING LETTERS	**relevant** not *revelant*
COMBINING SEPARATE WORDS	**a lot** not *alot* (22c-3)
USING IMPROPER FORMS	the **vanquished** enemy, not the *vanquish* enemy (22d-1)

Not all these patterns correspond to rules listed in the handbook. Patterns are often related simply to memory and not to stated rules. In fact, many people have their own particular misspelling patterns, unlike those of any other writer. Whatever your misspelling patterns, remember that your brain can handle five different *patterns* more easily than fifty-five different *words*. Not only is the number more manageable, but the concept of a pattern makes it easier for your brain to recognize possible misspelled words.

The most effective way to group your spelling errors into patterns is to keep a spelling chart. List on the chart all of the words you misspell, their correct spelling, the problem area, and the corresponding handbook section or pattern. Your chart should be set up like this:

INCORRECT	CORRECT	PROBLEM AREA	RULE OR PATTERN
recieve	receive	ie/ei	22d-2
writting	writing	tt/t	22d-1
labratory	laboratory	ra/ora	deleted syllable: 22c-4
immediatly	immediately	tly/tely	22d-1
Febuary	February	ua/rua	missing letter: 22c-4

▦‖ 22c
Solve spelling problems that arise from difficult words and word groups.

‖ ## 1
Recognize homonyms and commonly confused words.

Homonyms are words that sound exactly like others (*its/it's, morning/mourning*). Many other words sound almost alike so they are often confused for each other. The best way to distinguish between homonyms or other commonly confused words is to use mnemonic devices, like ones mentioned in 22b-2.

HOMONYMS AND COMMONLY CONFUSED WORDS

accept	to receive
except	with the exclusion of
advice	recommendation
advise	to recommend
affect	to produce an influence on *(verb)*; an emotional response *(noun)*
effect	result *(noun)*; to bring about or cause *(verb)*
aisle	space between rows
isle	island
allude	to make indirect reference to
elude	to avoid
allusion	indirect reference
illusion	false idea, misleading appearance
already	by this time
all ready	fully prepared
altar	sacred platform or place
alter	to change
altogether	thoroughly
all together	everyone or everything in one place

angel	supernatural being, good person
angle	the shape made by joining two straight lines at one end
are	plural form of *to be*
hour	sixty minutes
our	plural form of *my*
ascent	the act of rising or climbing
assent	consent
assistance	help
assistants	helpers
bare	nude, unadorned
bear	to carry; an animal
board	piece of wood
bored	uninterested
breath	air taken in
breathe	to take in air
brake	device for stopping
break	destroy, make into pieces
buy	to purchase
by	next to, through the agency of
canvas	heavy cloth
canvass	to poll
capital	major city
capitol	government building
choose	to pick
chose	past tense of *to choose*
cite	to point out
sight	vision
site	a place
clothes	garments
cloths	pieces of fabric
coarse	rough
course	path; series of lectures
complement	something that completes
compliment	praise, flattery
conscience	sense of morality
conscious	awake, aware
corps	regulated group
corpse	dead body
council	governing body
counsel	advice
dairy	place where milk products are collected, manufactured, and/or sold
diary	personal journal
descent	downward movement
dissent	disagreement

dessert	final, sweet course in a meal
desert	to abandon; dry, sandy area
device	a plan; an implement
devise	to create
dominant	commanding, controlling
dominate	to control
die	to lose life; one of a pair of dice
dye	to change the color of something
dyeing	changing the color of something
dying	losing life
elicit	to draw out
illicit	illegal
eminent	prominent
immanent	living within; inherent
imminent	about to happen
envelop	to surround
envelope	container for a letter or other papers
fair	light-skinned; just, honest
fare	money for transportation; food
formally	conventionally, with ceremony
formerly	previously
forth	forward
fourth	number four
gorilla	animal in ape family
guerilla	soldier specializing in unconventional, surprise attacks
hear	to sense sound by ear
here	in this place
heard	past tense of *to hear*
herd	group of animals
hole	opening
whole	complete; an entire thing
human	relating to the species *homo sapiens*
humane	compassionate
its	possessive form of *it*
it's	contraction for *it is*
know	to comprehend
no	negative
later	after a time
latter	second one of two things
lead	heavy metal substance; to guide
led	past tense of *to lead*
lessen	to decrease
lesson	something learned and/or taught
lightning	storm-related electricity
lightening	making lighter

loose	unbound, not tightly fastened
lose	to misplace
maybe	perhaps
may be	might be
meat	animal flesh
meet	to encounter
miner	a person who works in a mine
minor	under age
moral	distinguishing right from wrong; the lesson of a fable, story, or event
morale	attitude or outlook, usually of a group
of	preposition indicating origin
off	away from
passed	past tense of *to pass*
past	at a previous time
patience	forbearance
patients	people under medical care
peace	absence of fighting
piece	segment or part of a whole; musical arrangement
personal	intimate
personnel	employees
plain	simple, unadorned
plane	to shave wood; aircraft
precede	to come before
proceed	to continue
presence	being at hand; attendance at a place or in something
presents	gifts
principal	foremost (adjective); administrator of a school (noun)
principle	moral conviction, basic truth
quiet	silent, calm
quite	very
rain	water drops falling to earth; to fall like rain
reign	to rule
rein	strap to guide or control an animal (noun); to guide or control (verb)
raise	to lift up
raze	to tear down
respectfully	with respect
respectively	in that order
reverend	title given to clergy; deserving reverence or respect
reverent	worshipful
right	correct; opposite of *left*
rite	ritual
write	to put words on paper

road	path
rode	past tense of *to ride*
scene	place of an action; segment of a play
seen	viewed
sense	perception, understanding
since	measurement of past time; because
stationary	standing still
stationery	writing paper
straight	unbending
strait	narrow waterway
taught	past tense of *to teach*
taut	tight
than	besides
then	at that time; next
their	possessive form of *they*
there	in that place
they're	contraction for *they are*
through	finished; into and out of
threw	past tense of *to throw*
thorough	complete
to	toward
too	also
two	number following one
track	course, road
tract	pamphlet
waist	midsection of the body
waste	discarded material; to squander, to fail to use up
waive	forgo, renounce
wave	flutter, move back and forth
weak	not strong
week	seven days
weather	climatic condition
whether	if
where	in which place
were	past tense of *to be*
which	one of a group
witch	female sorcerer
whose	possessive form of *who*
who's	contraction for *who is*
your	possessive form of *you*
you're	contraction for *you are*
yore	long past

EXERCISE 2
From each group in parentheses, select the appropriate homonym.

Last week (are, our) county's governing (council, counsel) (passed, past) a new ordinance. As of July 1, no hazardous (waist, waste) dumping (cites, sights, sites) may be built within three miles of any populated area. Local factories will now have to ship (their, there, they're) refuse to another county or (choose, chose) to dispose of it in another way. We will (know, no) longer (accept, except) living in fear of poisons we might (breath, breathe). We are (know, no) longer willing (to, too, two) allow our water to be polluted. For example, a company (who's, whose) main branch is in our county is presently manufacturing (die, dye) for women's (clothes, cloths). The owners might try (to, too, two) have the regulations (waived, waved) for businesses (all ready, already) in existence, but the issue is (to, too, two) serious (to, too, two) permit any exceptions. Would you want a creek mixing red, blue, and green (all together, altogether) running (threw, through) (your, you're) backyard?

2
Know American versus British spellings and other preferred forms.

Many English words have two correct spellings: one British, one American. The variations often involve the following word endings:

AMERICAN		BRITISH	
-or	(vig**or**)	-our	(vig**our**)
-ize	(apolog**ize**)	-ise	(apolog**ise**)
-tion	(connec**tion**)	-xion	(conne**xion**)
-ed	(dream**ed**)	-t	(dream**t**)
-ment	(acknowledg**ment**)	-ement	(acknowledg**ement**)
-led	(revel**ed**)	-lled	(revel**led**)

In the United States, use American spellings. American college dictionaries differ in the ways they show variant spellings. Read your dictionarys' introductory pages to find out its method. As a general rule, any entry that is fully defined and not otherwise noted as a variant form is a word's most common (and usually preferred) form. In order to remain consistent, use one dictionary and stick to its preferred forms. Always use the same form throughout a paper.

EXERCISE 3

First underline the seven words spelled according to British rules. Then, write the preferred American form above each.

My friends often criticise me for my strange taste in ice cream. My favourite flavor is rum-berry-raisin, a magnificent concoction to be savoured only by the most ardent lovers of ice cream. This delicacy is too precious to be wasted on the ordinary ice cream fancier. To prevent even a drop of it from being spilt on a "Grandma's Little Angel" T-shirt, children should not be allowed near it. I consider this flavor food for the gods. I have travelled miles to taste the best rum-berry-raisin, and my judgement is impeccable. And I have the greatest respect for those who share my taste, because I consider good taste in ice cream to be a reflexion of one's overall character and zest for life.

3
Learn to tell apart words with multiple forms.

Some expressions may be written either as one word or two, depending on meaning:

> An **everyday** occurrence is something that happens **every day.**
> The guests were there **already** by the time I was **all ready.**
> When we were **all together,** there were five of us **altogether.**
> We were there **a while** when the host said dinner would be
>   **awhile** longer.
> **Maybe** the main course will be sushi, but it **may be** tofuburgers.
> When we went **in to** dinner, he walked **into** the table.

Memorize the two expressions that are always written as two words: *all right* (not *alright*), and *a lot* (not *alot*).

4
Avoid spelling problems based on faulty pronunciation.

Pronunciation can cause spelling problems for a number of reasons. Sometimes people have trouble hearing the differences between two forms of the same word. If you know what form of the word you need for the meaning you want your sentence to deliver, you can decide on the correct spelling. For example, *prejudice* can be a noun, *prejudiced* an adjective ("I am guilty of *prejudice* [noun] if I am a *prejudiced* [adjective] person"). *Advice* is a noun, *advise* a verb ("If I *advise* [verb] you, I hope you will take my *advice* [noun]").

Some expressions are often mispronounced. Here are three: **used to,** not *use to;* **supposed to,** not *suppose to;* **should have,** not *should of.*

Imprecise pronunciation often leads to misspelling familiar words. Some people, for example, add an extra syllable to the word *athletic,* spelling it with an extra *e.* On the other hand, some people delete a syllable from the word *privilege,* spelling it without the second *i.*

ask	not	*aks* or *axe*
athlete	not	*athelete*
disastrous	not	*disasterous*
environment	not	*enviorment* or *enviroment*
especially	not	*expecially*
etcetera	not	*eksetera*
February	not	*Febuary*
grievous	not	*grevious*
height	not	*heighth*
mischievous	not	*mischevious*
nuclear	not	*nucular*
prescribe	not	perscribe
privilege	not	privlege
represent	not	*repersent*
strength	not	*strenth*
width	not	*with*

Distinguishing between pronoun forms can also create spelling problems. Always consider the meaning of a pronoun. In general, the form containing an apostrophe is a contraction:

it's	=	*it is*
they're	=	*they are*
who's	=	*who is*
you're	=	*you are*

Note carefully that there is no word *its'*. The forms without contractions are possessive forms of the pronouns:

its	is the possessive form of *it*
their	is the possessive form of *they*
whose	is the possessive form of *who*
your	is the possessive form of *you*

■‖ 22d
Solve spelling problems within words.

‖ 1
Spell suffixes (word endings) carefully.

A **suffix** is an ending added to the basic (root) form of a word. For example, suffixes can change a present-tense verb to past tense *(talk, talked)*, an adjective to an adverb *(quick, quickly)*, a verb to a noun *(govern, govern**ment**)*, and a noun to an adjective *(courage, courag**eous**)*. Spelling problems can arise when different suffixes sound alike or when changes must be made in the base word before the suffix is added.

-d ending

The *-d* ending changes many present-tense verb forms into past tense and past participle forms *(change, changed)*. Spelling problems may arise if the *-d* ending is not clearly pronounced and therefore not written. Although you may hear "use to," write *used to*. Do not count on the way words sound in conversation to guide your spelling.

-able, -ible

The two *-ble* suffixes cause problems primarily because no consistent, reliable rules for their use exist. More words end in *-able: advisable, comfortable, culpable, inalienable, insurmountable, probable, treatable, washable.* Still, some common words end in *-ible: audible, forcible, fusible, irresistible.* The best rule to follow with these two endings is, "When in doubt, look it up."

-ally, -ly

Both *-ally* and *-ly* endings turn words into adverbs. The suffix *-ally* is added to words ending in *ic: logic + ally = logically; tragic + ally = tragically.* The suffix *-ly* is added to adjectives not ending in *ic: quick + ly = quickly; slow + ly = slowly.*

-ance, -ence, -ant, -ent

The *-nce* and *-nt* endings do not occur according to any rule. Some words end in *-ance: compliance, defiance, dissonance, observance, reluctance, resistance.* Other words end in *ence: convenience, correspondence, dissidence, existence, independence, prevalence.*

If a noun ends in *ance,* its adjective form ends in *-ant: compli-ance, compliant; defiance, defiant; resistance, resistant.* Similarly, if a noun ends in *-ence,* the adjective form ends in *-ent: confidence, confident; convenience, convenient; existence, existent; prevalence, prevalent.* Be careful of the spelling of the word *confident.* The sim-ilar word *confidant* is pronounced differently and has an entirely different meaning: *Confident* means "self-assured" and *confidant* means "a person confided in."

-cede, -ceed, -sede

Only one word ends in *-sede: supersede.* Three words end in *-ceed: exceed, proceed,* and *succeed.* All other words whose endings sound like these suffixes end in *-cede:* for example, *accede, concede, intercede, precede.* A very common misspelling involves *proceed:* its noun form drops an *e* from *-ceed* and is spelled *procedure.*

Final e

The basic rule for final *e* is this: drop it before a suffix begin-ning with a vowel, but retain it if the suffix begins with a conso-nant. Consider the word *require,* for example. If *-ing* is added to the word, the final *e* is dropped: *requiring.* If, however, *-ment* is added, the final *e* is retained: *requirement.* Other examples include *abate + ment = abatement; like + ly = likely; oblige + ation = obliga-tion; tribe + al = tribal.*

Some words retain final *e* to prevent confusing them with other words. For example, *dye + ing* is *dyeing* to avoid confusion with *dying (die + ing).*

For the few exceptions to the basic rule for final *e,* simply memorize their spelling: *argument, awful, truly,* and *wisdom,* for example.

Final y

When final *y* is preceded by a consonant, change the *y* to *i* before adding a suffix (unless the suffix begins with *i.*) For example, when adding *-ed* to the word *fry,* change the final *y* to *i: fried.* When *-ing* is added to a final *y,* however, the *y* is retained: *frying,* Here are other examples: *comply + ance =* compliance, *comply + ing =* complying; *supply + er = supplier, supply + ing = supplying.* If the final *y* is preceded by a vowel, retain the *y* when you are adding any suffixes: *destroy + er = destroyer, employ + ed = employed, joy + ous = joyous, stay + ing = staying.*

Doubling final consonants

When should you double a final consonant? If a one-syllable word ends in a consonant preceded by a single vowel, then double the final consonant before adding a suffix. For example, if you add -*ing* to the word *flip,* double the *p: flipping.* Here are more examples: *blot, blotted; cram, cramming; pit, pitted; quit, quitting.*

With two-syllable words, an additional rule applies: double the final consonant only if the last syllable is stressed. If you add -ing to *refer,* you should double the final consonant: *referring.* However, if you add -*ence,* do not double the final consonant: *reference.* The difference here is in pronunciation. In *referring,* the accent is on the last syllable of *refer,* while in *reference* the accent is on the first syllable. Here are more examples: *abut, abutting; control, controlled; omit, omitting; prefer, preferring.*

2
Know the *ie, ei* rule and exceptions.

The old rhyme for *ie* and *ei* is usually true: "*I* before *e,* except after *c,* or when sounded like *ay,* as in *neighbor* and *weigh.*"

IE   believe, field, grief

EI   ceiling, conceit, eight, neigh, receive, vein

Because there are so few exceptions, they are worth memorizing.

IE   conscience, financier, science, species

EI   counterfeit, either, foreign, forfeit, height, leisure, neither, seize, sleight, weird

EXERCISE 4
A. Add -*able* or -*ible* to each word.

1. contempt____
2. resist____
3. adore____
4. believe____
5. reverse____
6. adapt____
7. dispense____
8. use____

B. Add -*ant* or -*ent* to each word.

9. relev_____   12. immin_____
10. attend_____   13. reli_____
11. vari_____   14. resist_____

C. Add the given ending to each word, dropping final *e* as needed.

15. change + able   23. create + ion
16. change + ing   24. create + ing
17. manage + ment   25. complete + ly
18. manage + ing   26. complete + ion
19. revise + ion   27. note + able
20. revise + ing   28. note + ing
21. repulse + ive   29. include + ing
22. repulse + ion   30. include + ed

D. Add the given ending to each word, changing final *y* to *i* as needed.

31. play + ful   35. merry + ment
32. play + ing   36. supply + ed
33. study + ing   37. vary + ing
34. study + ous   38. vary + ous

E. Add the given ending to each word, doubling the final consonant as needed.

39. write + ing   42. trot + ed
40. stop + ed   43. begin + ing
41. start + ing   44. open + ed

F. Fill in the spaces correctly with *ie* or *ei*.

45. rel_____f   49. conc_____ve
46. br_____f   50. sl_____gh
47. dec_____ve   51. p_____rce
48. n_____ce   52. fr_____ght

3
Know how to use prefixes.

Prefixes are syllables placed in front of words, either changing or adding to the word's meaning. For example, the prefixes *un-* and *in-* turn a word into its opposite *(uncooperative, inadmissible);* re- adds the meaning "again" to a word *(recreate, reincarnation);* and *pre-* adds the meaning "before" to a word *(precook, predestination).* A prefix does not alter the spelling of the word to which it is added: for example, *un + reliable = unreliable; re + locate = relocate.* Some prefixes, however, do require hyphens, as is explained in 22e. For a complete list of prefixes, see 20c.

4
Know how to form plurals.

Plurals in English are formed in a number of different ways, but they are relatively easy to learn because the rules are fairly consistent:

Regular plurals (-s/-es)

In general, add -*s* to form a plural: *leg, legs; desk, desks; elephant, elephants; shoe, shoes.*

If a word ends in -*ch,* -*s,* -*sh,* -*x,* or -*z,* however, adding simply -*s* would cause pronunciation problems. Add -*es* to such words: *beach, beaches; iris, irises; ash, ashes; tax, taxes; topaz, topazes.*

Most words ending in *o* become plural with the addition of -*s: alto, altos; radio, radios; cameo, cameos; tobacco, tobaccos.* A few words ending in *o* become plural with the addition of -*es* (those that do so have a consonant before the final *o*): *hero, heroes; tomato, tomatoes; potato, potatoes; veto, vetoes.* A few words ending in *o* preceded by a consonant take either -*s* or -*es* (always be consistent in the form you use): *cargo, cargoes, cargos; volcano, volcanoes, volcanos; tornado, tornadoes, tornados; zero, zeroes, zeros.*

Words ending in f or fe

In general, change *f* to *v* before adding -*s* or -*es: leaf, leaves; loaf, loaves; life, lives; wife, wives.*

Three exceptions to this rule come up often: *belief, beliefs; motif, motifs; safe, safes.* These exceptions avoid confusion with the singular verbs *believes* and *saves* and with the plural noun *motives.*

When a word ends in *ff* or *ffe,* simply add -*s: giraffe, giraffes; staff, staffs.*

Compound words

In general, add -*s* or -*es* at the end of a compound word: *capful, capfuls; player-coach, player-coaches; nurse-midwife, nurse-midwives.* If, however, the major word in the compound is the first word, add the -*s* or -*es* to the first word: *mile per hour, miles per hour; professor emeritus, professors emeritus; sister-in-law, sisters-in-law.*

Internal changes

Some words change internally to form the plural: *child, children; foot, feet; man, men; mouse, mice; ox, oxen.* Fortunately, these plurals sound so different that they do not cause spelling problems, except in the case of *woman* and *women.* If you remember that these words add *wo-* to *man* and *men,* you should be able to spell them correctly.

Foreign plurals

Latin words ending in *-um* usually form their plurals by changing the *-um* to *-a; curriculum, curricula; datum, data; medium, media; stratum, strata.*

For Latin words ending in *-us,* the plural is *-i: alumnus, alumni; syllabus, syllabi.* Less common Latin forms and words borrowed from other languages usually form their plurals according to the rules of the language: *alumna, alumnae; criterion, criteria; axis, axes; thesis, theses.*

Plurals retaining singular form

Some words are spelled the same whether they are being used in a singular or plural sense. Usually they are the names of animals or grains: *deer, elk, fish, quail, rice, wheat.*

EXERCISE 5
Form the plurals of these words.

1. veto
2. brother-in-law
3. wolf
4. district attorney
5. march
6. stress
7. deer
8. tooth
9. child
10. self
11. bacterium
12. hero
13. spoonful
14. tomato
15. shelf
16. comrade-in-arms
17. life
18. trout
19. patio
20. monkey

22e
Use hyphens correctly.

1
Learn when and how to divide a word at the end of a line.

Unless the last word on a line would use up most of the right margin of your paper, do not divide it. If you absolutely must divide a word, remember not to divide the last word on the first line of a paper, the last word in a paragraph, or the last word on a page. When you must divide a word, follow these guidelines:

Never divide single-syllable words or very short words. No matter how long a word is, if it has only one syllable or is pronounced as one syllable, do not divide it—for example, *cleansed, drought, screamed, wealth.* Do not divide short words, even ones that have two or more syllables—for example, *area, every, envy.*

Always divide words between syllables. The dictionary listing of a word shows its syllables clearly. The dictionary shows *distinction,* for example, as *dis-tinc-tion,* so you should divide it after the *s* or after the *c,* but nowhere else.

Never leave or carry over only one or two letters. This guideline means that words like *alive* and *ocean* are not divided at all. It also means that a word like *he-li-cop-ter* can be divided after the *i* or the *p,* but not after the *e.*

Follow rules for double consonants. Suffixes (word endings) usually add syllables. If a base word ends in a double consonant, divide the word after the double consonant: *access-ible,* not *acces-sible; success-ful,* not *succes-sful; trespass-ing,* not *trespas-sing.* On the other hand, when you double a consonant only to add a suffix, divide the word between the double consonants: *omit-ting,* not *omitt-ing; regret-table,* not *regrett-able; swim-ming,* not *swimm-ing.*

Never violate pronunciation when you divide words. Not all word endings add pronounceable new syllables. The *-ed* ending, for example, often simply adds a *d* sound to the end of a word. If you divide such a word at the *ed,* a reader will read a syllable that the word's pronunciation does not reflect. For example, *cleared* should not be divided and *compelled* should be divided *com-pelled,* not *compel-led.* Also, do not divide a word like *issue,* because both its syllables are pronounced differently separated than they are together: *is-sue.*

‖ **2**
‖ **Divide words with prefixes and suffixes correctly.**

Most prefixes form **closed words,** or words written as one *(semi + sweet = semisweet).* When you divide a word that has a prefix of three or more letters, divide after the prefix rather than between other syllables: *mis-understand,* not *misunder-stand; non-conformist,* not *noncon-formist; super-impose,* not *superim-pose.*

Some prefixes must be followed by hyphens separating them from the base word. These prefixes fall into the following categories:

all-, ex-, quasi-, and self-

The prefixes *all-, ex-, quasi-,* and *self-* usually take hyphens: *all-inclusive, all-knowing, ex-husbamd, ex-president, quasi-judicial, quasi-psychological, self-assured, self-confidence.*

Selfish and *selfless* do not have hyphens because in each case *self* is a base word followed by a suffix, *-ish* and *-less,* respectively. Only when *self* is a prefix is it followed by a hyphen. It is never hyphenated when it is a suffix *(herself).*

Proper nouns and numbers

When the main word is a proper noun or a number, the prefix is followed by a hyphen: *all-American, anti-Communist, pro-Republican, pre-1950.*

Compound main words

When the main word is a compound, the prefix is followed by a hyphen: *anti-gun control, mini-baby boom, post-middle age.* Often, such compounds are not very clear, and you should revise, not so much to solve a hyphen problem as to make your meaning unambiguous for readers.

Avoiding confusion

Sometimes it is necessary to hyphenate a prefix in order to avoid confusion in meaning or pronunciation. If a prefix added to a word causes it to look exactly like another word, a hyphen after the prefix should help a reader understand which word you mean. For example, the hyphen in *re-dress* signals a reader that you mean "dress again" rather than "set right" *(redress).*

If the last letter of a prefix is the same as the first letter of the main word, or if adding a prefix results, in three vowels in a row, you may use a hyphen after the prefix: *anti-intellectual, re-*

ionize, semi-intensive. Some words are commonly spelled without this hyphen— *cooperation, preeminent,* and *reexamine,* for example.

Suspended hyphens

When you use two prefixes with one base word in a sentence, you may choose to write the base word only once, after the second prefix. But follow *both* prefixes with a hyphen: *pre- or post-test, pre- and post-war eras, two- and four-year colleges.* Note that the first hyphen is separated from the next word by a space.

3
Spell compound words correctly.

Many writers, professionals as well as students, have difficulty with compound words. Some terms, called **open compounds,** are written as two words: *cedar shingles, night shift, executive secretary, student union.* In compounds like these, the first term acts as an adjective modifying the second. Do not confuse open compounds with adjective-noun combinations such as *Central America* and *thatched roof.*

Other compounds, called **closed compounds,** are written as one word: *handbook, housewife, northeast, sunburn.*

The third type of compound is known as a **hyphenated compound.** Examples are *comparison-contrast, nurse-practitioner, secretary-treasurer, tractor-trailer.* In general, when terms of compound words are new or are coined for a specific purpose, they are spelled as open compounds. Once their use is widespread, however, they often come to be spelled as closed compounds. For example, the term *mini van* came into the language in the early 1980s. By the middle of the decade, *minivan* was the accepted spelling.

Some compounds require hyphens, either to make the meaning clearer or to make the compound easier to read. When a compound acts as a modifier° *before* a noun, it is usually hyphenated:

fast-paced lecture	soft-sided luggage
long-term commitment	twenty-page report

Usually, that same modifier is not hyphenated if it comes *after* the noun, however.

The lecture seems fast paced.	That luggage is soft sided.
My commitment is long term.	The report was twenty pages.

Some familiar terms are unambiguous and easy to understand and so do not require hyphens: for example, *genetic engineering laboratory, health insurance policy, junior high school, state sales tax.*

When the first word in a compound is an *-ly* adverb, when the first word is a comparative° or superlative°, or when the compound is a foreign phrase, the hyphen is omitted: **happily** *married couple,* **better** *fitting dress,* **least** *expected results,* **ex post facto** *law.*

Use a hyphen between the two components of a combined **unit of measurement:** for example, *degree-days, kilowatt-hours, light-years.*

Although most compound titles are not hyphenated *(state senator, vice principal),* many are. Hyphenated titles usually are nation names, actual double titles, or three-word titles: Anglo-Irish, Italian-American, broker-analyst, ambassador-at-large, father-in-law, forget-me-not.

‖ 4
‖ Use hyphens correctly in spelled-out numbers.

Fractions

Use a hyphen between the numerator and denominator of a fraction, unless a hyphen already appears in either or both: *three-hundredths* (3/100), but *two three-hundredths.* (2/300).

Double-digit numbers

Use hyphens between the two components of numbers from twenty-one through ninety-nine only. This rule holds whether those numbers are written alone or as part of larger numbers: *thirty-five, sixty-two, two hundred thirty-five, five hundred sixty-two.*

Combined numbers and words

When numbers and words are combined to form one idea or modifier, use a hyphen between the number and the word: for example, *50-minute class, 3-to-1 odds, 10-kilometer race.* If the word in the modifier is possessive, however, omit the hyphen: *5 days' vacation, 8 hours' pay, 1 week's work.*

EXERCISE 6
Write the correct form of the word in parentheses according to the way it is used in the sentence.

1. In (pre World War I) _____ America, a "red scare" gripped the nation.
2. Americans grew suspicious of foreigners, especially Slavs and (Eastern Europeans) _____.

3. (Anti Soviet) _____ feelings influenced every facet of American life.

4. The red scare (co incided) _____ with the rise of (labor unions) _____.

5. Many people viewed the unions as part of a (Bolshevik inspired) _____ plot to (over throw) _____ the government of the United States.

6. While some of the unions were (semi independent) _____ , many were branches of the Industrial Workers of the World, a socialist organization.

7. Often (pro and anti union) _____ forces met in violent confrontations.

8. Americans found (them selves) _____ injuring and killing their (fellow citizens) _____.

9. During the Lawrence, Massachusetts, Bread and Roses strike in 1912, more than (twenty five) _____ people were injured in street fighting.

10. After the strike was over, the people of Lawrence organized a parade "for God and country," to show the world that they were patriotic, (God fearing) _____ Americans.

EXERCISE 7

Each paragraph contains eleven misspelled words. Circle the words and enter them on a spelling chart as described in 22b-3. In the *Rule/Pattern* column, enter the page or code number of the appropriate section of this handbook. If the error does not fall under any particular section, describe the cause of the error in the Rule/Pattern column.

1. It seems that all we hear about now adays is the computer revolution. There are computers in librarys, schools, offices, and even in homes. Freinds of mine who once feared anything remotely associated with electronics now loudly sing the praises of word-processing, as if the typewriter were a product of the Stone Age. Last week I grew so weary of listening to them that I decided to see for myself exactly what these wonders of technology could do. As I cautiously approached my college's Writing Center, my ears were assalted by the click-click-click of keyboards, and an occassional screech from a printer. One of the tutors offerred me her assistants in learning to use the machine. Within a mere twenty-five minutes I was typing happily, thinking all the while that I should have tryed this much sooner. Just as I began the conclusion of my English paper, the entire building was plunged into silent darkness. I was dismayed at the thought of haveing to wait until the following day to see the printout. Then the tutor told me the bad news: I had lost the entire essay when the electricity went of. My draft no longer existed. With poise and grace, I felt my way to the exit.

2. Among the most effective voices for nonviolent resistance and civil disobediance in the twentieth century have been Mohandas Gandhi and Martin Luther King, Jr. Both were educated, middle-class men who found

407

themselfs the objects of discrimination because of they're race. Gandhi first encountered racism when he visited South Africa around the turn of the century. After forcing the goverment to modify parts of the racial code in that country, he returned to his homeland, India, were he began a long quest to rid it of British rule. His succeses as well as his failures influenced a young minister from Georgia, Martin Luther King, Jr., who fiercely opposed segregation in the United States. King embraced Gandhi's warning that oppressed people must resist the temptation to answer violence with violence. They both beleived that once the oppressed resort to violence they become no better than their oppressors. King's success in eliminateing legally sanctioned segregation in the South, like Gandhi's success in freeing India from the British, is testamony to the effectiveness of non-violent resistence. It is ironic that these two apostles of peace died in the same way: victims of assassins' bullets.

VI | PUNCTUATION AND MECHANICS

23
THE PERIOD, QUESTION MARK, AND EXCLAMATION POINT

The period, question mark, and exclamation point are called **end punctuation** because they occur at the end of sentences.

> I love you.
> I love you!
> Do you love me?

▉‖ 23a
Use a period at the end of a statement, a mild command, or an indirect question.

Unless a sentence asks a direct question (23c) or issues a strong command or emphatic declaration (23e), it ends with a period.

STATEMENT   A journey of a thousand leagues begins with a single step.   —LAO-TSU

MILD COMMAND   Put a gram of boldness into everything you do.   —BALTASAR GRACIAN

INDIRECT QUESTION   They wondered how many attempts have been made to climb Mt. Everest. [Compare with a direct question, which ends in question mark: *How many attempts have been made to climb Mt. Everest?*]

■‖ 23b
Use periods with most abbreviations.

Most **abbreviations** call for periods, but some do not. Typical abbreviations that include periods and that are acceptable in academic writing include *Dr., Mr., Ms., Mrs., Ph.D., M.D., R.N.,* and *a.m.* and *p.m.* with exact times such as *2:15 p.m.* Abbreviations not requiring periods include: address abbreviations for states, such as *CA* and *NY;* names of some organizations and government agencies, such as *CBS* and *FBI;* and acronyms (initials pronounced as words), such as *NASA* and *CARE.*

Ms. Yuan, who works at NASA, lectured to Dr. Arias's physics class yesterday at 9:30 A.M.

For a list of abbreviations and a discussion of their uses, see Chapter 30. ▋‖ PUNCTUATION ALERTS: (1) Abbreviations of academic degrees should usually be set off with commas. When they follow city names, abbreviations of states are set off with commas. (2) When the period of an abbreviation falls at the end of a sentence, the period serves also to end the sentence. ‖▋

■‖ 23c
Use a question mark after a direct question.

A **direct question** asks a question, in contrast to an **indirect question,** which reports a question and ends with a period (23a). A question mark follows a direct question.

What would life be if we had no courage to attempt anything?
                                                —VINCENT VAN GOGH

How many attempts have been made to climb Mt. Everest? [Compare with an indirect question: *They wondered how many attempts have been made to climb Mt. Everest.*]

411

■‖ PUNCTUATION ALERT: Do not combine a question mark with a comma, a period, or an exclamation point. ‖■

No   She asked, "How are you?."

Yes   She asked, "How are you?"

Questions in a series are each followed by a question mark, whether or not each question is a complete sentence.

The mountain climbers wondered whether they would reach the summit. Would they have good weather? Would they avoid accidents? Would everyone stay healthy?

After the fierce storm had passed, the mountain climbers debated what to do next. Turn back? Move on? Rest for a while?

If a request is phrased as a question, it does not always require a question mark.

Would you please send me a copy.

Would you please tell her I called.

■‖ 23d
Use a question mark in parentheses for a doubtful date or number.

When **information is unknown or doubtful** according to your very best research, you can use (?).

Mary Astell, an English author who was born in 1666 (?) and died in 1731, wrote pamphlets on women's rights.

The word *about* is often a graceful substitute for (?) within a sentence: *Mary Astell was born about 1666.*

Use language, not (?), to communicate irony or sarcasm.

No   Suffering from the flu is a delightful (?) experience.

Yes   Suffering from the flu is as pleasant as having a tooth drilled.

■‖ 23e
Use an exclamation point to issue a strong command or an emphatic declaration.

A **strong command** gives a very firm order, and an **emphatic declaration** makes a shocking or surprising statement.

Help!

John! Look out behind you!

"Oh no! There's been an accident!" cried my mother.

Mild commands, however, end with a period.

Don't worry about it.

▮ PUNCTUATION ALERT: Do not combine an exclamation point with a comma, a period, or a question mark. ▮

No   "You may not do that again!," ordered my mother.

Yes   "You may not do that again!" ordered my mother.

■‖ 23f

Do not overuse exclamation points.

In academic writing your choice of words, not exclamation points, is expected to communicate the strength of your message. Reserve exclamation points, therefore, for dialogue or, very rarely, for a short declaration within a longer passage.

What a new face courage puts on everything!
—RALPH WALDO EMERSON

Your writing will lose its punch if you use exclamation points more than very rarely, because your reader will think that your judgment of urgency is exaggerated.

No   Mountain climbing can be dangerous! You must learn correct procedures! You must have the proper equipment. Take rope! Wear spiked boots! Carry special picks designed for mountaineering.

Yes   Mountain climbing can be dangerous. Without knowing correct procedures, climbers quickly can turn an outing into a disaster. Absolute necessities for anyone mountaineering include rope, spiked boots, and special picks.

Similarly, use language, not (!), to communicate amazement or sarcasm.

No   At 29,141 feet (!), Mt. Everest is the world's highest mountain.

Yes   At a majestically staggering 29,141 feet, Mt. Everest is the world's highest mountain.

413

EXERCISE 1

Insert any needed periods, question marks, and exclamation points. Also, delete any unneeded ones.

EXAMPLE   Until World War II, few women were in the US military!

Until World War II, few women were in the U.S. military.

1. "When will women be encouraged to serve" many people asked.
2. During World War II, the Women's Army Corps, known as the WACs (!), was established.
3. Over 100,000 women became WACs!
4. Jeanne M Holm, a native of Portland, OR., moved up through the ranks and became a captain!
5. Captain Holm commanded a women's training regiment.
6. After World War II, she joined the US Air Force and began to increase women's career opportunities.
7. She became Director of Women and fought (?) to revise policies that discriminated (!) against women
8. Soon she was promoted to major!
9. In 1980, Major Holm had the pleasure of watching as 200 (?) women received active commissions upon graduation from military academies.
10. Women now serve in every branch of the American armed services. Some people wonder if women will ever be given combat duty?

EXERCISE 2

Insert needed periods, question marks, and exclamation points.

During World War II, US soldiers' mail was censored Specially trained people read the mail Many people wanted to know why this was necessary The censors had to make sure that no military information was disclosed Return addresses often read "Somewhere in the Pacific Area" to keep strategic positions secret Have you ever heard the story about the soldier who could not write his sweetheart for many months but finally had time He wrote her a long letter explaining the delay and telling her that he loved her very much All the woman received, however, was a tiny slip of paper that read: "Your boyfriend is fine He loves you He also talks too much Sincerely, The Censor."

24
THE COMMA

The comma is the most frequently used mark of punctuation, occurring twice as often as all other marks of punctuation combined. Rules for comma use abound because the comma *must* be used in certain places, it *must not* be used in other places, and it is *optional* in still other places. To help you sort through the various rules and get an overview of the uses of the comma, here is a summary of the material covered in this chapter.

The role of the comma is to group and separate sentence parts, helping to create clarity for readers. Consider how hard it is to understand the following paragraph, which contains all the punctuation it needs except commas.

> **No**   Among publishers typographical errors known as "typos" are an embarrassing fact of life. In spite of careful editing reviews and multiple readings few books are perfect upon publication. Soon after a book reaches the marketplace and reports of errors embarrassments to authors and editors alike start to come in. Everyone laughed therefore although no one thought it was funny when an English textbook was published with this line: "Proofread your writing carefullly."

Here is the same paragraph with commas included.

> **Yes**   Among publishers, typographical errors, known as "typos," are an embarrassing fact of life. In spite of careful editing, reviews, and multiple readings, few books are perfect upon publication. Soon after, a book reaches the marketplace, and reports of errors, embarrassments to authors and editors alike, start to come in. Everyone laughed, therefore, although no one thought it was funny, when an English textbook was published with this line: "Proofread your writing carefullly."

In the second paragraph, meaning is clear. Each comma is used for a specific reason according to a comma rule. Be guided by the comma rules, discussed in this chapter, to figure out when to use commas. Be wary of two practices that get inexperienced writers into trouble with commas: (1) As you are writing, do not insert a comma because you happen to pause to think before moving on; (2) as you reread your writing, do not insert commas according to your personal habits of pausing. Although a comma alerts a reader to a slight pause (except in dates and other conventional material), pausing is not a reliable guide for writers, because people's breathing spans, accents, and thinking stretches vary greatly.

■‖ 24a
Use a comma before a coordinating conjunction that links independent clauses.

The **coordinating conjunctions**—*and, but, or, nor, for, so,* and *yet*—can link two or more independent clauses° to create **compound sentences°**. Use a comma before the coordinating conjunction.

PATTERN FOR COMMAS WHEN COORDINATING CONJUNCTIONS LINK INDEPENDENT CLAUSES

Independent clause,   and   independent clause.
                     but
                     for
                     or
                     nor
                     so
                     yet

The sky was dark gray, **and** the air stilled ominously.

The November morning had just begun, **but** it looked like dusk.

Shopkeepers closed their stores early, **for** they wanted to get home.

Soon high winds would start, **or** thick snow would begin silently.

Farmers had no time to continue harvesting, **nor** could they round up their animals in distant fields.

The firehouse whistle blew four times, **so** everyone knew a blizzard was closing in.

People on the road tried to reach safety, **yet** a few unlucky ones were stranded.

When each independent clause° contains only a few words, writers sometimes omit the comma before the coordinating conjunction.

The storm ended **and** life returned to normal.

▌▌ COMMA CAUTION: Don't put a comma *after* a coordinating conjunction that links independent clauses°. ▐▌

No   The November morning had just begun **but,** it looked like dusk.

Yes   The November morning had just begun, **but** it looked like dusk.

▌▌ COMMA CAUTION: Don't use a comma when a coordinating conjunction links two words, phrases°, or dependent clauses°. (See 24c for information about commas with coordinating conjunctions in a series of three or more words, phrases, or clauses.) ▐▌

No   Learning a new language demands time, and patience.

Yes   Learning a new language demands time and patience.

No	Each language has a beauty of its own, and forms of expression which are duplicated nowhere else.
Yes	Each language has a beauty of its own and forms of expression which are duplicated nowhere else.

—Margaret Mead, "Unispeak"

▌COMMA CAUTION: To avoid creating a comma splice°, don't use a comma to separate independent clauses unless they are linked by a coordinating conjunction. ▐

No	Five inches of snow fell in two hours, one inch of ice built up when the snow turned to freezing rain. [The comma alone is insufficient. A coordinating conjunction must follow when the comma is used here.]
Yes	Five inches of snow fell in two hours, **and** one inch of ice built up when the snow turned to freezing rain. [The coordinating conjunction *and* links the two independent clauses.]
Yes	Five inches of snow fell in two hours. One inch of ice built up when the snow turned to freezing rain. [Independent clauses can become two separate sentences.]
No	The weight of the ice broke power lines, consequently, only places with their own generators had electricity. [*Consequently,* a conjunctive adverb°, must be preceded by a semicolon or a period when it comes between two independent clauses.]
Yes	The weight of the ice broke power lines; consequently, only places with their own generators had electricity.

When independent clauses containing other commas are linked by a coordinating conjunction, you can use a semicolon before the coordinating conjunction.

Because temperatures remained low all winter, the snow could not melt until spring; **and** some people wondered when they would see grass again.

EXERCISE 1

Insert commas before coordinating conjunctions that link independent clauses. If a sentence is correct, circle its number.

EXAMPLE   You and I make telephone calls almost every day yet we rarely think about the men and women who keep the telephone system functioning.

You and I make telephone calls almost every day, yet we rarely think about the men and women who keep the telephone system functioning.

418

1. Some people might say that anyone can be a directory assistance operator but only people with patience and a sense of humor can succeed.

2. Some callers whisper so that they can hardly be heard yet others shout commands in angry tones.

3. Callers may speak another language or they may use pedantic words or the latest slang.

4. Some people request a number and then they ask the operator to hold on while they get a pencil or answer the doorbell.

5. Many callers who want to reach a business number do not know the company's exact name nor do they know the address.

6. A few callers require very gentle and tactful treatment for their requests reveal that they have special needs.

7. An elderly woman called and asked the operator to sing "Happy Birthday" to her.

8. The operator lowered her voice and sang for the depressed and lonely sounding woman.

9. One young boy needed help with his homework so he called the operator to ask how to spell *Czechoslovakia*.

10. Operators say that the callers who take the cake are the ones who start cooking and then call an operator for advice about the recipe.

EXERCISE 2

Combine each pair of sentences using the coordinating conjunction shown in parentheses. When necessary, you can rearrange words. Insert commas before coordinating conjunctions that separate independent clauses.

EXAMPLE   Jurors usually believe eyewitness testimony. Eyewitnesses often give unreliable information. (yet)

Jurors usually believe eyewitness testimony, yet eyewitnesses often give unreliable information.

1. Someday you might be a juror or be accused of a crime. It is important to understand the ways in which eyewitnesses can be wrong. (so)

2. Eyewitnesses remember less accurately and completely than they think. They become more convinced and self-assured the more they are asked to repeat their information. (but)

3. One eyewitness viewed a lineup just after having glanced at a photograph on a detective's desk. The eyewitness promptly picked out the person in the picture—who was a suspect in another case and was in jail when the crime the eyewitness saw had taken place. (and)

4. A hypnotized eyewitness may describe the number and pattern of freckles or scars on a mugger's nose. The person who is eventually caught and confesses to the crime has neither freckles nor scars. (yet)

419

5. Most eyewitnesses strongly believe what they are saying is true. They would never go to the trouble of giving information to the police or offering testimony at a trial. (or)

6. After all, it is no treat to watch a crime being committed. It is not any pleasure to take the witness stand and undergo possibly nasty cross-examination. (nor)

7. A suspect's family or friends who insist that a suspect was with them often fail to convince a jury. Jurors usually believe the testimony of eyewitnesses. (for)

■‖ 24b

Use a comma after an introductory clause, phrase, or word.

When clauses°, phrases°, or words introduce an independent clause°, use a comma to signal the end of the introductory element and the beginning of the independent clause.

PATTERN FOR COMMAS WITH INTRODUCTORY CLAUSES, PHRASES, AND WORDS

Introductory clause,
Introductory phrase, ──────▶ independent clause.
Introductory word,

Some writers omit the comma when an introductory element is very short and the sentence is clear without the comma. If you are in doubt, use the comma; it is always correct.

‖ 1
Use a comma after an introductory adverb clause.

An adverb clause cannot stand alone as an independent unit because it starts with a subordinating conjunction. (Adverb clauses are discussed in 7e-2.) Subordinating conjunctions include *after, although, because, before, if, since, unless, until, when,* and *where.* When an adverb clause precedes the independent clause, separate the clauses with a comma.

> **When it comes to eating,** you can sometimes help yourself more
> by helping yourself less.   —RICHARD ARMOUR

Although most of us don't realize it, the foods of the future are already with us.
—LILA PERL, *Junk Food, Fast Food, Health Food*

When an adverb clause follows the independent clause, do not use a comma unless the adverb clause is long and complex.

The chimney made fearful sounds of protest **as it was invaded by the urgent gusts.**
—MAYA ANGELOU, *I Know Why the Caged Bird Sings*

Somehow he felt betrayed, **as he had when as a child he grew to discover that his father was dead.**
—RALPH ELLISON, "Flying Home"

‖ **2**
‖ **Use a comma after an introductory phrase.**

A **phrase** is a group of words that cannot stand alone as an independent unit; it lacks a subject, a predicate, or both. Use a comma to set off a phrase that introduces an independent clause.

Next to sugar, salt is the nation's leading food additive. [prepositional phrase°]
—JANE E. BRODY, Introduction to *Craig Claiborne's Gourmet Diet*

Beginning in infancy, we develop lifelong tastes for sweet and salty foods. [participial phrase°]

To satisfy a craving for ice cream, timid people sometimes brave midnight streets. [infinitive phrase°]

Eating being enjoyable, we tend to eat more than we need for fuel. [absolute phrase°]

‖ **3**
‖ **Use a comma after an introductory word.**

Conjunctive adverbs° and **transitional expressions** carry messages of a relationship between ideas in sentences and paragraphs. Transitional expressions include *for example* and *in addition* (complete list on page 84). Conjunctive adverbs include *therefore* and *however* (complete list on page 148). When these introductory words appear at the beginning of a sentence, follow them with a comma.

421

For **example,** fructose is fruit sugar, lactose is milk sugar, and maltose is malt sugar.

Therefore, no matter what their names, all sugars are metabolized into blood sugar.

Interjections convey surprise or other emotions. Typical interjections are *well* and *oh*. Interjections are uncommon in academic writing. Most interjections stand alone and are punctuated with an exclamation point. Use a comma after an interjection at the beginning of a sentence. If the interjection is meant to convey strong emotion, you may use an exclamation point after it. If you use an exclamation point, start the first word following it with a capital letter.

Oh, I did not realize you are allergic to cats.

Well, you didn't have to throw the cat outside.

Yes! Your sneezing annoys me.

EXERCISE 3

Insert commas where needed after introductory words, phrases, and clauses. If a sentence is correct, circle its number.

EXAMPLE Although everyone values a car for transportation few people realize that a car can help them survive danger.

Although everyone values a car for transportation, few people realize that a car can help them survive danger.

(1) To protect your life in certain life-threatening circumstances your car offers many resources. (2) Surprisingly it contains many items that can help you survive. (3) For example a car's horn can alert rescuers as far as a mile downwind. (4) To dig trenches or throw up an earth screen in a severe storm you can use the flat top of the air cleaner. (5) A reservoir of oil is available under the hood. (6) Burned in a hubcap a quart will spew a miniature cloud visible for miles. (7) While some people know that any hose in the car can be used as a siphon to get at gasoline few realize that windshield washer tubing can be used for a life-saving tourniquet. (8) When you need a fire that will not go out for three to four hours you can burn a tire. (9) In most situations your car can serve as a bunkhouse. (10) Yes survival experts know that giving people this information saves lives.

EXERCISE 4

Combine each set of sentences into one sentence that starts according to the directions in parentheses. You can add, delete, and rearrange words as needed. Be sure to use commas after introductory elements in the combined sentences.

EXAMPLE   You might be someone who is dieting for weight loss. You likely need to shed poor eating habits along with pounds. (clause beginning *if*)

If you are someone who is dieting for weight loss, you likely need to shed poor eating habits along with pounds.

1. You might want to lose weight very rapidly. Crash diets can endanger your health. (clause beginning *although*)

2. You need to diet wisely. You should begin with information about protein, vitamins, and minerals. (phrase beginning *to diet*)

3. Some dieters skip breakfast. They think they are saving calories. (clause beginning *when*)

4. You start the day with a balanced meal. Your body will soon demand food for energy. (clause beginning *unless*)

5. You have an empty stomach. You are more likely to snack before lunch. (phrase beginning *with*)

6. You might be tempted to eat a morning snack of doughnuts and coffee. You might be tempted at the office. (begin with *for example*)

7. Doughnuts are high in calories and low in nutrition. Other types of junk food are the same. (phrase beginning *along with*)

8. Some dieters like fad diets. Some fad diets consist of only one or two foods. (begin with *unfortunately*)

9. The nutrients in fad diets are very limited. You will weaken your body's ability to function well and fight illness. (clause beginning *because*)

10. Forget shortcuts and quick fixes. Your chances of losing weight and keeping it off are greatly increased. (phrase beginning *without*)

▮‖ 24c

Use commas to separate items in a series.

A **series** is a group of three or more elements—words, phrases, or clauses—that match in grammatical form and in importance in the same sentence.

Many **artists, writers, and composers** have indulged in daydreaming and reverie.

—EUGENE RAUDSEPP, "Daydreaming"

Culture is a way of **thinking, feeling, believing.**

—CLYDE KLUCKHOHN, *Mirror for Man*

A university should be a place **of light, of liberty, and of learning.**

—BENJAMIN DISRAELI

For real recreation I spent my slack afternoons and long evenings
**reading, playing Chinese checkers, and writing lies in my
diary.**

—PHYLLIS THEROUX

**The bearded vulture and the people survive there, the
Egyptian flourishes, and the great griffon swarms.**

—JOHN D. STEWART, "Vulture Country"

We have been taught **that children develop by ages and
stages, that the steps are pretty much the same for everybody, and that to grow out of the limited behavior of childhood,** we must climb them all.

— GAIL SHEEHY, *Passages*

Some writers omit the comma before the coordinating conjunction between the last two items of a series, but many do not. To
avoid misleading a reader, always use a comma unless the items in
the series are short and the way words are grouped is clear.

In a construction that repeats the coordinating conjunction in
a series of three or more words, writers usually omit the commas.

They were experts with hypersensitive powers of **sight and smell
and hearing.**

—ALAN MOOREHEAD, "A Most Forgiving Ape"

When the items in a series contain commas or other punctuation, or when the items are long and complex, separate them with semicolons instead of commas.

> If it's a bakery, they have to sell cake; if it's a photography shop, they have to develop films; **and** if it's a dry-goods store, they have to sell warm underwear.
> —ART BUCHWALD, "Birth Control for Banks"

Numbered or lettered lists within a sentence are items in a series. Use commas (or semicolons if the items are long) to separate them.

> To file your insurance claim, please enclose (1) a letter requesting payment, (2) a police report about the robbery, and (3) proof of purchase of the items you say are missing.

▊ COMMA CAUTION: Don't use a comma before the first item or after the last item in a series unless a different rule makes it necessary. ▊

YES   If we wanted **to find such a language, outfit it as a universal second language, launch it by satellite,** we could have the world speaking it in a decade. [The comma after *satellite* separates the introductory clause° *If we wanted . . .* from the independent clause°.]
—MARGARET MEAD, "Unispeak"

No   Many artists, writers, and composers, have indulged in daydreaming and reverie.

YES   Many artists, writers, and composers have indulged in daydreaming and reverie.

No   Such dreamers include, Miró, Debussy, Dostoevsky, and Brahms.

YES   Such dreamers include Miró, Debussy, Dostoevsky, and Brahms.

EXERCISE 5

Insert commas to separate items in series. If a sentence needs no commas, circle its number.

EXAMPLE   Car fumes industrial smoke and jet aircraft exhaust contribute to urban air pollution.

Car fumes, industrial smoke, and jet aircraft exhaust contribute to urban air pollution.

1. Governments industries and universities have attempted to find common ground for agreement about pollution control.
2. Experts compile statistics take photographs or run experiments to provide evidence about pollution.
3. Some businesspeople apply varying standards pursue different goals and offer diverse solutions concerning pollution.
4. Scientists discussing pollution point out that one part pollutant per million is equivalent to one inch in sixteen miles one minute in two years one penny in $10,000 or one adult mouthful over a lifetime.
5. Pollution is affecting animals that are suffering from diseases related to human illnesses and are dying in greater numbers than ever before.
6. A clinic in Florida has treated more than 5,000 birds suffering from illnesses deformities and injuries similar to those found in humans exposed to the same pollutants.
7. Many prominent people are trying to combat pollution because they know that sources of pollution are multiplying that too few people are taking the problem seriously and that the human race faces a serious threat to its well-being.

24d
Use a comma to separate coordinate adjectives.

Coordinate adjectives are two or more adjectives that equally modify a noun or noun group. Separate coordinate adjectives with commas or coordinating conjunctions.

> PATTERN FOR COMMAS WITH COORDINATE ADJECTIVES
>
> **coordinate adjective, coordinate adjective** noun

The **large, restless** crowd waited impatiently for the concert to begin.

Adjectives are coordinate if *and* can be inserted between them or if their order can be reversed without changing the meaning of the sentence. Meaning does not change when the example sentence says *large and restless crowd* or *restless, large crowd*. ▌COMMA CAUTIONS: (1) Don't put a comma after a final coordinate adjective and the noun it modifies—note that no comma comes between *restless* and *crowd* in the above example. (2) Don't put a comma between adjectives that are not coordinate. ▌

The program featured *several new* bands.

EXERCISE 6

Insert commas to separate coordinate adjectives. If a sentence needs no commas, circle its number.

EXAMPLE   A lively bright chimpanzee named Kanzi can communicate with humans.

A lively, bright chimpanzee named Kanzi can communicate with humans.

1. Kanzi communicates using a keyboard filled with complex geometric symbols.
2. Kanzi was not taught how to use the sophisticated intricate system.
3. The bright curious young chimp quickly and efficiently learned on his own by watching his mother being taught.
4. Kanzi has the most advanced linguistic abilities of any animal on record.
5. Kanzi sometimes can be an exasperating stubborn student who teases his teachers by doing exactly the opposite of what is asked.
6. He is not above giving his infant half-sister a sharp startling pinch if she is getting too much attention.
7. Most of the time, however, Kanzi is a cheerful alert spirited student with remarkable unending desire to learn.

24e
Use commas to set off nonrestrictive (nonessential) elements. Don't set off restrictive (essential) elements.

Restrictive and nonrestrictive elements are modifiers°. A **nonrestrictive element** is also called a **nonessential element** because the information it provides about the modified term is "extra." Although the extra information adds texture to the meaning, if a nonrestrictive element is dropped, a reader will still understand the full meaning of the modified term. Nonrestrictive elements are set off with commas.

PATTERN FOR COMMAS WITH NONRESTRICTIVE (NONESSENTIAL) ELEMENTS

Nonrestrictive element, independent clause.

Beginning of independent clause, **nonrestrictive element,** end of independent clause.

Independent clause, **nonrestrictive element.**

An eighteenth-century Englishman, Thomas Sedall grew the largest potato on record. [The nonrestrictive phrase *An eighteenth-century Englishman* adds information about Thomas Sedall, but the information is not essential for a reader to understand which Thomas Sedall is meant.]

Sedall dug the potato, which weighed 18.25 pounds, from his garden in 1795. [The reader can understand what potato is meant without the information about weight in the nonrestrictive clause.]

We can only imagine the reactions of his neighbors, who had never seen so large a potato.

When the nonrestrictive information in these examples is eliminated, the meaning of the modified terms does not change.

Thomas Sedall grew the largest potato on record.
Sedall dug the potato from his garden in 1795.
We can only imagine the reactions of his neighbors.

A **restrictive element** is essential to meaning. Notice what happens to the sentence *Sedall dug the potato, which weighed 18.25 pounds, from his garden in 1795* when we change *the potato* to *a potato* and *which* to *that:*

Sedall dug a potato that weighed 18.25 pounds from his garden in 1795.

In this sentence, the clause about weight specifies exactly which potato is meant of all the potatoes in the garden: the one weighing 18.25 pounds. The clause *that weighed 18.25 pounds* restricts the meaning of *potato* to one particular potato; it is essential to the meaning of *potato*. The clause is restrictive.

▎ COMMA CAUTION: A restrictive element is essential, not extra. Don't set it off from the rest of the sentence. ▎

Scientists **who study food production** experiment with many different growing conditions. [The noun *scientists* is limited by the restrictive element to only those scientists who study food production.]

Food **grown in the laboratory** is sometimes chemically produced without soil or water. [The noun *food* is limited to include only that grown in the laboratory.]

If you are unsure whether an element is nonrestrictive (non-essential) or restrictive (essential), consider it in the context of the whole sentence. If a term does not fully communicate your message without the modifier, the modifier is probably restrictive. On the other hand, if the modifier adds texture—interesting but not basic for your reader's comprehension—it is very likely a nonrestrictive element.

1
Use commas to set off nonrestrictive clauses and phrases.

Adjective clauses° modify nouns or pronouns and usually begin with *who, whom, that, which, when, where,* or *why*. When adjective clauses are nonrestrictive, set them off with commas.

NONRESTRICTIVE CLAUSES

Farming, **which is a major source of food production,** may not always be dependent on the weather. [Farming in this sentence is not meant to be restricted by *which is a major source of food production,* so the information is not essential and commas are used.]

Someday, food may be grown in places like Death Valley, **where temperatures of 120° have been recorded for 43 consecutive days.** Organic farmers, **who use only natural substances to produce food,** are appalled by the widespread use of chemicals in commercial agriculture.

RESTRICTIVE CLAUSES

Much food **that is canned or frozen** is grown by the same large companies **that process it for consumption.** [The first restrictive clause limits the general word *food* to only food that is canned or frozen; the second one restricts the large companies to only those that process the food for consumption. The information in both cases is essential.]

Cooling on the window might be a peach pie **whose steaming crust was made with bear grease.**
—EDWARD A. HOEY, "More Need for Elbow Room"

A **phrase** is a group of related words without a subject, a predicate, or both. Set nonrestrictive phrases off with commas.

429

NONRESTRICTIVE PHRASES

Farmers, **using pesticides and fertilizers,** try to enhance their crops' growth. [*Farmers* in this sentence is not meant to be limited by the phrase *using pesticides and fertilizers,* so the information is not essential and commas are used.]

Chemical pollutants affect all life forms, **including people.**

With their potential to harm human life, these chemicals create a serious health hazard.

RESTRICTIVE PHRASES

Farmers **retaining complete control over their land** are very hard to find these days. [The sense of *farmers* in this sentence is meant to be narrowed to only those retaining complete control over their land, so the information is essential.]

Corporations in agribusiness exercise considerable control over their farm investments.

2
Use commas to set off nonrestrictive appositives.

An **appositive** is a word or group of words that renames the noun or noun group preceding it. A **nonrestrictive appositive** is not essential for the identification of what it is renaming; it is set off by commas.

NONRESTRICTIVE APPOSITIVE

The agricultural scientist, **a new breed of farmer,** controls the farming environment so that food can be grown almost anywhere.

Most appositives are nonrestrictive. Once the name of something is given, words renaming it are not usually necessary to specify or limit it even more. In some cases, however, appositives are restrictive and are not set off with commas.

RESTRICTIVE APPOSITIVES

My parents **the farmers** dislike corporate control, but my parents **the investors** expect their shares to earn good dividends. [In the context of this sentence, the appositives *the farmers* and *the investors* specify essential information about what they rename—*my parents*—so they are restrictive and are not set off with commas.]

EXERCISE 7
Using your knowledge of restrictive and nonrestrictive clauses and phrases, insert commas as needed.

EXAMPLE   Farming which people developed about 10,000 years ago remains a major means of food production for the world's population.

Farming, which people developed about 10,000 years ago, remains a major means of food production for the world's population.

1. Farmers always chose seeds from the plants that were the strongest and most productive for the next season's crop.
2. In the 1860s, the few plant breeders who understood genetics started crossing varieties within the same species to create hybrids.
3. Modern farming particularly in the United States has become as technological as is the business world.
4. The tangelo a citrus fruit available in many modern markets is an example of such crossbreeding.
5. This fruit is a hybrid cross between two others, the orange and the tangerine.
6. Crossbreeding wheat an important practice in agricultural genetics has produced even more important results.
7. Some strains of wheat supported by the use of chemicals and irrigation yield enough grain to make underdeveloped nations nutritionally self-sufficient.
8. Research into the genetic makeup of plants which is almost as complex as the cellular coding found in humans promises to eliminate world hunger in the twenty-first century.
9. Scientists once limited to crossbreeding within a plant species are now transferring genetic material from one species to another to create new kinds of foods.
10. Scientists having spliced protein genes into potato cells hope to create a "meatato" that will contain the nutritional value of a whole meal.

■‖ 24f

Use commas to set off transitional and parenthetical expressions, contrasts, words of direct address, and tag questions.

Words, phrases, or clauses that interrupt a sentence but do not change its essential meaning should be set off, usually with

431

commas. (Parentheses or dashes—see Chapter 29—also set material off.)

Conjunctive adverbs such as *however* and *therefore* and **transitional expressions** such as *for example* and *in addition* sometimes express connections within sentences. When they do, they are set off with commas.

The American midwest, **therefore,** is the world's breadbasket.

California and Florida are important food producers, **too.**

▋ COMMA CAUTION: When a transitional expression links independent clauses°, use a semicolon or a coordinating conjunction°. A comma alone will create a comma splice. ▋

Parenthetical expressions are "asides," additions to sentences that the writer thinks of as extra.

American farmers, **according to U.S. government figures,** export more wheat than they sell at home.

Expressions of contrast are set off with commas.

Feeding the world's population is a serious problem, **but not an intractable one.**

We must work against world hunger continuously, **not just when emergencies develop.**

Words of direct address and tag questions, too, should be set off with commas.

Join me, **brothers and sisters of one world,** to end hunger. [direct address]

Worldwide response to the Ethiopian famine was impressive, **wasn't it?** [tag question]

EXERCISE 8

Add necessary commas to set off transitional, parenthetical, and contrasting elements, words of direct address, and tag questions. If a sentence is correct, circle its number.

EXAMPLE   Malaria according to recent World Health Organization reports is back on the list of epidemic diseases.

Malaria, according to recent World Health Organization reports, is back on the list of epidemic diseases.

1. Malaria is caused by organisms that mosquitoes carry not by malnutrition.

2. Almost eliminated in the 1960s to be sure malaria is reappearing in many parts of the world.
3. Mosquitoes are becoming resistant to pesticides not intended for them.
4. Insecticide on the crops originally succeeded in killing most malaria-carrying mosquitoes too.
5. Some mosquitoes survived however because they had developed immunity to the chemicals.
6. The immune mosquitoes sad to say began spreading malaria anew.
7. Agricultural specialists who were trying to solve the problem of malnutrition in underdeveloped nations unintentionally created as serious a problem with malaria didn't they?

24g
Use commas to set off quoted words from explanatory words.

Use a comma to set off quoted words from short explanations in the same sentence. This rule holds whether the explanatory words come before, between, or after the quoted words.

PATTERNS FOR COMMAS WITH QUOTED WORDS

Explanatory words, "Quoted words."
"Quoted words," explanatory words.
"Quoted words begin," explanatory words, "quoted words continue."

Speaking of ideal love, the poet William Blake wrote, "Love seeketh not itself to please."

"Happy I, that love and am beloved," said William Shakespeare about reciprocated love.

"I love no love," proclaimed poet Mary Coleridge, "but thee."

This is an especially important rule for reporting conversations or other direct discourse. Explanatory words like *she said, they replied,* and *he answered* are called **speaker tags,** and they are always set off from immediately following words of direct discourse in the ways shown in the pattern box.

433

When explanatory words have *that* just before the quoted words, however, do not use a comma after *that*.

> Shakespeare also wrote that "Love's not Time's fool."
> Shaw quipped that "Love is a gross exaggeration of the difference between one person and everybody else."

For information about capitalization in quotations, see 30c.

▉ COMMA CAUTION: When quoted words end with a question mark or an exclamation point, keep that punctuation even if explanatory words follow. ▉

QUOTED WORDS	"O, Romeo! Romeo!"
No	"O, Romeo! Romeo!," called Juliet as she stood at her window.
No	"O, Romeo! Romeo," called Juliet as she stood at her window.
YES	"O, Romeo! Romeo!" called Juliet as she stood at her window.
QUOTED WORDS	"Wherefore art thou Romeo?"
No	"Wherefore art thou Romeo?," continued Juliet as she yearned for her new-found love.
No	"Wherefore art thou Romeo," continued Juliet as she yearned for her new-found love.
YES	"Wherefore art thou Romeo?" continued Juliet as she yearned for her new-found love.

EXERCISE 9

Punctuate the following dialogue correctly. If a sentence is correct, circle its number.

EXAMPLE   "Has anyone called an ambulance?," shouted a bystander at the scene of an accident.

"Has anyone called an ambulance?" shouted a bystander at the scene of an accident.

1. "Let me through" said a man who was trying to push into the crowd.
2. A woman close to the victim said "First we have to loosen his collar and belt."
3. "I've had first-aid training! I'll do it" exclaimed the man.
4. "Excuse me" said the woman, tapping his shoulder.
5. "When you get to the part in your training where you call a doctor" she said "don't bother. I'm already here."

24h
Use commas in dates, names, addresses, and numbers according to accepted practice.

When you write dates, names, and numbers, be sure to use commas according to accepted practice.

RULES FOR COMMAS WITH DATES

1. Use a comma between the date and the year: **July 20, 1969.**
2. Use a comma between the day and the date: **Sunday, July 20, 1969**
3. Within a sentence, use commas after the day *and* the year in a full date.

   Everyone wanted to be near a television set on **July 20, 1969,** to watch Armstrong emerge from the lunar landing module.

4. Don't use a comma in a date that contains the month with only a day or a year or that contains only the season and year.

   The major news story during **July 1969** was the moon landing; news coverage was especially heavy on **July 21.**

5. An inverted date takes no commas: **20 July 1969.**

   People stayed near their television sets on **20 July 1969** to watch the moon landing.

RULES FOR COMMAS WITH NAMES, PLACES, AND ADDRESSES

1. When an abbreviated title (Jr., M.D., Ph.D.) comes after a person's name, use a comma between the name and the title—**Rosa Gonzales, M.D.**—and also after the title if it is followed by the rest of the sentence:

   The jury heard the expert testimony of **Rosa Gonzales, M.D.,** last week.

2. When you invert a person's name, use a comma to separate the last name from the first: **Troyka, David.**

3. Use a comma between a city and state: **Philadelphia, Pennsylvania.** In a sentence, use a comma after the state, as well:

   The Liberty Bell has been on display in **Philadelphia, Pennsylvania,** for many years.

4. When you write a complete address as part of a sentence, use a comma to separate all the items, with the exception of the zip code. The zip code follows the state after a space without a comma. A comma does not follow the zip code.

   I wrote to Mr. U. Lem, 10-01 Rule Road, Englewood Cliffs, New Jersey 07632 for the instruction manual.

RULES FOR COMMAS WITH LETTERS

1. For the opening of an informal letter, use a comma: **Dear Betty,**
   (The opening of a business or formal letter takes a colon.)

2. For the close of a letter, use a comma: **Sincerely yours, Love, Best regards, Very truly yours,**

RULES FOR COMMAS WITH NUMBERS

1. Counting from the right, put a comma after every three digits in numbers over four digits: **72,867   156,567,066**

2. In a number of four digits, a comma is optional for money, distance, and most other measurements and amounts as long as you use a consistent style within a given piece of writing.

$1776	$1,776
1776 miles	1,776 miles
1776 hours	1,776 hours
1776 cartons	1,776 cartons
1776 potatoes	1,776 potatoes

3. Don't use a comma for a four-digit year—**1990** (but **25,000 B.C.**); in an address of four digits or more—**12161 Dean Drive**; or in a page number of four digits or more—**see page 1338.**

4. Use a comma to separate related measurements written as words: **five feet, four inches**

5. Use a comma to separate a scene from an act in a play: **Act II, scene iv**

6. Use a comma to separate a reference to a page from a reference to a line: **page 10, line 6**

EXERCISE 10
Insert commas where they are needed. If a sentence is correct, circle its number.

EXAMPLE   Perhaps Eden Texas offers people an earthly paradise.
Perhaps Eden, Texas, offers people an earthly paradise.

1. Eden Texas lies 165 miles north of San Antonio Texas and has a population of 1400.
2. A researcher reported in the summer of 1983 that there are 16 Edens listed in the zip code book.
3. Eden Prairie Minnesota must be an attractive spot, for its population soared between January 1 1970 and January 1 1980 from 6938 to 16263.

4. The people of North Carolina's Edenton used a slight variation of the Eden name.
5. The citizens of Edenton North Carolina publish a brochure saying their town is the "South's Prettiest Town."
6. The brochure reports that the town is 135 miles from Raleigh North Carolina and has a population of 5264.
7. You can explore all the Edens by visiting them alphabetically throughout the United States from Eden Arkansas to Eden Wyoming.

■‖ 24i
Use commas to clarify meaning.

Sometimes you will need to use a comma to clarify the meaning of a sentence, even though no other rule calls for one.

No	Of the gymnastic team's twenty five were injured.
Yes	Of the gymnastic team's twenty, five were injured.
No	Those who can practice many hours a day.
Yes	Those who can, practice many hours a day.
No	George dressed and performed for the sellout crowd.
Yes	George dressed, and performed for the sellout crowd.

EXERCISE 11
Insert commas to prevent misreading. If a sentence is correct, circle its number.

EXAMPLE   Though controversial subliminal learning appeals to many people.
Though controversial, subliminal learning appeals to many people.

1. Using specially prepared tape recorders communicate hidden messages to listeners.
2. Some people who want to learn supposedly without effort by listening to the tape.
3. To prevent shoplifting, twenty major department stores started using subliminal tapes.
4. Of the twenty nine reported pilferage had decreased by about 37 percent.
5. Many people worry that governments or businesses might use subliminal learning to control people against their wills.

■‖ 24j
Avoid misusing the comma.

Don't overuse commas by inserting them where they don't belong. Common misuses are discussed throughout this chapter, signaled by COMMA CAUTION. A summary list of comma cautions begins
on page 440.

Besides the misuses of commas listed in the cautions, writers
sometimes unnecessarily separate major sentence parts with
commas.

No   Orville and Wilbur Wright, made their first successful
        airplane flights on December 17, 1903. [As a rule, don't
        let a comma separate a subject from its verb.]

YES   Orville and Wilbur Wright made their first successful
        airplane flights on December 17, 1903.

No   These inventors enthusiastically tackled, the problems of
        powered flight and aerodynamics. [As a rule, don't let a
        comma separate a verb from its object.]

YES   These inventors enthusiastically tackled the problems of
        powered flight and aerodynamics.

No   Flying has become, both an important industry and a
        popular hobby. [As a rule, don't let a comma separate a
        verb from its complement.]

YES   Flying has become both an important industry and a
        popular hobby.

No   Airplane hobbyists visit Kitty Hawk's flight museum
        from, all over the world. [As a rule, don't separate a
        preposition from its object.]

YES   Airplane hobbyists travel to Kitty Hawk's flight museum
        from all over the world.

Clauses and phrases that function as subjects, objects, or complements can be confusing. They may look like adjective clauses° or
adverb clauses° or phrases°—modifiers—that should be set off with
commas. When a clause or a phrase is doing the work of a noun,
though, don't set it off. (See 7e-2 for a discussion about noun
clauses.)

439

No   What appeals to many people about flying, is the pan-
oramic views. [The noun clause functions here as the
sentence subject. No comma should separate it from
the verb.]

Yes   What appeals to many people about flying is the panora-
mic views.

No   Hang gliders try, to find strong updrafts for long flights.
[The infinitive phrase° functions as an object. No comma
should separate it from the verb.]

Yes   Hang gliders try to find strong updrafts for long flights.

No   Their objectives are, soaring long times and covering
long distances. [The gerund phrases° function as complements. No comma should separate them from the
verb.]

Yes   Their objectives are soaring long times and covering long
distances.

Because the comma occurs so frequently, advice against overusing it sometimes clashes with a rule requiring it. In such cases,
follow the rule that calls for the comma.

Kitty Hawk, North Carolina, attracts thousands of tourists each
year. [Although the comma after *Carolina* separates the subject
and verb, using it is required.]

SUMMARY OF COMMA CAUTIONS

1. Don't use a comma *after* a
coordinating conjunction that
links two independent clauses.   See 24a, page 417

2. Don't use a comma when a
coordinating conjunction links
two words, phrases, or
dependent clauses.   See 24a, page 417

3. Don't use a comma to separate
independent clauses unless they
are linked by a coordinating
conjunction.   See 24a, page 418

4. Don't use a comma *before* the first item or *after* the last item in a series, unless a different rule makes it necessary.

See 24c, page 425

5. Don't use a comma after a final coordinate adjective and the noun it modifies.

See 24d, page 426

6. Don't use a comma between noncoordinate adjectives.

See 24d, page 426

7. Don't set off a restrictive element.

See 24e, page 428

8. When a transitional expression links independent clauses, use a semicolon or coordinating conjunction rather than a comma.

See 24f, page 432

9. When quoted words end with a question mark or an exclamation point, do not substitute a comma, even if explanatory words follow the quotation.

See 24g, page 434

10. Don't use commas to separate subjects from their verbs or verbs from their objects or complements.

See 24j, page 439

EXERCISE 12

Some commas have been deliberately misused and overused in these sentences. Delete or add commas as needed.

EXAMPLE   Airplanes started as little more than motorized, double-winged, gliders, and have advanced to supersonic transportation in less than a century.

Airplanes started as little more than motorized, double-winged gliders and have advanced to supersonic transportation in less than a century.

441

1. Wilbur, and Orville Wright proved that people could fly in 1903.
2. By 1943, U.S. engineers were building rocket planes for research.
3. The planes were built to withstand the intense air pressure, that is present at Mach 1, and to provide the necessary power to break the sound barrier.
4. Mach 1, is defined as the speed of sound, which is approximately 738 miles per hour, at sea level, and the term "sound barrier" applies to the resistance, experienced by planes as they near the speed of sound.
5. Finally, the Bell X-1, the product of many engineering challenges, was perfected.
6. In 1947, Air Force Captain, Charles E. Yeager, broke the sound barrier, in a Bell X-1 rocket plane.
7. This, was the first supersonic flight, in history.
8. At first, all supersonic jets were military, but Russia initiated commercial supersonic transport (SST), in 1968.
9. England and France, you may remember, cooperated with each other to build an SST, the Concorde.
10. Landings of the Concorde SST at American airports, has been a topic, of much debate, for no one knows, what long-term damage such planes might inflict on areas around the airports.

EXERCISE 13

Following the rules in this chapter, insert needed commas and delete misused ones. Some commas may be correct.

(1) In the United States disastrous tornadoes hurricanes floods fires earthquakes and volcanic eruptions, cause yearly damage estimated up to $7 billion of insured property. (2) In addition such dangerous destructive catastrophes have killed thousands of people, and left other thousands homeless in the past twenty years. (3) In spite of such devastation, most communities hit by a disaster, rebuild within one or two years. (4) "People bend" according to one leader of the American Red Cross "but they do not break." (5) Nevertheless, one place, that never recovered, is Baytown Texas, which was hit by hurricane Alicia in 1,983. (6) The wreckage was so complete that the federal government declared it unsafe purchased the land from its residents and created a park. (7) Compared with many other countries the United States handles catastrophes well however because of modern, expertly coordinated systems for early warning, and for emergency medical care. (8) Although hurricanes alone killed 1947 people in the United States between 1940, and 1985, a single cyclone that struck Bangladesh in 1970, killed 300000 people. (9) What surprised some people, was that anyone survived the cyclone.

25
THE
SEMICOLON

Most often used between two independent clauses°, the **semicolon** communicates greater separation than a comma but less than a period. A semicolon signals to a reader that the material on both sides is closely related in meaning.

■‖ 25a
You can use a semicolon between closely related independent clauses.

When independent clauses are related in meaning, you can separate them with a semicolon instead of a period.

SEMICOLON PATTERN I

Independent clause; independent clause.

The choice is yours in relation to the meaning you want your material to deliver. A period signals complete separation between independent clauses; a semicolon tells readers that the separation is softer.

> Knowledge is not a rock that we inherit from a geological past; it is a living, growing organism constantly in need of nourishment and renewal.
>
> —DANIEL J. BOORSTIN, Librarian of Congress,
> Congressional testimony, February 1986

> Our Constitution is in actual operation; everything appears to promise that it will last; but in this world nothing is certain but death and taxes. —BENJAMIN FRANKLIN

> This powerful sense of history constantly in the making, forever unfinished, is equally tangible in the 365 churches that dot the landscape surrounding the city of Choluda; they rise on the razed sites of an identical number of pre-Columbian temples.
>
> —CARLOS FUENTES, "Mexico"

▮▮ COMMA CAUTION: Do not use only a comma between independent clauses, or you will create the error called a comma splice (see Chapter 14). ▮

 ## 25b
Use a semicolon between related independent clauses that contain commas, even if a coordinating conjunction joins the independent clauses.

You will usually use a comma to separate independent clauses linked by a coordinating conjunction *(and, but, or, nor, for, yet, so)*. When the independent clauses already contain commas, however, use a semicolon instead. The semicolon makes plain to your reader where one independent clause ends and the next begins.

> **SEMICOLON PATTERN II**
>
> Independent clause, one that contains commas;
> coordinating conjunction independent clause.
> Independent clause; coordinating conjunction independent
> clause, containing commas.
> Independent clause, one that contains commas;
> coordinating conjunction independent clause, one that
> contains commas.

The U.S. Fish and Wildlife Service, after conducting its wildlife "census" in 1935, estimated the California condor population to be 60; but the 1985 count numbered only 6.

For anything worth having one must pay the price; and the price is always work, patience, love, self-sacrifice.

—JOHN BURROUGHS

◼‖ 25c

You can use a semicolon when conjunctive adverbs or other transitional expressions connect independent clauses.

Use a semicolon between two independent clauses when the second clause begins with a conjunctive adverb (*therefore, however,* and others, listed on page 148) or other transitional expressions (page 84). Your other option is to use a period, creating two sentences.

> **SEMICOLON PATTERN III**
>
> Independent clause; conjunctive adverb or other transition expression, independent clause.

The average annual rainfall in Death Valley is about two inches; **nevertheless,** hundreds of plant and animal species survive and even thrive there.

Patient photographers have spent years recording desert life cycles; all of us have, **as a result,** watched barren sands flower after a spring storm.

▮‖ COMMA ALERTS: (1) Do not use only a comma between independent clauses connected by a conjunctive adverb or other words of transition, or you will create the error called a comma splice, as explained in Chapter 14. (2) Use a comma *after* a conjunctive adverb or a transitional expression. Some writers omit the comma after short words, such as *then, next, soon.* (3) When you position a conjunctive adverb or a transitional expression somewhere after the first word in an independent clause, set it off with commas. See the example with *as a result,* above. ‖▮

◼‖ 25d

Use a semicolon between long or comma-containing items in a series.

When a sentence contains series of words, phrases°, or clauses°, commas usually separate one item from the next. When

445

the items are long and contain commas for other purposes, you can make your message much easier for readers to understand by using semicolons instead of commas to separate items. The semicolons show exactly where one item ends and the next begins.

SEMICOLON PATTERN IV

Independent clause that includes a series of items, each or all of which contain commas; another item in the series; another item in the series.

Everyone also remembers a few of the observances of childhood—wishing on the first star; looking at the moon over the right shoulder; avoiding the cracks in the sidewalk on the way to school while chanting, "Step on a crack, break your mother's back"; wishing on white horses, on loads of hay, on covered bridges, on red cars; saying quickly, "Bread and butter" when a post or a tree separated you from the friend you were walking with.
—MARGARET MEAD, *A Way of Seeing*

Functioning as assistant chefs, the students chopped onions, green peppers, and parsley; sliced chicken and duck meat into strips; started a delicious-smelling broth simmering; and filled a large, low, long-handled pan with oil before the head chef moved up to the stove.

25e
Avoid misusing the semicolon.

1
Don't use a semicolon between a dependent clause and an independent clause.

No   Although the new computers had arrived at the college; the computer lab was still being built.

Yes   Although the new computers had arrived at the college, the computer lab was still being built.

2
Don't use a semicolon to introduce a list; use a colon.

No   The newscast featured three stories; the latest pictures of Uranus, a speech by the president, and a series of brush fires in Nevada.

Yes   The newscast featured three major stories: the latest pictures of Uranus, a speech by the president, and a series of brush fires in Nevada.

EXERCISE 1

Insert semicolons where they are needed. If a sentence is correct, circle its number.

Example   The dangers of toxic wastes were first recognized over eight years ago today we face a serious environmental emergency.

The dangers of toxic wastes were first recognized over eight years ago; today we face a serious environmental emergency.

1. In 1980 Congress created a "superfund" of $1.6 billion, this money was earmarked to clean up thousands of dumps which were leaking toxic wastes.

2. The lawmakers' action seemed an excellent way to address the problem, however, the law providing the funds expired in 1985.

3. Meanwhile, fears about toxic wastes continue to grow because each day more and more communities discover that they are living on or near ground that has been contaminated, each day chemicals with names like dioxin, vinyl chloride, PBB, and PCB leach into the ground, each day lead, mercury, and arsenic poisoning threaten more households.

4. The Office of Technology Assessment (OTA) contends that there may be at least 10,000 hazardous-waste sites in the United States, not surprisingly, these dumps pose a serious threat to public health.

5. Cleanup costs, OTA estimates, could reach $100 billion, more than $1,000 per U.S. household.

6. The United States faces other grave environmental risks acid rain, smoggy skies, and lethal gases escaping from industrial plants are all threats to human, animal, and plant life.

7. The disposal of toxic wastes, however, is clearly the most pressing concern.

8. In the handling and production of chemicals, more than 1,500 people have been injured, 135 have died.

447

9. Knowing where to place the blame is difficult because each government agency blames the others, and each administration blames the one before it.

10. Placing blame is less important than cleaning up, otherwise, we will all suffer.

EXERCISE 2

Combine each set of sentences into one sentence containing two independent clauses. Use a semicolon between the two clauses. You may omit, add, revise, or rearrange words. More than one answer may be correct.

EXAMPLE   Postcards are more than a means of communication. They are miniature works of art. Some of them can be quite valuable.

Postcards are more than a means of communication; they are miniature works of art, some of them quite valuable.

1. Some postcards offer colorful views of exotic places. Some cards reproduce famous paintings. Others feature portraits of famous persons.

2. On postcard racks today you can find a wide variety of selections. You may find a classic scene from a Bogart film. On the other hand, you may see a giant cactus with sunglasses.

3. There are dinosaurs fighting Martians. There are great Olympic moments. There are also perennial favorites. These perennial favorites say such things as "Greetings from Fargo" or "Having a wonderful time in Hicksville."

4. Postcards have been popular for a long time. However, there was a so-called "Golden Age of Postcards." That lasted from the turn of the century to the Great Depression.

5. Today postcard sales are booming again. For example, in 1983 more than 2.5 billion cards were mailed to Americans. That was an increase of more than 100 million from the previous year.

6. Postcards are a popular means of communication for many reasons. Postcards cost from 15 cents to $1. That represents a bargain.

7. You may also send postcards for practical reasons. They give you a chance to show that you are enjoying the sun. Your friends who are shoveling snow get the message very quickly.

8. Some rare postcards are extremely valuable. A signed original by the artist Alphonse Mucha is a good example. One of these cards recently sold for $3,000.

9. The first postcard was designed in 1869. It was designed by Emmanuel Hermenn. Four years later the U.S. government began issuing specially designed "postal cards." These cards had an illustration on one side and a space for an address and stamp on the other.

EXERCISE 3

Insert needed semicolons in the following sentences, and delete unnecessary ones. If a sentence is correct, circle its number.

1. The sound of Muzak has invaded our banks, supermarkets, and elevators, furthermore, it often assaults our ears when we are placed on hold on a busy telephone line.

2. Muzak plays in government offices, in the White House, in the Pentagon, in Congress, it played during the Olympics, and it even played in the Apollo XI spaceship carrying Neil Armstrong to the moon.

3. The Muzak Corporation, now part of Westinghouse; estimates that its recordings are heard by 80 million people every day, and the company and its affiliates take in more than $150 million annually.

4. Not all listeners appreciate Muzak novelist Vladimir Nabokov, artist Ben Shahn, and composer Philip Glass have used adjectives such as "horrible," "abominable," "offensive," and "tormenting" to describe it.

5. The Muzak system was the creation of an unusual general, George Owen Squier; a West Pointer who devoted much of his army career to science.

6. During World War I, Squier invented a system for transmitting several messages simultaneously over electric power lines, in the era following the war, he took his ideas and patents to the North American Company, a utilities combine.

7. The company backed him in launching Wired Radio, Inc.; a kind of competitor to the booming fad for wireless radio.

8. The company wanted a catchy new name for this product; therefore, they combined the sound of the word "music" with the name of the manufacturer of popular cameras, Kodak.

9. The first customers for Muzak were residents of Cleveland however, a series of experiments in the late 1930s opened a much larger market.

10. These tests proved that Muzak could get more work out of people and animals, in factories, absenteeism was reduced, early departures were curbed, and morale was raised, on farms, cows gave more milk and chickens laid more eggs.

449

EXERCISE 4

Combine each set of sentences into one sentence containing two independent clauses. Use a semicolon between the independent clauses. You may
omit, add, revise, or rearrange words.

EXAMPLE   Some people live by the clock on the wall. All of us are governed
            by internal clocks. These clocks regulate hundreds of biological
            functions.

            *Some people live by the clock on the wall; however, all of us are
            governed by internal clocks which regulate hundreds of biological
            functions.*

1. Our inner clocks help determine our times of elation and depression.
   They also regulate our times of patience and irritability. Our inner clocks
   also regulate our precision and carelessness.

2. We need to understand how these clocks work. We need to know what
   they are. We need to know how they interact. We also need to know
   how they can be thrown off schedule.

3. Understanding these principles can help us to organize our lives. We will
   be able to maximize performance and pleasure. We will not waste energy
   fighting the body's natural inclinations.

4. Some valuable facts about the internal time clocks are already known.
   People are least likely to be alert, for example, after they have eaten
   lunch. In addition, calories consumed at breakfast are less likely to turn
   to body fat than those eaten at supper.

5. Many people find certain other facts useful. A high-protein breakfast enhances alertness. A high-carbohydrate supper helps induce sleep.

26
THE COLON

In sentence punctuation, the colon introduces what comes after it: a quotation, a summary or restatement, or a list. The colon has the effect of pointing a bit dramatically to what follows it. The colon has a few special separating functions as well.

▊‖ 26a
Use a colon to introduce quotations, summaries, lists.

Use a colon at the end of your words introducing a formal quotation.

COLON PATTERN I

Independent clause containing words that introduce a quotation: "Quoted Words."

Autumn is equally busy, as Eleanor Perenyi states in *Green Thoughts:* "As the natural world prepares to shut up shop, the gardener may be inclined to do the same. But as most of us know, fall is the busiest season of the year" (14).

E. B. White writes of his annual surge of interest in gardening: "We are hooked and are making an attempt to kick the habit."
— MARIE WINN, *The Plug-In Drug*

Your words introducing a quotation may be very short, but they should be a complete independent clause°. ▓ PUNCTUATION ALERT: When your words introducing a quotation are not an independent clause, use a comma between the introductory words and the quotation (see 24g). For advice on working quoted words smoothly into your writing, see 28a. ▓

You can use a colon to introduce statements that summarize, restate, or explain what is said in an independent clause.

> COLON PATTERN II
>
> Independent clause: summarizing or restating words.

The two-year-old rejects carrots, squash, pumpkin, segments of an orange, and apricot halves, but she accepts spinach, apples, celery, nuts, and slices of egg: She is rejecting the color orange, not food in general.

Perhaps it is this specter that most haunts working men and women: the planned obsolescence of people that is of a piece with the planned obsolescence of the things they make.
— STUDS TERKEL, *Working*

Anthropology provides a scientific basis for dealing with the crucial dilemma of the world today: How can peoples of different appearance, mutually unintelligible languages, and dissimilar ways of life get along peaceably together?
— CLYDE KLUCKHOHN, *Mirror for Man*

You can use a colon to lead into a final appositive—a word or group of words that renames or restates a noun or a pronoun.

The Metropolitan Museum in New York City now owns the best-known works of Louis Tiffany's studio: those wonderful stained-glass windows. [*Stained-glass windows* renames *best-known works*.]

452

Use a colon to introduce a list or a series of items announced by an independent clause°.

> **COLON PATTERN III**
>
> Independent clause: listed items.

If you really want to lose weight, you need give up only three things: breakfast, lunch, and dinner.

Laboratory experiments prove that tarantulas can distinguish three types of touch: pressure against the body walls, stroking of the body hair, and riffling of certain very fine hairs on the legs called trichobothria.

—ALEXANDER PETRUNKEVITCH, "The Spider and the Wasp"

When you use phrases like *the following* or *as follows,* a colon is usually required. A colon is not called for with the words *such as* or *including* (see 26c).

The students' demands included the following: an expanded menu in the cafeteria, better janitorial services, and more up-to-date textbooks.

▊ CAPITALIZATION ALERTS: (1) Use a capital letter to start a quotation introduced by a colon. (2) Use a lower-case letter for a list, an appositive, or any other set of words *not* an independent clause°—unless the first word after the colon is a proper noun. (3) Either a capital letter or a lowercase letter is correct for the first word of an independent clause or a question following a colon. Whichever practice you choose, be consistent throughout a paper. ▊

26b
Use a colon to separate standard material.

TITLE AND SUBTITLE

The Aquarian Conspiracy: Personal and Social Transformations in the 1980s
Charles Dickens: His Tragedy and Triumph

HOURS, MINUTES, AND SECONDS

The plane took off at 7:15 P.M.
She passed the halfway point at 1:23:02.

CHAPTERS AND VERSES OF THE BIBLE

Psalms 23:1–3

Luke 3:13

MEMO FORM

To: Dean Kristen Olivero
From: Professor Daniel Black
Re: Student Work-Study Program

SALUTATION OF FORMAL OR BUSINESS LETTER

Dear Ms. Beins:

MLA BIBLIOGRAPHIC FORMAT: CITY OF PUBLICATION AND PUBLISHER (BOOK)

Atwood, Margaret. *The Handmaid's Tale*. Boston: Houghton, 1986.

MLA BIBLIOGRAPHIC FORMAT: YEAR FROM PAGES (ARTICLE)

McGrath, Anne, "Books that Speak for Themselves." *U.S. News & World Report*. 14 July 1986: 49.

26c
Avoid misusing the colon.

A complete independent clause° must precede a colon except when the colon separates standard material (26b). Especially with listed items, take care that lead-in words make a grammatically complete statement. When they do not, do not use a colon.

No   The small boy bought: eggs, milk, cheese, and bread.

Yes   The small boy bought eggs, milk, cheese, and bread.

The words *such as* and *including* can be tricky: Do not let them lure you into using a colon incorrectly.

No   The health board discussed a number of problems, such as: water quality, the inefficiency of the sewage treatment system, and the lack of a backup water supply.

Yes   The health board discussed a number of problems, such as water quality, the inefficiency of the sewage treatment system, and the lack of a backup water supply.

454

YES   The health board discussed a number of problems: water quality, the inefficiency of the sewage treatment system, and the lack of a backup water supply.

No   Five dates were chosen, including: April 3, May 6, May 17, June 11, and July 6.

YES   Five dates were chosen, including April 3, May 6, May 17, June 11, and July 6.

YES   Five dates were chosen, including the following: April 3, May 6, May 17, June 11, and July 6.

Do not use a colon to separate a dependent clause° from an independent clause°.

No   After the drought ended: the mayor appointed a commission to plan water-saving measures for the future.

YES   After the drought ended, the mayor appointed a commission to plan water-saving measures for the future.

EXERCISE 1
Insert colons where they are needed. If a sentence is correct, circle its number.

EXAMPLE   Most gamblers ignore how slim their chances are of hitting the jackpot in a slot machine, about one in 2,000.

Most gamblers ignore how slim their chances are of hitting a jackpot in a slot machine: about one in 2,000.

1. Researchers at Washington University have discovered a startling new fact, not only do you dream approximately every 90 minutes when you are asleep, but you daydream approximately every 90 minutes when you are awake.

2. Among the forgers who have committed these crimes for hundreds of years, three continue to interest experts, William Henry Ireland, who forged a series of letters he claimed were written by Shakespeare; Hans Van Meegeren, who produced amazingly accurate copies of Jan Vermeer's paintings; and Clifford Irving, who convinced a New York publisher that he had been hired to ghost-write Howard Hughes's autobiography.

3. Writing about the problems of leadership, Barbara Tuchman reaches this conclusion "As witnesses of the twentieth century's record, comparable to the worst in history, we have little confidence in our species."

455

4. The worst insurance risks in the United States include astronauts, drivers of hydroplanes, race drivers in the Indianapolis 500, and drivers in Grand Prix auto races.

5. Many proper Victorians were shocked by Thomas Hardy's novel *Tess of the D'Urbervilles; A Virtuous Woman.*

6. Halley's comet made its predicted return in 1986, passing nearest to the sun on February 9, just before 1100 A.M. Greenwich time.

7. The text was based on Psalms 85,10, "Mercy and truth are met together: righteousness and peace have kissed each other."

8. Two characteristics aided Einstein in his work, his curiosity and his ability to concentrate.

9. Wills have been written in unusual places, napkins, wallpaper, hospital charts, and even the side of a corncrib.

10. For those who think there must be a pleasant way to lose weight, consider the following fact, you have to kiss 389 times to lose one pound.

27

THE
APOSTROPHE

The apostrophe plays three major roles: it helps to form the possessive of nouns and a few pronouns; it stands for one or more omitted letters; and it helps to form the plurals of letters and numerals. It does *not* help form plurals of nouns or the possessive case of personal pronouns.

▮‖ 27a
Use an apostrophe to form the possessive case of nouns and indefinite pronouns.

The **possessive case** serves to communicate ownership or close relationship.

OWNERSHIP	The writer's pen
CLOSE RELATIONSHIP	The novel's plot

Possession in nouns and certain indefinite pronouns can be communicated by an apostrophe in combination with an *-s* (*the instructor's comments*) or by phrases beginning with *of the* (*the comments of the instructor*).

1
When nouns and indefinite pronouns do *not* end in -*s*, add -'*s* to show possession.

The **dean's** duties included working closely with the resident assistants. [*dean* = singular noun not ending in -*s*]

In one more year I will receive my **bachelor's** degree. [*bachelor* = singular noun not ending in -*s*]

They care about their **children's** futures. [*children* = plural noun not ending in -*s*]

The accident was really **no one's** fault. [*no one* = indefinite pronoun not ending in -*s*]

2
When singular nouns end in -*s*, add -'*s* to show possession.

The tour **bus's** passengers switched to a train in Athens.

Chris's hand shook.

Lee **Jones's** insurance was cancelled.

Charles **Dickens's** story "A Christmas Carol" is a perennial favorite at Christmas time.

That **business's** system for handling complaints is inefficient.

3
When a plural noun ends in -*s*, use only an apostrophe to show possession.

The **boys'** bicycles are stored in the basement.

The **visitors'** comments included high praise for the park rangers at Yellowstone.

The newspapers have publicized several **medicines'** severe side effects recently.

4
In compound words, add -'*s* to the last word.

His **mother-in-law's** corporation just bought out a competitor.

The **tennis player's** strategy was brilliant.

They wanted to hear **somebody else's** interpretation of the rule.

5
In individual possession, add -'s to each noun.

Olga's and Joanne's books are valuable. [Olga and Joanne each own some of the valuable books; but they do not own the books together.]

After the fire, **the doctor's and the lawyer's** offices had to be rebuilt. [The doctor and the lawyer had separate offices.]

6
In joint or group possession, add -'s to only the last noun.

Olga and Joanne's books are valuable. [Olga and Joanne own the books together.]

Anne and Glen Smith's article on solar heating interests me. [More than one Smith wrote the article.]

■‖ 27b
Do not use an apostrophe with the possessive forms of personal pronouns.

Some pronouns have specific possessive forms. Do not use an apostrophe with these forms.

PRONOUN	POSSESSIVE FORM(S)
he	his
she	her, hers
it	its
we	our, ours
you	your, yours
they	their, theirs
who	whose

Be especially alert to *it's* and *its*, as well as *who's* and *whose,* which occur often in English and are frequently confused. (*It's* stands for *it is; its* is a personal pronoun showing possession. *Who's* stands for *who is; whose* is a personal pronoun showing possession.)

No   The government has to balance **it's** budget.

Yes   The government has to balance **its** budget.

No	This briefcase is mine and that one is **your's.**
Yes	This briefcase is mine and that one is **yours.**
No	The professor **who's** class was canceled is at a convention.
Yes	The professor **whose** class was canceled is at a convention.

▌ APOSTROPHE CAUTION: The following forms do not exist in English, so do not use them: *its', his', hers', yours', theirs', whos'.* ▐

◼‖ 27c

Use an apostrophe to stand for omitted letters, numbers, or words in contractions.

Contractions are words from which one or more letters have been intentionally omitted and in which apostrophes are inserted to signal the omission. Contractions are common in speaking and in informal writing, but many readers dislike them in formal writing. Always consider your proposed audience and the degree of formality you want to convey when you choose between a contraction and the full phrase.

COMMON CONTRACTIONS

I'm = I am
he's, she's, it's = he is, she is, it is
you're, we're, they're = you are, we are, they are
isn't = is not
aren't = are not
wasn't = was not
weren't = were not
he'll , she'll = he will, she will
you'll, we'll, they'll = you will, we will, they will
won't = will not
didn't = did not
I'd = I would
I've, we've = I have, we have
you've, they've = you have, they have
who's = who is
there's = there is
let's = let us
can't = can not or cannot
o'clock = of the clock

Contractions can help to show informal speech or dialect, especially in dramatic or fictional writing.

> Scout yonder's been **readin'** ever since she was born, and she **ain't** even started school yet. You look right puny for **goin'** on seven.
>
> —HARPER LEE, *To Kill a Mockingbird*

Apostrophes also indicate the omission of the first two numerals in years. Use this contraction only in informal writing.

> The class of '50 is having a reunion this year.
> They moved to Florida after the blizzard of '78.

∎‖ 27d
Use an apostrophe to form plurals of letters, numerals, symbols, and words used as terms.

> Billie always has trouble printing *W*'s.
> The address includes six *6*'s.
> The *for*'s in the paper were all misspelled as *four*'s.
> When the keys jammed, a series of *&*'s showed on the computer screen.

∎‖ UNDERLINING ALERT: Always underline letters as letters and words as words. In printed material, they are set in italic type; underlining is the way to show this distinction in typewritten or handwritten material. ‖∎

> Most of the first-graders consistently had trouble making 8's and trying to pronounce eight's phonetically.

For the plural form of years, two styles are acceptable: with an apostrophe (1980's) or without (1980s). Whichever form you prefer, use it consistently.

EXERCISE 1
Rewrite these sentences to insert *'s* or an apostrophe alone to make the words in parentheses show possession. Delete the parentheses.

1. At Pablo (Picasso) birth, two (midwives) errors nearly allowed him to be left for dead.
2. Luckily for Picasso, his cigar-smoking (uncle) quick act saved him.
3. The uncle filled his (nephew) lungs with a blast of much-needed, yet smoke-filled, air.

4. When (Paris) most celebrated beauty, Mme. Virginie Gautreau, was depicted by the painter John Singer Sargent as vain and immodest in a portrait entitled "Madame X," those who knew her agreed with the portrayal.

5. Nevertheless (the painting) notoriety and Madame (Gautreau) hysterics forced Sargent to leave for London.

6. (Max Jacob and Pablo Picasso) shared Paris apartment caused them some problems.

7. (Picasso) work habits included leaving paintings all over the floor, and many years later art (experts) skills were needed to remove (Jacob) footprints from (Picasso) valuable canvases.

8. The American painter Charles Willson Peale believed that (anyone) desire to paint could be fulfilled.

9. He acted on his belief and helped to develop his seventeen (children), and many (other), artistic talents.

10. His faith was rewarded: his sons Rembrandt and Raphaelle both earned their (contemporaries) praise.

EXERCISE 2
Rewrite these sentences so that each contains a possessive noun.

EXAMPLE   The Special Olympics is an international program promoting the physical fitness of mentally retarded children and adults.

The Special Olympics is an international program promoting mentally retarded children's and adults' physical fitness.

1. Athletic competition is encouraged in accordance with the age and ability of the participants.

2. The training of these athletes takes place in schools and other institutions.

3. Handicaps of the participants do not prevent them from competing in sports from basketball to gymnastics and ice skating to wheelchair exercise.

4. The sponsor of the program is the Joseph P. Kennedy, Jr., Foundation, which first sponsored the event in 1968.

5. The true beneficiary of the foundation is American society, for the aim of a democracy is equal opportunity and participation for all its members.

EXERCISE 3
Correct any errors in the use of apostrophes in the paragraph below.

(1) One of Albert Einsteins biographers tells about the famous physicists encounter with a little girl in his' neighborhood. (2) The little girl stared at Einstein's soaking wet feet and said, "Mr. Einstein, youve come out with-

out you'r boots again!'' (3) Einstein laughed and, pulling up his trousers, replied, ''Yes, and Ive forgotten my socks, too.'' (4) Most people arent as forgetful as Einstein, but sometimes our memories' let all of us down. (5) We may not be able to remember if our first job started in '81 or 82; we may forget whether our employers' husband spells his name with two ts or with one. (6) No one is absolutely sure how memory works. (7) Dr. Barbara Jones study of memory suggests that personality style's affect memory. (8) People with rigid personalities who's livelihoods depend on facts tend to have good memories. (9) Mr. Harry Lorayne and Dr. Laird Cermak's studies of memory each provide a different approach to improving that useful faculty. (10) Mr. Lorayne suggest's relating what you want to remember to something verbal or visual. (11) For instance, if you want to remember that your sister's-in-law's name is Rose, you would picture her wearing a rose corsage. (12) Dr. Cermaks suggestions include consideration of physiological factors. (13) He notes that doctors' are currently developing drugs that will prevent older people from losing the memories that are rightfully their's.

28
QUOTATION
MARKS

Most commonly, quotation marks enclose **direct quotations**—spoken or written words from an outside source. Quotation marks also set off some titles, and they can call attention to words used in special senses.

Always use quotation marks in pairs, and be especially careful not to omit the second (closing) quotation mark. **Double quotation marks** (" ") are standard. **Single quotation marks** (' ') are used only for quotation marks within quotation marks. In print, opening and closing quotation marks look slightly different from each other, but they look identical when made on a typewriter or computer printer. You will find examples of both print and of typewritten quotation marks in this chapter.

For information about the functions in quotations of brackets, see 29c; of the ellipsis, see 29d; of the slash, see 29e. For information about capital letters with quotations, see 30c.

When you quote the words of others in your writing, be sure to remain alert to these important matters:

- Incorporate quotations correctly and smoothly into your writing: see 31e-4.
- Avoid plagiarism—the use of another person's words as if they were your own: see Chapter 31.

- Document direct quotations correctly: for the MLA parenthetical system, see 32k; for the APA parenthetical system, see 34c-4; for a footnote or endnote system, see 34b-4.

■‖ 28a

Enclose direct quotations of not more than four lines in quotation marks.

Direct quotations are exact words copied from a print source or transcribed from a nonprint source.

‖ 1
Use double quotation marks to enclose short quotations.

A quotation is considered "short" if it can be typed or handwritten to occupy no more than four lines on a page. Short quotations are enclosed in double quotation marks. Longer quotations are not enclosed in quotation marks—they are **displayed.** A displayed quotation starts on a new line, and all typewritten lines indent ten spaces. (In the examples, parenthetical documentation is used—see 32k.)

SHORT QUOTATIONS

Hall explains the practicality of close conversational distances: "If you are interested in something, your pupils dilate; if I say something you don't like, they tend to contract" (47).

Personal space "moves with us, expanding and contracting according to the situation in which we find ourselves" (Fisher, Bell, and Baum 149).

LONG QUOTATION

Robert Sommer, an environmental psychologist, uses literary and personal analogies to describe personal space:

> Like the porcupines in Schopenhauer's fable, people like to be close enough to obtain warmth and comradeship but far enough away to avoid pricking one another. Personal space . . . has been likened to a snail shell, a soap bubble, an aura, and "breathing room." (26)

See Appendix B, Using Correct Manuscript Format, for a complete discussion of displaying quotations.

2
Use single quotation marks for quotations within quotations.

When you want to quote four lines or less and the original words already contain quotation marks, use double quotation marks at the start and end of the directly quoted words. Then, substitute single quotation marks (' ') wherever there are double quotation marks in the original source.

ORIGINAL SOURCE
Personal space . . . has been likened to a snail shell, a soap bubble, an aura, and "breathing room."
—ROBERT SOMMER, *Personal Space: The Behavioral Bases of Design,* page 26

SINGLE QUOTATION MARKS WITHIN DOUBLE QUOTATION MARKS
Robert Sommer, an environmental psychologist, lists comparisons of personal space to "a snail shell, a soap bubble, an aura, and 'breathing room' " (26).

If there are quotation marks in a quotation of more than four lines, display it without enclosing it in quotation marks. But be sure to use any quotation marks that appear in the original source. See Appendix B, Using Correct Manuscript Format, for a complete discussion of displayed quotations.

3
Use quotation marks correctly for short quotations of poetry and for direct discourse.

A quotation of poetry is "short" if it is no more than three lines of the poem. As with short prose quotations, use double quotation marks to enclose the material. If you quote more than one line of poetry, use a slash with one space on each side to show the line divisions (see 29e).

As W. H. Auden wittily defined personal space, "some thirty inches from my nose / The frontier of my person goes. . . ."

See Appendix B, Using Correct Manuscript Format, for a complete discussion of displayed quotations of poetry. ▮ CAPITALIZATION ALERT: When you quote lines of poetry, follow the capitalization of the version you are quoting. ▮

Quotation marks are also used to enclose speakers' words in **direct discourse.** Whether you are reporting the exact words of a real speaker or making up dialogue in, for example, a short story, quotation marks let your readers know which words belong to the speaker and which words do not. Use double quotation marks at the beginning and end of a speaker's words, and start a new paragraph each time the speaker changes.

> "I don't know how you can see to drive," she said.
> "Maybe you should put on your glasses."
> "Putting on my glasses would help you to see?"
> "Not me; you," Macon said. "You're focused on the windshield instead of the road."
>
> —ANNE TYLER, *The Accidental Tourist*

Indirect discourse reports what a speaker said, in contrast to direct discourse, which presents a speaker's exact words. Do not enclose indirect discourse in quotation marks.

DIRECT DISCOURSE
The mayor said, "I cannot attend the conference in San Antonio."

INDIRECT DISCOURSE
The mayor said that he could not attend the conference in San Antonio.

See 15a-4 for advice on revising incorrect shifts between direct and indirect discourse.

EXERCISE 1

Correct the use of double and single quotation marks in the following sentences. If a sentence is correct, circle its number.

EXAMPLE   According to J. F. Perkins, "O. Henry "solves" most of his short story plots with surprise endings.
According to J. F. Perkins, "O. Henry 'solves' most of his short story plots with surprise endings."

1. Canfield and Lebson write, No one understands the sleeping habits of these sharks.

2. In the last two lines of the poem, Dickinson creates a powerful contrast: Parting is all we know of heaven, / And all we need of hell.

3. "One can put up with "Service with a Smile" if the smile is genuine and not mere compulsory toothbaring," wrote Cornelia Otis Skinner. She did not, on the other hand, advocate 'Service with a Snarl.'

4. "Promises," said Hannah Arendt, are the uniquely human way of ordering the future.

5. According to Henry James, "Nothing . . . will ever take the place of the good old fashion of "liking" a work of art or not liking it."

6. Pauline Kael, the movie critic, notes that "certain artists can, at moments in their lives, reach out and unify the audience" and in so doing give people the opportunity for "a shared response.

7. Don't let anyone convince you that you can't fulfill your ambitions, warned the speaker, or you surely won't.

8. Why have women passion, intellect, moral activity—these three—and a place in society where no one of the three can be exercised? asked Florence Nightingale in the 1850s.

9. "In seven cases, the report continued, outlets with the lowest prices had the highest percentages of defective merchandise.

10. Leslie Hanscom reports about the latest volume of the *Oxford English Dictionary,* Most of the new words are originating in the USA.

EXERCISE 2

Indicate whether each sentence is direct or indirect discourse. Then rewrite each sentence in the other form.

EXAMPLE   In 1928 an elderly woman contacted a London auctioneer and asked, "Would you be interested in selling this manuscript?

(Direct discourse)

In 1928 an elderly woman contacted a London auctioneer and asked if he would be interested in selling a manuscript.

1. The auctioneer said that his company did sell manuscripts, but only original ones by famous authors.

2. "This manuscript is original," the woman replied.

3. "The author inscribed it with these words—'A Christmas gift to a dear child'—and I was that child," she continued.

4. Astonished, the auctioneer said, "Is this manuscript what I think it is?"

5. The woman acknowledged that it was the original Lewis Carroll manuscript of *Alice in Wonderland.*

 28b

Enclose certain titles in quotation marks.

When you refer to certain types of works by their titles, enclose the titles in quotation marks. Use quotation marks around the titles of short published works, like poems, short stories, essays, articles from periodicals, pamphlets, and brochures. Also use them around song titles and individual episodes of television or radio series.

> Discuss the rhyme scheme of Andrew Marvell's "Delight in Disorder." [poem]
>
> Have you read "Young Goodman Brown"? [short story]
>
> One of the best sources I found is "The Myth of Political Consultants," [magazine article]
>
> "Shooting an Elephant" describes George Orwell's experience in Burma. [essay]

Underlining (for italics) is used for titles of many other types of works, such as books and plays. A few titles are neither underlined nor enclosed in quotation marks. You will find useful lists showing how to present titles in 30e and 30f.

Do not put the title of your own paper in quotation marks either on a title page or at the top of a page. See 28d.

EXERCISE 3

Make the use of quotation marks correct in the following sentences. If a sentence is correct, circle its number.

1. Almost everyone who has had to make a difficult choice in life can relate to Robert Frost's poem The Road Not Taken.
2. On a *Twilight Zone* episode called Healer, the main character steals a magic artifact.
3. In her essay titled "In Search of Our Mothers' Gardens, Alice Walker says that she found her own garden because she was guided by a "heritage of a love of beauty and a respect for strength.
4. Unable to get enough peace and quiet to write songs, such as his famous Over There and You're a Grand Old Flag, George M. Cohan would sometimes hire a Pullman car drawing room on a train going far enough away to allow him to finish his work.
5. A snake gives Sherlock Holmes the clue he needs to solve a puzzling murder in the mystery story The Speckled Band.

▮‖ 28c

Words used in special senses or for special purposes may be enclosed in quotation marks.

Writers sometimes enclose in quotation marks words or phrases meant ironically or in some other nonliteral way.

The proposed tax "reform" is actually a tax increase.

The "wonderful companion for children" snarled menacingly.

Writers sometimes put technical terms in quotation marks and define them the first time they are used. No quotation marks are used once such terms have been introduced and defined.

"Plagiarism"—the unacknowledged use of another person's words or ideas—can result in expulsion. Plagiarism is a serious offense.

The translation of a word or phrase can be enclosed in quotation marks. (Underline words or phrases that require translation.)

My grandfather usually ended arguments with *de gustibus non disputandum est* ("there is no disputing about tastes").

Words being referred to as words can be either enclosed in quotation marks or underlined. Follow consistent practice throughout a paper.

Yes   Many people confuse "affect" and "effect."

Yes   Many people confuse *affect* and *effect*.

28d
Avoid misusing quotation marks.

Writers sometimes enclose in quotation marks words they are uncomfortable about using, such as slang in formal writing or a cliché. Do not use quotation marks around language you sense is inappropriate to your audience or your purpose. Take the time to find accurate, appropriate, and fresh words instead.

No   They "eat like birds" in public, but they "stuff their faces" in private.

Yes   They eat very little in public, but they consume enormous amounts of food in private.

Do not enclose a word in quotation marks merely to call attention to it.

No   "Plagiarism" can result in expulsion.

Yes   Plagiarism can result in expulsion.

470

In papers, when you refer to published or performed works by title, you will often need quotation marks (28b) or underlining (30f) to set the title off. When you put the title of your paper at the top of a page or on a title page, however, do not enclose the title in quotation marks.

No   "The Elderly in Nursing Homes: A Case Study"

Yes   The Elderly in Nursing Homes: A Case Study

The only exception is if the title of your paper refers to another title or a word that requires setting off.

No   Character Development in Shirley Jackson's The Lottery

Yes   Character Development in Shirley Jackson's "The Lottery"

Do not put a nickname in quotation marks unless you are giving a nickname with a full name. When a person's nickname is widely known and used, you do not have to give both the nickname and the full name. For example, use *Senator Ted Kennedy* or *Senator Edward Kennedy*, whichever is appropriate to your audience and purpose. You do not have to write *Senator Edward "Ted" Kennedy*.

EXERCISE 4

Make the use of quotation marks correct in the following sentences. If a sentence is correct, circle its number.

EXAMPLE   Many people confuse the spellings of "there," *their,* and *they're.*

Many people confuse the spellings of "there," "their," and "they're."

1. "Accept" and *except* sound enough alike to confuse many listeners.
2. "Mickey" Mantle, "Yogi" Berra, and Whitey Ford helped make the Yankees champions in the 1950s.
3. Although the district attorney thought it would be an "open and shut case," she found out that "life is full of surprises."
4. An "antigen" is any substance from outside the body that activates the body's immune system. Today scientists are focusing intensive research on "antigens."
5. *Valross,* whale-horse, is the Norwegian word from which we get *walrus.*

28e
Follow accepted practices for other punctuation with quotation marks.

1
Place commas and periods inside closing quotation marks.

> Because the class enjoyed F. Scott Fitzgerald's "The Freshest Boy," they were looking forward to his longer works.
> Ms. Rogers said, "Don't stand so close to me."
> Edward T. Hall coined the word "proxemics."

2
Place colons and semicolons outside closing quotation marks.

> We have to know "how close is close": we don't want to offend.
> Some experts claim that the job market now offers "opportunities that never existed before"; others disagree.

3
Place question marks, exclamation points, and dashes inside or outside closing quotation marks, according to the context.

If a question mark, exclamation point, or dash belongs with the words enclosed in quotation marks, put that punctuation mark *inside* the closing quotation mark.

> "Did I Hear You Call My Name?" was the winning song.
> "I've won the lottery!" he shouted.
> "Who's there? Why don't you ans—"

If a question mark, exclamation point, or dash belongs with words that are *not* included in quotation marks, put the punctuation *outside* the closing quotation mark.

> Have you read Nikki Giovanni's poem "Knoxville, Tennessee"?
> If only I could write a story like Erskine Caldwell's "The Rumor"!
> Weak excuses—"I have to visit my grandparents" is a classic—change little from year to year.

EXERCISE 5

Make the use of quotation marks and other punctuation with quotation marks correct in the following sentences. If a sentence is correct, circle its number.

1. One of the most famous passages in Shakespeare is Hamlet's soliloquy, which begins with the question "To be, or not to be"?

2. "Take this script", Rudyard Kipling said to the nurse who had cared for his first-born child", and someday if you are in need of money you may be able to sell it at a handsome price."

3. Ernest Hemingway claimed this was the source of his famous phrase "a lost generation:" in conversation with "Papa" Hemingway, a garage owner used the words to describe the young mechanics he employed.

4. After lulling the reader with a description of a beautiful dream palace in his poem Kubla Khan, Coleridge changes the mood abruptly: And 'mid this tumult Kubla heard from far / Ancestral voices prophesying war.

5. Syndicated disk jockey Dr. Demento offers this possibility for the worst song title of all time": I've Got Those Wake Up at Seven Thirty, Wash Your Ears They're Dirty, Eat Your Eggs and Oatmeal Rush to School Blues".

29

OTHER
MARKS
OF
PUNCTUATION

This chapter explains the uses of the dash, parentheses, brackets, ellipses, and slash.

■‖ 29a
Use the dash to emphasize interruptions in sentences.

The dash, or a pair of dashes, lets you interrupt a sentence's structure to add information—an explanation, examples, a definition, even a personal comment or reaction. Dashes are like parentheses in this function of setting off "asides," or extra material (see 29b for parentheses). Such asides can come at the beginning, in the middle, or at the end of a sentence. Unlike parentheses, dashes emphasize the interruptions. Use dashes sparingly—if you do use them—so that their impact is not diluted by overexposure.

In typed papers, make a dash by hitting the hyphen key twice. Don't put a space before, between, or after the hyphens. In handwritten papers, make a dash slightly longer than a hyphen, using one unbroken line for each dash.

1
Use a dash or dashes to emphasize explanations, including appositives°, examples, and definitions.

APPOSITIVES

On television, a cattle drive or a cavalry charge or a chase—the climax of so many a big movie—loses the dimensions of space and distance that made it exciting, that sometimes made it great.

—PAULINE KAEL, *Kiss Kiss Bang Bang*

Two of the strongest animals in the jungle are vegetarians—the elephant and the gorilla.

—DICK GREGORY, *The Shadow that Scares Me*

EXAMPLES

The care-takers—those who are helpers, nurturers, teachers, mothers—are still systematically devalued.

—ELLEN GOODMAN, "Just Woman's Work?"

Life, Look, the *Saturday Evening Post*—each went to its grave, later to undergo resurrection as a small-circulation ghost of its former self.

—ALVIN TOFFLER, "The De-Massified Media"

DEFINITIONS

From this analogy with sexism and racism I suppose the name for this malady is "speciesism"—the prejudice that there are no beings so fine, so capable, so reliable as human beings.

—CARL SAGAN, *Broca's Brain*

Personal space—"elbow room"—is a vital commodity for the human animal, and one that cannot be ignored without risking serious trouble.

—DESMOND MORRIS, *Manwatching*

Be sure to place the words you set off in dashes next to or near to the words they explain. Otherwise, the interruption will distract or confuse your reader.

No — The current argument is—one that parents, faculty, students, and coaches all debate fiercely—whether athletes should have to meet minimum academic standards to play their sports.

YES — The current argument—one that parents, faculty, students, and coaches all debate fiercely—is whether athletes should have to meet minimum academic standards to play their sports.

2
Use a dash or dashes to emphasize a contrast.

Tampering with time brought most of the house tumbling down, and it was this that made Einstein's work so important—and controversial.

—BANESH HOFFMANN, "My Friend, Albert Einstein"

Today a majority of men in this part of the country, especially in Texas, wear some type of "Western" hat—and so do a number of the women.

—ALISON LURIE, *The Language of Clothes*

3
Use a dash or dashes to emphasize an "aside."

"Asides" are writers' comments, within the structure of a sentence or a paragraph, on something they have written. Especially in writing that is otherwise meant to seem objective, asides let writers introduce their personal views or convey their attitudes. Writers who want to emphasize asides set them off with dashes.

These five passages have not been picked out because they are especially bad—I could have quoted far worse if I had chosen—but because they illustrate various of the mental vices from which we now suffer.

—GEORGE ORWELL, "Politics and the English Language"

In a world governed solely by the principle of "dog eat dog"—if indeed there ever was such a world—how many children a family had would not be a matter of public concern.

—GARRETT HARDIN, "The Tragedy of the Commons"

If the words you put between a pair of dashes would take a question mark or an exclamation point written as a separate sentence, use that punctuation before the second dash.

A first date—do you remember?—stays in the memory forever. Commas, semicolons, colons, and periods are not used next to dashes.

4
Use a dash to show hesitating or broken-off speech.

"Naturally," said Mr. Lorry. "Yes—I—"

After a pause, he added, again settling the crisp flaxen wig at the ears, "It is very difficult to begin."

—CHARLES DICKENS, *A Tale of Two Cities*

EXERCISE 1
Supply dashes in the following sentences.

EXAMPLE   In the Middle Ages nearly everyone believed as Aristotle had that the intellect was located in the heart.

In the Middle Ages nearly everyone believed—as Aristotle had—that the intellect was located in the heart.

1. The adult blue, or lycaenid, butterfly is tiny about big enough to cover a 20 cent stamp.
   —MATTHEW DOUGLAS, "The Butterfly Connection"

2. This personality so runs the erroneous belief will be revealed in all its splendor if the individual just forgets about courtesy. . . .
   —MARGARET HALSEY, "What's Wrong with 'Me, Me, Me'?"

3. They wanted to be moved, excited, inspired, consoled, uplifted in short, led!
   —MICHAEL KORDA, "What It Takes to Be a Leader"

4. Per capita, Japan has a twentieth of the lawyers and crime of America.
   —JOHN TRAIN, *Preserving Capital and Making It Grow*

5. Different as they were in background, in personality, in underlying aspiration these two great soldiers had much in common.
   —BRUCE CATTON, "Grant and Lee: A Study in Contrasts"

■‖ 29b
Use parentheses to enclose interrupting material in sentences, as well as for a few special purposes.

Parentheses let you interrupt a sentence's structure to add information of many kinds. Parentheses are like dashes in this function of setting off extra or interrupting words. Unlike dashes, which make interruptions stand out, parentheses deemphasize what they enclose.

DASHES	The books and journals—and tapes, filmstrips, even the people you want to interview—are all too often unavailable when you are ready.
PARENTHESES	The books and journals (and tapes, filmstrips, even the people you want to interview) are all too often unavailable when you are ready.

Do not use parentheses too frequently in any one piece of writing. They can be very distracting for readers.

1
Use parentheses to enclose interrupting words, including explanations, examples, and asides.

EXPLANATIONS

For a really big job of dictionary-writing, such as the *Oxford English Dictionary* (usually bound in about twenty-five volumes), millions of such cards are collected, and the task of editing occupies decades.

—S. I. HAYAKAWA, *Language and Thought in Action*

In *division* (also known as *partition*) a subject commonly thought of as a single unit is reduced to its separate parts.

—DAVID SKWIRE, *Writing with a Thesis*

EXAMPLES

Though other cities (Dresden, for instance) had been utterly destroyed in World War II, never before had a single weapon been responsible for such destruction.

LAURENCE BEHRENS and LEONARD J. ROSEN,
Writing and Reading Across the Curriculum

ASIDES

"Dreamlike and fantastic" is how Schell (correctly) dismisses the prospect of a pre-emptive Soviet missile attack on the U.S.'s supposedly vulnerable land forces.

—STROBE TALBOTT, "A Grim Manifesto on Nuclear War"

The sheer decibel level of the noise around us is not enough to make us cranky, irritable, or aggressive. (It can, however, affect our mental and physical health, which is another matter.)

—CAROL TAVRIS, *Anger: The Misunderstood Emotion*

2
Use parentheses for certain numbers and letters of listed items.

When you number listed items within a sentence, enclose the numbers (or letters) in parentheses.

These four items are on the agenda for tonight's meeting: (1) current membership figures, (2) current treasury figures, (3) the budget for renovations, and (4) the campaign for public contributions.

■ PUNCTUATION ALERT: Separate items of a run-in list (a list within the structure of a sentence) with commas or semicolons. ■

3

In business and legal writing, use parentheses to enclose a numeral repeating a spelled-out number.

The monthly rent is three hundred sixty-five dollars ($365).

We are confirming that your order of fifteen (15) gross was shipped today.

4

Use a question mark enclosed in parentheses for a doubtful date or number.

When information is unknown or doubtful despite your best attempts to determine it, you can use (?) after the number or fact. Using the word *about* is equally acceptable.

Sappho was born in 612 (?) B.C.

Sappho was born about 612 B.C.

5

Know how to use other punctuation with parentheses.

Never put a comma before an opening parenthesis even if what comes before the parenthetical material requires a comma. Put the parenthetical material in, and then use the comma immediately after the closing parenthesis.

No   Although radically different from my favorite film, *(Ben Hur) Citizen Kane* is an important film and one worth studying.

Yes   Although radically different from my favorite film *(Ben Hur), Citizen Kane* is an important film and one worth studying.

You can use a question mark or an exclamation point with parenthetical words that occur within the structure of a sentence.

Looking for clues (did we really expect to find any?) wasted four entire days.

Use a period, however, only when you enclose a complete statement in parentheses outside the structure of another sentence. In this case, use a capital letter as well.

No   Looking for clues (now I wonder whether we really expected to find any.) wasted four entire days.

Yes   Looking for clues wasted four entire days. (Now I wonder whether we really expected to find any.)

Yes   Looking for clues (now I wonder whether we really expected to find any) wasted four entire days.

EXERCISE 2

Supply needed or useful parentheses.

EXAMPLE   The universe is so large in relation to the matter it contains that it can be compared to a building of huge proportions twenty miles long, twenty miles high, and twenty miles wide that holds only a single grain of sand.

The universe is so large in relation to the matter it contains that it can be compared to a building of huge proportions *(twenty miles long, twenty miles high, and twenty miles wide)* that holds only a single grain of sand.

1. The four basic elements that make up all but one percent of terrestrial matter carbon, hydrogen, nitrogen, and oxygen are also the basic elements of the Milky Way.
2. A "shell" of television and radio signals carrying old radio and television programs for example, *Gangbusters, The Lone Ranger,* and *Howdy Doody* is expanding through the cosmos at the speed of light.
3. The first automobile to cross the United States took fifty-two days in 1903 to go from San Francisco to New York.
4. There are half a million 500,000 more automobiles in Los Angeles than there are people.
5. The most sensational thefts in history include 1 the theft of the British Crown Jewels from the Tower of London; 2 the Great Train Robbery near Cheddington, England, which netted the crooks over $7,368,715 in cash; and 3 the theft of the Mona Lisa from the Louvre in Paris on August 21, 1911.
6. Ts'ai Yen, who was born in 162 A.D. ? and who lived until about 239 A.D. is considered by many experts to be the first great Chinese female poet.
7. Dashes see Section 29a can sometimes, but not always, serve the same function as parentheses.
8. At the Safety Evaluation Conference called *Safecon* of the National Intercollegiate Flying Association, college flying teams compete in events such as 1 precision landing, 2 message drops, 3 navigation, and 4 accuracy with flight computers.

29c
Use brackets to enclose insertions into quotations or into parentheses.

1
Use brackets to enclose words you insert into quotations.

When you work quoted words into your own sentences (see 31e), you may have to change a word or two to make the quoted words fit into the structure of your sentence. Enclose any changes you make in square brackets.

ORIGINAL
Surprisingly, this trend is almost reversed in Italy where males interact closer and display significantly more contact than do male/female dyads and female couples.
—ROBERT SHUTER, "A Field Study of Nonverbal Communication in Germany, Italy, and the United States," page 305

QUOTATION WITH BRACKETS
Although German and American men stand farthest apart and touch each other least, "[this phenomenon] is almost reversed in Italy where males interact closer and display significantly more contact than do male/female dyads and female couples" (Shuter 305).

The same technique—enclosing your words in brackets—lets you add explanations and clarifications to quoted material.

ORIGINAL
This sort of information seems trivial, but it does affect international understanding. Imagine, for example, a business conference between an American and an Arab.

QUOTATION WITH BRACKETS
"This sort of information seems trivial, but it *does* affect international understanding [italics mine]."

Now and then you may find that an author or a typesetter has made a mistake in something you want to quote—a wrong date, a misspelled word, an error of fact. You cannot change another writer's words, but you do not want readers to think you made the error. You can show that you know about the error by inserting the Latin word *sic,* in brackets, next to the error. Meaning "so" or "thus," *sic,* in brackets says to a reader, "it is thus in the original."

> In the report, the construction supervisor points out one unintended consequence of doubling the amount of floor space: "With that much extra room per person, the tennants [sic] would sublet."

2
Use brackets to enclose very brief parenthetical material inside parentheses.

> From that point on, Thomas Parker simply disappears. (His death [c. 1441] is unrecorded officially, but a gravestone marker is mentioned in a 1640 parish report.)

29d
Use an ellipsis to signal omissions from quotations or to show hesitating or broken-off speech.

An **ellipsis** is a set of three spaced dots (use the period key on a typewriter). Its most important function is to show that you have left out some of the original writer's words in material you are quoting. Ellipses can also show hesitant or broken-off speech, as does the dash (29a-4).

1
Use an ellipsis to show that you have omitted words from material you are quoting.

ORIGINAL
Personal space is not necessarily spherical in shape, nor does it extend equally in all directions. (People are able to tolerate closer presence of a stranger at their sides than directly in front.) It has been likened to a snail shell, a soap bubble, an aura, and "breathing room."

—ROBERT SOMMER, *Personal Space:*
The Behavioral Bases of Design, page 26

SOME MATERIAL USED IN A QUOTATION
Surprisingly, Sommer has been able to define its dimensions: "Personal space . . . not necessarily spherical in shape . . . has been likened to a snail shell, a soap bubble, an aura, and 'breathing room' " (26).

If an omission occurs at the beginning of your quoted words, you do not need to use an ellipsis to show the omission. Also you do not need to use an ellipsis at the end as long as you end with a complete sentence. (Otherwise, almost everything you quote would require an ellipsis.)

> According to Sommer, it may not be "spherical in shape, nor does it extend equally in all directions" (26).

If you select for quotation two or more sentences separated by material you do not want to quote, show the omission with (1) the period that ends the sentence before the omission and (2) the three spaced periods of an ellipsis. Use this procedure for sentences in the same paragraph or in sequential paragraphs.

> Sommer explains, "Personal space is not necessarily spherical in shape, nor does it extend equally in all directions. . . . It has been likened to a snail shell, a soap bubble, an aura, and 'breathing room' " (26).

If you stop quoting before the end of the sentence in the original and your own sentence continues, you may use an ellipsis to show that the quoted sentence continues.

> Personal space "has been likened to a snail shell, a soap bubble, . . ." (Sommer 26), but the shape varies among cultures.

When a quotation comes at the end of your sentence but the quoted words are *not* the end of a sentence in the original source, you must use an ellipsis. If the quotation is not followed by parenthetical documentation, use (1) a sentence period after the last quoted word, (2) three spaced dots for the ellipsis, and then (3) closing quotation marks.

> ELLIPSIS AT END OF SENTENCE WITHOUT PARENTHETICAL DOCUMENTATION
> Still, on that same page Sommer says people have described personal space as "a snail shell, a soap bubble, an aura. . . ."

But if the quotation is followed by parenthetical documentation, use (1) three spaced dots for the ellipsis, (2) closing quotation marks, (3) the parenthetical reference, and then (4) the sentence period.

> ELLIPSIS AT END OF SENTENCE WITH PARENTHETICAL DOCUMENTATION
> Sommer says people have described personal space as "a snail shell, a soap bubble, an aura . . ." (26).

When you delete words immediately after an internal punctuation mark in the quotation, include that mark in your sentence and then add the three spaced dots for the ellipsis.

> It has been likened to a snail shell, . . . and "breathing room."

‖ 2
Use an ellipsis to show broken-off speech.

Like the dash (29a-4), an ellipsis shows a speaker's broken-off or interrupted speech.

> "And, anyway, what do you know of him?"
> "Nothing. That is why I ask you . . ."
> "I would prefer never to speak of him."
> —UMBERTO ECO, The Name of the Rose

■‖ 29e
Use the slash correctly for quoting poetry lines, for numerical fractions, and for and/or.

‖ 1
Use the slash to separate up to three lines of quoted ‖ poetry.

If you quote more than three lines of a poem in writing, set the poetry off with space and indentations as you would a prose quotation of more than four lines (see 28a and Appendix B). For three lines or less, quote poetry—enclosed in quotation marks—in sentence format, with a slash to divide one line from the next. Leave a space on each side of the slash.

> Consider the beginning of Anne Sexton's poem "Words": "Be careful of words, / even the miraculous ones."

Capitalize and punctuate each line as it is in the original, with this exception: End your sentence with a period, even if the quoted line of poetry does not have one.

‖ 2
In typed manuscripts, use the slash for numerical ‖ fractions.

If you have to type numerical fractions, use the slash to sepa-

rate numerator and denominator and a hyphen to tie a whole number to its fraction: *1/16, 1-2/3, 2/5, 3-7/8*. (See 30j for advice on using
spelled-out and numerical forms of numbers.)

3
Use the slash for *and/or*.

You will not use word combinations like *and/or* often for writing in the humanities, but where use is acceptable, separate the
words with a slash. Leave no space before or after the slash.

In the humanities, listing both alternatives in normal sentence structure is usually better than separating choices with a
slash.

No   The best quality of reproduction comes from 35mm
      slides/direct positive films.

Yes   The best quality of reproduction comes from 35mm slides
      or direct positive films.

EXERCISE 3
Supply needed dashes, parentheses, brackets, ellipses, and slashes. If a sentence is correct as written, circle its number.

Example   Every year in the United States, four times the amount of money
          spent on baby food is spent on pet food $1.5 billion.

          Every year in the United States, four times the amount of money
          spent on baby food is spent on pet food ($1.5 billion).

1. Albert Einstein's last words they were spoken in his native German will
   never be known because his attending nurse spoke only English.

2. During one five-week span in 1841, three different men served as President of the United States: 1 Martin Van Buren finished his term on
   March 3; 2 William Henry Harrison Van Buren's successor was inau-
   gurated on March 4; and 3 John Tyler who assumed the Presidency
   when Harrison died on April 6 after only thirty-two days in office.

3. Gold is so malleable that a single ounce can be beaten out into a thin
   film less than 1 282,000th of an inch that would cover 100 square feet.

4. To get at every ounce of gold, miners have dug as deep as 2-1/2 miles.

5. The American portrait artist Charles Willson Peale made George Washington an innovative set of dentures elks' teeth set in lead.

6. Henri Matisse's painting *Le Bateau* once hung in New York's Museum of

Modern Art for forty-seven days not to mention being viewed by about 116,000 people before someone noticed that it was hung upside down.

7. When Thomas Edison learned that one of the batteries his company manufactured was defective, he offered a refund to all buyers a pledge made good by $1 million from his own pocket.

8. In 1816 a strange chain of events (beginning with a volcanic eruption in the Dutch East Indies (now Indonesia) caused New England to experience snow in June and killing frosts through July and August.

9. Although the identity of the famous Jack the Ripper was never proven, when the convicted murderer Dr. Thomas Cream was hanged his last words were the unfinished sentence, "I am Jack the."

10. Maxine Kumin the winner of the 1973 Pulitzer Prize for Poetry wrote these memorable lines about calves as they are being born: "They come forth with all four legs folded in / like a dime-store card table."

EXERCISE 4
Follow the directions for each item. Use dashes, parentheses, ellipses, and slashes as needed.

EXAMPLE Write a sentence using dashes that exclaims about love.
    I am in love—again!

1. Write a sentence that quotes only three lines of Sonnet XLIII by Elizabeth Barrett Browning:
    How do I love thee? Let me count the ways.
    I love thee to the depth and breadth and height
    My soul can reach, when feeling out of sight
    For the ends of Being and ideal Grace.
    I love thee to the level of every day's
    Most quiet need, by sun and candlelight.
    I love thee freely, as men strive for Right;
    I love thee purely, as they turn from Praise.
    I love thee with the passion put to use
    In my old griefs, and with my childhood's faith.
    I love thee with a love I seemed to lose
    With my lost saints,—I love thee with the breath,
    Smiles, tears, of all my life!—and, if God choose,
    I shall but love thee better after death.

2. Write a sentence that includes a list of four numbered items.

3. Quote a few sentences from a source. Choose one from which you can omit a few words without losing meaning. Correctly indicate the omission. At the end, give the source of the quotation.

4. Write a sentence in which you use dashes to set off a definition.

5. Write a sentence in which you use parentheses to enclose a brief example.

30
CAPITALS, ITALICS, ABBREVIATIONS, AND NUMBERS

Capital letters, italics (shown as underlining in handwritten or typed material), abbreviations, and styles of writing numbers are sometimes referred to as **mechanics.** Knowing which forms to use and when to use them, however, is far from mechanical. Issues of mechanics involve making choices: Does a word start with a capital letter or a lower-case one? Does a group of words need to be underlined, put in quotation marks, or left alone? Is an abbreviation acceptable in a given case? When is a figure used rather than a number spelled out in words?

▰‖ CAPITALS

▰‖ 30a
Capitalize the first word of a sentence.

Always capitalize the first letter of the first word in a sentence, a question, or a command.

Records show that snow fell in Antarctica while the thermometer registered minus 65 degrees.

Does it ever get too cold to snow?

Verify that temperature immediately.

Practice varies for starting each question in a series of questions with a capital letter.

> **YES**   What facial feature would most people change if they could? Their eyes? Their ears? Their mouths?

> **YES**   What facial feature would most people change if they could? their eyes? their ears? their mouths?

Whichever practice you choose, be consistent throughout a piece of writing. Of course, if the questions are complete sentences, start each with a capital letter.

Practice also varies for using a capital letter for a complete sentence following a colon.

> **YES**   I need advice about what to do: The instructions give contradictory commands.

> **YES**   I need advice about what to do: the instructions give contradictory commands.

Whichever practice you choose, be consistent throughout a piece of writing.

A complete sentence enclosed in parentheses may stand alone or may fall within the structure of another sentence. Those that stand alone start with a capital letter. Those that fall within the structure of another sentence do not start with a capital letter. ▮
PUNCTUATION ALERTS: (1) When a complete sentence within parentheses stands alone, always end it with a period, question mark, or exclamation point—as needed for meaning. (2) When a complete sentence within parentheses falls within the structure of another sentence, use only a question mark or an exclamation point at the end if meaning calls for either; if meaning calls for a period, omit it. Both types of parenthetical sentences occur in the first example below. ▮

I didn't know till years later that they called it the Cuban Missile Crisis. But I remember Castro. (We called him Castor Oil and were awed by his beard—beards were rare in those days.) We might not have worried so much (what would the Communists want with our small New Hampshire town?) except that we lived 10 miles from an air base.

> —JOYCE MAYNARD, "An 18-Year-Old Looks Back on Life"

The journey from the first clues to the final interpretation was a long one (it took six years), and the route was not straightforward.

> —EVELYN FOX KELLER, *A Feeling for the Organism*

When you quote lines of poetry, follow the practice of the version you quote from concerning capital letters at the beginning of lines and within lines. (See 28a-3 for advice on formats for quoted poetry.)

■‖ 30b
Capitalize listed items correctly.

In a **run-in list,** the items are worked into the structure of a sentence or a paragraph rather than being set up vertically with each item on a new line. When the items in a run-in list are complete sentences, capitalize the first letter of each item.

> We found three reasons for the delay: (1) Bad weather held up delivery of raw materials. (2) Poor scheduling created confusion and slowdowns. (3) Lack of proper machine maintenance caused an equipment failure.

When the items in a run-in list are not complete sentences, do not begin them with capital letters.

> The reasons for the delay were (1) bad weather, (2) poor scheduling, and (3) equipment failure.

In a **displayed list,** the items are set up vertically, one below the other. Capitalize the first letter of all items in a displayed list if any item is a complete sentence. ■PARALLELISM ALERT: Make list items parallel in structure. If one item must be a sentence, make all the items sentences. ‖If the items are not sentences, you may either start all of them with capital letters or start all of them with lower-case letters. Whichever practice you choose, be consistent throughout a piece of writing.

Yᴇs   The reasons for the delay are as follows:
1. Bad weather
2. Poor scheduling
3. Equipment failure

Yᴇs   The reasons for the delay are as follows:
1. bad weather
2. poor scheduling
3. equipment failure

In a **formal outline,** each item must start with a capital letter (see 2e-5).

▣‖ 30c

Capitalize the first letter of an introduced quotation.

If you have made quoted words part of the structure of your own sentence, do not capitalize the first quoted word.

> Mrs. Saintonge says that when students visit a country whose language they are trying to learn, they "absorb a good accent with the food."
> Doris Lessing believes that "the way to learn a language is to breathe it in."

If the words in your sentence serve only to introduce quoted words or if you are directly quoting speech, capitalize the first letter of the quoted words.

> Mrs. Saintonge says, "Students should always visit a country when they want to learn its language. They'll absorb a good accent with the food."
> According to Doris Lessing, "The way to learn a language is to breathe it in."

Do not capitalize a quotation you resume within a sentence, and do not capitalize a partial quotation.

> "Persistence," says my supervisor, "is more important than quickness for this task."
> Winking, she encouraged me to try "very speedy persistence."

See Chapter 28 for full coverage of quotation marks.

▮‖ 30d
Capitalize the interjection *O* and the pronoun *I*.

I would drink from the river, which I would meet again and again.
> —MAXINE HONG KINGSTON, *The Woman Warrior*

Temper, O fair Love, Love's impetuous rage.
> —JOHN DONNE, "On His Mistress"

▮‖ CAPITALIZATION CAUTION: Do not capitalize *oh* unless it starts a sentence or unless it is capitalized in poetry you are quoting. ‖▮

▮‖ 30e
Capitalize nouns and adjectives according to standard practice.

Capitalize **proper nouns** (nouns that name specific people, places, or things) and **proper adjectives** (adjectives formed from proper nouns).

PROPER NOUNS	PROPER ADJECTIVES
Mexico	Mexican literature
Rome	the Roman legions
Shakespeare	a Shakespearean comedy

Notice that articles *(the, a, an)* in front of proper nouns or adjectives are not capitalized.

Do not capitalize common nouns (nouns that name general classes of people, places, or things) unless they start a sentence.

COMMON NOUNS
a state	people
the car	tomatoes
team	an exercise

▮‖ CAPITALIZATION CAUTION: A proper noun or adjective sometimes takes on a "common" meaning, losing its very specific "proper" word associations. When that happens, the word loses its capital letter as well. Examples include *arabic numeral, derringer, french fry, india ink, italics, oriental rug, panama hat, pasteurize.* ‖▮

Many common nouns are capitalized when names or titles are added to them. For example, *lake* is not ordinarily capitalized, but when a specific name is added, it is: *Lake Ontario.* Without the specific name, however, even if the specific name is implied, the common noun is not capitalized.

NO Canada and the United States cleaned up Lake Ontario in the 1970s, for the **Lake** was near death from industrial pollution.

YES Canada and the United States cleaned up Lake Ontario in the 1970s, for the **lake** was near death from industrial pollution.

The Capitalization Guide can help you with capitalization questions. Although it cannot cover all possibilities, you can apply what you find in the list to similar items.

This chapter shows you capitalization guidelines for academic writing in the humanities. In your reading, you will sometimes see capitalized words you are told here *not* to capitalize. How writers capitalize has a good deal to do with audience and purpose. A corporation's annual report will refer to *the Board of Directors* and *the Company,* not the *board of directors* and *the company.* The administrators of your school probably write *the Faculty* and *the College* or *the University,* words you would not capitalize in a paper. Capitalization is one convention you may need to adapt if you write for and about a particular group. The conventions set out here—and in dictionaries—apply to writing for a general audience.

CAPITALIZATION GUIDE

	CAPITALS	LOWER-CASE LETTERS
NAMES	Nikki Giovanni Bob Ojeda Mother Theresa Doc Holliday	my mother (*relationship*) the doctor (*role*)
TITLES	Chief Justice Earl Warren President Truman the President (*who is now in office*)	the chief justice a president

	CAPITALS	LOWER-CASE LETTERS
	Democrat (*a party member*)	democrat (*a believer in democracy*)
	Representative Marge Roukema	the congressional representative
	Senator Dole	the senator
	Professor Roberts	the professor
	Pope John XXIII	the pope
	Rabbi Gale Weiss	the rabbi
	the Reverend Allan Risden	the minister
	Queen Elizabeth II	the queen
GROUPS OF HUMANITY	Caucasian (*race*)	white (*also* White)
	Negro (*race*)	black (*also* Black)
	Oriental (*race*)	
	Muslim	
	Jewish	
ORGANIZATIONS	Congress	congressional
	the Ohio State Supreme Court	the state supreme court
	the Communist Party	the party
	the Rotary Club	the club
	Xerox Corporation	the corporation
	Eastman Kodak Company	the company
PLACES	Los Angeles	
	India	
	the South (*a region*)	turn south (*a direction*)
	Main Street	the street
	Hunter Avenue	the avenue
	Atlantic Ocean	the ocean
	the Atlantic	
	Orinoco River	the river
	the Gobi Desert	the desert
	the Australian continent	the continent

	CAPITALS	LOWER-CASE LETTERS
BUILDINGS	the Capitol (in Washington, D.C.)	the state capitol
	Union High School	the high school
	China West Cafe	the restaurant
	Highland Hospital	the hospital
SCIENTIFIC TERMS	Mars, Martian	
	Earth (*the planet*)	the earth (*where we live*)
	the Milky Way	the galaxy
		the moon
		the sun
	Streptococcus aureus	a streptococcal infection
	Amanita muscaria	fly amanita mushroom
	Gresham's law	the theory of relativity
LANGUAGES, NATIONALITIES	Spanish	
	Vietnamese	
	Chinese	
SCHOOL COURSES	Chemistry 342	the chemistry course
	History of the American Revolution	my history class
NAMES OF THINGS	the *St. Louis Post-Dispatch*	the newspaper
	Time	the magazine
	Purdue University	the university
	Campbell's vegetable soup	
	the Dodge Colt	

	CAPITALS	LOWER-CASE LETTERS
TIME NAMES	Friday August	
SEASONS		spring, summer, fall, autumn, winter
HISTORICAL PERIODS	World War II the Great Depression (*in the 1930s*) the Reformation	the war the cold war the depression (*any economic depression*) an era, an age the eighteenth century fifth-century manuscripts the civil rights movement
RELIGIOUS TERMS	God Buddhism the Torah the Koran the Bible	a god, a goddess
LETTER PARTS	Dear Ms. Tauber: Sincerely yours, Yours truly,	
TITLES OF WORKS	"The Lottery" *A History of the United States to 1877* *Catcher in the Rye*	[Capitalize the first word and all other words except articles°, short prepositions°, and short conjunctions°]

	CAPITALS	LOWER-CASE LETTERS
COMPOUND WORDS	un-American post-Victorian Mexican-American native American Indo-European	
ACRONYMS	IRS FBI NATO UCLA AFL-CIO IBM NAACP CUNY	

EXERCISE 1

Add needed capital letters and change incorrect capitals to lower-case letters.

1. President Abraham Lincoln's Secretary, whose name was Kennedy, and President John F. Kennedy's Secretary, whose name was Lincoln, advised these ill-fated Presidents not to go out just before their assassinations.
2. The first child of European Parents to be born in north America was Snorro, whose mother was the Widow of Leif Erickson's Brother.
3. The Ancient Egyptians, the first to embalm their Dead Citizens, also embalmed their Dead Crocodiles.
4. In 1659 Massachusetts outlawed christmas and fined anyone celebrating the Holiday five Shillings.
5. Mark Twain, the author of "the Celebrated jumping frog of Calaveras county," once refused to invest in a friend's invention, calling it a "Wildcat speculation." The invention was the Telephone!
6. An artificial hand invented in 1551 by a frenchman (His name was Ambroise Tare) had Fingers that moved by cogs and levers, thus enabling a handless member of the Cavalry to grasp the reins of his Horse.
7. "Take care, o traitor," roared the hero, "Or your Villainy will do you in!"
8. Researchers at the Institute for policy studies of Harvard university discovered that the following jobs are considered most boring by those

who hold them: (1) Assembly line worker, (2) elevator operator, (3) pool typist, (4) Bank Guard, (5) Housewife.

9. What is the most common item in a family medicine chest? Is it Aspirin? adhesive bandages? a thermometer? an antibacterial agent?

10. "I don't care what you do, my dear," the Actress mrs. Patrick Campbell is supposed to have said, "as long as you don't do it in the Street and frighten the horses!"

▮‖ ITALICS (UNDERLINING)

In printed material, **roman type** is the standard; type that slants to the right is called **italic**. Words in italics contrast with standard roman type, so italics create an emphasis readers can see. In typewritten and handwritten manuscripts, underlining stands for italics.

HANDWRITTEN   *Catch 22*

TYPED   <u>Catch 22</u>

TYPESET   *Catch 22*

▮‖ 30f

Follow standard practice for underlining titles and other words, letters, or numbers.

Underlining is conventional for titles of long written works, names of ships and some aircraft, film titles, titles of television series, titles of works of graphic art and sculpture, and titles of long musical compositions, such as operas. Underlining also calls the reader's attention to words in languages other than English and to letters, numbers, and words that are mentioned as such. For examples, refer to the Guide to Underlining. The list also points out which titles call for quotation marks. It gives standard treatments for titles in notes and bibliographies. For other treatments of titles in documentation, consult Chapters 32–34.

GUIDE TO UNDERLINING

TITLES

UNDERLINE	DO NOT UNDERLINE
<u>The Bell Jar</u> [a novel]	
<u>Death of a Salesman</u> [a play]	
<u>Collected Works of O. Henry</u> [a book]	"The Last Leaf" [one story in the book]
<u>Simon & Schuster Handbook for Writers</u> [a book]	"Thinking Critically" [one chapter in the book]
<u>Contexts for Composition</u> [a collection of essays]	"Science and Ethics" [one essay in the collection]
<u>The Iliad</u> [a long poem]	"Nothing Gold Can Stay" [a short poem]
<u>The African Queen</u> [a film]	

the <u>Los Angeles Times</u> [a newspaper. Note: Even if *The* is part of the title printed on a newspaper, don't use a capital letter and don't underline it in your paper. In documentation°, omit the word *The*.]

<u>Scientific American</u> [a magazine]	"The Molecules of Life" [an article in a magazine]
<u>The Barber of Seville</u> [title of an opera] <u>Symphonie Fantastique</u> [title of a long musical work]	Concerto in B-flat Minor Symphony No. 8 in F [identification of a musical work by form, number, and key. Use neither quotation marks *nor* underlining]
<u>Twilight Zone</u> [a television series]	"Terror at 30,000 Feet" [an episode of a television series]
<u>The Best of Bob Dylan</u> [a record album or a tape]	"Blowin' in the Wind" [a song or a single selection on an album or a tape]

OTHER WORDS

UNDERLINE	DO NOT UNDERLINE
the <u>Intrepid</u> [a ship; don't underline preceding initials like U.S.S. or H.M.S.]	aircraft carrier [a general class of ship]

498

<u>Voyager 2</u> [names of specific aircraft, spacecraft, and satellites]

<u>summa cum laude</u> [term in a language other than English]

What does <u>our</u> imply? [a word referred to as such]

the <u>abc</u>'s; confusing <u>3</u>'s and <u>8</u>'s [letters and numbers referred to as themselves]

Boeing 747 [general names shared by classes of aircraft, spacecraft, and satellites]

burrito, chutzpah [widely used and commonly understood words from languages other than English]

■‖ 30g
Underline sparingly for special emphasis.

Professional writers use italics to clarify a meaning or stress a point.

> Many people we *think* are powerful turn out on closer examination to be merely frightened and anxious.
> —MICHAEL KORDA, *Power!*

Meanings can change when the emphasized word changes.

> *Isabella* ordered Ferdinand to outfit the ships.
> Isabella *ordered* Ferdinand to outfit the ships.
> Isabella ordered *Ferdinand* to outfit the ships.

Instead of counting on underlining to deliver impact, try to make word choices and sentence structures convey emphasis. Excessive underlining makes writing seem immature.

> No   One hundred and fifty years ago in England working men were *not allowed* to wear moustaches. The moustache was a privilege reserved *exclusively* for aristocrats. When some feisty tradesmen *defied* tradition by growing moustaches, members of the upper class were *furious*. They called the popularization of the moustache a *profound threat* to national institutions.

499

EXERCISE 2
Cross out unneeded underlining and quotation marks and add needed underlining. Correct capitalization if necessary.

1. The first rule in an old book about Rules of Etiquette reads, "Do not eat in mittens."
2. When he originated the role of Fonzie in the television series "Happy Days," Henry Winkler earned about $750 per episode.
3. The Monitor and the Merrimac were the first iron-hulled ships to engage in battle.
4. Iowa's name comes from the Indian word ayuhwa, which means "sleepy ones."
5. The New York Times does not carry comic strips.
6. Judy Garland was the second lowest paid star in the film classic The Wizard of Oz; only the dog who portrayed Toto was paid less.
7. For distinguished accomplishments of people over age 70, we should look to Goethe, who finished the poem "Faust" at age 80; Verdi, who wrote the song "Ave Maria" at age 85; and Tennyson, who wrote the short poem "Crossing the Bar" at age 80.
8. Handwriting experts say personality traits affect the way an individual dots an i and crosses a t.
9. The Italian word ciao is both a greeting and a farewell.
10. A sense of danger develops slowly in Shirley Jackson's short story The Lottery.

■|| ABBREVIATIONS

■|| 30h
Use abbreviations in the body of a paper according to standard practice.

What you are writing and who will read that writing affect whether you should abbreviate or spell a word out. A few abbreviations are standard in any writing circumstances.

A.M. AND P.M. WITH SPECIFIC TIMES
    7:15 a.m.   3.47 p.m.

A.D. AND **B.C.** WITH SPECIFIC YEARS
A.D. 977 [A.D. precedes the year]
12 B.C. [B.C. follows the year]

TITLES OF ADDRESS BEFORE NAMES

Dr. D. K. Gooden	Ms. S. R. Odell
Mr. Charles Piatagorski	Mrs. Edna Cheek

ACADEMIC DEGREES AFTER NAMES

D. K. Gooden, Ph.D.	S. R. Odell, M.D.
Charles Piatagorski, J. D.	Edna Cheek, M.S.W.

▌▌ ABBREVIATION CAUTION: Don't use a title of address before a name *and* an academic degree after the name. Use one or the other. ▌▌

NO   Dr. Joyce A. Brown, M.D.

YES   Dr. Joyce A. Brown

YES   Joyce A. Brown, M.D.

If you use a long name or term frequently in a paper, you can abbreviate it. The first time you use it, give the full term, with the abbreviation in parentheses right after the spelled-out form. After that you can use the abbreviation alone.

Spain recently voted to continue as a member of the North Atlantic Treaty Organization (NATO), to the surprise of most other NATO members.

You can use *USSR* without giving the spelled-out form first. You can abbreviate *U.S.* as a modifier (the U.S. ski team, a U.S. government official); spell out *United States* when you use it as a noun, however.

NO   Lousiana is one of the few places in the **U.S.** where rice can be grown.

YES   Louisiana is one of the few places in the **United States** where rice can be grown.

Other than these cases, you should seldom use abbreviations in the body of a paper you write for a course in the humanities.

NO   Robt. Frost taught at Amherst Col. in Amherst, Mass., where Doctor Eliz. Adams (my lit. prof.) taped an interview with him in Sept. 1957.

YES   Robert Frost taught at Amherst College in Amherst, Massachusetts, where Dr. Elizabeth Adams (my professor of literature) taped an interview with him in September 1957.

▮ ABBREVIATION CAUTION: If you include a full address—street, city, and state—in the body of a paper, you can use the postal abbreviation for the state name (see 30i for a list), but spell out any other combination of a city and a state. ▮

NO   The Center for Disease Control in **Atlanta, GA,** sometimes quarantines livestock.

YES   The Center for Disease Control in **Atlanta, Georgia,** sometimes quarantines livestock.

Abbreviations in documentation° are common in the humanities. See 30i for a list. In the social and natural sciences, abbreviations are common in the body of a paper as well as in documentation. For guidance, see the *Publication Manual of the American Psychological Association,* 3rd edition, the *CBE Style Manual,* 5th edition, or ask instructors.

Like other abbreviations, symbols are seldom used in the body of papers written for courses in the humanities. You can use a percent symbol (%) or a cent sign (¢), for example, in a table, graph, or other illustration, but in the body of the paper spell out *percent* and *cent.* You can, however, use a dollar sign with specific dollar amounts: $23 billion, $7.85. As with other decisions, let common sense and your readers' needs guide you. If you mention temperatures once or twice in a paper, spell them out: *ninety degrees, minus twenty-six degrees.* If you mention temperatures throughout a paper, use figures and symbols: 90°, −26°.

▰▮ 30i

Use abbreviations in documentation according to standard practice.

Documentation styles are discussed in Chapters 32 (for English composition) and 34 (for the humanities, social sciences, and natural sciences). The list of scholarly abbreviations below gives forms you may find in the sources you consult as well as those you will need to document your own work. Use the postal abbreviations and month abbreviations as needed in your lists of works cited.

SCHOLARLY ABBREVIATIONS

anon.	anonymous
b.	born
c. *or* ©	copyright
c. *or* ca.	about (with dates)
cf.	compare
col., cols.	column, columns
d.	died
ed.; eds.	editor, edited by; editors
e.g.	for example
esp.	especially
et al.	and others
f., ff.	and the following page, pages
i.e.	that is
ms., mss.	manuscript, manuscripts
n.b.	note carefully
n.d.	no date (of publication, for a book)
p., pp.	page, pages
pref.	preface
rept.	report, reported by
sec., secs.	section, sections
v. *or* vs.	versus (legal case)
vol., vols.	volume, volumes

POSTAL ABBREVIATIONS

AL	Alabama	IL	Illinois
AK	Alaska	IN	Indiana
AZ	Arizona	IA	Iowa
AR	Arkansas	KS	Kansas
CA	California	KY	Kentucky
CO	Colorado	LA	Louisiana
CT	Connecticut	ME	Maine
DE	Delaware	MD	Maryland
DC	District of Columbia	MA	Massachusetts
FL	Florida	MI	Michigan
GA	Georgia	MN	Minnesota
HI	Hawaii	MS	Mississippi
		MO	Missouri
ID	Idaho	MT	Montana

503

NB	Nebraska	RI	Rhode Island
NV	Nevada	SC	South Carolina
NH	New Hampshire	SD	South Dakota
NJ	New Jersey	TN	Tennessee
NM	New Mexico	TX	Texas
NY	New York	UT	Utah
NC	North Carolina	VT	Vermont
ND	North Dakota	VA	Virginia
OH	Ohio	WA	Washington (state)
OK	Oklahoma	WV	West Virginia
OR	Oregon	WI	Wisconsin
PA	Pennsylvania	WY	Wyoming

MONTH ABBREVIATIONS

Jan.	January	July	
Feb.	February	Aug.	August
Mar.	March	Sept.	September
Apr.	April	Oct.	October
May		Nov.	November
June		Dec.	December

EXERCISE 3

Make needed changes so that abbreviations are used correctly.

1. All of the world's ten largest cities are in the Union of Soviet Socialist Republics.
2. The ice over the Arctic Ocean is seven or more ft. thick in most places.
3. Did you know that more births and deaths occur in the a.m. and more growth hormone is produced in the p.m. while people sleep?
4. After an extended study, Doctor Derel L. Abrams and Dr. Norton G. Waterman, M.D., of the U. of Louisville Sch. of Med. in KY found almost half the paper $'s they tested to be contaminated with germs.
5. If the age of the earth were one yr., humans would have lived on it for only fifteen mins.
6. Pres. Harry Truman was the first U.S. pres. to travel in a submerged submarine.

7. He made his trip in a captured German sub. on Nov. 21, 1946.
8. At 20,300 ft., McKinley is the highest mt. in No. America.
9. When the ms. of his book on the Fr. Revolution was used to feed a fire, the great Eng. historian Thomas Carlyle rewrote every page from memory.
10. Some political analysts believe that SE Asia will be the area of greatest economic growth in the twenty-first century.

■‖ NUMBERS

■‖ 30j
Use figures and spelled-out numbers according to standard practice.

Depending on how often numbers occur in a paper and what they refer to, you will sometimes express the numbers in words and sometimes in figures. The guidelines here, like those in the *MLA Handbook for Writers of Research Papers,* 2nd edition, are suitable for writing in the humanities. For the guidelines other disciplines follow, ask your course instructors or consult other style manuals. The *Publication Manual of the American Psychological Association,* 3rd edition, and the *CBE Style Manual,* 5th edition, will guide you for the social sciences and natural sciences respectively.

If conveying numerical exactness to your readers is not a prime purpose in your paper and if you mention numbers only a few times, you may spell out numbers that can be expressed in one or two words.

Emma O'Brien was twenty-six years old when she emigrated to the United States.

Iceland's population increases by more than one percent a year, but that gain translates into fewer than three thousand individuals.

■‖ HYPHENATION ALERT: Use a hyphen between spelled-out two-word numbers from *twenty-one* through *ninety-nine.* ‖■
If you use numbers fairly frequently in a paper, spell out numbers from *one* to *nine* and use figures for numbers *10* and above.

505

Never start a sentence with a figure. If a sentence starts with a number, spell it out.

> Three hundred seventy-five dollars per credit is the tuition rate for nonresidents.
>
> Nineteen twenty-nine saw the stock market crash, wiping out speculators and conservative investors alike.

In practice, you can usually revise a sentence so that the number does not come first.

> The tuition rate for nonresidents is $375 per credit.
>
> The stock market crashed in 1929, wiping out speculators and prudent investors alike.

Do not mix spelled-out numbers and figures in a paper when they both refer to the same thing. Use figures for all the numbers.

No   In four days, our volunteers increased from five to eight to 17 to 233.

YES   In four days, our volunteers increased from 5 to 8 to 17 to 233. [All the numbers referring to volunteers are given in figures, but *four* is still spelled out because it refers to a different quantity—days.]

Give specific numbers—dates, addresses, measurements, identification numbers of many kinds—in figures. The following list shows examples in major categories.

DATES	August 6, 1941 1732–1845 34 B.C. to A.D. 230
ADDRESSES	10 Downing Street 237 North 8th Street Export Falls, MN 92025
TIMES	8:09 a.m.; 3:30 [but *six o'clock*, not 6 *o'clock*]
DECIMALS AND FRACTIONS	5.55; 98.6; 3.1416; 7/8; 12-1/4 [but *three quarters*, not 3 *quarters*]

CHAPTERS AND PAGES	Chapter 27, page 245
SCORES AND STATISTICS	a 6-0 score; a 5 to 3 ratio; 29 percent
IDENTIFICATION NUMBERS	94.4 on the FM dial; call 1-212-555-0000
MEASUREMENTS	2 feet; 67.8 miles per hour; 1.5 gallons; 2 level teaspoons, 3 liters; 8-1/2″ × 11″ paper or 8-1/2 × 11-inch paper
ACT, SCENE, AND LINE NUMBERS	act II, scene 2, lines 75–79
TEMPERATURES	43° F; 4° Celsius
MONEY	$1.2 billion; $3.41; 25 cents

EXERCISE 4
Revise so that numbers are in correct form—spelled out or in figures.

1. The film *Quo Vadis* used thirty thousand extras and 63 lions.
2. The best time to use insecticides is four p.m. because that is when insects are most susceptible.
3. People in the United States spend six hundred million dollars a year on hot dogs.
4. 4/5 of everything alive on this earth is in the sea.
5. The earliest baseball game on record was played in 1846 on June nineteenth for a final score of 23 to one in 4 innings.
6. Aaron Montgomery Ward started the first mail order company in the United States in 1872 at eight hundred twenty-five North Clark Street in Chicago.
7. The record for a human's broad jump is about twenty-eight feet, one-quarter inch, and the record for a frog's broad jump is 13 feet, 5 inches.
8. 250 words per minute is the reading speed of the typical reader.
9. The yearly income of the average family in the United States in nineteen fifteen was six hundred and eighty-seven dollars.
10. 3 out of 4 people who wear contact lenses are between 12 and 23 years of age.

VII | WRITING SPECIAL ASSIGNMENTS

31

PARAPHRASING, SUMMARIZING, QUOTING

The core of every writing project is its content. In many writing assignments, the source of that content is expected to be your own thinking. For many other assignments, however, you are expected to draw upon outside sources—such as books, articles, films, and interviews—to explain and support your ideas. **Paraphrasing, summarizing,** and **quoting** are three techniques that writers use both to take notes from sources and to incorporate into their own writing the ideas and sometimes the words of sources—always according to accepted academic practice.

CORRECT PRACTICES FOR USING OUTSIDE SOURCES IN YOUR WRITING

1. Avoid plagiarism by always attributing ideas and words that are not yours to their source.
2. Document sources accurately and completely.
3. Know how and when to use the techniques of paraphrase, summary, and quotation.

■‖ 31a
Avoid plagiarism.

To plagiarize is to present another person's words or ideas as if they were your own. Plagiarism is like stealing. The word *plagiarize* comes from the Latin word for kidnapper and literary thief. Plagiarism is a serious offense that can be grounds for failure of a course or expulsion from a college. Plagiarism can be intentional, as when you deliberately incorporate the work of other people in your writing without mentioning and documenting the source. Plagiarism can also be unintentional—but no less serious an offense— if you are unaware of what must be acknowledged and how to go about documenting. All college students are expected to know what plagiarism is and how to avoid it. If you are not absolutely clear about what is involved, take time *now* to learn the "rules of the game" so that you never expose yourself to charges of plagiarism.

What do you *not* have to document? You are not expected to acknowledge information that is considered *common knowledge*— for example, that Columbus's ships landed in America in 1492 or that Einstein's theory of relativity is represented in the formula $E = mc^2$. You might have to look up and remind yourself about the date on which the Titanic sunk or Neil Armstrong walked on the moon, but such material is common knowledge nevertheless. Similarly, you do not document *personal knowledge*—for example, that your mother was born June 6, 1906, or that a blizzard crippled your city last January for 48 hours.

What should you document? You must acknowledge the source of any words you quote. Along with your documentation, you must always use quotation marks or, if the material is more than three lines, an indented format. For an example of a paragraph that uses quotation marks for some material and an indented format for other material, see paragraph 3 of the research paper in Chapter 33.

In addition, you must acknowledge your source when you paraphrase or summarize someone else's ideas. Writing the words of others in your own words does not release you from your obligation to attribute the material to its originator. When you write a paper that draws on outside sources, you are expected to use your own thinking to formulate the thesis and to organize your material, but when you use outside sources in support of your thesis, you are expected to document. For an example of a paper that has these characteristics, see the student research paper in Chapter 33. Note that the student, Amy Brown, presents her own thesis but uses outside sources—all of which she acknowledges through correct documentation—to support her ideas.

Plagiarism can slip into your work unless you keep careful notes as you look for supporting material from outside sources. (For guidelines on evaluating sources, see 32d-2. For guidelines on selecting material for notetaking, see 32f.) Here are practices that help assure researchers that they will avoid plagiarism.

1. *Use a consistent note-taking system.* Good notes give you more than a report of what you have read. **To avoid the risk of plagiarism, you must always be able to tell what in the notes is yours and what belongs to an outside source.** You must keep three things separate: (1) material you have paraphrased or summarized; (2) quotations from a source; and (3) your own thoughts triggered by what you are reading. For quotations, always write very large quotation marks that you have no chance of missing later. Color coding can help you keep material separate. Stores stock different colors of cards, inks, highlighter pens, and clips. A more cluttered but acceptable method is to underline one type of material, circle another, and leave the third unmarked.

2. *Record complete documentation information.* Become entirely familiar with the documentation style you intend to use in your paper (31b). Make a master list of the documentation facts required for each source.

3. *Record documentation information as you go along.* Never forget to write down documentation facts as you take notes. Use very clear handwriting. Do not expect to retrace your steps and get documentation facts after you finish taking notes or writing your paper. **Your chances of unintentional plagiarism increase sharply if you have to recreate your research process. Do not expect to be able to relocate your sources or to reconstruct what came from the source and what was your own thinking.** In addition to increasing your risk of plagiarizing, retracing your steps wastes your time. You also risk not being able to find a source again—someone else might be using it.

∎‖ 31b

Understand the concept of documentation.

Basic to paraphrasing, summarizing, and quoting is the concept and practice of **documentation**—acknowledging your sources by giving full and accurate information about the author, title and date of publication, and related facts.

Documentation styles vary among the disciplines. Some use a system of footnotes or endnotes, and others place reference information in parentheses within the text. Some styles abbreviate and capitalize differently than others; and each style sequences information and punctuates it a little differently. In each course for which you write using outside sources, find out what documentation style you are expected to use. Chapters 32 and 34 explain and illustrate documentation styles you may be required to use. Here is a chart to help you locate what you need for the discipline in which you are writing.

DOCUMENTATION STYLES DISCUSSED IN THIS HANDBOOK

FOR ENGLISH AND OTHER SUBJECTS IN THE HUMANITIES

Parenthetical system (MLA)	pages 562–74; 579–85
Endnote or footnote system	pages 631–40

FOR THE SOCIAL SCIENCES

Parenthetical system (APA)	pages 647–50

FOR NATURAL SCIENCES AND TECHNOLOGIES

Varies; see pages 650–58

■‖ 31c
Paraphrase accurately.

When you **paraphrase,** you make a detailed restatement of someone else's words in your own. The word *paraphrase* combines the Greek word for "tell" with the Greek prefix *para-,* meaning "alongside." Thus, *paraphrase* describes a parallel text, one that goes alongside an original writing. When you paraphrase, you precisely restate in your own words a passage written by another author (or spoken by someone interviewed, or heard on a film). Your paraphrasings offer an account of what various authorities have to say, not in their words but in yours. (For advice about identifying authoritative sources in a subject, see 32d-2.) The ideas of authorities can give substance and credibility to your message, and they can offer support for your thesis°.

Equally important, the process of writing a paraphrase helps you untangle difficult passages and gain domination over a thought. Paraphrasing forces you to read closely and to extract precise meaning from complex passages. The process of paraphrasing helps you come to know material on at least two levels of reading: the literal and the inferential (both are explained in Chapter 5).

Select for paraphrase only the passages that carry ideas that you will need to reproduce in detail. Because paraphrase calls for very close approximation of a source, it is not practical to paraphrase whole chapters—or indeed much more than a page. Usually, two or three paragraphs in a chapter are the most you should attempt to translate in the detail required by paraphrase; use summary (31d) for the rest.

1
Restate the material completely.

When you paraphrase, you restate the material—and no more. You do not skip points, you do not guess at meaning, and above all, you do not insert your own opinions or interpretations The source's thinking is paramount, in both order and emphasis.

You may later select what parts you want to use in your writing, but do not make those decisions when you are taking the notes. Recast the source's message just as it appears. If the source's words trigger your own thinking, do not lose your thought or assume you will recall it later. *Be sure, however, to write down your thought so that it is physically separate from your paraphrase:* put it in the margin, use an alternate color ink, or circle it clearly so that you will know it does not belong in the paraphrase.

2
Use your own words, not the source's.

To paraphrase, translate the writer or speaker's language into your own. If you do not use your own words, you will be quoting, not paraphrasing. Use words that come naturally to you. Use synonyms for the source's words wherever you can, and then always read over your sentences to be sure that your paraphrase makes sense and does not distort the meaning.

Sometimes, synonyms are not advisable. For example, if you are dealing with basic concepts such as *water* or *politics,* synonyms such as *aqua* or *the science and art of political government* might make the material seem strained. Consider how each synonym fits into the flow of your sentence. Also, do not rename terms that the author identifies as coined; quote them. For example, in paragraph 2 of the student research paper in Chapter 33, no synonym is used for Edward Hall's word "proxemics," because he originated it. When you use someone else's special terms in a paraphrase, be certain to put the words in quotation marks and then to give a definition in your own words enclosed in parentheses.

In paraphrasing, the farther you get from the original phrasing, the more likely you are to sound like yourself. Do not be surprised, therefore, to find that when you change language you might also have to change word order, sentence length and style, punctuation, verb tense, and voice°.

As you turn someone else's words into your own, you can expect your material to be as long as or longer than the source's. To paraphrase well, you must use as many words as you need to extract every drop of meaning. Authors are usually forced to condense their material as they polish it for publication. Conciseness is a virtue in writing (see Chapter 16), but it runs counter to the nature of paraphrase. Your paraphrase should be accurate and complete, not necessarily concise.

3
Avoid plagiarizing when you paraphrase.

Be sure to recast your source material so that you are not plagiarizing. Compare these three passages: an original, a paraphrase that plagiarizes, and an acceptable paraphrase that uses many synonyms and some alternate sentence structures.

SOURCE
Smith, Hedrick. *The Russians*. New York: Quadrangle, 1976: 260.*

ORIGINAL
The fact that power and authority derive from above, not below, has made Soviet society far more rank-and-hierarchy conscious than Western societies—strange as that may seem for a state that preens itself as the protagonist of the proletariat. The crucial test, in Lenin's blunt formula, is *Kto-Kogo?*, literally, "Who-Whom" but more meaningfully "Who can do what to whom?" It is an unspoken question Russians have in mind constantly as they deal with each other. Hence the enormous attention paid to the pecking order at all levels of Soviet society. It is the inordinate care that the Soviet leadership itself devotes to de-

*Source information throughout this chapter is adapted from MLA style for bibliographic entries.

ciding who stands where in official photographs or on top of the Lenin Mausoleum which gave birth to the Western art of Kremlinology.

UNACCEPTABLE PARAPHRASE (ITALICIZED WORDS ARE PLAGIARIZED)

Power and authority derive from above which has led Soviet society to be *more conscious of rank-and-hierarchy than Western societies.* This is surprising because Soviet society *preens itself as the protagonist of the proletariat.* The major point is what Lenin called *"Kto-Kogo?"* which means *"Who can do what to whom?"* This is the silent question Russians think about *constantly as they deal with each other.* As a result, they pay a great deal of attention to "the pecking order at all levels of Soviet society." The *Soviet leadership use inordinate care* to determine who will stand where in *official photographs or on top of the Lenin Mausoleum which gave birth to the Western art of Kremlinology.* (Smith 260)*

ACCEPTABLE PARAPHRASE

Power and rank come from above in Soviet society. Russians are more concerned with status than are people from Western societies. This is surprising in light of the communists' bragging that the state represents the interests of the common people—those with the lowest status in the society. The major point is what Lenin called *"Kto-Kogo?"* which means "What can anyone do to anyone else?" In interpersonal dealings, everyone thinks about this question. As a result, people always think about "the pecking order at all levels of Soviet society." For example, Soviet leaders spend much time determining who will stand where in official photographs or at ceremonies at the Lenin Mausoleum. In the Western world, this fact provides the basis of the study of the government, foreign policy, and related matters in the Soviet Union. (Smith 260)

The first attempt to paraphrase fails because the writer has simply changed a few words here and there. What remains contains much plagiarized material because the passage keeps most of the original's language and sentence structure. Of course, the Russian Word *"Kto-Kogo"* had to be used because no English-speaking student would be expected to know a synonym.

The second paraphrase is acceptable. It captures the essence of the original in the student's own words. A distinctive phrase from the original is placed in quotation marks. No one would charge this student with plagiarism.

*Unless otherwise noted, parenthetical references are in MLA style. This documentation system is fully described in Chapter 32.

GUIDELINES FOR WRITING A PARAPHRASE

1. Say what the source says, but no more.
2. Reproduce the source's order of ideas and emphases.
3. Use your own words and phrasing to restate the message. If certain synonyms are awkward, quote the material—but resort to this very sparingly.
4. Read over your sentences to make sure that they make sense and do not distort the source's meaning.
5. Expect your material to be as long as, and possibly longer than, the original.
6. Avoid plagiarism.
7. Write down all documentation facts so that you can document your source when you use it in your writing.

Here are two more examples of acceptable paraphrase. Both were written by the student doing research for the paper in Chapter 33.

SOURCE
Morris, Desmond. *Manwatching*. New York: Abrams, 1977: 131.

ORIGINAL
Unfortunately, different countries have different ideas about exactly how close is close. It is easy enough to test your own "space reaction": when you are talking to someone in the street or in any open space, reach out with your arm and see where the nearest point on his body comes. If you hail from western Europe, you will find that he is at roughly fingertip distance from you. In other words, as you reach out, your fingertips will just about make contact with his shoulder. If you come from eastern Europe you will find you are standing at "wrist distance." If you come from the Mediterranean region you will find that you are much closer to your companion, at little more than "elbow distance."

ACCEPTABLE PARAPHRASE
People from different nations think that "close" means different things. You can easily see what your reaction is to how close to you people stand by reaching out the length of your arm to measure how close someone is as the two of you talk. When people from Western Europe stand on the street and talk together, the space between them is the distance it would take one person's fingertips to reach to the other person's shoulder. People

from Eastern Europe converse at a wrist-to-shoulder distance. People from the Mediterranean, however, prefer an elbow-to-shoulder distance. (Morris 131)

SOURCE

Worchel, Stephen, and Joel Cooper. *Understanding Social Psychology* 3rd ed. Homewood, IL: Dorsey, 1983: 535. (The material from Worchel and Cooper shows the APA style of parenthetical documentation. APA style is described in Chapter 34.)

ORIGINAL

One of the more consistent findings in the personal-space literature is that females have smaller personal spaces than males (Willis, 1966; Aiello & Aiello, 1974; Edwards, 1972; Heckel & Hiers, 1977; Evans & Howard, 1973). Further, smaller personal space zones are found between male–female pairs than between same-sex pairs. We can speculate about the reasons for these differences. In Western cultures there are strong taboos against homosexuality, especially male homosexuality. Children are often punished by their parents for touching or caressing another child of the same sex. However, direct teaching and available models inform children that heterosexual behavior is accepted. Hence, children's spatial behavior may result in part as a response to norms about permitted sexual behavior. Children learn, however, that such behavior with members of the opposite sex is all right under some circumstances.

In light of this speculation, it is interesting to note that stable personal-space norms do develop around the time that the child reaches puberty. Investigations reveal that children do not begin to exhibit consistent spatial behavior before the age of four or five (Eberts & Lepper, 1975). After that age, the size of personal space increases until the age of 12 or 13 when it stabilizes (Aiello & Aiello, 1974; see Figure 13–2).

ACCEPTABLE PARAPHRASE

People do differ as to how much private space they need around them, depending on whether they are male or female and on how old they are. Many scientists have confirmed that men feel more comfortable with more space around them while women maintain less private space. It is also true that between any two people, a male and a female will approach each other more closely, each person maintaining less personal space, than a male will approach a male or a female, a female. Why do these differences exist? In the West, society clearly forbids homosexual behavior, among men in particular. Many parents punish their children if they catch them behaving in any intimate way with others of the same sex.

Until children reach the beginning of sexual maturity, they do not settle into consistent patterns with regard to how much private space they need and how far they should keep from males and females until they approach sexual maturity in their early teens. Before they are four or five, children act in all sorts of different ways with regard to how near they come to people. After four or five, they gradually seem to expand their private space until they are twelve or thirteen. After that, their behavior changes very little (Worchel and Cooper 535).

EXERCISE 1

A. For a paper proposing that drug and chemical companies have rushed too fast into the new technology of genetic engineering, paraphrase this paragraph. End your paraphrase with this parenthetical reference to the source that conforms to the MLA documentation style explained in Chapter 32: (DeDeuve 362–63).

Some of the initial objections to genetic engineering arose largely from the fear that some bacteria, unwittingly transformed into highly pathogenic species, might escape into the environment. This risk appeared particularly hazardous because the most widely used bacterium is E. coli, a normal inhabitant of the human digestive track. At first, strict physical containment of the facilities used was imposed as a safeguard against such conjectural accidents. Nowadays, reliance is put mostly on biological containment, itself a product of genetic manipulation (by conventional procedures). Mutant strains of E. coli have been produced that have strict temperature and nutritional requirements, absolutely incompatible with their survival in the human body, or in any environment other than the highly specialized conditions provided in the culture vats.
—Christian DeDeuve, *A Guided Tour of the Living Cell*

B. Write a paraphrase of a paragraph of at least 150 words from one of the sources you are using for a paper assigned in one of your courses. If you have no such assignment, choose any material suitable for a college-level paper.

■‖ 31d

Summarize accurately.

A **summary** reviews the main points of a passage and gets at the gist of what an author or speaker says. A summary condenses the essentials of someone else's thought in a few general statements.

Writing summaries is probably the most frequently used technique for taking notes and for incorporating sources into your writing. To summarize a paragraph, a chapter, or a statement, isolate its separate points and, in your own words, write a statement that digests the material. To do this, you must discover the material's main ideas and their relation to one another. The length of your summary should be in proportion to the length of the passage you are summarizing: a general guide is one sentence per paragraph, though sometimes more is needed when the material is particularly complex. In a formal summary—the type to use in your writing— you are expected to tie together your summarizing sentences with appropriate transitional expressions°. In an informal summary—the type you use to take notes—you can pay less attention to transitions, but you still need to record connections among ideas so that the material is clear to you when you consult it at a later time.

As you likely know from experience, writing summaries of your lecture notes or your chapter assignments in preparation for a test helps you study. Writing summaries is an excellent way to learn material because the process helps you lock information into your memory. Summarizing forces you to read closely and to comprehend clearly.

1
Isolate the main points.

A summary must capture the entire sense of a paragraph in very little space, so you must read through (or listen to) all the content before you write. A good summary reports only the main points contained in a passage. Isolating the main points involves making decisions. These are the controlling questions: What is the subject? What is said about it? You have to take in the complete message, and then you must differentiate between main ideas and supporting facts, examples, or reasons. A summary excludes more than it includes, so you must make substantial deletions.

Sometimes, but not often, the points for your summary are available in topic sentences°. If so, you must rewrite the topic sentences in your own words, and you must make sure that the connections among the ideas are clear. If you find no topic sentences, your summary serves to supply their equivalent.

Condensing information into a table is another option you can use to summarize, particularly when you are summarizing numerical data. For an example, see paragraph 5 of the sample research paper in Chapter 33: Table 1 summarizes ten pages of a source.

‖ 2
‖ Condense without losing meaning.

As you summarize, you will be tracing a line of thought. This involves deleting peripheral ideas and sometimes transposing certain points into an order more suited to summary. A summary is always significantly shorter than the original. In fact, it should reduce the original by at least half. The essential content should take no more than one or two sentences per paragraph. If your summary is too long, summarize it.

Until you are experienced at writing summaries, you will likely have to revise them more than once. Always be firm in your resolve to see that any summary accurately reflects the source and its emphases.

As you summarize, you may be tempted to interpret something the author says or make some judgment about the value of the argument. Your own opinions do not belong in a summary, but you do not have to lose a good thought. Jot down your ideas immediately, but *be sure to place them in your notes so that they are physically separate from your summary*—in the margin, an alternate color ink, or clearly circled so they stand out.

‖ 3
‖ Avoid plagiarizing when you summarize.

In summarizing, use your own language. If you have no alternative but to use a source's key terms because synonyms would not work, be sure to use quotation marks. When you copy exact words from a source, use quotation marks written large. If you do not, you will surely forget whose words are whose when you incorporate your summary into your paper—and your summary will be plagiarizing words from the author.

Compare these three passages: an original, a summary that plagiarizes, and an acceptable summary.

Source
Smith, Hedrick. *The Russians*. New York: Quadrangle, 1976: 16.

Original
What makes the Soviet false fronts so much more misleading than those of other countries is the lack of public controversy and independent information to provide a corrective context. The

visitor can peer in vain at power stations, truck factories, or private cars for an understanding of Soviet Russia. It is not a monolith, but it can wear a pretty monolithic facade, and the outsider can miss entirely the intangibles and the invisible mechanisms that set it and its people apart from America, the West, and even Eastern Europe.

UNACCEPTABLE SUMMARY (ITALICIZED WORDS ARE PLAGIARIZED)
Soviet false fronts are misleading especially because no *corrective context* is available from public debate or *independent information* (Smith 16).

ACCEPTABLE SUMMARY
The outsider cannot get behind the "false fronts" in Soviet Russia because public debate is not permitted and confirming evidence from independent sources is not available (Smith 16).

The unacceptable summary does isolate the main point, but it plagiarizes because the writer has taken almost all the language from the source. The only substitute is "debate" for the source's "controversy" in "public controversy."

The second summary is acceptable because it not only isolates the main idea but also recasts it in the student's words. One phrase, "false fronts" is borrowed, but it is set off in quotation marks. No one would charge this student with plagiarism.

‖ **4**
‖ **Turn long paraphrases into summaries to use in your writing.**

When a paraphrase is too long and involved to use in your paper, condense your paraphrase by summarizing it. Here is a summary written from the paraphrase of the Worchel and Cooper material on page 518–19. You can see it in its final form in paragraph 8 of the student research paper in Chapter 33.

People have different needs for interpersonal space, depending on their sex and age. Males need more space than females, and males in pairs keep farther apart than they do when with a female; females keep farther apart when paired together and approach males more closely. This may be because same-sex intimacy is forbidden by Western cultures. In fact, until children are four or five, they seem to be unaware of personal space boundaries, but after that they become more aware until they reach puberty, when their behavior conforms to cultural standards (Worchel and Cooper 535).

1. Identify the main points.
2. Condense the main points without losing the essence of the material.
3. Use your own words to condense the message. If certain synonyms are awkward, quote the words.
4. Keep your summary short.
5. Avoid plagiarism.
6. Write down all documentation facts so that you can document your source when you use it in your writing.

Here is a summary written for the sample research paper in Chapter 33.

SOURCE
Hall, Edward T. *The Hidden Dimension.* New York: Doubleday, 1966: 109.

ORIGINAL
The general failure to grasp the significance of the many elements that contribute to man's sense of space may be due to two mistaken notions: (1) that for every effect there is a single and identifiable cause; and (2) that man's boundary begins and ends with his skin. If we can rid ourselves of the need for a single explanation, and if we can think of man as surrounded by a series of expanding and contracting fields which provide information of many kinds, we shall begin to see him in an entirely different light. We can then begin to learn about human behavior, including personality types. . . . Concepts such as these are not always easy to grasp, because most of the distance-sensing process occurs outside the awareness. We sense other people as close or distant, but we cannot always put our finger on what it is that enables us to characterize them as such. So many different things are happening at once it is difficult to sort out the sources of information on which we base our reactions.

ACCEPTABLE SUMMARY
Human beings make the mistake of thinking that events have single causes and that people are limited by the boundaries of their bodies. Most people are unaware of the "distance-sensing process," nor do they know that the concept of interpersonal dis-

tance exists and contributes to their reactions to other people (Hall 109).

EXERCISE 2
A. For a paper defending the potential benefits to farming from genetic engineering, summarize this material. End your summary with this parenthetical reference to the source that conforms to the MLA documentation style explained in Chapter 32: (Schneiderman 52).

With genetic engineering, scientists can take one or several genes from one organism—a corn plant or an animal—and insert them into a completely different organism, such as a bacterium, to produce a bacterium with those new genes. Each new gene inserted into the bacterium carries instructions to manufacture a new protein. It is now commonplace, for example, to insert the human gene for insulin, a protein native only to humans, into bacteria to produce insulin by the pound for fermentation tanks. Plant breeding has provided plants with resistance to major diseases and to some insect pests. But genetic engineering will be able to accelerate plant breeding and confer traits such as resistance to insects on soybeans, wheat, corn, rice, alfalfa, and cotton.   —H. A. SCHNEIDERMAN, "Altering the Harvest"

B. Write a summary of your paraphrase of the DeDeuve material in Exercise 1. End it with the parenthetical reference given.
C. Write a summary of one or two paragraphs, totaling about 200 words. Take it from a source you are using for a paper assigned in one of your courses, or select material suitable for a college-level paper.

■‖ 31e
Use quotations well.

Quotations are the exact words of a source—in written form set off in quotation marks. (See Chapter 28 for rules on using quotation marks.) Quotations lend special credibility and support to your statements. If you choose quotations for their particularly apt language and if you use them in moderation, quotations add impact to your paper. Whereas paraphrase and summary distance your reader one step from your source, quotations give your reader the chance to encounter directly the words of your source.

When you use quotations in your writing, however, you confront two conflicting demands. You want the effect and support of quotations, but you also want your writing to be fluent, coherent, and readable. You gain authority by quoting experts on the topic, but if you use too many quotations, you lose coherence, as well as control of your own paper. Rather than a single piece of carefully woven fabric, you get a patchwork quilt. As a general rule, if more than a quarter of your paper consists of quotations, your instructor and other readers will assume that you have done little thinking on your own. A paper overloaded with quotations becomes what some people call a "scotch tape special." Your words and thinking about the subject are paramount. Use quotations sparingly, therefore. When you want to draw on support from an authority, rely mostly on paraphrase and summary. (In contrast, when you write a literary analysis which rests on examination of specific passages, you are expected to use fairly extensive quotations: for an example see pages 623–25.)

Well-chosen quotations should support, not make, your points. Draw on authorities to confirm what you are saying, not to deliver the message of your thesis or main ideas. Use quotations only when (1) the language is especially striking, (2) the thought is particularly difficult to rephrase accurately, (3) the authority conveyed by the quotation is especially important for your thesis or main ideas, or (4) the source's words could be open to alternate interpretations, so your reader needs direct access to the words.

1
Quote accurately.

Be very careful not to misquote a source. Always check your quotations against the originals—and then recheck. It is very easy to make mistakes when you are copying from the source into your notes or from your notes into your paper. If you photocopy material, be sure to mark off on the copy the exact place that caught your attention; otherwise, you might forget your impressions and will have to spend time trying to reconstruct your thought processes.

If you have to add a word or two to a quotation so that it fits in with your prose, put those words in brackets (see 29c) and make sure that your additions do not distort the meaning of the quotation. The student writer of the sample research paper in Chapter 33 added *North* to *American* in paragraph 13 to make it clear that the source was not referring to South Americans or Central Americans. The student's addition helps the reader understand the material, but the added words do not intrude on the source's meaning.

> If the [North] American moves away, the Arab feels that the American is being cold and hostile, while the American finds the Arab, who keeps moving closer, is being pushy and aggressive (Charles G. Morris 516).

Similarly, if for the sake of conciseness and focus, you delete a portion of a quotation, indicate the omission with an ellipsis (see 29d). When using ellipses, make sure that the remaining words accurately reflect the source's meaning. Also, make sure that the sentence structure does not become awkward. The author of the sample research paper in Chapter 33, wanted to quote only some of Robert Sommer's words on page 26 of *Personal Space: The Behavioral Bases of Design.*

ORIGINAL   Like the porcupines in Schopenhauer's fable, people like to be close enough to obtain warmth and comradeship but far enough away to avoid pricking one another. Personal space is not necessarily spherical in shape, nor does it extend equally in all directions. (People are able to tolerate closer presence of a stranger at their sides than directly in front of them.) It has been likened to a snail shell, a soap bubble, an aura, a "breathing room." (Sommer 26)

WITH ELLIPSES   Like the porcupines in Schopenhauer's fable, people like to be close enough to obtain warmth and comradeship but far enough away to avoid pricking one another. Personal space . . . has been likened to a snail shell, a soap bubble, an aura, a "breathing room." (Sommer 26)

2
Select quotations that are from accepted authorities and that fit your meaning.

Whom you choose to quote is as important as the words you choose. Your message is enhanced only when you use authorities who bring credibility to your discussion. For example, the student author of the research paper in Chapter 33 about personal space correctly included Edward T. Hall. If she had not, she would have been missing a basic source because Hall founded the field of "proxemics." Any paper that ignores a key figure in a field under discussion is missing something crucial. (For advice on how to select sources when doing research, 32d-2.)

Similarly, the words you choose to quote are important. They must fit your context. Never hunt for a quotation simply because you want to include a person's words, and don't resort to a quotation because you do not want to take the time to paraphrase or summarize. If you force a quotation to fit your material, your reader will quickly discern the manipulation.

3
Keep long quotations to a minimum.

When you use a quotation, your purpose is to supply evidence or support your assertion, not to reconstruct someone else's argument. Occasionally, however, you may need to present a complicated argument in detail and thus quote long passages. Make sure every word in the quotation counts. Edit out irrelevant parts (using an ellipsis to indicate deleted material) while maintaining proper sentence structure.

When you must use a long quotation, prepare your reader by explaining its importance. Otherwise, chances are your reader will simply skip over it.

4
Work quotations smoothly into your own prose.

The greatest risk you take when you use quotations is that you will end up with choppy, incoherent sentences in which the quoted portions do not quite mesh with the style, grammar, or logic of your prose. Guard against this possibility by reading the combined material aloud. Listen and try to hear whether the language flows smoothly and gracefully.

> While the genetic [engineering] gold rush was getting under way, Apple happened to read an article about plant breeding. "It clicked in my mind that this was the big opportunity in genetic engineering," he says. "Everyone else was thinking about medical applications." Having started a medical-instruments company while a college student, Apple decided to travel the entrepreneurial path once again. He wrote a plan for a research institute, focusing on the idea of transplanting a protein gene into potato cells to create a "meatato" full of valuable protein—equivalent, he says, "to having lamb chops grow on trees."
> —STEPHEN SOLOMON, "Green Genes"

Equally important, avoid tossing disembodied quotations into your paper. Help readers concentrate on your message by mentioning the author's name as you introduce a quotation. If the flow of language is not seriously interrupted, also give the title of the source you are quoting. Moreover, if the source is an eminent figure, you can give additional authority to your message by referring to his or her credentials as part of this introductory tag.

NAME

As Adam B. Ulam argues, "For some time now, the United States and Russia have been struggling not so much against each other as against phantoms, their own fears of what each might become unless it scored points over the other. . . ."

NAME AND BOOK TITLE

As Adam B. Ulam argues in *The Rivals,* "For some time now, the United States . . . ."

NAME, CREDENTIALS, AND BOOK TITLE

As Adam B. Ulam, Harvard University Professor of Government, argues in *The Rivals,* "For some time now . . . ."

Occasionally quotations speak for themselves, but often they do not. The chances are that you have seen the words you are quoting as part of a larger piece, so connections may be obvious to you; however, they might not be clear to your reader, who may have to puzzle over why you included the quotation. Avoid this problem by giving a brief introductory analysis that tells your readers what you want them to notice about the quotation:

GUIDELINES FOR WORKING QUOTATIONS INTO YOUR WRITING

1. Set off quotations with quotation marks—otherwise you will be plagiarizing.
2. Do not use quotations in more than a third of your paper; rely mostly on paraphrase and summary to report information from sources.
3. Use quotations to *support* what you say, not to present your thesis and main points.
4. Choose a quotation if
   a. its language is particularly apt.
   b. its thought is particularly difficult to rephrase accurately.
   c. the authority of the source is especially important to support your thesis and main ideas.
   d. the source's words are open to interpretation.
5. Quote accurately.
6. Select quotations from authorities in your subject.
7. Select quotations that fit your meaning.
8. Keep long quotations to a minimum.
9. Work quotations smoothly into your writing.
10. Document your source.

NAME AND INTRODUCTORY ANALYSIS
But Adam B. Ulam does not think that the tension between the superpowers is based on objective information: "For some time now, the United States . . . ."

A good variety of verbs is available to help you weave quotations into your writing smoothly, without any strain of style. Many are used in the student research paper starting on page 594. Some of these verbs have rather specific meanings while others are general enough to use in most situations, so choose them according to the meaning you want your sentences to deliver:

allege	conclude	insist	reveal	think
argue	deduce	maintain	say	volunteer
assert	describe	note	show	write
claim	explain	observe	speculate	
complain	find	offer	suggest	
concede	grant	report	suppose	

EXERCISE 3

A. For a paper explaining that the science of genetic engineering has advanced dramatically in recent years, write a three- to four-sentence passage that includes your own words and a quotation from this material. After the quoted words, use this parenthetical reference to the source that conforms to the MLA documentation style explained in Chapter 32: (Lax 32).

"We used to do genetics with our eyes closed," [Ron] Cape [founder and chief executive officer of the Cetus Corporation] says late one afternoon in his office. "Now we can do it with our eyes open. We can redesign genes, not at random but actually knowing the genetic coding material. It's unfortunate that people use the term 'genetic genes' as a flip joke, because it's accurate. The genetic code is almost precisely as an engineer would have designed it. It's almost impossible to communicate the wonder and yet simplicity of it." ·

—ERIC LAX, "Banking on the Biotech Industry"

B. For a paper that urges cautious control of genetic engineering, write a three- to four-sentence passage that includes your own words and a quotation from the DeDeuve material in Exercise 1.

C. Write a three- to four-sentence passage that includes your own words and a quotation from a source you are using for a paper assigned in one of your courses. If you have no such assignment, choose any material suitable for a college-level paper.

32
WRITING
RESEARCH

Conducting research for the purpose of writing helps you gain authority over knowledge and join yourself to groups of people recognized as experts. *Research* literally means repeated *(re-)* going over or looking through to find something *(search)*. Research is, therefore, a process that seeks to answer a question—to move from the known to the unknown. Seeing research as a quest for an answer makes clear that you cannot know whether you have found something unless you know what it is you are looking for.

Not all research assignments in college are given in the form of questions, but all imply that you will need to search for answers. Research questions, explicit or implicit, and the processes needed to answer them vary widely. You might be asked to explain information: "How does penicillin destroy bacteria?" You might be asked to argue one side of an issue: "Is Congress more important than the Supreme Court in setting social policy?"

To attempt to answer such questions, you must conduct experiments or track down information from varied sources. *Attempt* is an important word in relation to research. Not all research questions lead to a final, definitive answer. The question about penicillin, for example, leads to a definitive answer—the antibiotic destroys the cell walls of some bacteria (though researchers did not learn this information until the electron microscope was invented). The question about social policy, on the other hand, does not lead to a definitive answer. It invites an informed opinion based on evidence gathered from research.

Some research assignments, like the one about penicillin, may require you to conduct experiments and make direct observations. Such activities are called *primary research*. The reports written from such research are one type of **primary source.** Primary sources include original works of an author—novels, poems, short stories, autobiographies, diaries, first-hand reports of observations and of research, and so on. When you use primary sources, no one comes between you and your direct exposure to the author's own words. For many research assignments, primary sources provide invaluable information and offer excellent material for quotation, paraphrase, and summary (techniques explained in Chapter 31).

Secondary sources, also important for writing research, talk about someone else's original work. The information comes to you second-hand, influenced by the intermediary between you and the primary source. Secondary sources explain events, analyze information, and draw conclusions. The question about social policy, for example, calls for an informed opinion based on your reading of secondary sources. Consulting secondary sources gives you the opportunity to read closely—and listen closely, if you interview authorities—and thereby work to understand what scholars and other experts know about your subject. But some caution is needed also, for you want to avoid distorted reports and biased analyses..

Whether you use primary or secondary sources, or a combination, research is an engrossing and creative activity. By gathering information and composing a synthesis of it, you come to know your subject deeply. You make fresh connections and gain unexpected insights. Equally important, you sample the pleasures of being an independent learner. Little is more rewarding than the realization that you have the self-discipline and intellectual resources to locate and understand information on your own.

This chapter shows you methods for doing secondary research and writing research papers about it. To help you further, Chapter 33 presents a student research paper and a commentary on it and the research that produced it.

32a

32a
Understand what a research-paper project involves.

A "research paper," sometimes called a "library paper" or a "term paper," involves two processes. You conduct the research, and you write the paper based upon it. Both processes take time. If you are aware of the steps involved in a research-paper project, you will be able to plan ahead and budget your time intelligently.

SAMPLE SCHEDULE FOR A RESEARCH-PAPER PROJECT

FINISH BY

Assignment received (date) _____

1. Choose a suitable topic (32b). _____
2. Determine purpose and audience (32c). _____
3. Prepare to conduct research.
   a. Gather equipment (32d-1). _____
   b. Know how to evaluate sources (32d-2). _____
   c. Determine documentation style (32d-4). _____
4. Use a search strategy (32e), keep a research log (32f-1), take notes (32f-2), and make bibliographic cards (32g). *Use whichever steps fit the situation.*
   a. Get a broad overview (32e-1). _____
   b. Draft a preliminary thesis statement (32h). _____
   c. Decide whether to interview experts (32e-2). _____
   d. Decide whether to send for information (32e-3).
   e. Use reference books (32e-5). _____
   f. Use indexes to periodicals and read periodicals (32e-6). _____
   g. Use the card catalog and read books (32e-7). _____
   h. Use computerized databases (32e-8). _____
5. Compile a bibliography (32g). _____
6. Draft and revise a final thesis statement (32h). _____
7. Outline as required (32i). _____
8. Draft paper (32j). _____
9. Use parenthetical references (32k). _____
10. Revise paper (32j). _____

11. Assignment due (date) _____

The processes of researching and of writing are interwoven throughout a research-paper project. The **writing process** for a research paper is much like the writing process for all academic papers. As discussed in Chapter 1 of this book, you begin by thinking about your paper's purpose, audience, and sources. As discussed in Chapters 2 and 3, you plan, draft, revise, edit, and proofread. The **research process** is an added dimension to consider throughout. In planning, you are involved in choosing a suitable topic, refining it into a research question, using a search strategy to find sources of information, evaluating those information sources, and taking notes on useful sources. In drafting and revising, you are involved in integrating sources into the paper by paraphrasing, summarizing, and quoting. (These techniques are the subject of Chapter 31.) Also, during revising, you are watching for sections that need additional support from sources.

Once you know what is involved, you can design your research-paper project according to the limits of time and information resources available. As soon as your instructor gives a research-paper assignment, work out a schedule for finishing each step. You might need one day for a number of steps and two weeks for another. For example, if your assignment gives the topic and specifies the sources, you do not have to choose or narrow a suitable topic. If interim deadlines are part of your assignment, plan your work around them. The more you do research-paper projects, the more skilled you will become at mapping out the work and handling it efficiently. The schedule shown here lists typical steps in a research-paper project (the parentheses give the section in which each step is discussed). No two research-paper projects are alike. The steps do not proceed in a straight line, but often loop back or work in concert. This chapter covers all major steps, but you have to adapt them to your assignment and personal work style.

 32b

Choose and narrow a topic suitable for a research-paper project.

Instructors assign research-paper topics in different ways. Some assign the specific topic that they want you to research. Others expect you to find a suitable topic. Still others assign a general subject area but expect students to narrow it to a limited, researchable topic. Whenever you are responsible for choosing a topic or for narrowing a general subject area into a researchable topic, remember that not every topic is suitable for a research-paper project.

32b

1
Choose a sufficiently narrow topic.

Two characteristics make a topic sufficiently narrow. First, the topic must work within the time allotment and word limit set by your instructor. For example, in five weeks and 1500 to 2000 words, you could not do justice to the history of skyscrapers—or even to the history of all the skyscrapers in San Francisco. A sufficiently narrow topic would relate to the question: "How have new San Francisco skyscrapers been built to withstand earthquakes?"

Second, a topic must be specific enough to allow for sufficient detail to make your paper more than a collection of generalizations. For example, in a paper of 1500–2000 words, you could include too few details if your topic covered all aspects of the risks and benefits of nuclear energy. Your topic would still be too broad if it were in response to the question: "What are the effects on unborn children of overexposure to radiation?" The word *effects* needs to be narrowed, as does *children,* and *radiation.* Sufficient detail would be possible if you narrowed the topic to answer this question: "What were the birth defects in children born in Hiroshima up to eight months after the atomic bomb was dropped?"

Communication was the general topic assigned to Amy Brown, the student who wrote the paper in Chapter 33. Her instructor required a paper of 1800 to 2000 words to be written in five weeks based on about twelve secondary sources. To get started, Brown borrowed two textbooks from a friend, one an introduction to psychology and the other an introduction to business communications. Browsing through the textbooks helped Brown make her first major choice. She decided to focus on *nonverbal communication.* To further narrow her focus, Brown read a book that a psychology professor recommended during an interview. She then began to concentrate on *personal space,* a topic that particularly caught her interest. She was fascinated to learn that cultures have unspoken standards for the accepted distances between people who are conversing and interacting. Brown also liked the topic of personal space because her college had excellent sources to which she could refer. As she began to read closely on the topic, Brown evolved her research question: "How do standards for personal space differ among cultures?" The flow chart (p. 535) illustrates Brown's process of narrowing the topic. Although this chart makes each decision look as if it flowed smoothly from the one before, the process looks clear-cut only after all the thinking, debating, and choosing is over. The process in action is rarely neat and tidy. As you think through your topic, do not be surprised if you have to back out of dead ends and make some

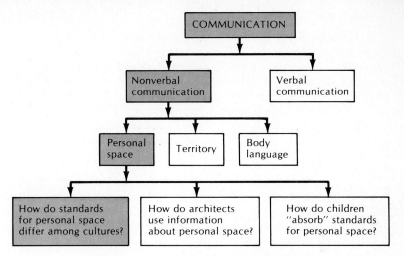

Flow Chart of Amy Brown's Narrowing Process

sharp turns to new avenues. To help yourself define your choices and find a suitable path to a research question, try charting your decision process as you go along.

2
Choose a topic neither too narrow nor too current.

Extremely specific topics are usually so narrow that an extensive search will turn up only a few fragments of information. Imagine looking at your general subject area with a zoom lens. You can survey the whole terrain, zoom in part way, look around for a point of interest, and zoom in yet closer. If, however, you zoom in yet again, you might be focusing on a small detail. You will know you are being overly specific if your topics resemble these: "The Doves in the Altarpieces of Guarineto di Arpo" or "The Effect of Muddy Infields During the 1974 Baltimore Orioles Season."

Also, avoid topics that have suddenly come to public attention in current newspapers or magazines. They tend to move in and out of vogue quickly. Most of all, they cannot lead you to the diversity of sources you need to represent a thorough search.

This warning does not mean that you should avoid current publications to provide support for what you are saying. Indeed, you might well refer to a current event—for example, a recent accident at a nuclear power plant—as an example of a point you are making.

535

3
Choose a topic worth researching.

When choosing a topic, do not rush. Keep in mind that a good research topic should give you the chance to investigate related ideas or bring together conflicting concepts. The topic should not be too trivial for a college-level research paper. For example, recent marriages among Hollywood stars is not suitable for a research-paper project. Such a subject not only lacks importance but also prevents you from demonstrating that you can grapple with ideas and their implications.

A topic worth researching has a number of characteristics. First, it allows you to draw from varied sources rather than one or two books or articles. Second, it gives you the chance to delve into material worth time and attention from you and your reader. Third, it is complex enough to stimulate you to think critically (see Chapter 5) and gain new insight.

When considering topics, try to find one that interests you sufficiently to spend time on it. You might select an aspect of a major you are considering (or have chosen) so that you can get to know it better. You might select a worthwhile topic that you wish you knew more about but have not had the time to get to know well. If you cannot think of a topic, try browsing in the library to find books and articles that catch your attention.

32c
Determine your paper's purpose and audience.

Your research process involves making decisions about your paper's purpose and audience. Purposes and audiences for writing are discussed extensively in Chapter 1, which you might want to review at this time.

The two major purposes for writing academic papers are *to inform* and *to persuade*. The question that guides your research process helps determine your paper's purpose. If the question asks for facts or information, your purpose is to inform. The question "How do standards for personal space differ among cultures?" requires an answer that calls for informative writing. On the other hand, if the question raised by a topic asks for an informed opinion supported with evidence, your purpose is to persuade. The question "Why should people be aware of intercultural differences in standards for personal space?" calls for persuasive writing. A paper's purpose may shift during the research process. Remain open-minded as you work.

By the time you are writing your paper, however, be sure to have defined your purpose.

The audience for your college writing is primarily (but perhaps not exclusively) your instructor. When you think of writing for your instructor, remember that he or she is both a member of the general reading public and a person responsible to see how well you have learned your material and the forms for presenting it. Sometimes the audience for a research paper includes other people—students in your class or even specialists on your topic. For a fuller understanding of writing for various audiences, see 1c.

32d
Prepare to conduct your research.

Before you start your research, you need to prepare. You need equipment to facilitate your work. You need also to be familiar with

---

BASIC EQUIPMENT FOR CONDUCTING RESEARCH

1. A copy of your assignment.
2. A separate notebook to use for a research log. This important tool is explained in 32f.
3. Pens—several different colors—for taking notes. Writing in pencil tends to blur when notes are shuffled and handled often.
4. Index cards for two purposes. Cards that measure 4 × 6″ give you more room for notes. The 3 × 5″ size is fine for bibliographic data. Use one index card per source to record bibliographic information (see 32d-4 and 32g). Also, use a separate index card for each idea you take down in notes. (See 32f about taking notes, and see Chapter 31 for avoiding plagiarism by learning to paraphrase, summarize, and quote sources.) Index cards give you flexibility in moving information around; pages in a notebook do not.
5. Dimes, quarters, or whatever coins you need for the library's copying machines. (See 32f about the uses and limitations of photocopying.)
6. Paper clips, a small stapler, or rubber bands to help you organize index cards and other papers.
7. A book bag if you intend to check out books from the library. Librarians joke about researchers with wheelbarrows. You might need a backpack.

two key concepts in research—evaluating sources and using headings or key words.

1
Equip yourself.

Experienced researchers use equipment that helps them work efficiently. Gather the materials listed in the chart on page 537 and keep them separate from your regular books and materials so that you can locate them easily.

Color coding is an option many researchers find helpful in establishing categories for information. For example, you might use one color of index cards or colored clips for notes and another for bibliographic information. You might use one color ink for summarized information, another for quotations taken from sources, and a third for your own comments on a source.

2
Know how to evaluate sources.

A source is any information-providing person, book, article, document, or other form of communication. But not all sources are equally valuable. Before you start to gather information from sources, learn how to evaluate them. Follow the guidelines on page 539. If you are using a secondary source, also see the Checklist for Evaluating a Secondary Source in 5c.

3
Start to compile a list of headings or key words.

Researchers use headings and key words to look up information. **Headings** are subject categories in books and periodicals. **Key words**—sometimes called *descriptors* or *identifiers*—identify subject categories in periodicals and computerized databases.

Knowing how to locate headings and key words is central to the research process. The people who prepare reference books, catalog cards, and indexes to periodicals do not have the resources to maintain an infinite number of headings. In fact, their job is to group information into categories and arrange efficient retrieval systems. Your paper constructs its own category of information. Your job, therefore, is to locate the headings and key words that lead you to books and articles on your topic. For example, the topic *nuclear energy* is identified with various headings or key words: *energy, nuclear; atomic energy; energy, atomic; nuclear power; power, nuclear;* and so on. You have to "break the code" to figure out what

GUIDELINES FOR EVALUATING SOURCES

1. **Authoritative:** Check encyclopedias, textbooks, articles in academic journals, and bibliographies, and ask experts. If a particular name or a specific work is mentioned often, that source is probably recognized as an authoritative one on your topic. Also, to check if the author of a source has a background that makes him or her an authority, consult one of the biographical references listed on pages 546–47.

2. **Reliable:** Check different sources. If the same information appears, the material is likely to be reliable.

3. **Well Supported:** Check that each source supports assertions or information with sufficient evidence. If the material expresses the source's point of view but offers little to back up that position, turn to another source.

4. **Balanced Tone:** Read a source critically, as explained in Chapter 5. If the tone is unbiased and if the reasoning is logical, consider the source to be balanced.

5. **Current:** Check that the information is up-to-date. Sometimes long-accepted information is replaced or modified by new research. Check indexes to journals or computerized databases to see if anything newer has come along.

words identify the category you are seeking in each source. As you conduct your research, keep an ongoing list in your research log of headings and key words that relate to your topic. Then when you approach a new source, your search process will be more efficient.

4
Determine your documentation style.

The term **documentation style** refers to various systems for providing information about the sources you have used in a research paper. Documentation styles vary among the disciplines. Some styles use footnotes or endnotes; others put reference information in parentheses within the text. Styles also differ in requirements for the complete list of sources at the end of a paper.

Before you start consulting sources, know what documentation style you will be using in your paper. If your assignment does not specify a documentation style, ask your instructor which to use. Be aware of what information the style calls for about each source. Then as you take notes on each source, keep a record of that information so that you can document your sources correctly and fully.

The **Modern Language Association (MLA)** has developed the documentation styles used most often in the humanities. Before 1984, "MLA style" called for footnotes or endnotes, and the list of sources was named Bibliography. Current MLA style, introduced in 1984, calls for parenthetical references instead of footnotes or endnotes. It also changed the name of the list of sources used to Works Cited. If your instructor tells you to use MLA style, see 32k to find out how to use parenthetical references and see 32g about the Works Cited list. If your instructor tells you to use a footnote or endnote system of documentation, see 34b-4.

The **American Psychological Association (APA)** has developed another documentation system commonly used for research papers, especially in the social sciences. Like MLA style, APA style uses parenthetical references and a list of sources. If your instructor tells you to use APA style, see 34c-4.

■‖ 32e
Use a search strategy to conduct your research.

Inexperienced researchers can easily feel overwhelmed by a seemingly limitless choice of source. Researchers can interview experts, send for information by mail, and—most of all—use the resources of a library. Experienced researchers use a **search strategy** for working systematically through these sources. A search strategy is an organized procedure that leads step-by-step from general to specific sources. A structured approach helps you use time efficiently and cover the necessary territory. No two research processes are exactly alike, so the search strategy explained here should serve as a guide to your personally tailored strategy. A search strategy is rarely as tidy as it seems to be when described in a textbook. Expect to adapt the explanation here to your needs in each research project.

‖ 1
‖ Get a broad overview and narrow your topic.

If you have to choose a topic of your own or narrow a subject into a researchable topic, start by getting a broad overview. For advice on how to think about narrowing a topic, see 32b.

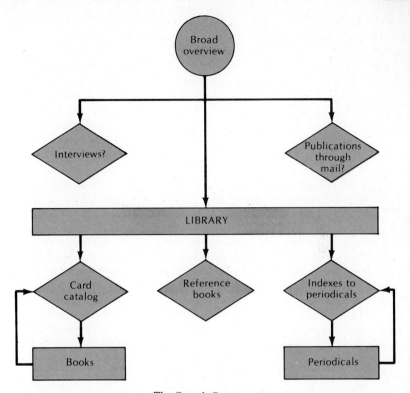

The Search Strategy

SUGGESTIONS FOR GETTING A BROAD OVERVIEW

1. Confer briefly with a professor in your general field of interest (psychology, biology, literature, and so on). Ask for advice in narrowing your topic. Also ask for names of major books and authorities on your topic.

2. Browse through a textbook in your field of interest. Look for material that points toward ways to narrow your topic. Also look for names of major books and authorities on your topic.

3. Read an encyclopedia article about your field of interest or subcategories of the field. Get basic information that might help you narrow your topic. Look for the names of major books and authorities. *Do not, however, stop with the encyclopedia.* College-level research demands a thorough search of a variety of sources.

2
Decide whether to interview experts.

As you pursue a broad overview, you might decide to interview experts on your subject, either in person or on the telephone. An expert can often offer valuable leads or advice. If your topic relates to an event that your family or friends lived through, they qualify as experts, and access to them will likely be easy. If you want to interview other people, start early. It takes time to set up appointments and fit your research needs into other people's schedules. You may not always be granted the interviews you seek. Still, many people remember their own experiences doing research in school or college and try to help.

The faculty at your college or nearby colleges have special expertise about many topics. Corporations and professional organizations can often suggest experts in many fields. (When you call a large company, ask to be connected with the public relations department or its equivalent.) Public officials are sometimes available for interviews. Many federal and state government offices have employees who specialize in providing information to the public.

Carefully evaluate any information you get from interviewing experts, using the guidelines in 32d-2. Even the information of experts may be slanted to suit special interests. For example, what are your chances of getting unbiased information about the dangers of smoking from the executive of a tobacco company?

Prepare questions that use time efficiently. Know why you are interviewing the person and what you want to know. Ask questions that elicit information, not merely a "yes" or "no" answer. Be constructive and avoid language that shows bias or a hostile attitude. For example, if you are researching toxic waste disposal, a good question to ask a government official is "What long-range plans are being made to dispose of toxic wastes?" A loaded question not likely to yield useful information is: "Why doesn't the government or your office do anything about the proper disposal of toxic wastes?"

Always follow up an interview, no matter how short, with a brief note of thanks. Aside from its being polite, this courtesy helps pave the way for the next student who might ask for an interview.

3
Decide whether to send for information.

As a result of getting a broad overview, you might decide to send for publications or other kinds of information available by mail. A month or more can go by before your inquiry is processed, so send early and leave time in your schedule to use the material. Never depend entirely on mail-order sources for your research. The material might not arrive in time or might turn out to be unsuitable. Also, a well-handled research-paper project draws on a variety of sources, including those found in a library.

When researching a question about business, you might write to companies involved with matters related to your topic. Target your request to the material you need. If you are unsure of what is available, call the company and talk with someone in its public relations office (or the equivalent). Evaluate the material carefully for bias and promotion of special interests. To be useful, corporate publications must go well beyond the kinds of information usually written for consumers. Large libraries sometimes have corporate reports and specialized technical reports on file, so check with a reference librarian *before* you order through the mails.

United States government publications are available in an almost astounding variety. You can get information on population figures, weather patterns, agriculture, national parks, and much more. Large libraries often have many government documents on file, so ask a reference librarian before you order. To find out what publications are available and how to order them, consult one of these directories in the reference section of a large library.

The *Monthly Catalog of United States Government Publications* is an up-to-date listing of all offerings. Items are cataloged according to subject.

American Statistics Index (ASI) is published in two volumes. The *Index* catalogues all statistical documents produced by government departments. The *Abstracts* gives concise summaries of the documents' contents.

CIS, published by the Congressional Information Service, indexes all the papers produced by congressional panels and committees. These documents include the texts of hearings (for example, testimony about the plight of the homeless) and reports (for example, a comparative study of temporary shelters for the homeless).

4
Be ready to use all the resources of the library.

Using the library as a resource for a research-paper project takes time. In his work as Chief of the General Research Division of the New York Public Library, Rodney Phillips has become extremely familiar with the time needed to prepare a good undergrad-

uate research paper. Division staff receives an average of 2,000 in-
quiries per day, and many of them are from students like you who
want to know how to find information for their papers. To do a decent job, Mr. Phillips says, you will want to gather and look over at
least 25 different items. Some you will need to skim, and some you
will need to read slowly. You will need to take notes on many. "Plan
to spend at least 15 hours in the library," Mr. Phillips says. "You
will sometimes be frustrated to find that others have been there
before you and taken books you want. Then you'll have to look further, just as they probably did. You will find that titles you thought
were promising will not give you what you were after. Other
sources might pay off enormously." Mr. Phillips says the typical un-
dergraduate, new to research writing, expects to obtain a paper
from one book and two or three other sources. These students, he
states flatly, are not budgeting anywhere near the time they need
to do a good job.

Librarians are information experts. They are highly skilled at
searching for and finding information. Reference librarians seek to
help people learn how to use library resources well. Nevertheless,
the research task remains yours. Professor Mary Cope, chief of the
reference division of the library at the City College of the City University of New York, says she holds "reference interviews" with students "to determine what they want to learn. We direct them, then,
to the resources and tell them to return if they need more guidance." Professor Cope thinks that the best assistance she offers is to
point out different aspects of subjects covered in reference sources.
By doing so, she helps students narrow their topics.

Many college and large public libraries prepare written guides
to their resources. Find out if your library has such a guide. With
or without a guide, get to know your library well. Wander around
and browse. Libraries differ slightly from each other, in physical
layout and in the breadth and depth of resources.

5
Know how to use reference books.

Reference books range from general sources to specialized
ones. Reference books summarize or list much important information. You can choose from encyclopedias, yearbooks and almanacs,
atlases, dictionaries, biographies, bibliographies, indexes, and other
reference books. Some of these are general references; others focus
on a particular subject.

Eugene P. Sheehy's *Guide to Reference Books* is a valuable resource. It covers reference works in all fields, describing general

ones first, and then specialized ones. This book, or another like it, is worth getting to know well.

Encyclopedias

Articles in general encyclopedias summarize information about a wide variety of subjects. The articles are most useful for a broad overview but not as major sources for college-level research. They are written by specialists for nonspecialist readers. Many articles end with a brief bibliography of major works on the subject. Because encyclopedias take long to write and publish, some kinds of information in them—about technology, for example—quickly becomes outdated. Look for up-to-date editions and annual supplements. Even so, general encyclopedias are not the place to look for reports on recent events or current research.

Collier's Encyclopedia, Encyclopaedia Britannica, and *Encyclopedia Americana* are among the respected multivolume general encyclopedias. They are all widely available.

One-volume general encyclopedias cover subjects very briefly. You may want to consult one, such as *The New Columbia Encyclopedia* or the *Random House Encyclopedia,* to see whether a general subject area interests you enough for further research. A one-volume encyclopedia may also be useful when something comes up in your research that you need not explore fully but do need to understand in a general way.

Specialized encyclopedias exist in many fields. See the list (pp. 547–50) of specialized reference works arranged by academic discipline.

Almanacs, Yearbooks, Fact Books

Almanacs—books such as *The World Almanac and Book of Facts*—briefly present a year's events and data in government, politics, sports, economics, demographics, and many other categories. *Facts on File* covers world events in a weekly digest and in an annual one-volume *Yearbook.*

Congressional Record and *Statistical Abstract* contain a wealth of data about the United States. *Demographic Yearbook* and *United Nations Statistical Yearbook* carry worldwide data. Other specialized yearbooks and handbooks are named in the list of reference works below, arranged by academic discipline.

Atlases

Atlases contain maps—and remember that seas and skies and even other planets have been mapped. You have probably looked up places in a geographical atlas, such as *National Geographic Atlas of the World*. These comprehensive books contain many kinds of geographic information: topography, climates, populations, migrations, natural resources, crops, and so on.

Dictionaries

Dictionaries define words and terms. The kinds of dictionaries described in Chapter 20 define words in the English language and give various other information about these words. As a reference work, no other dictionary is more comprehensive or scholarly than the *Oxford English Dictionary*. Unless you are researching word origins, however, you will likely find the other dictionaries discussed in Chapter 20 sufficient. They give extensive definitions and also report information on usage, slang, regional forms, and other categories of English.

Specialized dictionaries exist in many fields, among them literature, music, folklore, economics, and the sciences. These dictionaries define the words and phrases specific to a field. For specialized dictionaries, see the reference works below arranged by academic discipline.

Biographies

Biographical reference books give brief information about the major events in many famous people's lives. Various *Who's Who* series cover noteworthy people, male or female, living or dead. *Current Biography: Who's News and Why*—well-described by its title—is published monthly, with six-month and annual cumulative editions. *Dictionary of American Biography* and *Webster's Biographical Dictionary* are very widely available.

Specialized biographical reference books focus on artists, musicians, important people of various historical periods or nationalities, and so on. See the list below of specialized reference works arranged by academic discipline.

Bibliographies

Bibliographies name books. *Books in Print* lists all books in print—that is, available through their publishers and sometimes other sources—in the United States. This multivolume work classifies its entries by author name, by title, and by general subject headings, but it does not describe a book's content in any way.

The *Book Review Digest* excerpts book reviews. If a book has been reviewed in major newspapers and magazines, you can find out what those critics thought of it. These excerpts can help you evaluate a source (see also 32d-2). This digest is published every year.

The reviews appear in the volume that corresponds to the year a book was published or the one immediately following. The *Book Review Index* and *Current Review Citations* list *where* reviews have appeared but do not carry the actual reviews.

Consulting specialized bibliographies—ones that list many books on a particular subject—can be very helpful in your research process. Annotated or critical bibliographies describe and evaluate the works they list and so are especially useful. You will find some specialized bibliographies in the following list of reference works arranged by academic discipline.

Specialized Reference Works

As you work into a research topic, you should look for increasingly specific and focused information. First, get an overview from general reference works, and then consult specialized ones. Here are some titles, grouped by general academic disciplines.

BUSINESS AND ECONOMICS
Accountant's Handbook, Lee. J. Seidler and Douglas R. Charmichael
A Dictionary of Economics, Harold S. Sloan and Arnold Zurcher
Encyclopedia of Advertising, Irwin Graham
Encyclopedia of Banking and Finance, G. G. Munn
The Encyclopedia of Management, Carl Heyel, ed.
Handbook of Modern Marketing, Victor P. Buell, ed.

FINE ARTS
Bryan's Dictionary of Painters and Engravers, Michael Bryan
Crowell's Handbook of World Opera, Frank L. Moore
The Dance Encyclopedia, Anatole Chujoy and P. W. Manchester
Dictionary of Contemporary Music
Dictionary of Contemporary Photography
Encyclopedia of Painting
Encyclopedia of World Architecture, Henri Stierlin
Harvard Dictionary of Music, Willi Apel
International Cyclopedia of Music and Musicians, Oscar Thompson and N. Slonimsky
The Lives of the Painters, John E. Canaday
New Dictionary of Modern Sculpture, Robert Maillard, ed.
Oxford Companion to Art, Harold Osborne
Oxford Companion to Music, Percy A. Scholes
Popular Music: An Annotated List of American Popular Songs

HISTORY AND POLITICAL SCIENCE
Cambridge History of China, John K. Fairbank and Denis Twitchett

547

A Biblographic Guide to the History of Indian-White Relations in the United States, Francis P. A. Prucha

Dictionary of American Biography

Dictionary of American History

Encyclopedia of American History

An Encyclopedia of Latin-American History, Michael R. Martin et al.

An Encyclopedia of World History, William L. Langer

Foreign Affairs Bibliography

Harvard Guide to American History, Frank Freidel and Richard K. Showman, eds.

The Literature of Political Science, Clifton Brock

The Negro in America: A Bibliography, Elizabeth W. Miller and Mary Fisher

New Cambridge Modern History

Political Handbook and Atlas of the World

Political Science Bibliographies, Robert W. Harmon

The Study of the Middle East: Research and Scholarship in the Humanities and Social Sciences, Leonard Binder, ed.

LITERATURE

American Authors, 1600–1900, S. F. Kunitz and Howard Haycraft

Cassell's Encyclopedia of World Literature

Columbia Dictionary of Modern European Literature

Contemporary Authors

The Contemporary Novel: A Checklist of Critical Literature on the British and American Novel Since 1945, Irving Adelman and Rita Dworkin

Dictionary of Literary Biography

A Dictionary of Literary Terms

European Authors, 1000–1900, S. J. Kunitz and Vineta Colby

Funk & Wagnall's Guide to Modern World Literature

A Handbook to Literature, C. Hugh Holman

Harvard Guide to Contemporary American Writing, Daniel Hoffman, ed.

Literary History of the United States: Bibliography, Robert E. Spiller

MLA International Bibliography of Books and Articles on the Modern Languages and Literature

Modern Drama: A Checklist of Critical Literature on the Twentieth Century Plays, Irving Adelman and Rita Dworkin

New Cambridge Bibliography of English Literature, George Watson, ed.

The Oxford Companion to American Literature, James D. Hart, ed.

The Oxford Companion to English Literature, Margaret Drabble, ed.

The Oxford Companion to the Theatre, Phyllis Hartnoll, ed.

Poetry Explication, Joseph M. Kuntz

The Reader's Encyclopedia, William Rose Benet

MYTHOLOGY

Bulfinch's Mythology, Thomas Bulfinch
Funk & Wagnall's Standard Dictionary of Folklore, Mythology, and Legend
Larousse World Mythology

PHILOSOPHY AND RELIGION

The Concise Encyclopedia of Western Philosophy and Philosophers
Dictionary of the Bible, F. C. Grant and H. H. Rowley
Eastern Definitions: A Short Encyclopedia of Religions of the Orient, Edward Rice
Encyclopedia of Judaica
Encyclopedia of Philosophy, Paul Edwards, ed.
An Encyclopedia of Religion, Vergilius Ferm
New Catholic Encyclopedia
The Oxford Dictionary of the Christian Church, F. L. Cross and E. A. Livingston
A Reader's Guide to the Great Religions, Charles Adams, ed.
Twentieth-Century Encyclopedia of Religious Knowledge

SCIENCE AND TECHNOLOGY

American Men and Women of Science
Biological Abstracts
Chamber's Technical Dictionary
Dictionary of Physics
A Dictionary of Science Terms, G. Speck and B. Jaffe
The Encyclopedia of the Biological Sciences, Peter Gray, ed.
Encyclopedia of Chemistry, Douglas M. Considine and Glenn D. Considine
Encyclopedia of Computer Science and Technology, J. Belzer et al., eds.
The Encyclopedia of Oceanography, Rhodes W. Fairbridge, ed.
Encyclopedia of Physics
Handbook of Chemistry and Physics
Introduction to the History of Science, George Sarton
The Larousse Encyclopedia of Animal Life
McGraw-Hill Encyclopedia of Science and Technology
Universal Encyclopedia of Mathematics
Van Nostrand's Scientific Encyclopedia

SOCIAL SCIENCES

The American Negro Reference Book, John P. Davis, ed.
Dictionary of Anthropology, Charles Winnick
Dictionary of Education, Carter V. Good
Encyclopedia of Human Behavior: Psychology, Psychiatry, and Mental Health

549

Encyclopedia of Psychology, Hans Jurgen Eysenck

International Encyclopedia of the Social Sciences, David L. Sills, ed.

Reference Encyclopedia of the American Indians, Barry T. Klein, ed.

Sources of Information in the Social Sciences, Carl Milton White et al.

Women: A Bibliography of Bibliographies, Patricia K. Ballou

TELEVISION AND FILM

International Encyclopedia of Film

International Television Almanac, C. S. Aaronson, ed.

New York Times Film Reviews, 1913–1970

World Encyclopedia of the Film, Tim Cawkwell and John Milton Smith, eds.

6
Know how to use indexes to periodicals.

Periodicals are magazines and journals published at set periods during a year. **Indexes to periodicals** list articles written between the dates on the cover on each edition. Many indexes are kept up-to-date with supplements between editions. Some indexes include abstracts—brief summaries—of each article. Classification systems vary among indexes, so take time to learn how to decipher the codes and abbreviations in the index you need. Most indexes include a guide for readers in the front or back of each volume and supplement. As you learn to use an index, update your list of headings and key words (32d-3) for future reference.

Indexes are packaged in a variety of ways. Some are in print, with yearly bound volumes and interim paperback updates. Some indexes are on microfilm or microfiche—film strips or film cards with miniature reproductions of the print pages. Machines called *readers* project the pages full size or larger onto a screen. Get to know how these machines work. Some machines come with an instruction diagram; if you need help, ask a librarian. Many indexes are also part of computerized databases (see 32e-8).

General Indexes

General indexes list articles in magazines and newspapers. Headings and key words on the same subject vary among indexes, so think of every possible way to look up the information you seek. Large libraries have many general indexes. Almost all libraries have these two major indexes:

The *New York Times Index* catalogs all articles that have been printed in this encyclopedic newspaper since 1851. Supplements are published every two weeks in paperbound volumes. The supplements are organized into volumes (bound or on microfilm) periodically.

The *Readers' Guide to Periodical Literature* is the most widely used index to over 100 magazines and journals with general (rather than specialized) readers. Paperback supplements are published every two weeks. These supplements are organized into volumes (bound or on microfilm) periodically. This index does not include scholarly journals, so its uses are often limited for college-level research. It can be useful, however, for getting a broad overview and for ways to narrow a subject. Illustrated is an entry from *Readers' Guide* showing listings for Communication, the subject of Amy Brown's research-paper assignment.

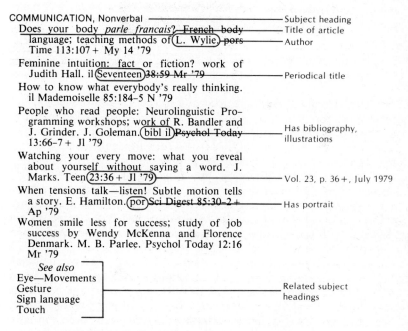

Annotated Excerpt from *Readers' Guide to Periodical Literature*

Specialized Indexes

Specialized indexes list articles published in academic and professional periodicals. When researching a college-level paper, you will often find the material in specialized indexes more appropriate than that in general indexes. Many specialized indexes carry an abstract (a summary) of each listed article.

Depending on their resources, libraries stock many or few specialized indexes. Commonly available specialized indexes include *America: History and Life,* published every four months; *Applied Science and Technology Index,* published monthly; *Art Index,* published every three months; *Biological Abstracts,* published monthly; *Biological and Agricultural Index,* published monthly; *Business Periodicals Index,* published monthly; *Education Index,* published monthly; *General Science Index,* published monthly and cumulative editions published every three months; *Humanities Index,* published every three months. (Before 1974, it was part of the *Social Sciences and Humanities Index.* Before 1965, the *Social Sciences and Humanities Index* was called the *International Index.*); *MLA International Bibliography of Books and Articles in the Modern Languages and Literatures,* published annually; *Music Index,* published monthly; *Psychological Abstracts,* published monthly.

7
Know how to use the card catalog.

The **card catalog** is a record of all books—and most periodicals—available in a library. Information is organized alphabetically in three categories: authors' names, book titles, and subjects. In some libraries, authors and titles are in one file, subjects in another. In other libraries, the three types of information are filed together.

Each card from the card catalog contains much useful information. The **call number** is most important. Be sure to copy it down *exactly* as it appears, with all numbers, letters, and decimal points. The call number tells where the book is located in the stacks. If you are working in a library with open stacks (one where you can go into the book collection yourself), the call number leads you to the area in the library where all books on the same subject can be found. Being there is an excellent search strategy in itself, even though some books might have been checked out and other books might be at the reserve desk. The call number is also crucial in a library with closed stacks. In this case, to get a book, you must fill in a call slip, hand it in at the call desk, and wait for the book to arrive. If you have filled in the wrong number or an incomplete number, your wait will be in vain.

Libraries classify books according to one of two systems. You can tell what system a particular library uses from the call numbers on the catalog cards. Cards in the **Library of Congress system** have call numbers that start with a letter. Each letter indicates a major classification of information: *A* stands for general works, *B* for philosophy, *C* and *D* for history, and so on. Cards in the **Dewey Decimal system** have call numbers that start with three-digit numbers. Each number indicates a major classification of information: 0–99 signals general works, 100–199 philosophy, 200–299 religion, and so on. Find out what system your library uses and ask for a complete list of the classifications.

Tracers are another important feature of cards in the card catalog. Tracers are words, numbered and in fine print below a book's publication data. Tracers give other headings used to classify information related to the subject of the card. They are valuable hints for other topics to look up in the subject file of the card catalog when you want to find more about a subject. As you find tracers, be sure to add them to your list of headings and key words (see 32d-3).

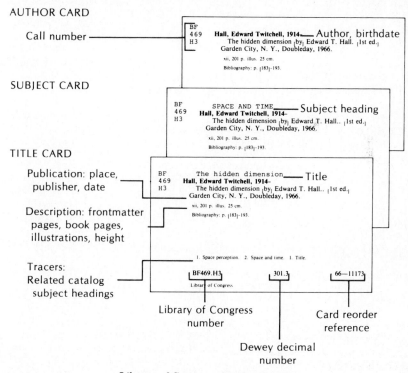

Library of Congress Catalog Cards

553

At libraries that use the Library of Congress cataloging systems, the multi-volume *Library of Congress Subject Headings (LCSH)* is an excellent guide. Available in the reference or reserve section of a library, it is a catalog of the subject headings (not title or author) used in the card catalog.

This valuable resource helps you in three ways. First, you can look up your subject without having to go through the cards. Second, if the term you are using is not in the card catalog, it might be in the *LCSH* with a cross reference to the term used in the card catalog. The expense and time is enormous to change subject headings in the card catalog, so the terms are not always up-to-date. For example, until recently, sources related to "World War I" were filed in the card catalog under "The European War." People who consulted the *LCSH* easily found out that the old term for "World War I" was still in effect, and they could continue with their research. Third, at each subject heading, you can find a list of tracers—related headings that can lead you to additional sources. As a bonus, the *LCSH* also lists related terms (marked by *x*) that are *not* used to classify information in the system; knowing these terms will help you avoid unproductive searching. All the terms in the *LCSH* suggest alternate key words you can use when searching through other sources. Amy Brown, whose research paper appears in Chapter 33,

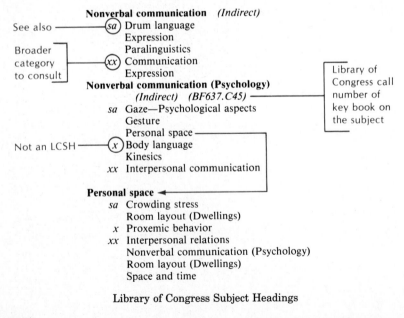

Library of Congress Subject Headings

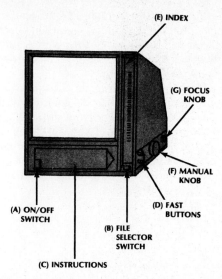

(E) INDEX

(G) FOCUS KNOB

(F) MANUAL KNOB

(D) FAST BUTTONS

(A) ON/OFF SWITCH

(B) FILE SELECTOR SWITCH

(C) INSTRUCTIONS

The COMCAT (Computer Output Microform CATalog)

found this when she looked up "nonverbal communication" as well as "personal space," the two entries shown in the illustration.

Many libraries today have card catalogs "on-line." These computerized access systems often list millions of titles, some of which are in the library you are using. On-line systems vary, so if your library has one, learn how to use it to best benefit. (See also 32e-8.)

Many libraries today have transferred their card catalogs from cards in drawers to alphabetical listings on microfilm. The microfilm entries have exactly the same information that would appear on a card in a drawer. Some libraries offer a mixture of cards and microfilm. To use microfilm, you need to operate a machine called a *reader*. Learn how to turn it on and off, focus the picture, and search at fast and slow speeds. Many such readers are currently on the market. *Comcat,* shown in the illustration, is a widely used one.

8
Know how to use computerized databases.

A **computerized database** is a bibliographic computer file of articles, reports, and—less often—books. Each item in a computerized database provides information about title, author, and pub-

555

lisher. If the database catalogs articles from scholarly journals, the entry might also provide a summary—called an *abstract*—of the material. Once you locate an entry that seems promising for your research, you must then locate the source itself. A computerized database entry is only the beginning.

The idea of letting a computer do the work is very attractive, but for a computerized database to be useful, you as a researcher have to lay much groundwork. To use a database, you must know how to search by consulting a list of key words (as explained in 32d-3). Cast a net too widely and you can get far too many entries; cast a net too narrowly and you can get too few. Most computerized databases are complicated to use, so you likely will need a reference librarian to guide you at first.

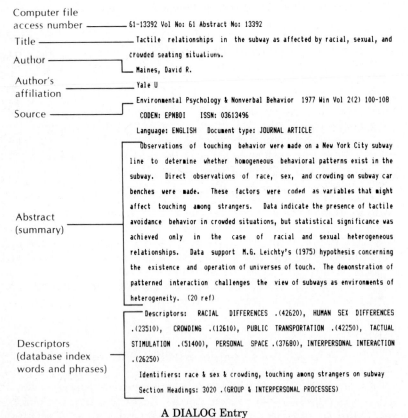

Computer file access number —— 61-13392 Vol No: 61 Abstract No: 13392

Title —— Tactile relationships in the subway as affected by racial, sexual, and crowded seating situations.

Author —— Maines, David R.

Author's affiliation —— Yale U

Source —— Environmental Psychology & Nonverbal Behavior 1977 Win Vol 2(2) 100-108
CODEN: EPNBDI   ISSN: 03613496
Language: ENGLISH Document type: JOURNAL ARTICLE

Abstract (summary) —— Observations of touching behavior were made on a New York City subway line to determine whether homogeneous behavioral patterns exist in the subway. Direct observations of race, sex, and crowding on subway car benches were made. These factors were coded as variables that might affect touching among strangers. Data indicate the presence of tactile avoidance behavior in crowded situations, but statistical significance was achieved only in the case of racial and sexual heterogeneous relationships. Data support M.G. Leichty's (1975) hypothesis concerning the existence and operation of universes of touch. The demonstration of patterned interaction challenges the view of subways as environments of heterogeneity. (20 ref)

Descriptors (database index words and phrases) —— Descriptors: RACIAL DIFFERENCES .(42620), HUMAN SEX DIFFERENCES .(23510), CROWDING .(12610), PUBLIC TRANSPORTATION .(42250), TACTUAL STIMULATION .(51400), PERSONAL SPACE .(37680), INTERPERSONAL INTERACTION .(26250)

Identifiers: race & sex & crowding, touching among strangers on subway
Section Headings: 3020 .(GROUP & INTERPERSONAL PROCESSES)

A DIALOG Entry

Most computerized databases are operated by commercial companies. Libraries pay a fee for computer time and for each entry. Often that charge is passed on to the user—you. Find out the arrangement at your library. The cost of locating entries can vary from nothing to over one dollar per entry, with a set minimum charge. The cost of a printout is extra per entry.

Amy Brown, the student who wrote the research paper in Chapter 33, used the DIALOG Information System to search for sources. DIALOG contains over 100 million references—mostly journal articles and reports—combined from over 200 smaller databases in the humanities, the social sciences, business, the sciences and technology, medicine, economics, and current events. A librarian helped Brown choose key words. Brown's topic was *personal space,* an area of nonverbal communication. Brown started with *nonverbal communication,* but the librarian soon discovered that the term was too general. It would have yielded 1,486 citations. The expense of such a list, as well as its lack of focus, led Brown to limit her search to the journal *Psychological Abstracts* (called *PsycINFO* in the DIALOG system). To get the number of entries down to manageable size, Brown crossed *nonverbal communication* with other key words such as *conversation, personal space, social perception,* and *ethnic values.* One of those citations is illustrated here, with an explanation of its parts.

■‖ 32f
Keep a research log and take useful notes.

Your research process includes locating sources, taking notes on them, and recording your ideas along the way.

‖ 1
Keep a research log.

A **research log** is like a diary. Keep it in a notebook reserved exclusively for your research project. A thorough research log helps you think about your evolving material. Your log is a history of your search strategy and ideas that occur to you during the research process. It keeps you from having to retrace your steps or reconstruct your thoughts unnecessarily. It is *not* for notes about content of sources: put notes on index cards, as explained in 32f-2. Rereading your log can help you make decisions about the next research step or about the content of your paper. Although much of your log will not find its way into your paper, its entries become valuable

> Nov. 15: Found Sommer and made a biblio. card. Excellent source. He is an environmental psychologist. Tone is calm, seems to be unbiased. I now realize that I was overlapping two concepts: territory and personal space. Territory refers to the places we carve out as "our own" — a chair in a classroom, a room in a house. Personal space is the "bubble" of space we carry around with us. We don't like intrusions in our bubbles. Sommer's description on page 26 is the best I've seen. I photocopied the page and marked off the part I will probably quote in my paper.

Excerpt from Amy Brown's Research Log

aids when you move from gathering material to organizing information to writing the paper. An entry from Amy Brown's log is shown above.

2
Take useful notes.

Taking good notes is the key to using sources well in your research paper. Together with your research log and bibliography cards, your notes give you a complete record of your research and the information you found.

Notetaking is a decision-making process. The first decision concerns whether a source related to your topic is worth taking notes on. To decide, evaluate it according to the guidelines in 32d-2. If it seems to be a good source, take notes. If it does not, record its title and location in your research log—along with a message to yourself about why you rejected it. What seems useless one day might have potential if you revise your focus or narrow your topic.

The second decision concerns what to put into your notes. Knowing how to select material for notes comes with experience.

Dive in and get that experience. Use critical reading skills (as explained in Chapter 5) to sort out major information from minor information as it relates to your topic. Do not get bogged down in unimportant details. At the same time, do not overlook important material. Try for a reasonable balance.

When you begin, if you have only a general sense of your topic, read and take notes widely. Stay alert for ways to narrow your topic. Use your research log to keep track of your thoughts—ideas tend to pop in and out of mind during a selection process. Topic narrowing takes time and patience (for advice, see 32b). Do not get discouraged. All researchers cast about at first. Once you have narrowed your subject, take notes focused within the boundaries of your choice.

The third decision in the notetaking process concerns the form of your notes. **You must use procedures that prevent plagiarism.** This matter is so important that Chapter 31 is devoted to the skills of paraphrasing, summarizing, and quoting. To plagiarize is to steal someone else's words and pass them off as your own. To avoid the risk of plagiarism, always be able to tell from your notes what is yours and what belongs to a source.

To take notes, use index cards. You can write more on a 4 × 6″ than on a 3 × 5″ card. Cards, in contrast to pages in a notebook, provide flexibility for organizing information to write your paper. Never put notes from more than one source on the same index card.

Hall, *Hidden*, p. 109

Awareness of personal space

Summary: Most people are unaware that interpersonal distances exist and contribute to peoples' reactions to one another.

A Note Card Summarizing a Source

Sommer, p. 26

> The best way to learn the location of invisible boundaries is to keep $\big\}$ *I'll paraphrase this*
> walking until somebody complains. Personal space refers to an area
> with invisible boundaries surrounding a person's body into which in-
> truders may not come. [Like the porcupines in Schopenhauer's fable,
> people like to be close enough to obtain warmth and comradeship but $\big\}$ *I'll quote this with ellipses*
> far enough away to avoid pricking one another. Personal space ~~is not~~
> ~~necessarily spherical in shape, nor does it extend equally in all direc-~~
> ~~tions. (People are able to tolerate closer presence of a stranger at their~~
> ~~sides than directly in front.) It~~ has been likened to a snail shell, a
> soap bubble, an aura, and "breathing room."] There are major differ-
> ences between cultures in the distances that people maintain—English-
> men keep further apart than Frenchmen or South Americans. Reports

Photocopy of Source, with Annotations

If your notes on a source require more than one index card, number the cards sequentially. (If, for example, you use the labels "1 of 2" and "2 of 2" for two cards, you will know each card's number and the total number of cards in your records). If you take notes on more than one idea or topic from a particular source, start a new card for each new area of information. Head each index card with identifying information that clearly relates to one of your bibliographic cards. Include the source's title and the number of the page or pages from which you are taking notes. Also, clearly identify the *type* of note on the card: paraphrase, summary, or quotation. Think of note cards as one half of a set of cards—the second half is the bibliographic card. Without bibliographic information you cannot write parenthetical references (32k) or a final bibliography. A note card written by Amy Brown, the student whose paper is in Chapter 33, is shown on page 559.

Photocopying can save you time if you want a word-for-word record of a source. Photocopying, however, can be a seductive trap for researchers. It is a waste of time and money to photocopy everything you come across. Write your paraphrases and summaries as you go along. When you do photocopy, always mark the paper with (1) identifying information and (2) notations about what you consider important and why. Do not merely pile up stacks of photocopies without any record of your thought processes. A photocopy Amy Brown made and annotated is shown above.

■‖ 32g
Make a working bibliography and include a final list of sources in your paper.

Informing readers about the sources you have used for a research paper is an important part of documentation. A working bibliography helps you to keep careful track of all sources you take notes on. A list of sources submitted with your research paper gives readers bibliographic facts for the evidence you use.

1
Make a bibliographic card for each source you take notes on.

To create a working bibliography, write out a bibliographic card for every source you take notes on (*Bibliography* literally means "description of books.") Include on each card all the bibliographic information you need to fulfill the requirements of the documentation style you are using (see 32d-4). Also, for each card on a library source, write the call number in the upper lefthand corner,

HM
285
H3

Hall, Edward T. *The Hidden Dimension.* New York: Doubleday, 1969.

Martin, Judith. "Here's Looking at You." *Newsday* 27 Jan. 1981, Section 2: 9-13

being careful to copy it exactly. When the time comes to compile a final list of sources for your research paper, you can easily arrange bibliographic cards in correct order. Two of Amy Brown's bibliographic cards are shown, one for a book and one for an article.

As you organize and write your paper, you may find that you have not drawn on certain sources at all, even though you took notes on them. In MLA documentation, presented in this chapter, and APA documentation, presented in 34c-4, include only the sources you mention in your paper. If you are *not* using either MLA or APA documentation, ask your instructor whether your source list should include all the sources you consult or only sources you refer to.

2
Compile a Works Cited list according to MLA guidelines.

In Modern Language Association (MLA) documentation style, a final list of sources is called Works Cited. (See 34c-4 about the References list in American Psychological Association—documentation style and 34d-4 for information about other styles.) Works Cited is a list of all sources referred to in your paper and arranged alphabetically by author name. The list includes only the sources from which you use paraphrases or summaries or quotations. It does not include sources you consulted but did not actually refer to in the paper. This list follows any endnotes* and begins on a new page, numbered sequentially with the rest of the paper. Entries are alphabetized according to the author's last name. If the author's name is unknown, the entry is alphabetized by the first significant word of the title (not by *A, An,* or *The*). Each entry starts at the left margin, and the second and any subsequent lines indent five spaces. Double spacing is used within and between entries. Citations include information to help a reader easily locate a source.

The following pages present examples of patterns for citing various sources in a Works Cited list. If you have further questions about citations or parenthetical references, consult Joseph Gibaldi and Walter S. Achtert, *MLA Handbook for Writers of Research Papers,* 2nd ed., New York: MLA, 1984.

---

*MLA style calls for notes not for documentation purposes, but for commentary or other information that would interrupt the discussion in your paper. See page 585.

Citing books

Citations for books have three main parts: author, title, and publication information (place of publication, publisher, and date of publication). Each part is followed by a period and two spaces.

    Didion, Joan. Salvador. New York: Simon, 1983.

Many sources need additional items of information included in the citation.

    Chester, Laura, and Sharon Barba, eds. Rising Tides:
        Twentieth Century American Women Poets.
        Intro. Anäis Nin. New York: Simon, 1973.

You can find most of this information on the title page or copyright page (reverse of the title page). If several cities are listed for the place of publication, give only the first. If the city might be unfamiliar to a reader, add an abbreviation of the state, Canadian province, or country. You can shorten the publisher's name as long as the shortened version is easily identifiable. (*Prentice-Hall* can be *Prentice; Oxford University Press* can be *Oxford UP, Simon & Schuster* can be *Simon.*) Give the latest copyright date for the edition you are using. If the book has had several printings (rather than editions), use the original publication date. The examples of various book citations on the following pages show and explain this format.

BOOK WITH ONE AUTHOR

    Welty, Eudora. One Writer's Beginnings. Cambridge:
        Harvard UP, 1984.

This citation follows the basic pattern of author (last name first, for alphabetizing), full title, and publication information (place, publisher, and date). Each part is followed by a period and then two spaces before entering the next part. Note the abbreviation of *University Press* as *UP.*

BOOK WITH TWO OR THREE AUTHORS

    Leghorn, Lisa, and Katherine Parker. Woman's Worth.
        Boston: Routledge, 1981.

Kelly, Alfred H., Winfred A. Harbison, and Herman Belz.

The American Constitution: Its Origins and

Development. 6th ed. New York: Norton, 1983.

Give only the first author's name in reversed order; give other authors' names in normal order. Use commas to separate authors' names, including a comma before the *and* preceding the last name in the series. Give the names in the order they appear on the title page of the book; note that authors' names are not always listed alphabetically on the title page. Note the shortened version of the publisher's name.

BOOK WITH MORE THAN THREE AUTHORS

Moore, Mark H., et al. Dangerous Offenders: The Elusive

Target of Justice. Cambridge: Harvard UP, 1984.

Use only the first author's name, in reversed order; *et al.* ("and others") indicates the other three or more authors' names.

TWO OR MORE BOOKS BY THE SAME AUTHOR(S)

Morris, Desmond. Manwatching: A Field Guide to Human

Behavior. New York: Abrams, 1977.

---, ed. Primate Ethology. London: Wiedenfeld, 1967.

When citing two or more books by the same author(s), give the name(s) in the first entry only. In the second and subsequent entries, use three hyphens to stand for exactly the same name(s). If the person served as author of subsequent books, put a period and two spaces following the three hyphens. If the person served as editor or translator, put a comma and the appropriate abbreviation (ed. or trans.) following the three hyphens. Alphabetize the works listed according to book title, regardless of such labels as *ed.* or *trans,* and regardless of the chronological order in which they were published.

BOOK BY A CORPORATE AUTHOR

The Boston Women's Health Collective. Our Bodies,

Ourselves. New York: Simon, 1986.

Cite the full name of the corporate author first. If the author is also the publisher, the name may be abbreviated.

ANONYMOUS BOOK

> The Chicago Manual of Style. 13th ed. Chicago:
>
> U of Chicago P, 1982.

If there is no author's name on the title page, begin the citation with the title. Alphabetize the entry according to the first significant word of the title (not *A, An,* or *The*).

ANTHOLOGY OR COLLECTION

> Valdez, Luis, and Stan Steiner, eds. Aztlan: An
>
> Anthology of Mexican American Literature.
>
> New York: Knopf, 1972.

The name of the editor follows the same pattern as book authors, but after the name place a comma, a space, and the abbreviation *eds.*

ONE SELECTION FROM AN ANTHOLOGY OR A COLLECTION

> Galarza, Ernesto. "The Roots of Migration." Aztlan:
>
> An Anthology of Mexican American Literature.
>
> Ed. Luis Valdez and Stan Steiner. New York:
>
> Knopf, 1972. 127-132.

Give the author and title of the selection first. Place titles of essays, short stories, or short poems in quotation marks. Underline the title of a book or a play. Then give the full title of the anthology. Follow it with the editor(s). Note that the editors' names are preceded by *Eds.* (you would use *Ed.* for only one editor) and are given in normal order. End the citation with the inclusive page numbers of the selection. Just put the number(s); do not use the abbreviation *p.* or *pp.*

TWO SELECTIONS FROM ONE ANTHOLOGY OR COLLECTION

> Gilbert, Sandra M., and Susan Gubar. The Norton Anthology
>
> of Literature by Women. New York: Norton, 1985.
>
> Kingston, Maxine Hong. "No Name Woman." Gilbert
>
> and Gubar 2337-2347.
>
> Morrison, Toni. "The Bluest Eye." Gilbert and
>
> Gubar 2067-2184.

If you cite more than one selection from the same anthology, you can avoid repeating all the bibliographic facts. List the anthology as a separate entry, complete with all the publication information. Also list each selection from the anthology by author and title of the selection, but then give only the names of the editor(s) of the anthology and the page number(s) of the selection.

ARTICLE IN A REFERENCE BOOK

> Holt, Robert R. "Freud, Sigmund." <u>International Encyclopedia</u>
>
> <u>of the Social Sciences</u>. Ed. David L. Sills. 18 vols.
>
> New York: Macmillan, 1968.
>
> "Ireland." <u>Encyclopaedia Britannica</u>. 1974 ed.

Treat articles in an encyclopedia and dictionary entries like selections in an anthology. If no author is named, give the title first. If articles are alphabetically arranged in the work, omit the volume and page numbers. If the reference book is frequently revised, give only the edition and year of publication. If a reference book is probably not well known, however, give full publication information.

BOOK WITH AN AUTHOR AND AN EDITOR

> Brontë, Emily. <u>Wuthering Heights</u>. Ed. David Daiches.
>
> London: Penguin, 1985.
>
> Daiches, David, ed. <u>Wuthering Heights</u>. By Emily Brontë.
>
> London: Penguin, 1985.

If what you refer to in your paper is the work of the book's author, begin the citation with the author's name. If you are citing instead the work of the editor, begin the citation with the editor's name.

TRANSLATION

> Freire, Paulo. <u>Pedagogy of the Oppressed</u>. Trans. Myra
>
> Bergman Ramos. New York: Seabury, 1970.

Cite the author's name first, and then cite the work's title. Then put Trans. followed by the translator's name.

WORK IN SEVERAL VOLUMES OR PARTS

> Jones, Ernest. <u>The Last Phase</u>. Vol. 3 of <u>The Life and</u>
>
> <u>Work of Sigmund Freud</u>. 3 vols. New York:
>
> Basic, 1957.
>
> Randall, John Herman, Jr. <u>The Career of Philosopy</u>. 2 vols.
>
> New York: Columbia UP, 1962.

If the work has two or more volumes, state the total number of volumes between the title and the publication information or between the editor and the publication information. If you are citing only one volume of a multivolume work, place this information after the publication date. For example:

```
New York: Columbia UP, 1962.  Vol. 1.
```

If you are citing one volume of a multivolume work that has its own title, state that title first and then state the volume number of the work. Note that the MLA recommends using arabic numerals, even if the source uses roman numerals *(Vol. 6* for *Vol. VI)*.

EDITION

```
Mandell, Maurice I.  Advertising.  4th ed.  Englewood
        Cliffs, NJ: Prentice, 1984.
```

When a book is not the first edition, the edition number appears on the title page. Place this information between the title and the publication information. An edition may also mean an edition of a particular author's work, involving an author and an editor (see the citation for a book with an author and an editor). If there is an edition number as well as a citation for an editor, that number should follow the editor's name.

REPRINT OF AN OLDER BOOK

```
Hurston, Zora Neale.  Their Eyes Were Watching God.  1937.
        Urbana: U of Illinois P, 1978.
```

A republished book may be the paperback version of a book originally published as a hardbound, or it may be the reissuing of a book. Republishing information can be found on the copyright page. Give the date of the original version before the publication information for the version you are citing.

INTRODUCTION, PREFACE, FOREWORD, OR AFTERWORD

```
Mead, Margaret.  Preface.  Patterns of Culture.  By Ruth
        Benedict.  1934.  Boston: Houghton, 1959.
```

If you are citing an introduction, preface, foreword, or afterword, give its author's name first and then the name of the part cited. Capitalize the first letter of the part cited, but do not underline it nor put it in quotation marks. If the writer of the introduction, preface, foreword, or afterword is different from the author of the book, give that author's full name after the title. Give the inclusive page numbers of the part you are citing after the publication information. Note that such prefatory page numbers are in roman numerals just as they appear in the work.

BOOK IN A SERIES

McClave, Heather. <u>Women Writers of the Short Story</u>.
Twentieth Century Views Series. Englewood Cliffs,
NJ: Prentice, 1980.

Place the title of the series, found on the title page, between the title of the work and the publication information.

BOOK WITH A TITLE WITHIN A TITLE

Lumiansky, Robert M., and Herschel Baker, eds. <u>Critical</u>
<u>Approaches to Six Major English Works: Beowulf Through</u>
<u>Paradise Lost</u>. Philadelphia: U of Pennsylvania P, 1968.

When a book title includes the title of another work that is usually underlined (such as a novel, play, or long poem), do *not* underline the incorporated title. If the incorporated title is usually enclosed in quotation marks (such as a short story or short poem), keep the quotation marks and underline the complete title of the book.

GOVERNMENT PUBLICATION

United States. Cong. House. Committee on the Judiciary.
<u>Immigration and Nationality with Amendments and Notes</u>
<u>on Related Laws</u>. 7th ed. Washington: GPO, 1980.

If such a publication has no stated author, use the government, governmental body, and/or government agency as the author, with periods and two spaces separating the parts. "GPO" is the standard abbreviation for Government Printing Office.

PUBLISHED PROCEEDINGS OF A CONFERENCE

Harris, Diana, and Laurie Nelson-Heern, eds. <u>Proceedings of</u>
<u>NECC 1981: National Educational Computing Conference</u>.
17-19 June 1981. Iowa City: Weeg Computing Center,
U of Iowa, 1981.

Treat published proceedings of a conference like a book. Add any important information, such as the date of the conference, which does not appear in the title.

Citing articles

Like citations for books, citations for articles in periodicals (such as journals, magazines, and newspapers) contain three major parts: author, title of article, and publication information. For articles, however, the publication information usually includes the periodical title, volume number, year of publication, and inclusive page numbers.

```
Maines, David R.  "The Sand and the Castle: Some Remarks

    Concerning G. P. Stone's Critique of Small Group Research."

    Studies in Symbolic Interaction 5 (1984): 23-24.
```

In the citation for an article, each part is followed by a period and two spaces. Additional items of information may be required, depending on the source. In citations for articles, arrange information in the following order:

1. Author's name
2. Title of the article
3. Name of the periodical
4. Series number or name
5. Volume number
6. Date of publication
7. Page numbers

You can usually find this information on the cover and/or title page of the periodical and sometimes on the first page of the article. Examples of various citations on the following pages show and explain this format.

ARTICLE IN A JOURNAL WITH CONTINUOUS PAGINATION

```
Cochran, D. D., W. Daniel Hale, and Christine P. Hissam.

    "Personal Space Requirements in Indoor versus Outdoor

    Locations."  Journal of Psychology 117 (1984): 132-133.
```

To cite an article in a journal with continuous pagination, follow the basic format of author (last name first), title of the article, and publication information (journal title, volume number, year of pub-

569

lication in parentheses followed by a colon, and inclusive page numbers). Separate each part with a period and two spaces. If a journal pages its issues continuously through an annual volume, give only the volume number, not the issue number, and the page numbers. (*National Geographic* is such a journal. If the first issue of a volume ends on page 224, for example, the second issue starts on page 225.) Notice that all numbers, even the volume, are arabic numerals.

ARTICLE IN A JOURNAL THAT PAGES EACH ISSUE SEPARATELY

> Wacker, J. F., and R. K. Teas. "Starting Salaries of the
> College of Business Graduates." Review of Business and
> Economic Research 15.1 (1979): 70-81.

Some journals page each issue of an annual volume separately. (Each issue begins with page 1.) To cite articles from such journals, give both the volume number and the issue number (15.1 because 15 is the volume and 1 is the issue).

ARTICLE FROM A WEEKLY OR BIWEEKLY MAGAZINE OR NEWSPAPER

> Randolph, Barbara. "Hailing the Eureka Factor." Time 21
> Feb. 1986: 65.

If a periodical is published every week or every two weeks, cite the complete date in place of the volume and issue number. Cite the year of publication without parentheses. First cite the day, then the month (abbreviated if necessary), and finally, the year. Always drop an introductory *A, An,* or *The* from the title of a periodical.

ARTICLE FROM A MONTHLY OR BIMONTHLY PERIODICAL

> Hogan, Patti. "Setting the Pace." Ms. Aug. 1985: 20-32.

If a periodical is published monthly or every two months, cite the month(s) and year instead of volume and issue numbers and year of publication.

ARTICLE FROM A DAILY NEWSPAPER

> Dullea, Georgia. "Literary Folk Look for Solid Comfort."
> New York Times 16 April 1986: C14.
> "Hospitals, Competing for Scarce Patients, Turn to
> Advertising." New York Times 20 April 1986: 47.

If an author's name appears, give the author's name, last name first. If no author's name is given, begin the entry with the title. As with books, alphabetize the entry according to the first main word of the title. Cite the title of the newspaper exactly as it appears on the masthead, omitting any introductory *A* or *The* (Boston Globe, New York Times). If the city of publication is not in the title of the periodical, add it in square brackets after the title, not underlined: for example, Patriot Ledger [Quincy, MA]. The day, month, and year of the issue are given instead of volume and issue numbers. Be sure to give the section letter as well as the page number, if appropriate: for example, C14. If an article does not run on consecutive pages (if, for example, it starts on 23 and continues on 42), give the first page number and add a plus sign (23+).

ARTICLE FROM A COLLECTION OF REPRINTED ARTICLES

> Ryan, Bill. "Nuclear Waste Crisis--Don't Dump on Us." In
>
> Social Issues Resources Series. Pollution. Vol. 3 Article
>
> 14. Boca Raton, FL: Social Issues Resources Series, 1984.

EDITORIAL, LETTER TO THE EDITOR, REVIEW

> Childress, Glenda Teal. Letter. Newsweek 9 June 1986: 10.
>
> Linebaugh, Peter. "In the Flight Path of Perry Anderson."
>
> Rev. of In the Tracks of Historical Materialism,
>
> by Perry Anderson. History Workshop 21 (1986):
>
> 141-46.
>
> "Prayer Meetings in Public School?" Editorial. Washington
>
> Post 27 March 1986: A20.

To cite editorials, letters to the editor, and reviews, follow the same format as for previous citations. In addition, add descriptive labels *(Editorial, Letter,* or *Rev.)* to identify the kind of work clearly.

ABSTRACT FROM *Dissertation Abstracts* **OR** *Dissertation Abstracts International*

> Huber, Elaine Clare. "Women and the Authority of Inspiration."
>
> DAI 45 (1984): 315A. U of California, Berkeley.

Dissertation Abstracts (DA) became *Dissertation Abstracts International (DAI)* with volume 30 (1969). The letter at the end of the page number (3691A) indicates which paginated series (humanities, social sciences, or European dissertations) is being cited. Give the degree-granting institution at the end of the citation.

UNPUBLISHED DISSERTATIONS OR ESSAYS

```
Geissinger, Shirley Burry.   "Openness versus Secrecy in
     Adoptive Parenthood."  Diss. U. of North Carolina
     at Greensboro, 1984.
```

To cite an unpublished dissertation or essay (your own or another person's), state the author's name first, then the title in quotation marks (not underlined), then a descriptive label (such as *Diss.* or *Unpublished essay*), then the degree-granting institution (for dissertations), and finally the date.

Citing other sources

Citations for computer software, films, or maps are treated similarly to printed books and articles. The particular nature of each source dictates what information is available and what items of information should be included.

PUBLISHED AND UNPUBLISHED LETTERS

```
Lapidus, Jackie.   Letter to her mother.  12 Nov. 1975.
     Between Ourselves: Letters Between Mothers & Daughters.
     Ed. Karen Payne.  Boston: Houghton, 1983.  323-26.
```

Treat a published letter like a selection in an anthology, adding a descriptive label (if there is no title), the date of the letter, and the number (if one is assigned in the text). For unpublished letters, cite the author, a descriptive label, and the date.

INTERVIEW

```
Atwood, Margaret.  Telephone interview.  4 Feb. 1984.
```

For personal interviews, cite the person interviewed, a descriptive label, and the date.

COMPUTER SOFTWARE

> SuperCalc. Computer software. Sorcim, 1981. CP/M-based
> microcomputer, disk.

To cite computer software, give the writer of the program (if known), the title (underlined), a descriptive label, the distributor, and the year of publication. Add any other important information, such as the computer on which the program can be used, number of kilobytes or units of memory, the operating system, and the form of the program (cartridge, cassette, or disk).

INFORMATION SERVICE

> Beam, Paul. COMIT English Module. ERIC ED 167 189.

To cite material from an information service, give the writer, the title, full details of original publication (if published previously), and the name of the service and identifying number within the service.

MAPS AND CHARTS

> The Caribbean & South America. Map. Falls Church,
> VA: AAA, 1982.

Begin the citation for a map or chart with the title. Name the type of visual (map or chart) between the title and the publication information.

RADIO AND TELEVISION PROGRAMS

> The Little Sister. Writ. and dir. Jan Egleson. With
> Tracy Pollan and John Savage. Prod. Rebecca Eaton.
> American Playhouse. PBS. WGBH, Boston. 7 April 1986.

To cite radio or television programs, include all information shown in the example: the title of the program (underlined); the network; the local station and its city; and the date of the broadcast. For a series also supply the title of the specific episode (in quotation marks) before the title of the program and the title of the series (neither underlined nor in quotation marks).

RECORDINGS

```
Handel, George Frederick.  Water Music.  Cond. Pierre Boulez.

    Hague Philharmonic Orch.  Nonesuch, H-71127, n.d.

Turner, Tina.  "Show Some Respect."  Private Dancer.

    Capitol, ST-12330, 1983.
```

Begin the citation of a recording with either the composer, conductor, or performer, depending on whom or what you are emphasizing in your paper. Then give the information shown in the examples.

FILMS

```
Erendira.  Writ. Gabriel Garcia Marquez.  Dir. Ruy Guerra.

    With Irene Pappas.  Miramax, 1984.
```

To cite a film, include the title (underlined), the director, the distributor, and the year of issue. Add any other pertinent information about the writer or actors after the title. Begin the citation with the title or the director, the writer, or the performer, depending on what or whom you are emphasizing in your paper.

LIVE PERFORMANCE

```
The Real Thing.  By Tom Stoppard.  Dir. Mike Nichols.  With

    Jeremy Irons and Glenn Close.  Plymouth Theatre, New

    York.  3 June 1984.
```

To cite a performance (stage play, concert, ballet, or opera) include the title; pertinent information about the playwright, conductor, performers; the theater, city, and the date of the performance. Begin with the title or a particular individual (for example, writer, conductor, or director) depending on the emphasis in your paper.

WORKS OF ART

```
Cassatt, Mary.  La Toilette.  Art Institute of Chicago,

    Chicago.
```

To cite a work of art (painting or sculpture), give the artist's name (last name first), the title (usually underlined), and the institution housing the work (for example, a museum, private collection) and its city.

■|| 32h
Draft a thesis statement

A **thesis statement** in a research paper is like the thesis statement in any essay: it tells the central theme. (Thesis statements are discussed thoroughly in 2e.) Any paper must fulfill the promise of its thesis statement. Because readers expect unified material, the theme of the thesis must serve as a connecting thread throughout a paper.

The research process and the writing process are interwoven throughout a research-paper project, as explained in 32a. Drafting a thesis statement for a research paper is the beginning of the transition between the research process and the writing process. Some researchers draft a **preliminary thesis statement** before or during their research process. They know that they will revise the thesis somewhat after their research, but they use the preliminary version as a useful focus while they search for sources. Other researchers draft a thesis statement after the research process.

No matter at what point you draft your thesis statement, expect to write many alternatives. Your goal is to draft the thesis carefully so that it delivers the message you intend. In writing any **revised thesis statement,** take charge of your material. Reread your research log. Reread your notes. Look for categories of information. Rearrange your note cards into logical groupings. Begin to impose a structure on your material. (For an example, see how Amy Brown accomplished these processes in Chapter 33.)

In addition to presenting the central theme of a paper, a thesis statement reflects a writing purpose—*to inform* or *to persuade* (see 32b). Also, a thesis statement implies the amount of expertise in the subject expected from an audience. For example, when writing for people who likely have little background about your topic, your thesis cannot be too technical.

To check your thesis statement, go back to the research question that guided your research process. Your thesis statement should be one answer to the question. Here are examples of subjects narrowed to topics, then focused into research questions, and then cast as thesis statements. The thesis statements are written on the assumption of a nonspecialist audience.

SUBJECT	Rain forests
TOPIC	The importance of rain forests
RESEARCH QUESTION	What is the importance of rain forests?

THESIS STATEMENT (informative)	Rain forests provide the human race with many resources.
THESIS STATEMENT (persuasive)	Rain forests must be preserved because they offer the human race many irreplaceable resources.
SUBJECT	Nonverbal communication
TOPIC	Personal space
RESEARCH QUESTION	How do standards for personal space differ among cultures?
THESIS STATEMENT (informative)	Everyone has expectations concerning the use of personal space, but accepted distances for that space are determined by each person's culture.
THESIS STATEMENT (persuasive)	To prevent intercultural misunderstandings, people must be aware of cultural differences in standards for personal space.

As you draft a thesis statement, remember that one of your major responsibilities in a research paper is to support the thesis. Be sure that the material gathered during the research process offers effective support. If it does not, revise your thesis or conduct further research, or both. Never stray from the unifying effect of your thesis. Do not move too far afield from the material in your notes.

▦‖ 32i
Know how to outline your paper.

Outlining is explained in detail in Chapter 2; you might want to review that material. To organize your evidence, you can make an **informal outline.** Look over your note cards and group them into piles of related information. You likely started this process in preparation for writing your thesis statement. If the content of one note relates to more than one category, make a new card that contains the material so that each topic's pile of cards will be complete.

Make a list of the categories of information represented by the piles. Then look over the list to see if material needs to be regrouped. During this process, you might find that you lack sufficient material for some categories. If so, go back to your sources or research new sources to fill in what you need. Once you feel comfortable with your list, look within each pile for subcategories of information. Group the subcategories. Then list them and regroup as needed.

Your instructor may ask you to submit a **formal outline** with your research paper. Writing a formal outline before drafting helps some people plan. Writing a formal outline after drafting helps some people check a paper's organization. Do the main ideas clearly relate to each other? Do the subordinate ideas offer support clearly connected to their main ideas?

A formal outline is headed with the title of the paper and followed by the paper's thesis statement. It can be a **topic outline,** a format that requires words or phrases for each item. It can be a **sentence outline,** a format that requires full sentences for each item. It cannot be a mixture of the two types. See Chapter 33 for a sentence outline of Amy Brown's research paper on personal space. A sentence outline has the advantage of having complete thoughts in its items. A reader can tell not only what topics are covered but also what is said about those topics.

A formal outline uses rankings for levels of information. It goes into detail according to the material it covers. If you outline only main and subordinate ideas, your outline has entries for Roman numeral and capital letters. If you go into more detail, your outline includes lower-case letters. Always follow one important principle: subdivide information only when you have at least two entries to make. In a formal outline, you cannot have an *A* without a *B,* a *1* without a *2,* and so on.

I. Main idea
   A. Subordinate idea
   B. Subordinate idea
      1. Example of subordinate idea
      2. Example of subordinate idea
         a. Supporting detail
         b. Supporting detail
II. Main Idea

■‖ 32j

Draft and revise your paper.

Drafting and revising a research paper have much in common with the processes for writing any type of paper. (See Chapters 2 and 3.) But more is demanded. You must demonstrate that you have followed the research steps in this chapter. You must demonstrate an understanding of the information you have located. You must organize for effective presentation. You must integrate sources into your writing without plagiarizing, by properly using the techniques of paraphrase, summary, and quotation described in Chapter 31. And you must use parenthetical references (32k) to document your sources. These special demands take extra time for drafting, thinking, redrafting, and rethinking.

Expect to write a number of drafts of your paper. Successive drafts help you to gain authority over the information you learn from your research. The **first draft** is your initial attempt to structure your notes into a unified whole. It is also a chance to discover new insights and fresh connections. Only the act of writing makes such discovery possible. A first draft is a rough draft. It is a prelude to later work at revising and polishing. Here are some alternative ways to write the first draft of a research paper.

1. Some researchers work with their notes in front of them. They use the organized piles made for drafting a thesis statement (32h) and for outlining (32i). They spread out each pile and work according to the categories of information that have emerged from their material. They proceed from one pile to the next. They expect this process to take time, but they are assured of a first draft that includes much of the results of their research.

2. Some researchers gather all their information and then set it aside to write a **partial first draft,** a quickly written first pass at getting the material under control. Writing this way helps researchers get a broad view of the material. The second step is to go back and write a **complete first draft** with research notes at hand. They go over their partial draft slowly to correct information, add material left out, and—most important—insert parenthetical references (32k).

3. Some researchers write their first draft quickly to get words down on paper when they feel "stuck" about what to say next. When they have a clear idea of how to proceed, they slow down and use their notes.

Your **second and subsequent drafts** are the results of reading your first draft critically and revising it. If at all possible, get some distance from your material by taking a break of a few days (or few hours, if you are pressed for time). Then, reread your first draft and get a fresh look at it. Think how it can be improved. You also might ask friends or classmates to read it and react.

Some researchers photocopy their first drafts and cut up the paper to move paragraphs and sentences around. If the researchers like a new order that suggests itself, they tape the paper together in its new form.

Here are some questions to guide your reading and revising of each draft. If any answer is "no," you need to rework your material.

Are you fulfilling the promise of the thesis statement?

Do the ideas follow from one another?

Do you stay on the topic?

Are important questions answered?

Do you avoid bogging down the paper with irrelevent or insignificant information?

Do you avoid leaving gaps in information?

Have you integrated source material without plagiarizing?

Have you used paraphrases, summaries, and quotations well?

Do not try to talk yourself out of uneasy feelings. Pay attention to those instincts and work on refining your drafts. Good writing is rewriting.

The **final draft** shows that you have revised well. It shows also that you have edited and proofread for correct grammar, spelling, and punctuation. No amount of careful research and good writing can make up for a sloppy manuscript. Strive to make the paper easy to read. If any page is messy with corrections, retype it. If your instructor accepts handwritten papers, use ruled white paper that has *not* been torn out of a spiral notebook. (If at all possible, however, type your work because it will present itself better.) Use black or blue ink and write very legibly.

For an example of the writing process in action for research writing, and for a sample research paper, see Chapter 33.

■‖ 32k
Know how to use parenthetical references in MLA style.

As you draft and revise your research paper, be sure to use parenthetical references. The purpose of parenthetical references is to lead your readers to the sources you have used. In the past, you may have used footnotes or endnotes to document your paraphrases, summaries, and quotations of sources. In the MLA style mentioned throughout this chapter, brief **parenthetical references** within the text of papers replace footnotes or endnotes. (A note system of documentation is explained in 34b-4.)

32k

1
Understand the MLA system of parenthetical references.

In the MLA system of parenthetical references, you may still use footnotes or endnotes for certain explanatory purposes, as discussed on page 585. In general, this MLA system of parenthetical references and the Works Cited list (described in 32g-2) are simpler and more efficient for both writers and readers.

Parenthetical references within a paper have three functions:

1. They signal places in your paper where you have paraphrased, summarized, or quoted ideas or words from another source.
2. They say exactly where that material is located in the source.
3. They often give information enabling a reader to find the source in the Works Cited (32g-2) list.

When you quote fewer than four handwritten or typewritten lines, you integrate the quoted material into your own sentence or paragraph.

SHORT QUOTATIONS

> Political economists have identified two main categories
> of corporate women: "Those who have corporate positions in
> major industrial enterprises and those who own their own
> business" (Berch 151).

> Because Berch recognizes that housework has traditionally
> been defined by many people as "just puttering around the
> house" (92), she provides detailed tables to demonstrate
> the time required to keep a household running efficiently.

In the first example, the author's name and the page number are cited in parentheses after the quotation marks but before the period. The author's name, which is usually what a reader needs to find in an entry in the Works Cited list, is provided in the parenthetical reference because it is not mentioned anywhere else in the sentence. No punctuation separates the author's name from the page number.

In the second example, only the page number is given as a parenthetical reference because the author's name is mentioned in the sentence. The page number is placed at the end of the quoted words but before the comma. Placing the page reference immediately after the quotation signals that the rest of the sentence does not paraphrase or summarize Berch; it is the paper-writer's own words.

When you quote more than four hand-written or typewritten lines, you set the quoted material off from your own writing by indenting it ten spaces from the left margin and double-spacing it. You do not put quotation marks around a long, indented quotation.

LONG QUOTATION

Bettina Berch suggests self-employment to be one of the most promising developments for women:

> Self-employed women are engaged in businesses, from the mundane to the spectacular. There are the free-lance inventors and writers as well as the more straightforward businesses, ranging from banks to record companies. Of course, not all of these businesses are all-female, but they do offer a growing number of women the satisfaction of trying out their ideas, without unnecessary interference. While self-employment is difficult financially, it may provide women with some needed autonomy in the future. (205)

This example shows how to document a quotation that is set off from the rest of the text. The reference is in parentheses at the end of the quotation and *after* the final period. Again, because the author's name is mentioned in the sentence that introduces the quotation, it is not given in the parenthetical reference. Only the page number is supplied in parentheses.

The quotations above all come from one book. The entry for this book in the Works Cited (32g-2) list looks like this:

Works Cited

Berch, Bettina. The Endless Day: The Political Economy of Women and Work. New York: Harcourt, 1982.

Make parenthetical references brief and accurate. When you are deciding what information to include in a reference, you need to consider what information about the source already appears in the sentence or the immediate context. Sometimes you may mention an author and refer to the entire work being cited in the sentence. Then *no* parenthetical reference is necessary.

> Bettina Berch's careful research, which she presents in
> every chapter of <u>The Endless Day</u>, makes a significant
> contribution to our understanding of women's work.

Most references are not as straightforward as these examples, however. Some sources name multiple authors or corporate authors or even no author. Some sources have several volumes or are reprinted from another source. Always consider such factors so that you can identify sources and the uses you make of them briefly and accurately. To avoid lengthy parenthetical references, get in the habit of putting into your sentence or the immediate context enough information about a source so that readers can locate it in the Works Cited list.

The following cases discuss format and methods for handling long citations within a paper. All the works mentioned in these examples are shown as Works Cited entries in 32g-2.

Works by more than one author

Suppose you have used a source written by more than one author, such as one book by Lisa Leghorn and Katherine Parker. You have the option of providing the names in the parenthetical reference—(Leghorn and Parker 115)—or providing the names in the sentence itself, followed by just the page number in parentheses. If a book is by two or three authors, you must give all the names. If a book is by more than three authors, such as Mark Moore, et al., you can use the author's last name plus *et al.* either in the parenthetical reference—(Moore, et al. 275)—or in the sentence. *Et al.* means "and others." Notice that there is never a period after *et* (because it is the complete Latin word for *and*); however, there is always a period after *al.* (because it is an abbreviation of the Latin word *alii,* meaning "others").

An author with two or more works

Suppose you have used several works by Desmond Morris in your paper. To refer to one of those works, supply the author's last name, an abbreviated title of the work, and the relevant page numbers—(Morris, <u>Manwatching</u> 95). Notice that a comma separates the author and underlined title, but no punctuation separates the title and page number. To shorten the parenthetical reference, use the author's name and the title of the work in your sentence and give only the page number in parentheses.

Two or more authors with the same last name

Suppose your list of works cited contains sources by Edith Johnson and Samuel Johnson. To cite either source, you must supply the author's first and last names—(Edith Johnson 278–81). Notice that no comma separates the author from the page numbers. To shorten the parenthetical reference, you can include the author's complete name in the sentence itself and give only the relevant page numbers in parentheses—(278–81).

Corporate authors

Suppose you are referring to a source by the Boston Women's Health Collective. The author's name is the name of the corporation. A parenthetical reference might use the corporate author's name and relevant page number—(Boston Women's Health Collective 11). Whenever possible, however, follow the MLA's recommendation to incorporate long names in your sentence to avoid a long parenthetical reference. The parentheses will contain only the relevant page number—(11).

Works cited by title

Suppose you have used a source with anonymous authors, such as The Chicago Manual of Style. Substitute the title or abbreviated title for the author's name in the parenthetical reference—(Chicago 305)—or in the text itself. Notice that the title is underlined. If you use a shortened version of the title, be sure it starts with the word by which the source is alphabetized in the Works Cited list.

Multivolume works

Suppose you have used both volumes of a work by John Herman Randall, Jr. To cite a reference from one volume, indicate the volume number as well as the page number in the parenthetical reference—(Randall 1:64). Notice that a colon and a space separate the volume number and the page number. If the entry in the Works Cited list refers only to one volume of a multivolume work, give only the page number, not volume number too, in the parenthetical citation—(Byron 130). If you include the author's name in your sentence, supply only the page number—(130)—or the volume and page number in the parenthetical reference—(1:64).

Literary works

Suppose you are referring to an edition of a classic novel, play, or poem. Because there are usually multiple editions of such classic literary works, the MLA recommends that you give more information than a page reference. (Readers might be using other editions.) For prose works, in addition to a page number to your edition, give additional information about parts, sections, or chapters—(3; pt. 1, ch. 1). Notice that a semicolon separates the page number from other information. Use standard abbreviations, such a *pt.* (part); *sec.* (section); and *ch.* (chapter). For classic verse, plays, and poems, the MLA recommends that you omit page references altogether and cite divisions (canto, book, part, act, or scene and line), using periods to separate the various numbers:

Il. 9.19 [book 9, line 19 of Homer's *Iliad*]

King Lear 4.1.5–6 [act 4, scene 1, lines 5–6 of Shakespeare's *King Lear*]

Never use the lower-case letter *l* to abbreviate *lines* in reference to poetic works, since these abbreviations may be confused with the numeral "one" (1). As in the reference to *King Lear,* the MLA recommends the use of arabic rather than roman numerals; however, some instructors still prefer roman numerals for citing acts and scenes—King Lear IV.i.

References to more than one source

Suppose more than one source has contributed to an idea or opinion in your paper. To acknowledge multiple sources, put all necessary information for each source in the parenthetical reference, and separate the sources with a semicolon—(Morris, Intimate 193; Mead 33). Because multiple references tend to interrupt the flow of your prose, the MLA recommends that you put them in footnotes or endnotes.

Article in a book

Suppose you quote an article that appears in a book. Cite the name of the author of the article, not the editor of the book. If you were quoting from Ernesto Galarza's "The Roots of Migration," which appears in a book edited by Luis Valdez and Stan Steiner, you would use the following citation form: (Galarza 127).

An indirect source

Suppose you are quoting an author who has been quoted by another author. Indicate both names: (Cather qtd. in Mc-

584

Clave). This form tells the reader that you are quoting the words of Willa Cather, that you found them in McClave's work, and that the Works Cited entry is in McClave's name.

2
Understand how to use notes with the MLA system of parenthetical references.

In MLA's system of parenthetical references, footnotes or endnotes serve two specific purposes. You can use them for commentary that does not fit into your paper but is still worth relating.

TEXT OF PAPER

> Eudora Welty's literary biography, <u>One Writer's</u>
> <u>Beginnings</u>, shows us how both the inner world of self
> and the outer world of family and place form a writer's
> imagination.[1]

ENDNOTE WITH COMMENTARY

> [1] Welty, who values her privacy, has resisted
> investigation of her life. However, at the age of 74,
> she chose to present her own autobiographical
> reflections in a series of lectures at Harvard University.

You can also put into notes extensive lists of bibliographic information supporting points you make in a paper. Otherwise, such information interrupts the flow of your paper.

TEXT OF PAPER

> Barbara Randolph believes that enthusiasm is contagious
> (65).[2]   Many psychologists have found that panic, fear,
> and rage spread more quickly in crowds than positive
> emotions do, however.

ENDNOTE WITH ADDITIONAL SOURCES

> [2] Others agree with Randolph. See Thurman 21, 84,
> 155; Kelley 421-25; and Brookes 65-76.

33
OBSERVING
A STUDENT
WRITING
RESEARCH

This chapter explains Amy Brown's processes of conducting research and writing a research paper based on her findings. This chapter also shows Brown's paper with annotations that draw your attention to its key elements. Here is the assignment Brown worked from.

Assignment for a research paper

This assignment for a research paper will involve you in two interrelated processes. One process calls for you to conduct research according to the procedures explained in Chapter 32 of the *Simon & Schuster Handbook for Writers*. In particular, you will (1) narrow the subject of the assignment to a suitable topic and research question; (2) determine your purpose and audience; (3) use a search strategy to yield information—mostly from sources in the library—that answers your research question; and (4) take notes so that you have a record of information and can avoid plagiarism.

The second process calls for you to write a paper based on your research findings. To do this, you have to integrate your researched information into your writing. Carefully consult Chapter 31 of the *Simon & Schuster Handbook for Writers,* which explains how to avoid plagiarism and how to use the techniques of paraphrase, summary, and quotation.

The general subject for this assignment is "communication." Your paper should be 1,800 to 2,000 words based on about twelve different sources. It is due in five weeks. Use MLA documentation style presented in the *Simon & Schuster Handbook for Writers,* sections 32g and 32k. Interim deadlines for parts of your work will be announced.

Brown made many decisions as she worked on this assignment. First, she set up a project schedule like the one in 32a. Next, she narrowed the subject of communication to a suitable topic. She decided to concentrate on nonverbal communication because she had heard the expression "body language," and the idea of unspoken messages among people interested her.

The memory of a personal experience helped Brown narrow the topic further. She remembered how she felt when a cousin had come for a weekend and stayed three weeks while looking for a new job. Brown's family lived in a small apartment. Brown liked her cousin and wanted to help, but she felt she had lost her "space." Brown remembered this reaction when she read Edward T. Hall's *The Hidden Dimension,* the book recommended by a professor when Brown was getting a broad overview of her subject. Hall talks about the concept of personal space. Personal space concerns the amount of physical distance people expect during social interaction. Hall discusses the fact that cultures differ in their standards for personal space. Although the topic of personal space was not directly related to the crowding Brown felt during her cousin's visit, the idea of space as a part of communication interested Brown. She therefore chose personal space as her topic. She decided that her research question would focus on intercultural differences: "How do standards for personal space differ among cultures?" (For a flow chart that shows Brown's narrowing process, see 32b.)

Next Brown thought about her purpose and audience. She chose a general audience (rather than a specialized one) because she assumed her readers would know little about the topic. Brown's choice of purpose was more complicated. She started with one and later switched. At first, she wanted to argue that people from different cultures can have trouble communicating unless they are aware of varying expectations concerning personal space. While conduct-

587

ing her research, however, Brown decided to change from persuasive writing to informative writing. She found that she could not explain basic concepts *and* argue a position within the assignment's length and time limits.

While narrowing her topic, Brown had already begun her search strategy. (For a discussion and flow chart of a search strategy, see 32e.) Brown had looked over two textbooks and had talked with a professor who recommended Hall's book. Reading Hall helped Brown narrow her topic and formulate her research question.

While knowing that Hall would be an important source in her paper, Brown started to search for additional sources. Hall called the study of personal space *proxemics*. Brown assumed it was a key word (for an explanation of key words, see 32d-3) and went to the library to look for books and articles. She drew several blanks. Nowhere could she find the term *proxemics*, not in the *Readers' Guide*, in any of the encyclopedias, or in any dictionary. Hall had evidently made up the term himself based on the word *proximity*. Finally, Brown had a breakthrough. The *Social Sciences Index* listed proxemics in a cross-reference: "See personal space." She did, and there were numerous articles exploring aspects of the topic.

The key words *personal space* produced an important title from the library's card catalog: Robert Sommer's *Personal Space: The Behavioral Basis of Design*. Brown also looked in the card catalog under the key words *body language* and found the book *Body Language* by Julius Fast. At the back of Fast's book she found a bibliography of key references. She was delighted to find Hall's book and Sommer's book listed. This helped her confirm that Hall and Sommer were authoritative and reliable sources. (For guidelines on evaluating sources, see 5c and 32d-2.)

To find more articles on personal space, Brown used the computerized databased system called DIALOG. She searched the *Psychological Abstract Index*—called PsycINFO in the DIALOG system. (For a description of this search and a sample from DIALOG, see 32e-8.) Two articles that Brown found became references in her paper.

Now Brown had a working bibliography. Using MLA documentation style, she had made bibliography cards on three key books, fifteen articles, and two textbooks. It was time to read closely and take notes. Brown carefully headed each index card with the author of the source. Making sure to avoid plagiarism, she paraphrased, summarized, and copied quotations according to the techniques described in Chapter 31 of this handbook. Whenever she used an author's exact words, Brown wrote oversized quotation marks so that she would be sure to see them when using her notes.

While taking notes, Brown realized that some of the articles she had found were not as useful as she had thought. Later as she was writing her paper she dropped a few more. She ended up with fourteen references.

In organizing her paper, Brown looked through her notes and saw that they fell into two piles: standards for personal space in North America and standards in other countries. She tried to outline the material, and quickly realized that she had to start with a definition of personal space. Going back through her cards, she created a third pile for definitions. Her thesis statement was next. Brown knew that her thesis statement would be the last sentence of her introductory paragraph. She drafted a number of versions to answer her research question, and revised the thesis further as she drafted her paper. Here is an early draft of Brown's introduction:

```
People know unconsciously how close is close when they

stand near other people during conversations. This relates

to the concept of personal space--the amount of physical

distance people expect during social interaction. Stand-

ards for personal space vary among cultures.
```

Brown knew that the paragraph was flawed. It lacked interest, the word "this" was a vague pronoun reference, and the thesis statement did not give a full picture of the paper. She showed her draft to three friends and asked them to react. One friend who was majoring in psychology had a newspaper clipping in his files that gave Brown the opening she needed. Then as Brown worked on drafts of her paper, she refined her thesis statement. For the result, see page 1 of Brown's paper.

In writing her paper. Brown composed three drafts. In addition to rewriting her opening paragraph, Brown made other improvements as she revised. Her first draft lacked clear signals to readers about the material's organization. In her second draft, Brown used topic sentences to start many of her paragraphs. Her first draft relied too much on quotation. In her second draft, Brown used paraphrase and summary—techniques explained in Chapter 31 of this handbook. She used quotations only when an author's language was particularly apt. In her third draft, Brown polished her word choice, corrected her grammar and spelling, and reworked her conclusion. Brown wanted the conclusion to be a "call to action," urging people to become sensitive to the concept of personal space and thereby avoid intercultural misunderstandings. In her first and second drafts, her concluding paragraph was quite long, so in her final draft she divided it into two and added a particularly relevant quotation.

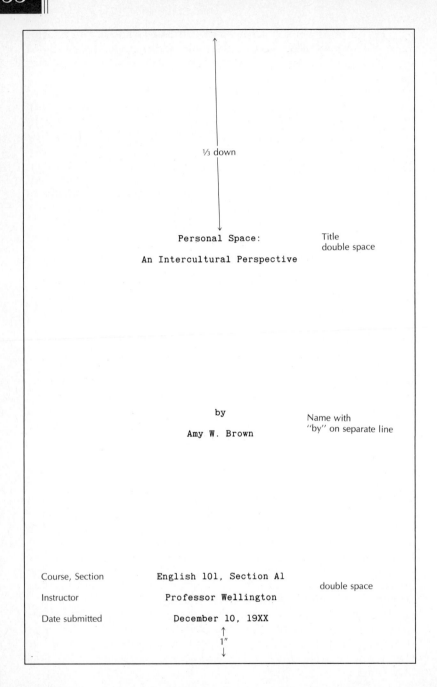

⅓ down

Personal Space:

An Intercultural Perspective

Title
double space

by

Amy W. Brown

Name with
"by" on separate line

Course, Section   English 101, Section A1

Instructor   Professor Wellington

Date submitted   December 10, 19XX

double space

1″

Cover page. If your instructor requires a cover page, use the format and types of information shown on the opposite page. Then on page 1 of your paper, repeat only the paper's title.

First page. If your instructor does not require a cover page, follow the Modern Language Association style shown below for heading your first page. If you use a cover page, omit this heading and put the title at the top of page 1. Always leave a quadruple space between the title and the first line of your paper.

HEADING FOR FIRST PAGE WITHOUT COVER PAGE   1

Amy W. Brown   Name

Professor Wellington   Instructor

English 101, Section A1   Course, Section

10 December 19XX   Date submitted

                                                double space

Personal Space:

An Intercultural Perspective

                                                quadruple
                                                space

     When she returned home after a year in South America,

Judith Martin, a North American writer, began to have a

problem. People kept interpreting her behavior as

flirtatious, but she was not flirting. Fairly soon she

Outline

Thesis statement: Everyone has expectations concerning the use of personal space, but accepted distances for that space are determined by each person's culture.

I. Observations about personal space began about twenty years ago.

    A. Most people are unaware that interpersonal distances exist.

    B. Personal space depends on invisible boundaries.

    C. Personal space moves with people as they interact.

    D. People do not like anyone to trespass on their personal space.

II. Research reveals North Americans' expectations for personal space.

    A. Hall identified four zones.

        1. "Intimate" is the smallest zone.

        2. "Personal" is next.

        3. "Social" is next.

        4. "Public" is the largest zone.

    B. Subcultures help determine expectations for personal space.

    C. Age affects how people use personal space.

    D. Gender influences people's use of personal space.

III. Research reveals standards for personal space in countries other than the United States.

    A. Conversational distances vary.

        1. Western Europeans use a fingertip-to-shoulder distance.

Brown ii

      2. Eastern Europeans use a wrist—to—shoulder

         distance.

      3. Mediterraneans use elbow—to—shoulder distances.

   B. Permitted amounts of touching vary.

   C. Arabs prefer close interpersonal distances.

   D. Japanese do not prefer close interpersonal

      distances.

Outline. Brown uses a formal outline. It is also a sentence outline, in that all items are complete sentences. (For information about outlining, see 32i.) Outline pages precede page 1 of the paper, so they are numbered in lower-case roman numerals; the student's last name is also given.

     Note that in Brown's paper, Section I corresponds to paragraphs 2 through 4; Section II corresponds to paragraphs 5 through 8; Section III corresponds to paragraphs 9 through 12. The conclusion consists of the last two paragraphs.

1

A

B

Personal Space:

An Intercultural Perspective

1

C

When she returned home after a year in South America, Judith Martin, a North American writer, began to have a problem. People kept interpreting her behavior as flirtatious, but she was not flirting. Fairly soon, she figured out what was happening. When most South Americans talk to each other face-to-face, they stand closer together than do North Americans. Martin had not readjusted to North American distances (9). She had forgotten about the phenomenon known as "personal space"— the amount of physical distance people expect during social interaction. Everyone has expectations concerning the use of personal space, but accepted distances for that space are determined by each person's culture.

D

2

Observations about personal space began about twenty years ago. Anthropologist Edward T. Hall was a pioneer in the field. He conducted research to find out precisely what distances were acceptable when people interacted. In his aptly titled book The Hidden Dimension, Hall coined the word "proxemics" to describe people's use of space as a means of communication (1). As Hall's book title indicates, most people are unaware that interpersonal distances exist and contribute to people's reactions to one another (109).

E

F

General Note: Amy Brown has followed the new MLA Style for format and documentation (see 32g and 32k).

A. **Page number.** In the upper righthand corner Brown typed the number 1; on continuation pages, the page number is preceded by her last name.

B. **Title.** Brown's title prepares readers for the paper in two important ways. It gives the paper's major term (personal space) and the focus of the paper's discussion (more than one culture). In an earlier draft, Brown's title was "Proxemics: An Intercultural Perspective on the Need for Space." She rejected it because "space" was too general and "proxemics" was too technical. She then tried "Being Close: An Intercultural Perspective." She liked the second half because it was an accurate description of her focus, but the first half had multiple meanings.

C. **Introductory device.** In her introductory paragraph, Brown uses an anecdote. (Introductory devices are discussed in 4e.) She felt the ancedote served four functions: to make the abstract concept of personal space concrete and familiar; to tie into the paper's title; to lead into the thesis statement; and to capture readers' interest.

D. **Thesis statement.** The last sentence of Brown's introductory paragraph is the paper's thesis statement. The thesis presents the central idea of the paper. Emerging from the paper's title and opening anecdote, the thesis prepares readers for what to expect—a discussion of expectations concerning personal space and how those expectations differ among cultures.

E. **Evaluation of source:** Brown establishes Hall as an expert by identifying him as an anthropologist and as a pioneer on the subject of personal space.

F. **Parenthetical reference to author and book named in the text.** Brown uses two sources by Edward T. Hall (see "Works Cited" on Brown's page 10). When referring to the two works, Brown has to be sure to keep them separate. In this paragraph, therefore, she mentions Hall's name and the title of the work she is referring to. Her two parenthetical references, therefore, include only the page numbers. They are inserted before the periods that end the sentences. Brown uses quotation marks to set off the coined word "proxemics," but she uses no other quotation marks because she has summarized the material. The other work by Hall is cited in paragraph 11.

Brown 2

3

Personal space depends on invisible boundaries. Those boundaries move with people as they interact. Personal space "moves with us, expanding and contracting according to the situation in which we find ourselves" (Fisher, Bell, and Baum 149). Robert Sommer, an environmental psychologist, uses literary and visual analogies to describe personal space:

G

H

> Like the porcupines in Schopenhauer's fable, people like to be close enough to obtain warmth and comradeship but far enough away to avoid pricking one another. Personal space . . . has been likened to a snail shell, a soap bubble, an aura, a "breathing room." (26)

I

4

People do not like anyone to trespass on their personal space. As Worchel and Cooper explain, invasions of personal space elicit negative reactions that range from mild discomfort to retaliation to walking out on the situation (539–40). The poet W. H. Auden threatened a uniquely negative reaction to intrusions in his space.

J

> Some thirty inches from my nose
> The frontier of my Person goes
> And all the untilled air between
> Is private pagus or demesne
> Stranger, unless with bedroom eyes
> I beckon you to fraternize
> Beware of rudely crossing it
> I have no gun but I can spit.
>
> (qtd. in Worchel and Cooper 539)

K

G. **Quotation within sentence.** Brown fits a quotation into her prose. She uses quotation marks to avoid plagiarism.

H. **Parenthetical reference to author not named in the text.** The source of the definition (author and page) is added in parentheses.

I. **A long quotation.** A quotation of more than four typewritten lines, is set off from the rest of the text. Brown introduces it with a colon because she has written a complete sentence (compare with paragraph 13). She indents the material 10 spaces and does not paragraph indent the first line. In the fourth line Brown uses a three-dot ellipsis to indicate the place where she omitted words (the full original source is shown on page 560). The page reference for the quotation is given in parentheses after the punctuation that ends the quotation. The words "breathing room" are in quotation marks because they appear this way in the original source.

J. **Use of an unexpected source.** Brown realizes that W. H. Auden is not a likely expert on personal space. She uses his poem nonetheless because (a) she discovered it reprinted in a discussion of personal space by social psychologists, so she decided its content had credibility for her paper, and (b) she decided that it would suit her audience well, given the paper was for her freshman English class.

K. **Parenthetical reference for an indirect source.** Brown did not find the poem in its original source. After she found it, she tried to locate the book in which the poem was first published, but her library did not have a copy. So she relied on the indirect source. In her parenthetical reference, she used *qtd. in,* the abbreviation for "quoted in."

Brown 3

5   Research provides information about the distances
that North Americans prefer when interacting. The
pioneering work was done by Hall. He observed the
behavior of a group of middle-class adults in business and
professions in the northeastern United States. He saw
four zones of personal space; they are summarized and
explained in Table 1.

Table 1   **L**

Hall's "Distance Zones"[a]

	Intimate	Personal	Social	Public
Close	0 to 6"	1½' to 2½'	4' to 7'	12' to 25'
Far	6" to 1½'	2½' to 4'	7' to 12'	25' +

Source: Discussion in Hall, Hidden 110–20; also Henley 32–   **M**
33; Fisher, Bell, and Baum 153.

[a]Selected illustrations of each zone are: Close
Intimate: lovers, children with parents; Far Intimate:
strangers in crowds; Close Personal: husband and wife
talking on the street; Far Personal: friends talking on
the street; Close Social: boss and subordinate at a
meeting; Far Social: receptionist and people in a large
waiting room; Close Public: teacher and students in a
classroom; Far Public: actors or public speakers with
audiences.

L. **Table.** A table is an excellent way to summarize complex information that involves numbers and/or repeated categories. A table should be placed as close as possible to the paragraph in which it is first mentioned. If a table cannot fit in the space remaining on the page, it can be placed on the following page after the end of the first paragraph on that page. Some instructors permit students to put tables on a separate page at the end of the paper, before "Notes," if any, or before "Works Cited." Brown uses the format described in the *MLA Handbook:* the table number and title at the left margin, a lettered—not numbered—footnote, and source information immediately below the data, before the footnote.

M. **Source identification.** Because Brown uses two works by Hall, she includes a shortened title *(Hidden)* so that readers will know which Hall work she is referring to. Semicolons are used to separate each item in a series of multiple references. The other Hall work is cited in paragraph 11.

Brown 4

6   Researchers working with Hall's data found that
accepted interpersonal distances in the United States also
depend on other factors. For example, subcultures help
determine expectations concerning personal space. Fisher,
Bell, and Baum report that groups of Hispanic—Americans
generally interact more closely within their subculture
than Anglo—Americans do within theirs. They further
explain that in general "subcultural groups tend to
interact at closer distances with members of their own
subculture than with nonmembers" (158).   **N**

7   Age also affects how people use personal space.
North American children seem unaware of boundaries for
personal space until the age of four or five, according to
Worchel and Cooper. As the children get older, however,
they become more aware of standards for personal space. By
the time they reach puberty, they have completely adapted
to their culture's standards for interpersonal distances
(535–37).   **N**

8   Gender also influences people's use of personal
space. For example, North American males' most negative   **O**
reaction is reserved for invasions of their personal space
that come directly in front of them. Females, on the
other hand, feel most negative about approaches from the
side (Worchel and Cooper 535). Also, females have smaller
interpersonal distances than do males, although same—sex
pairs communicate across larger spaces than do male—female

N. **Placement of parenthetical references.** Parenthetical references go immediately after a quotation or after the end of a set of information.

O. **Paraphrase of original source.** In paragraph 8, Brown paraphrases Worchel and Cooper, page 535. The original reads: "Males responded most negatively to frontal invasions of their space, whereas females reacted most negatively to invasions from the side." Brown uses her own words for almost all words except "males," "females," and "from the side."

Brown 5

pairs (Worchel and Cooper 535–537). The gender factor
shifts, however, in high density situations such as
crowded subways or elevators in the United States. As
Maines reports, when people have some choice about where
they stand or sit in crowded settings, they gravitate to
people of the same sex (100).

9   Expectations concerning personal space exist in all
cultures, but such expectations vary greatly from culture
to culture (Fast 29). Research reveals standards for
personal space in countries other than the United States.
For example, conversational distances vary between people   P
from different countries, according to Desmond Morris, a
British zoologist. He notes that when people from Western
Europe stand on the street and talk together, the space
between them is the distance it would take one person's
fingertip to reach the other's shoulder. People from
Eastern Europe converse at a wrist-to-shoulder distance.
People from the Mediterranean, however, prefer elbow-to-
shoulder distance (131).

10   Permitted amounts of touching also illustrate   Q
intercultural differences in standards for personal space.
Touching while conversing differs in Germany, Italy, and
the United States, reports Robert Shuter, a communications
specialist. His research shows that Germans and North
Americans behave alike in that males stand farther apart
and touch less when talking than do male-female pairs or

P. **Summary of original source.** In paragraph 9, Brown summarizes Desmond Morris, page 131. Here is the original, which uses British—not American English—conventions for quotation marks.

> Unfortunately, different countries have different ideas about exactly how close is close. It is easy enough to test your own 'space reaction': when you are talking to someone in the street or in any open space, reach out with your arm and see where the nearest point on his body comes. If you hail from western Europe, you will find that he is at roughly fingertip distance from you. In other words, as you reach out, your fingertips will just about make contact with his shoulder. If you come from eastern Europe you will find you are standing at 'wrist distance'. If you come from the Mediterranean region you will find that you are much closer to your companion, at little more than 'elbow distance'.

Q. **Transferring information from note to paper.** In paragraph 10, Brown uses the summary from her notes. Here is her note card:

> _Shuter_, p. 305
> <u>Intercultural differences</u>
> <u>Summary</u>:
> Germans and N. Americans behave alike in that males stand farther apart and touch less while talking than do male-female pairs. The opposite is true in Italy, where males interact more closely and touch more during conversations than do male-female pairs or female pairs. Thus, Italian males expect to use personal space as females do in Germany and the United States.

female pairs. The opposite is true in Italy, where males interact more closely and touch more during conversations than do male—female pairs or female pairs. Shuter concludes that Italian males expect to use personal space as females do in Germany and the United States (305). In another experiment, adults were asked to put dolls in position for what was called "comfortable interaction." People from Italy and Greece placed the dolls closer together than did people from Sweden, Scotland, or the United States (Worchel and Cooper 536). Also, in doctors' waiting rooms, Australians were less likely to start conversations with strangers than were Indonesians (Worchel and Cooper 536).

11   Arabs prefer close interpersonal distances. Polhemus explains that Arab students move close together more often, confront each other directly, and touch each other frequently when talking than do American students. (21). In an interview called "Learning the Arabs' Silent Language," Hall explains that Arabs know the practicality of close conversational distances: "If you are interested in something, your pupils dilate; if I say something you don't like, they tend to contract" (47).[1]   **R** Conversational distances of two feet—that preferred by many Arabs—permits people to see each other's pupils better than does the typical North American distance of five feet (48).

R. **Comment in an endnote.** Brown uses an endnote to comment on her information. She wants to make a related observation about the use of sunglasses. Because the point does not fit into her paragraph, she uses an endnote. The number for the endnote is raised slightly above the line after the period ending the sentence. The endnote is on Brown's page 9.

Brown 7

12   Japanese do not prefer close interpersonal distances. Because the island of Japan is quite small for its population of about 120 million, public places are often very crowded. To cope, the people remain formal and aloof even when in very close proximity to one another (Fast 38).

13   People can easily be misunderstood if they are insensitive to how people from another culture use personal space. Clearly, what is considered obnoxious in one culture might be considered polite in another (Fisher, Bell, and Baum 167). As Hall explains, virtually everything people are and do

S

> is associated with the experience of space. . . . Therefore, people from different cultures, when interpreting each other's behavior, often misinterpret the relationship, the activity, or the emotions. This leads to alienation in encounters or distorted communications. (<u>Hidden</u> 171)

T

In the next few years, more studies will be undertaken to uncover information about cultural differences in matters such as personal space (Davis and Skupien, xix). The information will be important. International understanding cannot thrive unless people recognize and accept such disparities, according to Charles G. Morris, a professor of psychology:

S. **Concluding device.** In paragraphs 13 and 14, Brown concludes her paper with a "call for action" (concluding devices are discussed in 4e).

T. **Combined quotation from two paragraphs in original source.** Brown combines into one quotation material from two paragraphs in Hall. She uses no punctuation to lead into the quotation (compare to colon used before next quotation). She does this because her lead-in is an incomplete sentence that is completed by the quotation. Brown uses a four-dot ellipsis to show that the quotation is taken from two paragraphs. Here is the original source (Hall, *Hidden* 171):

> This book emphasizes that virtually everything that man is and does is associated with the experience of space. Man's sense of space is a synthesis of many sensory inputs: visual, auditory, kinesthetic, olfactory, and thermal. Not only does each of these constitute a complex system—as, for example, the dozen different ways of experiencing depth visually—but each is molded and patterned by culture. Hence, there is no alternative to accepting the fact that people reared in different cultures live in different sensory worlds.
>
> We learn from the study of culture that the patterning of perceptual worlds is a function not only of culture but of *relationship, activity,* and *emotion.* Therefore, people from different cultures, when interpreting each other's behavior, often misinterpret the relationship, the activity, or the emotions. This leads to alienation in encounters or distorted communications.

Brown 8

This sort of information seems trivial, but it does affect international understanding. Imagine, for example, a business conference between a [North] American and an Arab. The American prefers to have about three or four feet between them, while the Arab is inclined to stand closer.[2] If the American moves away, the Arab feels that the American is being cold and hostile, while the American finds that the Arab, who keeps moving closer, is being pushy and aggressive. (516)

U

14

As international travel and commerce increase, intercultural contact is becoming commonplace. Soon, perhaps, cultural variations in expectations for personal space will be as familiar to everyone as are cultural variations in food and dress. Until then, people need to make a special effort to learn one another's expectations concerning personal space. Once people are sensitive to such matters, they can stop themselves from taking the wrong step—either away from or toward a person from another culture.

U. **Words inserted in a quotation.** Brackets are used to show words that do not appear in the original quotation. Brown inserts the word "North" to clarify that Morris is talking about North Americans, not South Americans. She inserts it the first time only, assuming that each subsequent use of "American" will be read as "North American."

½"

Brown 9   V

1"

Notes

¹ This explains why some Arab leaders wear sunglasses
indoors.

² Both Morris and Hall agree that North Americans
prefer larger conversational distances than do Arabs.
They do not, however, seem to agree on the precise distances. Morris says the distance is three to four feet.
Hall says five feet. These differences do not detract,
however, from the central point concerning the contrasts
in cultural preferences.

Brown 10

Works Cited

Davis, Martha, and Janet Skupien, eds. Body Movement and   A
    Nonverbal Communication: An Annotated Bibliography
    1971–1981. Bloomington, IN: Indiana UP, 1982.

Fast, Julius. Body Language. New York: Evans, 1970.   B

Fisher, Jeffrey D., Paul A. Bell, and Andrew Baum. Envi-   C
    ronmental Psychology. 2nd ed. New York: Holt, 1984.

V. **Comment notes.** On a separate numbered page headed "Notes," Brown provides commentary that does not fit into the text of her paper. Contents notes in MLA style can comment upon, explain, or clarify material written in the text. Each note starts with a number raised a half line and indented five spaces, paragraph style. Double spacing is used within and between all comment notes.

General Format. A bibliography, called "Works Cited," is used in MLA documentation style (see 32g). Entries are in alphabetical order by author's last name, with a 5-space indention after the first line of each entry. Punctuation and spacing between words and lines are as shown. Double spacing is used within and between entries. Two spaces occur after each period in an entry.

A. **Entry for edited book.** Inverted order for name of first editor (last name, first name), but regular order for second name. *University Press* abbreviated *UP*.

B. **Entry for book by a single author.**

C. **Entry for book by three authors.** Inverted order (last name, first name) for name of first author, but regular order for others. [*Note:* In a work with three or fewer authors, all names are listed; in a work by four authors or more, the first author is followed by *et al.*] *Second edition* abbreviated to *2nd ed.* Publisher abbreviated from *Holt, Rinehart and Winston* to *Holt*.

611

Hall, Edward T. The Hidden Dimension. New York: Doubleday, 1966.

---. Interview. "Learning the Arabs' Silent Language." With Kenneth Friedman. Psychology Today Aug. 1979: 44–54.

Henley, Nancy M. Body Politics: Power, Sex, and Nonverbal Communication. Englewood Cliffs: Prentice, 1977.

Maines, David R. "Tactile Relationship in the Subway as Affected by Racial, Sexual, and Crowded Seating Situations." Environmental Psychology and Nonverbal Behavior 2 (1977): 100–108.

Martin, Judith. "Here's Looking at You." Newsday 27 Jan. 1981, sec. 2: 9+.

Morris, Charles G. Psychology: An Introduction. 4th ed. Englewood Cliffs: Prentice, 1982.

Morris, Desmond. Manwatching: A Field Guide to Human Behavior. New York: Abrams, 1977.

Polhemus, Ted. "Social Bodies." The Body as a Medium of Expression. Ed. Jonathan Benthall and Ted Polhemus. New York: Dutton, 1975. 13–35.

Shuter, Robert. "A Field Study of Nonverbal Communication in Germany, Italy, and the United States." Communication Monographs 44 (1977): 298–305.

Sommer, Robert. Personal Space: The Behavioral Bases of Design. Englewood Cliffs: Prentice, 1969.

Worchel, Stephen, and Joel Cooper. Understanding Social Psychology. 3rd ed. Homewood, IL: Dorsey, 1983.

D
E
F
G
H
I
J

D. **Second work by same author.** Three hyphens and a period stand for the repetition of the preceding author's name. [*Note:* In such instances, works by the same author are listed alphabetically by title, not chronologically according to date of publication.]

E. **Entry for an interview published in a magazine.** Entry listed by person interviewed, not by the person doing the interviewing. The page numbers are not preceded by *pp.*

F. **Entry for an article in a journal with continuous pagination.** Article title in quotation marks. Journal title underlined. Then volume number, year (in parentheses), and page numbers without *pp.*

G. **Entry for article in a daily newspaper.** Title of article in quotation marks. Name of newspaper underlined. Date of newspaper in this order: day, month (abbreviation permitted), year. Then newspaper section, columns, and page numbers without *pp.*

H. Publisher abbreviated from *Prentice-Hall* to *Prentice.*

I. **Entry for article in a book.** Author of article heads the entry. Editors of book, with names in regular order, follow book title. Title of article in quotation marks. Title of book underlined. Page numbers—without *pp.*—after city of publication and publisher.

J. **Entry for book by two authors.** Inverted order (last name, first name) for name of first author, but regular order for second name. Place of publication includes city *and* two-letter postal abbreviation for state because many readers might not know that Homewood is in Illinois.

34
WRITING
IN
OTHER
DISCIPLINES

Writing assignments are given in most college courses. A literature instructor may require you to write an analysis of a poem or a research paper on literary critics' reactions to Ernest Hemingway's *The Sun Also Rises;* a psychology instructor may require you to write a case study based on your observations of a person or write a research report that synthesizes various experts' observations about the causes of divorce or the problems of the homeless; a biology instructor may require you to write a laboratory report or a formal scientific paper.

When college instructors give writing assignments, they assume that you have the requisite reading and writing skills to complete college-level assignments. Instructors also expect your writing to conform to the standards for content, style, and format common to each separate discipline. This chapter discusses standards for writing—especially research writing—in academic disciplines other than English composition.

34a
Recognize similarities and differences among the disciplines.

Each field of study—the humanities, social sciences, and natural and technological sciences—has its own perspectives on the world and its own philosophies about academic thought and research. To understand some of the differences among the disciplines, consider these three quite different paragraphs about a mountain.

HUMANITIES

The mountain stands above all that surrounds it. Giant timbers—part of a collage of evergreen and deciduous trees—conceal the expansive mountain's slope, where cattle once grazed. At the base of the mountain, a cool stream flows over rocks of all sizes, colors, and shapes. Next to the outer bank of the stream stands a shingled farmhouse, desolate, yet suggesting its active past. Unfortunately, the peaceful scene is interrupted by billboards and chairlifts, landmarks of a modern, fast-paced life.

SOCIAL SCIENCES

Among the favorite pastimes of American city dwellers is the "return to nature." Many outdoor enthusiasts hope to enjoy a scenic trip to the mountains, only to be disappointed. They know they have arrived at the mountain that they have traveled hundreds of miles to see because huge billboards are directing them to its base. As they look up the mountain, dozens of people are riding over the treetops in a chairlift, littering the slope with paper cups and food wrappers. At the base of the mountain stands the inevitable refreshment stand, found at virtually all American tourist attractions. Land developers consider such commercialization a way to preserve and utilize natural resources, but environmentalists are appalled.

SCIENCES

The mountain is approximately 5,600 feet in height. The underlying rock is igneous, of volcanic origin, composed primarily of granites and feldspars. Three distinct biological communities are present on the mountain. The community at the top of the mountain is alpine in nature, dominated by very short grasses and forbs. At middle altitudes, a typical northern boreal coniferous forest community is present, and at the base and lower altitudes, deciduous forest is the dominant community. This community has, however, been highly affected by agricultural development along the river at its base and, more recently, by recreational development.

Though such examples cannot demonstrate all differences among the disciplines, they do show clearly that each discipline has its writing traditions and preferences. The paragraph written for the humanities describes the mountain from the individual perspective of the writer—a perspective both personal and yet representative of a general human response. The paragraph written for the social sciences focuses on the behavior of people as a group. The paragraph written for the sciences reports observations of natural phenomena.

SIMILARITIES AND DIFFERENCES IN WRITING FOR VARIOUS DISCIPLINES

SIMILARITIES

1.	Consider your purpose and audience.	Chapters 1–2
2.	Use the writing process to plan, shape, draft, revise, edit, and proofread.	Chapters 2–3
3.	Develop a thesis.	Chapters 2–3
4.	Arrange and organize your ideas.	Chapter 2
5.	Use supporting evidence.	Chapters 2–4
6.	Develop paragraphs thoroughly.	Chapter 4
7.	Think critically, and use correct reasoning and logic.	Chapter 5
8.	Write effective sentences.	Chapters 16–19
9.	Choose words well.	Chapters 20–21
10.	Use correct grammar.	Chapters 6–15
11.	Spell correctly.	Chapter 22
12.	Use correct punctuation and mechanics.	Chapters 23–30

DIFFERENCES

1. Conduct research and select sources according to the discipline.
2. Select a style of documentation appropriate to the discipline.
3. Follow special format requirements, if any, in each discipline.
4. Use specialized language, when it is needed, in each discipline.

No matter what differences exist among the disciplines, all subject areas interconnect and overlap. When you study biology in your biology class, literature in your literature class, and psychology in your psychology class, you will likely notice that distinctions among fields of study are not absolutely rigid. For example, in a humanities class you might read *Lives of a Cell,* a collection of essays about science and nature, by Lewis Thomas, both a noted physician and prize-winning author, but you will also be thinking deeply about biology and other sciences. Similarly, if you write a research paper on senility for your psychology class, you might refer to medical texts and scientific journals for some information.

Writing is the one activity that unites all the disciplines. You will have to write often for most of your college courses. Writing is the principal means of communication between you and your instructor, and writing is a way for you to learn material and gain authority over knowledge.

The chart on the opposite page summarizes similarities and differences in writing for different disciplines.

1
Conduct research and select sources according to the discipline.

Research methods differ among the disciplines when **primary sources** are used. Primary sources offer you first-hand exposure to information. No one comes between you and the exciting experience of discovering and confronting material on your own. No one else's interpretation or description can color your reactions when you confront primary sources "raw." In the humanities, existing documents are primary sources; the task of the researcher is to analyze and interpret these primary sources. Typical primary-source material for research could be a poem by Dylan Thomas, the floor plans of Egyptian pyramids, or early drafts of music manuscripts. In the social and natural sciences, primary research involves the design and undertaking of experiments involving direct observation. The task of the researcher in the social and natural sciences is to conduct the experiments or to read the first-hand reports of experiments and studies written by people who conducted them.

Secondary sources—articles and books about a primary source—are also important in all disciplines. In the humanities, you can learn much from the examples of others who have analyzed and interpreted primary sources. In the social sciences, secondary sources can usefully synthesize findings in many areas and draw parallels that offer new insights. In the natural sciences, if some primary sources are outdated by the time they are published, review articles and monographs can be useful for making connections among studies and bringing major questions into focus.

Because a secondary source puts one step or more between you and the primary source, many instructors prefer that whenever possible you work with primary sources for certain assignments. At other times, instructors assign secondary sources so that you can get a more comprehensive perspective. Secondary sources can even be worth investigating or analyzing in their own right. For example, reading nineteenth-century reviews for the reactions of his contemporaries to Edgar Allen Poe's early writing might lead you to try to determine whether this criticism influenced Poe's later works. Similarly, a fifty-year-old anthropological study can highlight changes in a group you are studying today.

2
Select a style of documentation appropriate to the discipline.

Writers use **documentation** to give credit to the sources they have used. A writer who does not credit a source is guilty of **plagiarizing**—a serious academic offense discussed at length in Chapter 31. Styles of documentation differ among the disciplines. The major styles are presented in this handbook, as indicated in the chart on the opposite page.

3
Follow special format requirements, if any, in each discipline.

Because of the differences among disciplines, different formats are expected in each for presentation of material. These special formats have evolved to communicate a writer's purpose, to emphasize content by eliminating distracting variations in format, and to make the reader's work easier. Writing in the humanities (34b) is less often subject to set formats, although your writing is expected to be well organized and accepted documentation formats are expected. Writing in the social sciences (34c) and natural sciences (34d) often calls for using fixed special formats for specific types of writing. For example, if you are writing a case study (for a sample, see pages 644–45) or a laboratory report (for a sample, see pages

DOCUMENTATION STYLES DISCUSSED IN THIS HANDBOOK

FOR ENGLISH AND OTHER SUBJECTS IN THE HUMANITIES

Parenthetical system (MLA)	pages 562–74; 579–85
Endnote or footnote system	pages 631–40

FOR THE SOCIAL SCIENCES

Parenthetical system (APA)	pages 647–50

FOR NATURAL SCIENCES AND TECHNOLOGIES

Varies; see pages 650–58

654–56), you are expected to use the formats always used for such writings.

4
Use specialized language, when it is needed, in each discipline.

All disciplines use specialized language to some degree. The specialized terms in the natural and social sciences are generally more technical and less accessible to nonspecialists than are those in the humanities. The more important observable or theoretical exactness is to a discipline, the more likely there will be many words with very special meanings. For example, consider the word *niche.* It has two generally known meanings: "a place particularly suitable to the person or thing in it," and "a hollowed space in a wall for a statue or vase." *Niche* in the natural sciences, however, has a very specialized meaning: "the set of environmental conditions—climate, food sources, water supply, enemies—that permit an organism or species to survive." The extent to which you define the specialized language in your writing depends on your readers' level of expertise. (For more about audience awareness, see 1c).

The acceptability of the active voice° or passive voice° in writing varies with the disciplines. Writers in the humanities generally prefer the active voice *(John Priestley discovered oxygen in 1774),* while writers in the social and natural sciences often use the passive voice *(Oxygen was discovered in 1774)* to report facts and observations. The use of the passive voice in the sciences occurs when a writer wishes to emphasize the observation rather than the observer: "The gorillas were observed in their natural setting" focuses on the gorillas, not on the person observing the gorillas. In science writing when the focus can be on the observer, however, the writer uses the active voice: "Susan Kohn Green observed Lulu and Patty Cake, mother and daughter gorillas in New York City's Central Park Zoo, for one and a half years." (For a full discussion of active and passive voices, see 8j and 16a-2.)

■‖ 34b
Understand writing in the humanities.

Disciplines in the humanities include literature, language, philosophy, religion, and other subject areas. (Some colleges consider history to be part of the humanities, while other colleges consider it part of the social sciences; similarly, art and music are sometimes included in the humanities and sometimes not.)

‖ 1
Understand methods of inquiry in the humanities.

The humanities are concerned with questions that focus on human values. Reading, writing, and discussing—sometimes referred to as *discourse*—are key activities in the pursuit of answers to questions in the humanities. From the perspective that the well-reasoned thoughts of one person are typical of a general human response, the humanities draw on individual engagement and personal point of view. Thinking critically (Chapter 5) is crucial; for inquiry in the humanities seeks to locate "truth" based on values, ideas, and interpretations that relate to the human condition. Such inquiry must avoid emotionalism in favor of balanced, unbiased exploration.

Some questions in the humanities ask you to deal with material in its literal level. You might be asked what a passage says, or to describe the major tenets of a particular religion or philosophy. Other questions in the humanities call for inferential and evaluative thinking—looking "between the lines" and "beyond the lines," as explained in 5b. You might be asked to discuss the relative merits of abstract and representational art or your personal interpretation of Jean-Paul Sartre's statement "life is absurd." Your answers must be thorough, well-reasoned, and informed by knowledge of the material and the major issues at hand.

2
Understand writing purposes and practices in the humanities.

The major purposes of writing in the humanities are to inform and to persuade. **Informative writing** includes explaining what a passage means or what constitutes the key features of a philosophy. **Persuasive writing** includes arguing the merits of an opinion or interpretation. To those ends, writers synthesize, analyze, interpret, and evaluate.

In the humanities, some instructors ask students to use first person *(I, we, our)* to write about their own points of view or personal evaluations, and the third person *(he, she, it, they)* for all other assignments. Other instructors prefer students to write always in the third person. Be sure to inquire about and adapt to your instructor's requirements. In research papers for the humanities, the first person is generally acceptable only when you present your personal experience, your own conclusions, or your personal views contrasted with those of the sources you consult and document.

As discussed in Chapter 31, the techniques of paraphrasing and summarizing the words of others—with proper documentation so that plagiarism is avoided—are called upon frequently by writers in the humanities. For example, if you are assigned a review or a report, you often cannot assume that your readers have read or seen the work you are referring to, so you must provide a short summary of the work.

3
Recognize different types of papers in the humanities.

The types of papers in the humanities described in this section focus on literary works, but you can adapt the principles to other works as well. Before you write a paper that asks you to refer or react to a literary work, be sure to read the work closely. To read well, use your understanding of the reading process (5a) and critical reading skills (5b).

Analyses and Reviews

Analysis, the examination of the relationship of a whole to its parts, is a common method of development in writing about literature (as well as films, plays, works of art, architecture, and music). In a literary analysis, you discuss your well-reasoned ideas about a work of fiction, poetry, or drama. To get to know the work well and to gather ideas for your analysis, you read closely—reading thoroughly again and again while being *on the lookout for patterns in all the aspects of literary analysis* listed on the chart below. Look up or consult with other people about any word, reference, allusion, or idea you do not understand. Keep notes as you go along so that you have a record both of the patterns you find in the material and of your reactions to the patterns and the whole work.

Use this brief list of major aspects of literary works as an introductory guide to what to look for, think about, and seek to understand in a literary work.

MAJOR ASPECTS OF LITERARY WORKS TO ANALYZE

PLOT	The story and its emphases
THEME	Central idea or message
STRUCTURE	Organization and relationship of parts to each other and to the whole
CHARACTER(S)	Traits, thoughts, and actions of the person(s)
SETTING	Time and place of the action
POINT OF VIEW	Perspective or position from which the material is presented—sometimes by a narrator or a main character
STYLE	How words and sentence structures present the material
IMAGERY	The pictures created by the words (similes, metaphors, figurative language)
TONE	The attitudes expressed through the choice of words and the imagery
SYMBOLISM	The meaning beneath the surface of the words and images
RHYTHM AND RHYME	Beat, meter, repetition of sounds, etc.

Starting on the next page, you will find an example of literary analysis. The student writer decided from a close reading of Alfred Lord Tennyson's poem "Break, Break, Break" that the poet was using indirect techniques to convey emotions. To support this thesis, the student analyzes the poem's imagery and style.

SAMPLE LITERARY ANALYSIS PAPER

Chris Johns

Professor Perkins

English 105

April 22, 19XX

Emotion in Alfred Lord Tennyson's

"Break, Break, Break"

1   In Tennyson's "Break, Break, Break," the poet avoids direct
description of his feelings of grief. Instead he allegorizes,
alludes to, and only suggests his essential emotion.
Tennyson uses two vehicles to convey his feelings: sea imagery
and personal musings. These personal musings are not descriptions of what Tennyson is feeling, but rather are statements of
what he is thinking: "But the tender grace of a day that is dead /
Will never come back to me."[1] From the knowledge of these
thoughts the reader can infer the content and intensity of
Tennyson's feelings.

2   The imagery also suggests the poet's feelings. This is
obvious from the line structure of the poem and from the quality
of the image. In the first, third, and fourth stanzas the imagery
is presented in the first two lines, while Tennyson's thoughts are
given in the second two lines (which are also the last lines,
because each verse is composed of four lines). In the second
stanza the relationship between the imagery and Tennyson's
thoughts is closest: All four lines are devoted to Tennyson's
reaction to an image:

[1] All quotations in this paper are from Tennyson's poem
"Break, Break, Break." The complete poem is shown in the Appendix.

O well for the fisherman's boy

That he shouts with his sister at play!

O well for the sailor lad

That he sings in his boat on the bay!

3   Every element in the poem is designed to define and modify
Tennyson's grief. The images are controlled and simple and
always clear. Tennyson deals with each image separately; there
is no pictorial confusion. In the first and last verses the
image is clearly of breaking waves:

Break, break, break,

On thy cold gray stones, O Sea!

. . . .   Indicates
skipped lines

Break, break, break

At the foot of thy crags, O Sea!

The third verse's image is equally specific: "And the stately
ships go on / To their haven under the hill; . . ."

4   Images rather than direct statement of feeling are
Tennyson's resource:

Break, break, break,

On thy cold gray stones, O Sea!

I would that my tongue could utter

The thoughts that arise in me.

As the waves beat against the rocks, so does Tennyson's grief
beat against his heart; as the rocks can find no refuge, so
Tennyson's tongue cannot release the feelings from his heart.
The reader can sense the intensity of Tennyson's grief and can
then construct the pain and what lies behind it.

Start new page

Appendix

Break, Break, Break

Alfred Lord Tennyson

Break, break, break,

  On thy cold gray stones, O Sea!

And I would that my tongue could utter

  The thoughts that arise in me.

O well for the fisherman's boy

  That he shouts with his sister at play!

O well for the sailor lad,

  That he sings in his boat on the bay!

And the stately ships go on

  To their haven under the hill;

But O for the touch of a vanished hand,

  And the sound of a voice that is still!

Break, break, break,

  At the foot of thy crags, O Sea!

But the tender grace of a day that is dead

  Will never come back to me.

Interpretations

An interpretation discusses either what the author means by the work or what the work means personally to the reader. When you are writing an interpretation paper, always consider these questions.

625

1. What is the theme of the work?
2. How are particular parts of the work related to the theme?
3. If patterns exist in various elements of the work, what do they mean?
4. What message does the author convey through the work's setting, characters, narrator, etc.?
5. What symbols are used, and what do they mean?
6. Why is the ending what it is?

Book reports

A book report informs readers about the content of a book—by summarizing its plot and its theme and by discussing (1) the book's significance and purpose, (2) how the book presents its content, and (3) who might be most interested in the book. Your discussion of the book's significance should relate to your field of study. For example, if the book is a classic in children's literature, your focus for a literature class would differ somewhat from your focus for a course in psychology or education.

Reaction papers

A reaction paper presents the writer's thoughts, reactions, and feelings about a work of literature, or about an idea or an interpretation related to a work (or group of works). In a reaction paper, you might ask and try to answer a central question that the work made you think about, criticize a point of view in the work, or present a problem that you see in the work. For example, if you are asked to respond to a play, you might write about why you did or did not enjoy reading the play, how the play does or does not relate to your personal experience or to your view of life, what the play made you think about and try to puzzle through. You can focus on the entire play or on a particular scene, character, or set of lines.

Research papers

In a research paper for the humanities, you consult outside sources to learn what they have to say about a subject or a work of literature. After reading and perhaps talking with experts, you then evolve a thesis° whose purpose is either to inform or to persuade (see Chapter 1). In writing your research paper, you must draw on the sources to support your thesis° and help develop its main points. To do this, you draw heavily on the techniques of paraphrase, summary, and quotation, as explained in detail in Chapter 31.

Research in the humanities always calls for you to use library resources to obtain books and articles other people have written about your topic. You will find a list of reference works for subjects in the humanities in 32e-5. For a complete discussion of conducting research for writing, see Chapters 32 and 33. Remember that when your research subject concerns written works of literature, you have to read them closely—reading thoroughly again and again to evolve your thesis and then to find material that specifically supports it.

Starting below you will find a student paper written for a humanities course. The student's thesis is that the Greek myth of Icarus has strongly influenced other works of art and literature.

This paper uses a note system of documentation, as is required in some humanities courses. In most English courses, the MLA parenthetical system of documentation is used. It is presented and explained in Chapter 32.

SAMPLE HUMANITIES RESEARCH PAPER

Theresa A. Shannon

Professor Anderson

Humanities 32

March 10, 19XX

The Influence of the Myth of Icarus

We cannot know exactly why the Greeks included the myth

of Icarus in their mythology or why Ovid wrote the myth down

and included it in the Metamorphoses.[1] However, the impor-

tance of the myth is evident by its obvious influence on

other works of art and literature. These influences can be

seen in Brueghel's painting Landscape with the Fall of Icarus[2]

and in Stephen Spender's poem "Icarus."[3] Even psychologists

---

have named a personality that exhibits a particular pattern of behavior the Icarus complex.[4] The fact that the Icarus myth has generated so many other works indicates that it is more than an interesting story.

2   According to the myth, Daedalus, Icarus' father, designs wings of wax and feathers for himself and his son so that they may fly to freedom. Daedalus warns Icarus to fly directly between the sun and the ocean to prevent damage to the wings from either of these elements. Icarus ignores his father's warning and flies too close to the sun, causing the wax to melt. Icarus then plunges into the ocean and drowns. After Icarus' death, Daedalus offers a sacrifice of appeasement to the sun god, Apollo.

3   Pieter Brueghel's painting, Landscape with the Fall of Icarus, is not merely a representation of Icarus' death. Brueghel shows Icarus falling from the sky on a typical day near an average village. A ploughman either does not notice Icarus falling or chooses to ignore the event. A nearby sailing ship continues on its route. The poet W. H. Auden interpreted the painting as a representation of human suffer-ing. In "Musée des Beaux Arts," a poem about Brueghel's painting of Icarus, Auden writes about suffering: "they were never wrong, / The Old Masters: how well they understood / Its human position."[5] He continues to describe the plough-man's reaction to Icarus' fall: "But for him it was not an important failure;" and observes how the ship "Had somewhere to go and sailed calmly on."[6]

Shannon 3

4   Stephen Spender's poem, on the other hand, focuses on Icarus instead of on those who observed his death. He presents Icarus as a bold and arrogant boy who "almost had a War on the sun." He writes:

> This aristocrat, superb of all instinct,
>> With death close linked
> Had paced the enormous cloud, almost had won
>> War on the sun.[7]

5   Although these are not the only allusions in art and literature to the myth of Icarus, they are representative of the importance of the myth as an influence to artists. The myth of the fall of Icarus, like any other myth, serves to educate us, not just to entertain us. Artists will undoubtedly continue to interpret the myth according to their own insights, perhaps viewing it from a perspective that only the future can offer.

Start new page   Shannon 4

Notes

[1] Publius Ovidius Naso, "Icarus and Daedalus," in Metamorphoses (Amsterdam: Wetstein and Smith, 1932), I, 257–260.

[2] Pieter Brueghel, Landscape with the Fall of Icarus, Musée des Beaux Arts, Brussels, Belgium.

[3] Stephen Spender, "Icarus," in The Norton Anthology of Poetry, eds. Richard Ellman and Robert O'Clair (New York: W. W. Norton and Company, 1973), p. 790.

[4] Daniel Ogilvie, "The Icarus Complex," Psychology Today, 20, No. 6 (1976), 31–4, 67.

[5] W. H. Auden, "Musée des Beaux Arts," in The Norton Anthology of English Literature, eds. M. H. Abrams et al. (New York: W. W. Norton and Company, 1979), p. 2396.

[6] Auden, p. 2397.

[7] Spender, p. 790.

Start new page   Bibliography   Shannon 5

Auden, W. H. "Musée des Beaux Arts." In The Norton
        Anthology of English Literature. Eds. M. H. Abrams
        et al. New York: W. W. Norton and Company, 1979,
        pp. 2396–2397.

Brueghel, Pieter. Landscape with the Fall of Icarus.
        Musée des Beaux Arts, Brussels, Belgium.

Ogilvie, Daniel. "The Icarus Complex." Psychology
        Today, 20, No. 6 (1976), 31–4, 67.

Ovidius Naso, Publius. "Icarus and Daedalus." In
        Metamorphoses. Amsterdam: Wetstein and Smith, 1932,
        pp. 257–260.

Spender, Stephen. "Icarus." In The Norton Anthology of
        Poetry. Eds. Richard Ellman and Robert O'Clair. New
        York: W. W. Norton and Company, 1973, p. 790.

4

Know documentation style in the humanities.

Writers use **documentation** to give credit to the sources they have used. (A writer who does not credit a source is guilty of **plagiarizing**—a serious academic offense discussed at length in Chapter 31.) Styles of documentation differ among the disciplines. A very commonly used documentation style is the so-called parenthetical system developed by the Modern Language Association (MLA), an organization of scholars and teachers in language and literature. This system is discussed and illustrated in Chapters 32 and 33. Some humanities instructors require the documentation system developed by the American Psychological Association (APA). See 34c-4 for APA documentation. Some humanities instructors require a note system of documentation. Such a system, based on the Modern Language Association system before 1984, is explained here.

GUIDELINES FOR NOTE NUMBERS IN A PAPER

1. Put the number as near as possible to whatever you are referring to: at the end of a quotation, either direct or indirect, but after any punctuation that goes with whatever you are quoting.
2. Raise these numbers a little above the line of words.
3. Leave no extra space before a number.
4. Leave one space after the number except at the end of a sentence. Leave two spaces after the number before starting a new sentence.

EXAMPLE

We cannot know exactly why the Greeks included the myth of Icarus in their mythology or why Ovid wrote the myth down and included it in the Metamorphoses.[1] However, the importance of the myth is evident by its obvious influence on other works of art and literature. These influences can be seen in Brueghel's painting "Landscape with the Fall of Icarus"[2] and in Stephen Spender's poem "Icarus."[3]

GUIDELINES FOR FORMATTING ENDNOTES

1. Center the word *Notes* two inches from the top of a separate page at the end of the paper. Do not put *Notes* in quotation marks, and do not underline it.
2. Skip four lines before starting the first note.
3. Indent the first line of each note five character spaces, but if a note has more than one line, start the second line (and any following lines) at the left margin.
4. Raise each note number a little above the words.
5. Leave one space between the note number and the first word.
6. Double space within *and* between endnotes.
7. Do not number the first page of endnotes, but number the second page and any other pages in continuous sequence with the text of your paper.

EXAMPLE

Notes

[1] Publius Ovidius Naso, "Icarus and Daedalus," in Metamorphoses (Amsterdam: Wetstein and Smith, 1932), I, 257–260.

[2] Pieter Brueghel, Landscape with the Fall of Icarus, Musée des Beaux Arts, Brussels, Belgium.

[3] Stephen Spender, "Icarus," in The Norton Anthology of Poetry, eds. Richard Ellman and Robert O'Clair (New York: W. W. Norton and Company, 1973), p. 790.

Put documenting information in notes either at the bottom of pages (footnotes) or on a separate page or pages following the end of your paper (endnotes). The content is the same, whether you use footnotes or endnotes. Unless your instructor requires footnotes, use endnotes because they are easier to manage when you are typing a paper. Consecutive numbers raised a little above the words alert readers to the information you are documenting in a note.

Here are guidelines for inserting note numbers in a paper and for formatting endnotes and footnotes. To illustrate each set of guidelines, an example is shown from the student paper that begins on page 627.

GUIDELINES FOR FORMATTING FOOTNOTES AND FITTING THEM ON PAGES

1. Be aware that footnotes differ from endnotes in only one way: single space within footnotes and double space between them.
2. Be prepared to allot space at the bottom of each page for footnotes.
3. Estimate space on each page this way: Each time you use a footnote number in the text of your paper, know that you will need room at the bottom of the page for four lines (the space required between text and the first note) *plus* three lines for each note. Stop typing text and start your footnotes according to your estimate.
4. Retype a page if a footnote runs more than two or three lines short or long.
5. Remember that four spaces are required between the end of the text and the start of the footnotes.
6. If the content of a footnote runs more than six or eight lines, you can continue the note on the next page. On the new page (but not on the page where the content note started), type a line across the page, one line below the text. Then skip four more lines before beginning the first line of the continued note.

EXAMPLE

[1] Publius Ovidius Naso, "Icarus and Daedalus," in Metamorphoses (Amsterdam: Wetstein and Smith, 1932), I, 257–260.

[2] Pieter Brueghel, Landscape with the Fall of Icarus, Musée des Beaux Arts, Brussels, Belgium.

If your paper refers to only one or two sources, you may be permitted to use simplified documentation. (Such papers typically are about one or two works of literature, like the student paper beginning on page 623.) In such cases, keep the documentation as simple as possible. A single note tells where quotations come from. For example, this note tells that the entire work is given in the paper's appendix:

34b

but rather are statements of what he is thinking: "But the
tender grace of a day that is dead / Will never come back
to me."[1]

[1] All quotations are from Tennyson's poem "Break,
Break, Break." A copy of the full text is in the appendix
at the end of this paper.

If the poem were not included with the paper, the note would give
full publication information:

[1] All quotations are from Alfred Lord Tennyson,
"Break, Break, Break," in <u>Literature: An Introduction to
Reading and Writing</u>, Edgar V. Roberts and Henry E. Jacobs.
Prentice-Hall, 1986, p. 629.

In either case, a separate list of sources is unnecessary. When
a paper refers to two or three sources, the following system works
well:

the similarities between Frost's "The Onset" and "Stopping
by Woods" and Aiken's "Winter for a Moment Takes the
Mind."[1]

[1] Quotations from "The Onset" are followed by (1);
those from "Stopping by Woods" by (2); and from "Winter
for a Moment Takes the Mind" by (3). The versions referred to are collected in <u>The Pocket Book of Modern
Verse</u>, Oscar Williams, ed. (New York: Pocket Books, 1954),
pp. 233-34, 240, 360-62.

First-reference note form

In a note system of documentation, the first time you refer to a source in your writing, the note gives complete bibliographic facts as well as the specific place you are referring to or quoting from in that source. Here are first-reference note forms for common sources.

BOOK WITH ONE AUTHOR

[1] Joan Didion, <u>Salvador</u> (New York: Simon & Schuster, 1983), p. 64.

BOOK WITH TWO OR THREE AUTHORS

[2] Irving Wallace, David Wallechinsky, and Amy Wallace, <u>Significa</u> (New York: Dutton, 1983), p. 177.

BOOK WITH A CORPORATE AUTHOR

[3] Music Educators' National Conference, <u>Music in the Senior High School</u> (Washington: Music Educators' National Conference, 1959), 42.

WORK IN SEVERAL VOLUMES OR PARTS

[4] Robert Kelley, <u>The Shaping of the American Past</u>, II (Englewood Cliffs, NJ: Prentice–Hall, 1975), 724–25.

WORK IN AN ANTHOLOGY OR A COLLECTION

[5] Wayne Tosh, "Computer Linguistics," in <u>Linguistics Today</u>, ed. Archibald A. Hill (New York: Basic Books, 1969), p. 200.

ARTICLE IN A REFERENCE WORK

[6] "Fraudulence in the Arts," <u>The New Encyclopaedia Britannica</u>, 1979 ed.

ARTICLE FROM A JOURNAL WITH CONTINUOUS PAGINATION

[7] William A. Madden, "Wuthering Heights: The Binding Passion," Nineteenth-Century Fiction, 27 (1972), 151.

ARTICLE FROM A JOURNAL THAT PAGES EACH ISSUE SEPARATELY

[8] Michael C. T. Brookes, "A Dean's Dilemmas," Journal of Basic Writing, 5, No. 1 (1986), 65.

ARTICLE FROM A WEEKLY OR BIWEEKLY MAGAZINE OR NEWSPAPER

[9] Barbara Randolph, "Hailing the Eureka Factor," Time, 21 April 1986, p. 65.

ARTICLE FROM A MONTHLY PERIODICAL

[10] Patti Hogan, "Setting the Pace," Ms., Aug. 1985, p. 20.

ARTICLE FROM A DAILY NEWSPAPER

[11] Georgia Dullea, "Literary Folk Look for Solid Comfort," New York Times, 16 April 1986, Sec. 3, p. 6, col. 5.

FILM

[12] Bernardo Bertolucci, dir., Last Tango in Paris, with Marlon Brando, United Artists, 1972.

INTERVIEW

[13] Personal interview with professor Shirley Stearns, 17 July 1985.

WORK REPRINTED IN ANOTHER WORK

[14] W. H. Auden, "Prologue: The Birth of Architecture," About the House (New York: Random; London: Faber and Faber), 1965; rpt. in Understanding Social Psychology, 3rd ed., Stephen Worchel and Joel Cooper (Homewood, IL: Dorsey, 1983), p. 539.

Note forms for second and subsequent references

After the first note for a source, you should shorten all further references to the source. If you are citing only one work by the author, the author's last name and the page references are enough:

[15] Hogan, p. 31.

If you are citing more than one work by the same author, you must include a shortened form of the title of the particular book—along with the author's last name and the page reference.

[16] Didion, Salvador, p. 45.

[17] Didion, Common Prayer, pp. 92–94.

List of sources

Bibliographies list all sources consulted for a research paper, not just the sources referred to or quoted from. Because first-reference notes give full bibliographic data for each source, your instructor may not require you to submit a separate list of sources. If your instructor requires a list of sources, ask whether you should include in it all sources consulted or only those cited. You can follow the format here for a list of *all* sources consulted. Follow the advice in 32g-2 for a list of only sources cited.

GUIDELINES FOR FORMATTING A BIBLIOGRAPHY

1. Center the word *Bibliography* two inches from the top edge of the paper. Leave four lines of space before starting the list.
2. Arrange the entries alphabetically by author's last name.
3. In general, give this information: author's last name, author's first name (if more than one author, use first–last order for the second and other authors); title; and publishing data. Follow each block of information with a period.
4. Start each item at the left margin, but if the item has two or more lines, indent all lines after the first line five spaces.
5. Double-space within *and* between entries.

6. If you use endnotes, place the bibliography on a new page after them. If you use footnotes, put the bibliography on a new page after the end of the text of your paper.
7. Do not number the first page of the bibliography, but number second and subsequent pages in continuous sequence with the text of your paper.

EXAMPLE

Bibliography

Thurman, Judith. Isak Dinesen: The Life of a Storyteller.
    New York: St. Martin's, 1982.
Zigrosser, Carl. The Book of Fine Prints, revised ed. New
    York: Crown, 1966.

Below are bibliographic entries for the note forms shown on pages 635–37.

BOOK WITH ONE AUTHOR

Didion, Joan. Salvador. New York: Simon & Schuster, 1983.

BOOK WITH TWO OR THREE AUTHORS

Wallace, Irving, David Wallechinsky, and Amy Wallace,
    Significa. New York: Dutton, 1983.

BOOK WITH A CORPORATE AUTHOR

Music Educators' National Conference. Music in the Senior
    High School. Washington: Music Educators' National
    Conference, 1959.

WORK IN SEVERAL VOLUMES OR PARTS

Kelley, Robert. <u>The Shaping of the American Past</u>, 2 vols.
Englewood Cliffs, N.J.: Prentice-Hall, 1975.

WORK IN AN ANTHOLOGY OR A COLLECTION

Tosh, Wayne. "Computer Linguistics." In <u>Linguistics Today</u>.
Ed. Archibald A. Hill. New York: Basic Books, 1969,
pp. 198–206.

ARTICLE IN A REFERENCE WORK

"Fraudulence in the Arts," <u>The New Encylopaedia Britannica</u>,
1979 ed.

ARTICLE FROM A JOURNAL WITH CONTINUOUS PAGINATION

Madden, William A. "<u>Wuthering Heights</u>: The Binding Passion."
<u>Nineteenth-Century Fiction</u>, 27 (1972), 127–154.

ARTICLE FROM A JOURNAL THAT PAGES EACH ISSUE SEPARATELY

Brookes, Michael C. T. "A Dean's Dilemmas." <u>Journal of Basic
Writing</u>, 5, No. 1 (1986), 65–76.

ARTICLE FROM A WEEKLY OR BIWEEKLY MAGAZINE OR NEWSPAPER

Randolph, Barbara. "Hailing the Eureka Factor." <u>Time</u>, 21
April 1986, p. 65.

ARTICLE FROM A MONTHLY PERIODCAL

Hogan, Patti. "Setting the Pace." <u>Ms.</u>, Aug. 1985, pp. 20–32

ARTICLE FROM A DAILY NEWSPAPER

Dullea, Georgia. "Literary Folk Look for Solid Comfort." <u>New
York Times</u>, 16 April 1986, Sec. 3, p. 1, col. 1; p. 6,
cols. 1–6.

FILM

Bertolucci, Bernardo, dir. <u>Last Tango in Paris</u>. With Marlon
Brando. United Artists, 1972.

INTERVIEW

Stearns, Shirley. Personal interview. 17 July 1985.

WORK REPRINTED IN ANOTHER WORK

Auden, W. H. "Prologue: The Birth of Architecture." In <u>About
the House</u>. New York: Random; London: Faber and Faber),
1965. Rpt. in <u>Understanding Social Psychology</u>, 3rd ed.,
Stephen Worchel and Joel Cooper. Homewood, IL: Dorsey,
1983, p. 539.

■‖ 34c
Understand writing in the social sciences.

Disciplines in the social sciences include subject areas such as
economics, education, geography, political science, psychology, and
sociology.

‖ 1
Understand methods of inquiry in the social sciences.

The social sciences ask questions that focus on the behavior of
people as individuals and in groups. As researchers and writers,
social scientists—such as economists and psychologists—want to
know what people do and why. To find out, they usually follow a
procedure that involves observation, investigation, and collection of
data.

Observation is a common method for research in the social sciences (as well as the natural sciences). If social scientists want to study how aggression emerges in small children, for example, they might observe a group of children at play. If you are asked to make observations, take along whatever tools or equipment you might need in order to work: writing or sketching materials, and perhaps recording or photographic equipment. As you make your observations, take very accurate and complete notes about what you see. If you use your own system of abbreviations to speed your note taking, make sure you can go back to your notes and understand them when the time comes to write up your observations. In your report, be sure to indicate what tools or equipment you took along and how you used it—because your method might have influenced what you saw (for example, taking photographs may make people too self-conscious to act as they usually do).

Interviewing is another common technique that social scientists use for collecting information. They are useful for gathering people's opinions and impressions of events. Remember, however, that interviews are not always a reliable way to gather factual information because people's memories are not precise. If your only source for facts is interviews, be sure to interview as many people as possible so that you can cross-check the information. As with observation, if you have scheduled an interview, be prepared with

GUIDELINES FOR WRITING QUESTIONS FOR A QUESTIONNAIRE

1. Know clearly what you want to find out.

2. Make questions easy to understand.

3. Make the questions fair—do not use slanted language (see 21a-5) or imply to people what *you* want to hear.

4. Test your questions on a small group of people before you use them for gathering data. If any question turns out to be hard for people to understand, or if it can be interpreted in more than one way, revise and retest it.

5. Use a sufficient number of people when you administer the final form of the questionnaire. You cannot generalize from small samples.

whatever note-taking tools you might need. Practice with those tools so they do not intrude on the interview process.

Questionnaires are often useful for gathering information in the social sciences. If you are asked to write questions for a questionnaire, you need to make sure that you get the information you are looking for. The way you phrase the questions will determine if your data are a true reflection of what people are thinking.

2
Understand writing purposes and practices in the social sciences.

Social scientists write to inform and to persuade by classifying, analyzing, or explaining a human problem or condition. They most often use rhetorical strategies such as definition, analogy, and analysis of a problem and its solution.

Definition is extremely important in the social sciences when ambiguous social issues and terms are the topic of discussion. For example, if you are writing a paper on substance abuse in the medical profession, you first have to define *substance* and *medical profession*. By *substance* do you mean alcohol and drugs or only drugs? When you refer to the medical profession, are you including nurses and lab technicians or just doctors? Without defining these terms, you can confuse your readers or lead them to the wrong conclusions.

Analogy helps social scientists make unfamiliar ideas clearer to their readers. When an unfamiliar idea is compared with one that is more familiar, the unfamiliar idea becomes easier to understand. For example, when sociologists talk of the "culture shock" that people feel when they live in a society very new to them, they might compare it to the reaction someone living today might have when moving suddenly hundreds of years into the future or the past.

Analysis can be helpful when social scientists write about problems and their solutions. For example, an economist studying a major automobile company in financial difficulties might analyze the situation to define a problem and ultimately to offer a solution. The economist might break the situation into parts, analyzing employee salaries and benefits, the selling price of cars, costs of doing business, and other aspects, to show how these parts relate to the financial status of the whole company. Then the economist might speculate about how specific changes in these parts would contribute to solving the automobile manufacturer's financial problems.

In college courses in the social sciences, some instructors ask students to write their personal reactions to information or experiences, in which case the first person *(I, we, our)* is acceptable. In most writing for the social sciences, however, writers use the third person *(he, she, it, they)*. Also, because the emphasis is on people or groups being observed rather than on the person doing the observing, the passive voice° is a frequent characteristic of such writing. An economist is likely to write, "The audits of The Frazzle Company were studied for indications of mismanagement and waste" instead of "I studied the audits of The Frazzle Company for indications of mismanagement and waste." Nevertheless, some material can be written about in the less austere active voice°: "The Frazzle Company seems eager to improve its methods of operation" and "The audits revealed that The Frazzle Company needs major overhauling."

3
Recognize different types of papers in the social sciences.

Two major types of papers in the social sciences are case studies and research papers.

Case studies

A case study is an intensive study of one group or individual. It is usually presented in a relatively fixed format, but the specific parts and order of case study formats vary. Most case studies contain the following components: (1) basic identifying information about the individual or group; (2) a history of the individual or group; (3) observations of the individual's or group's behavior; and (4) conclusions and perhaps recommendations as a result of the observations.

On pages 644–45 are parts of the first and last sections of a case study written by a student. Omissions are noted in the paper. The purpose of the case study was to determine if a young child was having trouble socializing in her day-care center.

SAMPLE CASE STUDY (EXCERPTS)

Case Study: Child Observation

Theresa L. Cox

Basic Information

Name: Molly

Setting: Early Education Center

Age: 3 years

Sex: Female

Time: 10:30 to 11:00 A.M.

Date: 6-30-85

Activity: Painting and play

Observations

Molly stretched her arms out and stated "Me" as the teacher was giving another child a paint pencil. She watched as the other child began painting, reached for this child's paint pencil and then turned to the teacher and stated "Me want some." Molly painted with a paint pencil, squeezed the paint pencil, and periodically touched the paint with her finger. She observed the other children frequently. Molly made marks on another girl's paper, and after being reprimanded, she returned to her paper. Molly marked another girl's arm and smiled broadly, until she was reprimanded. Molly then marked on the same child's arm a second time and placed in "time-out." She crossed her arms, looked down, frowned, and muttered "I'm mad."

[A section on background omitted here]

Conclusion

Molly expressed her independence and demonstrated a self-centered attitude in practically everything she did. She often

Cox 2

returned to activities for which she had earlier been

reprimanded, thus nonverbally (and sometimes verbally)

objecting to what she was told. Cognitively, Molly is

progressing from the sensorimotor stage to the stage of

symbolic thought. She frequently observed her environment,

was very expressive and imitative, and showed imagination in

her play. Molly's actions primarily met her needs, but she did

alter her behavior at times to avoid punishment. Overall, Molly

exemplifies the behavior of one type of typical toddler.

The case study begins with basic information and moves to a detailed account of Molly's activities. The study concludes with an interpretation of Molly's actions as compared to those of other children her age. The information in the observation section is actual observed activities. The conclusion contains ideas and interpretations of the observer based on the observed activities.

In writing a case study, always be sure to differentiate between the things you observed and the things you conclude or surmise—facts versus opinions. For example, if you are observing patients in a nursing home and you notice that several of them lie in bed in the afternoon facing the door, describe the situation; do not interpret it by saying that the patients are watching for visitors. The fact could be that medicines are administered by injection in the right hip every afternoon and the patients are therefore more comfortable if they lie on the left hip, causing them to face the door.

Research papers

Research papers are common in the social sciences. In some social science courses you may conduct an experiment or do other **primary research** that offers you first-hand exposure to information. Papers that report primary research often have fixed formats, depending on the subject area; be sure to ask your instructor if a specific format is required.

You may also be assigned a research paper based on your consulting **primary** and **secondary sources**—articles and books that report, summarize, and otherwise discuss the findings of primary research. You will find a list of reference works for subjects in the social sciences in 32e-5.

645

SAMPLE SOCIAL SCIENCE RESEARCH PAPER (EXCERPT)

America's Street People

Douglas Franklin

The number of homeless people in the cities of the United
States is a social problem that has grown larger over the last
few years. Estimates range from 250,000 (Huntley and Thorton,
1985) to 2–3 million (Bassuk, 1984; Fustero, 1984) people
living in the streets of the United States. One fact experts
agree on, however. The stereotypical "skid–row bum" is being
replaced by a large assortment of people (Bassuk). As Fustero
(1984) reports, the homeless now include "runaway children,
immigrants, bag ladies, displaced families, a growing number of
unemployed, alcoholics and drug abusers, and the mentally ill"
(p. 58).

These changes in the size and nature of the homeless
population have many causes. Two stand out. First, the
deinstitutionalization of the mentally ill (Bassuk; Fustero)
led to a huge outpouring of people unable to take care of
themselves. This trend of releasing people from mental
institutions "followed the widespread introduction in the
1950s of psychoactive drugs, which seemed to offer the
possibility of rehabilitating psychotic people within a
community setting" (Bassuk, p. 41). Second, availability of
low–cost housing in the cities has dropped sharply since
single–room occupancy and other modest facilities have given
way to urban development projects (Fustero).

Franklin 6

References

Bassuk, E. L. (1984, July). The homelessness problem.
Scientific American, pp. 40–45.

Fustero, S. (1984, February). Home on the street. Psychology
Today, pp. 56–63.

Huntley, S., & Thorton, J. (1985, December 9). Shielding the
homeless from a deadly winter. U.S. News and World
Report, p. 79.

Here is an excerpt from a social science research paper by a student. It uses the style of documentation established by the American Psychological Association (APA), described in detail in 34c-4. Its purpose is to inform readers about the problem of homeless people living in cities of the United States.

4
Know documentation style in the social sciences.

Writers use **documentation** to give credit to the sources they have used. (A writer who does not credit a source is guilty of **plagiarizing**—a serious academic offense discussed at length in Chapter 31.) Styles of documentation differ among the disciplines.

In the social sciences, the American Psychological Association (APA) style is a common method of documentation. APA style uses parenthetical citations to refer briefly to a source and a References list to give detailed information on all sources referred to in the paper. All citations in your paper must have equivalent entries listing bibliographic facts in the References list, and no items can appear in References that have not been cited in your paper. Notes serve only to convey content information not included in your paper.

Here are basic guidelines to help you use APA parenthetical citations and references. For complete information covering all types of citations, see the *Publication Manual of the American Psychological Association* (1983, or later if available).

GUIDELINES FOR PARENTHETICAL CITATIONS IN APA STYLE

1. If a parenthetical citation comes at the end of your sentence, place the sentence's period after the parentheses.
2. If you are paraphrasing or summarizing material and you do *not* mention the name of the author in your text, do this: (Jones, 1982).
3. If you are quoting and you do *not* mention the name of the author in your text, do this: (Jones, 1982, p. 65).
4. If you are paraphrasing, summarizing, or quoting material and *do* mention the name of the author in your text, do this: (p. 65).
5. If you use more than one source written in the same year by the same author(s), assign letters (*a, b,* etc.) to the works in the References list and do this for a parenthetical reference: (Jones, 1983a).
6. If you refer to a work more than once, give the author's name and year only the first time; then use only the name.
7. If you cite several sources in one place, put them in alphabetical order by authors' last names and separate the sources with a semicolon: (Bassuk, 1984; Fustero, 1984).

GUIDELINES FOR THE APA REFERENCES LIST

1. Arrange the list of sources cited alphabetically by author's last name. For two or more works by an author, arrange the works by date, most recent first.
2. Start with an author's last name, followed by initials for the author's first and middle names. If there is more than one author, name them all (up to six authors)—again starting with the last name and using initials for first and middle names. If there are over six authors, use only the first author and the words *et al.*
3. Put the date of publication in parentheses immediately after the author's name. If you list two works by the same author published in the same year, assign letters (*a, b,* etc.) to the year: (1984a), (1984b).

4. Put the title after the year of publication. Capitalize only the first word and any proper names in a title or subtitle. Do not put articles in quotation marks. Underline titles.
5. Put the city of publication and the publisher next. Use short forms for the names of well-known publishers: New York: Harper.
6. Put page numbers next, but use *p.* or *pp.* only for page numbers of articles in newspapers or popular magazines. Do not use *p.* or *pp.* with page numbers of articles in professional journals. In contrast, parenthetical references to specific pages, always include *p.* or *pp.*—no matter what type of source.
7. Start each item at left margin, but if the item has two or more lines, indent all lines after the first line five spaces.

Here are sample references in APA style for common types of source material.

BOOK WITH ONE AUTHOR

Toynbee, A. (1939). <u>A study of history</u>. New York: Oxford University Press.

BOOK WITH TWO OR THREE AUTHORS

Smith, R. E., Sarason, I. G., & Sarason, B. R. (1982). <u>Psychology: The frontiers of behaviors</u>. New York: Harper.

WORK IN AN ANTHOLOGY OR A COLLECTION

Ambrose, J. A. (1961). The development of the smiling response in early infancy. In B. M. Foss (Ed.), <u>Determinants of infant behavior</u>. New York: Wiley.

ARTICLE IN A REFERENCE WORK

Family and marriage (1979). <u>Encyclopaedia Britannica</u>.

A BOOK WITH A CORPORATE AUTHOR

U.S. Department of Commerce (1985). <u>Statistical</u> <u>abstract</u> <u>of</u>
<u>the</u> <u>United</u> <u>States</u>. Washington, DC: U.S. Government
Printing Office.

ARTICLE FROM A JOURNAL WITH CONTINUOUS PAGINATION

Bernstein, B. (1960). Language and social class. <u>British</u>
<u>Journal of Sociology</u>, <u>11</u>, 271–276.

ARTICLE FROM A JOURNAL THAT PAGES EACH ISSUE SEPARATELY

Maines, D. R. (1977). Tactile relationships in the subway as
affected by racial, sexual, and crowded seating
situations. <u>Environmental</u> <u>Psychology</u> <u>and</u> <u>Nonverbal</u>
<u>Behavior</u>. <u>2</u>(2), 100–109.

**AN ARTICLE FROM A WEEKLY, BIWEEKLY, OR MONTHLY MAGAZINE, OR
WEEKLY NEWSPAPER**

Jarmulowski, V. (1985, February). Blended families: A
growing American phenomenon . . . Who are they?
<u>Ms.</u>, pp. 33–34.

ARTICLE FROM A DAILY NEWSPAPER

Castillo, A. (1980, November 2). Mystery resurfaces. <u>The</u>
<u>Courier–Journal</u>, p. A22.

■|| 34d
Understand writing in the natural and technological sciences.

Disciplines in the natural and technological sciences include
astronomy, biology, chemistry, engineering, geology, physics, computer science, health sciences, and electrical or mechanical technology.

1
Understand methods of inquiry in the sciences.

The natural and technological sciences ask questions about natural phenomena. The sciences adhere to key principles of research: observation, collection, and organization of physical and factual material. The purpose of scientific investigation is discovery; scientists observe and attempt to explain natural phenomena. To do this, scientists formulate and test hypotheses in order to explain cause and effect systematically and objectively.

The **scientific method,** commonly used in the sciences to make discoveries, is a procedure for gathering information related to a specific hypothesis. A hypothesis is a tentative explanation for an observed phenomenon. In an attempt to confirm or reject the hypothesis, scientists do one or all of these: collect data related to the hypothesis, test the hypothesis through experimentation, form further hypotheses and investigate them. Scientists then draw conclusions about the hypothesis based on the data from their observations. The information gathered by observing natural events is known as **empirical evidence.** Ideas or opinions, even those stated by experts, never constitute empirical support for a scientific report. Here is a basic guide to the scientific method:

GUIDELINES FOR USING THE SCIENTIFIC METHOD

1. Formulate a hypothesis or question, defined as specifically as possible.
2. Collect "known" (previously published) information related to the hypothesis or question.
3. Plan a method of investigation to uncover unknown information.
4. Experiment, exactly following the investigative procedures you have outlined.
5. Analyze the results of the investigation.
6. Apply the results to the hypothesis or question and arrive at conclusions—and perhaps suggest additional hypotheses.

2
Understand writing purposes and practices in the sciences.

Scientists usually write to inform their audiences about some piece of research or to relate factual information about some topic. Sometimes a scientific paper's thesis is implied in the paper's statement of purpose. For example, when a geologist describes a rock formation for other geologists who are not able to visit the formation themselves, the writer's purpose is to inform, not to present the writer's own ideas or hypotheses. Similarly, a chemist describes an experiment in detail so that others may evaluate the scientific procedure or may duplicate the experiment to compare results.

Exactness is extremely important in scientific writing. Readers expect precise descriptions of procedures and findings, free of personal biases. Scientists expect to be able to *replicate*—repeat step-by-step—the experiment or other process and get the same outcome as the writer.

Completeness is another essential characteristic of scientific writing. A scientist who makes an observation does not always know what information might become important at a later date. For example, a researcher describing observations of the types of food brought to baby robins by their parents also should report other information, such as the times feedings occur, the behavior of the nestlings when food is presented, and the identity of the parent offering the food. Having recorded all this information, the researcher may gain unexpected insights. For example, the researcher may realize that food types tell only part of the story because the food presented depends on the parents' hunting preferences, the food available at a specific time of day, or the nestlings' preference. Unless complete information is available, the researcher and the readers can come to wrong conclusions about what determines the diet of nestling robins.

Because the sciences generally focus on the experiment rather than the experimenter, and on objective observation rather than subjective interpretation, scientific report writing is often written in a style that distances a subject from both writer and reader. As a result, the passive voice° is common in scientific and technical reports because the observer of the action is often either unimportant or understood to be present. Therefore, do not refer to *the experimenter* or *the technician* unless that person is the focus of the discussion. For example, readers expect to see "The robins were observed feeding over a 24-hour period" rather than "I observed the robins over a 24-hour period." Unless you are writing a personal-reaction paper for a college course, generally avoid the first person (*I, we, our*).

When writing for the sciences, often you are expected to follow fixed formats, which are designed to summarize a project and its results efficiently. Even though the format establishes the overall organization, you must organize the presentation of information within each section. Also, writers in the sciences often use charts, graphs, tables, diagrams, and other illustrations to present material to readers. In fact, illustrations sometimes show complex material more clearly than words can.

3
Recognize different types of papers in the sciences.

Two major types of papers in the sciences are scientific reports and scientific review papers.

Scientific reports

Scientific reports tell about observations and experiments. A formal scientific report must accurately represent the procedures and results. Imprecise or inexact reports mislead other researchers. Formal reports include the seven sections (plus the title) described below; less formal reports, such as are sometimes assigned in introductory college courses, might not include an abstract or a review of the literature. Be sure to ask your instructor which sections to include if you are assigned a scientific report. Here are the sections of a scientific report, listed in the order in which they should appear.

The **title** should be exact and should include the main idea of your research. If the work gets published, it will be catalogued according to its key words. If your title is not descriptive of your main point, your work will not be found when other scientists do library research.

An **abstract** is a very condensed summary of the report. Its purpose is to give the reader a rapid overview and understanding of the contents without the reader's having to go through the entire presentation of methods, data, and conclusions.

The **introduction** states the purpose of the research, explains the problem addressed by the hypothesis, states the hypothesis, and gives the reasons for investigating the problem. The introduction also may include two other matters: any background information necessary to explain the hypothesis or to interpret the research, and a "review of the literature," which presents previous references that relate to the hypothesis. In some courses students are not required to include a literature review.

The **methods and materials** section describes the equipment, materials (such as chemicals), and procedures used in the experiment or investigation.

The **results** section provides information obtained from experiments, tests, and observations. (In some reports this section is combined with the discussion section.) For ease of reading, the information is presented from most-to-least important or—less frequently—chronologically. Charts, graphs, and photographs can be included as needed to explain material.

The **discussion** section evaluates the results and examines what the experiment means. The section starts with a statement that reports whether the hypothesis was supported by the research. Questions underlying the rest of the discussion might include: (1) Do the results agree with the results of previous experiments discussed in references? (2) If the results do not support the hypothesis, what reasons can be suggested? (3) If the experiment failed, how did it happen and why? All general statements here must be supported by concrete evidence.

The **conclusions** section lists conclusions about the hypotheses and the outcomes, with particular attention to any theoretical implications that can be drawn from the work. Also this section can include *specific* suggestions for further research, but it should avoid vague statements such as "further research is suggested."

References cited lists references cited in the review of the literature in a report's introduction. Its format conforms to the requirements of the documentation style in the discipline (see 34d-4). Students are sometimes not required to review the literature and therefore do not give a reference list.

SAMPLE SCIENCE REPORT (EXCERPTS)

An Experiment to Predict Vestigial Wings

in an F_2 Drosophila Population

by Avery Bird

INTRODUCTION

The purpose of this experiment was to observe second filial generation (F_2) wing structures in Drosophila. The hypothesis was that abnormalities in vestigial wing structures would follow predicted genetic patterns.

METHODS AND MATERIALS

On February 7, four Drosophila (P_1) were observed.
Observation was made possible by etherizing the parents
(after separating them from their larvae), placing them on a
white card, and observing them under a dissecting
microscope. The observations were recorded on a chart.

On February 14, the larvae taken from the parents on
February 7 had developed to adults (F_1) and they were
observed as on February 7. The observations were recorded
on the chart started on February 7.

On February 19, the second filial generation (F_2) was
supposed to be observed. This, however, was impossible
because they did not hatch. The record chart had to be
discontinued.

RESULTS

No observations of F_2 were possible. For the F_1
population it is interesting to note that according to the
prediction, no members should have had vestigial wings.
According to the observations, however, some members of F_1
did have vestigial wings.

[Discussion section omitted]

CONCLUSIONS

Two explanations are possible to explain vestigial
wings in the F_1 population. Perhaps members from F_2 were
present from the F_1 generation that was observed. This is
doubtful since the incubation period is 10 days, and the
time between observations was only 8 days. A second
possible explanation is that the genotype of the male P_1 was
not WW (indicating that both genes were for normal wings)
but rather heterozygous (Ww). If this were true the
following would be the first filial products:

P_1 Ww × ww

F_1 Ww ww   in a 1:1 ratio.

Thus, the possibility for vestigial wings would exist. The problem remains, however, that according to the observations the ratio was not 1:1 2:1 (i.e., 24 normal to 12 abnormal). One explanation could be that the total number was not large enough to extract an average. This experiment should be repeated to get F_2 data. Also, a larger F_1 sample should be used to see if the F_1 findings reported here are repeated.

Scientific reviews

A scientific review is a paper about published information on a scientific topic or issue. The purpose of the review is to inform readers about the current knowledge about the topic or issue. Sometimes the purpose of a scientific review is to suggest a new interpretation of the old material. Any reinterpretation is based on a synthesis of old information with new, more complete information. In such reviews, the writer must marshal evidence to persuade readers that the new interpretation is valid.

If you are assigned a review, do this: (1) choose a very limited scientific issue currently being researched; (2) use information that is current—the more recently published the articles, books, and journals you consult, the better; (3) accurately summarize and paraphrase material—as explained in Chapter 31; and (4) document your sources, as explained in 34d-4. You will find a list of reference works for the sciences in 32e-5. You can use headings to help your reader understand your paper's organization and progression of ideas.

4
Know documentation style in the sciences.

Writers use **documentation** to give credit to the sources they have used. (A writer who does not credit a source is guilty of **pla-**

giarizing—a serious academic offense discussed at length in Chapter 31.) Styles of documentation differ among the disciplines.

The documentation styles of the various fields within the natural and technological sciences may vary slightly from one another. Many fields have manuals (see list below) that explain the documentation style common to their professional journals. If you are writing in a field that does not have a style manual, refer to a journal in the field and imitate its documentation style. Most style manuals also provide useful information about writing practices in the field, covering such matters as abbreviations, spelled-out numbers versus numerals, special formats, literature citation, writing standards, and format issues.

In each course, ask your instructor what documentation style is required. If the choice is yours, use the style of your major field so that you can practice it, or follow the style of the subject of your course. Here is a list of some style manuals in the sciences.

BIOLOGY

Council of Biology Editors Style Manual Committee. *CBE Style Manual.* 5th ed. Bethesda, MD: Council of Biology, 1983.

CHEMISTRY

American Chemical Society. *Handbook for Authors of Papers in American Chemical Society Publications.* Washington, DC: American Chemical Society, 1978.

GEOLOGY

U.S. Geological Survey. *Suggestions to Authors of Reports of the United States Geological Survey.* 6th ed. Washington, DC: Department of the Interior, 1978.

PHYSICS

American Institute of Physics. *Style Manual for Guidance in Preparation of Papers.* 3rd ed. New York: American Institute of Physics.

To take an example, the *CBE Style Manual* suggests documentation much like the American Psychological Association (APA) system explained on pages 647–50. Brief information about a reference is given in parentheses in the text, and full bibliographic information is given in a Literature Cited list at the end of the paper.

On the next page is a paragraph and part of a reference list from a student paper that follows conventions given in the *CBE Style Manual.* Notice that in the paragraph scientific names are underlined, and that the genus is capitalized and the species is not *(Passer griseus).* Name–year parenthetical references are given within the text—except in the last sentence, where only the year of publication is given because the source author's name is part of the sentence.

In the Literature Cited, notice that (1) the entries are typed "block style" (without indentations); (2) single spacing is used within a reference and double spacing is used between the references; (3) the list is alphabetical according to author's last name; (4) titles are neither underlined nor put in quotation marks; (5) only the first word and proper names are capitalized in titles; and (6) only initials are used for author's first and middle names.

SAMPLE SCIENCE RESEARCH (EXCERPT)

Brian D. Anderson

The genus _Passer_ is believed to have arisen on the African savanna during the late Miocene or early Pliocene (Johnston and Klitz 1977). Ten species occur in Africa, seven of these in Africa exclusively. Consequently, an African origin seems reasonable. Morphologically, all are similar and are primarily adapted for grain and seed eating. One might reasonably expect a group such as this to have arisen in a savanna biotope. Summers-Smith (1963) suggested that the ancestor form may have been very much like _Passer griseus_ (Gray-headed sparrow), which currently inhabits the sub-Saharan grasslands.

Literature Cited

Johnston, R. F.; Klitz, J. Variations and evolution in a grainivorous bird: the house sparrow. In: Pinowski, J.; Kendeigh, S. C., eds. Grainivorous birds in ecosystems. Cambridge, England: University press; 1977.

Summers-Smith, J. D. The house sparrow. Cambridge, England: University Press; 1963.

35
BUSINESS WRITING

Business writing requires of you what other kinds of writing call for: understanding your audience and your purpose. When you write for the business world—perhaps a letter asking for a job interview or a memo or report for an employer—keep five points in mind.

- Consider your audience's needs and expectations.
- Show that you understand the purpose for a business communication and the context in which it takes place.
- Put essential information first.
- Make your points clearly and directly.
- Use conventional formats.

■|| 35a
Understand how to write and format a business letter.

Business letters are clear, usually short communications written to give information, to build good will, or to establish a foundation for discussions or transactions. Experts in business and government agree that the letters likely to get results are short, simple, direct, and human. As part of International Paper Company's series of advertisements "The Power of the Printed Word," Malcolm Forbes of *Forbes* magazine gave these recommendations for effective business letters:

1. Call the person by name.
2. Tell what your letter is about in the first paragraph.
3. Be honest.
4. Be clear and specific.
5. Use accurate English.
6. Be positive and natural.
7. Edit ruthlessly.

For business letters and envelopes, you can use the standard formats shown on pages 664 and 665.

■‖ 35b

Understand how to write and format a job-application letter.

One important type of business letter is the job-application letter. (See the sample job-application letter written by a student, Lee Franco, on page 666.) Specific advice about each part of the letter is given in the chart below.

GUIDELINES FOR JOB APPLICATION LETTERS	
YOUR ADDRESS	To the right, type your address as you would on an envelope. Be sure to give as your address a place where you can be reached **by letter.** Be sure to give the zip code.
DATE	Put the date below your address.

INSIDE ADDRESS	(1) Direct your letter to a specific person. You can phone a company to find out the name of the personnel director or a department head, if you know what department the job is in. (2) Be accurate. With a misspelled name or the wrong address, your letter may never get to its destination. If it does, inaccuracies make you seem careless.
SALUTATION	Again, be accurate. No one likes to see his or her name misspelled. If you are replying to an ad that gives only a post-office box number (no personal or company names), omit the salutation. Start the opening paragraph right below the inside address.
INTRODUCTORY PARAGRAPH	State your purpose for writing and the source of your information about the job.
BODY PARAGRAPH(S)	Interest the reader in the skills and talents you offer by mentioning whatever personal experience you have that relates to the job. Say that you have enclosed your resume, but do *not* summarize it.
CLOSING PARAGRAPH	Suggest an interview, stating when you are available for one and when you will call to make arrangements.
CLOSING	*Sincerely* is generally appropriate for a job-application letter.
NAME LINES	Type your full name below your signature.
NOTATION	If you are enclosing any other materials with your letter of application, type *Enc.:* and briefly list what you are enclosing.

▉‖ 35c
Understand how to write and format a résumé.

A **résumé** is an easy-to-read, factual document that presents your qualifications for employment. (The résumé that Lee Franco enclosed with her job-application letter is shown on page 667.) All résumés cover certain standard items:

> name, address, phone number; education; past experience; skills and talents; publications, awards, honors, membership in professional organizations; list of references or a statement that they are "available upon request."

A résumé gives you an opportunity to present a positive picture of yourself to a prospective employer. You are expected to give information about your skills, your experience, and your education. Employers understand that college students may have limited experience in the business world. Think of headings that allow you to emphasize your strengths. For example, if you have never done paid work, do not use *Business Experience*. You can use *Work Experience* if you have done volunteer or other unpaid work. If the experience you can offer an employer is that you have run school or social events, you might use *Organizational Experience*. If your greatest strength is your academic record, put your educational attainments first.

You may choose to arrange your résumé with the most important information first and the least important last. Lee Franco's is a good example of an emphatic résumé. Or you may choose to arrange information in chronological (time) order, a sequence that is good for showing a steady work history or solid progress in a particular field. Stephen Schmit's résumé (see page 668) is chronological.

▉‖ 35d
Understand how to write and format a memo.

A **memo** can call for action or document action; it can provide a written record of a conversation; it can make a brief, informal report. A sample memo, its parts labeled, is shown. You can follow it for format guidance. When you are writing a memo, determine who should receive the information by evaluating the audience and deciding the memo's goals. At the **"to" line** list the person or people who need to act on the information in the memo. List for **distribution** anyone else you think should be informed.

Use the **subject line** to define and limit the memo's contents. The subject line should also set the tone for the message, signaling to the reader your attitude toward the subject. A subject line is like an essay title.

In the **message,** give the most important information first. Give additional information or secondary points in decreasing order of importance, but include them only if they are essential to the picture. If you expect action of some kind from the memo, end the memo with a clear statement of your expectations—about the action and about the time the action should take place.

MEMO FORMAT

Date	12 March 19XX
"To" Line	To: Len DeBeers
Sender	From: Ann Soukolov
Subject Line	Subject: Annual Meeting Publications Support
Message	For the annual meeting of our stockholders on April 3 we need the active participation of the following people:

```
                    —speech writer
                    —graphic artist
                    —graphics production specialist
                    —one copy editor
                    —typists and proofreaders
```

We will use the office space on the second floor of the office building next to the auditorium. Word processing equipment should be in place by Monday. Six phones were installed today.

Art Smith, the meeting manager, will be here on Monday for a kick off meeting at 10:00 a.m.

Please prepare a detailed list of critical items for that meeting.

Typist's Notation	AS/ls
Distribution	Dist: A. Adams
	R. Traub
	T. Ziff-Smith

BUSINESS LETTER FORMAT

AlphaOmega Industries, Inc.   Letterhead
123456 Motor Parkway
Fresh Hills, CA 55555

December 28, 19xx   Date

Ron R. London, Sales Director   Inside
Seasonal Products Corp.   address
5000 Seasonal Place
Wiscasset, ME 00012

Subject: Spring Promotional Effort   Subject line

Dear Ron: Salutation

Since we talked last week, I have completed plans for
the Spring promotion of the products that we market
jointly. AlphaOmega and Seasonal Products should
begin a direct mailing of the enclosed brochure
on January 28th.

I have secured several mailing lists that contain the
names of people who have a positive economic profile   Message
for our products. The profile and the outline
of the lists are attached.

Do you have additional approaches for the promotion?
I would like to meet with you on January 6 to discuss
them, and to work out the details of the project.

Please call me and let me know if a meeting next week
at your office accommodates your schedule.

Sincerely,   Closing

Alan Stone   Signature

Alan Stone, Director of Special Promotions   Name, Title

AS/kw   Typist's
                                               notation

Copy to: Ken Lane, V.P. Marketing
Encl.:   Brochure; Mailing Lists;   Other
          Customer Profile   notations

BUSINESS ENVELOPE FORMAT

```
AlphaOmega Industries, Inc.
123456 Motor Parkway
Fresh Hills, CA 55555



          Ron R. London, Sales Director
          Seasonal Products Corp.
          5000 Seasonal Place
          Wiscasset, ME 00012
```

GUIDELINES FOR BUSINESS LETTER AND ENVELOPE

LETTERHEAD	If printed stationery is not available, type the company name and address centered at top of opaque white paper, 8½ × 11″.
DATE	Place the date at left margin under letterhead, when typing in block form as shown in the example. If using paragraph indentations, type date to end at right margin.
INSIDE ADDRESS	Direct the letter to a specific person. Be accurate in spelling the name and in the address. If unsure of your information, call the company and ask questions.
SUBJECT LINE	Type at left margin. Be concise; in a few words inform your reader of the subject.
SALUTATION	Use a first name only if you know the person. Otherwise, use *Mr.* or *Ms.* or whatever title is applicable.
CLOSING	*Sincerely* is generally appropriate unless you know the person very well and wish to use *Cordially*. Leave about four lines for your signature.
NAME LINES	Type your name and title. The title can be on the same line as your name or on the next line.
ENVELOPE	Use block form. If printed envelope is not available, type the company name and return address in the upper left corner of a 9½ × 4″ envelope. In the center of envelope, type the name and address of the person to receive your letter.

JOB-APPLICATION LETTER

422 Broward
University of Texas at Arlington
Arlington, Texas 75016
May 15, 19XX

Rae Clemens, Director of Human Resources
Taleno, Ward Marketing, Inc.
1471 Summit Boulevard
Houston, Texas 78211

Dear Ms. Clemens:

I am answering the advertisement for a marketing trainee
that Taleno, Ward placed in today's <u>Houston Chronicle</u>.

Marketing has been one of the emphases of my course work
here at the University of Texas, Arlington, as you will
see on my enclosed résumé. This past year, I gained some
practical experience as well, when I developed marketing
techniques that helped to turn my typing service into a
busy and profitable small business.

Successfully marketing the typing service (with flyers,
advertisements in college publications, and even a two-
for-one promotion) makes me a very enthusiastic novice. I
can think of no better way to become a professional than
working for Taleno, Ward.

I will be here at the Arlington campus through August 1.
You can reach me by phone at 555-1976. Unless I hear from
you before, I'll call on May 25 about setting up an
interview.

Sincerely,

Lee Franco

Lee Franco

Enc.: Résumé

EMPHATIC RÉSUMÉ

```
                                          MARKETING TRAINEE

                    Lee Franco
                    422 Broward
          University of Texas at Arlington
              Arlington, Texas 75016


                   713:555-1976

The experience I acquired marketing my typing service
provided me with a good practical background for a
position as a marketing trainee.

MARKETING EXPERIENCE (program for campus typing service)
     Evaluated typing-service capabilities; analyzed market
     for service; drew up and implemented marketing plan;
     produced 2-color flyer, designed print ads and wrote
     copy, developed and ran special promotion. August 19XX
     to February 19XX

BUSINESS EXPERIENCE
     Type-Right Typing Service: Ran campus typing service
     for two years. Duties included word processing
     (Wordstar, Displaywrite, SuperCalc), proofreading,
     billing and other financial record-keeping, and
     customer contact. August 19XX to present

     Archer & Archer Advertising: Worked as general
     assistant in the copy department under direct
     supervision of John Allen, Director. Duties included
     proofreading, filing, direct client contact. June 19XX
     to August 19XX

ADDITIONAL EXPERIENCE
     Coordinated student-employment service at Hawthorne
     High School, Baton Rouge, Louisiana. Duties included
     contacting students to fill jobs with local employers,
     arranging interviews, and writing follow-up reports on
     placements.

EDUCATION
     University of Texas, Arlington
     B.A. May 19XX, Psychology, Marketing

EXTRACURRICULAR
     Marketing Club, Computer Graphics Society

References available upon request.
```

CHRONOLOGICAL RÉSUMÉ

STEPHEN L. SCHMIT
5230 ST. STEPHENS STREET
BOSTON, MASSACHUSETTS 02188
617–555–8165

CAREER QUALIFICATIONS
Technical writer trained in preparation of technical definitions and descriptions, manuals, catalogues, part lists, and instructional materials. Experienced in evaluating and editing computer documentation containing syntax formats.

WORK EXPERIENCE
Northeastern University, Boston, Massachusetts
Reading and Writing Specialist, English Language Ctr.
March–July 1987, January–March 1988

Created individual lesson plans for each student assigned to the Reading and Writing Laboratory. Designed materials for use in the Laboratory. Ran the Laboratory for approximately one hundred students for twenty hours each week, maintained records of students' work, and prepared written and oral reports on student progress and the operation of the Laboratory.

Tutor of Foreign Students, September 1985–Present

Integrated foreign students into a large urban school and community while being a positive role model educationally and socially.

William M. Mercer, Incorporated Boston, Massachusetts, September–December 1984

Data Processing and general office duties. Initiated and implemented a CRT search system for office personnel.

American Architect Magazine, New York, N.Y., 1981–1984
Student intern.

SPECIAL SKILLS
BASIC programming. PASCAL, Editing and Graphics courses to be completed June 1988.

EDUCATION
Northeastern University, Boston, Massachusetts
Bachelor of Arts, June 1986

Concentration: English with minors in Technical Communications and Economics.
Activities: Selected to serve on the Residence Judicial Board, an impartial group of faculty, staff and students who adjudicate discipline problems; Northeastern News; Northeastern Yearbook staff.

APPENDIX A
WRITING
ESSAY
TESTS

Writing answers for essay tests is one of the most important writing tasks in college. Essay tests give you the chance to synthesize and apply your knowledge, thereby helping your instructor determine what you have learned.

Common in the social sciences and humanities, essay tests are becoming increasingly common in the natural sciences as well. Essay tests demand that you recall information and also put assorted pieces of that information into contexts that lead to generalizations you can support. For example, from your reading and lecture notes, you may know many facts about the battles in the Korean War, but the facts become significant when you use them to show one side's superior military strength, or a general's brilliant tactics, or a pattern of defeats from seemingly inconsequential misjudgments.

Most essay questions contain what is sometimes called a **cue word,** a word of direction that tells what the content of your answer is expected to emphasize. Knowing the major cue words and their meanings can increase your ability to plan efficiently and to write effectively. Be guided by the following list of cue words and sample essay-test questions.

669

CUE WORDS FOUND IN QUESTIONS FOR ESSAY TESTS

Analyze means to separate something into parts and discuss the parts.

> Analyze Socrates's discussion of "good life" and "good death."

Clarify means to make clear.

> Clarify T. S. Eliot's idea of tradition.

Classify means to arrange into groups on the basis of shared characteristics.

> Classify the different types of antipredator adaptations.

Compare and contrast means to show similarities and differences.

> Compare and contrast the reproductive cycles of a moss and a flowering plant.

Criticize means to give your opinion concerning the strengths and weaknesses of something.

> Criticize the architectural function of the modern football stadium.

Define means to give the definition of something and in so doing to separate it from similar things.

> Define the term "yellow press."

Describe means to explain features to make clear an object, procedure, or event.

> Describe the chain of events that constitutes the movement of a sensory impulse along a nerve fiber.

Discuss means to consider and evaluate as many details as possible concerning an issue or event.

> Discuss the effects of television viewing on modern attitudes toward violence.

Evaluate means to give your opinion about the value of something.

> Evaluate Margaret Mead's contribution to the field of anthropology.

Explain means to give reasons for something.

> Explain how the amount of carbon dioxide in the blood regulates rates of heartbeat and breathing.

Illustrate means to give examples of something.

> Illustrate the use of symbolism in Richard Wright's novel *Native Son*.

Interpret means to explain the meaning of something.

> Give your interpretation of Robert Frost's poem "Fire and Ice."

Justify means to show or prove that something is valid or correct.

> Justify the existence of labor unions in today's economy.

Prove means to present evidence that cannot be refuted logically or with other evidence.

> Prove that smoking is a major cause of lung cancer.

Relate means to show the connections between two or more things.

> Relate increases in specific crimes in 1932-33 to the prevailing economic conditions.

Review means to reexamine, summarize, or reprise something.

> Review the structural arrangements in proteins to explain the meaning of the term *polypeptide*.

Show means to point out or demonstrate something.

> Show what effects the second law of thermodynamics predicts for Halley's comet.

Summarize means to repeat briefly the major points of something.

> Summarize the major benefits of compulsory education.

Support means to argue in favor of something.

> Support the position that passage of the equal rights amendment must occur at the national rather than the state level.

Each essay question also has one or more **key words** that tell you the information, topics, and ideas you are to write about. For example, in the question "Criticize the architectural function of the modern football stadium," the key words are "architectural function" and "football stadium." To answer the question successfully, you must define "architectural function," then describe the typical modern football stadium (mentioning major variations when important), and then you must discuss how well the typical football stadium meets the principles you named in your definition of "architectural function." Similarly, in the question, "Classify the different types of antipredator adaptations" you need to define "antipredator adaptations" by dividing them into groups based on their shared characteristics.

Here are two answers to the question, "Classify the different types of antipredator adaptations." The first one is successful; the second is not. The sentences are numbered for your reference.

ANSWER 1

(1) Although many antipredator adaptations have evolved in the animal kingdom, they all can be classified into four major categories according to the prey's response to the predator. (2) The first category is hiding techniques. (3) These techniques include cryptic coloration and behavior in which the prey assumes characteristics of an inanimate object or part of a plant. (4) The second category is early enemy detection. (5) The prey responds to alarm signals from like prey or other kinds of prey before the enemy can get too close. (6) Evasion of the pursuing predator is the third category. (7) Prey that move erratically or in a compact group are displaying this technique. (8) The fourth category is active repulsion of the predator. (9) The prey kills, injures, or sickens the predator, establishing that it represents danger to the predator.

ANSWER 2

(1) Antipredator adaptations are the development of the capabilities to reduce the risk of attack from a predator without too much change in the life-supporting activities of the prey. (2) There are many different types of antipredator adaptations. (3) One type is camouflage, hiding from the predator by cryptic coloration or imitation of plant parts. (4) An example of this type of antipredator adaptation is the praying mantis. (5) A second type is the defense used by monarch butterflies, a chemical protection that makes some birds ill after eating the butterfly. (6) This protection may injure the bird by causing it to vomit, and it can educate the bird against eating other butterflies. (7) Detection and evasion are also antipredator adaptations.

Here is an explanation of what happens, sentence by sentence, in the two responses.

	ANSWER 1	**ANSWER 2**
Sentence 1	Sets up classification system and gives number of categories based on key word	Defines key word
Sentence 2	Names first category	Throwaway sentence—accomplishes nothing
Sentence 3	Defines first category	Names and defines first category
Sentence 4	Names second category	Gives an example for first category
Sentence 5	Defines second category	Gives an example for second (unnamed) category
Sentence 6	Names third category	Continues to explain example
Sentence 7	Defines third category	Names two categories
Sentence 8	Names fourth category	
Sentence 9	Defines fourth category	

Answer 1 sets about immediately answering the question by introducing a classification system as called for by the cue word, *classify.* Answer 2, on the other hand, defines the key word, a waste of time on a test that will be read by an audience of specialists. Answer 1 is tightly organized, easy to follow, and to-the-point, whereas answer 2 rambles, never manages to name the four categories, and says more around the subject than on it.

Remember that your purpose in answering essay exam questions is to show your instructor what you know in a clear, direct, and well-organized way. Most essay tests have a time limit, so you will do well to use well-developed strategies. Try to follow this plan:

STRATEGIES FOR WRITING ESSAY TESTS

1. Do not start writing immediately.
2. If the test has more than one question, read them all at the start. If you know from the beginning what you will have to answer, you will know what to expect and you will have a better sense of how to budget your time by either dividing it equally or allotting more for some questions. If you have a choice, select questions about which you know the most—and the ones whose cue words you can work with best.
3. Reread each question you are going to answer and then underline the cue and key words to determine exactly what the question asks for.
4. Use the writing process as much as possible within the constraints of the time limit. Try always to find time to plan and revise. For a one-hour test of one question, take about 10 minutes to jot down preliminary ideas about content and organization, and save at least 10 minutes to reread your answer and to revise and edit it. For a one-hour test with more than one question, divide your time for planning, drafting, and revising accordingly. If you suddenly become pressed for time— but try to avoid this—consider skipping a question you cannot answer well or a question that counts less on your total score.
5. Organize and develop your answer to provide what a question's cue and key words ask for.

The more you use these strategies, the better you will be able to use them to your advantage. Try to practice them, making up questions that might be on your test and timing yourself as you write the answers. Doing this offers you another benefit: if you study by anticipating possible questions and writing out the answers, you will be very well prepared if one or two of them show up on the test.

APPENDIX B
USING
CORRECT
MANUSCRIPT
FORMAT

▪‖ B1

Follow standard practices for typing or handwriting marks of punctuation.

PERIOD, QUESTION MARK, EXCLAMATION POINT   **. ? !**   **. ? !**
Do not space before these marks. Space twice after each mark when it ends a sentence.

```
I do.  Do you?  You do!  I know you do.
```

In typing initials used in personal names, leave one space after each period.

```
B. A. Jones
W. E. B. Du Bois
```

Practice varies both for the use of periods and for spacing after periods in other abbreviations. An up-to-date dictionary can guide you.

COMMA, SEMICOLON, COLON   , ; :   , ; :

Do not space before these marks. Space once after them in sentences. (See 26b for cases where the colon separates numbers with no space before or after.)

```
Usually, I call first; however, I failed to do so today.   My
reason is this: I saw you peeking through the curtains.
```

APOSTROPHE   '   '

Do not space before or after an apostrophe within a word.

```
Isn't that Ken's car?
```

Space once after a final apostrophe followed by another word.

```
He must be using the Clarks' garage.
```

When an apostrophe ends the word that ends a sentence, do not leave a space between the apostrophe and the final period, question mark, or exclamation point. Put the apostrophe before the final mark of punctuation.

```
Those cars in the driveway are the Clarks'.
```

QUOTATION MARKS   " "   ' '   " "   ' '

Do not space between quotation marks and whatever they enclose. Do not space between double and single quotation marks.

```
I said, " 'Here Comes the Sun' makes me smile whenever I hear
it."
```

Space once after a closing quotation mark unless it ends a sentence. In that case, space twice.

```
He said "plaster."  I heard "blister," but I guess I was wrong.
```

HYPHEN   -   -

Do not space before or after a hyphen except to use one space after a "suspended" hyphen—that is, a hyphen showing that two prefixes or suffixes refer to one root word.

```
Many athletes trade the agony of defeat for pre- and post-game
shows.
```

When a hyphen occurs at the end of a line, always make it the last mark on the line. Do not carry the hyphen over to start a new line.

Dash − −   ▬

In typed manuscripts, make a dash by striking the hyphen key twice, with no space between. In handwritten manuscripts, make a dash with a single line a little longer than a hyphen. Do not space before or after a dash.

```
All of us--all of us!--think sentimentally about adolescence.
```

Slash /   /

Do not space before or after a slash except when you use the slash to separate no more than three lines of quoted poetry.

```
and/or     1/16
```

When separating lines of poetry, space once before and once after the slash.

```
Consider these lines from Shakespeare's "Sonnet 30": "When to
the sessions of sweet silent thought / I summon up remembrance
of things past."
```

Brackets, Parentheses [ ] ( )   [ ] ( )

Do not space between brackets or parentheses and whatever they enclose.

```
The letter continued, "Parrish was borne [sic] June 30, 1830. At
least that's what Ada Jencks (my great grandmother) wrote."
```

Ellipses . . .   . . .

Use three evenly spaced dots for an ellipsis. Use one space before, between, and after the dots.

```
"Turning away . . . they began to laugh."
```

Use four dots to indicate the omission of one or more sentences. Because the first dot is the period at the end of the sentence, leave no space before it. After the first dot, use three evenly spaced dots.

```
"The shopper felt crowded. . . . Moving away was natural."
```

See 29d for information about using other punctuation with ellipses.

Underlining (Italics)
When you underline more than one word, you may use either style shown here—with or without breaks between words. Whichever style you choose, use it consistently throughout a paper.

```
Zen and the Art of Motorcycle Maintenance
Zen and the Art of Motorcycle Maintenance
```

▌▌ B2
Follow standard practices when you prepare the final copy of a paper.

The appearance of a paper sends important messages to your instructor. Although no paper will earn an *A* only because it looks exceptionally neat and shows your attention to the conventions of manuscript format, a first-rate appearance suggests to the instructor that you took the assignment seriously and that you value what you have written.

Appearance
Paper: For typed papers, use 8-1/2 × 11-inch white, standard typing paper. Do not use onionskin or erasable paper: onionskin is for copies only, and erasable paper smudges easily and resists handwritten corrections. Type on only one side of each sheet of paper.

If your instructor accepts handwritten papers, use ruled 8-1/2 × 11-inch standard white, lined paper. Do not use colored paper or paper torn from a spiral-bound notebook. Write on only one side of each sheet of paper. Write on every other line, so that you will have space to make neat corrections and so that your instructor will have space to make comments.

Ink: Use a black typewriter ribbon, and keep the typewriter keys clean so that the letters will be clear, not blurred.

For handwritten papers, use dark blue or black ink, not red, green, brown, or other colors. Do not use pencil.

Computer printouts: If a printer has both capital and lowercase letters and produces an easy-to-read type, most instructors accept papers prepared on word processors. Ask first, however. When you submit the paper, tear off the hole-punched edges and separate the pages.

First page: In this appendix you will find reproduced a paper's first page with the endorsement (name, date, course, and other information your instructor may specify) in MLA-recommended spacing; a later page with name and page number at the top and a long prose quotation; and the first page of a Works Cited list. Note the 5-character indent for paragraphs and for second and subsequent lines of Works Cited entries.

Formats for long quotations: Set off a prose quotation of four or more lines by starting the quotation on a new line. Indent this first line and all other lines of the quotation ten spaces from the left. See the examples in this appendix, in 28a, and in 33.

When you quote more than three lines of poetry, set the quotation off from your own words. Start a new line and lay the quoted poetry out so that it looks as much as possible like the printed version you are quoting from. If indenting ten spaces from the left causes you to have to break lines, you can indent less than ten spaces or not at all.

```
O Captain! my Captain! our fearful trip is done,
The ship has weather'd every rack, the prize we sought is won,
The port is near, the bells I hear, the people all exulting,
While follow eyes the steady keel, the vessel grim and daring;
     But O heart! heart! heart!
       O the bleeding drops of red,
          Where on the deck my Captain lies,
            Fallen cold and dead.
```

You will find other examples in 33 and 34b-3.

WHERE TO FIND DOCUMENTATION FORMATS

Parenthetical MLA documentation	32g, 32k
Footnotes or endnotes	34b-4
APA documentation	34c-4
CBE (natural sciences) documentation	34d-4

■|| B3

Make careful handwritten corrections and insertions in typed papers.

Your typewriter may lack special characters, such as accent marks. If you need them, you will have to handwrite them. You can also make a few handwritten corrections in a paper you intend to hand in (see list below). But if you have more than three handwritten corrections on a page, you should retype the page.

Draw one line through words you want to take out.

These ~~extra words~~ are deleted.

To insert words, make a caret ($\wedge$) where the missing words should be, and then write them in above the caret.

A caret shows *where words* should be inserted.

To transpose letters, use a mark like this:

squiggle

You can transpose words in a similar way:

Transpose in the words wrong order.

You can indicate the start of a new paragraph like this:

Molly's actions primarily met her needs. ¶ Overall, Molly exemplifies the behavior of one type of typical toddler.

You can close up space between letters this way:

Avoid in correct spacing.

You can open space between letters this way:

Leave one space between words in a sentence.

You can drop a letter and close up the remaining letters this way:

Some spellers have trouble with double letters.

FIRST PAGE WITHOUT COVER PAGE

Amy W. Brown	**Name**
Professor Wellington	**Instructor**
English 101, Section A1	**Course, Section**
10 December 19xx	**Date submitted**

} **Quadruple space**

Personal Space: } **Double space**

An Intercultural Perspective

} **Quadruple space**

When she returned home after a year in South America, Judith Martin, a North American writer, began to have a problem. People kept interpreting her behavior as flirtatious, but she was not flirting. Fairly soon she figured

Brown 7

personal space. Clearly, what is considered obnoxious in one culture might be considered polite in another (Fisher, Bell, and Baum 167). As Hall explains, virtually everything people are and do

> is associated with the experience of space. . . .

10 space indent for displayed quotation

> Therefore, people from different cultures, when interpreting each other's behavior, often misinterpret the relationship, the activity, or the emotions. This leads to alienation in encounters or distorted communications.
>
> (Hidden 171)

In the next few years, more studies will be undertaken to uncover information about cultural differences in matters

↕ ½″

**Indent 5 spaces after
first line of entry**

Works Cited

**Double space
throughout**

Davis, Martha, and Janet Skupien, eds. <u>Body Movement and</u>

    <u>Nonverbal Communication: An Annotated Bibliography</u>

    <u>1971–1981</u>. Bloomington, IN: Indiana UP, 1982.

Fast, Julius. <u>Body Language</u>. New York: Evans, 1970.

Fisher, Jeffrey D., Paul A. Bell, and Andrew Baum.

    <u>Environmental Psychology</u>. 2nd ed. New York:

    Holt, 1984.

Hall, Edward T. <u>The Hidden Dimension</u>. New York:

    Doubleday, 1966.

———. Interview. "Learning the Arabs' Silent Language."

    With Kenneth Friedman. <u>Psychology Today</u> Aug. 1979:

    44–54.

Henley, Nancy M. <u>Body Politics: Power, Sex, and Nonverbal</u>

    <u>Communication</u>. Englewood Cliffs: Prentice, 1977.

USAGE
GLOSSARY

A **glossary** is a list of words or phrases singled out for special attention. This glossary relates to **usage,** the customary manner of using particular words or phrases.

The term "customary manner" refers to usage by educated people, as demonstrated especially in books, newspapers, and speeches. "Customary manner," however, is not as firm in practice as the term implies. Indeed, little demonstrates as dramatically as does a usage glossary that standards for language use change. Some words slip away from usage: for example, *thee* and *thou* are no longer used in everyday life. Some constructions considered nonstandard a decade ago are accepted as standard today; for example, *shall* used to be required for the first-person future *(I **shall** finish the work tomorrow),* but today most dictionaries and usage surveys report that *shall* and *will* can be used interchangeably in such constructions.

This Usage Glossary, which contains over 200 entries in alphabetical order, reflects customary practice for academic writing—as of the date this handbook was published. If you think that any information reported here might have changed, consult one of the dictionaries discussed in Chapter 20 with a publication (or revision) date later than this handbook's. The entries in this Usage Glossary cover matters of usage as well as many frequently confused homonyms and commonly confused words. Additional homonyms and commonly confused words appear in Chapter 22.

You will find this glossary easier to use if you understand two terms used frequently in the discussion: *Informal* indicates that the word or phrase occurs commonly in speech but should be avoided in academic writing. *Nonstandard* indicates that the word or phrase is unacceptable for standard spoken English and for writing.

This glossary can help you in at least two ways: (1) You can browse through it to become familiar with the words and phrases that are subject to usage constraints in academic writing. (2) You can consult it as a reference when you are editing your writing to make sure that you are using the words or phrases correctly.

As in the rest of this book, words marked here with a degree symbol (°) are defined in the Glossary of Grammatical and Selected Composition Terms.

a, an Use *a* before words beginning with consonant sounds: *a dog, a grade, a harbor.* Also, use *a* before words beginning with vowels that sound like consonants: *a unit, a one-page paper, a European.* Use *an* before words beginning with vowel sounds or a silent *h: an apple, an onion, an hour.*

accept, except To *accept* means "to agree to" or "to receive." To *except* (verb°) means "to exclude or leave out"; *except* (preposition°) means "leaving out."

Except [preposition] for one or two details, the striking workers were ready to **accept** management's offer. The workers wanted the no-smoking rule **excepted** from the contract.

advice, advise *Advice* (noun°) means "recommendation"; to *advise* (verb°) means "to give a recommendation".

I **advise** you to follow your doctor's **advice.**

affect, effect To *affect* means "to influence" or "to arouse the emotions"; to *effect* means "to bring about"; *effect* (noun°) means "result or conclusion."

One **effect** of the weather is that it **affects** some people's moods. We **effected** some changes in our system for weather forecasting.

aggravate, irritate *Aggravate* is used colloquially to mean *irritate.* Use precisely: to *aggravate* means "to intensify or make worse"; to *irritate* means "to annoy or make impatient".

The executive was **irritated** by her assistant's carelessness, for it further **aggravated** the company's financial problems.

ain't is a nonstandard contraction for *am not, is not, are not, has not,* and *have not.*

all ready, already *Already* means "before or by this time"; *all ready* means "completely prepared."

The athletes were **all ready;** the warmup had **already** begun.

all right is two words, never one (not *alright*).

all together, altogether *All together* means "in a group, in unison"; *altogether* means "entirely or thoroughly."

The sopranos, altos, and tenors were supposed to sing **all together,** but the outcome was not **altogether** successful.

allude, elude To *allude* means "to refer to indirectly or casually"; to *elude* means "to escape notice of."

The researchers **alluded** to budget cuts when they discussed why the identification of the virus had **eluded** them.

684

allusion, illusion An *allusion* is an indirect or casual reference; an *illusion* is a false impression or idea.

> The candidate wanted to create the **illusion** that he was sympathetic to the poor, so he made a snide *allusion* to his rival's wealth.

a lot (two words, not *alot*) is informal for *a great deal* or *a great many* and should be avoided in academic writing.

a.m., p.m. (or A.M., P.M.) are used only with numbers, not as substitutes for the words *morning, afternoon,* or *evening.*

> Our class, which usually meets early in the **morning** [not *a.m.*], will meet at 7:10 **p.m.** tomorrow.

among, between Use *among* for three or more people or things; use *between* for two people or things.

> The problem was discussed **among** the three students. They had to choose **between** staying in school and getting full-time jobs.

amount, number Use *amount* for concepts or things that are collective rather than separate (wealth, work, happiness); use *number* for anything that can be counted (coins, jobs, joys).

> A large **number** of people had to do a great **amount** of work.

an, and *An* is an article° (see *a, an*) and should not be confused with *and,* which is a conjunction°.

> They saw **an** eagle **and** its chicks in the nest.

and/or occurs in business or legal writing when either one or both of the items it connects can apply.

anybody, any body *Anybody* is any person not specified; *any body* is a specific person, object, or group.

> The purity of **any body** of water can be tested by **anybody** with the correct materials.

anyone, any one. See *anybody, any body.*

anyplace is informal for *any place* or *anywhere.* Avoid it in academic writing.

anyways, anywheres are nonstandard for *anyway, anywhere.*

apt, likely, liable See *likely, apt, liable.*

as, like, as if
1. Use *like,* not *as,* in a comparison when resemblance but not equivalence is suggested.

> Mexico, **like** [not *as*] Argentina, is a Spanish-speaking country.

2. Use *as,* not *like,* in a comparison when equivalence is suggested—that is, when the subject equals the description.

> John served **as** [not *like*] the chef at our barbecue. [John = the chef]

3. *As* functions as a subordinating conjunction° or a preposition°, depending on the meaning of the sentence. *Like* functions only as a preposition. To start a clause°, *as* is required.

> That hamburger tastes good, **as** [not *like*] a hamburger should. [subordinating conjunction]
>
> That hamburger tastes **like** chopped leather. [preposition]

685

4. Use *as if,* not *like,* with the subjunctive mood.°
 This hamburger tastes **as if** [not *like*] it has been grilled for an hour.

assure, ensure, insure To *assure* means "to promise or convince"; to *ensure* or to *insure* means "to make certain." *Insure* is reserved for financial or legal certainty, especially related to insurance.
 The insurance agent **assured** me that I could **insure** my life, but he explained that no one could **ensure** that I would have a long life.

as to should be avoided as a substitute for *about.*
 The pilot was unsure **about** [not *as to*] the airplane's safety.

awful, awfully *Awful* (adjective°) means "causing fear" or "inspiring awe"; it should not be used as a substitute for intensifiers such as *very* or *extremely.* *Awfully* (adverb°) is informal for *very* or *extremely* and should be avoided in academic writing.
 The cyclone was an **awful** phenomenon to watch. It caused serious [not *awful*] damage. It came **very** [not *awfully*] close to our house.

a while, awhile *A while* is an article° and a noun°; it functions as a subject° or object°. *Awhile* is an adverb°; it modifies verbs°. In a prepositional phrase°, the correct form is *a while: for* **a while,** *in* **a while,** *after* **a while.**
 We waited **awhile** for our friends to arrive, but after **a while** we had to leave.

bad, badly *Bad* is an adjective° (*bad* feelings); it is used after linking verbs° such as *feel* or *felt* (*He felt* **bad**). *Badly* is an adverb° and is nonstandard after linking verbs. For more information, see 12d.
 The farmers felt **bad** [not *badly*]. [*Felt* in this example is a linking verb.]
 The **bad** drought had **badly** damaged the crops.

been, being *Been* is the past participle° of *to be; being* is the progressive form° of *to be.*
 Alcohol abuse has **been** [not *being*] on the rise recently. We see lives **being** [not *been*] ruined by drinking.

being as, being that are nonstandard for *because* or *since.*
 Because [not *being as* or *being that*] the catcher injured his arm, he had to leave the game.

beside, besides *Beside* (preposition°) means "next to or by the side of "; *besides* (when functioning as a preposition) means "other than or in addition to"; *besides* (when functioning as an adverb°) means "also or moreover."
 With keys in her hand, she stood **beside** the new car. No one **besides** her had a driver's license. **Besides,** she owned the car.

better, had better Used in place of *had better, better* is informal. Avoid it in academic writing.
 We **had better** [not *we better*] be careful.

between, among See *among, between.*

breath, breathe *Breath* is a noun°; *breathe* is a verb°.
 The jogger had to rest and **breathe** rapidly before he could catch his **breath.**

bring, take Use *bring* for movement from a distant place to a near place; use *take* for any other movement.

The coach will **bring** her team to our college, and then she will **take** the team on a tour of the campus.

broke is nonstandard for past participle° *broken*. Avoid it in academic writing, except as the past tense°.

The jogger's ankle was **broken** [not *broke*]. He **broke** it yesterday.

burst, bust To *burst* means "to break apart suddenly and violently"; its principal parts are *burst, burst, burst,* (not *bursted*). To *bust* is slang for to *burst* and should be avoided in academic writing.

The bubble **burst** [not *busted* or *bursted.*]

but, however, yet Use *but, however,* and *yet* alone, not in combination with each other.

The economy is strong, **but** [not *but yet* or *but however*] unemployment is still high.

but that, but what are nonstandard for *that.* Avoid them in academic writing.

The supervisor does not doubt **that** [not *but that* or *but what*] the job can be done.

calculate, figure, reckon are informal for *imagine* or *expect.* Avoid such informal uses in academic writing.

The farmers **expect** [not *figure* or *reckon*] that they will have a good crop.

can, may *Can* indicates ability or capacity; *may* requests or grants permission. In the negative, however, *can* is acceptable in place of *may.*

May I leave the room so that I **can** have a cigarette?

Why **can't** I?

can't hardly, can't scarcely are double negatives and are nonstandard; use *hardly* and *scarcely* only. For more information, see 12c.

They can **hardly** [not *can't hardly* or *can't scarcely*] see through the fog.

censor, censure To *censor* means "to judge" or "to delete objectional material"; to *censure* means "to condemn or officially reprimand."

The town council **censured** the mayor for permitting a citizen's committee to **censor** books in the public library.

chairman, chairperson, chair Usage is changing concerning *chairman,* which has a masculine implication. The gender-free terms *chairperson* and *chair* often are preferred, although *chair* seems to be more widely used at this time.

choose, chose *Choose* is the simple form of *to choose; chose* is the past tense of *to choose.*

Today I will **choose** the college I will attend. Yesterday she **chose** the college she will attend.

cloth, clothe *Cloth* (noun°) means "fabric"; to *clothe* (verb°) means "to dress" or "to cover with garments."

The king wanted to **clothe** himself with garments made of fine **cloth.**

complement, compliment To *complement* means "to complete" or "to supplement"; to *compliment* means "to express praise or flattery."
The instructor **complimented** the student for her research project, saying that it **complemented** work done twenty years before.

conscience, conscious *Conscience* (noun°) means "a sense of right or wrong"; *conscious* (adjective°) means "being aware or awake."
The thief was **conscious** that his **conscience** was bothering him.

consensus of opinion is a redundant phrase. Use *consensus* only.

continual, continuous *Continual* is occurring repeatedly; *continuous* is going on without interruption in space or time.
Although all essential systems of the spacecraft were expected to operate **continuously,** the astronauts **continually** checked their instrument panels.
The washing machine **continually** breaks down, and then it makes a **continuous** humming sound.

couple, couple of are nonstandard for *a few* or *several.*
You should rest for **a few** [not *a couple* or *a couple of*] minutes before you begin again.

data is the plural of *datum,* a rarely used word. Informal usage now treats *data* as singular, but it should be treated as plural in academic writing.
These [not *this*] **data show** [not *shows*] that the virus is spreading.

different from, different than *From* is the preferred preposition after *different,* although *than* is commonly used in speech.
Football is **different from** [not *different than*] soccer.

disinterested, uninterested *Disinterested* means "impartial"; *uninterested* means "indifferent or not concerned with."
They were **uninterested** in hearing my side of the story, so we agreed to ask a **disinterested** person to settle our dispute.

done is a past participle°; it cannot substitute for the past tense *did.*
The farmers raised [not *done* raised] a fine crop. They **did** [not *done*] a good job.

don't is a contraction for *do not,* not for *does not (doesn't).*
She **doesn't** [not *don't*] like loud music.

due to is informal as a preposition° meaning "because of." *Due to* is always acceptable after a form of *to be.*
He was late **because of** [not *due to*] an accident. [There is no noun for *due to* to modify.] His lateness was **due to** an accident. [*Due to* modifies *lateness.*]

emigrate from, immigrate to See *immigrate to, emigrate from.*

ensure, assure, insure See *assure, ensure, insure.*

enthused as an adjective° is nonstandard for *enthusiastic.*
The student was **enthusiastic** [not *enthused*] about going to college.

especially, specially *Especially* and *specially* are not interchangeable. *Especially* means "mainly or particularly"; *specially* is for a special purpose.

Because the quarterback was **especially** tired, he could not attend the **specially** organized party celebrating his team's victory.

etc. is the abbreviation for the Latin *et cetera,* meaning *and the rest.* Do not use it in academic writing; acceptable substitutes are *and the like, and so on,* or *and so forth.*

everyday, every day *Everyday* is an adjective°; it means "daily" and modifies nouns. *Every day* is an adjective-noun combination that functions as a subject° or object°.

I missed the bus **every day** last week. Arriving at work late has become an **everyday** occurrence.

everywheres is nonstandard for *everywhere.*

except, accept See *accept, except.*

explicit, implicit *Explicit* means "directly stated or expressed;" *implicit* means "implied or suggested."

The warning on cigarette packs is **explicit:** Smoking may be dangerous to your health. The warning's **implicit** message is that people should not smoke.

farther, further are used interchangeably, although many writers prefer to use *farther* for geographical distances and *further* for all other cases.

fewer, less Use *fewer* for anything that can be counted (**fewer** *dollars,* **fewer** *jobs,* **fewer** *joys*); use *less* for concepts or things thought of collectively, not separately (**less** *money,* **less** *work,* **less** *happiness*).

figure, calculate, reckon See *calculate, figure, reckon.*

fine, find *Fine* is an adjective° *(She bought a **fine** electric drill);* it is nonstandard for *well* or any other adverb° (not *The new electric drill worked* **fine**). *Find* is the simple form of the verb *to find (We **find** the defendant "not guilty").*

former, latter When two ideas or things are referred to, *former* refers to the first of the two, and *latter* refers to the second of the two. When more than two ideas or things are referred to, do not use these words.

Brazil and Ecuador are two Latin American countries. The **former** is Portuguese-speaking, the **latter** Spanish-speaking.

gender, sex *Gender* is attributed to words, *sex* to people and animals.

Today, many writers prefer to use **gender-free** not [*sex-free*] language, like *chair* instead of *chairman.*

given, giving *Given* is the past participle° of *to give; giving* is the progressive° form.

A reward was **given** to a citizen for **giving** the police valuable help in preventing a robbery.

goes, says *Goes* is nonstandard for *says.*

He **says** [not *goes*] we will have a test tomorrow .

gone, went *Gone* is the past participle° of *to go; went* is the past tense° of *to go.*

They **went** [not *gone*] to the concert after their friends **had gone** [not *had went*] home.

689

good and is nonstandard for *very.*
>He was **very** [not *good and*] sorry.

good, well *Good* is an adjective° (*good idea*); it is nonstandard as an adverb; *well* is an adverb° (*run* **well**). For more information, 12d.
>The **good** writer spoke **well.**

got, have *Got* is the past tense° of *to get (He* **got** *an A)* and is also one of the past participles° of *to get (She has* **got**—or **gotten**—*excellent grades). Got* is nonstandard in place of *have; got to* is nonstandard as a substitute for an intensifier such as *must.*
>What do we **have** [not *got*] for dinner?
>You **must** [not *got to*] help me.

great is an informal adjective meaning "good," "wonderful," "skillful," or "clever." Reserve it for its precise meaning: "a high degree of," "eminent," "large," "grand."
>No She has a **great** personality.
>Yes Einstein was a **great** scientist.
>Yes Her work gave her **great** satisfaction.

had best, had better are nonstandard for *ought* or *should.*
>She **ought** to [not *had best* or *had better*] call home.

had ought, hadn't ought are nonstandard for *ought* and *ought not.*
>He **ought** [not *had ought*] to call home.

hanged, hung Use *hanged* only to refer to executions *(The prisoner was* **hanged** *this morning).* Use *hung* for all other meanings.

have, got See *got, have.*

have, of *Have,* not *of,* should be used after such verbs as *could, may, might, must, should.*
>They *could* **have** [not *of*] telephoned. They *may* **have** [not *of*] tried to call.

he, she, he or she Using *he* to refer to both males and females is avoided by many people today. Many writers use *he or she* or, if it's at all possible for the meaning of the sentence, they switch to plural nouns and pronouns. For more information, see 21a-3.
>If **they** want [not *he* wants] to avoid accidents, **drivers** [not a driver] should drive defensively.

himself, herself See *myself, yourself, himself, herself.*

hisself is nonstandard for *himself.*

hopefully means "with hope"; it is nonstandard if used to mean "it is hoped that."
>No **Hopefully,** the plane will land safely.
>Yes They waited **hopefully** for her safe return.

however, yet, but See *but, however, yet.*

hung, hanged See *hanged, hung.*

if, whether *If* is a subordinating conjunction°. *Whether* occurs in three situations: (1) in an indirect question *(She asked* **whether** *I had heard from the hikers),* (2) to express doubt *(She was not sure* **whether** *they would be safe* *in the storm),* and (3) to express alternatives with or without *or not (I did not know* **whether** [or *whether or not*] *to search for them).*

illusion, allusion See *allusion, illusion.*

immigrate to, emigrate from To *immigrate to* means "to enter a new country to live there"; to *emigrate from* means "to leave one country to live in another."

> After the ballet star **emigrated from** Russia, he **immigrated to** the United States to start a new life.

implicit, explicit See *explicit, implicit.*

imply, infer To *imply* means "to hint or suggest without stating outright"; to *infer* means "to draw a conclusion from what has been written or said." Speakers and writers *imply;* listeners and readers *infer.*

> The governor **implied** that she might not seek reelection, and the reporters **inferred** that she had decided to run for president.

incredible, incredulous *Incredible* means "extraordinary" or "not believable"; *incredulous* means "unable or unwilling to believe." A person would be *incredulous* in response to something that is *incredible.*

> Their families were **incredulous** as the freed hostages told of the **incredible** cruelty they had suffered while captives.

illusion See *allusion, illusion.*

individual, person, party are not interchangeable in academic writing. Use *individual* to emphasize the uniqueness of a single human being; otherwise use *person.* Use *party* only for a group of people.

> The Constitution guarantees every **individual** certain rights.
> Each **person** received a written invitation.
> The governor and his **party** entered the room together.

infer, imply See *imply, infer.*

inside of, outside of See *outside of, inside of.*

insure, assure, ensure See *assure, ensure, insure.*

irregardless is nonstandard for *regardless.*

irritate, aggravate See *aggravate, irritate.*

is when, is where In giving definitions, *is* should not be followed by *when* or *where.*

> Defensive driving means that [not *is when*] drivers stay on the defense against accidents that might be caused by other drivers.

its, it's *Its* is a personal pronoun in the possessive case. *(The dog lost its bone). It's* is a contraction of *it is* (**It's** *a warm day).*

-ize is a suffix used to change a noun° or adjective° to a verb° *(hospital +* *ize = hospitalize, brutal + ize = brutalize).* Be careful not to attach *-ize* indiscrimiately to create new words rather than using good words that already exist. When in doubt, check your dictionary to see if a word ending in *-ize* is acceptable.

kind, sort are singular words and should therefore be paired with *this,* not *these. These* can be paired with *kinds* or *sorts.*

kind of (a), sort of (a) *Kind of* and *sort of* are nonstandard if used as adverbs° meaning "in a way" or "somewhat." Also, the *a* with these phrases is nonstandard.

The hikers were **somewhat** [not *kind of*] tired when they got home. That **kind of** [not *kind of an*] exercise is healthy.

later, latter *Later* means "after some time" or "subsequently;" *latter* refers to the second of a pair of ideas or things.

That restaurant opens **later** than we had thought. It serves lunch and dinner, the **latter** starting at 7 p.m.

latter, former See *former, latter.*

lay, lie *Lay* (principal parts: *laying, laid*) is always followed by a direct object°. As a substitute for *lie* (principal parts: *lying, lay, lain*), *lay* is nonstandard. For more information, see 8d.

Lay the blanket on the beach so you can **lie** [not *lay*] down and rest.

learn, teach *Learn* is nonstandard for *teach.* Students *learn;* teachers *teach.*

The instructor will **teach** us [not *learn* us] chemistry.

leave, let To *leave* means "to depart"; to *let* means "to permit." *Leave* is nonstandard for *let* unless *leave* is followed by *alone.*

I had to **leave** the classroom early because I was ill. My instructor will **let** [not *leave*] me take a retest tomorrow. She will have to find a proctor, because she cannot **leave** a student **alone** during an exam.

likely, apt, liable *Likely* and *apt* are loosely interchangeable. Strictly, however, *apt* is used to indicate a tendency or inclination; and *likely* is used to indicate a reasonable expectation that something will happen. *Liable* means "having undesirable consequences."

Although the roads are **apt** to be icy, you **likely** will arrive on time. However, you are **liable** to have an accident if you speed on icy roads.

loose, lose, loss *Loose* means "not tight;" to *lose* means "to be unable to find"; *loss* means "that which cannot be found or retrieved."

Before I **lose** this **loose** belt, I had better tighten it. The **loss** from the fire included most of his clothing.

lots, lots of, a lot of are informal for *many, much, a great deal of.*

Many [not *lots of*] bees were in the hive.

may, can See *can, may.*

may be, maybe *May be* is a verb phrase°; *maybe* is an adverb°.

Our team **may be** out of practice, but **maybe** we will win anyway.

media is the plural of *medium* and therefore requires a plural verb.

The **media** *cover* [not *covers*] the elections, but the **medium** that reaches most people is television.

mighty is a nonstandard substitute for *extremely* or *very.*

mind, mine *Mind* is a noun° *(She had a good* **mind***); mine* is a personal pronoun° *(That key is* **mine***).*

morale, moral *Morale* (noun°) means "a mental state relating to courage, confidence, or enthusiasm." *Moral* (noun) means "the conclusion of, or lesson from, a story"; *moral* (adjective°) means "right in conduct or character."

692

The president's good **moral** character boosted the country's **morale**.
The **moral** of that story is that people should be kind to animals.

most is nonstandard for *almost*.

Ms. is the title free of reference to marital status for women; it is equivalent to the male title *Mr.* Unless a woman specifically requests *Miss* or *Mrs.*, use *Ms.*

myself, yourself, himself, herself are reflexive pronouns° *(I told myself to stay home)* and intensive pronouns° *(I myself will volunteer)*. They are nonstandard when used as a subject° or an object in a prepositional phrase.°
The dean and **I** [not *myself*] will explain the facts to the president. First, however, the class has to explain them to the dean and **me** [not *myself*].

nothing like, nowhere near are nonstandard for *not nearly*.
Last month's rain was **not nearly** [not *nowhere nearly*] enough.

nowheres is nonstandard for *nowhere*.

number, amount See *amount, number*.

of, have See *have, of*.

off of is nonstandard for *off*.
He fell **off** [not *off of*] the chair.

OK, O.K., okay are acceptable, but avoid them in academic writing in favor of a word more specific to the meaning of the sentence.
The weather was *satisfactory* [not *okay*] for the race. Course officials gave the *approval* [not *okay*] for the final lap.

on account of is wordy for *because, because of*.
Because of [not *on account of*] the rainy weather, we stayed home.

outside of, inside of are nonstandard when used with *of (She waited **outside** [not *outside of*] the dormitory)*. Also, *inside of* is nonstandard when referring to time *(She waited **about** [not *inside of*] five minutes)*.

party, individual, person See *individual, person, party*.

per The Latin word *per* is reserved for technical terms *(miles **per** hour, **per** capita income)*. Use English equivalents in academic writing.
He earned $200 **a** [not *per*] month **as explained in** [not *per*] your letter.

percent, percentage *Percent* is used with specific numbers *(two percent, 95 percent)*. *Percentage* is used with descriptive words or phrases (a *small percentage*), but only for amounts that have been expressed as percentages. Do not use it as a synonym for *part, portion, number, amount,* or other words denoting quantity
Several people in my class are bilingual [not *A percentage* of my class is bilingual].
A large **percentage** of the voters watch the presidential debates on television.

693

person, individual, party See *individual, person, party.*

photocopy, Xerox® To *photocopy* (verb°) means "to make a copy on a copier machine"; *photocopy* (noun°) is the copy. *Xerox®* is a registered trademark, not a synonyn for either the noun or the verb *photocopy.*

plenty is nonstandard for words such as *quite* and *very (She was* **very** (not *plenty) tired from the workout).* When used as a noun meaning *a large amount, plenty* must be followed by *of (They must have* **plenty of** *food for the winter).*

plus is a preposition° meaning "in addition to" *(She had talent* **plus** *good work habits). Plus,* however, is nonstandard (1) as a substitute for *and* between independent clauses and (2) as a transitional word such as *besides, moreover, in addition.*

> He studied hard, **and** [not *plus*] he played hard. **In addition** [not *plus*], he had a long commute between his home and campus.

p.m., a.m. See *a.m., p.m.*

practical, practicable *Practical* means "useful or sensible"; *practicable* means "capable of being put into practice."

> The mayor wanted a **practical** evacuation plan, but none of the proposals was **practicable** for a large city.

precede, proceed To *precede* means "to come before"; to *proceed* means "to continue."

> The attorney **preceded** her client to court and then **proceeded** to unpack her briefcase.

pretty is informal for words such as *rather, quite, very,* and *somewhat.* Avoid such use in academic writing.

> The flu epidemic was **quite** [not *pretty*] severe.

principal, principle *Principle* means "a basic truth or rule." *Principal* (noun°) means "chief person" or "main or original amount"; *principal* (adjective°) means "most important."

> The school **principal** paid interest on the **principal** of her bank loan. One of the **principal** values in the United States is the **principle** of free speech.

raise, rise *Raise* (principal parts: *raised, raising*) needs a direct object° *(Please* **raise** *your hand); rise* (principal parts: *rose, risen, rising*) does not take a direct object *(The run will* **rise***).* Using these verbs interchangeably is nonstandard. For more information, see 8d.

> The governor will **rise** [not *raise*] to speak after we **raise** [not *rise*] the flag.

rarely ever is an informal expression for *rarely* or *hardly ever;* avoid it in academic writing.

> He **rarely** [not *rarely ever*] came to class, so I **hardly ever** (not *rarely ever*) saw him.

real is nonstandard for intensifiers such as *really* (informal) or *very.*

really is informal for intensifiers such as *very* and *extremely.*

reason is should not be used in combination with *because.*

> The **reason is** [not *the reason is because*] we want to lower taxes.

reason why is redundant; drop *why*.

> The **reason** [not *reason why*] they left home is a mystery.

reckon, calculate, figure See *calculate, figure, reckon*.

regarding, in regard to, with regard to are used in some legal and technical writing but are too stiff for most academic writing. Useful substitutes are words such as *about* and *concerning*.

> The committee members asked **about** [not *regarding, in regard to,* or *with regard to*] the plan for a new park.

respectful, respectfully; respective, respectively *Respectful* and *respectfully* relate to showing respect; *respective* and *respectively* refers to items that are in the given sequence.

> The staff **respectfully** requested that the dean hear their complaints. He suggested that the typist and telephone operators go back to their desk and switchboards, **respectively.** They then returned to their **respective** jobs.

right is nonstandard for intensifiers such as *very* or *extremely*.

> The workers were **very** [not *right*] pleased to hear that the factory will reopen.

says, goes See *goes, says*.

seen is a nonstandard substitute for *saw. Seen* is the past participle° of *to see* and must be used with an auxiliary verb° such as *have, has,* or *had*.

> They **saw** [not *seen*] the film. I **had seen** [not *I seen*] it last week.

set, sit *Set* (principal parts: *set, setting*) is nonstandard as a substitute for *to sit* (principal parts: *sat, sitting*). *Set* means "to place" and is followed by a direct object°. *Sit* means "to be seated." For more information, see 8d.

> After you carefully **set** [not *sit*] the rare Chinese vase on the table, please **sit** [not *set*] down.

sex, gender See *gender, sex*.

shall, will Use *shall* for questions in the first person *(Shall I leave?)* or in very formal settings *(The judge **shall** render her verdict after hearing the testimony)*. In all other cases, *will* is now accepted for the future tense in first, second, and third persons.

should, would Use *should* to express obligation *They **should** practice what they preach)* or condition *(If you **should** need advice, call me)*. Use *would* to express a wish *(I wish my family **would** buy a VCR)* or habitual action *(I **would** tape all the comedy specials)*.

sit, set See *set, sit*.

so is colloquial as an intensifier like *very* and *extremely*.

some is both nonstandard and vague as a substitute for modifiers such as *somewhat, a little,* and *remarkable*.

> That was **a remarkable** [not *some*] performance.

somebody, some body See *anybody, any body*.

someone, some one See *anybody, any body*.

sometime, sometimes, some time *Sometime* means "at an unspecified future time"; *sometimes* means "now and then"; *some time* is a span of time.

Sometime next semester we have to take qualifying exams.
Sometimes I worry about the tests. I need **some time** to get used to the pressure.

somewhereas is nonstandard for *somewhere*.

sort, kind See *kind, sort.*

sort of (a), kind of (a) See *kind of (a), sort of (a).*

specially, especially See *especially, specially.*

stationary, stationery are not interchangeable. *Stationary* means "standing still"; *stationery* refers to paper and related products.

such is informal and overused as an intensifier such as *very* or *extremely*. Avoid it in academic writing, unless it is part of a comparison including *that*.
> No It was **such** a poorly written play.
> Yes It was a **very** poorly written play.
> Yes It was **such** a poorly written play **that** no one went to see it.

supposed to, used to The final *d* is essential in both expressions.
> The weather is **supposed to** [not *suppose to*] improve. It **used to** [not *use to*] be sunny this time of year.

sure is nonstandard when used an an adverb° meaning *surely* or *certainly*.
> I **surely** [not *sure*] hope to go to college.

take, bring See *bring, take.*

teach, learn See *learn, teach.*

than, then *Than* indicates comparison *(One is smaller **than** two)*. *Then* relates to time *(He tripped and **then** fell)*.

that there, then there, this here, these here are nonstandard for *that, those, this*, and *these*, respectively.

that, which Use *that* with restrictive (essential) clauses°; *which* can be used today for both restrictive and nonrestrictive (nonessential) clauses°, but most writers prefer to use it only with nonrestrictive (nonessential) clauses.
> We visited the house **that** Jack built. Jack built the house, **which** is on Beanstalk Street, for his large plant collection.

their, there, they're *Their* is possessive; *there* means "in that place" or serves as an expletive°; *they're* is a contraction of *they are*.
> The students attended **their** classes in the lecture hall, which is over **there**. At this college, **there** are many courses to take, but **they're** all scheduled in the morning.

theirself, theirselves, themself are nonstandard for *themselves*.

them is nonstandard when used for *these* or *those*.
> *Let's buy* **those** [not **them**] *strawberries.*

then, than See *than, then.*

thusly is nonstandard for *thus*. Because *thus* is already an adverb°, the *-ly* ending is not needed.

till, until are both acceptable, although most writers prefer *until* in academic writing. Avoid the contraction *'til* in academic writing.

to, too, two *To* is a preposition°; *too* is an adverb°; *two* is the number.
> They went **to** the game. They ate at a restaurant, **too.** The check was not **too** expensive for the **two** of them.

toward, toward, are both acceptable, although some writers prefer *toward*.

try and, sure and are nonstandard for *try to* and *sure to*.
> She wanted to **try to** [not *try and*] get a part-time job. Therefore, she had to be **sure to** [not *sure and*] prepare a résumé.

type is nonstandard for *type of*.

uninterested, disinterested See *disinterested, uninterested*.

unique is an absolute word and therefore cannot be modified by intensifiers such as *very* or *most*.
> Her talent was **unique** [not *very unique* or *most unique*].

used to, supposed to See *supposed to, used to*.

wait on is informal for *wait for*.

ways is colloquial for *way*.
> California is a long **way** [not *ways*] from New York.

well, good See *good, well*.

went, gone See *gone, went*.

what is nonstandard when used for *that* or *who*.
> The house **that** [not **what**] Jack built contains a beanstalk.

where is nonstandard when used for *that*.
> I read in the newspaper **that** [not *where*] tuition will be increased.

where . . . . at is redundant; drop *at*.
> **Where** is the house [not *house at*]?

whether, if See *if, whether*.

which, that See *that, which*.

which, who Use *which* to refer to things or ideas; use *who* to refer to people.

who, whom Use *who* for the subjective case° *(The person **who** can type has an easier time in school)*. Use *whom* for the objective case° *(I asked to **whom** my professor was speaking)*. For more information, see 9d.

who's, whose *Who's* is the contraction of *who is; whose* is possessive.
> **Who's** going to run for mayor?
> **Whose** campaign is well organized?

will, shall See *shall, will*.

-wise The suffix *-wise* means "in a manner, in a direction, or in a position" *(clockwise, sidewise)*. Be careful not to attach *-wise* indiscriminately to create new words rather than using good words that already exist. When in doubt, check your dictionary to see if a word ending in *-wise* is acceptable.
> The **weather** [not *Weatherwise, the*] outlook is excellent.

would, should See *should, would*.

Xerox®, photocopy See *photocopy, Xerox*®

Xmas is an abbreviation for *Christmas;* avoid using it in academic writing.

yet, however, but See *but, however, yet.*

your, you're *Your* is possessive; *you're* is the contraction of *you* are.
> **You're** generous to share **your** food with us.

yourself, See *myself, yourself, himself, herself.*

GLOSSARY
OF GRAMMATICAL
AND SELECTED
COMPOSITION
TERMS

The first time that a term is used in this handbook, it is defined. After that when the term is used, it is marked with a degree symbol (°) to signal that it is defined in this glossary. Also, when a definition in this glossary uses terms that are themselves defined here, the terms are marked with a degree symbol. In addition, each definition concludes with a reference, in parentheses, to the handbook section(s) or chapters where the term is most fully discussed.

abstract A condensed summary of a report, especially used in research papers in the social sciences and in theses and dissertations. (34d-3)

abstract noun A noun° that names things not knowable through the five senses: *idea, guilt*. (6a)

absolute phrase A phrase containing a subject° and a participle° and modifying an entire sentence: *Summer being over,* we left the seashore. (7d)

acronym A word made up of the first letters of other words that acts as an abbreviation for those words: *NASA*. (30h)

active voice The form of a verb° in which the subject° performs the action named by the verb. This voice° emphasizes the doer of the action, in contrast to the passive voice°, which emphasizes the action. (8j)

adjective A word that describes or limits (modifies) a noun° or pronoun° or word group functioning as a noun: *silly, three*. (6e, 12)

adjective clause A dependent clause° that usually begins with a relative pronoun° and that modifies nouns° or pronouns°. (7e-2)

adverb A word that describes or limits (modifies) verbs°, adjectives°, other adverbs, or whole sentences: *wearily, very.* (6f, 12)

adverb clause A dependent clause° that begins with a subordinating conjunction° and that modifies verbs°, adjectives°, adverbs°, or whole sentences. (7e-2)

agreement The match in expressing number° and person° required between a subject° and its verb° or a pronoun° and its antecedent°. For pronouns and antecedents, expressions of gender° must match as well. (11)

analogy An explanation of the unfamiliar in terms of the familiar, analogy compares objects or ideas from different classes, things not normally associated with each other. Analogy is also a method of developing one or more paragraphs. (4d, 34c-2)

analysis A thinking process, analysis divides something into its component parts to make clear the relationship between the whole and the parts. Sometimes called *division,* analysis is also a method of developing one or more paragraphs. (4d)

antecedent The noun° or pronoun° to which a pronoun refers. (10)

agreement The match in expressing number° and person° required between a subject° and its verb° or a pronoun° and its antecedent°. For pronouns and antecedents, expressions of gender° must match as well. (11)

appositive A word or group of words that renames a noun° or words functioning as a noun: *my favorite month,* **October.** (7c-3)

argumentative writing See *persuasive writing.*

articles The words *a, an,* and *the.* Also called *limiting adjectives, noun markers* or *noun determiners.* (6a)

audience The readers to whom a piece of writing is directed. Knowledge of the educational level, age, cultural background, interests, economic status, political philosophy, and religious beliefs of the audience can help the writer shape the message so that it will effectively inform or persuade the reader. (1c)

auxiliary verb Also known as a *helping verb,* an auxiliary verb is a form of *be, do, have, can, may, will,* and others that combine with main verbs° to make verb phrases°. Auxiliary verbs help main verbs to express tense°, mood°, and voice°. (6c, 8a, 8c)

balanced sentence A sentence that uses parallelism° to enhance the message of similar or dissimilar ideas. (18b-3)

base form See *simple form.*

brainstorming An invention technique° that calls for listing all the ideas that come to mind in connection with a topic and then grouping the ideas according to patterns that emerge. (2d-3)

bureaucratic language Stuffy, overblown language that tries to impress by sounding important and official when, in fact, it is wordy, ambiguous, and often evasive. (21d-5)

case The way a noun° or pronoun° changes form to show whether it is functioning as a subject°, an object°, or a possessor: *she, her, hers.* (9)

cause-and-effect analysis Examination of the relationship between outcomes (effects) and the reasons for them (causes). Cause-and-effect analysis can be used to develop one or more paragraphs°. (4d, 5d)

chronological order An arrangement of ideas according to a time sequence. Paragraphs, essays, and larger works may be in chronological order. Narrations and descriptions of processes are usually in chronological order. (2e-2, 4c)

clarifying sentence See *limiting sentence.*

classification A method of developing a paragraph° or a larger piece of writing in which separate categories that share some characteristics are grouped together. Classification is often used along with analysis°. (4d)

clause A group of words containing a subject° and a predicate°. A clause that delivers full meaning is called an *independent clause°* (or main clause). A clause that needs another sentence structure to deliver full meaning is called a *dependent clause°* (or subordinate clause). (7e)

cliché An overused, worn-out phrase that has lost its capacity to communicate effectively: *smooth as silk, ripe old age.* (21c)

climactic order An arrangement of ideas in a paragraph° or larger piece of writing from least important to most important. Climactic order is sometimes called *emphatic order.* (2e-2, 4c)

climactic sentence See *periodic sentence.*

coherence The clear progression from one idea to another in a piece of writing. Transitional expressions°, pronouns°, selective repetition, and parallelism° enhance coherence. A piece of writing is coherent when its parts relate to one another not only in content but also grammatical structures and choice of words. (3b, 4b)

collective noun A noun° that names a group of people or things: *family, pride* (of lions). (6a, 11g, 11o)

colloquial language Language characteristic of conversation and informal writing. (21a-4)

comma fault See *comma splice.*

comma splice The error that occurs when only a comma connects two independent clauses°. (14)

common noun A noun° that names general groups, places, people, or things: *dog, house.* (6a)

comparative The form of an adjective° or adverb° that reflects a different degree of intensity between two: *bluer, more easily.* See also *positive* and *superlative.* (12e-1)

comparison and contrast A pattern for developing a paragraph° or whole essay in which the writer considers the similarities (comparison) and differences (contrast) of subjects. (4d)

complement A word or group of words in the predicate° of a sentence that renames or describes a subject° or object° in that sentence. (7c-1)

complete predicate See *predicate.*

complete subject See *subject.*

complex sentence A sentence containing one independent clause° and one or more dependent clauses.°. (7f-3)

compound-complex sentence A sentence containing at least two independent clauses° and one or more dependent clauses°. (7f-4)

compound predicate See *predicate.*

compound sentence A sentence containing two or more independent clauses° joined by a coordinating conjunction. (7f-2)

compound subject See *subject.*

concrete noun A noun° that names things that can be seen, touched, heard, smelled, or tasted: *smoke, sand.* (6a)

conjunction A word that connects words, phrases°, or clauses°, including coordinating conjunctions°, correlative conjunctions°, and subordinating conjunctions°. (6h)

conjunctive adverb A kind of adverb° that creates logical connections between independent clauses°: *therefore, however.* (6f)

connotation The emotional associations suggested by a word that, along with its denotation°, make up its complete meaning. (20b)

coordinate adjectives Two or more adjectives that equally modify a noun° or pronoun°. They are separated by a comma: *heavy, round* paperweight. (24d)

coordinating conjunction A conjunction that joins two or more grammatically equivalent structures. The seven coordinating conjunctions are *and, or, for, nor, but, so,* and *yet.* (6h)

coordination The technique of using grammatically equivalent forms to show a balance or sequence of ideas. (17)

correlative conjunction A pair of words that joins equivalent grammatical structures, including *both . . . and, not only . . . but also, either . . . or, neither . . . nor,* and *whether . . . or.* (6h)

cumulative sentence A sentence that begins with the subject° and verb° and then adds modifiers°—the most common kind of sentence. Also known as a *loose sentence.* (19d-2)

dangling modifier A modifier° that describes something implied but not stated: ***Walking down the street,*** *the Sears Tower came into view.* (15c)

deadwood Empty words and phrases that increase the word count but do not add to the meaning. Also called *padding.* (16b)

declarative sentence A sentence that makes a statement: *I walked home.* (7)

deduction The process of reasoning from general claims to a specific instance. (5e-2)

demonstrative pronoun A pronoun° that points out the antecedent°. The demonstrative pronouns are *this, these, that,* and *those.* (6b)

denotation The dictionary definition of a word. (20b)

dependent clause A clause° that cannot stand alone as an independent grammatical unit, usually preceded by a relative pronoun° or subordinating conjunction°. (7e-2)

descriptive adjective An adjective° that describes the condition or properties of the noun° it modifies and has comparative° and superlative° forms: *round, rounder, roundest.* (6e)

descriptive adverb An adverb° that describes the qualities of the verb° and has comparative° and superlative° forms: *happily, more happily, most happily.* (6f)

diction Word choice. (20a, 20b)

dictionary form A term relating to verbs. See *simple form.*

direct discourse In writing, words that repeat speech or conversation exactly, requiring the use of quotation marks. (15a-4, 28a-3)

direct object A noun° or pronoun° or group of words functioning as a noun that receives the action—that is, completes the meaning—of a transitive verb°. (7b, 8d)

direct question A sentence that asks a question and ends with a question mark: *Are you going?* (23c)

direct quotation Spoken or written words from an outside source; such words must be enclosed in quotation marks. (28a, 31e)

division See *analysis.*

documentation Acknowledging the sources used in any piece of writing, by giving full and accurate information about the source's author, title, and the work's date of publication, and related facts. (31-b, 32d-4)

documentation style Any of various systems for providing information about the sources other than oneself used in writing others read. Some cite information in parentheses at appropriate places within the text; others use footnotes or endnotes. The form of the bibliography also varies from one style of documentation to another. Two of the most widely used styles are those of the Modern Language Association (MLA) and the American Psychological Association (APA). (31b, 32d-4)

doublespeak Evasive language intentionally used to hide the truth. (21d-4)

double negative A nonstandard statement that contains two negative modifiers°, the second of which repeats the message of the first. (12c)

drafting A part of the writing process° in which writers compose ideas in sentences and paragraphs. (2a, 3b)

edited American English Also called *standard English,* the language that conforms to established rules of grammar, sentence structure, punctuation, and spelling. (21a-2)

703

editing A part of the writing process° in which writers check the technical correctness of their grammar, spelling, punctuation, and mechanics°. (2a, 3d)

elliptical clause See *elliptical construction.*

elliptical construction A sentence structure, such as a clause° or phrase°, that deliberately omits words that have already appeared in the sentence and can be inferred from the context. (7e-2, 15e-1)

euphemism Language that attempts to avoid the harsh reality of some truths by using more pleasant-sounding, "tactful" words. (21d-3)

evaluative reading A part of the reading process in which the reader determines the author's tone, differentiates between fact and opinion, and assesses the author's reasoning. (5b-3)

evidence Facts, statistical information, examples, and opinions of others used by a writer to support assertions and conclusions. (5c)

exclamatory sentence A sentence that expresses strong emotion by making an exclamation: *That's ridiculous!* (7, 19b)

expletive A term that describes the function of *there* and *it* when they combine with a form of the verb *to be* to postpone the subject of the sentence: *It is Harold whom we must convince.* (6j, 11e)

expository writing See *informative writing.*

extended definition A definition that includes in addition to the denotation° of a word or phrase, its connotations° as well as concrete details to clarify abstract terms. An extended definition may require an entire paragraph° or essay. (4d)

faulty predication An error that occurs when a subject° and its predicate° do not make sense together. (15d-2)

finite verb A verb° form that shows tense°, mood°, voice°, person°, and number° while expressing an action, occurrence, or state of being. (8a-1)

first person See *person.*

freewriting Writing nonstop for a specified time in order to generate ideas by free association of thoughts. Freewriting that starts with a set topic is called "focused freewriting." As an invention technique°, freewriting often helps writers discover interesting ideas or patterns of thought to develop. (2d-2)

fused sentence The error of running independent clauses° together without a semicolon or a comma and a coordinate conjunction° between them. Also called a *run-on* or *run-together sentence.* (14)

future perfect progressive tense The form of the future perfect tense° that describes an action or condition ongoing until some specific future time: *they will have been talking.* (8g, p. 193)

future perfect tense The tense° indicating that an action will have been completed or a condition will have ended by a specified point in the future: *they will have talked.* (8f, p. 193)

future progressive tense The form of the future tense° showing that a future action will continue for some time: *they will be talking.* (8g, p. 193)

704

future tense The form of a verb, made with the simple form° and either *shall* or *will,* expressing an action yet to be taken or a condition not yet experienced: *they will talk.* (8c, p. 193)

gender Concerning languages, the labeling of nouns° and pronouns° as masculine, feminine, or neutral, a division in English only in third person singular personal pronouns *(he, she, it)* and in a few nouns *(prince, princess).*

gerund A verbal°, the present participle° functioning as a noun°: **Walking** *is good exercise.* (6d)

gerund phrase A verbal° phrase functioning as a noun° and containing a gerund° and its modifiers°. (7d, 8a-1)

helping verb See *auxiliary verb.*

highly formal level of language A level of language characterized by multisyllabic Latinate words and stylistic flourishes such as extended or complex figures of speech. (21a-1)

homonyms Words spelled differently that sound alike: *to, too, two.* (22c)

illogical predication See *faulty predication.*

imperative mood The mood° that expresses commands and direct requests: *Go.* It uses the simple form° of the verb. (8h-2)

imperative sentence A sentence that gives a command: *Go home now.* (7)

indefinite pronoun A pronoun° that refers to nonspecific persons or things but that takes on meaning in context: *any, few.* (6b, 11f)

independent clause A clause° that can stand alone as an independent grammatical unit. (7e-1)

indicative mood The mood° of verbs° used for statements about real things, or highly likely ones, and questions about fact: *I think Grace will be there.* (page 202)

indirect discourse Discourse that reports speech or conversation and is not enclosed in quotation marks because it does not give the speaker's exact words. (15a-4, 28a-3)

indirect object A noun° or pronoun° or group of words functioning as a noun that tells *to whom* or *for whom* the action expressed by a transitive verb° was done. (7b-2)

indirect question A sentence that reports a question and ends with a period: *I wonder whether you are going.* Also see *direct question.* (23c)

induction The process of arriving at general principles from particular facts or instances. (5e-1)

inferential meaning The meaning gained in the part of the reading process when a reader reads "between the lines," understanding what is implied but unstated. (5b-2)

infinitive A verbal° made of the simple form° of a verb and usually, but not always, *to.* It functions as a noun°, adjective°, or adverb°. (6d, 8a-1, 9g)

infinitive phrase An infinitive° and its modifiers°. It functions as a noun°, adjective°, or adverb°. (7d)

informal language Word choice that creates a tone° appropriate for casual conversation or letters to friends. The words may be slang°, colloquial language°, or regional language°. (21a-1)

informative writing Also known as *expository writing,* informative writing gives information and, when necessary, explains it. In contrast to persuasive writing°, informative writing focuses on the subject being discussed rather than the reader's reaction to the information. (1b-1)

intensive pronoun A *-self* form of a pronoun°, which intensifies the antecedent. (6b, 9h)

interjection A word (or words) conveying surprise or another strong emotion. (6i)

interrogative pronoun A pronoun° that asks a question, such as *whose* or *what.* (6b)

interrogative sentence A sentence that asks a question: *Did you see that hat?* (7)

intransitive verb A verb that does not take a direct object° and is not a linking verb°. (8d)

invention techniques Ways writers gather ideas. Some techniques are keeping an idea book or journal, freewriting°, brainstorming°, using the journalist's questions, mapping°, and reading. (2d)

irony Suggesting the opposite of the usual sense of the words. (21b-4)

irregular verb A verb that forms the past tense and past participle° in some way other than by adding *-ed* or *-d: see, saw, seen.* (8b)

jargon Specialized vocabulary of a particular field or group that people outside the group would not understand. The unnecessary use of jargon creates pretentious language°. (21d-2)

limiting adjective An adjective° that limits the noun° it modifies by pointing out, questioning, enumerating, showing possession, or showing its relation to other words in the sentence. (6a, 6e)

limiting sentence A sentence that follows the topic sentence in a paragraph and narrows the focus of the paragraph; sometimes called a clarifying sentence. (4a-1)

linking verb A main verb° that connects a subject° with a subject complement°. Linking verbs indicate a state of being, relate to the senses, or indicate a condition. (6c, 11h, 12d)

literal meaning The meaning gained in the reading process, when a reader reads "on the line," getting information from facts, points in an argument, or details of plot or character. It does not include inferential meaning° or opinions about the material. (5b-1)

logical fallacies Flaws in reasoning that leads to illogical statements. Common fallacies are hasty generalization, false analogy, circular reasoning, *non sequitur, post hoc,* self-contradiction, red herring, *ad hominem,* bandwagon, appeal to false authority, special pleading, the either-or fallacy, taking something out of context, appeal to ignorance, and ambiguity and equivocation. (5f)

706

loose sentence See *cumulative sentence.*

main clause See *independent clause.*

main verb A verb that expresses action, occurrence, or state of being. It shows mood°, tense°, voice°, number°, and person°. (6c, 8a)

mapping An invention technique° for generating ideas. This process is also called *webbing.* (2d-5)

mass noun A noun° that names "uncountable" things: *furniture, weather.* (6a)

mechanics Conventions regarding the use of capital letters, italics, abbreviations, and styles of writing numbers. (30)

medium level of formality A level of language that is neither too scholarly nor too casual. This level, which uses standard vocabulary, conventional sentence structure, and few or no contractions, is acceptable for academic writing. (21a-1)

metaphor A comparison between otherwise dissimilar things. It does not use a word like *like* or *as* to form the comparison, as a simile° does, but directly equates the things being compared. (21b)

metonomy A figure of speech that uses a name associated with something to refer to anything in that class. (21b)

misplaced modifier A modifier° that is incorrectly positioned in a sentence, thus distorting meaning. (15b)

mixed construction A sentence that begins by setting up one grammatical form but switches unintentionally to another, thus garbling the meaning of the sentence. (15d-1)

mixed metaphors Incongruously combined images. (21b)

modal auxiliary verbs Auxiliary verbs° that have only one form: *can, could, may, might, should, would, must,* and *ought.* They add a sense of needing, wanting, or having to do something, a sense of possibility, likelihood, obligation, permission, or ability. (8c)

modifier A word or group of words that describes or limits other words, phrases°, or clauses°. The most common modifiers are adjectives° and adverbs°. (7c-2)

mood The ability of verbs° to convey the attitude that the writer or speaker is expressing toward the action. English has three moods: indicative°, imperative°, and subjunctive°. (8i)

nonessential element See *nonrestrictive element.*

nonfinite verb A participle° or infinitive° functioning as a noun° or modifier°. Also known as a *verbal°.* (8a-1)

nonrestrictive element A limiting or descriptive word, phrase°, or dependent clause° that provides information not essential to understanding the element it modifies. A nonrestrictive element, sometimes called a *nonessential element,* is set off by commas. (24-e)

nonsexist language See *sexist language.*

noun The name of a person, place, thing, or idea. Nouns can be classified as proper°, common°, concrete°, abstract°, collective°, or mass°. Nouns function as subjects°, objects°, and complements°. (6a)

noun clause A dependent clause° that functions as a subject°, object°, or complement°. (7e-2)

noun phrase A noun° and its modifiers° functioning as a subject°, object°, or complement°. (7d)

number Relates to how many subjects act or experience an action, one (singular) or more than one (plural). (page 176)

object complement A noun° or adjective° that immediately follows a direct object° and either describes or renames it. (7c-1)

objective case The case° of the pronoun° functioning as direct object°, indirect object°, object of a preposition°, or object of a verbal°. (9)

object A noun° or pronoun° or group of words functioning as a noun or pronoun that receives the action of a verb° (direct object°), tells to whom or for whom something is done (indirect object°), or completes the meaning of a preposition° (object of a preposition°). (7b, 6g)

onomatopoeia The use of a word or words to imitate the sound the word denotes: *the rat-a-tat of a woodpecker*. (21b)

oxymoron The technique of combining opposites for a seeming contradiction or paradox: *the burning winter wind*. (21b)

padding See *deadwood*.

paragraph A group of sentences that work together to develop a unit of thought. Introductory paragraphs° prepare the reader for what will follow in a piece of writing. Concluding paragraphs° bring a sense of completion to a piece of writing. Transitional paragraphs° link major sections within a piece of writing. Most paragraphs are topical paragraphs°, stating a main idea and offering specific, logical support of that idea. (4)

paragraph development The arrangement and organizational pattern a writer chooses to elaborate on or to support the topic° of a paragraph°. Methods of paragraph development include general to specific, specific to general, climactic order°, problem to solution, spatial order°, chronological order°, narration, description, process, example, definition, analysis°, classification°, comparison and contrast°, analogy°, and cause-and-effect analysis°. (4)

parallelism The use of equivalent grammatical forms or matching sentence structures, to express equivalent ideas. (18)

paraphrase A restatement of someone else's ideas in language and sentence structure different from those of the source. (31c)

parenthetical documentation Information enabling a reader to identify the source of ideas or of direct quotations°. This information is placed in parentheses close to that quotation or information, usually at the end of the sentence in which the material appears. (32k)

parenthetical reference See *parenthetical documentation*.

participial phrase A phrase containing a present participle° or past participle°, and any modifiers, that functions as an adjective° or adverb°. (7d)

passive construction See *passive voice.*

passive voice The form of a verb° in which the subject° is acted upon. If the subject is mentioned in the sentence, it usually appears as the object of the preposition° *by.* This voice° emphasizes the action, in contrast to the *active voice°,* which emphasizes the doer of the action. (8j)

past participle The third principal part° of the verb°. In regular verbs°, it adds -*d* or -*ed* to the simple form° and is identical to the past tense°. In irregular verbs°, it often differs from the simple form and the past tense. To function as a verb, it must have an auxiliary verb°. Used alone, it functions as an adjective°. (6d, 8a-1)

past perfect progressive tense The past perfect tense° form that describes an ongoing condition in the past that has been ended by something stated in the sentence: *I had been talking.* (8g)

past perfect tense The tense° that describes a condition or action that started in the past, continued for a while, and then ended in the past: *I had talked.* (8f)

past progressive tense The past tense form° that shows the continuing nature of a past action: *I was talking.* (8g)

past tense form The second principal part of the verb°. It shows an action or occurrence or state of being completed in the past. The past tense of regular verbs° add -*ed* or -*d* to the simple form°: *watched.* The past tense of irregular verbs° changes in spelling or uses a different word than the simple form°: *wrote.* (8a-1)

perfect tenses The three tenses—the present perfect°, the past perfect°, and the future perfect°—that show complex time relationships in the present, past, and future. (8f)

periodic sentence A sentence that begins with modifiers° and ends with the independent clause°, thus saving the main idea—and the emphasis—for the end of the sentence. Also called *climactic sentence.* (19d-2)

person Who or what acts or experiences an action. First person is the one speaking *(I, we);* second person is the one being spoken to *(you, you);* and third person is the person or thing spoken about *(he, she, it; they).* (page 231)

personal pronoun A pronoun° that refers to people or things, such as *I, you, them, hers,* and *it.* (6b, 9)

personification A type of figurative language that gives human traits to non-human things: *Mother earth.* (21b)

persuasive writing Also known as argumentative writing, persuasive writing seeks to convince the reader about a matter of opinion. It focuses on the reader, whom the writer wants to influence. (1b-2)

phrase A group of related words that does not contain a subject° and predicate°, and thus cannot stand alone as an independent grammatical unit. A phrase functions as a noun°, verb°, or modifier°. (7d)

plagiarism A serious offense, like stealing. A form of intellectual dishonesty that can lead to failure or expulsion, plagiarism occurs when a writer presents another person's words or ideas without giving credit to that person. Writers must use documentation° to give proper credit to their sources.

planning An early part of the writing process° in which writers gather ideas, often using invention strategies°. Along with shaping°, planning is sometimes called *prewriting*°. (2a–2d)

plural See *number*.

positive The form of an adjective° or adverb° when it is not being compared. Also see *comparative, superlative*. (12e-1)

possessive case The case° of a noun° or pronoun° that shows ownership or possession. (9)

predicate The part of the sentence that contains the verb° and tells what the subject° is doing or experiencing or what is being done to the subject. A *simple predicate* contains only the main verb° and auxiliary verb°, if any. A *complete predicate* contains the verb and all its modifiers°, objects°, and other related words. A *compound predicate* contains two or more verbs and their objects and modifiers. (7a-2)

predicate adjective An adjective° used as a subject complement°. (7c-1)

predicate nominative See *subject complement*.

prefix One or more syllables in front of a root word° that modify its meaning. (20c, 22d-3)

premise In the syllogism of a deductive argument, the first premise is an assumption and the second premise is either a fact or another assumption based on evidence. These two premises are followed by a conclusion. (5e-2)

preposition A word that shows a relationship between a noun° or pronoun° and other words in the sentence. A preposition is followed by a noun or pronoun object°. (6g)

prepositional phrase A preposition° and its object° and any modifiers° of its object. A prepositional phrase often shows a relationship in time or space. Prepositional phrases function as adjectives° or adverbs°. (6g)

present participle Used with one or more auxiliary verbs° in a main verb phrase°, shows action, occurrence, or state of being: *I am running*. As a verbal°, the *-ing* form of the verb° functioning as an adjective° (*running* water) or a noun° (*running* pleases me). (6d, 8a-1)

present perfect progressive tense The present perfect tense form° that describes something ongoing in the past that is likely to continue into the future. *I have been talking*. (8g)

present perfect tense The tense° indicating that an action or its effects continue into the present though begun or perhaps completed in the past: *I had talked*. (8f)

present progressive tense The present tense° form of the verb° that indicates something taking place at the time it is written or spoken about: *I am talking*. (8g)

710

present tense The tense that describes what is happening, what is true at the moment, and what is consistently true. It uses the simple form° *(I talk)* and in the third person singular, it uses the *-s* form° *(she talks)*. (8a-1, 8a-2, 8d)

pretentious language Showy, overblown writing that calls attention to itself with complex sentences and long words for their own sakes. (21d-1)

prewriting A term for all activities in the writing process before drafting°. See *planning* and *shaping*.

primary evidence First-hand evidence from direct observation by the writer or an authoritative reporter. (5c)

primary source An original work of an author—novels, poems, short stories, autobiographies, diaries—and first-hand reports of observations and of research. (32)

progressive forms Verb forms made in all tenses° with the present participle° and forms of *to be*. These forms show that an action is ongoing. (8g)

pronoun A word that takes the place of a noun°. Types of pronouns are personal°, relative°, interrogative°, demonstrative°, reflexive°, intensive°, reciprocal°, and indefinite°. Pronouns function in the same ways that nouns° do. (6b)

pronoun-antecedent agreement The match in expressing number°, person°, and gender° required between a pronoun° and its antecedent°. (11l–11o)

pronoun case The way a pronoun changes in form to reflect its use as the agent of action (subjective case°), the thing being acted upon (objective case°), or the thing showing ownership (possessive case°). (9b–9h)

pronoun reference The relationship between a pronoun° and its antecedent°. (10)

proofreading The final step in the writing process°, proofreading calls for the writer to read the final copy a piece of writing to find and correct typing errors or handwriting illegibility. (2a, 3e)

proper adjective An adjective° formed from a proper noun°: *Victorian, American*. (6e, 30e)

proper noun A noun° that names a specific person, place, or thing: *St. Louis, Toni Morrison, Corvette*. (6a, 30e)

purpose The goal or aim of a piece of writing: to express oneself, to provide information, to persuade, or to create a literary work. (1b)

quotation The use in written form of words another person has spoken or written. Direct quotation° repeats the words of the source exactly and encloses them in quotation marks. Indirect quotation° reports what the source said, without the requirement for using quotation marks unless some of the source's words are repeated as well. Quotation requires documentation° of the source. (31)

reciprocal pronoun A pronoun° that refers to individual parts of a plural antecedent°: *each other, one another*. (6b)

reflexive pronoun A *-self* form of the pronoun° that reflects the antecedent°. A reflexive pronoun cannot substitute for subjects° or objects°. (9h)

regional language Language specific to a geographic area. (21a-4)

regular verb A verb° that forms its past tense° and past participle° by adding *-ed* or *-d* to the simple form°. Most English verbs are regular. (8b)

relative clause See *adjective clause*. (7e-2)

relative pronoun A pronoun° that introduces certain noun clauses° and adjective clauses°, for example, *who, which, that, what,* and *whomever.* A relative pronoun is a subordinating word°. (6b, 7e-2)

restrictive appositive An appositive° renaming a noun° or pronoun° by giving information that is essential to distinguish it from other things in its class: *my brother **John.***

restrictive clause A dependent clause° that limits a noun° or pronoun° by giving information necessary to distinguish it from others in its class. In contrast to a nonrestrictive clause°, this kind of dependent clause is never set off with commas. (24e)

restrictive element A word, phrase°, or dependent clause° that provides information essential to the understanding of the element it modifies. Restrictive elements are never set off by commas. (24e)

revision A part of the writing process° in which writers evaluate their rough drafts and, based on their decisions, rewrite by adding, cutting, replacing, moving, and often totally recasting material. (2a, 3c)

rhetoric The area of discourse that focuses on arrangement of ideas and choice of words as a reflection of the writer's purpose° and sense of audience°. (1)

root word The central part of a word to which a prefix° and/or suffix° is added. (20c-2)

run-on (run-together) sentence See *fused sentence.*

second person See *person.*

secondary evidence Evidence° from experts, reliable sources in their fields. Reliable secondary evidence appears in respected publications, is current, and is stated in relatively objective language. (5c)

secondary source A source that talks about someone else's original work. It explains events, analyzes information, and draws conclusions. (32)

sentence See *simple sentence, compound sentence, complex sentence, compound-complex sentence.*

sentence fragment A portion of a sentence that is punctuated as though it were a complete sentence. (13)

sexist language Language that unfairly assigns roles or characteristics to people on the basis of sex. Language that avoids stereotying according to sex is called *nonsexist language* (21b-3)

shaping An early part of the writing process° in which writers consider ways to organize their material. Along with planning°, shaping is sometimes called prewriting°. (2e)

simile A comparison, using *like, as,* or *as if,* between otherwise dissimilar things. (21b)

simple form The form of the verb° that shows action (or occurrence or state of being) taking place in the present for first and second person° singular and for first, second, and third persons plural. It is also the first principal part° of a verb. The simple form is also known as the *dictionary form* or *base form.* (8a-1)

simple predicate See *predicate.*

simple sentence A single independent clause° with no dependent clauses°. The subject° or predicate° or both may be compound. (7f-1)

simple subject See *subject.*

simple tenses The present°, past°, and future tenses°, which divide time into present, past, and future. (8e)

singular See *number.*

slang Coined words and new or extended meanings for established words, which quickly pass in and out of use. Inappropriate for any but the most informal communications. (21a-4)

slanted language Biased or emotionally loaded language. (21a-5)

spatial order A description of objects according to their physical relationship to one another, often in terms of a central reference point. Spatial order is a pattern that may be used to organize a paragraph°. The topic sentence° usually establishes a location that serves as the orientation for all other places mentioned. (2e-2, 4c)

speaker tag Explanatory words that identify the speaker of directly quoted words: *"Stay,"* **said the trainer.** (24g)

standard English See *edited American English.*

subject The word or group of words in a sentence that acts, is acted upon, or is described by the verb°. A *simple subject* includes only the noun° or pronoun°. A *complete subject* includes the noun or pronoun and all its modifiers°. A *compound* subject includes two or more nouns or pronouns and their modifiers. (7a-1)

subject complement Also called a *predicate nominative,* a noun° or adjective° that follows a linking verb° and describes or renames the subject° of the sentence. (7c-1, 8c)

subject-verb agreement The match of the subject° and verb° in expressing number° and person° required between a subject° and its verb°. (11a–11k)

subjective case The case° of the pronoun° functioning as subject°. (9)

subjunctive mood The verb mood° that expresses wishes, recommendations, indirect requests, and speculations: *I wish I* **were going.** (8i)

subordinate clause See *dependent clause.*

subordinating conjunction A conjunction that introduces an adverbial clause°, showing its relationship to the independent clause°. (6h, 7e-2)

subordination The technique of using grammatical structures to reflect the relative importance of ideas. A sentence with subordinated information contains an independent clause° to express important ideas in the sentence, and it contains dependent clauses° or phrases° to express ideas of lesser importance. (17d–17g)

suffix A syllable or syllables added to the end of a root word° that modify its meaning. (20c-2, 22d-1)

summary A condensed version of the essentials of ideas originally expressed in a longer version. (31d)

superlative The form of the adjective° or adverb° when three or more things are being compared: *greenest, most quickly.* (12e-1)

syllogism The structure of an argument reflecting deduction°. It has two premises°, the first one an assumption and the second a fact or an assumption based on evidence°. The conclusion, which is about a specific instance, follows logically from the premises. (5e-2)

synecdoche A kind of figurative language that substitutes a part for the whole or a whole for the part. (21b)

synthesis A component of critical thinking in which one makes connections among ideas. (page 114)

tense The time at which the action of the verb° occurs—in the past, present, or future. (8h)

tense sequence The accurate matching of verbs° to reflect the logical time relationships in sentences that have more than one verb. (8h)

thesis A statement of the central theme of an essay that makes clear the main idea of the essay, the writer's purpose, and the focus of the topic. It may also suggest the organizational pattern of the essay. (2e-4, 3c-2)

third person See *person.*

tone The writer's attitude towards his or her material and reader, especially as reflected in the writer's choice of words. (1c-1, 2e-3, 5b-3, 21a)

topic The subject of a piece of writing. A writer should consider both audience° and purpose° in choosing a topic. (2c)

topical paragraph See *paragraph.*

topic sentence The sentence in a paragraph° that contains the main idea of the paragraph. Not all paragraphs have topic sentences. (4a-1)

transition The logical connection of one idea to another in a piece of writing. Transition is achieved through the use of transitional expressions°, pronouns°, parallelism°, and the repetition of key words and phrases. (4b)

transitional expressions Words and phrases that signal connections among ideas and create coherence. A transitional expression lets the reader know how one idea connects to the next. (4b-1)

transitional paragraph See *paragraph.*

transitive verb A verb° that takes a direct object. (8c, 8d)

transitional words See *transitional expressions.*

understatement Also called *litotes,* a rhetorical device in which something is deliberately stated as being less than it is. (21b)

unity The close relationship of the parts of a piece of writing to one another. In a college essay, all parts should relate to the thesis° of the essay and all parts of a paragraph° should relate to the topic sentence° or main idea of the paragraph. Also called coherence°. (4a, 4b)

valid A term applied to an argument based on deduction° when the conclusion logically follows from the premises°. Validity has to do with the structure of the argument, not the truth of the premises. An argument based on untrue premises is valid if the conclusion follows from those premises. (5e-2)

verb The part of the predicate° in a sentence that acts or describes a state of being. Verbs change form to show time (tense°), attitude (mood°), and role of the subject (voice°). Verbs can be main verbs° or auxiliary verbs°, and they appear in verb phrases°. Verbs can be described as transitive° or intransitive° depending on whether they take a direct object°. (7d, 8)

verb phrase A verb° and its modifiers°. A verb phrase functions as a verb in the sentence. (7d, 8a)

verbal phrase A group of words that contains a verbal°—an infinitive°, participle°, or gerund°—and its modifiers°. Verbals function as nouns° or modifiers° rather than as verbs°. (7d)

verbals Verb parts functioning as nouns°, adjectives°, or adverbs°. Verbals include infinitives°, present participles°, past participles°, and gerunds°. (6c)

voice An attribute of a verb° showing whether the subject° acts (active voice°) or is acted upon (passive voice°). (8j)

webbing See *mapping.*

writing process A series of stages in which a writer gathers and shapes ideas, organizes material, expresses those ideas in a rough draft, evaluates the draft and revises it, and edits the writing for technical errors, and proofreads it for typographical mistakes or illegibility. See planning°, shaping°, drafting°, revising°, editing°, and proofreading°. (2, 3)

INDEX

A degree symbol (°) after an index entry signals that the term is defined in the Glossary of Grammatical and Selected Composition Terms. An entry in boldface italics (*advice, advise*, for example) is discussed in the Usage Glossary. Section numbers are in boldface type and page numbers in regular type. The listing **6a**: 142 thus refers you to page 142, which is in Section **6a**.

Evaluation
and critical thinking, **5**: 114
of evidence, **5c**: 125–26
in reading, **5b-3**: 120–23
of sources, **5c**: 128, **32d-2**: 538, 539
Evaluative reading, **5b-3**: 120–23
every
agreement of pronoun with, **11l**: 243
agreement of verb with, **11c**: 234
everyday, every day, **22c-3**: 395
everywheres
Evidence°
guidelines for using, **5c**: 125–26
primary, **5c**: 126–28
secondary, **5c**: 128
Exact words, **20b**: 362–66
Exactness in scientific writing, **34d-2**: 652
Examples
as cause of comma splices or fused
sentences, **14a**: 273
as clue to word meaning, **20c-2**: 370
emphasizing with dashes, **29a-1**: 475
for paragraph development, **4a-2**: 81–82,
4d: 99
in parentheses, **29b-1**: 478
transitional expressions for, **4b**: 84
except, accept, **22c-1**: 389
Exclamation points
with commands, **8**: 202, **19b**: 344, **23e**:
412–13
with emphatic declarations, **23e**: 412–13
with exclamations, **19b**: 344
with interjections, **6i**: 152, **24b-3**: 422
with other punctuation, **23e**: 413, **24g**:
434; dashes, **29a-3**: 476; parentheses,
29b-5: 479; question marks, **23c**: 412
overuse of, **23f**: 413
in quotations, **24g**: 434
Exclamatory sentences°, **7**: 154, **19b**: 344
Experts
false or irrelevant, **5f**: 137
interviewing, **32e-2**: 542
quoting from, **31e-2**: 526
as a source of secondary evidence, **5c**:
128
Explanations. *See* Examples
Expletive constructions
overuse of *it*, **10d**: 226–27
revising for conciseness, **16a-1**: 303–4
subject-verb agreement, **11e**: 236–37
Expletives°, **6j**: 152–53
explicit, implicit
Expository writing°, **1a**: 3, **1b-1**: 4–5. *See
also* Informative writing
Extended definitions°, **4d**: 99–100

-f, -fe, plurals of words ending in, **22d-4**: 401
Facts
books of, and almanacs, **32e-5**: 545
conditions contrary to, **8i-1**: 203
vs. opinions, **5b-3**: 122–23
fair, fare, **22c-1**: 391
Fallacies. *See* Logical fallacies
False analogy, **5f**: 135–36
False authority, **5f**: 137
False dilemma, **5f**: 137
farther, further
Faulty parallelism, **18**: 331
Faulty predication°, **15d-2**: 295–96
fewer, less, **12e-2**: 254

Figurative language, **21b**: 377–78
figure, calculate, reckon
Figures. *See* Numbers
Films
bibliographic citations: MLA
parenthetical-references style, **32g-2**:
574; MLA note style, **34b-4**: 639
documentary note references, **34b-4**: 636
reference works on, **32e-5**: 550
titles of, italics for, **30f**: 497, 498
Final draft
proofreading, **3e**: 70–71
of research paper, **32i**: 579
Final thesis statement, **2e-4**: 34. *See also*
Preliminary thesis statement
fine, find
Fine arts, reference works on, **32e-5**: 547
Finite verbs°, **8a-1**: 179
First draft, **3b**: 46–48
of research paper, **32i**: 578
First person°
conventions for use in various disciplines:
humanities, **34b-2**: 621; natural and
technological sciences, **34d-2**: 652;
social sciences, **34c-2**: 643
shall with, **8c**: 188
subject-verb agreement, **11**: 231
Focus
of essay, **2b**: 15
of sentence, **19c**: 346
Focused freewriting, **2d-2**: 23–24, **3a**: 46
Footnotes, formatting, **34b-4**: 633. *See also*
Notes; Parenthetical references
for, as coordinating conjunction, **6h**: 151,
17: 317, **24a**: 416–17
Foreign words and phrases
American English and, **20**: 355–56
in italics (underlined), **30f**: 497, 499
plural forms, **22d-4**: 402
formally, formerly, **22c-1**: 391
Formal language level, **21a-1**: 372–73
Formal outlines, **2e-5**: 39–43
conventions, **2e-5**: 39–41
parallel structures in, **18e**: 337–38
for research papers, **32i**: 577, **33**: 592–93
topic vs. sentence type, **2e-5**: 41–43
Formal tone, **2e-3**: 33
Format, manuscript, 675–82
former, latter
forth, fourth, **22c-1**: 391
Fractions
figures vs. spelled-out form, **30j**: 506
hyphenation of, **22e-4**: 406
slash with, **29e-2**: 484–85
Fragments. *See* Sentence fragments
Freewriting, **2d-2**: 23–24
Fused sentences°, **14**: 271–79
correcting: with coordinating conjunction, **14c**: 275; by revising an independent clause to a dependent clause, **14d**:
276–77; with semicolons or periods,
14b: 274, **14e**: 278–79
leading causes, **14a**: 273
recognizing, **14a**: 272–73
Future perfect progressive tense°, **8g**:
196
Future tense°, **8**: 192, 193
formation of, **8c**: 188
and simple form of verb, **8a-1**: 178
and tense sequences, **8h-1**: 198, 199

Indentation
in bibliographic lists, **32g-2**: 562, **34b-4**: 637
of displayed quotations, **28a-1**: 465
in formal outlines, **2e-5**: 40
of notes, **32b-4**: 632
to signal paragraphing, **4**: 73
Independent (main) clauses°, **7e**: 165; **7e-1**: 166
colons after, **26a**: 451–53
comma spliced or fused, **14**: 271–79
conjunctive adverbs joining, **6f**: 148, **12**: 248, **14e**: 278–79, **25c**: 445
coordinating conjunctions joining, **14c**: 275, **17**: 316–20, **24a**: 416–18
modified by adverb clauses, **7e-2**: 167
revising as dependent clauses, **14d**: 276–77
semicolons between, **14b**: 274, **14e**: 278–79, **25a,b,c**: 443–45, **25e**: 446
and subordinated information, **17**: 322–28
in various sentence types, **7f**: 172–73
Index cards
for bibliographic data, **32g-1**: 561–62
for note taking, **32f-2**: 559–60
as a research tool, **32d**: 537
Indexes to periodicals, **32e-6**: 550–52
Indicative mood°, **8**: 202, **15a-3**: 286
Indirect discourse°
quotation marks not used with, **28a-3**: 467
and unmarked shifts to direct, **15a**: 286–87
Indirect objects°, **7b-2**: 158, **9**: 209
Indirect questions°, **23a**: 410–11
Indirect requests, **8i-3**: 204
Indirect sources, parenthetical references, **32k-1**: 584–85, **33**: 597
Indirect titles, **3c-2**: 53
individual, person, party
Induction°. *See* Inductive reasoning
Inductive reasoning, **5e-1**: 132–33
compared with deductive reasoning, **5e**: 132
and position of topic sentence, **4a-1**: 78
in specific-to-general arrangement of paragraph, **4c**: 91
summary, **5e-1**: 132
Inferential meaning, **5b-2**: 119–20
Infinitive phrases°, **7d**: 163–64, **24j**: 440
introductory, comma with, **24b-2**: 421
Infinitives, **6d**: 145, **8a-1**: 178
objective case with, **9f**: 218
repetition of *to* in parallel forms, **18c-3**: 334
split, **15b-3**: 290
and tense sequences, **8h-2**: 200
Informal language level°, **21a-1**: 372–73
Informal outlines, **2e-5**: 38–39
for research paper, **32i**: 576–77
Informal tone, **2e-3**: 33
Information
background, **4e**: 107
sending for, **32e-3**: 542–43
for which documentation is not required, **31b**: 511
Information services, bibliographic citations, **32g-2**: 573
Informative writing°, **1b-1**: 4–5
in the humanities, **34b-2**: 621

thesis statements, **2e-4**: 34–35
topical paragraphs, **4**: 74
Inquiry, methods of
in the humanities, **34b-1**: 620
in the natural and technological sciences, **34d-1**: 651
in the social sciences, **34c-1**: 640–42
inside of, outside of
Instructor as audience, **1c-2**: 10
insure, assure, ensure
Intensive pronouns°, **6b**: 143, **9h**: 220
Interjections°, **6i**: 152
capitalization of, **30d**: 491
punctuation with, **6i**: 152, **24b-3**: 422
Interpretation papers, **34b-3**: 625–26
Interrogative adjectives, **6e**: 147
Interrogative pronouns°, **6b**: 143
case forms, **9d**: 215, **9d-2**: 217
vs. relative pronouns, **13a**: 264
Interrogative sentences°, **7**: 154, **19b**: 344. *See also* Questions
Interruptions
dashes with, **29a**: 474–76
in parentheses, **29b-1**: 478
Interviews
bibliographic citations: MLA style, **32g-2**: 572, **33**: 613; old MLA style, **34b-4**: 639
conducting, **32e-2**: 542, **34c-1**: 641–42
documentary note references, **34b-4**: 636
in to, into, **22c-3**: 395
Intransitive verbs°, **8d**: 190–91
Introductions
bibliographic citations, **32g-2**: 567–68
in scientific reports, **34d-3**: 653
See also Introductory paragraphs
Introductory devices. *See* Introductory paragraphs
Introductory elements
commas after, **24b**: 420–22
for variety, **19d**: 349
Introductory paragraphs, **4e**: 106–9
content not included in formal outline, **2e-5**: 41
devices for, **4e**: 107, **33**: 595
in job application letters, **35b**: 661
what to avoid, **4e**: 109
Invention techniques°. *See* Gathering ideas
Inverted order
dates, **24h**: 435
for emphasis, **19e**: 350–51
names, **24b**: 436
and subject-verb agreement, **11e**: 236–37
Irony°, **21b**: 378
irregardless
Irregular adjectives, **12e-2**: 254–55
Irregular adverbs, **12e-2**: 254–55
Irregular verbs°, **8a-1**: 178
principal parts, **8b**: 181, **8b-2**: 182–85
tenses, **8**: 193
Irrelevant authority, **5f**: 137
irritate, aggravate
isle, aisle, **22c-1**: 389
Issue numbers, **32g-2**: 570
is when, is where (faulty predication), **15d-2**: 296
it
in expletives: **6j**: 152–53, **10d**: 226; and subject-verb agreement, **11e**: 236
in idiomatic expressions, **10d**: 226
indefinite use of, **10c-4**: 226

Multivolume works
bibliographic citations: MLA parenthical-
references style, **32g-2**: 566–67; MLA
note style, **34b-4**: 639
documentary note references, **34b-4**: 635
parenthetical references, **32k-1**: 583
Musical compositions
bibliographic citations for recordings and
performances of, **32g-2**: 574
titles of, italics for, **30f**: 497, 498
must, **8c**: 188–89
myself, yourself, himself, herself
Mythology, reference works on, **32e-5**: 549

Names of persons
with academic degrees or titles, **23b**: 411,
24h: 436, **30h**: 501
capitalization of, **30e**: 492
inverted, **24h**: 436
nicknames, **28d**: 471
using to develop paragraphs, **4a-2**: 81–82
See also Author names
Narration, **1a**: 3, **4d**: 97
Narrowing an assigned topic, **2c-2**: 18–20,
32b: 533–36
Nationalities, capitalization of, **30e**: 494
Natural sciences. *See* Scientific writing
Negative modifiers, double, **12c**: 249–50
neither. . .nor, double negative with, **12c**:
249. *See also* Correlative conjunctions
never, avoiding double negative with **12c**:
249–50
Newspaper articles
bibliographic citations: APA style, **34c-4**:
650, MLA parenthetical-references
style, **32g-2**: 570–71, **33**: 613, **34b-4**:
639, 640
documentary note references, **34b-4**: 636
Newspaper names, **30f**: 498, **32g-2**: 571
Nicknames, **28d**: 471
no
double negative with, **12c**: 249–50
homonym of *know,* **22c-1**: 391
Nominative. *See* Subjective case
none, double negative with, **12c**: 249–50
Nonessential elements°. *See* Nonrestrictive
elements
Nonfinite verbs°, **8a-1**: 179
Nonrestrictive elements°, **24e**: 427–30
commas with, **7e-2**: 168, **7f-4**: 173, **17**:
323, **14d**: 277, **24e**: 427–30
use of *which* with clauses, **7e-2**: 168, **10f**:
228–29
Nonsexist language°, **11n-2**: 244–45, **21a-3**:
373–75
Non sequitur fallacy, **5f**: 136
nor, **6h**: 151, **17**: 317
pronoun agreement with antecedents
joined by, **11m**: 243
verb agreement with subjects joined by,
11d: 235–36
not
contractions of, **12c**: 250, **27c**: 460
double negative with, **12c**: 249–50
Notes
content: APA style, **34c-4**: 647, with MLA
parenthetical references, **32k-1**: 580,
32k-2: 585, **33**: 611
documentary (old MLA style): formatting,
34b-4: 632–33; first references, **34b-4**:

635–37; second and subsequent
references, **34b-4**: 638; text references
to, **34b-4**: 631; when few sources are
used, **34b-4**: 633–64
Note taking, **32f-2**: 558–60
to avoid plagiarism, **31b**: 512
recording bibliographic data, **32g-1**:
561–62
nothing, double negative with, **12c**: 249–50
nothing like, nowhere near
not only. . .but (also). See Correlative
conjunctions
Noun clauses°, **7e-2**: 170
punctuation with, **24j**: 439–40
Noun determiners. *See* Articles
Noun markers. *See* Articles
Noun phrases°, **7d**: 162, 163
Nouns°, **6a**: 141–42
abstract, **6a**: 141
as appositives, **7c-3**: 161–62
collective, **6a**: 141, **11g**: 238, **11o**: 245
common, **6a**: 141, **30e**: 491–92
as complements, **6a**: 141, **7c-1**: 159
concrete, **6a**: 141
formed from verbs, **16a-4**: 308
infinitives as, **8a-1**: 179
mass, **6a**: 141
matching pronoun case to, **9b**: 213
modified by adjectives, **6e**: 146, **7c-2**: 160,
12: 248
as modifiers, **12f**: 256–57
as objects, **6a**: 141
plural forms, **6a**: 141, **11a**: 232–33
possessive forms, **6a**: 141, **27a-1,2**: 458
present participle as, **8a-1**: 179
proper, **6a**: 141, **30e**: 491–96
as subjects, **6a**: 141
suffixes with, **20c-1**: 368
verbal phrases as, **7d**: 163–64
verbs functioning as, **6d**: 145
nowheres
Number
avoiding shifts in, **15a-1**: 283
of nouns, **6a**: 141
of personal pronouns, **9**: 209
pronoun agreement, **11**: 242–45
subject-verb agreement, **11**: 230–41
of verb, **8**: 176
Numbers, **30j**: 505–7
combined with words, hyphenation with,
22e-4: 406
commas with, **24h**: 437
decimals, **30j**: 506
doubtful, **23d**: 412, **29b-4**: 479
in formal outlines, **2e-5**: 40
with list items, **24c**: 424, **29b-2**: 478
omitted, apostrophes for, **27c**: 461
prefixes with, **22e-2**: 404
spelled out, **30j**: 505–6, followed by
numeral, **29b-3**: 479; hyphenation of,
22e-4: 406
used as terms: italics for, **30f**: 497, 499;
plural form, **27d**: 461
using to develop paragraphs, **4a-2**: 81
See also Fractions, Page numbers, Roman
numerals, Statistics, Volume numbers
Numerical adjectives, **6e**: 147

o, oh, **30d**: 491
Object complements°, **7c-1**: 159

Plurals° (*cont.*)
of foreign words, **22d-4:** 402
of letters, numerals, symbols, and words
used as terms, **27d:** 461
possessive forms, **27a-3:** 458
-s and *-es* endings, **11a:** 232–33
subjects connected by *and*, **11c:** 234–35
that retain singular form, **22d-4:** 402
of words ending in *-f* or *-fe*, **22d-4:** 401
of years, **27d:** 461
plus
P.M., **23b:** 411, **30h:** 500
Poetic usage, **20a-1:** 358
Poetry
quotations from, **28a-3:** 466; capitalization in, **30a:** 489; slashes in, **29e-1:** 484
titles of, quotation marks for, **28b:** 468–69
Point-by-point structure, for comparison and contrast, **4d:** 101–2
Political science, reference works on, **32e-5:** 547–48
Positive form of adjectives and adverbs°, **12e-1:** 253, **12e-2:** 255
Possessive adjectives, **6e:** 147
Possessive case°
apostrophes in, **27a:** 457–59
instead of nouns as modifiers, **12f:** 256–57
before gerunds, **9g:** 218–19
of nouns, **6a:** 141; avoiding pronoun reference to, **10c-1:** 224
of personal pronouns, **9:** 210, **27b:** 459–60; vs. contracted forms, **22c-4:** 396
Postal abbreviations of states, **30h:** 502, **30i:** 503–4
post hoc, ergo propter hoc fallacy, **5f:** 136
practical, practicable
precede, proceed, **22c-1:** 392
Predicate adjectives°, **7c-1:** 159
Predicate nominatives°, **7c-1:** 159
Predicates°, **7a-2:** 156
in clauses, **7e:** 166, 167
compound, **7a-2:** 156
simple, **7a-2:** 156
in sentence outlines, **2e-5:** 39
See also Complements; Objects; Verbs
Predication, faulty, **15d-2:** 295–96
Predicting, during reading, **5a:** 114–15
Prefixes°, **20c-1:** 366, 367–68
hyphenated, **22e-2:** 404–5
spelling, **22d-3:** 400
and word division, **22e-2:** 404
Prejudice, **5b-3:** 122
Preliminary thesis statement, **2e-4:** 34, **32h:** 575
Premises°
contradictory, **5f:** 136
in deductive reasoning, **5e-2:** 133
Prepositional phrases°, **6g:** 149, **7d:** 163
instead of nouns as modifiers, **12f:** 256–57
case of pronouns in, **9a:** 212
expanding basic sentences with, **19d-1:** 347
as sentence fragments, **13c:** 267–68
between subject and verb, **11b:** 233
Prepositions°, **6g:** 149–50
inadvertant omission of, **15e-3:** 299–300

objects of, **6g:** 149, **9a:** 212
repetition of, in parallel forms, **18c-3:** 334
Present participles°, **8a-1:** 179
phrases with, **7d:** 164
in progressive forms, **8g:** 195, **6d:** 145
Present perfect progressive tense°, **8g:** 196
Present perfect tense°, **8:** 193, **8f:** 194–95
and tense sequences, **8h-1:** 198, 199
Present progressive tense°, **8g:** 195
Present subjunctive, **8i:** 203
Present tense°, **8:** 192, **8e:** 193–94
-s form, **8a-2:** 179–80
and tense sequences, **8h-1:** 198, 199
Pretentious language°, **21d-2:** 381
pretty
Prewriting strategies°. *See* Gathering ideas
Primary evidence°, **5c:** 126–28
Primary research, **34c-3:** 645–46
Primary sources°, **32:** 531, **34a-1:** 617
in the social sciences, **34c-3:** 646
principal, principle, **22c-1:** 392
Principal parts of verbs, **8a-1:** 177–79
of *be, do,* and *have*, **8c:** 187
of irregular verbs, **8b-2:** 182–85
Problem-to-solution arrangement, **4c:** 92
Process description, **4d:** 98–99
Process, writing. *See* Writing process
Progressive forms (of verbs), **8a-1:** 179
tense, **8:** 193
use, **8g:** 195–96
Pronoun antecedent agreement°, **11:** 242–45
with antecedents joined by *and*, **11l:** 243
with antecedents joined by *or* or *nor*, **11m:** 243
with collective noun antecedents, **11o:** 245
with indefinite pronoun antecedents, **11n-1:** 244
using masculine pronoun appropriately, **11n-2:** 244–45
Pronoun case°. *See* Case
Pronoun reference°, **10:** 221–29
avoiding indefinite use of *you*, **10e:** 227
avoiding overuse of *it*, **10d:** 226–27
choosing *who, which,* or *that*, **7e-2:** 168, **10f:** 228–29, **17:** 322–23
making pronoun refer to a definite antecedent, **10c:** 224–25
making pronoun refer to a single antecedent, **10a:** 222, **10c-2:** 225
placing pronoun close to antecedent, **10b:** 222–23
See also Pronoun agreement
Pronouns°, **6b:** 42–43
antecedents of, **6b:** 142, **10:** 221–29, **11:** 242–45
case forms, **6b:** 142, **9:** 209–20
as cause of comma splices and fused sentences, **14b:** 273
demonstrative, **6b:** 143, **10c-3:** 225, **11a:** 232
inadvertent omission of, **15e-3:** 299
indefinite, **6b:** 143, **11a:** 232, **11f:** 237–38, **11n:** 244–45, **27a-1:** 458
intensive, **6b:** 143, **9h:** 220
interrogative, **6b:** 143, **9d:** 215, **9d-2:** 217, **13a:** 264
modified by adjectives, **6e:** 146, **12:** 248
personal, **6b:** 143, **9:** 209–10, **11a:** 232, **27b:** 459–60

LYNN QUITMAN TROYKA received her Ph.D. from New York University in 1973. She started teaching in 1960 and joined the faculty of Queensborough Community College of the City University of New York (CUNY) in 1967. There she became a professor (specializing in writing) in 1976. At CUNY she also has taught at the Center for Advanced Studies in Education at the Graduate School and has been a research associate at the Instructional Resource Center.

Currently, Dr. Troyka is editor of the *Journal of Basic Writing,* and she serves on the editorial board of *College Composition and Communication (CCC)* and as a reviewer for *College English* and *Research in the Teaching of English.* Her articles have appeared in journals such as *CCC, College English,* and *Writing Program Administration* and in books from Southern Illinois University Press and Boynton/Cook.

She is the co-author of *Steps in Composition* (Prentice-Hall), now in its fourth edition; author of *Structured Reading* (Prentice-Hall), now in its second edition; co-author of *Taking Action* (Prentice-Hall), a book based on her doctoral dissertation; and editor of *Guide to Writing* (Harper & Row).

Dr. Troyka has been a consultant to federal agencies including the National Endowment for the Humanities, the National Institute of Education, and the Fund for the Improvement of Post Secondary Education; and to testing agencies including the College Board, Educational Testing Service, and American College Testing. She has been a guest lecturer at dozens of colleges and universities. She is a past chair (1981) of the Conference on College Composition and Communication, and she is currently chair of both the College Section of the National Council of Teachers of English and the Division on the Teaching of Writing of the Modern Language Association.

KEY LISTS, GUIDELINES, AND SUMMARIES